Ninth Edition

Literacy Development in the Early Years

Helping Children Read and Write

Lesley Mandel Morrow
Rutgers, The State University of New Jersey

Director and Publisher: Kevin Davis
Portfolio Manager: Drew Bennett
Managing Content Producer: Megan Moffo
Content Producer: Yagnesh Jani
Portfolio Management Assistant: Maria Feliberty
Executive Development Editor: Linda Bishop
Executive Product Marketing Manager: Krista Clark
Managing Digital Producer: Autumn Benson
Digital Studio Producer: Lauren Carlson
Digital Development Editor: Kim Norbuta
Procurement Specialist: Deidra Headlee
Cover Design: Pearson CSC, SPi Global
Cover Art: FatCamera/E+/Getty Images
Full Service Vendor: Pearson CSC
Full Service Project Management: Pearson CSC, Vanitha Puela
Editorial Project Manager: Pearson CSC, Clara Bartunek
Printer-Binder: LSC Communications
Cover Printer: LSC Communications
Text Font: PalatinoLTPro-Roman
For related titles and support materials, visit our online catalog at www.pearsonhighered.com

Library of Congress Cataloging-in-Publication Data
Names: Morrow, Lesley Mandel.
Title: Literacy development in the early years: helping children read and write / Lesley Mandel Morrow.
Description: Ninth Edition. | Hoboken, New Jersey: Pearson Education, Inc., [2018]
Identifiers: LCCN 2018045762 | ISBN 9780134898230 | ISBN 0134898230
Subjects: LCSH: Reading (Early childhood)—United States. | Language arts (Early childhood)—United States. | Literacy—United States.
Classification: LCC LB1139.5.L35 M67 2018 | DDC 372.4—dc23 LC record available at https://lccn.loc.gov/2018045762

Printed in the United States of America

4 2021

ISBN 13: 978-0-13-489823-0
ISBN 10: 0-13-489823-0

Brief Contents

Contents

About the Author

LESLEY MANDEL MORROW is a distinguished professor of literacy at Rutgers University's Graduate School of Education, where she is director of the Center for Literacy Development. She began her career as a classroom teacher, then became a reading specialist, and later received her Ph.D. from Fordham University in New York City. Her area of research deals with early literacy development and the organization and management of language arts programs. Her research is carried out with children and families from diverse backgrounds.

Dr. Morrow has more than 300 publications, including journal articles, book chapters, monographs, and books. She has received Excellence in Research, Teaching, and Service Awards from Rutgers University. She was the recipient of the International Literacy Association (ILA) Outstanding Teacher Educator of Reading Award and the William S. Gray Citation of Merit, and the IRA (now ILA) Special Service Award. She also received Fordham University's Alumni Award for Outstanding Achievement. In addition, Dr. Morrow has received numerous grants for research from the federal government and has served as a principal research investigator for the Center of English Language Arts, the National Reading Research Center, and the Center for Early Reading Achievement. She was an elected member of the board of directors and president of the International Literacy Association (ILA), an organization at the time of her presidency of 80,000 educators from 100 countries. Dr. Morrow was elected into the Reading Hall of Fame and was president of the Hall of Fame as well. In 2010 she received the Literacy Research Association's Oscar Causey Award for research that has added knowledge to and caused change in literacy practice.

Dr. Morrow is proud of the Center for Literacy Development that she created, and the work it has done. She has provided professional development for the Rutgers Reading Club and after-school program for struggling readers, which is training she created with Susan Dougherty. Dr. Morrow, has also provided professional development at conferences she organized with well-known speakers from around the country and abroad. Most recently, she works with pediatricans from Rutgers Medical School on the Reach Out and Read Organization. They do research to help children from "at risk" backgrounds and share information with pediatricians on how they can help with literacy in their practice. In addition, she is the proud grandmother of James Ethan and Natalie Kate.

List of Contributors

Christina Boyland is a sixth grade Language Arts Teacher in Bernards Township, NJ. She takes pride in her work of teaching students to read and write on a daily basis, while emphasizing the importance of individual creativity. Christina has created a welcoming classroom environment that encourages her students to collaborate and express themselves in ways that go beyond books. While she enjoys the challenges and new learnings that come with teaching Middle School, Christina has a dream, now goal, to become a Reading Specialist. She hopes to help elementary students develop a strong and ongoing appreciation for literature as they grow into young individuals both inside and outside the classroom.

Dr. Jennifer Renner Del Nero is an Assistant Professor with the Special Education, Language and Literacy Department at The College of New Jersey (Ewing, NJ) where she teaches literacy education to pre-service teachers. She has numerous articles published in The Reading Teacher, Journal of Adolescent & Adult Literacy, and Reading Improvement. Dr. Del Nero has presented at numerous national conferences and previously served as a literacy coach and teacher in NJ public schools.

Lucia Oubina Laka is an ESL instructional coach for kindergarten through 8th grade for the Red Bank Borough Public Schools. She supports teachers by helping them implement strategies to meet the needs of their English Language Learners. A large part of Lucia's role includes training teachers to use the Sheltered Instruction Observation Protocol (SIOP) instructional model. Leading workshops for cohorts of teachers, Lucia then follows up with coaching visits to model SIOP strategies in various classrooms and observes how teachers utilize SIOP strategies. Additionally, Lucia supports the ESL teachers at the primary school through the implementation of a vertical professional learning community (PLC).

Pooja Rajan is a graduate student at the Rutgers Graduate School of Education and is currently enrolled in the 5-Year Elementary Education (K-6) with Preschool through Grade 3 (P-3) Certification dual program. She will receive a master's degree along with a Special Education endorsement in May 2019. She has been working under Dr. Lesley Morrow for the past year, leading to her newfound passion in Literacy. In January 2018, she along with other graduate students took a trip to Yucatán, Mexico, where she collaborated with the UADY School of Education in efforts to engage in projects with Mexican pre-service teachers through conversation cafes and community-based education. She has been a substitute teacher in the West Windsor-Plainsboro School District as she completes her graduate studies and truly enjoys any opportunity she has to inspire children. Pooja has a passion for teaching and hopes to better our educational system and continue on this endeavor throughout her career.

Stephanie Rosato is a fifth grade English Language Arts teacher in Edison, New Jersey. She supports readers and writers through the implementation of a balanced literacy program encompassing Reading Workshop, Writing Workshop, and Word Study. Through the balanced literacy approach, Ms. Rosato fosters a literature rich environment, where students acquire the necessary skills to increase comprehension. She also encourages students to build strong reading lives, and works hard to inspire a love of reading within each child. As a teacher, Ms. Rosato understands the tremendous impact reading makes on a child. Therefore, the next step within her career is to achieve a Reading Specialist Certification that will allow her to provide further individualized and focused instruction to young readers and writers who need extra support and motivation.

Melissa Stawicki is an Interventionist at Bloomfield High School, where she works with students and teachers in need of support and oversees a variety of student programs. Previously, she taught English Language Arts to students in grades nine through twelve for more than a decade. Melissa has presented at multiple conferences throughout the country on topics in literacy and educational leadership. She holds two master's degrees in leadership and is currently a doctoral candidate in Literacy Education at Rutgers University.

Foreword

Literacy Development in the Early Years: Helping Children Read and Write was published in its first edition in 1989. With the publication of this ninth edition, it has now been in print for 30 years. New features were added to each of the previous editions, as they are in this new edition. In the ninth edition, material dealing with what was research-based best practice 30 years ago was retained, and other material was updated based on current research, policy, and practice. This book was one of the first on the topic of early literacy and has prevailed as one of the most utilized texts of its kind in the country.

The first edition of *Literacy Development in the Early Years* appeared when research on emergent literacy was just beginning to be implemented. We once thought that children learned to speak and listen during their early years and later learned to read and write at 6 and 7 years of age. We also believed that early childhood was a time to learn to read and the elementary grades were a time to read to learn. We now know that children begin to develop early forms of language and literacy ability concurrently and from the day they are born. We now know that learning to read and reading to learn go hand in hand. We have discovered that excellent strategies are good for all children at all ages. Excellent literacy instruction is created in literacy-rich environments in social contexts through immersion in literacy experiences, explicit instruction, practice, and modeling by teachers—all with constructive feedback. Lesley Mandel Morrow based her book on her own research as well as that of others and her practical experience as a classroom teacher, reading specialist, researcher, mother, and now grandmother. She took a look at historical theories and philosophies about how children learn. As time passed and policy changes in teaching reading were legislated, Morrow took these developments into account and shared this very important information. With these new laws came new challenges, especially in the area of testing. There is a great deal about assessment in this edition so that teachers can assess children's needs by doing a case study with all materials in this new volume.

English learners (ELs) make up a large portion of our school population. Morrow has added more material to the chapter covering diversity and has incorporated the label, *Teaching English Learners*, to call out specific activities throughout the book that work particularly well with children who are English learners. Morrow demonstrates the value of involving children in many types of language and literacy experiences. She provides insightful examples of children's approximations of writing and reading as she establishes the necessity of giving them unlimited opportunities to practice. Further, she illustrates the ways in which adults provide models, explicit instruction, and feedback for young learners as they attempt to read and write. Morrow takes a comprehensive perspective toward literacy instruction by selecting the best techniques based on sound learning theories, such as a constructivist model with a problem-solving approach to more explicit instruction.

Children's literature plays an important role in Lesley's literacy environment. Literature serves as a model for language learning and provides strong motivation for learning to read and write. It is a springboard for many literacy-related activities. Most important, literature is a way of knowing. It is shaped around story whether it is narrative or expository—a primary act of human minds. She is also aware that in early literacy development, materials designed for instructional purposes are necessary for skill development and to attain national, state, and local standards for literacy learning.

Dr. Morrow recognizes the importance of parents, siblings, grandparents, and other caregivers reading to children and enjoying books together. She shows how reading to babies influences their grasp of language and story patterns that serve them well as they learn to read and write. She illustrates how children learn concepts about print, book handling, and conventions of stories as they interact with books. She establishes that adults teach by example as they enjoy shared reading and shared writing with children. She shows the impact of having a literacy center in a classroom and the effects of storybook reading aloud by a teacher. She illustrates that when children know authors and illustrators as real people, they want to read their work and write in a manner similar to them. Morrow states that storytelling is similar to reading aloud in its impact on children. She also recognizes the necessity of skills that involve learning concepts about print and books. For example, children need to develop phonological and phonemic awareness, alphabetic principles, and phonics for reading success. They also must learn to construct meaning from text by learning strategies for comprehension. Speaking from her own experiences as a teacher, researcher, parent, and grandparent, Morrow charts a path that leads to successful literacy learning.

Lesley has taken a long view of literacy development in the early years, showing its historical roots. She also knows and draws on the research of today's leaders because she is a member of that research community. She succinctly summarizes language theories and relates current research to shape sound practices. She has conducted much of the original research herself, testimony to the fact that she can bridge the gap among theory, research, and practice. Her examples are anchored in real classroom experiences—her own and those of other teachers with whom she works collaboratively. The examples are authentic and add credibility to the content of this book.

Morrow spends a significant amount of time on organizing and managing language arts throughout the day. In case studies and outlines, she takes the reader step by step to show what exemplary literacy instruction looks like. This edition puts a great deal of emphasis on the use of technology in the early childhood literacy classroom, differentiated instruction, response to intervention, and content-area literacy instruction. She has added information about looking at schools as "Communities of Learning" that have a positive mindset for success. She addresses the need for teachers to look at the social, emotional, physical and intellectual parts of a child and what that means for literacy instruction. Her book is filled with photographs, figures, and illustrations that take the reader into classrooms, and reproducible strategies for the classroom are sprinkled throughout the book. There also are online video clips where students can see strategies come to life in the classroom.

Lesley Morrow's treatment of literacy development is on the cutting edge of current knowledge. She is well informed about her subject and makes connections among all aspects of literacy learning. She is a sensitive observer and writer, letting children and teachers speak for themselves through their work.

Dr. Morrow states that few children learn to love books by themselves. Someone must lure them into the wonderful world of the written word. She shows us how to do that and enriches our lives and the lives of children through her work. Her contribution to the literacy development of children from birth through grade 3 is a lasting one.

Linda B. Gambrell, Ph.D.
Distinguished Professor of Education
Clemson University
Distinguished Professor Emeritus

Preface

Literacy Development in the Early Years, ninth edition, is for teachers, reading specialists, administrators, students in teacher education programs, and parents. It is appropriate for graduate, undergraduate, and professional development courses in early literacy, and it complements texts on teaching reading in the elementary school, children's literature, child development, early childhood curriculum, and teaching language arts.

I wrote the book because of my special interest in literacy development in early childhood. I taught in preschool, kindergarten, and the primary grades; I was a reading specialist; and then I taught early childhood curriculum and literacy courses at the university level. My research has focused on instructional strategies in early literacy. Over the years, research in early literacy has generated new theory. It has implications for new instructional strategies and reinforces older practices based on little or no research to establish their validity. The book describes a program that nurtures literacy development from birth through third grade.

The ideas in the book are based on research. They have been tried and they have worked, but not all are appropriate for all teachers or all children. The good teacher functions most effectively with strategies he or she feels most comfortable with. The teacher needs to be a decision maker who thinks critically about the design of his or her literacy program and the selection of materials. Children come to school with diverse social, emotional, physical, and intellectual abilities and achievement levels. They have diverse cultural backgrounds, experiences, and exposures to literacy. All must be addressed appropriately.

Underlying this book is the merging of the art and the science of teaching. The science involves theories based on research findings that have generated instructional strategies. The book is also based on current standards for teaching literacy and current policy. Most of the book contains descriptions of strategies and steps for carrying them out. But the research does not necessarily take into account individual differences among teachers and children. The art of teaching concentrates on those human variables. This book provides a comprehensive and balanced approach to early literacy instruction. Constructivist ideas that involve problem-solving techniques are blended with explicit direct instructional approaches so that teachers can decide what works best for the children they teach. There is a strong emphasis on learning to read through the integration of reading, writing, listening, speaking, and viewing. There is also a strong emphasis on the integration of these literacy skills into content-area learning. Differentiation of instruction is a major theme. That theme suggests that teaching must be directed to the individual needs of every child and, in addition, there is a strong emphasis on the diverse nature of children.

Chapter Organization

Chapter 1 places you in an early childhood classroom immediately. Its purpose is to provide you with an exemplary model of excellent literacy instruction. It provides the student with a look at what can be in an excellent early literacy classroom. It lays the groundwork for the rest of the book, which looks at each part of an exemplary literacy day.

Chapter 2 provides a framework of theory, research, and policy from the past and present that has influenced strategies for developing early literacy.

Chapter 3 covers the important issues of assessment and provides you with concepts for authentic assessment, portfolio assessment, and standardized assessment. This chapter emphasizes how assessment must guide instruction and how they are connected. With this philosophy in mind, strategies for assessment are integrated into all chapters. There is also a look at standards to see how they influence what we teach.

Chapter 4 is about the diversity in our classrooms. The chapter has been expanded because of the diverse nature of our classrooms. There is an emphasis on English learners (ELs) as well as discussions of special learning needs such as learning disabilities, physical disabilities, gifted children, and others. This chapter provides strategies for teaching children who are diverse in many ways. However, meeting the needs of these individuals is a special focus throughout the book.

Chapters 5 through 10 deal with emergent literacy skills and strategies, oral language and vocabulary development, word study, comprehension, and writing. These chapters discuss theory and research—specifically, developmental trends, instructional strategies, and methods for assessment. The book views the development of literacy skills (reading, writing, oral language, listening, and viewing) as concurrent and interrelated; the development of one enhances the development of the others. Furthermore, the theories, stages, acquisition, and strategies associated with each are similar, and it is difficult to separate them entirely. To make the volume more readable, however, I have treated the various areas of literacy in different chapters.

Chapter 11 places a strong emphasis on the importance of children's literature in literacy development as well as creating rich literacy centers in classroom.

Chapter 12 focuses on motivation through the integration of literacy throughout the school day. The topics discussed are technology and literacy, content areas and literacy, and playfulness in school. Thematic instruction and project-based instruction are discussed.

Chapter 13 provides the organization and management of the components presented in the book that are organized to create a successful program. The best strategies will fall apart if the school day is not organized well. Ways of scheduling the school day are discussed, as well as descriptions of how to organize whole-group, small-group, and individualized instruction. An area of extreme importance to teachers is how children can learn to work independently at centers while teachers instruct small groups to meet achievement needs. This is accomplished through differentiation of instruction.

Chapter 14 discusses the strong influence of the home on the development of literacy, especially in a child's earliest years. It discusses broad perspectives concerning family literacy, such as integrated home and school programs, intergenerational programs, and sensitivity to cultural differences to provide programs that are not intrusive but build on the strengths of the families being served.

Each chapter begins with expected outcomes to focus on while reading the text. Important vocabulary in the chapter is listed at the beginning of each chapter. The questions and vocabulary are followed by theory and research, a great deal of practice and assessment. Each chapter has multiple and reproducible strategies throughout. The chapters end with a summary that focuses on the expected outcomes with questions and activities for further study. The appendices supplement the text with lists of materials that teachers use in carrying out a successful program to develop early literacy. Appendix E offers the instructor ideas for his or her college classroom. Key words dealing with early literacy development are defined in the glossary at the end of the book.

What's New in the Ninth Edition

New features of the ninth edition include the following:

- There are 14 chapters instead of 10 in this edition. The purpose was to make chapters shorter with less information but more targeted information in each one. This was done to make the book more student-friendly. New chapters are Chapter 5, Early Childhood Language Development: Birth to Age 2; Chapter 6, Language and Vocabulary Development: Preschool Through Grade 3; Chapter 7, Emergent Literacy Skills and Strategies: Helping Children Figure Out Words; and, Chapter 8, Phonological Awareness and Phonics Instruction.
- There is an emphasis on creating a community of learners in literacy instruction by embracing a positive mindset of "*You can do it*," "*We can do it*" and "*I will do it*".
- There is an emphasis on the use of informational text, integration of literacy throughout the curriculum, a look at close reading, and text complexity.
- More strategies than ever before are embedded within the book followed by vignettes to illustrate how to put them into practice.
- Appendix B provides a new Integrated Language Arts Thematic Unit entitled Healthy Bodies, Healthy Minds. This unit not only covers content to encourage healthy living but identifies how to seamlessly integrate reading and writing strategies into lesson planning and meet Common Core standards.
- Continued emphasis is placed on research and policy in early literacy development, including findings from the National Reading Panel, the National Early Literacy Panel, Preventing Reading Difficulties, Reading First, the Rand Report, the implications of the No Child Left Behind legislation, Race to the Top, and the Common Core State Standards.
- Updated photographs, as well as tables and illustrations enhance the text.
- There are additional strategies for developing literacy in writing workshops, reading workshops, independent and partner reading, organizational methods, and comprehension development.
- Appendices for children's literature, early literacy software, and multiple websites for teachers and children have been updated.
- There are additional assessment tools for carrying out a very complete case study of a child's abilities and needs in literacy development and an emphasis on assessment guided instruction.
- Emphasis is placed on school reievance and motivation.
- There is a strong focus on how to organize children with similar needs for small-group instruction.

MyLab Education

One of the most visible changes in the ninth edition, and also one of the most significant, is the expansion of the digital learning and assessment resources embedded in the eText and the inclusion of MyLab Education in the text. MyLab Education is an online homework, tutorial, and assessment program designed to work with the text to engage learners and to improve learning. Within its structured environment, learners see key concepts demonstrated through real classroom video footage, practice what they learn, test their understanding, and receive feedback to guide their learning and to ensure their mastery of key learning outcomes. Designed to bring learners more directly into the world of K–12 classrooms and to help them see the real and powerful impact of early literacy concepts covered in this book, the online resources in MyLab Education with the Enhanced eText include:

- **Video Examples.** About two or three times per chapter, an embedded video provides an illustration of an early literacy principle or concept in action. These video examples most often show students and teachers working in classrooms, and sometimes they show students or teachers describing their thinking or experiences.

- **Self-Checks.** In each chapter, self-check quizzes help assess how well learners have mastered the content. The self-checks are made up of self-grading multiple-choice items that not only provide feedback on whether questions are answered correctly or incorrectly, but also provide rationales for both correct and incorrect answers.

- **Application Exercises.** These exercises give learners opportunities to practice applying the content and strategies from the chapters. The questions in these exercises are usually constructed response. Once learners provide their own answers to the questions, they receive feedback in the form of model answers written by experts.

Acknowledgments

I extend my heartfelt appreciation to those who helped with the ninth edition. These individuals always said yes to whatever request I had and worked tirelessly on many parts of the book with me. They are Christina Boyland, Jennifer Renner Del Nero, Lucia Oubina Laka, Melissa Stawicki, Pooja Rajan, and Stephanie Rosato. I extend my appreciation to Drew Bennett the Acquisitions Editor at Pearson for supporting the ninth edition of this book, and for the guidance he offered during the revision process. I would also like to thank Clara Bartunek and Vanitha Puela for their careful attention during the editing process. Also thanks to Linda Bishop and thanks to the CSC composition team for all their help.

Thank you to students, teachers, and administrators who worked on the other eight editions: Paula Batsiyan, Lisa Mullin, Kathy Minto, Sara Stofik, Doug Bushell, Elizabeth Freitag, Stefanie Lederman, Stacy Stannzel, Joellen Surace, Thu Win, Danielle Wintringham, Julie Anastasi, Lara Heyer, Kristen Valvanis, Patricia Addonizio, Susan Burks, Kathleen Cunningham, Katie Farrell, Mary Ann Gavin, Laura Babarca, Tricia Lyons, Melody Olsen, Michele Preole, Mary Joyce Santoloci, Sari Schnipper, Karen Szabo, Patricia DeWitt, Erica Erlanger, Michael Gravois, Katherine Heiss, Pamela Kelliher, Lisa Lozak, Stacey Rog, Monica Saraiya, Amy Sass, Connie Zauderer, Stephanie Adams, Ellen Abere, Bonita Bartholomew, Maxine Bell, Lynette Brenner, Karen Buda, Pat Burton, Barbara Callister, Heather Casey, Jennifer Castio, Melissa Colucci, Shannon Corcoran, Tom DelCasale, Judy DeVincenzo, Fran Diamente, TamiLyn Eisen, Gina Goble, Arlene Hall, David Harris, Lori Harrje, Catherine Hickey, Joanne Jacobson, Adriann Jean-Denis, Noreen Johnson, Tracy Kahn, Linda Keefe, Sheryl King, Gail Martinez, Nancy Mason, Joyce McGee, Carna Meechem, Dennis Monaghan, Stephanie Moretti, Joyce Ng, Susan Nitto, Ellen O'Connor, Catherine Ogletree, Lucy Oman, Barbara Oxfeld, Mary Payton, Tammye Pelovitz, Cynthia Peters, John Quintaglie, Robert Rosado, Sonia Satterwhite, Joyce Schenkman, Linda Schifflette, Christine Temple, Patty Thaxton, Marcia Wesalo, Susan Yoder, Margaret Youssef, Andrea Shane, Milton Mandel, Howard Manson, Cheryl Devine, Kate Brach, Danielle Lynch, Lynn Cohen, Lisa Rosenfeld, Jennifer Chiaramida, Kelly Lamar, Amy Sass, Michael Gravois, Kenneth Kunz, Marilyn Burnbaum, Lisa Bratas, Jen Chen, Jennifer DelNero, Maureen Hall, Jennifer Kamm, Patricia Tait, Ghina Molinari-Schiano, Bethany Reichwein, Christina Speizio, Sharon Weldon, Jennie Dzurrila, and Cathy Kobylarz.

Thank you to the children I taught, my college students, and the excellent teachers I have observed and from whom I've learned so much. I am grateful to the researchers in early literacy who have provided exciting information in the field. I consider this book a cooperative effort as a result of the contributions of so many in both direct and indirect ways.

To those who reviewed the eighth edition of the book, especially Rosemary Geiken of East Tennessee State University, and offered suggestions for what to include in the ninth edition, I appreciate your thoughtful comments. To the college professors, college students, teachers, and parents who purchased earlier editions and demonstrated their support for the publication, the ninth edition was made possible by you.

Finally, I thank my parents, Mary and Milton Mandel, who provided a literacy-rich environment for me and a work ethic that gave me the ambition to take on this task. Thank you to my family, Stephanie M. Bushell, Doug Bushell, and Bob Janney for their support and my grandson James and granddaughter Natalie for demonstrating the validity of many of the concepts expressed in the book.

L. M. M.

James and Natalie, you light up my life.

Chapter 1

Looking at an Exemplary Early Literacy Classroom

Photo credit: Lesley Mandel Morrow

In this chapter, I describe an early childhood teacher and her students in the beginning of first grade. The purpose of this introduction is to give you an idea of what an exemplary early childhood classroom in which literacy is emphasized looks like. This will give you a framework for what you will read in the rest of the book.

This chapter presents information you should know and be able to create in your classroom after reading the book. By previewing this case study, you will have some background knowledge about what is to come. The rest of the book will look at each part of the day and skills being taught. You will find new vocabulary in the chapter that is unfamiliar. These words will be defined in the chapters to come. In the description of this classroom, many of the critical components, materials, and routines of an exemplary literacy instruction will be discussed. After completing the book, come back to Chapter 1 and read it again.

Introduction to the Teacher and Students

Wendy Hayes has been teaching first grade for the past seven years. Recently, she completed a master's degree with a reading specialist certification. She teaches in a working-class community. She has 22 students in her class, including 7 African American,

6 Caucasian, 5 Hispanic, 2 from Korea and 2 children from India. Nine of Wendy's children speak one of four languages at home: English, Spanish, Korea, and Hindi. Twelve students are girls and ten are boys. There is a full-time aide assigned to one student who is physically disabled and uses a wheelchair.

Wendy's philosophy of teaching includes integration of the curriculum so that students can build connections between content areas. She purposefully integrates literacy skill development in reading, writing, listening, speaking, and viewing with her social studies and science themes as much as possible. Her small-group literacy instruction emphasizes her belief in differentiated instruction. In the small groups, she teaches skills in an explicit manner. Ms. Hayes uses both narrative and informational texts. She is spending more time on informational books than she has in the past since she recognizes that children gain background knowledge and vocabulary from this material. She is aware that people read a variety of informational texts such as how-to manuals, applications, instructions, recipes, and websites. Consequently, Ms. Hayes understands that children must be introduced to multiple genres at a young age. She uses standards from her state in her early literacy program.

Setting the Stage for Wendy's Teaching

Wendy's classroom is warm and inviting, with well-defined stations. The displays on the walls clearly reflect the theme being studied. They also show considerable evidence of the children's growing literacy development. The displays include charts that Wendy wrote with the children and samples of children's writing and artwork. Wendy has an easel with chart paper for the morning message, a calendar, a weather chart, a temperature graph, a helper chart, a daily schedule, a pocket chart, a word wall and an anchor chart that lists classroom rules made by the teacher and children. All of this is in the area where she teaches the whole group.

Wendy's largest station is the literacy station that has a rug for independent reading and whole-class meetings. The area includes lots of space for storing books. One set of shelves holds books organized in two different ways. There are baskets of books leveled for difficulty coordinating with Wendy's small-group guided reading instruction. For example, students reading books in the green basket during small-group instruction know that these are the books for instruction. Other shelves hold baskets of books of many different levels organized by themes, such as dinosaurs, sports, and weather. Wendy rotates books in the baskets monthly. Colored stickers on the books and baskets assist students in returning them to the correct spot. Student-made class books and stories are displayed in another basket. Books about the current theme are on an open-faced shelf.

The literacy station has a felt board and characters, a magnetic board with magnetic characters, puppets, and props for storytelling. There is a rocking chair for the teacher and other adults to use to read to the class. The children use the rocking chair to read independently and to each other. The listening area in the literacy center has a CD player for listening to stories. The literacy center also has manipulative materials for learning about print, etc. Wendy has an electronic white board for presenting lessons in word study and comprehension as well as activities for students to do on their own. Finally, she embeds the use of technology in her teaching with digital texts, by accessing information from the Internet, and posting information on the class website. She and the children also create PowerPoint presentations and videos; these are programs that enhance literacy and engage children, such as Animoto and Puppet Pals.

In this video, students work independently at a writing station, before sitting in the author's chair to present their work.

The writing station is an extension of the literacy station. There is a round table for small groups of children to meet with the teacher. Shelves hold many types of paper (lined and unlined), a stapler, markers, crayons, colored pencils, dictionaries, alphabet stamps, and ink stamp pads. A word wall in the writing center has the letters of the alphabet taped on horizontally. When the children learn a new word, it is written on a card and taped under the letter it begins with on the word wall. Children use the words when they need the spelling of a word or to practice reading. During instruction, children are asked to think of words that begin with the same letter and sound as a word on the word wall, or to think of words that rhyme with a word on the word wall. Wendy puts her students' names on the word wall. She also puts high-frequency sight words that her children are expected to learn.

Content area stations are difficult to find space for. Wendy wants to make sure all areas of the curriculum are visually apparent in her room. The next set of stations are spaces she finds to display materials such as shelves, window, sills and doors.

Wendy's science station provides a home for the class guinea pig and hermit crabs. Equipment in this center includes plants, magnets, magnifying glasses, and objects that sink or float. Materials are added to match the themes being studied, and there are always new hands-on experiments for students to complete.

The dramatic play station includes a table, chairs, and a bookshelf. Changes are made to the area to reflect the themes studied during the year. This center has been converted into a restaurant where children take orders and read menus. The restaurant helps with learning about multicultural food and customs. This year the area has been an Italian restaurant, Indian, Mexican, Japanese, and a Jewish Deli. Dramatic-play settings also include a newspaper office, a post office, and a travel agency.

There is a construction station which includes blocks of all sizes and shapes and other items for construction, such as Legos®. There are trucks, cars, trains, people, and animals in this area with labels designating where each toy goes. Also supplied are 5 × 8 cards and tape for labeling structures created by the children. There are signs written by children such as "Please Save" on buildings under construction and signs naming finished structures. Children sign their names on the labels.

Located near the sink is the art station, which contains an easel, table, and chairs. There are scissors, markers, crayons, and paper of many colors, types, and sizes. Collage materials such as cotton balls, doilies, foil, wallpaper, stickers, and glue are also included.

The math station contains math manipulatives for counting, adding, measuring, weighing, graphing, and distinguishing shapes. There are felt numbers to use on the felt board, magnetic numbers for magnetic boards, numbers to sequence in a pocket chart, and geometric shapes, such as squares, triangles, cylinders, and rectangles.

The children sit at tables clustered together. In a quiet corner of the room, there is a kidney-shaped table that Wendy uses for small-group instruction. Shelves near the table have materials for small groups, such as letters of the alphabet, rhyming cards, leveled books, sentence strips, index cards, white boards, markers, and word-study games.

Assessing Students to Determine Instructional Needs

To provide instruction to meet the varied reading and writing levels of her students, Wendy spends considerable time assessing them with formal and informal measures. In September, January, and June, she assesses students' phonemic awareness, phonics knowledge, their ability to read sight words, vocabulary development, their reading comprehension, fluency, and writing ability. She plans instruction based on the needs she identifies. She also looks at daily performance samples. Wendy takes monthly running records for children who are reading and checks knowledge of concepts about books and print (CAP) for those not yet reading. These early assessments are called *formative assessments* to help the teacher identify the types of errors that children make, the decoding strategies they use, and their comprehension and reading grade level. A comparison of previous running records to new ones and CAP tests indicate student progress and how well her teaching strategies are working. These are called summative assessments. Wendy writes anecdotal notes about child behavior that indicates achievement and what help is needed. She collects samples of children's writing, evaluates them, and places these in student portfolios. Wendy also observes students for social, emotional, and physical development.

Small-Group Guided Reading Instruction

Wendy developed a schedule that allows her to work with small groups of children to develop reading skills. Using the collected assessment information, she places students with similar needs together for small-group guided reading instruction. As she works with children, she takes careful notes regarding progress in literacy and adjusts the members of her various groups as needed. While in small groups, Wendy provides skills instruction for the children. She could work on phonics, comprehension, fluency writing or vocabulary development. Wendy currently has four small groups and meets with each group from once a week to at least four times a week depending on the group's needs.

Wendy's Daily Schedule

8:45 - When children arrive at school, they have a Do Now time:

Carry out their jobs
Partner read
Make entries in their journals
Complete unfinished work

9:00 to 9:15 - The group meets as a whole for

Morning greetings
The calendar and weather are discussed
The schedule for the day is reviewed

9:15 to 10:00 - Vocabulary morning meeting

There is a vocabulary lesson to match the theme being studied. Vocabulary words from the theme are reviewed and some new ones added to the list. With a partner, the children create sentences with the new vocabulary. In this vocabulary period, grade-level vocabulary is also introduced. Engaging vocabulary lessons will happen here.

10:00 to 10:20 - Reading comprehension workshop

The teacher does a read-aloud based on the theme being studied and does a mini-lesson to build comprehension using either an informational or narrative book. After the lesson, children select from a group of books the teacher has provided. They read with a partner to practice the skill taught. The teacher moves around the room and conferences with children about their reading, offering guidance when necessary. The class as a whole shares what each student learned from partner reading based on the comprehension skill taught in the read aloud.

10:20 to 11:10 - Small-group guided reading instruction and station activities to differentiate instruction

The teacher meets with small groups and does explicit instruction for the needs of the group. Literacy activities in stations are assigned and children are required to complete three tasks.

11:15 to 12:00 - Writing workshop

The teacher does a mini-skill lesson for the whole group focusing on one writing skill. The children write alone or with a partner to practice the skill. The teacher holds conferences with the children as they write. The children share their writing.

12:00 to 12:45 - Lunch and indoor or outdoor play

12:45 to 1:15 - Word study session

1:00 to 1:40 - Math

1:40 to 2:15 - Theme or project based-related activities in social studies or science in which reading and writing activities are purposefully embedded

2:15 to 2:50 - Creative arts, music, or gym (specials or classroom teacher-related to classroom theme studied and tied into literacy skills provided by the classroom teacher)

Wrap up: Read-aloud or silent reading

Sharing and reviewing the most important things learned that day
Planning for tomorrow

A Typical Day in Wendy's Classroom

Wendy and her students are studying dinosaurs. In her classroom, reading, writing, listening, speaking, and content-area subjects are integrated into the dinosaur theme. On Monday, she organizes activities for the week.

It is Monday morning and Wendy's room is filled with quiet chatter as her students arrive. Classical music plays in the background as children complete their morning routines. Children move their name tags on the attendance board from the side labeled "Not here" to "Here" and place their name stickers into the "Buy lunch" or "Milk" can. Some children cluster around the easel, where Wendy has written the morning message and included the question for the day. The message says, "Good morning, children. Today is Monday, April 3rd. We will have art today as our special. Our question for today is how many dinosaur names do you know? Write them in your journal and we will talk about it later."

Children check the helper chart for jobs such as feeding the animals, watering plants, and recording the temperature and day's weather on the weather graph. Wendy puts pictures next to each step to help with reading the chart. This is particularly useful for struggling readers and English learners (EL).

Students know it is "Do Now" time and write their weekend news in their journals. On other days of the week, they partner read three times and journal write one more time. Wendy greets each child as she circulates among the readers or writers. A two-minute warning bell rings, letting children know that it is time to gather on the rug for the morning meeting.

Morning Message and Vocabulary Meeting

Wendy says, "Good morning," and the children repeat the greeting to each other and shake hands around the circle. Because they are starting with April as a new month, they echo read and then choral read a poem about the month that Wendy showed on the digital white board. She gives the children a paper copy of the poem to put in their poem books, along with other poems for each month.

Next, Wendy leads the class in reading the morning message together. She asked the children to look at the morning message and read it together. It said, "Good morning, children. Today is Monday, April 3rd. We will have art today as our special. What dinosaurs did you write down? Can you tell me something about them?" The morning message is used to develop vocabulary. They discussed the dinosaurs and Wendy brought pictures of them to show as they are mentioned. New dinosaur names were added to the themed word wall to continue vocabulary development. The children talk about the one characteristic of the new dinosaurs that is different from the others. The new 'characteristic' word is also added to the word wall to help children engage in a discussion about the characteristics of the dinosaurs and identify the differences among them.

Reading Comprehension Workshop

In this video, a kindergarten teacher models a read aloud for an informational text. https://www.youtube.com/watch?v=Oyb-OjQmM1M

Wendy has her class move to another portion of the room for reading comprehension workshop. She will do a read-aloud and comprehension mini-lesson. The book is an informational book about dinosaurs. They look through the pages together and decide what the book will be about. It seems it might be about plant-eating dinosaurs. Wendy tells them to listen for all the types of plants that the animals eat. She tells the children to compare characteristics of meat-eating dinosaurs they read about recently and the plant-eating dinosaurs she was going to read about today. The children have copies of the book and follow along as the teacher reads. After reading, they discuss the facts in the book and compare the meat eaters to the plant eaters.

After the discussion, children choose a book to read from a selection of dinosaur books. The books are about meat-eating dinosaurs and plant eaters. Children are to remember facts about the meat-eating dinosaurs and the plant-eating dinosaurs to compare. While they read with a partner, the teacher circulates and listens to readers. She offers assistance if needed. She may even conference with some who seem to need additional help.

After their partner reading, the class shares and compares facts together. They discuss the differences between plant-eating dinosaurs and meat-eating dinosaurs on a Venn diagram and discuss things they have in common.

Station Time

Wendy spends a few minutes reviewing the center activities and describing new ones placed in the centers for the exploration of dinosaurs. Stations have materials that are in place over a period of time, and they are enriched with activities that reflect the current theme and skills that need to be practiced. All of the stations require students to engage in literacy activities. A description of what has been added to each station related to the dinosaur theme follows.

- **Writing station:** Dinosaur-bordered writing paper, dinosaur-shaped books, a dinosaur dictionary, a dinosaur-shaped poster with words about dinosaurs, pencils, crayons, colored pencils, and markers.
- **Literacy station:** Fiction and nonfiction dinosaur books, dinosaur books with accompanying CDs, a dinosaur vocabulary puzzle, a dinosaur concentration memory game, and a teacher-made dinosaur lottery game.
- **Computer station:** Find information on different types of dinosaurs, and watch a video about fossils and list important facts.
- **Science station:** Small skulls and old animal bones, along with a magnifying glass and rubber gloves to examine the bones and draw what they think the entire animal may have looked like; dinosaur pictures to sort into meat eaters and plant eaters; other pictures to be sorted into "walked on two feet" and "walked on four feet." There are recording sheets for all activities.
- **Math station:** Measuring tools in a basket and sheets to record the measurement of various plaster bones of dinosaurs; dinosaur counters; little plastic dinosaurs in an estimation jar; and a basket containing 50 little dinosaurs numbered from 1 to 50 to be put in sequential order.
- **Blocks center:** Toy dinosaurs, trees, bushes, and some dinosaur books.

- **Art center:** Dinosaur stencils, dinosaur stamps, clay models of dinosaurs, and many pictures of dinosaurs to help students make their own sculptures. There are cards for labeling each dinosaur with its names.
- **Dramatic play station:** The dramatic-play area is transformed into a paleontologist's office with chicken bones embedded in plaster of Paris, carving tools and small hammers to remove the bones, safety goggles, paper and pencils for labeling bones, trays to display them, dinosaur books, and posters of fossils and dinosaurs.

After Wendy reviews station activities, she assigns her students to activities. The work in the stations is reinforcing skills that students need practice in, such as matching pictures with letters to reinforce long and short vowel sounds. When they complete the "have to" activities, children may select any station.

Small-Group Guided Reading Instruction: Differentiation of Lessons to Meet the Needs of All Children

Station time allows the teacher to work with small groups and individuals while the children are working independently. Wendy's first group is reading a new book. She does a quick book walk to introduce the children to the difficult words and interesting pictures. During the book walk they discuss the names of the dinosaurs in the book. Wendy asks the children to whisper read the book and words that are new to them. They also discuss the names of the animals in the book. Wendy reads the story to the children first. Next, the children are asked to read the book orally at their own pace. As the group whisper reads, Wendy notices that one student reads the book quickly without making any errors. Wendy makes a note to think about moving him to a more challenging reading group. After the children finish reading, Wendy asks everyone to turn to page eight. "I noticed that James read, 'We saw the pot bear' and then changed it to 'polar bear,' since he looked back at the letters and took into account the meaning of the sentence. He remembered that the words have to match the letters and what you read has to make sense."

While the children were reading, Wendy did a running record on one child. She noted that this student read "tooth" instead of "teeth" and said "winds" instead of "wings." Wendy will help this child pay more attention to the print when working with him.

Wendy's next group is reading a different and more difficult book. This group is more advanced than the first. The group has worked with this book before; therefore, the lesson that Wendy will carry out will help her children become more independent readers. She will teach them how to figure out unknown words by using the meaning of a sentence and by looking at the letters in the words. They begin with a game called "Guess the Covered Word," similar to an activity they used during the morning meeting. This time, the covered word in the sentence "I can ☐ fast" is the word "run." The children are encouraged to select a word that makes sense in the sentence and then look at the letters in the word to see which is the correct word. Words generated for the missing word were: *walk, eat, hop, sleep, and run.* The activity is repeated in other sentences throughout the book.

The next group is reading another book. In this lesson, Wendy **focuses** on teaching the children to look at ending sounds to figure out words. Wendy wrote, "I am *go* to the store" on the chart. She reads the sentence and the children quickly point out that it does not sound right. Joan writes a second sentence, "I am *going* to the store." They identify the difference in the two sentences by pointing to the words *go* and *going*. Wendy reminds the children to look at the ends and beginnings of words when reading. They read the book with special attention to the word endings. After the first reading, she starts a discussion to demonstrate their ability to infer and asks them if they could think of another way to end the story.

A Quick Snack

For a snack there are dinosaur animal crackers and what Wendy refers to as "dinosaur juice." Children read independently when finished with the snack.

Writing Workshop

The children gather for writing in the whole-class meeting area. Wendy prepares them for a school-wide activity. They will survey all students in the school to find out what their favorite dinosaurs are. Wendy does an interactive writing activity to draft a letter asking the teachers and children in other classrooms to participate. She begins by reviewing the format of a letter, which was introduced during a previous unit on the post office. They discuss how to begin and end a letter. Using chart paper, Wendy asks the children to offer suggestions to start the letter and write the letter. The children and their teacher compose the text. Wendy types the letter and distributes it to each classroom. The original shared writing chart will be posted on the cafeteria door.

Next, Wendy introduces the writing activity for the week. The children will be writing informational texts about dinosaurs. They are each to select their favorite dinosaur and answer the following questions before they begin their writing:

> What are the parts of your dinosaur? What does your dinosaur eat? Where did your dinosaur live? What else do you know about your dinosaur?

Each child selects a partner to work with and a dinosaur to study. Jamal and Damien chose a tyrannosaurus. Wendy has provided books for looking up information in the categories outlined and has identified websites for children to review. Each child takes two sections of the book on which to write.

Through this initial activity, the children have learned that brainstorming is a crucial step in the writing process. Brainstorming helps children decide what they will write. On Tuesday, they will continue to browse through dinosaur books for information and start to draft. Children will write the facts collected in informational stories and illustrate them. When the activity is completed at the end of the week, children will share their informational dinosaur stories.

Lunch and Play

Lunch is in the cafeteria. After eating, if weather permits, the children play outside. If not, they play in the gym or their classroom.

Word Study Session

The school where Wendy teaches has a phonics program that makes sure children systematically learn the skills they need to read automatically and independent. This program includes many manipulative materials that engage children in building words using initial consonant blends and digraphs, and creating word families. In addition to using the phonics program, Wendy always adds something that brings meaning to the lesson. For example, with the study of dinosaurs as meat eaters and plant eaters, she points out that the word "meat" follows the rule she has taught that says, "when two vowels go walking, the first one does the talking." She asks the children for other words with *ea* that follows that rule. Children mention "treat," "seat," and "beat." They also look at the word "plant" to notice the blend at the beginning of the word. They think of other words that have the *pl* blend at the beginning, such as place, plot, and play.

Math

There is a specific math curriculum that Wendy follows in her school. She also ties her math to her theme and literacy. Children are working on subtracting a one-digit number from a two-digit number. After working on the skill, she asks the children to write a word problem that involves subtraction and dinosaurs. James wrote the following, "Fifteen dinosaurs went for a walk in the forest. They were plant eaters and munching on plants along the way. Five of them at the end of the line got lost. How many dinosaurs were left in the big group."

Science: Theme Activity and Center Time

Wendy has planned a theme-related art activity. Everyone will contribute to a mural and construct a habitat environment for dinosaur sculptures the children will create with the art teacher. To introduce the mural and habitat activity, everyone listens as Wendy explains the details. Children talk about a piece of the mural they would like to work on, such as trees, vines, a cave, a river, or plants. Wendy writes the children's names on a chart with the item they would like to draw with markers.

One-third of the students remain on the carpet to work on the mural. These children huddle around books depicting plants and trees from the time of the dinosaurs. Animated discussions take place as each child draws food, shelter, water, and other elements necessary to sustain dinosaur life. The rest of the children use this time to complete unfinished journal writing or station work. If they have completed all their work, they can select any station activity they wish. Students who did not get to work on the mural will have a chance another day during the week.

Art, Music, and Gym

At this time of day, the class goes to a special teacher for art, music, or gym. Wendy has coordinated with these teachers about the current class theme so the art teacher is working on papier-mâché dinosaur sculptures with the children.

The music teacher has found some great dinosaur songs and one about habitats as well. The gym teacher has thought of some movement activities to help the students walk like dinosaurs.

Wrap Up

At the end of the day, students gather in the meeting area for a read-aloud and a review of the day. Wendy has selected an informational book about dinosaurs. This book will provide children with more facts and vocabulary that they can use in their writing and for the mural habitat they are creating. Before she reads it, she points out some of the features of this informational book. There is a table of contents that includes each chapter and glossary of new words. There are labels on figures, captions describing pictures, headings introducing new topics, and new vocabulary written in a bolder and bigger print than the rest of the words. Wendy knows this book will introduce children to a topic not yet discussed in class: The differences between dinosaurs that were plant eaters and those that were meat eaters. After reading, Wendy helps children list the characteristics of plant-eating and meat-eating dinosaurs on an interactive writing chart. There were new dinosaur terms to learn, such as armored plates, carnivore, and extinct.

In another shared reading at the end of the next day, Wendy focused on finding facts in the informational text. When she read, she asked the children to listen for the facts about dinosaurs and the elements in the book that make it informational.

After reading, Wendy asked, "What elements made this book an informational story?"

Student 1: There aren't characters that have a story to tell.

Student 2: It is about real things.

Student 3: You learn a lot of facts.

After the discussion, Wendy made a web that included the facts in the text. She drew a circle on a chart with the word *dinosaurs* written in the center. Then she drew lines radiating out from the center circle. Next, she drew smaller circles connected to each line radiating out from the larger circle.

As children recalled facts about dinosaurs, Wendy wrote the words in one of the smaller circles. After writing the web, Wendy and the children read it: Dinosaurs: big, scary, vegetarians, meat eaters, dangerous, extinct.

Wendy talked about how informational texts are also called nonfiction because everything is real instead of make-believe. One student raised her hand and said:

Student 1: I think the book is make-believe, because the pictures are drawings. If it was an informational book, there would be photographs that we take with cameras.

Student 2: But they can't have real photographs because dinosaurs are dead, and they didn't have photographs since they had no cameras when they were alive. We don't have any more dinosaurs. What is that word, they are? Oh yeah, they are *extinct*.

The teacher gives each child a sticky note to write the three most important things they learned. They put the sticky notes on a bulletin board and make a copy to bring home. This reinforces what was learned and lets parents and guardians know what was learned as the children share the sticky note with their families.

Tuesday: Learning More about Dinosaurs

Tuesday's schedule is the same as Monday, but with new books and assignments. During the rest of the week, the children followed the same routines with morning messages, vocabulary meeting, reading comprehension workshop, with a shared story book reading, etc. whole-group skills lessons, and reading practice. There is small-group instruction, center work, writing workshop, and theme-related activities in social studies, science, math, art, music, and play.

Summary

Wendy's classroom allows children to have the opportunity to explore and experiment while also receiving explicit instruction. They are expected to complete work assigned to them during small-group instruction or during whole-group lessons. However, they also have choices in the selection of activities a few times during the day. A lot of information is introduced during whole- and small-group lessons, and information is repeated and reviewed all week long. Children's individual needs are met during small-group reading instruction, writing workshop, and station time. Reading and writing are integrated in content-area learning. Children in Wendy's classroom read and write all day long in all of the content areas. Her classroom is arranged so the children have access to varied materials and books. Most importantly, Wendy's children are engaged in literacy from the time they walk into the classroom in the morning until they leave in the afternoon.

Chapter 2
Foundations of Early Literacy: From the Past to the Present

Courtesy of Douglas Bushell

LEARNING OUTCOMES

After reading this chapter, you should be able to:

2.1 Discuss the historical roots of early childhood education.

2.2 Discuss the evolution of theory and practice in early childhood education across the twentieth century.

2.3 Identify key approaches to early literacy instruction.

2.4 Describe the effects of evidence-based research, governmental policies, and legislation on early childhood literacy.

VOCABULARY

Accommodation
Assimilation
Child-centered curriculum (progressive education)
Constructivist
Emergent literacy
Explicit instruction
Integrated language arts
Reading readiness
Scaffolding
Schema
Whole-language instruction

Sylvia Ashton-Warner wrote in her book *Spinster* "What a dangerous activity reading is: teaching is. All this plastering of foreign stuff. Why plaster on at all when there's so much inside already? So much locked in? If only I could draw it out and use it as working material. If I had a light enough touch, it would just come out under its own volcanic power" (Ashton-Warner, 1963, p. 14). What Sylvia Ashton-Warner said is true. The issue is how do we unlock what is inside the right way? Following is a vignette that a mom helps a child who has a lot locked inside and helps her daughter with a light touch to draw it out.

Four-year-old Natalie and her mother were in the mall and doing some errands. As they approached one store, Natalie said, "Look, Mommy, I can read those letters: T-A-R-G-E-T. Those letters spell Marshalls." Natalie's mother smiled and said, "That was great, Natalie. You got every letter right. Now, I'll read the sign for you; it says Target. This is another store like Marshalls. You did some good thinking when you tried to read that word since the stores look alike. Do you see any letters in the word "Marshalls" that you have in your name?" Natalie looked and then said, "I have an **A** and so does Marshalls, and I have an **L**."

Not too long ago, we would have chuckled at Natalie's remarks as cute, but incorrect. Today, we realize that she is demonstrating a great deal of literacy knowledge that needs to be recognized. First, she knows what letters are, and she can identify the ones on the sign. Next, she knows that letters spell words. She knows that words are read and have meaning. Although she did not read the word correctly, she made an informed guess. Through utilizing background knowledge, Natalie was aware that this building was a department store. Even though she had never been to this one, she called it by a store name she was familiar with. Her mother offered encouraging reinforcement for what Natalie did know and helped her with the correct response when she needed help. Her mother continued the learning experience by asking Natalie if any of the letters in Marshalls were in her name.

Babies begin to acquire information about literacy from the moment they are born. They continue to build their knowledge of oral language, reading, and writing as they grow. A great deal of attention must focus on literacy development in early childhood. Research demonstrates that teachers, parents, and administrators must view young children as having literacy skills even though the literacy demonstrated by them is not conventional like adults. Early literacy behaviors have implications for instructional practice and later reading success.

MyLab Education
Video Example 2.1
Literacy Development
In this video, Dr. Lesley Morrow discusses literacy development. http://www.youtube.com/watch?v=c8A38PdipDc

Like a child's first words and first steps, learning to read and write should be exciting and rewarding. This book draws on research and blends it with theory, policy, and practice that have proved successful in developing literacy. It presents a program for developing children's literacy from birth to 9 years. This book takes into account the joint position statement of the International Reading Association (IRA) and the National Association for the Education of Young Children entitled *Learning to Read and Write: Developmentally Appropriate Practices for Young Children* (1998) and the position statement by the IRA, *Literacy Development in the Preschool Years* (2006). It also considers the *National Reading Panel Report* (2000), *National Early Literacy Report* (National Center for Family Literacy, 2004), *Common Core State Standards* (CCSS, 2011), and the concept of mindset (Dweck, 2007) The rationale for the book includes the following beliefs:

1. Literacy learning begins in infancy.
2. Families need to continuously provide a literacy-rich environment and literacy experiences at home to help children acquire skills.
3. Children come to school with unique and prior knowledge about reading and writing and teachers need to build on their existing information.
4. Literacy learning requires a supportive environment that builds positive feelings about self and literacy activities. There must be a mindset established that says to the child, "You can do this."

5. Literacy learning requires a school environment rich with accessible materials and varied experiences.
6. Teachers must serve as models for literacy behavior by scaffolding or demonstrating strategies to be learned.
7. Children should socially interact during literacy experiences, share information and learn from one another.
8. Reading and writing experiences must motivate children by being engaging, concrete, relevant, and evidenced-based best practice.
9. Early reading and writing experiences need to provide systematic and explicit instruction.
10. Literacy development should focus on experiences that integrate reading, writing, listening, speaking, and embed these language arts into content areas such as social studies, science, and so on.
11. Diversity in culture and language backgrounds must be addressed in early literacy development.
12. Differences in literacy development will vary and must be addressed with small-group and one-to-one differentiated instruction.
13. Struggling readers must be provided with early intervention programs in addition to the regular literacy instruction.
14. Assessment of achievement should be frequent and guide instruction. Multiple formats for evaluating a student's literacy development should be used.
15. For children to read fluently by the end of third grade, standards for early literacy grade-level must be acknowledged.
16. Instruction must be age appropriate for the development of children, with high and achievable expectations.

This book incorporates the work of philosophers, educators, psychologists, and researchers who have described how young children learn and what they need to be taught. The book emphasizes that literacy development occurs in prepared, literacy-rich environments where planned experiences facilitate development in reading, writing, listening, speaking, and viewing in coordination with content-area subjects. Although some chapters concentrate on language, reading, or writing, an important concern at all times is the integration of all these literacy dimensions. In early childhood, literacy instruction should occur all day long. It should be explicit, embedded, and spontaneous.

Literacy development must focus on both learning and teaching. Teachers must explicitly instruct children while also encouraging them to be actively involved in collaborative learning experiences, using materials with which they can explore and experiment. A major focus of the book is to motivate children to view reading as a relevant act and associate it with pleasure. Children must understand that reading is a source of information that is valuable for them to learn to succeed in life. According to statistics from the U.S. Department of Education, Justice, and Health and research by Assel, Landry, Swank, and Gunnewig (2007), those who are functionally illiterate are likely to:

- Drop out of high school
- Have behavior and social problems that result in being incarcerated
- Be chronically ill
- Live in poverty
- Have children who are likely to be illiterate.

Alternatively, those who learn to read are likely to:

- Graduate from high school and possibly college
- Have strong social skills

- Enjoy a healthier life
- Earn a living to support themselves and a family
- Have children who are literate

Ninety percent of the children who are below grade level in reading at the beginning of fourth grade, although they can improve, will never reach grade level. Therefore the early childhood teacher has a tremendous responsibility.

Historical Roots of Early Childhood Education: How the Theories Effected Literacy Instruction

Early childhood education is not a recent development. Since the 1700s, philosophers, theorists, psychologists, and educators have addressed appropriate educational practice for learning in early childhood. They address the issue of whether learning to read is a matter of nature or nurture, both of which have implications for early literacy instruction in contemporary education.

Rousseau (1712–1778)

Jean-Jacques Rousseau was a philosopher, writer, and composer in the 1700s. In his work titled *Émile* (1762), Rousseau recommended that a child's early education be natural. That is, children should only be asked to learn things for which they are developmentally

Photo courtesy of Lesley Mandel Morrow

According to Pestalozzi, Froebel, Dewey, as well as other philosophers and theorists, learning in early childhood occurs when youngsters have the opportunity to explore, experiment, and play at real-life experiences.

ready. Rousseau advocated abandoning contrived instruction in favor of allowing children to learn with the freedom to be themselves. According to Rousseau, children learn through curiosity. He believed that children have individual ways of learning and that formal instruction can interfere with development. Rousseau's philosophy suggests that there should be little adult intervention as possible for young children.

Pestalozzi (1746–1827)

Johann Heinrich Pestalozzi (Rusk & Scotland, 1979) believed in natural learning, but he added another dimension. He developed principles for learning that combined natural elements with informal instruction. He found it unrealistic to expect children to learn to read completely on their own, he believed that it was necessary for teachers to create the conditions in which the reading process grows. He suggested that children develop through sensory manipulative experiences, so he designed lessons that involved manipulating objects he called "gifts." Children learned about them through touch, smell, language, size, and shape.

Froebel (1782–1852)

Friedrich Wilhelm August Froebel also believed in the natural unfolding of a child; and followed Pestalozzi's ideas by providing plans for instructing young children (Rusk & Scotland, 1979). Froebel stressed the importance of play in learning. He felt that the benefits of playing to learn required adult guidance and a planned environment. The teacher was a designer of playful activities that facilitate learning. He was the first educator to design a systematic curriculum for young children that included objects and materials. In handling and playing with these materials, children learned about shape, color, size, measurement, and comparison. Many of Froebel's strategies are used in early childhood classrooms today, such as circle time when the class sings songs and learns new ideas through discussion. He coined the term *kindergarten*, which means "children's garden." This illustrated his philosophy that, such as seeds, children grow if they are tended to and cared for by the gardener, or teacher.

MyLab Education Self-Check 2.1

The Evolution of Theory and Practice in Early Childhood Education across the Twentieth-Century

Out of the philosophies of the eighteenth and nineteenth centuries evolved the theories and practices that defined early childhood education across the twentieth and twenty-first centuries. Of course there were and are still numerous other theories to mention.

Teaching English Learners

Dewey's thoughts about building on children's interests through themes is helpful with English Language Learners.

Dewey—Progressive Education

John Dewey's (1966) philosophy of early childhood education led to the concept of the **child-centered curriculum**, or *progressive education* as it was called. Dewey believed that curriculum should be built around the interests of children and that children learn through play in real-life settings. He maintained that social interactions encourage learning and that themes of interest to children, such as learning about dinosaurs, are the vehicles for learning information and skills. Dewey rejected the idea of teaching skills as ends unto themselves. He also believed that learning is maximized through integrating content areas.

Dewey influenced programs in United States early childhood education. Classrooms reflecting Dewey's ideas contained centers for different activities and content areas. Shelves held various sizes and shapes of blocks, toy trucks, and figures of people. An art area had easels with paint, crayons, paste, scissors, construction paper, clay, scraps of fabric, pipe cleaners, and so on. The dramatic-play center looked like a kitchen, with a sink, oven, refrigerator, empty food boxes, table and chairs, telephone, mirror, dolls, and some clothing for dressing up. A science area revealed a water-play table, tables with shells, rocks, plants, a class animal, and magnets. The music area had a piano, rhythm instruments, and, at that time, a record player. There was a rug for children to sit on when they came to sing by the piano. One corner of the room had a shelf of children's literature and soft pillows to lie on when looking at books.

The day in kindergarten began as children played with quiet toys. Then circle time on a rug to talk about the weather and the calendar. The conversation focused on a theme being studied with a social studies or science topic, for example: animals or community helpers. Children sang about the theme. Circle time was commonly followed by a period of free play in which children could use the materials in the different areas of the room. There was minimal guidance during free play. A snack was followed by a rest period. The day included a special lesson in art, social studies, or science appropriate to the theme being studied. Outdoor play allowed children to run and climb. The teacher read a story daily, and related it to a class theme.

Reading and mathematics were not taught formally or as isolated skills. Instead, the teacher might ask a child to count out enough cookies for the children in the class, to name the date on the calendar, or to compare the sizes of different children. In the area of language arts she might list some of the words used in the theme and discuss them. There were no workbooks or commercial reading materials. Teachers led informal activities that could lead to reading, but they did not explicitly teach children to read. The letters of the alphabet could be strung across the wall, the days of the week pointed out on a calendar, children's names written on their cubbies, and other items in the room labeled with words. The goal was to accustom children to school routines and make them comfortable in this environment. The focus was on social, emotional, physical, and intellectual development of the children as a whole with minimal formal instruction in reading and writing.

Skinner—Behaviorism

At about the same time that Dewey was advocating progressive education, behaviorists were taking a different approach to learning. According to behaviorists, the outcome of learning is a permanent change in behavior that is caused by a response to an experience or stimulus (Slavin, 1997). Behaviorists suggest that we learn through imitation *and* association, and *through* conditioning, or a series of steps that are repeated so that the response becomes automatic. B. F. Skinner (1954) found that human learning was not automatic and unintentional, as it required explicit instruction. Skinner's research demonstrated that positive reinforcement for a desired behavior increased the use of that behavior. Skills are acquired in a series of steps, small enough to avoid failure, with rewards at each level. A *behaviorist learning perspective* includes an organized program presented in a systematic and direct manner. Learning requires time on task, structure, routines, and practice. Behaviorist programs are skill based, with little time for social, emotional, or physical development; the main concern is the acquisition of cognitive skills. The materials are rated according to difficulty and are often programmed sequential lessons. The programs provide objectives for learning and then a script for the teacher using direct instruction as demonstrated below (Engelmann & Bruner, 1969):

Teacher:	*sh, sh, sh.* What sound is this?
Wait for Response:	*sh, sh, sh.* Good.
Teacher:	*sh, sh, sh.* Now you say *sh.*
Wait for Response:	Yes, *sh, sh.* Good.

Some reading programs that use behaviorist methods are DISTAR: Direct Instruction System for Teaching Arithmetic and Reading (Englemann & Bruner, 1969), Programmed Reading Series (Sullivan & Buchanan, 1963), and Success for All (Slavin, 1997).

We all use behaviorism in classrooms with routines and rules however the theory of learning just discussed is often not viewed as child-friendly. There are ways to use the **explicit instruction** in an engaging manner. At the end of the chapter is a behavioristic child-friendly lesson from a classroom that demonstrates explicit instruction done well.

Montessori—Senses and Systems

Maria Montessori (1965) believed that children needed early, orderly, systematic training in order to master skills. She created an environment supplied with materials for learning concepts to meet specific objectives. The use of the materials is modeled by the teacher, which the child imitates. The materials were manipulatives and self-correcting; therefore, the children could determine their errors and make corrections. There are precise steps to complete each task correctly. Materials were stored in their own containers, on a particular shelf, and in order of difficulty. According to Montessori, the teacher is a guide who prepares an environment with materials designed to teach specific skills.

Montessori materials had children using their five senses of touch, taste, smell, hearing, and sight, children learn about size, color, and shape by manipulating materials designed to teach these skills. The curriculum includes learning reading and math, which are taught using manipulative materials. Early reading instruction includes learning the sounds of letters more than the names of letters, with the help of cards that have raised textured letters. Children trace the cards as they make the sound. Sight words are taught using real objects and pictures. Montessori's curriculum is based on behaviorist theory. Children's curiosity and exploration are of less concern than working with a material to achieve a goal.

Piaget—Cognitive Development

Jean Piaget's (Piaget & Inhelder, 1969) theory of cognitive development describes the intellectual capabilities of children at their different stages of cognitive development. The stages are as follows:

1. **Sensorimotor period (0–2 years):** Thoughts are determined by sensory explorations as a baby hears, sees, tastes, and feels.
2. **Preoperational period (2–7):** A child's language develops, and thinking is concrete. The child begins to organize his world.
3. **Concrete operational period (7–11):** The child begins his thought processes in the concrete and is able to eventually move into some abstract ideas.
4. **Formal operations period (11–adult):** This high level of thinking involves using language to deal with abstract thought.

Piaget believed that a child acquires knowledge by interacting with the world. Educators who have applied his theories involve children in natural problem-solving situations where they learn through assimilation and accommodation. **Assimilation** means that the child incorporates new information into existing schemes. That is, she interprets new information she has from the past. For example, when Michael saw a cat for the first time, he said, "Look at the dog, Mommy." Michael used what he knew about four-legged animals from his experience with dogs and applied it to the cat, an animal he had never seen. **Accommodation** requires changing existing schemes to incorporate new information. A child accommodates when a new situation is unfamiliar. In this situation, the child has to create a new response. Michael, for example, knows what dogs do and look like, such as bark and have four legs. When he perceived a cat to be a dog, he had assimilated the new experience with reference to his present comprehension level. The complementary process of accommodation may be engaged when the child finds that the new object is not a dog,

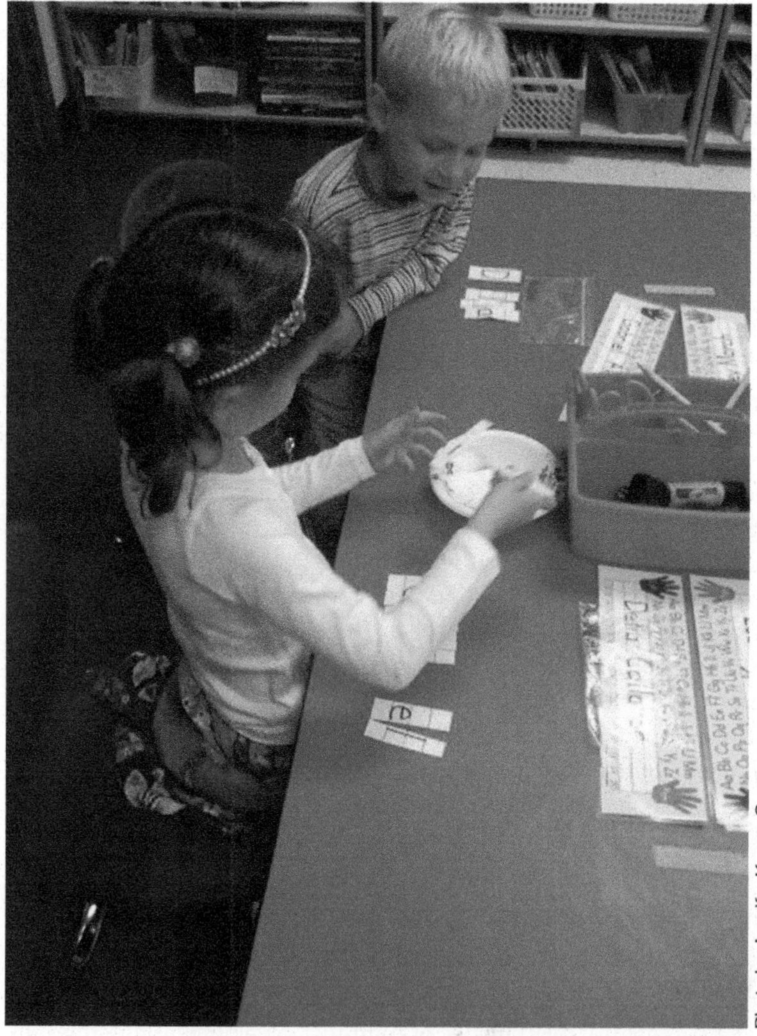

Piaget stressed that learning occurs when children interact with peers and adults in a social setting as they act on the environment.

Photo by Jennifer Kamm Greco

MyLab Education
Video Example 2.2
Piaget's Cognitive Development
In this video, a Piagetian preschool curriculum, High Scope, is discussed. https://www.youtube.com/watch?v=4oGnvxzOqDw

but rather a cat, and that the cat meows and doesn't bark. His conceptual understanding of "cat" must be refined due to the incongruity; he accommodates his thoughts to fit the reality more accurately. According to Piaget, children need to be active participants in their learning by changing and reorganizing their knowledge. Learning occurs when children interact in their environment with peers and adults. Educators who have incorporated Piaget's theories in curricula have designed constructivist type programs: a setting with many real-life materials, including the opportunities to play, explore, experiment, and use language. A Piagetian preschool curriculum, called High Scope, encourages decision making, problem solving, self-discipline, goal setting, planning one's own activities, and cooperating with teachers and peers. Piaget agreed that young children should use their curiosity and spontaneity to learn. His theories do not stress content-area centers such as math and science. The Piaget curriculum has centers that involve children in cognitive activities such as:

1. **Language development:** Talking, listening to stories, and describing.
2. **Classifying:** Describing attributes of objects, to notice sameness and (differences, sort, match, and so on).
3. **Seriating:** Placing objects in a particular order, typically by size.
4. **Representing in different modalities:** Learning about something in many different ways; for example, to learn about an apple, eat an apple, make applesauce, draw an apple, write and read the word *apple*, sing a song about apples, and so on.
5. **Spatial relations:** Children are asked to put things together, take things apart, rearrange things, reshape things, see things from a different point of view, describe direction or distance, and so on.

Vygotsky—Schema Acquisition

Lev S. Vygotsky's (1978) general theory suggest that learning occurs as children acquire new concepts. The new concepts are considered **schema** which are mental structures where people store information. When needed, we call the stored information to mind to help make predictions, generalizations, or inferences. According to Vygotsky, new concepts are acquired as children interact with others who provide feedback for their thoughts. This interaction helps them complete a task they could not do alone. Parents and teachers who are more knowledgeable need to *scaffold* how to complete new tasks for children by modeling what it looks like. The **scaffolding** directs a children's attention to what they need to know and do. Children learn by internalizing the activities and language of others into their world. Vygotsky speaks of the "zone of proximal development" when a child can do some parts of a task but not all. This is when the adult steps back and allows the child to take responsivity to practice on his own to internalize the task. (Ankrum, Genest, & Belcastro, 2014; Muhonen, Rasku-Puttonen, Pakarinen, Poikkeus, A., & Lerkkanen, 2016).

MyLab Education
Video Example 2.3
Vygotsky's Zone of Proximal Development

In this video, Vygotsky's concept of zone of proximal development is explained and reviewed. http://www.youtube.com/watch?v=0BX2ynEqLL4

MyLab Education Application Exercise 2.1

Reading Readiness

Developmental psychologists advocated maturation as the most important factor in learning to read. Preschool and kindergarten teachers were told to avoid reading instruction because such young children were not ready to read. Morphett and Washburne's (1931) research found that children who were developmentally 6 years and 6 months were old enough for reading instruction. They would make better progress. Uncomfortable about waiting for children to mature, educators began to provide experiences they believed would help prepare children for reading.

In the 1930s and 1940s, standardized tests were developed that included sections of specific skills used to indicate whether a child had reached the maturity to be ready to learn to read. The term **reading readiness** became popular; instead of waiting for a child's maturation to unfold, educators focused on nurturing that maturation through instruction in skills seen as prerequisites for reading. Skills identified in Reading Readiness are skills that students need. Some of the large motor skills such as walking a balance beam and skipping aren't required before teaching children to read .The skills included are:

1. **Auditory discrimination:** the ability to identify and differentiate familiar sounds, similar sounds, rhyming words, and the sounds of letters;
2. **Visual discrimination:** including color recognition, shape, and letter identification;
3. **Visual motor skills:** such as left-to-right eye progression, cutting on a line with scissors, and coloring within the lines of a picture; and
4. **Large motor skills:** such as skipping, hopping, and walking on a line. The reading-readiness model implies that children prepare for literacy by acquiring these four skills.

These skills are taught systematically on the assumption that all children are at a similar level of development when they come to preschool or kindergarten with little concern for experiences and information that children may already have. However, educators discovered that some children could read without the knowledge of many of the skills outlined, and some children mastered the skills but had difficulty learning to read. Some of these skills were indicators of readiness for reading, others were not.

The Research Era

Between the 1960s and the 1980s, researchers investigating early childhood literacy development brought about many changes in practice. Investigators looked at the cognitive development of the child using varied research methodologies such as experimental studies with treatment and control groups, correlational research, interviews, observations, videotapes, and case studies. The research was done in diverse cultural and socioeconomic settings. It took place in classrooms and homes, rather than in laboratories, as in the past. Research in the areas of oral language development, family literacy, and early reading and writing had a strong impact on educators understanding the processes involved in becoming literate, how children learn, and how to teach initial reading and writing.

MyLab Education Self-Check 2.2

Key Approaches to Early Childhood Literacy

In early childhood literacy, two approaches shared the stage. The **constructivist** theory views learning as an active process by which children construct knowledge by problem solving, guessing, and approximating. In contrast, explicit instruction views learning as a teacher-directed activity with emphasis on teaching a task and the specific steps needed to master it; for example teaching reading through phonics. The balanced comprehensive approach attempts to blend these two key approaches for more effective outcomes.

The field of literacy tends to vacillate about theories and method. For a period of time, educators embraced constructivist thinking and promoted exploration and experimentation on the part of the child. Then, either switched to championing direct, explicit instruction or rely more heavily on phonics and other direct methods. These swings often include widespread changes in instructional materials and instructional strategies.

Emergent Literacy

To acquire literacy skills, children need models to emulate and to create their own forms of reading, writing, and speaking. This is called an **emergent literacy** perspective in preschool and kindergarten. The emergent literacy perspective exposes children to books early; it is a child-centered approach where social interaction and problem solving is emphasized with less direct instruction of skills.

Emergent literacy, a phrase first used by Marie Clay (1966), assumes that the child acquires some knowledge about language, reading, and writing before coming to school. Literacy development begins early in life and is ongoing. There is a relationship among the communication skills (reading, writing, oral language, and listening) because each influences the other in the course of development. Development occurs in everyday contexts of the home, community, and school through meaningful and functional experiences that require the use of literacy in natural settings. For example, when a child "pretend reads" a book that is a sign of emergent literacy behavior. The settings for the acquisition of literacy are often social, with adults and children interacting through collaboration and modeling. To provide meaning and purpose, literacy activities occur and are embedded within content areas such as art, music, play, social studies, and science. For example, in art, children are given directions to read for making play dough.

At every age, children possess certain literacy skills, but these skills are not as yet fully developed or conventional (Baumann, Hoffman, Duffy-Hester, & Rowe, 2000; Morris & Slavin, 2003). Emergent literacy acknowledges a child's scribble marks on a page as rudimentary writing, even if not one letter is discernible. The child who knows the difference between such scribbles and drawings knows the difference between writing and illustrations. Similarly, when children narrate familiar storybooks while looking at the pictures and print and give the impression of reading, we acknowledge the activity as literacy behavior, but not conventional reading. Emergent literacy accepts children at the level they are functioning and provides a program for instruction based on individual needs.

MyLab Education Application Exercise 2.2

Constructivism and Whole-Language Instruction

Whole-language instruction is similar to the emergent literacy perspective, but it considers children who are reading conventionally. Advocates of whole language support the constructivist perspective and natural approaches to learning. In a whole-language approach, literacy learning is child centered because it is designed to be meaningful, relevant, and functional. Learning to read is based on a child's life experiences at home, his interests, or those created in school. For example, if a beehive is discovered at school and removed by an exterminator, children may be interested in discussing, reading, or writing about bees. Although learning about bees is not a part of the curriculum, the teacher allows children to pursue this teachable moment (Collins & Shaeffer, 1997; Fingon, 2005).

Literacy activities are integrated into the learning of content-area subjects such as art, music, social studies, science, math, and play. The use of social studies and science themes connects literacy and content area experiences. Skills are taught when they seem appropriate; for example, in the unit on farms, when the class hatches baby chicks in an incubator, journals may be kept on the progress of the chicks, and the digraph *ch* could be emphasized. In art, children draw farms, sing farm songs, visit a farm, and learn *some* scientific and social studies information about the farm. Topics are selected by the children and teacher, or spontaneously based on something of interest that occurs in school, in someone's home, or in the world.

Equal emphasis is placed on teaching reading, writing, listening, and oral language, because all of these components help create a literate individual. In the past, this program has been referred to as an **integrated language arts** approach. Themes are studied through the use of varied genres of children's literature that provides the main source of reading material for instruction. Classrooms are rich with literacy materials throughout the room and housed in literacy centers. This design is often called a *rich-literacy environment* (Gelzheiser, Hallgren-Flynn, Connors, & Scanlon, 2014).

In a classroom that uses holistic strategies, teachers place more emphasis on learning than on teaching. Learning is self-regulated and individualized, with self-selection and choices of literacy activities. Rather than teach lessons in literacy, teachers provide experiences that engage children in literacy activities. Social interaction is encouraged with children along with opportunities for peer tutoring. Children learn through practice by engaging in long periods of independent reading and writing and sharing what is learned—by reading to others and presenting written pieces to an audience. A major objective of this approach is an emphasis on the joy of reading and the development of lifelong readers.

In classrooms that use holistic approaches, skills are taught when they are relevant and meaningful. In whole-language classrooms, themes (such as the rain forest) are studied. The teacher may focus on some letters and sounds found in the vocabulary of the current theme (such as names of animals in the rain forest). In early implementation of whole-language programs, some individuals thought that skills were not to be taught in any systematic way; children would acquire necessary skills by being immersed in experiences with reading children's literature and writing. Certainly, skills are assimilated through this immersion approach, but specific skills, such as decoding strategies, require explicit instruction by the teacher.

Commercial materials do not dictate the instructional program, although they may be used. Literacy learning is embedded throughout the curriculum during the school day. Large blocks of time are needed for projects. Children often read independently;

however, there was little accountability for what was read. Whole language, the integrated language arts approach, and emergent literacy are similar in practice and use a social constructivist approach to learning with very limited explicit instruction.

Explicit Instruction and Phonics or Sound–Symbol Relationships

During the mid-1980s and early 1990s, whole-language instruction began to be criticized because test scores seemed to indicate that children were not acquiring literacy skills needed to become fluent readers. Many educators misunderstood the philosophy and thought that whole language meant teaching children only as a whole class. Thus, teachers stopped meeting with small groups of children for instruction to handle individual needs. Many educators also made the incorrect presumption that whole language meant you shouldn't teach phonics (sound symbol relationship, e.g., *t* has the sound of *tuh*). Phonics would be learned through immersion into literature with spontaneous and contextual teaching of skills instead of explicit instruction. As a result of the misinterpretations, many children received little or no instruction in phonics. *Many schools did not follow or monitor a scope or sequence of skill development.* Because of misinterpretation, inadequate professional development, and incorrect implementation, many children did not develop skills they needed to become fluent, independent readers.

The pendulum began to swing again to those who favored an approach to early literacy development with more explicit use of phonics; these individuals cited many studies to substantiate their claims. According to Juel (1989), as children begin to experiment with reading and writing, they need to focus on the sounds that make up words. As a precursor to learning how to use *phonics* (sound–symbol relationships), children need the ability to rhyme words, hear syllables or parts of words, know that words are made up of individual sounds, segment sounds out of the words, and blend them together. These skills are called *phonological awareness* and *phonemic awareness*. Phonological and phonemic awareness instruction in preschool, kindergarten, and first grade strengthens reading achievement (Byrne & Fielding-Barnsley, 1993, 1995; Stanovich, 1986). With phonological and phonemic awareness, children can then learn principles of phonics, including (1) alphabetic knowledge (knowing that words are composed of letters) and (2) sound–symbol relationships (knowing that there is a relationship between printed letters and spoken sounds). Research results report that knowledge of sound–symbol relationships, or phonics, is necessary for learning to read and write (Anthony & Lonigan, 2004; Lonigan, 2006). Chapter 8 covers phonological awareness, phonemic awareness, and phonics in greater detail.

A behaviorist or direct-skills approach for literacy instruction proposes the use of a strong phonics programs in early literacy. The materials for instruction provide systematic, explicit instruction of skills with scripted guides for teachers.

Statistics surrounding achievement, coupled with current political beliefs and school leadership, determine the type of reading instruction that is adopted. Research has proven, however, that no single approach produces better results than another. First-grade studies (Bond & Dykstra, 1967a, 1967b) tried to answer the question: Which method is best for early literacy development? This classic research pooled the findings from 27 independent studies conducted from 1964 to 1967. Bond and Dykstra ultimately concluded that no one method was more effective than another such that it should be used exclusively. What has been found is that exemplary teachers are the key to successful literacy instruction (Pressley, Allington, Wharton-McDonald, Block, & Morrow, 2001).

Balanced Comprehensive Approach

The International Reading Association's (now called the International Literacy Association) wrote *Position Statement: Using Multiple Methods of Beginning Reading Instruction* (1999), which suggests that no single method or single combination of methods can successfully teach all children to read. Teachers must know the social, emotional, physical, and intellectual status of the children they teach. They must also be well versed in the various processes involved and methods for reading instruction. Only then can educators develop a comprehensive plan for teaching reading to meet individual needs. This perspective on literacy instruction, which emerged as a result of the whole language versus phonics discussion, is a *balanced comprehensive approach (BCA)*. The use of a BCA includes careful selection of the best theories and research based practices available and matches teaching to the learning styles of individual children to help them learn to read. Both skill-based explicit instruction and holistic constructivist ideas, which include problem-solving strategies, might be used (Morrow & Tracey, 1997). Explicit teaching of skills is a start for constructivist problem-solving activities, and constructivist activities permit consolidation and elaboration of skills. One method does not preclude the other (Pressley, 1998). Figure 2.1 outlines a balanced comprehensive approach to literacy.

A BCA is not a random combination of strategies, nor is it a formula that uses whole-class, small-group, and one-on-one instruction in the same format continuously. A teacher must select strategies from different learning theories to provide appropriate balance. One child, for example, may be a visual learner who derives little benefit from instruction in phonics; another child, whose strength may be auditory learning, will

Teaching English Learners

Teachers need to know many strategies for teaching children to read and select ones that work for individual children. Children who are EL for example, might need more time with vocabulary instruction than others.

Figure 2.1 Strategies and Structures in a Balanced Comprehensive Approach

SOURCE: Adapted from L. M. Morrow, D. S. Strickland, and D. G. Woo, *Literacy Instruction in Half- and Whole-Day Kindergarten: Research to Practice* (Fig. 2, p. 76). Newark, DE: International Reading Association. Copyright © 1998 by the International Reading Association

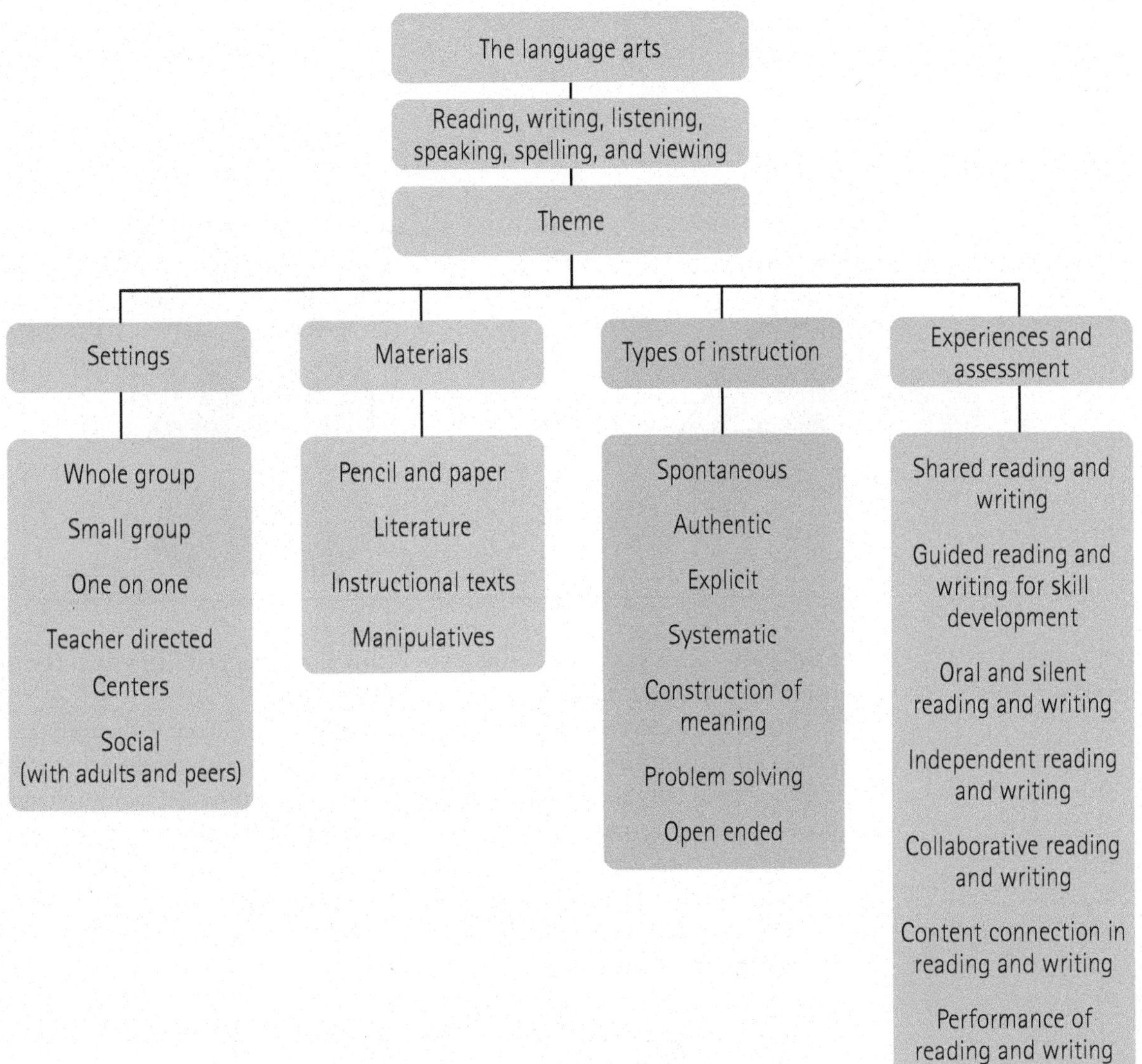

Figure 2.2 Constructivist and Explicit Behaviorist Lesson Plans for "The Three Bears"

DIRECTIONS: Photocopy, color, and laminate figures on firm paper. Cut and then paste felt on the back and tell the story to the children using the figures and a felt board. Have the children retell the story as they heard it. Next, ask the children to tell the story again but create a new ending.

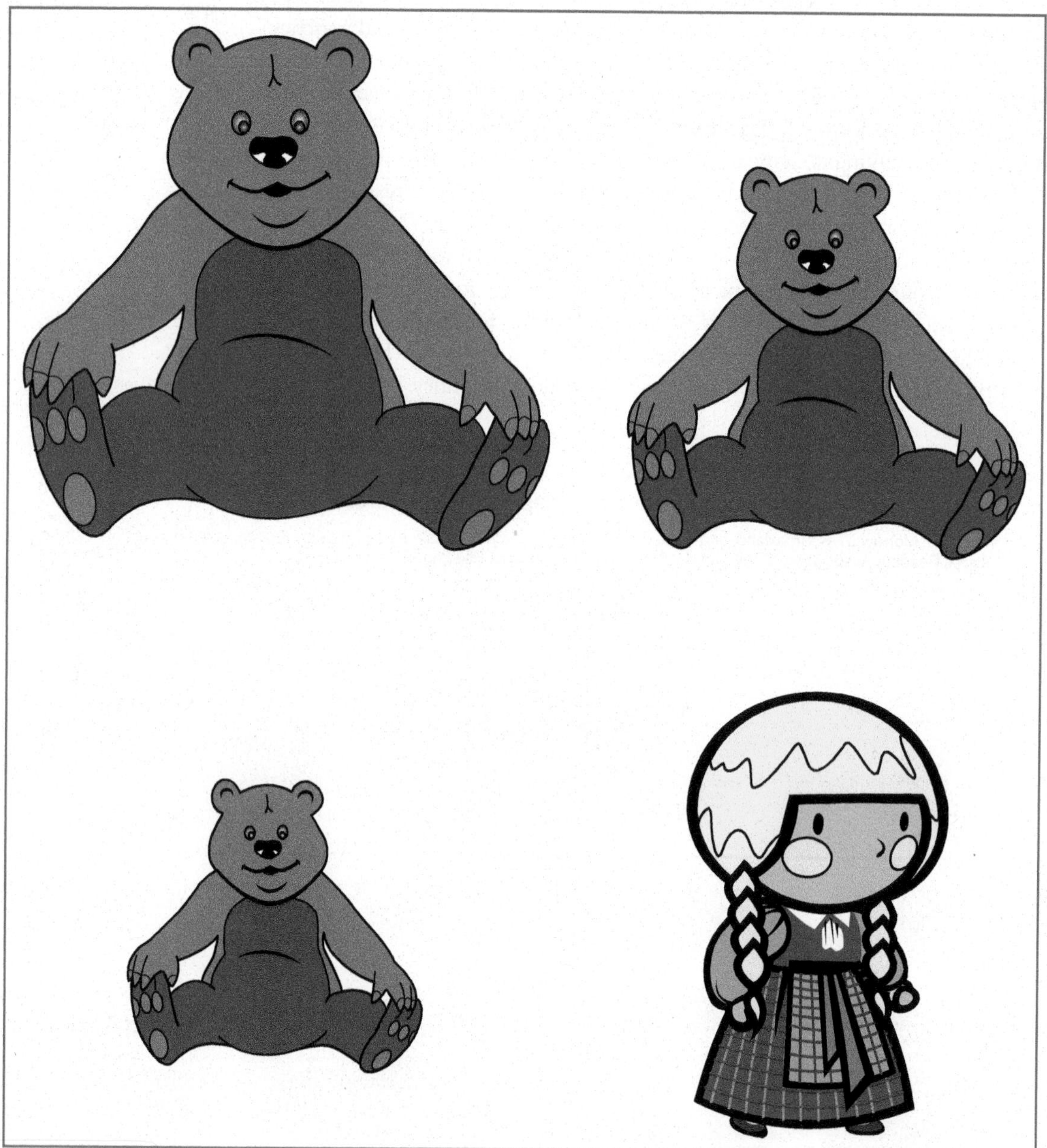

learn best from a great deal of phonics instruction. The BCA approach focuses more heavily on what is important for individual children.

Balanced instruction is grounded in a rich model of literacy learning that encompasses the elegance and complexity of literacy processes. This model acknowledges the importance of both form (phonics and mechanics) and function (comprehension, purpose, and meaning) of the literacy processes. This type of instruction is characterized by meaningful literacy activities that provide children with both the skill and motivation to become proficient and lifelong literacy learners (Snow & Matthews, 2016).

Figures 2.2 and 2.3 illustrate a lesson that engages children in both explicit and constructivist activities.

MyLab Education Self-Check 2.3

Figure 2.2 Constructivist and Explicit Behaviorist Lesson Plans for "The Three Bears" (*continued*)

Figure 2.3 Sequencing Strips for "The Three Bears"

Directions: Cut out strips and arrange them in the correct order of events. Technology Link: Video record children in an explicit instruction lesson and in a constructivist setting. Note the differences in how they pay attention (or don't) and how involved they are (or aren't)

Once upon a time, Goldilocks was wandering through the woods.

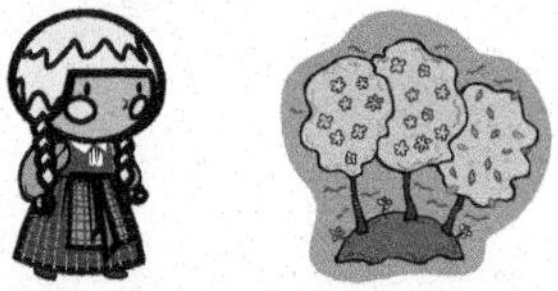

She came across the three bears' house and walked inside.

First she saw three bowls of porridge.

She tried the first bowl, but it was too cold.

She tried the second bowl, but it was too hot.

She tried the third bowl and it was just right.

Next she saw three chairs.

She sat in the first chair, but it was too small.

She sat in the second chair, but it was too big.

She sat in the medium-size chair and it was just right.

Figure 2.3 Sequencing Strips for "The Three Bears" (*continued*)

Then Goldilocks went into the bedroom and saw three beds. 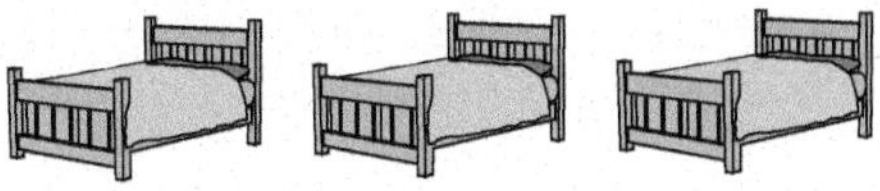
The first bed was way too big. 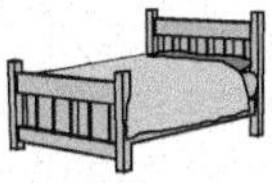
The second bed was way too small. 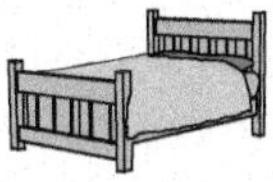
The third bed was just right, so she fell asleep. 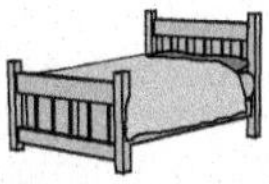
Soon after, the three bears came home. 
They noticed that someone had been sitting in their chairs. 
They noticed that someone had been eating their porridge. 
They noticed that someone had been sleeping in their beds. 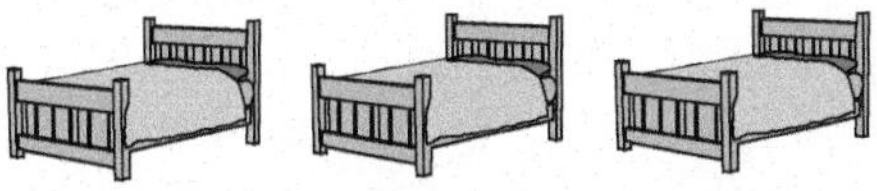
Little Bear found Goldilocks in his bed and screamed! Goldilocks woke up, ran out the door, and never came back again. 

The Effects of Evidence-Based Research and Public Policy on Early Literacy

Throughout the twentieth century until about the 1960s, federal educational policy was mostly voluntary. Schools were governed locally; with varied teaching models accepted with limited accountability, especially to the federal government. As time passed, documents that came from the federal government became more prescriptive. The federal government also engaged in more of its own research as a way to improve policy decisions. As a result, today there is more centralized authority and greater accountability. Evidence-based research and public policy have had significant effects on early literacy initiatives and practices.

Teaching English Learners

It is important to use research-based strategies with English Language Learners.

National Reading Panel Report

The National Reading Panel Report (2000) was a significant meta-analysis that revealed key elements to literacy success. The report presents findings about the most effective strategies for teaching children to read in grades kindergarten through third grade. The panel reviewed more than 100,000 studies to come up with its results. Panelists admit, however, that some areas that may be important to literacy instruction, such as writing development and motivation for reading, were not studied because of a lack of adequate numbers of high-quality investigations to analyze. In addition, only randomized experimental studies with treatment and control groups were selected for analysis. Other research designs, such as qualitative or case study and correlational, were not included because the designs did not meet with the panel's criteria. Although the report was published in 2000 it still has a strong effect on early literacy instruction. The results of the report indicate that learning the following processes were crucial to becoming a fluent reader by the end of third grade:

- Phonemic awareness (individual sounds are in words)
- Phonics (sound–symbol relationships)
- Vocabulary (learning the meaning of many words in order to understand what is read)
- Comprehension (being able to understand what is read)
- Fluency (reading with expression and appropriate speed).

Writing, independent reading, and motivation were not studied because there wasn't enough scientifically based research to determine if these were predictors of literacy success. However, it is generally accepted among literacy researchers that these elements are necessary for successful literacy development.

National Early Literacy Panel Report

The National Early Literacy Panel (2008) studied existing scientifically based research to identify the skills and abilities of young children from birth through age 5 that predict later achievement in reading. After identifying the variables, the panel determined environments, settings, programs, and interventions that contribute to or inhibit the skills that are linked to later outcomes in reading. The variables the panel identified as those that needed to be acquired by the end of kindergarten were:

Teaching English Learners

When working with young English Language Learners we are more likely to be successful in their acquisition of the second language than when they are older.

- Knows the letters of the alphabet and sounds of the letter.
- Knows that words are made up of individual sounds, this is called *phonological awareness.*
- Can rapidly name letters and numbers.
- Can identify colors, can remember names of a set of pictures.
- Can write their name and letters.
- Can remember what was said to them for a while.
- Knows that words are read from left to right, books are read from front to back, can show you the cover of a book, the text, and so on.
- Can produce or comprehend spoken language.

One important conclusion from the report is that involving children in appropriate activities will help them develop in these listed areas. Schools whose students do not score well on measures testing for these variables will be identified as needing help. There were Early Reading First grants for schools to improve preschool and kindergarten programs.

No Child Left Behind

Federal research into early childhood literacy influenced policy decisions. In January 2001, the No Child Left Behind Act (NCLB) was passed by the Bush administration. This nonpartisan program had extensive involvement of the federal government with grants to improve literacy in grades K–3 with strong accountability required. The goal of NCLB was for every child in the United States to become a fluent reader by the end of grade 3. The legislation was designed to close the achievement gap in literacy development between socioeconomic classes and prevent literacy problems early. To qualify for these grants, states had to identify the reading assessments and programs in use and demonstrate that the programs were reliable, valid, and scientifically or evidence based.

The use of financial incentives for districts to achieve continued under the Obama administration, which launched the 2010 Race to the Top grant program for underachieving schools.

As with the Reading First grants, Race to the Top grants include teachers were specified components to enhance educational outcomes. In Race to the Top (RTT), for example, grant recipients were held accountable for student scores on standardized tests and were obligated to implement merit pay for teachers whose children scored well. Many believe that these initiatives intensified test-preparation activities because teachers were evaluated on their outcomes. The educational community, concerned that using one test as the measure for success, would have a negative effect on the curriculum. The RTT program was discontinued in 2016.

Common Core State Standards

Standards are a staple of American schools and curriculum since the late 90s. Schools find their academic lives shaped by whatever standards become a priority where they live. There was an effort to develop national standards that creates a clear statement of what students should know and be able to do at various developmental levels. Standards attempt to outline the typical progression of student performance, assessments, and curricular schemes. Some states adopted the CCSS, others didn't. There has been variability in the content and quality of standards, and assessments used across states. (Bandeira de Mello, 2011; Polikoff, Porter, & Smithson, 2011). The Common Core State Standards Initiative (2010) was an attempt to reduce that variability.

The Common Core State Standards (CCSS) are a set of goals initiated under the auspices of the National Governors Association (NGA) and the Council of Chief State School Officers (CCSSO). The CCSS attempt to ensure that at the end of K–12, students are prepared to enter either college or the workforce and take their place as knowledgeable, contributing members of the American economy and society. The CCSS were intentionally designed to improve upon the standards of individual states by creating clear, consistent, and rigorous standards for the country, globally, and in a digital world.

The CCSS were established by looking closely at standards and curriculum in consistently high-achieving United States sites and in other countries that are high achievers in literacy.

The CCSS highlights the need for developing literacy and language proficiencies by extending the involvement of the English language arts in the language arts classroom and in content area classrooms as well. The CCSS suggests that an integrated approach should be taken by those teaching English language arts (reading, writing, listening, and speaking) not as separate entities but rather elements to build on each other (Caspergue, 2017).

The CCSS are not a curriculum or methods. Schools and teachers, teach the goals to be attained in their own way and there are assessments to measure achievement. The CCSS have been in effect for a while. Some states have modified them to suit their needs, others continue to use them as written. We will always have standards. Exactly how they will change in the future cannot be determined at the time this book is being written. Different administrations create policy about the teaching of reading.

Teaching English Learners

Kindergarten restaurants demonstrates respect for other cultures as the restaurant changes from one country to another.

MyLab Education Self-Check 2.4

Learning the Initial Consonant *P* (Explicit Instruction)

Explicit Modeling for Children

Teacher: Today we are going to learn about the sound of *P*. Who has a name that starts with a *P*?

Peter: My name does.

Teacher: You are right. Let's everyone say *Peter*.

Class: Peter.

Teacher: Now put your hand up to your mouth and say *Puh, Puh, Puh.*

Class: *Puh, Puh, Puh.*

Teacher: How did it feel?

Nancy: I felt air, and it was warm.

Teacher: Good. I'm going to tell you a story that has a lot of *P* words in it. I will use felt figures to tell the story. Listen and remember your favorite two *P* words so you can tell your neighbor about them after the story. You might hear pig, party, pizza, panda, plums, or purple. The story is called *The Pig's Party.* (See the characters in Figure 2.4. Photocopy, color, laminate, and put felt on the back for use on a felt board or magnets for use on a white board. The characters and items in the story are numbered here and in Figure 2.4.)

Figure 2.4 The Pig's Party

Pink Pig was having a party. He wanted it to be a perfect party. He had invited Patty Pig (1), his favorite pig person, Panda Bear (2), and Proud Peacock (4). He had petunias on the table and there were pizza for dinner and popsicles for dessert. Panda Bear came to the party first, and Pink Pig asked, "How can I look special for Patty Pig?" Panda Bear said, "Borrow my panda bear suit, and you will look perfect." So Pink Pig put on Panda Bear's suit, and he thought he looked perfect (3). Then Proud Peacock came to the party. Pink Pig asked him, "How can I look perfect for the party?" Proud Peacock said, "Take my purple plumes and put them on, and you will look perfect." So he did (4, 5, and 6). Everyone agreed he looked perfect. Patty Pig (7) knocked on the door. Pink Pig opened it. She screamed when she saw Pink Pig; she thought she saw a monster with his purple plumes and panda bear suit, and she ran away. Pink Pig gave back the suit to Panda Bear and the plumes to Proud Peacock and took a petunia to run to find Patty Pig (1 and 8). He found her hiding behind the porch. When she saw Pink Pig she said, "Thank goodness it is you Pink Pig," and they had a perfect party.

Guided Practice

Teacher: Tell your partner the two words you liked the most that started with a *P* in the story.

Josh to Jen: I liked *plumes* and *Patty*.

Jen to Josh: I liked *petunia* and *pizza*.

Teacher: How many of you had the same two words? (Only a few children raise their hands.) How many of you had one word the same? (A few more raise their hands.) How many had two different words? (Most of the class raise their hands.)

Independent Practice

Teacher: I will put the pig story and the felt characters in the literacy center in this plastic baggie and you can tell the story or read the story and write down the *P* words you remember and like the most. There is paper for you to write your words on.

An Idea from the Classroom

Out to Eat: Kindergarten Restaurateurs (Constructivist Theory)

At the end of a unit on nutrition, students in my kindergarten class have the opportunity to create their own restaurant menu. Regardless of the menu they create, students are encouraged to include healthy foods. Students draw on their knowledge of different foods and their personal experiences at various restaurants. As a result, our classroom is filled with menus for Italian restaurants, Mexican restaurants, diners, breakfast bistros, and more. Our kindergartners write and illustrate their own menus, using invented and conventional language.

During our morning meeting each day, several students have the opportunity to share their menus with the class and use persuasive language to try to convince their classmates to visit their restaurant. Then, each week, one or two students set up their "restaurant" for classmates to visit during dramatic play or centers. I assist students by making copies of their menus for their classmate patrons and helping them locate or create the foods they will need using the kitchen area of our classroom. Not only are many speaking and listening standards addressed as students take on the role of restaurant owner, chef, or guest, but students utilize what they've learned in our nutrition unit when deciding what to order!

Amy Monaco, kindergarten teacher

Summary

2.1 Discuss the historical roots of early childhood education.

Theories of early childhood began in the 1700s with Jean-Jacques Rousseau and continued into the 1800s through the work of Johann Heinrich Pestalozzi and Friedrich Froebel. Rousseau advocated abandoning contrived instruction in favor of allowing children to grow and learn with the freedom to be themselves. He believed that education follows the child's own development and readiness for learning. Pestalozzi combined Rousseau's natural learning philosophy with elements of informal instruction, including sensory work with manipulatives. Froebel continued the work of Pestalozzi with an added emphasis on the role of play in learning.

2.2 Discuss the evolution of theory and practice in early childhood education across the twentieth century.

Many theories define the evolution and practice of early childhood education in the twentieth century. Progressive education, advocated by John Dewey, argued that curriculum should be built around the interests of the child and that learning is maximized through integrating content areas into instruction. The behaviorist learning perspective was built on the research of B. F. Skinner and advocated an organized program presented in a structured, routine, systematic, and direct manner. Maria Montessori also embraced a systematic approach but one coupled with specific concepts, objectives, and sensorial experiences. Cognitive development theories advanced by Jean Piaget argued that the content of instruction should be appropriate for the child's developmental stage and that children acquire knowledge through interacting with the world. Lev Vygotsky argued that learning occurs as children acquire new concepts or schemas, so parents and teachers need to scaffold new ideas for children. Reading readiness involves nurturing children through instruction that helps them develop skills needed for reading: auditory discrimination, visual discrimination, visual motor skills, and large motor skills.

2.3 Identify key approaches to early literacy instruction.

Three key approaches in early childhood literacy are constructivist theory, explicit instruction, and the balanced comprehensive approach, which blends the two. Emergent literacy and whole-language instruction are built around the constructivist approach. Emergent literacy recognized that behaviors children participated in prior to reading authentically were actual reading activities that needed to be recognized and acknowledged. Whole language advocated the use of real children's literature and emphasized the joy of reading, the use of narrative text, and understanding about what was read. An explicit (direct-skills) approach for literacy instruction includes a strong phonics program that incorporates a systematic, explicit instruction of skills with scripted guides for teachers. The balanced comprehensive approach includes careful selection of the best theories available and matches learning strategies based on these theories to the learning styles of individual children to help them learn to read. Both skill-based explicit instruction and holistic constructivist ideas might be used.

2.4 Describe the effects of evidence-based research and governmental policies and legislation on early childhood literacy.

Throughout most of the twentieth century, federal educational policy was mostly voluntary and symbolic. As policies became more prescriptive, the federal government engaged in its own research to support those policy decisions. The National Reading Panel Report (2000) was a significant meta-analysis that revealed key elements to literacy success: phonemic awareness, phonics, vocabulary, comprehension, and fluency. The National Early Literacy Panel (2008) studied existing scientifically based research to identify the skills and abilities of young children from birth through age 5 that predict later achievement in reading, such as the ability to decode and comprehend. This research created the context for the No Child Left Behind Act, which requires all U.S. children to become fluent readers by grade 3. Grants were awarded to districts to accomplish this goal. The Bush administration created Reading First grants, and the Obama administration created Race to the Top grants. Common Core State Standards (CCSS) were adopted in 2011 as a way to reduce the variability of standards from state to state and to raise the level of expectation to bring it in alignment with the most competitive nations in the world. CCSS cover English language arts as well as other disciplines.

Activities and Questions

1. The emergent literacy and whole-language philosophies are constructivist approaches to literacy instruction. How do constructivists believe that children learn?
2. Select a constructivist mentioned in the chapter and a behaviorist. Create a lesson on any topic that uses both theories in the plan.
3. Observe an early childhood classroom (preschool through third grade). Decide which theoretical influences have determined the type of practices carried out. Document your findings with specific anecdotes illustrating the theory.
4. Figures 2.3 and 2.4 offer a basic look at teaching using constructivist and explicit approaches to instruction. Is one of these types of teaching better than another and why?
5. What is the purpose of having standards?
6. How have policies influenced classroom practice? Explain.

Chapter 3

Assessment in Early Literacy

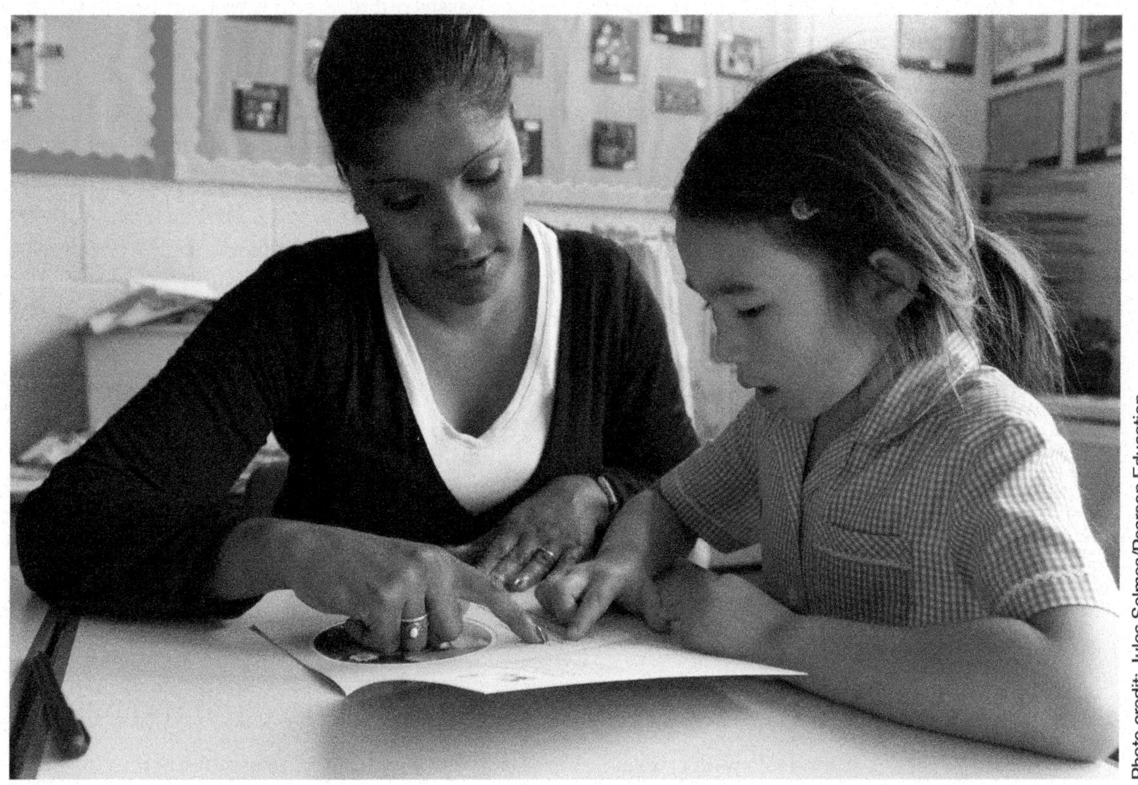

Photo credit: Jules Selmes/Pearson Education

Learning Outcomes

After reading this chapter, you should be able to:

3.1 Explain the role of assessment in early literacy development.

3.2 Define authentic assessment and describe several techniques for conducting it.

3.3 Identify and describe in-depth measures of assessment.

3.4 Discuss the pros and cons of standardized tests.

3.5 Discuss standards and explain how they can affect the literacy curriculum.

3.6 Describe standards and assessment tools designed to measure outcomes against them.

VOCABULARY

Standards
Standardized tests
High-stakes assessment
Informal reading inventories
Portfolio assessment
Running records

The following is a quote from the book *First Grade Takes a Test.* (Miriam Cohen. First Grade Takes a Test, pp 9–10, Star Bright Books. Copyright © 2006 Star Bright Books, Inc.)

> On the test there was a picture of Sally and Tom. Sally was giving Tom something. It looked like a baloney sandwich. Underneath it said:
>
> Sally is taller than Tom. ______________________
>
> Tom is taller than Sally. ______________________

Jim wondered what being tall had to do with getting a baloney sandwich.

And was it really a baloney sandwich? It might be tomato. Jim took a long time on that one (Cohen, 1980, pp. 9–10).

In the book it explains how the teacher passes out tests and how one child was very nervous since she only knew a little English but, in Spanish she was fluent and read very well. She filled in boxes with an *X* as she was supposed to but really didn't understand the questions to make a good decision for the answer. The author went on and talked about another child whose name was George. He read a question about rabbits and what they eat. The answer choices were sandwiches, lettuce, and meat. He knew that rabbits needed to eat carrots to keep their teeth from growing too long. He had a rabbit once, and they told him that at the pet store. He didn't know what box to check, so he drew a carrot in the test booklet and put an *X* next to it.

In both incidents, children answered questions incorrectly on the standardized test but for different reasons. George, related his own experience to the question at hand, and actually had a more sophisticated answer than those provided. His answer was marked incorrect because his background experience with rabbits was different from that of the person who wrote the test. In addition, George was not familiar with how to take the test, by filling in the box beside the best answer provided. Rosa could not comprehend the test in English. Although she was reading at grade level in Spanish, she was jeopardized because of her language background. In both incidents, children answered incorrectly, but not because they did not know the answer.

Assessing Early Literacy Development

This chapter deals with critical issues facing early childhood educators: achieving standards by assessing the needs of children. Assessment must be sensitive to children's different backgrounds, abilities, and needs in order for teachers to select appropriate instructional strategies.

This chapter covers many issues relating to the topic of assessment in detail, including basic assessment instruments. The practical applications for assessment of children's performance will be discussed in the chapters that deal with the various skills and instructional strategies. The purpose of assessment in early childhood is to generate data that can be used to create more effective instruction. That is, assessment is about information-gathering.

Early literacy educators must take into consideration children's interests, learning styles, and different achievement levels; therefore, they think about instruction as being guided by assessment. Administering a single standardized paper-and-pencil test is insufficient for assessing everything teachers need to know about each child. Nor can one measure be the only source for evaluating a child's progress. Teachers need to test children and assess their performance in many areas and under many conditions. Assessment should help the teacher, child, and parent determine a child's strengths and weaknesses and plan appropriate instructional strategies; it should also match educational goals and practices. To meet the needs of all children, there must be multiple measures to see how a child performs in different settings.

The International Literacy Association (ILA) and the National Association for the Education of Young Children (NAEYC) issued a joint position statement on learning to read and write (1998) that recommends using culturally and developmentally appropriate assessment measures. Additionally, the assessments should align with the instructional objectives, while always keeping in mind best practices for the total development of the child. Quality assessment should be drawn from real-life reading and writing tasks and should continuously follow a range of literacy activities.

MyLab Education Self-Check 3.1

Authentic Assessment: Measures and Strategies

Authentic assessment is defined as assessment activities that represent and reflect the actual learning and instructional activities of the classroom and out of school world. Several objectives emerge from an authentic assessment perspective (Johnston & Costello, 2005; Purcell-Gates, Duke, & Martineau, 2007; Risko & Walker-Dalhouse, 2011).

MyLab Education
Video Example 3.1
Five Keys to Comprehensive Assessment
In this video, Linda Darling-Hammond reviews different types of assessment and highlights best practices.
https://www.youtube.com/watch?v=HFimMJL3Wz0

Objectives for Assessment

- Assessment should be based on a variety of measures.
- Assessment should be observations of children engaged in authentic classroom reading and writing tasks, daily performance samples, standardized tests, and standards-based tests.
- Assessment should focus on children's learning based on the goals of curriculum and standards.
- Formative assessment is the continual collection of many assessments of children's work over a learning period.
- Assessment should take into account the diversity of students' cultural, language, and special needs.
- Assessment should be collaborative and include the participation of children, parents, and teachers.
- Summative assessment is at the end of a learning period to evaluate the child's progress, how well the instruction helped the child to improve. It is a guide for designing future instruction.

To accomplish these goals, assessment often called formative assessment, is frequent with varied measures. The main goal is to observe and record actual behavior that provides the broadest possible picture of a particular child (McKenna & Dougherty-Stahl, 2009; Fountas & Pinnell, 2012). Every chapter in this book that deals with a specific area of literacy development contains a section with suggestions for collecting assessment data for particular skills. In this chapter, we provide general assessment measures that will help paint a comprehensive picture of a child. Educators should integrate a variety of authentic assessment methods into their instruction. Some of the more common and more useful types include: anecdotal observation forms, daily performance samples, audio recordings, videos, pencil-and-paper forms, student evaluations, surveys and interviews, conferences, and checklists (Dennis, Rueter, & Simpson, 2013).

Figure 3.1 Sample Observation Form

SOURCE: From Morrison, *Fundamentals of Early Childhood Education,* 5th edition. © 2008.

Teacher's Name: ______________________________

Child's Name: ______________________________

Date: __________ Time: __________ Location of Observation: __________

Purpose for Observing:

Significant Events During Observation:

Reflective Analysis of Significant Event (this reflection should include what you have learned):

List at least three ways you can use or apply what you observed to your future teaching:

Anecdotal Observation Forms

Authentic observation forms are prepared forms or teacher-made forms used for observing and recording children's behavior. Observation forms usually have broad categories with large spaces for notes about children's activities. Goals for observing should be planned and forms designed to meet those goals. Teachers can write down interesting, humorous, and general comments about the child's behavior in the classroom. Observations should focus on one particular aspect of the child's performance, such as oral reading, silent reading, behavior while listening to stories, or writing. Within the descriptions of behavior, dialogue is often recorded, for example:

> Although Janet read orally without errors, her reading was without expression. She read, "The big bad wolf ran away" and every word was said in the same tone. I asked her to listen to me read the sentence and then echo read it or read it as I did after me and she did. She said, "I like doing that. Can we try it again?"

Figure 3.1 presents a sample form that can be used for several different types of observations—for example, oral reading behavior, writing, and more.

Daily Performance Samples

These are samples of the child's work in all content areas that are done on a daily basis. Daily performance samples provide data points about how the child is learning and mastering the content. This data allows teachers to track learning trends for each student individually, as well as the class as a whole. Various types of samples from different content domains should be collected periodically (refer to Figure 3.2).

Figure 3.2 A Daily Performance Sample of Nicole's Writing at the End of Her Kindergarten Year

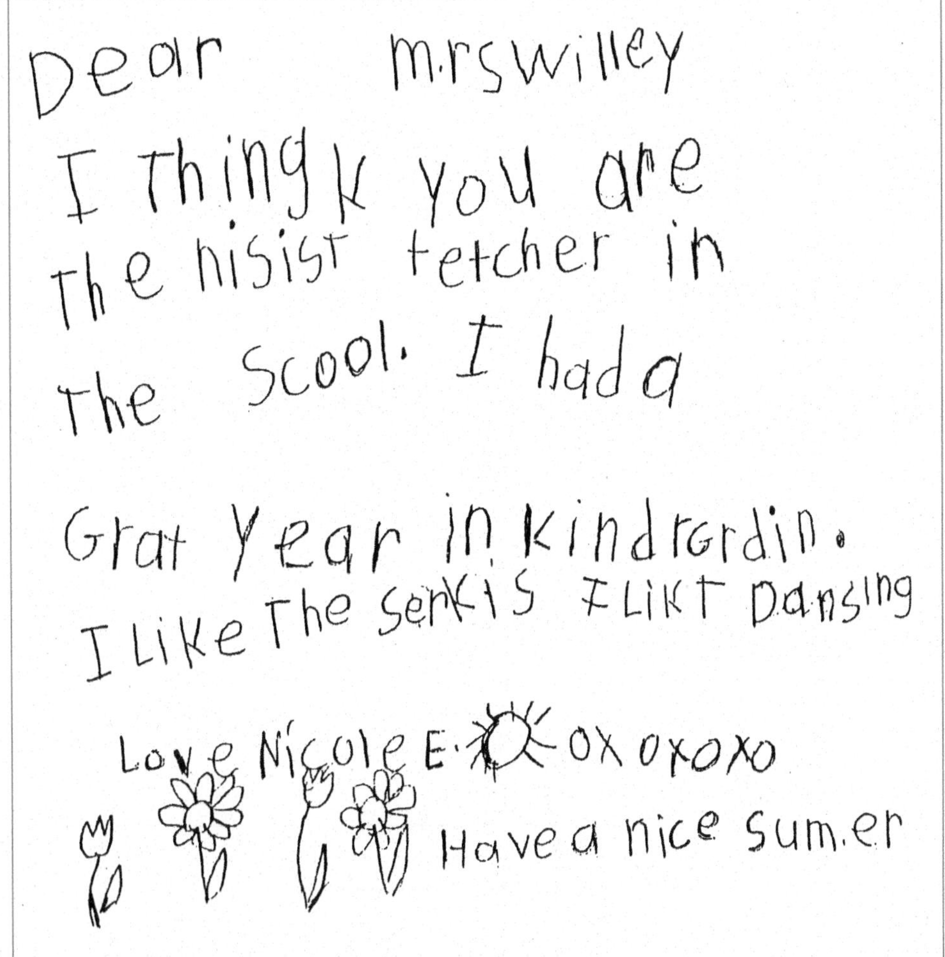
Dear m.rs Willey
I thingk you are
The hisist tetcher in
The Scool. I had a
Grat Year in kindrGrdin.
I Like The senkis I LikT Dansing
Love Nicole E. oxoxoxo
Have a nice sum.er

Audio and Video Recordings

Both audio and visual assessments represent digital literacies that provide authentic audiences and purposes. Students enjoy the act of performing and having their efforts recorded; thus, these digital literacies simultaneously accomplish the goals of authentic assessment and student participation in intrinsically motivating practices.

Audio Recordings. Audio recordings are an assessment that can determine language development, comprehension through a recorded retelling of a story, progress in the fluency of oral reading, and so on. By recording discussion sessions related to responses to literature, the teacher can better understand how youngsters function in a group. Audio recordings can also be used as a type of self-assessment. Children can listen to their own recordings to evaluate both their story retellings and fluency. Chapter 6 and Chapter 9 on comprehension provides a transcription of a child's recorded retelling and an accompanying assessment tool.

Videos. Videos allow teachers to view and review their students in action. Videos are an excellent and rich form of assessment because the teacher can hear the child as well as see the child's facial expressions and body movements. Teachers can also use videos to assess their own teaching performance.

Because of the wealth of information contained in assessment videos, teachers need to have a specific purpose in mind when choosing video as an assessment tool and collected recordings should be evaluated with a checklist or observation form.

Teacher-made Pencil-and-Paper Tests

As the name suggests, teachers design these tests to match instruction. Because it's customized, this type of assessment can closely follow the progress of the students and what they are actually learning.

Student Evaluation Forms

Children should regularly evaluate themselves by collecting samples of their work and discussing them with their teacher, parents, and other children. In addition, children should use student evaluation (self-evaluation) forms to evaluate their own

Figure 3.3 Reading Interview for Children

Name: ______________________ **Date:** ______________

Ask questions that are age appropriate for the child you are interviewing.

1. What is a book?
2. What do people do with books?
3. What can books be about?
4. What is your favorite book? Why?
5. What is your least favorite book? Why?
6. What is fun about reading?
7. What is hard about reading?
8. Do you like to read outside of class?
9. What kinds of things do you read outside of class?

performance. Completing self-evaluation forms allows children to reflect on their learning experience and helps them become intentional learners and start to develop metacognitive skills. Self-evaluations should be an integral part of authentic assessment.

Surveys and Interviews

Teachers can prepare surveys to assess children's attitudes about how they think they are learning or what they like or dislike in school. Surveys can be in the form of questionnaires or interviews with written or oral answers. Chapter 12 provides a motivation survey in the form of a multiple-choice questionnaire that asks for open-ended responses. (Note the sample surveys about literacy in Figures 3.3 and 3.4.)

Figure 3.4 Writing Interview for Children

Name: ______________________ **Date:** ______________

Ask questions that are age appropriate for the child you are interviewing.

1. What is writing?
2. What do people write about?
3. What is the most fun to write about?
4. What is the least fun to write about?
5. What is your favorite thing about writing?
6. What is hard about writing?
7. If you wrote a book, what would you write about?
8. Do you like to write outside of class?
9. What kinds of things do you write about outside of class?

Conferences

Conferences allow the teacher to meet with a child one-to-one to assess skills such as reading aloud, discuss a child's progress, talk about steps to improve, provide individual instruction, and prescribe activities. Children should take an active role in evaluating their progress, and parents should be involved in conferencing with teachers about their child's progress—both with and without the child present. Read the following interaction between Janice and her teacher Ms. Hall. Notice how the teacher and child contribute to learning.

Ms. Hall: Janice, that was excellent reading. You used expression, and you used the illustrations to help you know what was written.

Janice: I remember how you read it when we did echo reading with this book and I used the expression I learned from you. The pictures help a lot. I like to look at them first to get an idea what that page will be about.

Ms. Hall: Janice, I noticed you had a problem figuring out one of the words at the end of the book and I helped you. The word was *prepared* and the sentence was, "Mother prepared spaghetti for dinner." What was the problem?

Janice: I couldn't sound it out and didn't know what else to do.

Ms. Hall: So, I asked you to read the sentence and look at the picture and fill in a word that made sense. You said, "It might say Mother *made* spaghetti for dinner." That makes sense but the first letter of the word is *p* so the word "made" wasn't right. So, I asked you to try and sound out the word now by making sense and also looking at the letters in the word.

Janice: Oh and I looked at the picture which helped so I finally got it.

Ms. Hall: Great job "Janice" you are using all of the strategies we learned to figure out words.

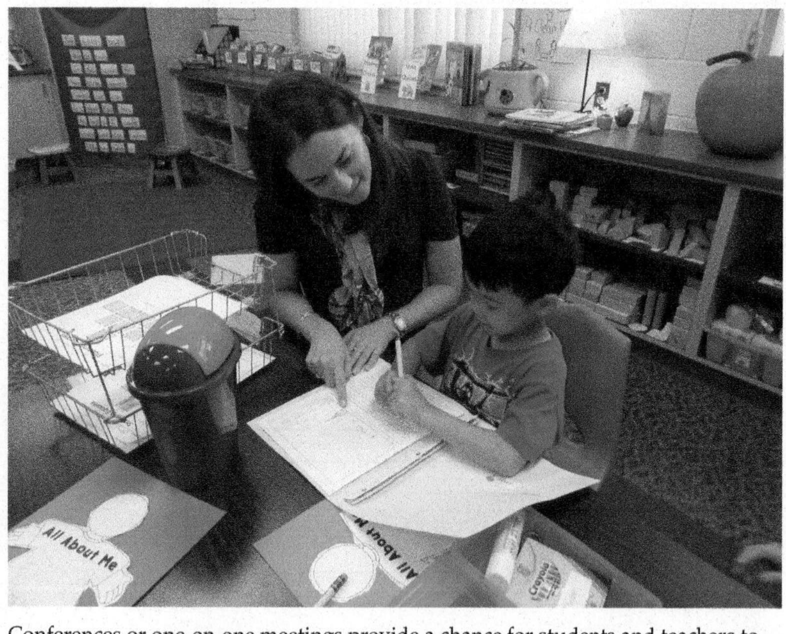

Photo credit: Jennifer Kamm Greco

Conferences or one-on-one meetings provide a chance for students and teachers to have interactive assessments, which help the teacher and child discuss what he or she has learned and what is needed to learn more.

Checklists

Checklists and inventories include lists of developmental behaviors or skills for children to accomplish. The checklist should be based on objectives a teacher may have for instruction and designed to determine whether goals set forth have been accomplished. Figure 3.10 at the end of the chapter organized the developmental characteristics of children and can be used as a checklist to determine how children are developing socially, emotionally, physically, and cognitively based on their age. In several chapters of the book, checklists for skills are presented.

MyLab Education Self-Check 3.2

More In-depth Measures of Assessment

The assessment tools discussed to this point have offered ways to take a snapshot of a student's performance at a particular moment. As informative as they are, however, teachers also need to incorporate more in-depth tools into their assessment programs, for example, running records, informal reading inventories (IRIs), and portfolio assessments.

Running Records

Marie Clay (1993a) created **running records** for observing and recording children's oral reading and for planning instruction. In this analysis, what a child can do and the types of errors the child makes when reading are recorded. Running records can be useful in determining the appropriate material to use for instructional purposes and for independent reading, and they can also help the teacher identify a student's frustration level. The data collected from a running record, specifically the numbers and types of errors students make, should inform the level of material the teacher uses for instruction and the types of instructional strategies used to deliver it. Having the instruction reflect the information gathered from running records is crucial. One drawback of running records, however, is that they devote more time indicating types of errors students make in oral reading than evaluating their ability to comprehend text.

MyLab Education
Video Example 3.2
Running Record Assessment
In this video, a teacher discusses how to analyze a running record. It is part of an 18-video series on Running Records. https://www.youtube.com/watch?v=QHrHS6wGOko

Using running records is straightforward. In taking a running record, the child is asked to read a short passage of 100 to 200 words from a book the child has not read before. Younger children have shorter passages, and older children have longer ones. Select a book you believe is at the independent level for a child, that is, a book that she or he can read easily. If the child gets each word correct, then select a book that is a bit more difficult. The teacher and the student each have a copy of the passage. As the child reads, the teacher makes the running record by marking the passage using the prescribed coding system to indicate whether words are read correctly and what types of errors are made. The types of errors recorded are insertion of a word, omission of a word, repeating a word, substituting one word for another, reversal, refusal to pronounce a word, and an appeal for help. Self corrections are recorded but are not considered errors (refer to Figure 3.5). For the running record to be a valid representation of the student's ability, the teacher must know the difficulty level of the materials being used and match students to the appropriate level. Leveled books for difficulty are discussed later as commonly used materials.

After collecting the raw data by marking up the passage, the teacher needs to analyze the data by organizing it on a running record form such as the one in Figure 3.6. The form allows the teacher to systematically review the errors the students made and classify them as meaning (M), structure (S), or visual (V) errors.

1. **Meaning error (Does it make sense?).** When you look at an error, figure out if the child is using meaning cues in identifying the word. If the child is using information from the text, picture clues, or context clues and reads, "The boy *took* the leaf from the tree" instead of "The boy *pulled* the leaf from the tree," he has made an error but the meaning is intact. This error should be marked with an M. The child knows how to use the context to get the word but needs to look more closely at the print.
2. **Visual errors (use of phonics).** When a child makes a visual error, she knows how to use phonics to decode but doesn't pay attention to the meaning of the text. This child reads, "I *stepped* the milk," instead of "I *spilled* the milk."

   This error is marked with a V. In this situation, ask the child if what she read makes sense and emphasize that it is important to think about the meaning of the sentence when reading, as well as look carefully at the words.
3. **Structure error (Is the syntax correct?).** The child makes a structure or syntax error when he intuitively understands the syntax in sentences. For example, if a child

Figure 3.5 Running Record Coding System

From *Teaching Children to Read* by D. Ray Reutzel and Robert B. Cooter. Copyright © 2013.

Reading Behavior	Notation	Explanation
Accurate reading	✓✓✓✓✓✓	*Notation:* A check is noted for each word pronounced correctly.
Self-Correction	✓✓✓✓ attempt | sc / word in text	The child corrects an error himself. This is not counted as a miscue. *Notation:* "SC" is the notation used for self-corrections.
Omission	—— / Word in text	A word or words are left out during the reading. *Notation:* A dash mark is written over a line above the word(s) from the text that has been omitted.
Insertion	Word inserted / ——	The child adds a word that is not in the text. *Notation:* The word inserted by the reader is placed above a line and a dash placed below it.
Student Appeal and Assistance	—— | A / Word from text	The child is "stuck" on a word he cannot call and asks (verbal or nonverbal) the teacher for help. *Notation:* "A" is written above a line for "assisted" and the problem word from the text is written below the line.
Repetition	✓✓✓R✓✓✓	Sometimes children will repeat words or phrases. These repetitions are not scored as an error, but *are* recorded. *Notation:* Write an "R" after the word repeated and draw a line back to the point where the reader returned.
Substitution	Substituted word / Word from text	The child says a word that is different from the word in the text. *Notation:* The student's substitution word is written above a line under which the correct word from text is written.

reads, "I *went* to the zoo," instead of "I *ran* to the zoo," the English grammar or syntax is correct because a verb goes in that spot, but the word chosen is not correct. As a result, you mark this error with an S and know the child understands the sentence structure but needs to look more closely at the print.

MyLab Education Application Exercise 3.1

After categorizing the child's errors, the teacher can calculate an accuracy rate:

$$\frac{\textit{Total words} - \textit{Errors}}{\textit{Total words}} \times 100 = \%\ \textit{Accuracy}$$

Figure 3.6 Running Record Form

SOURCE: Adapted from M. Clay, *Running Records for Classroom Teachers*. Reprinted by permission of Pearson New Zealand.

Name: ______________________ **Date:** ________

Book: ______________________ **Book level:** ______

Words: **Error rate:** **Accuracy rate:**

Errors:

Self-correction rate:

Cues used

			E—errors			SC—self-correction		
E	SC	Text	M	S	V	M	S	V

M—meaning, S—structure, V—visual, E—error, SC—self-correction

Reading level

Independent: 95% to 100% accuracy
Instructional: 90% to 95% accuracy
Difficult (or Frustration): 89% or less accuracy

Reading proficiency: fluent______ word by word______ choppy ______

Retelling

Setting: characters______ time ______ place ______

Theme: problem or goal ______

Events: number included ______

Resolution: solved problem______ achieved goal ______ ending ______

In other words,

1. Record the number of words in the testing passage (e.g., 70 words).
2. Count the number of errors made by the child and subtract that from the total number of passage words (e.g., 5 errors subtracted from 70 equals 65).
3. Divide that number (65) by the total words in the passage (70).
4. Multiply that by 100; the result equals the percent of accuracy for the passage read (about 93% in this example).

If a child reads 95 to 100% of the words correctly (generally 0 to 3 errors in the passage), the material is at his or her independent level; if 90 to 95% of the words are correct (roughly 4 to 10 errors in the passage), the material is at the instructional level; less than 90% of the words read correctly (more than 11 errors) is the child's frustration level. If a child is at the frustration level with the first book he or she tries, for kindergarten, stop testing. If an older child is at frustration level for the first passage, go down as many levels as necessary until you arrive at the appropriate instructional material.

MyLab Education Application Exercise 3.2

Keep in mind that although leveled books are good for small group reading instruction, they are not meant to replace literature. Leveled books are mostly for instruction. Standards have recommended that, from time to time, teachers use books above a child's grade level to help the child strive to reach higher goals. When using books that are more difficult for a child than his or her current instructional level, the teacher should be reading the book to the child. Although they may not be able to read the book alone, they can learn new vocabulary and have sophisticated discussions about it. Often listening comprehension is greater than reading comprehension. If the child wishes to read the book, she can follow along in their own copy as the teacher reads. The teacher needs to model, and provide a lot of support, when the child is reading a text that is difficult for him.

The running record form also contains a place to indicate if the child's reading was fluent, word by word, or choppy. Teachers can also ask children to retell stories read to determine comprehension of text (Kuhn, 2007; Stahl & Heubach, 2005; Bellinger & DiPerna, 2011).

MyLab Education
Video Example 3.3
Running Record Analysis
In this video, two teachers discuss the purpose of a running record and model how to use it with a student (1:48). At 7:55, they model how to analyze it to plan instruction.
https://www.youtube.com/watch?v=AxJxp9bT0yA&t=118s

Running records should be done about at least once every other month for all early childhood students. Teachers should talk to children about the types of errors they make in a running record; teachers should also provide children with strategies such as listening to the meaning of a sentence and looking at the letters in the word to figure out a word.

Children who cannot yet read sentences in the first-leveled books can be evaluated for their progress with a letter recognition test. This test shows the letters of the alphabet printed out of order in uppercase and lowercase. Children are asked to read the letter names one row at a time as the teacher records correct and incorrect letters. The test can go one step further, to determine whether students know sound–symbol correspondence, by asking children if they know the sound that particular letters make and a word that begins with each letter or sound and then recording their responses. In addition, high frequency word recognition assessment can be done. Chapter 7 is a high-frequency word list. The list can be divided by grade level according to which words are considered most difficult. The teacher asks children to read words from the list beginning with what are considered to be the easiest first. If they are successful, the next group of words for the next grade level is tried. Vocabulary word lists will be discussed more in Chapter 7.

Informal Reading Inventories

Informal reading inventories (IRIs) are similar to running records, but they place a larger emphasis on comprehension. The purpose of this type of inventory is to determine a student's reading level, such as first, third, or sixth grade. This is done by having children read graded word lists. They may also read graded reading passages orally and silently to help determine if the materials are at their (1) independent reading level

Figure 3.7 Sample Reading Inventory and Scoring Guide

Adapted with permission of Kendall Hunt Publishing, from Johns, J. (2012). *Basic reading inventory; pre-primer through grade twelve and early literacy assessment.* Dubuque, IA: Kendal Hunt Publishing Company.

First Grade	**Miscues**						
Spotty Swims	Substitution	Insertion	Omission	Reversal	Repetition	Self-Correction	Meaning Change
One day Spotty went for a walk.							
The sun was warm. Spotty walked to							
the pond. There he saw a frog. The							
frog was on a log. Spotty wanted to							
play. Spotty began to bark. The frog							
jumped in the water.							
Then Spotty jumped into the water.							
But poor Spotty did not know what to							
do. The water was very deep. The water							
went way over his head. Spotty moved							
his legs. Soon his head came out of the							
water. He kept moving. He came to							
the other side of the pond. That is how							
Spotty learned to swim.							
Total							

Comprehension Questions

T 1. ____ What is the story about?

F 2. ____ Where did Spotty go?

F 3. ____ What did Spotty see?

F 4. ____ What happened when Spotty saw the frog?

F 5. ____ What did the frog do when Spotty barked?

F 6. ____ What did Spotty do when the water went over his head?

F 7. ____ What did Spotty learn in the story?

I 8. ____ Who was Spotty?

E 9. ____ Why do you think Spotty wanted to play with the frog?

V 10. ____ What is a "pond"?

Comprehension Scoring Guide	
Questions Missed	Level
0–1	Independent
1.5–2	Ind./Inst.
2.5	Instructional
3–4.5	Inst./Frust.
5+	Frustration

Word Recognition Scoring Guide		
Total Miscues	Level	Significant Miscues
0–1	Independent	0–1
2–4	Ind./Inst.	2
5	Instructional	3
6–9	Inst./Frust.	4
10+	Frustration	5+

(when they don't need help); (2) instructional reading level (when they can read the material but need some scaffolding from the teacher; or (3) frustration level (when the material is too difficult for them to read). After reading, children answer several types of comprehension questions. Students should read both narrative and informational text. The comprehension questions focus on main ideas, inferences, and vocabulary (refer to Figure 3.7).

As with the running record, when teachers listen to the oral reading, they use a coding system to identify and record the types of errors the children make. For example, these codes will indicate if the students omit words, repeat words, reverse words, self-correct, add words, substitute words, and so on. This information helps to guide instruction. One of the most important elements of the IRI, however, is the assessment of comprehension when a child reads or listens to a story (Flippo, Holland, McCarthy, & Swinning, 2009). Children can be tested reading orally and silently. Errors are counted and an accuracy percentage is calculated which indicates if the book the child is reading is at his or her independent, instructional, or frustration level.

When we read to children, sometimes the material should be above their reading level but at their level of comprehension. With the use of the IRI, comprehension questions can determine if what is being read is too easy or too difficult for the child's listening comprehension (Gunning, 2003; Hasbrouck & Tindal, 2006; Tompkins, 2003). Teachers can make their own IRI tests, but there are also published tests. Some of these tests are:

- Johns, J. (2012). *Basic Reading Inventory; Pre-primer through Grade Twelve and Early Literacy Assessment*. Dubuque, IA: Kendal Hunt Publishing Company.
- Leslie, L. & Caldwell, J. S. (2011). *Qualitative reading inventory-5*. Boston, MA: Allyn & Bacon.
- Mariotti, A. & Homan, S. (2001). *Linking reading assessment to instruction: An application worktext for elementary classroom teachers* (5th ed.). New York, NY: Routledge.
- Wheelock, W., Silvaroli, J. & Campbell, C. (2005). *Classroom reading inventory* (12th ed.). New York, NY: McGraw-Hill.
- Woods, M. J. & Moe, A. (2011). *Analytical reading inventory: Comprehensive standard based assessment for all students including gifted and remedial* (9th ed.). Boston, MA: Allyn & Bacon.

The children are to read the passage. As they read you can determine the types of oral reading errors made, and when they answer the comprehension questions you can see how well they understand the text. If using this as a retell, for oral and silent reading, have them retell it first and then ask them the comprehension questions. Scoring procedures for retelling are in Chapter 9 on comprehension, scoring for types of oral errors are in this chapter, and scoring for comprehension is on the page with the passage. If a child gets 0 to 4 questions correct, the material is at the appropriate level for his independent level of reading. Five questions correctly correspond to his instructional level and five to 10 incorrect reflects his frustration level. The graded passages tell you what the child's reading grade level is. Chapter 13 discusses the concept of leveling books for instructional purposes in more depth.

Portfolio Assessment

Portfolio assessment provides a way for teachers, children, and parents to collect representative samples of children's work. It can include work in progress and completed samples. A portfolio provides a story of where children have been and what they are capable of doing now, to determine where they should go from this point forth. The teacher's portfolio should include work selected by the child, teacher, and parent. It should represent the best work that children can produce and illustrate difficulties they may be experiencing. The physical portfolio is often a folder that is personalized with a drawing by the child, a picture of the child, and his or her name.

Currently, many teachers are opting to create digital portfolios where all of the students' work is electronic. Computerized assignments can simply be transferred into an electronic folder, and projects that are done by hand can be scanned into a computer file and added to that same folder. A separate digital folder can be used for each child. One obvious benefit of a digital portfolio is that it is easy for the student, teacher, parents, and future teachers to obtain copies, as the folders can be attached

Figure 3.8 Schedule for Collecting Portfolio Samples and Tests

*Not applicable for Pre-K. **SOURCE:** Copyright (c) Pearson Education

Student: ______________________ **Grade:** __________

School: ______________________ **Teacher:** __________

Tests are given in September, January, and May. Record the test when given in the space provided.

"Grade"	Sept. "Pre-K"	Jan. "Pre-K"	May "Pre-K"	Sept. "K"	Jan. "K"	May "K"	Sept. "1"	Jan. "1"	May "1"	Sept. "2"	Jan. "2"	May "2"
1. Child interview												
2. Parent interview												
3. Self-portrait												
4. Concepts about print test												
5. Story retelling/ reenactment												
6. Written retelling*												
7. Free writing												
8. Letter recognition												
9. Running record*												
10. High-frequency sight words												
11. Observation comments												

and sent in an email or transferred to removable storage drives. Digital portfolios also reduce the amount of paperwork stored in the classroom and make organizing and tracking items easier.

Whether a teacher opts for a physical or digital portfolio, it should include grade appropriate work such as:

- Daily work performance samples
- Anecdotes about behavior
- Audio and video of oral reading
- Analyzed language samples
- Analyzed story retellings
- Checklists recording skill development
- Interviews
- Standardized and standards-based test results
- Child's self-assessment form
- Evaluated expository and narrative writing samples.

MyLab Education Application Exercise 3.3

Some schools have formal schedules for collecting portfolios and administering tests (refer to Figure 3.8). A portfolio should be prepared by the teacher with the child. Children usually take them home at the end of the school year. Occasionally, teachers pass a portfolio on to the next teacher the child will have (McKenna & Dougherty-Stahl, 2009). With all of this information the teacher should write a narrative about the child's formative assessment early in the school year and his summative assessment at the end of the year. These reflections discuss what the child can do and needs to do (Gullo, 2013). Following is such a reflection.

September: First Grade
Student: DJ
Teacher: Ms. Murray
Recommendations for Instructions Based on Multiple Measures of Assessment (Courtesy of Lesley Mandel Morrow)
DJ recognizes most of the letters of the alphabet but must learn to recognize all of the letters specifically upper and lower case and their sounds. This will help him with figuring out unknown words in both reading and writing. When reading, he needs to learn to self-monitor—that is, remember the strategies he has learned and use them. If one strategy doesn't work than he should be able to use another. In this way he will begin to self-monitor his reading.

DJ's reading is word by word. He needs help with automaticity and expressions. I will need to select texts on his independent level so he can practice fluency and gradually move up to texts at his instructional level. I need to model fluent reading for him and do some echo reading.

When writing DJ needs to leave appropriate space within a word and between words, and match sounds of letters when writing words. He has a similar problem in reading text. He does not seem to be able to focus on a word to figure it out and will read words out of sequence in a sentence.

Now in September, DJ's reading level is in an A text. My goal is for him to reach beginning second grade level reading by the end of first grade.

Recommendations for Instructions Based on Multiple Measures
February 2: Grade 1
Student: DJ
Teacher: Ms. Murray
DJ has mastered recognition of all of the letters in the alphabet both upper and lower case. He knows all the regular letter sounds and the hard and soft *c* and *g*. He still has trouble with vowel sounds. He is demonstrating strong word solving skills. He still hesitates for a long time for figuring out unknown words. More work with phonics, reading pictures for clues, and figuring out the word by selecting one that makes sense with the context and the sounds in the word. I will also try and increase his sight word vocabulary.

DJ can identify a variety of text structures. He also uses visual information, including familiar word families or patterns within words, to solve unknown words. DJ uses multiple strategies to figure out unknown words such as the meaning of the sentence, picture clues, clues from the syntax of a sentence and phonics skills.

When writing DJ is now able to compose varied, compound sentences with good detail. His spacing in writing has improved enormously. His sentences sometimes run on. Continued instruction will teach him how to break up his sentences so they are more easily read and grammatically correct.

From September until February, DJ has become a confident reader and uses strategies learned to help him with decoding and understanding the text. He monitors his fluency and will repeat a sentence when the pace and expression don't seem quite right to him. He is ready to work on developing many strategies to help him comprehend.

DJ has demonstrated steady growth in his independent use of reading strategies. He is now reading in a Level G book.

MyLab Education Self-Check 3.3

Standardized Tests: The Pros and Cons

In addition to the informal assessments, teachers are also responsible for administering formal assessments. **Standardized tests** often start in third grade. However there is more and more testing in preschool and kindergarten than in the past. Standardized tests are prepared by publishers and are norm referenced; that is, they are administered to large numbers of students when they are created to develop norms. Norms are the average performance of students who are tested at a particular grade and age level. When selecting a standardized test, it is important to check its validity for your students. That is, does the test evaluate what it says it tests for, and does it match the goals you have for your students? The reliability of the test is important as well. In other words, are scores accurate and dependable when given over and over again? Other features of standardized tests are as follows:

1. Grade equivalent scores are raw scores converted into grade level scores. For example, if a child scores a grade equivalent of 2.3, in first grade, it means as a first grader the child reads on a 2.3 grade level.
2. Percentile ranks are raw scores converted into a rank according to where the child ranked as compared to all children who took the test at the same grade and age level. Therefore, if a youngster received a percentile rank of 80, it would mean that she scored better than or equal to 80% of students taking the test in the same grade and age level and that 20% of the children taking the test scored better.

Although many criticisms are associated with standardized measures, they do present another source of information about a child's performance. Parents like receiving the information from the test because it is concrete information regarding where their child ranks among others in the same grade. It must be emphasized, however, that standardized scores are just one type of information and no more important than all the other measures discussed earlier.

Concerns Associated with Standardized Testing

Because standardized tests represent only one form of assessment, their use must be coordinated with that of other assessment measures. Some standardized tests for early literacy evaluate children on skills such as auditory memory, rhyme, letter recognition, visual matching, school language, and listening. Less commonly covered by standardized tests are many practices that nurture early literacy, such as measuring a child's prior knowledge, book concepts, attitudes about reading, association of meaning with print, and characteristics of printed materials. Additionally, one child might pass all portions of a standardized test and still not be ready to read. Another child might not pass any portion of the test but already be reading.

Some standardized tests do not match the instructional practices suggested by the latest research and theory on early literacy. Because school districts are often evaluated on how well children perform on the standardized tests, teachers may feel pressured to teach to the test. This situation is often referred to as **high-stakes assessment** because major decisions are being made from the results of one test score. For example, a teacher's competency might be judged based on test scores; these scores may also factor into the decision to retain or promote a child to the next grade. Some schools prepare children for standardized tests by drilling them on sample tests similar to the real ones. The sample tests are graded, and instruction is geared to remedy student weaknesses. If teachers do not prepare children for the test with practice sessions and do not teach to the test, their children may not score well. However, children must have the advantage of knowing what the test is like and some test taking strategies. They need to be able to:

- Follow the directions and how to fill in the answers.
- They need to know to read the entire question and all of the answers before selecting the answer.
- If the test allows, answer easier questions in a section first and then go back to the more difficult ones.
- If the test is multiple choice and you aren't sure about the answer eliminate answers you know aren't right and then you can more easily figure out which is the right answer.

- Don't change your answer, your first response is likely to be correct.
- Remember the test is timed so don't spend too much time on something very difficult for you. Skip it and answer as many questions as possible.

Standardized tests, on which high stakes decisions are based, can potentially yield inaccurate information. Figure 3.9 illustrates hypothetical subscores and overall percentile ranks of three kindergarten children on a typical standardized test. The example illustrates the need for teachers to use multiple assessment measures and also take into account the whole child when determining academic strengths and weaknesses (Im, 2017).

Student A scored well in auditory and visual skills and poorly in language skills. The child's overall score is at the 50th percentile. Student B has good auditory skills, poor visual skills, and good language skills, and also scored overall at the 50th percentile. Student C scored fairly consistently across visual, auditory, and language skills, and likewise scored overall at the 50th percentile. These three children are very different in ability yet have scored at the same overall percentile on a standardized test. All three children will go to the first grade and could be placed in the same reading group, even though Student A has a possible language deficit and is missing one of the most important ingredients for reading success—a strong language base. It is very unlikely that the three will achieve similar success in reading, although they might be expected to on the basis of their test scores.

Figure 3.9 Hypothetical Subtest Profiles on Three Kindergarten Children Achieving about the Same Test Performance Rating

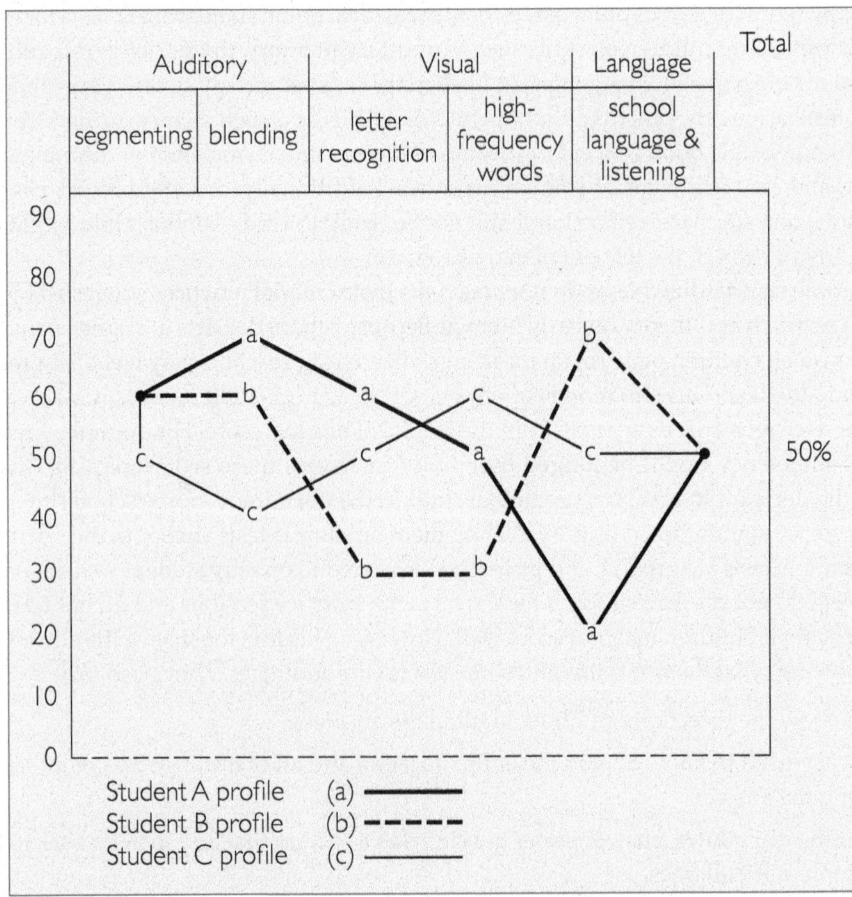

Standardized test scores are less reliable with younger children than with older children, and some tests are still biased in favor of white, middle class children despite genuine attempts to alleviate the problem. Their use tends to place rural, African American, and English learners at a disadvantage. Prior knowledge plays a large role in how well children will do on the test. Children from white, middle-class homes tend to have experiences that lead to better achievement on the tests. The joint International Literacy Association ILA/NAEYC position statement, *Learning to Read and Write: Developmentally Appropriate Practices for Young Children* (1998), suggests that evaluative procedures used with young children be developmentally and culturally appropriate and that the selection of measures be based on the objectives of an instructional program. Standardized tests and multiple authentic assessments, such as interviews, anecdotal records, checklists, and so on, will provide a complete picture of a child's progress (International Literacy Association ILA, 1999). Parents, community members, and policy makers need to be made aware of the value of classroom-based assessment (Howard, Woodcock, Ehrich, & Bokosmaty, 2017).

MyLab Education Self-Check 3.4

Literacy Standards and Shifts in the Literacy Curriculum

As a result, professional literacy organizations, the federal government, and individual states have outlined standards for achievement. The purpose of **standards** is to articulate what students need to learn at each grade level in the English/Language Arts. In 1996 and again in 2010, the ILA and National Council of Teachers of English (NCTE) published *Standards for the English Language Arts*, one of the first attempts at national standards in literacy for the United States (1996). The Standards also asked for a higher level of achievement on the part of students. The document advanced a set of general standards to do the following:

1. Prepare students for literacy now and in the future with specific concerns about how technology will change the manner in which we deal with literacy in the future.
2. Ensure that students attain the vision of parents, teachers, and researchers about expectations for their achievement in the language arts.
3. Promote high expectations for literacy achievement among children and bridge inequities that exist in educational opportunities for all (From IRA and NCTE. (1996). Standards for the English Language Arts. Newark, DE: International Reading Association, and Urbana, IL: National Council of Teachers of English. Reprinted with permission.)

Standards are assessed with a test that matches them. Potentially everyone could pass standards based tests since they are based on a certain number of questions answered correctly. This differs from standardized tests, which are based on norms, and 50% of the population will pass and 50% will fail. To help students become fluent readers, we must have standards beginning with preschool.

Standards for Prekindergarten

The National Institute of Literacy and the National Center for Family Literacy (2004) created a panel called the National Early Literacy Panel. Its purpose was to determine (from scientifically-based research) what precursors, predictors, and foundational or emergent literacy skills children needed from birth to age 5 to predict success in reading and writing. Several variables were found as predictors of later literacy and could be considered standards to accomplish in preschool literacy. They include:

- **Alphabet knowledge (AK):** knowledge of the names and sounds associated with printed letters
- **Phonological awareness (PA):** ability to detect, manipulate, or analyze the auditory aspects of spoken language (including the ability to distinguish or segment words, syllables, or phonemes)
- **Rapid automatic naming (RAN) of letters or digits:** ability to rapidly name a sequence of random letters or digits
- **RAN of objects or colors:** ability to rapidly name a sequence of repeated random sets of pictures, objects (e.g., car, tree, or house), or colors
- **Writing or writing name:** ability to write letters in isolation on request or to write one's own name, and write a short sentence
- **Phonological memory:** ability to remember spoken information for a short period of time
- **Concepts about books and print:** knowledge of the title of the book, author, cover, back, front, print, and pictures
- **Print knowledge:** combination of alphabetic knowledge, concepts of print, vocabulary, memory, and phonological awareness
- **Oral language:** ability to produce or comprehend spoken language, with appropriate vocabulary and grammar
- **Visual processing:** ability to match or discriminate visually presented symbols.

(There will be more detailed discussion of these goals in Chapters 4 and 6)

The panel also found that interventions and intentional instruction in literacy in preschool and at home was important.

Standards in K–3 Common Core State Standards for English Language Arts. As mentioned there must be standards to provide goals for achievement in all content areas and of course in the language arts. Many states have had standards for a while. The Common Core State Standards (CCSS) in English language arts were adopted as national standards in 45 states. States that didn't adopt them created their own but they are similar. The standards describe what children should be able to demonstrate at the end of each grade. Now states have carved out their own standards however they are very similar to the Common Core. Here are examples of standards for grades K–3:

1. **Key ideas and details:** reading (fiction and nonfiction texts)
   a. Read closely to determine what the text says explicitly and to make logical inferences from it; cite specific textual evidence when writing or speaking to support conclusions drawn from the text.
   b. Determine central ideas or themes of a text and analyze their development; retell and summarize the key supporting details and ideas.
   c. Analyze how and why individuals, events, and ideas develop and interact over the course of a text.
2. **Craft and structure**
   d. Interpret words and phrases as they are used in a text, including determining technical, connotative, and figurative meanings, and analyze how specific word choices shape meaning or tone in different types of text.
   e. Analyze the structure of texts, including how specific sentences, paragraphs, and larger portions of the text (e.g., a section, chapter, scene, or stanza) relate to each other and to the whole.
   f. Assess how point of view or purpose shapes the content and style of a text.
3. **Integration of knowledge and ideas**
   g. Integrate and evaluate content presented in diverse media and formats, including visually and quantitatively, as well as in words.

h. Delineate and evaluate the argument and specific claims in a text, including the validity of the reasoning as well as the relevance and sufficiency of the evidence.
i. Analyze how two or more texts address similar themes or topics in order to build knowledge or to compare the approaches the authors take.

4. **Range of reading and level of text complexity**
   j. Read a range of difficult text fluently and comprehend complex literary and informational texts independently, orally, in collaboration with others, and proficiently.

Standards should include all of the language arts, for example there needs to be an emphasis on

- Comprehension of informational text
- Comprehension of narrative text
- Learning foundational skills
- Writing
- Speaking, listening, and language development.

These processes of communication are closely connected and should be taught concurrently.

MyLab Education Self-Check 3.5

Implementing and Assessing the Standards

Standards are important in schools. In addition to the skills involved in reading and comprehending literature and informational text, the other skills covered include foundational skills, writing skills, speaking and listening skills, and language skills.

Assessing Standards

Assessments for standards are similar to standardized tests. The common core has two similar tests. One is called the *Partnership for Assessment of Reading for College and Career (PARCC)*. The other one is called *SMARTER Balanced Assessment Tool*. Different states have chosen to use one or the other. They are very similar. The tests involve children in the following:

1. Formative assessment to plan instruction.
2. The test are tightly links assessment to standards.
3. Assesses each child's achievement in relationship to him or herself.
4. Assesses each child in relationship to his or her group (compare to their class and to select groups for explicit instruction).
5. Assesses select areas of need and competence across the whole group (to adjust the curriculum if needed).

   Children will not be tested until third grade.

Now that states have adopted their own standards the assessments in states are changing. They are still standardized tests however to test what the standards suggest we should teach.

MyLab Education Self-Check 3.6

Stages of Child Development

Early childhood education has always been concerned about the physical, social, emotional, and cognitive development of the child. The curriculum, therefore, should emphasize all four areas. One cannot discuss early literacy without being concerned with the total child. This information is needed when preparing instructional environments and activities. This knowledge will also help determine whether children have special needs related to learning disabilities, giftedness, or communication disorders, for example. Considering the total development of the child, and not just the cognitive, has been and always should be a hallmark in early childhood education and must influence early literacy development as well. Figure 3.10 describes the developmental characteristics of children from birth through 8 years (Seefeldt & Barbour, 1998, pp. 63–69). It can be used as a reference throughout this book in teaching and assessing child development. The chart can be used as a checklist for evaluating child development.

Figure 3.10 Developmental Characteristics of Children during Stages of Development

SOURCE: From Seefeldt and Barbour, Early *Childhood Education: An Introduction*, 4th edition, pp. 63–69. © 1998. Reprinted and Electronically reproduced by permission of Pearson Education, Inc., Upper Saddle River, New Jersey.

Birth through 12-Months-Old

Physical

Develops rapidly.
Changes from waking because of hunger and distress to sleeping through the night with two naps during the day.
Changes eating patterns from every 3 hours to regular meals three times a day.
Develops control of muscles that hold up the head. By 4 months enjoys holding up head.
Focuses eyes and begins to explore the environment visually.
Begins to grasp objects at about 16 weeks. Can grasp and let go by six months.
Rolls over intentionally (4 to 6 months).
Holds own bottle (6 to 8 months).
Shows first tooth at about 6 months. Has about 12 teeth by age 1.
Sits well alone, can turn and recover balance (6 to 8 months).
Raises body at 9 months. May even pull self up to a standing position.
Starts to crawl at 6 months and to creep at nine or ten months.
May begin walking by age 1.

Social

Begins to smile socially (4 or 5 months).
Enjoys frolicking and being jostled.
Recognizes mother or other significant adult.
Notices hands and feet and plays with them.
By 6 months likes playing, alone or with company.
Begins to be wary of strangers.
Cooperates in games such as peek-a-boo and pat-a-cake.
Imitates actions of others.

Emotional

Differentiates crying according to specific discomforts, such as being hungry, cold, or wet.
Shows emotions by overall body movements, such as kicking, arm waving, and facial expressions.
Begins to show pleasure when needs are being met.
By 6 months shows affection by kissing and hugging.
Shows signs of fearfulness.
Pushes away things not liked.

Cognitive

First discriminates mother from others; later discriminates familiar faces from those of strangers.
Explores world through looking, mouthing, grasping.
Inspects things for long periods.
As a first sign of awareness, protests disappearance of objects.
Discovers how to make things happen and delights in doing so by repeating an action several times.
Between 6 and 12 months becomes aware of object permanency by recognizing that an object has been taken away and by looking for a hidden object.
Begins intentional actions by pulling at an object or removing an obstacle to get at an object.
Becomes increasingly curious about surroundings.

One- and Two-Years-Old

Physical

Begins to develop many motor skills.
Continues teething until about 18 months; develops all 20 teeth by age 2.
Develops large muscles. Crawls well, stands alone (at about a year), and pushes chair around.
Starts to walk at about a year to 15 months.
Places ball in and out of box.
Releases ball with thrust.
Creeps down stairs backward.
Develops fine motor skills. Stacks two blocks, picks up a bean, and puts objects into a container. Starts to use spoon. Puts on simple things—for instance, an apron over the head.
By end of 18 months, scribbles with a crayon in vertical or horizontal lines.
Turns pages of book.
During the second year, walks without assistance.
Runs but often bumps into things.
Jumps up and down.
Walks up and down stairs with one foot forward.
Holds glass with one hand.
Stacks at least six blocks and strings beads.
Opens doors and cupboards.
Scribbles spirals, loops, and rough circles.
Starts to prefer one hand to the other.
Starts day control of elimination.

Social

At age 1, differentiates meagerly between self and others.
Approaches mirror image socially.
By 18 months, distinguishes between terms *you* and *me*.
Plays spontaneously; is self-absorbed but notices newcomers.
Imitates behavior more elaborately.
Identifies body parts.
Responds to music.
Develops socialization by age 2. Is less interested in playing with parent and more interested in playing with a peer.
Begins parallel play, playing side by side, but without interaction.
By age two learns to distinguish strongly between self and others.
Is ambivalent about moving out and exploring.
Becomes aware of owning things and may become very possessive.

Figure 3.10 Developmental Characteristics of Children during Stages of Development (*continued*)

Emotional

At age 1 is amiable.
At 18 months is resistant to change. Often suddenly—won't let mother out of sight.
Tends to rebel, resist, fight, run, hide.
Perceives emotions of others.
At age 1, shows no sense of guilt. By age 2, begins to experience guilt and shows beginnings of conscience.
Says no emphatically. Shows willfulness and negativism.
Laughs and jumps exuberantly.

Cognitive

Shows mental imagery: looks for things that are hidden, recalls and anticipates events, moves beyond here and now, begins temporal and spatial orientation.
Develops deductive reasoning: searches for things in more than one place.
Reveals memory: shows deferred imitation by seeing an event and imitating it later.
Remembers names of objects.
Completes awareness of object permanence.
By age 2 or 3 distinguishes between black and white and may use names of colors.
Distinguishes one from many.
Says "one, two, three" in rote counting, but not often in rational counting.
Acts out utterances and talks about actions while carrying them out.
Takes things apart and tries to put them back together.
Shows sense of time by remembering events. Knows terms *today* and *tomorrow* but mixes them up.

Three- and Four-Years-Old

Physical

Expands physical skills.
Rides a tricycle.
Pushes a wagon.
Runs smoothly and stops easily.
Climbs jungle gym ladder.
Walks stairs with alternating feet forward.
Jumps with two feet.
Shows high energy level.
By four can do a running broad jump.
Begins to skip, pushing one foot ahead of the other.
Can balance on one foot.
Keeps relatively good time in response to music.
Expands fine motor skills, can do zippers and dress oneself.
Controls elimination at night.

Social

Becomes more social.
Moves from parallel play to early associative play. Joins others in activities.

Emotional

Begins enjoying humor. Laughs when adults laugh.
Develops inner control over behavior.
Shows less negativism.
Develops phobias and fears, which may continue until age 5.
At four may begin intentional lying but is outraged by parents' white lies.

Cognitive

Begins problem-solving skills. Stacks blocks and may kick them down to see what happens.
Learns to use listening skills as a means of learning about the world.
Still draws in scribbles at age 3, but in one direction and less repetitively.
At age 4, drawings represent what child knows and thinks is important.
Is perceptually bound to one attribute and characteristic. "Why" questions abound.
Believes everything in the world has a reason, but the reason must accord with the child's own knowledge.
Persists in egocentric thinking.
Begins to sort out fantasy from reality.

Five- and Six-Years-Old

Physical

Well controlled and constantly in motion.
Often rides a bicycle as well as a tricycle.
Can skip with alternating feet and hop.
Can control fine motor skills. Begins to use tools such as toothbrush, saw, scissors, pencil, hammer, needle for sewing.
Has established handedness well. Identifies hand used for writing or drawing.
Can dress self but may still have trouble tying shoelaces.
At age 6 begins to lose teeth.

Social

Becomes very social. Visits with friends independently.
Becomes very self-sufficient.
Persists longer at a task. Can plan and carry out activities and return to projects next day.
Plays with two or three friends, often for just a short time only, then switches play groups.
Begins to conform. Is very helpful.
By age 6 becomes very assertive, often bossy, dominating situations and ready with advice.
Needs to be first. Has difficulty listening.
Is possessive and boastful.
Craves affection. Often has a love–hate relationship with parents.
Refines sex roles. Has tendency to type by sex.
Becomes clothes conscious.
Becomes aware of racial and sexual differences.
Begins independence.
By four shows growing sense of initiative and self-reliance.
Becomes aware of basic sex identity.
Not uncommonly develops imaginary playmates (a trait that may appear as early as two and a half).

Emotional

Continues to develop sense of humor.
Learns right from wrong.
At age 5 begins to control emotions and is able to express them in socially approved ways.
Quarrels frequently, but quarrels are of short duration.
At age 6 shifts emotions often and seems to be in emotional ferment.
New tensions appear as a result of attendance at school all day. Temper tantrums appear.
Giggles over bathroom words.
At age 5 develops a conscience but sees actions as all good or all bad.
At age 6 accepts rules and often develops rigid insistence that they be obeyed.
May become a tattletale.

Figure 3.10 Developmental Characteristics of Children during Stages of Development (*continued*)

Cognitive

Begins to recognize conservation of amount and length.
Becomes interested in letters and numbers. May begin printing or copying letters and numbers. Counts.
Knows most colors.
Recognizes that one can get meaning from printed words.
Has a sense of time, but mainly personal time. Knows when events take place in the child's own day or week.
Recognizes own space and can move about independently in familiar territory.

Seven- and Eight-Years-Old

Physical

Great variation in height and weight, but rate of growth slows.
Masters physical skills for game playing and enjoys team sports.
Is willing to repeat a skill over and over to mastery.
Increases in fine motor performance—can draw a diamond correctly and form letters well.
Has sudden spurts of energy.
Loss of baby teeth continues and permanent teeth appear.
Physique begins to change. Body more proportionately developed and facial structure changes.

Social

Beginning to prefer own sex—has less boy/girl interaction.
Peer groups begin to form.
Security in sex identification.
Self-absorption.
Begins to work and play independently.
Can be argumentative.
At age 7 still not a good loser and often a tattletale.
By 8 plays games better and not as intent on winning.
Conscientious—can take responsibility for routine chores.
Less selfish. Able to share. Wants to please.
Still enjoys and engages in fantasy play.

Emotional

Difficulty in starting things but will persist to end.
Worries that school might be too hard.
Beginning of empathy—sees other's viewpoint.
Sense of humor expressed in riddles, practical jokes, and nonsense words.
Discriminates between good and bad, but still immature.
Is sensitive and gets hurt easily.
Has sense of possession and takes care of possessions (makes collections).

Cognitive

Attention span is quite long.
Can plan and stay with a task or project over a long period.
Interested in conclusions and logical ends.
Aware of community and the world.
Expanding knowledge and interest.
Some sevens read well and by eight really enjoy reading.
Can tell time—aware of passage of time in months and years.
Interested in other time periods.
Conscious of other's work and their own. May comment, "I'm good at art, but Sue is better at reading."
Differences in abilities widening.

An Idea from the Classroom

Teacher-Designed Informal Assessment

I like my second-grade students to reflect on and evaluate what they have learned on a daily basis, so I have my children maintain an ongoing record that chronicles knowledge they have constructed over time. I created a chart that hangs on the wall with one pocket for each student on the chart. There is a stack of index cards in a pocket for this purpose. At the end of each day, I set aside 10 minutes for the children to complete the evaluation task. They are to take an index card and for 2 to 3 minutes, review what they thought was the most important thing they learned that day and tell it to a partner. Then they are to write for 5 minutes what they discussed. After they write these concepts, they "pair and share" with their partner. When the children leave the class, they put the index cards into their pockets on the chart. I review the cards. This gives me insight into what concepts the children have understood and recalled correctly. Cards are sent home at the end of a week so parents are kept up to date about what their children are learning. I encourage children and parents to discuss the contents of the cards and to extend the learning at home.

I have gotten good parental feedback from this activity. When parents ask their children, "What did you do in school today?" the children no longer say, "Nothing." They share what they have written on their index cards. Reviewing at the end of the day helps the children remember things they've done.

Christina Spiezio, Second Grade Teacher

Summary

3.1 Explain the role of assessment in early literacy development.

Assessment in early literacy development is used for guiding instruction first and therefore is a crucial element in the design of a program for children. At this stage, assessment is as much about information gathering as it is about evaluation—educators need to collect information to determine how to create more effective instruction. Assessment at this stage should also seek to be panoramic. That is, assessment needs to align with instructional objectives and, at the same time, take into account the total development of the child.

3.2 Define authentic assessment and describe several techniques for conducting it.

Authentic assessment activities represent and reflect the actual learning from inside and outside the classroom. The different authentic assessment models allow educators to determine what a child knows and needs to learn. Educators should integrate a variety of authentic assessment methods into their instruction. Some of the more common and more useful types include anecdotal observation forms, daily performance samples, audio recordings, videos, pencil-and-paper forms, student evaluations, surveys and interviews, conferences, and checklists.

3.3 Identify and describe in-depth measures of assessment.

Unlike the performance snapshots provided by authentic assessment tools, in-depth measures of assessment allow educators to track a student's longitudinal progress. Running records involve recording on a monthly basis errors and error types and tracking a child's accuracy rate. Informal reading inventories are similar to running records but also track comprehension. Portfolio assessment involves collecting pieces of work that, over time, paint an almost complete picture of the child's literacy achievement. The information in a portfolio should be shared with the child, parents, and school personnel.

3.4 Discuss the pros and cons of standardized testing.

Standardized tests are prepared by publishers and are norm referenced. Raw scores are converted into grade level scores and into percentile ranks that allow for a child's performance to be compared to his or her larger group of cohorts. Scores and rankings provide simple and understandable measures of performance. There are, however, many concerns about using standardized tests: they only test one modality; they may not reflect instructional best practices; teachers may feel pressured to teach to the test; quantitative results do not qualitatively reflect the strengths and weaknesses in the aggregate score; and standardized tests produce less reliable results with younger children.

3.5 Discuss standards and explain how they can affect the literacy curriculum.

Literacy standards articulate what students need to learn at each grade level in English/Language Arts. CCSS describe what children should be able to demonstrate at the end of each grade and are organized into four levels: key ideas and details, craft and structure, integration of knowledge and ideas, and range of reading and level of text complexity. Standards have been adopted by 45 states and provide uniform expectations for student outcomes across the country. The standards do however, leave room for each state to determine how to reach the standards. The CCSS emphasize helping each child become a reader who can understand critically analyze materials read, so the standards emphasize the use of nonfiction materials and project-based instruction.

3.6 Describe the assessment tools designed to measure outcomes.

Standardized assessment should have a formative component tightly linked to standards. The test should assess each child's individual progress, asses each child's progress in relationship to his or her peers, and assess groups across specific areas of need. This is a way to determine the effectiveness of the curriculum.

Activities and Questions

1. Select a child from your field placement or from your own classroom. The child can be a relative or a friend's child. The child should be between the ages of 4 and 8. Begin a portfolio for this child and collect the following pieces of work over a three month period of time:

   a. An analyzed language sample (Chapter 6)
   b. Concepts about books and conventions of print (Chapter 7)
   c. Letter recognition (Chapter 7)
   d. Phonological awareness test (Chapter 8)
   e. Phonics test (Chapter 8)
   f. Frequently used words (Chapter 7)
   g. Story retelling for sequence, details, and story structure (Chapter 9)
   h. Assessment of writing samples (Chapter 10)
   i. Running record for grade level and types of errors (Chapter 3)
   j. Assessment of comprehension of text (Chapter 9)
   k. Child interviews about reading and writing (Chapter 3)
   l. Promoting early literacy at home, parent interview (Chapter 14)

2. Imagine that the parents in your district are not pleased with the authentic measures for assessment being used. They want to know if their children are doing as well as others. Based on standardized test scores, they want to know if their child is above, below, or at grade level. You are convinced that authentic assessment is the right way to evaluate children. What can you do to help parents understand and accept the authentic assessment strategies? Plan a parent workshop to inform them about standards and how you link your instruction and assessment to them.

3. Design your own assessment that you could potentially use in your classroom. Outline the components of the assessment and align them with the corresponding standards in this chapter. Provide a brief rationale for what this assessment is measuring and how its student results could impact future lessons.

   a. Child interviews about reading and writing (Chapter 3)
   b. Promoting early literacy at home, parent interview (Chapter 14)

Chapter 4

Literacy and Diversity: Teaching Children with Different Needs

Photo credit: Cathy Yeulet/123RF

Learning Outcomes

After reading this chapter, you should be able to:

4.1 Describe the impact of shifting demographics and cultural diversity on literacy.

4.2 List ways to help English learners communicate in school.

4.3 Describe strategies for teaching children with exceptionalities.

4.4 Summarize how to address diversity through differentiated instruction.

4.5 Explain the importance of practicing empathy for diversity in the literacy environment.

VOCABULARY

Cultural diversity
Dialect
English learner (EL)
Gifted
Inclusion
Pull-out programs
Reading Recovery
Response to Intervention (RTI)

In the beginning of our country our founders understood the need for a literate population and that we needed to start educating children from the time they were very young. Thomas Jefferson talked about three fundamental characteristics that needed to become a part of our national beliefs and they were: "*(1) the ability of every citizen to read is necessary to the practice of democracy, (2) it is therefore the duty of the general public to support the teaching of reading for all youngsters, and (3) reading should be taught during the earliest years of schooling.*" He continued with the following: "*none is more important, none more legitimate, than of rendering the people safe, as they are the ultimate guardians of their own liberty.*" "Thomas Jefferson, The Life and Selected Writings of Thomas Jefferson" (Koch & Penden, 1998)

Quality literacy instruction is necessary for all children. Small-group settings are particularly critical for children with diverse needs. Such settings encourage communication and meaningful, natural conversation. **English learners (EL)** will pick up a lot of English from informal conversations and interactions with their peers. More capable children can help struggling readers to learn in small groups and centers. Stations are small areas in a classroom that provide children with activities to do independently or in collaboration with another child. Activities in centers focus on practicing skills learned in literacy or in content areas.

Mr. Abere's second-grade children were working independently and collaboratively during station time. He described the following incident with a English learner: Juanita never spoke in class. One day, Mr. Abere observed Juanita acting as a teacher with a group of children she organized. These three children sat in a circle; each child had a copy of the same book. Juanita, acting as the teacher, asked different children if they wanted to read.

Mrs. Nash had station time where small groups of children had the opportunity to work together independent of the teacher. She modeled the materials so they would know how to use them. When speaking with Mrs. Nash, it became apparent that children with special needs greatly benefited from independent work during literacy center time. Mrs. Nash described a specific incident involving a struggling reader in her classroom whose work was well below grade level. According to Mrs. Nash, Charlene never read aloud. One day, Mrs. Nash noticed her reading aloud to a rag doll while another child was listening. Mrs. Nash bent over and said quietly "Nice reading, Charlene." The reading aloud continued daily during literacy station time.

Marcel was a gifted child in Mrs. Rosen's classroom with many low achievers. He worked alone most of the time. About two months after literacy center time was initiated in his classroom, he participated with other children in literacy activities. The first time Mrs. Rosen observed him with others, he was reading the newspaper and checking out the weather in other parts of the country. Patrick asked Marcel if he could look too. Marcel was pleased, and then David joined them. Together, they read and discussed how hot and cold it was in various locations throughout the country.

Numerous anecdotes from station time describe how children are able to find ways to participate in spite of some challenges they may have. One teacher commented, "There seems to be something that every child can find to do during station time and the social interaction causes collaboration no matter what the achievement of the children involved."

The Impact of Shifting Demographics and Cultural Diversity on Literacy

Early childhood education has always been child centered and concerned with the social, emotional, physical, and intellectual needs of children. In early childhood, every youngster is seen as a unique individual; however, now, more than ever, there is greater diversity in today's classrooms; differentiating instruction to meet the individual needs of all children is a necessity.

Identification of special needs makes educators more aware that differences exist; this helps in determining the implications for instructional programs and successfully meeting individual needs. According to the Common Core Standards (2010), learning goals are the same for all children although not all will be able to achieve them. That means we need to adjust instruction for each student. Best practice is usually appropriate for all, with some modifications for those with special needs (Banks & Banks, 2009; Delpit, 1995). In addition to this chapter, more strategies are offered on diversity throughout this book.

The Role of Shifting Demographics

The demographics of the U.S. population are becoming more racially and ethnically diverse. Statistics show that one in every three children is from a different ethnic or racial group. Today, the United States is serving about 15 million children who come from households in which English is not the primary language. It is projected that by 2030, 40 percent of the school-age population in the United States will be English learners (Brock & Raphael, 2005). More than 400 different languages are reported to be spoken in the United States.

Spanish is the most widespread, but there are other languages spoken such as Korean, Arabic, Russian, Navajo, Mandarin, and Japanese, to name just a few (Brock & Raphael, 2005). A major concern is that about 85 percent of the country's teachers speak English only (Gollnick & Chinn, 2008). However, most effective strategies for teaching early literacy development to native English speakers are also effective with EL students.

Much of the research on academic achievement in the United States demonstrates that if English is not a child's first language, that is, if the child is an EL that child is less likely to be successful than a native English student (Donahue et al., 2001; Rossi & Stringfield, 1995). Some of the reasons for this gap are the lack of acceptance and inclusion of a student's home culture in schools, the complex nature of learning a second language, and the limited literacy ability of many of the families who do not speak English as a first language (Banks & Banks, 2009).

In the past, diversity was disregarded in the United States; children were expected to ignore their unique cultural backgrounds and language differences and to learn English and American customs. If we are to live in harmony in a pluralistic society and provide a worthwhile educational experience for all children, it is imperative that educational leaders accept the charge to provide a relevant education for all students. Educators must be sensitive toward cultural and language differences and recognize that children can and should maintain their cultural heritage and native language, while simultaneously learning standard English and American cultural values (George, Raphael, & Florio-Ruane, 2003; Templeton, 1996).

MyLab Education
Video Example 4.1
Cultural Experiences
In this video, children learn about cultural dances during Black History Month. The video shows 5th graders but the activity can be adapted for all grade levels. https://www.youtube.com/watch?v=cBByA9PMg78

Responding to Cultural Diversity

Multiculturalism is a complicated issue, referring not only to race and ethnicity but also to class, culture, religion, sex, and age. The multiracial, multiethnic, multicultural, and multilingual nature of our dynamic society mandates that we teach understanding of differences as an ongoing process involving self-reflection, self-awareness, increasing knowledge, and while developing relevant skills (Schickedanz, York, Stewart, & White, 1990). We must welcome **cultural diversity** in our schools; it adds a rich dimension to the classroom and to topics of study. Most importantly, every child has the right to be respected and to receive a quality educational experience. By recognizing students' diverse backgrounds, we will enhance their self-images. Differences should be the norm rather than the exception.

Goals for classrooms in our multicultural society include:

1. An improved understanding of cultural differences and their effect on lifestyle, values, worldviews, and individual differences.
2. An increased awareness of how to develop strategies to enhance learning in a multicultural environment.
3. A framework for conceptualizing ways to create a climate conducive to learning and development.

The goals we need to pursue for children in culturally diverse classrooms and for children whose language is other than English are as follows:

1. Children need to feel comfortable with their ethnic identities.
2. Children need to learn to function in other cultures, particularly in the dominant culture.
3. Children need to relate positively with individuals from various ethnic backgrounds.
4. Children must learn English however they should also retain and value their first language(s) and culture(s)

Teachers must develop their own understanding of the multiethnic groups they serve and respect their students' ethnic identities, heritages, and traditions. Teachers must also be aware of their own ethnic heritages, traditions, and beliefs (Barone, 1998; Bauer & Manyak, 2008; Tabors, 1998).

MyLab Education Self-Check 4.1

Helping English Learners Communicate at School

A major instructional concern in early childhood literacy programs is the varied language backgrounds of the children who come to day-care centers, preschools, kindergartens, and first, second, and third grades. Any given group may contain children using words, syntax, and language patterns very different from those of standard English. Just within the United States, there are many different forms of English usage; for example, there are distinct grammars and accents in rural New England, Appalachia, and in some African American communities. Even similar languages of children, whose families have immigrated from Latin America, the Middle East, or Asia, can differ greatly.

In addition to speaking different languages, children also come to school speaking different dialects. A **dialect** is an alternative form of one particular language used in a different cultural, regional, or social group (Jalongo, 2007; Leu & Kinzer, 1991; Otto, 2006). Such differences can be so significant that an individual from a region with one English dialect may have difficulty understanding someone from another region because the pronunciation of letter sounds is so different. Dialects are not inherently superior to one another; however, one dialect typically emerges as the standard for a given language and is used by the more advantaged individuals of a society. Teachers must be aware of different dialects and help youngsters with the comprehension of standard dialects. Children should not be degraded or viewed as less intelligent for speaking different dialects.

The following categories represent the diverse language abilities of young children (Fromkin & Rodman, 2010; Galda, 1995).

Diverse Language Abilities of Children

1. Children who are recent immigrants with little or no English.
2. Children who come from homes in which the language is something other than English, but who speak some English because of their experiences with television and their contacts outside the home.

3. Children who speak both English and another language fluently. These children are usually easily assimilated into the majority group. Often, English becomes the major language with which they communicate.
4. Children who speak mainly English but who have poor skills in their parents' or family's language. Often, these children speak English at home, but their parents speak to them in another language.
5. Children who speak nonstandard English because the English spoken at home is not fluent or is a dialect. These children need to learn to speak and read standard English. However, they must not be made to feel that their home language is inferior or asked to abandon it.
6. Children who are monolingual in English.

All six categories represent major concerns because a firm base in oral language is strongly linked to literacy development. In addition to skill development, teachers need to consider emotional concerns. Unfortunately and often unintentionally children with language differences are looked down on and classified as students with potential learning problems. Some teachers have low expectations for English learners and assign low-level tasks.

Differences do *not* mean deficits. Teachers need to respect language differences and help children take pride in their backgrounds. Diversity in language and heritage should be shared to enrich the classroom experience (Meier, 2004). It is however crucial for all children to learn to speak and write in standard English to succeed in our society.

Children's Responses to Language Differences

Children tend to choose playmates who speak the same language, presumably because it is easier to communicate. However, they usually do not reject those who speak a different language and will use gestures and other means of communication when interacting with them. Allowing children natural opportunities in the classroom to communicate with one another is a crucial component of helping EL students. Much of the research on dual-language acquisition suggests that we *acquire,* or naturally and subconsciously internalize, a new language through informal situations that warrant real communicative needs. Providing students time to acquire a second language along with *learning,* which is defined by more conscious learning and more direct instruction about rules and conventions, is crucial.

MyLab Education
Video Example 4.2
Supporting ELs and Families
In this video, best practices are shown in a comprehensive and engaging way to help ELs develop language skills.
https://www.youtube.com/watch?v=09PrmLppQ1A

Creating language-rich instruction for English learners is important as well. Bilingual children will often act as interpreters for their parents and friends who are less skilled in the language of the classroom. Although children are curious about differences in speech and will often "correct" one another, they have not developed the biases that adults have toward nonstandard usage.

Preschool and kindergarten children will acquire the language easily when immersed in language-rich classrooms where there are good models of English and sensitive teachers. This is particularly true of children whose native language is well developed. Children whose first language is not English and whose first language is not well developed will have difficulty learning English as easily as those who have a command of their first language (Meier, 2004). For that reason, it is important for children to feel good about their first language. To support them in that regard:

- Include some print in the classroom that is from the children's first language.
- Suggest that EL students create books in their first language and share their stories.
- Be sure that children from different language backgrounds have the opportunity to read and write with others who speak their language, such as parents, aides, and other children in the school (Freeman & Freeman, 2006; Griffin, 2001; Otto, 2006; Roskos, Tabor, & Lenhardt, 2009).

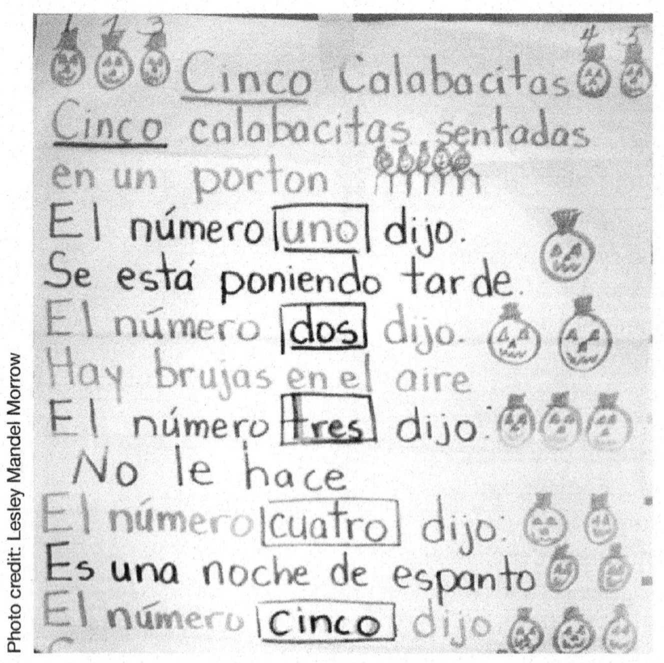

Photo credit: Lesley Mandel Morrow

Encourage EL students to create and share books and materials in their native languages as a means to respect and learn about their home culture.

Respecting the Different Cultural Backgrounds of Children at School

It is crucial that teachers show that they respect the cultural heritages and *value* the native languages of their students from the moment they walk into their classrooms. Imagine how scary it is for a young child to come into a place where everyone speaks a different language. Teachers need to show interest in their students' native languages and try to learn at least a few key phrases in each of the languages represented in their classrooms (Xu, 2003). It is helpful to talk with parents about their child's level of familiarity with English. Teachers should have a translator during conferences if the family wants one and agrees to have one. Whenever possible, schools should communicate with the parents to create a connection between home and school (International Reading Association, 2001). Encourage parents to participate in their children's classroom and share their culture and language.

The classroom should have plenty of words, phrases, and texts in the native languages of the EL students. These include translations of favorite books, newspapers, menus, and other everyday texts that a student might encounter at home. This will allow teachers to connect each child's home and school literacy experiences (Au, 2001; Xu & Drame, 2008). If teachers become familiar with each student's cultures, the teachers are more likely to respond effectively to all students' needs (Allen, 2017).

In some cultures children are encouraged to participate in classroom discussions; in others, children are encouraged not to speak in class. Making eye contact with someone of authority while he or she is speaking is regarded as a sign of respect in some cultures, whereas this practice is viewed as disrespectful in others. In some cultures, children eat with their hands; in others, they use chopsticks or forks, knives, and spoons. We cannot expect children to engage in manners or activities that conflict with what they learn at home. It is imperative that teachers keep this in mind when designing classroom rules and procedures so that all students feel at ease. If teachers are unaware of these cultural traditions, they can easily be misinterpreted as rude or indifferent behavior.

The questionnaire shown in Figure 4.1 assists teachers in obtaining important information from parents about their children. This will help you better understand their culture, respond to their behavior in an appropriate manner, and make the child feel comfortable and respected in your classroom (Hadaway & Young, 2006).

Strategies for Teaching English Learners to Read and Write

Four well-known types of instruction for English learners are:
(1) English immersion, (2) English as a second language (ESL), (3) bilingual education, and (4) primary language instruction.

English immersion, or English-only instruction, is effective with young children who are able to acquire new languages easily. Students may learn English through interaction with peers and teachers in school. There isn't a special program other than respecting the child's background, making them feel comfortable, and using bits of their language in the classroom.

In an *English as a second language (ESL)* program, children are taken out of their classroom by a different teacher and taught English. Students learn through direct linguistic instruction as well as through the interactions they have with their peers and other teachers throughout the day.

Figure 4.1 Helping Me Learn about You and Your Child

Information about your child

Child's Name and Country of Origin: ____________________

Mother's Name and Country of Origin: ____________________

Father's Name and Country of Origin: ____________________

Name of caregiver if not the mother or father: ____________________

Language or Languages spoken at home: ____________________

Does your child speak English? ____________________

Does your child speak the language spoken at home if it isn't English? ____________________

What types of food is eaten at home? ____________________

What utensils are used to eat? Fork, chop sticks, Hands? ____________________

Do you live in a house?, apartment? ____________________

How many people live with you? ____________________

Are there brothers and sisters? How Many? ____________________

Is the child the oldest, youngest, etc? ____________________

Do you help your child with homework? ____________________

What does your child like most in school? ____________________

What doesn't your child like at school? ____________________

Does your child have friends they see after school? ____________________

What does your child do when he/she is a alone? ____________________

Does your child like to read? ____________________

What does he/she read? ____________________

What are the most important things you want your child to learn in school? ____________________

There are several approaches to *bilingual education*. The *transitional approach* promotes subtractive bilingualism, in which English eventually replaces the student's native language in school. The goal of the *maintenance approach* is additive bilingualism, which means that students learn English while maintaining their first language. The two languages have equal value. The *two-way bilingual approach* can be used in classrooms with a mix of English speakers and non-English speakers (Gollnick &

Chinn, 2008). Roughly half of the curriculum is taught in English, and half is taught in the language of the child.

Primary language instruction for EL students develops literacy in the primary language first, before shifting to bilingual or English-only instruction. Children are taught concepts, knowledge, and skills in their primary language as English skills are gradually incorporated into instruction (Gollnick & Chinn, 2008).

There is research to support all of these approaches. Several investigations show that programs that provide initial literacy instruction in a child's primary language and promote long-term primary language development have proved effective with English learners (Gunning, 2003; International Reading Association, 2001). The Committee on the Prevention of Reading Difficulties in Young Children recommends that children learn to read in their first language while learning to speak English over time (Snow, Burns, & Griffin, 1998). Two-way bilingual instruction has also been successful.

Research supported by the U.S. Institute of Education Sciences, the U.S. National Institute for Child Health and Human Development, and the U.S. Office of English Language Acquisition found that:

- Knowledge of vocabulary in English is much more important in learning to read for EL students than learning to decode.
- Bilingual education has the most positive impact on English reading when English is introduced early at all grade levels.
- Teaching the components of literacy—phonemic awareness, phonics, fluency, vocabulary, comprehension, and writing—is essential.
- Effective programs for native speakers are also effective for EL students.
- Instruction must be differentiated based on children's needs.
- Effective instruction for EL students utilizes multiple strategies such as dual and bilingual approaches, as well as use of the home language.
- Effective instruction uses all content areas to teach English.

Because there are many factors at play in each EL student's educational development, there is no one perfect method of instruction for *all EL* students. Teachers need to decide with other professionals and parents what is best for each child.

There are numerous strategies for attending to ELs in the classroom. Many of these strategies are effective in promoting literacy for *all* students, not just English learners. Good literacy practice is good practice for all.

English learners may be very timid and nervous when they first enter an English-speaking classroom, so it is crucial that teachers have a warm smile which is a universal sign of welcome. Additionally, teachers may want to have someone who speaks the child's language record a welcoming greeting to be played on the first day of class. Teachers can help their native-speaking students develop empathy for the non-English-speaking child by having someone come into the class and teach a lesson in an unfamiliar language (Shore, 2001). In fact, if the EL student is comfortable, the student could act as "teacher for a day" and immediately foster a sense of belonging for them.

Share some words from the EL child's native language. This activity would reinforce the message that knowing another language is something to be celebrated and will place the EL student in the role of expert to help foster self-esteem. This experience will help the English-speaking children to better understand how a non-English-speaking child feels in an English-only classroom.

1. Making EL's comfortable
2. Strategies to the EL's learn to read and
3. Parent involvement

Some elements to helping EL students feel comfortable are:

Photo credit: Nailia Schwarz/Fotolia

Dramatic play with stories, rhymes, and props is helpful with students.

- Make your classroom predictable with routines that will help EL students feel safe and accepted in their new environment. Do things at the same time each day. Next to the components of the daily schedule, provide a visual reference for EL students.
- Tasks should involve students as active participants. For example, assign a EL student nonverbal class jobs, such as passing out folders or watering the plants, at the beginning of the year so he or she can contribute immediately.
- Assign a classmate (ideally a bilingual student) as a buddy of each EL child. This buddy should be friendly, knowledgeable, respectful, and eager to show the EL student around and provide help when necessary.
- Engage the EL student in peer-assisted learning with older children working with younger children. Instructional content should utilize student diversity.
- Label various classroom objects in English and in the EL child's native language.
- The classroom library should contain a variety of texts in English as well as in the primary language of EL. Include newspapers, menus, and other environmental print in multiple languages in the class library.
- Speak slowly and use good diction; you do not have to speak loudly.
- Demonstrate sincere interest in learning about your EL child's native language, customs, and traditions. Allow this discussion to play an important role in your activities.

To help EL students with language and literacy development:

- Provide intensive small-group language and literacy instruction (Gersten et al., 2007).
- Provide daily and extensive vocabulary instruction.
- Vocabulary development is the key to learning English and learning to read. For example, select greetings, games, and familiar words and phrases to introduce, such as playground, cafeteria, bathroom, gymnasium, centers, books, pens, and pencils (refer to Figures 4.2 and 4.3) (Cappellini, 2005).
- Use visuals (such as pictures or graphic organizers), model language, then engage in extended conversations with EL students, read multiple genres of children's literature to EL (such as picture story books, fables, folk tales, poems, and informational books). Preview what you believe is new vocabulary before reading (Gunning, 2003; Xu, 2003).
- ELs should participate in interactive word games, such as picture puzzles and action Jeopardy!
- Have EL children collect new vocabulary on their Very Own Words cards kept in a container. On one side, write the word in English, and on the other, write it in their native language. Use an accompanying picture for reinforcement. (See the Glossary and Chapter 5 for a description of Very Own Words.)

Figure 4.2 Spanish and English Words

These are familiar school words. Enlarge them and color or copy them on firm colored paper, laminate them, and hang them around the room. Talk about them before and after hanging them and refer to them often. Add to the list using clip art from the Internet.

Figure 4.2 Spanish and English Words (*continued*)

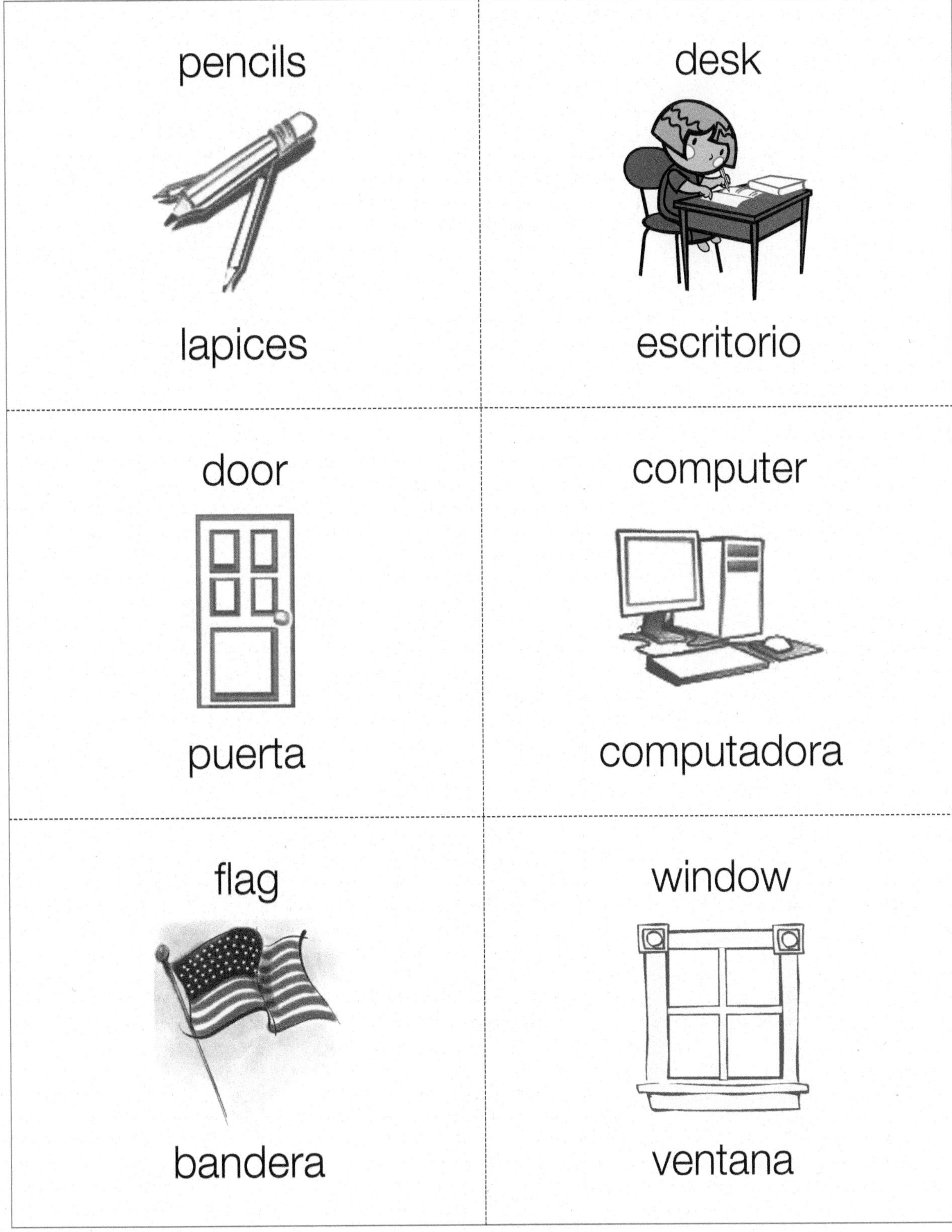

Figure 4.3 Spanish and English Phrases

These are familiar phrases. Enlarge them and color or copy them on firm colored paper, laminate them, and hang them around the room. Talk about them before and after hanging them and refer to them often. Add to the list using clip art from the Internet.

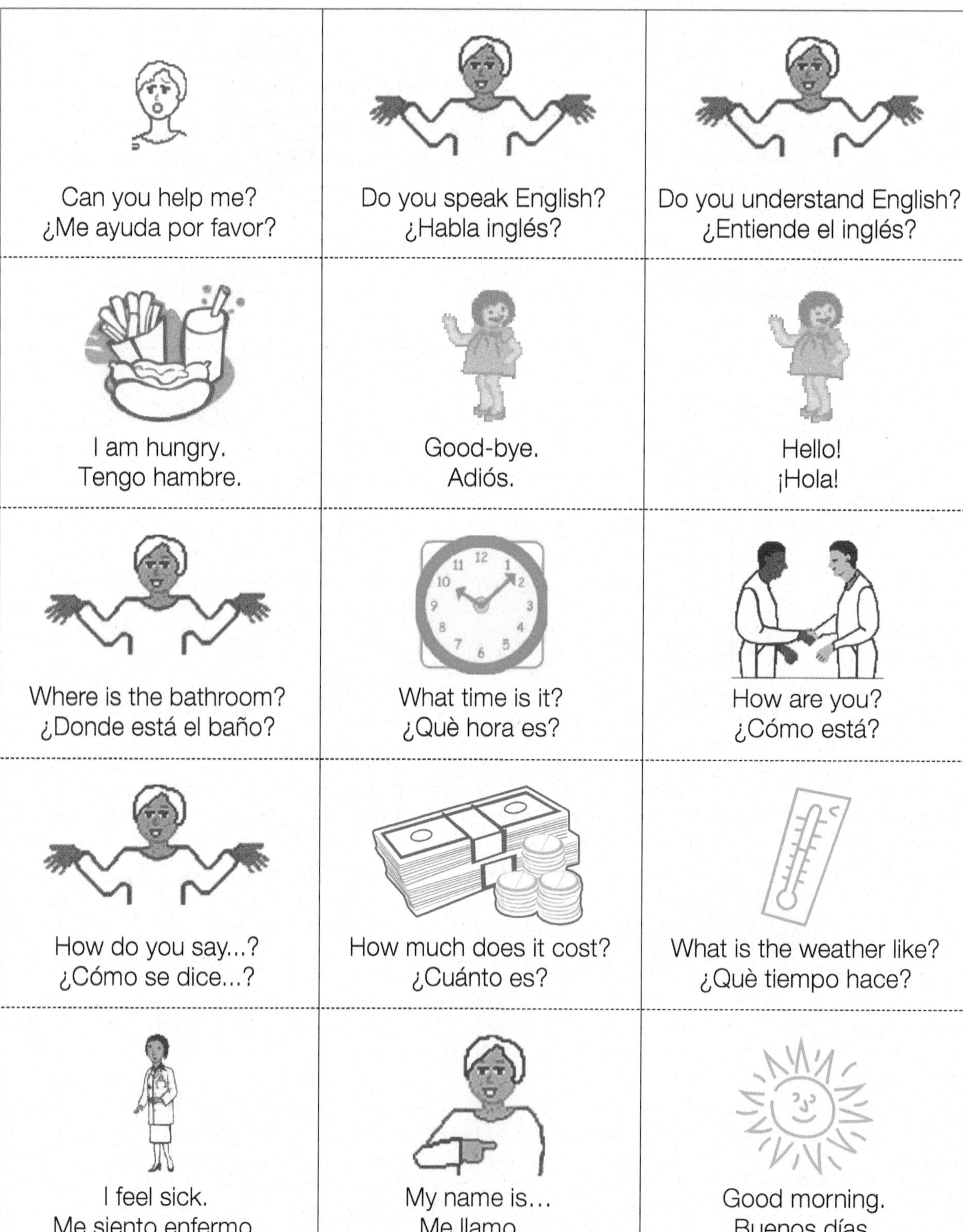

Can you help me?
¿Me ayuda por favor?
Do you speak English?
¿Habla inglés?
Do you understand English?
¿Entiende el inglés?
I am hungry.
Tengo hambre.
Good-bye.
Adiós.
Hello!
¡Hola!
Where is the bathroom?
¿Donde está el baño?
What time is it?
¿Què hora es?
How are you?
¿Cómo está?
How do you say...?
¿Cómo se dice...?
How much does it cost?
¿Cuánto es?
What is the weather like?
¿Què tiempo hace?
I feel sick.
Me siento enfermo.
My name is...
Me llamo...
Good morning.
Buenos días.

- Teachers can use *sheltered English* that involves using simple language, slow and repeated phrases, gestures, and visual references (Shore, 2001).
- Use high-interest picture books with predictable patterns.
- Give children as many language clues as possible through visuals, gestures, voice tone, expressions, and repetitive phrases. Repetition should be encouraged through songs, rhyming, dramatic play with stories, and props.
- Involve EL students in creating their own books about subject matter that is familiar to them. Original text is not bogged down in unfamiliar vocabulary, syntax, or cultural references, so it is easier for them (Gunning, 2003; Xu, 2003).
- Buddy and partner reading and writing are especially useful when one person is proficient in English and has some knowledge of the language spoken by the non-English-speaking child.
- Teachers can take dictation from EL students and write down their stories when they cannot write them down themselves. Stories can include a mixture of English and the native language of the children (Gunning, 2003).
- Whenever possible, allow EL students to utilize a computer for additional support and literacy motivation. Many digital programs and games are available to support such students. For example, Gmail (Google mail) has a "Google Translator" device that can translate emails into many languages.
- Research Internet sites that can support EL. A few that have been recommended are teachchildrenesl.com, eslkidstuff.com, and everythingesl.net.
- Engage EL students in visual media projects. Mixbooks.com is a website that allows students to create a digital scrapbook of visuals to communicate a story or message. Because the visuals are universal, they allow English learners more communicative opportunities.
- Repeated exposure to the English alphabet is necessary.
- Use explicit instruction in literacy lessons. In addition, model for children the use of picture cues and "picture walks." Picture walks are looking at each page of the book, reading the pictures first and then going back to read the words.
- Use the cloze procedure. Write a sentence or two and leave out a word or put the first letter of the word and leave the rest out. Have the children figure out the word from the meaning of the sentence. For example, after reading a simple story, have the children fill in the missing letters.

  Once upon a time there were th________little pigs.

  They lived with their mother and f________, but wanted to leave home. They said good-bye and each one left to build themselves a h________.

  The first pig built a house of st________w.

  The second pig built a house of st________ks.

  The third pig built a house of br________.
- Use manipulative materials, such as puppets and figures.
- Engage EL students in repeated readings. You read a story first and then the child reads it

  Choral reading is a useful strategy for EL.

  Echo reading is a useful strategy for EL.
- Record simple stories and have EL follow the text as the story is read.
- Cut up short stories into sentences for children to sequence.
- Cut up sentences into words to be sequenced into the sentences.

Photo credit: Erin Kramer

Use visual figures such as felt characters or puppets when telling stories to help students with vocabulary.

Show the similarity between some English and Spanish words—for example:

accident	accidente
intelligent	intelligente
marvelous	maravilloso

All activities should maximize the opportunity for language use.

Involving parents:

- Demonstrate strategies for parents so they can reinforce your literacy instruction at home.
- Encourage parents and family members to come into the classroom to share their culture and customs through a story, song, artifact, or traditional food.

Empower the parents of EL students by ensuring that they are informed about important school procedures, routines, and events. (Caesar & Nelson, 2014).

Remember the cultural heritage of children whose families have been in the United States for generations. Don't forget to recognize that their native land is the United States.

Throughout this book, when an activity or strategy is particularly helpful for use with EL students, a note with the head, Teaching English Learners, will be placed in the margin. Books written by the following authors cited in this chapter and referenced in the bibliography are devoted to dealing with English language learners: Akhavan (2006); Cloud, Genesee, and Hamayan (2009); Freeman and Freeman (2006); Herrera, Perez, and Escamilla (2010); and Herrell and Jordan (2011).

MyLab Education Self-Check 4.2
MyLab Education Application Exercise 4.1

Strategies for Children with Exceptionalities

Diversity in the classroom doesn't stop at cultural and linguistic differences. Students come to the classroom with a variety of individual competencies that need to be addressed in the learning situation. There are gifted students, students with learning disabilities, children from adverse environments, and students with physical impairments all with unique learning needs. In the next few sections we discuss how the teacher accommodates all of these differences by differentiating classroom instruction to meet the needs of these types of diversity. Differentiated instruction may take place in pull out resource rooms or within the reguar classroom, practicing *inclusion*–or educating all children in the same classroom including those with special education needs.

Gifted Students

Children who are **gifted** are often identified as having an intelligence quotient (IQ) of approximately 130 or more. For example, those who develop other skills, such as playing a musical instrument at an ability level far above that which is expected of a same-age child, are also considered gifted.

Gifted children are often leaders. Their special talents need to be encouraged, but not at the expense of recognizing their social, emotional, and physical needs. Differentiating assignments to make them more challenging for the ability levels of these children will accommodate their special talents.

There have been pull out programs where a few times a week a child in a gifted program goes to another classroom for enrichment activities. Some school districts round up all their gifted children and they have a day together in another school to work on projects.

With tremendous concern for the achievement gap, the gifted are often forgotten. In the 1980s, there were multiple programs to challenge gifted children. With growing concerns for struggling readers and English language learners, many programs for gifted children have unfortunately been canceled under the assumption that these children will do well regardless. There is a glimmer of new interest in the gifted and hopefully good programs will be restored.

Teachers must look to alter assignments and activities for the gifted to ensure they are being challenged. This does not mean that teachers should simply give these children additional busy work to complete. Instead, if a gifted child finishes an assignment early, he or she could opt to read a choice book, assist struggling students with their assignments, or work on an ongoing project of interest. Similarly, assignments could be designed with a basic portion and an enrichment or extension portion that allows the gifted student to delve more deeply into the topic.

Without the challenge of an appropriate program, many of these children will not reach their full potential and some will lose interest in school because of the lack of stimulation; therefore, maintaining challenge and motivation for highly motivated, very bright children is crucial to their ongoing development.

Students with Learning Disabilities

Children who have **learning disabilities** are those who perform below age and/or grade level. They are usually of normal intelligence but perform below their ability level. Children have learning disabilities for a variety of reasons. Some cannot process language easily; they have trouble speaking, writing, or understanding language. Some conditions associated with learning disabilities are perceptual and some are related to processing problems, dyslexia, or a brain injury causing minimal brain dysfunction. Children with learning disabilities have normal intelligence but there is some issue causing them difficulty in learning to read.

Children with learning disabilities are often easily distracted and have short attention spans. For these students, assignments and class procedures may require modification. For example, a student with a short attention span might have preferential seating in proximity of the classroom teacher who can subtly redirect attention as necessary. An emphasis on quality over quantity with regard to assignments is also important, as well as maintaining contact with the child's parents. These children are likely to need additional instructional time. With appropriate instruction, children who have learning disabilities can achieve success in school.

MyLab Education
Video Example 4.3
Special Education K-2 Teacher
In this video, a K-2 Special Education teacher talks about what her day is like. https://www.youtube.com/watch?v=an3ngVFbJC0

Attention deficit hyperactivity disorder (ADHD) also can cause learning issues. It is a condition causing children to have trouble focusing, paying attention, sitting still, and staying on task. The problem is usually due to a chemical imbalance and causes learning problems. *Attention deficit disorder (ADD)* is similar to *ADHD*; however, these children are not hyperactive; they are often the opposite. They tend to be quiet and often seem to be elsewhere, as their ability to concentrate is minimal.

Programs for children with learning disabilities and children with *ADHD* or *ADD* need to be highly structured, with short periods of direct instruction. In addition, programs must provide students with materials that will be of interest to them. Regular breaks throughout the day may also help these children maintain attention and focus in the classroom. Many of the strategies discussed throughout the book will be effective for teaching children who have learning disabilities.

Students with Physical Impairments

Physical impairments include visual or hearing impairments, communication disorders, and orthopedic impairments. **Inclusion** is a term that suggests that children with impairments become a part of the regular classroom, even if they have severe problems, with the necessary assistance provided.

Children with *visual impairments* are considered legally blind, have no useful vision, or have very limited sight. For these children, strategies that include auditory and tactile experiences are important. Learning materials are available in large print for low-vision children. Children with no vision must learn to read through the use of Braille, a system of reading for the blind consisting of characters represented by raised dots on paper. These materials are available in basal readers from the American Printing House for the Blind (Ward & McCormick, 1981). For the most part, only children with minimal visual problems will be included in the regular classroom.

Children who are *hearing impaired* are completely deaf or have some useful limited hearing. Some of these youngsters can be helped through the use of a hearing aid, which amplifies sounds for them. Children likely to be included in regular classrooms will be those with some hearing ability. Visual and tactile methods for learning are encouraged with these students. Those who are deaf or have very limited hearing may use sign language to communicate, so some knowledge of signing would help classroom teachers better connect with their students who are hearing impaired.

Mobility impairment in this context refers to disabilities that are often congenital or acquired during childhood through such as cerebral palsy, muscular dystrophy, spina bifida, and rheumatoid arthritis. Effective learning strategies for these youngsters will be similar to those used with all children. If the ability to use fine motor control is compromised, alternative methods for writing will be needed. These children may benefit from regular computer use or having a teacher, paraprofessional or peer take dictation. Youngsters with conditions that cause mobility problems may need more time to complete assignments because of motor coordination problems. Because their disability is more obvious than others, an important goal is for the classroom teacher to nurture a positive attitude toward these children, especially with those students who have no special needs. Open communication surrounding disabilities will often help.

Children with *communication disorders* are also included in the regular classroom. These children have speech or language difficulties. Speech impairments include problems in articulation or pronunciation, a lisp, voice disorders (abnormal loudness, pitch, or voice quality), and fluency disorders such as stuttering.

Children with *language disorders* have difficulty acquiring and using language. Children who have language delays are significantly behind their peers in both the production and comprehension aspects of language development. These children likely will go to special classes for additional support. For the most part, strategies that are appropriate for all children will be appropriate for these youngsters in the regular classroom. Chapters 4 and 6, which deals with language development, discusses instructional contexts appropriate for children with minimal language problems.

Techniques for instruction need to be concrete and include active involvement. Helping these youngsters stay on task is an important goal. Activities that will grasp their attention are those that are most likely to be successful. Working with them on an individual basis is crucial to finding out the best ways for these children to learn. As with gifted children, differentiating regular classroom activities to meet their ability levels will accommodate their needs.

When trying to meet the special needs of children, focusing on the instructional goal is important. A team of school personnel needs to be involved in preparing plans for disabled youngsters. This team needs to figure out how to help these children compensate for their disabilities so that they will be able to carry out activities successfully. For example, a child who has an attention deficit disorder and moves too quickly during independent station work from one task to the next can be paired with a peer who is known to be able to stay focused. This peer can read directions for the student who has the disability, thus providing explicit instruction about the activity.

Parents can be an excellent resource for informing the teacher about a child's strengths, weaknesses, and interests. The collective guidance of other children, special education consultants, and aides will support the children with special needs.

All those involved in working with children with special needs must have a tolerance for differences. Thinking of children with differences as less fortunate is not conducive to learning. Teachers must focus on how to assist children in compensating for their disabilities so that they can learn to function independently with their strengths (Erickson & Koppenhaver, 1995).

The following instructional guidelines are helpful when dealing with children who have physical impairments or developmental learning differences:

1. Observe students regularly for indications that they may have some physical impairment or developmental learning differences. For example, a child who seems to have difficulty seeing the chalkboard, who copies things incorrectly, and who squints to see things may have visual problems needing attention.
2. Seek help from your district's support services with children you find are experiencing problems. Be sure you have concerns identified and appropriate assistance given to children in need.
3. When you find out the problem a child may be experiencing, become informed about it by discussing it with special education teachers and other staff members.
4. Use learning principles that are successful with all youngsters, such as encouragement, praise, and a positive mindset.
5. Adapt instruction to meet special needs. Good strategies are often good for all children, with minor adaptations needed to meet their individual differences.
6. Remain in regular contact with parents of children with special needs. Discuss the help the school is providing, inform them of additional help they might seek outside the school environment, and enlist their help with activities they can do with their youngsters at home.
7. When a child cannot handle his or her needs independently, physically or intellectually, you may consider requesting that a special teacher be assigned to your classroom to offer the individual attention that child needs.

MyLab Education Application Exercise 4.2

At-Risk Students

Children considered at risk are affected by several factors that have been identified. Such students may speak a language other than English, have a learning disability, have physical difficulties, or live in poor, disadvantaged homes with or without parents. Poverty does not mean that children cannot be successful in school; however, research on literacy achievement illustrates that about 55 percent of children below the poverty level read below grade level (Donahue, Doane, & Grigg, 2000). This is often due to limited literacy ability of their family, or the lack of awareness of the importance of literacy to succeed as an adult.

Research illustrates that children who attend preschool are more successful in school. It is crucial to start early with children at risk; many are already behind at 3 and 4 years of age. Teachers need to select activities in which children can experience success. When children are successful, they want to try more. If they are not successful, they often want to quit.

Children at risk often lack literacy background experiences; this limitation affects their vocabulary and language development, which in turn affects their literacy learning. Many have limited literacy materials in their homes; thus, positive literacy experiences may be few and far between for these students outside of school. Providing classroom experiences that stimulate discussion are helpful in building vocabulary. Motivational variables are particularly crucial to these children and will be discussed at length in a later chapter. Having access to a variety of print and digital materials of interest to your children will nurture positive literacy experiences in the classroom.

In a speech given at a National Reading Conference meeting, Lisa Delpit ("Delpit, 1995") spoke about teaching "other people's children." She discussed general characteristics for a successful literacy program in urban school settings with children from diverse and disadvantaged backgrounds. Here are some of the main points in her presentation:

1. Learn and respect the child's home culture.
2. Do not teach less content to children from disadvantaged backgrounds. They can learn as all other children learn. Teachers, parents, children, and the community should recognize children's ability and teach them accordingly.
3. Whatever instructional program or methodology is used, critical thinking should be a goal. Children achieve because of teachers who believe in them. Poor children often practice the use of critical skills on a regular basis because they have had to be independent and have many home responsibilities.
4. All children must gain access to basic skills, conventions, and strategies that are essential to succeed in U.S. education and life.
5. Help children view themselves as competent and worthy.
6. Use familiar metaphors and experiences from children's lives to connect what they already know to school knowledge. If you cannot justify what you are teaching, you should not be teaching it.
7. Create a sense of family and nurture a caring attitude in your classroom. Make the children your own while you have them. Tell them they are the smartest children in the world and expect them to be. Children rise to the bar you set for them. Then they will learn for the teacher, not just from the teacher.
8. Monitor and assess needs and then address them with a wealth of diverse strategies.
9. Recognize and build on strengths that children and families already have.
10. Foster a connection between the child and the community so that learning experiences are relevant and inspirational. Help children understand that they go to school for their community and predecessors. If they fail, they fail not only for themselves but also for their community; if they succeed, they succeed for all.

MyLab Education Self-Check 4.3
MyLab Education Application Exercise 4.3

Addressing Diversity Through Differentiated Instruction

Meeting individual needs is a major concern for teachers. In this chapter, we have discussed dual language learners, children who are gifted, those with learning disabilities, those who are struggling readers, and children with physical disabilities. Many of these children are at risk for success at learning to read, yet all children need differentiated instruction to meet their individual needs. Let's continue the discussion of diversity by examining best practices for differentiated instruction in the classroom.

Steps for Differentiating Instruction

If educators have learned one thing from implementing the many programs throughout the years to help children with special concerns, it is that differentiation of instruction requires time with a teacher and child working together. With small group or one-on-one instruction, teachers are able to assess the child and differentiate instruction to meet individual needs.

> Savannah is reading at a second-grade level and is very immature. Her Mom works long hours and is tired when she gets home. However, she doesn't know that she should be reading to Savannah or take her to the library. Savannah only reads in school. José just came from Mexico and speaks no English. He knows only math facts and has no access to books. Nathaniel reads at the fourth-grade level. His mom and dad are both teachers and provide lots of literacy experiences for him. He has a large collection of books at home and goes to the library often. He has many experiences with his family on vacation and at museums and reads a lot at home. Ashley is an excellent creative writer who reads at the third-grade level. She often doesn't pay attention to what is going on at school and does her own thing. Finally, Jenny is a struggling reader with language and visual processing problems. She is not fluent in English. All these children are in Ms. Callihan's second-grade classroom. She also has 20 more children each having her or his own special needs. These children are in need of differentiated instruction.

When teachers differentiate instruction, they:

- Assess students to design the instruction to meet their needs.
- Keep their instruction flexible and make quick changes if necessary.
- Respond to student differences.
- Respond to student interests.
- Respond to student achievement levels and learning needs.

Quality instruction includes whole-class lessons that build on background knowledge, are linked to the standards of the grade level, are research based, and include a variety of activities to learn skills. This is often referred to as *tier 1* teaching.

Next, to account for the differences children have in one classroom, the teacher will have small-group instruction targeted at the needs of the group. Each group's instruction is different; this is referred to as *tier 2* teaching and it includes:

- Small groups
- Working directly with the teacher, with peers, or independently.
- Accelerated work for those who are most capable.
- Reinforcement of particular skill needs for those who are struggling.
- Materials for instruction driven by children's interests and achievement levels.
- Instruction tailored to students' learning styles.

Tier 3 is geared toward students who still need additional instruction after tiers 1 and 2. It is the most targeted approach and the most intensive instruction provided to children who are struggling with learning to read. Tier 3 has been called *response to intervention*. Tier 3 involves:

- Children receive small-group systematic and explicit instruction in addition to tier 1 and tier 2 instruction.
- Instruction aims at preventing children from needing special education services by providing more flexible education options.
- Students receive their regular reading instruction in tiers 1 and 2, but they also have additional small-group or one-to-one literacy work in their classroom or in a pull-out setting.

Tier 3 can be used with gifted children to enhance their experiences, for dual language learners, and children with other issues.

When teachers differentiate instruction, they select appropriate materials and move at an appropriate pace. Instruction must be as interesting for the struggling child as it is for the gifted child. An example activity that provides differentiated instruction is finding little words in big words.

> *Assume the word is Thanksgiving. The more capable children will find more words and more difficult words; the less capable will find fewer words and less sophisticated words, but the activity and goals are the same.*

Teachers believe that differentiation of instruction is important. However, many feel they lack appropriate materials and time. Teachers also need more professional development and additional instructors in their classroom to carry out differentiation successfully. The organization and management of differentiated instruction is more thoroughly dealt with in Chapter 13.

Intervention Programs

Early intervention programs are a form of differentiated instruction. The intervention is preventive rather than reactive. The goal is to fix the problem early before it creates long-term problems for the student. These programs are based on the premise that more can be done and needs to be done in school to support young children's literacy learning. Many children from at-risk populations could be successful if early intervention was available (Bufalino, Wang, Gómez-Bellengé, & Zalud, 2010; Tomlinson, 2004; Walpole & McKenna, 2007).

The term *early intervention* refers to programs that encourage literacy instruction that is developmentally appropriate. The purpose is to improve and enhance the literacy development of children entering school who have not had literacy experiences that have made them ready for school. Research illustrates that these programs can bring children up to level. As a result, they do not fall behind their peers and experience failure (O'Connor, Harty, & Fulmer, 2005; Shonkoff & Meisels, 2000; Foorman, Dombek, & Smith, 2016).

Educators have questioned whether it is more appropriate for early intervention to occur in the classroom with the support of special teachers or whether **pull-out programs** are more successful, in which youngsters go to a special teacher to work on skill improvement. The ultimate goal of such programs is to provide supplemental instruction to accelerate literacy development with the use of quality instruction in reading and writing in the most inclusive classroom environment.

There are those who prefer to integrate the intervention into the regular classroom, rather than taking children out of class. The rationale for this trend, is to limit the movement of children in and out of the classroom during the school day and for the special instruction to be an integral part of the regular classroom instruction. This way, children do not miss what is going on in the regular classroom, and the special instruction is coordinated with their classroom instruction. The stigma of being taken out for special help is eliminated, and the classroom teacher and a special teacher work together. Whether a child is pulled out or the teacher comes into the room most likely depends on the child and his or her difficulties. The size of the regular classroom which has a lot of movement in it and more noise than a resource room might not be optimal for some children who need the calm and small environment to focus. For others, being in their own classroom might be more important for them. There isn't a single best way; the decision should be based on the individual needs of the child (Wise Lindeman, 2013).

A well-known early intervention pull-out program is **Reading Recovery**, developed in New Zealand (Clay, 1987) and studied extensively at The Ohio State University (Pinnell, Freid, & Estice, 1990). Reading Recovery is a program for young readers who are experiencing difficulty learning to read during first grade. In Reading Recovery, children receive daily 30-minute, one-to-one instructional sessions in addition to their regular classroom reading instruction. These lessons are tailored to the special needs of children, contain authentic literacy experiences that are collaborative and active between teacher and child, and use specific skill instruction. Some Reading Recovery strategies within a lesson include the following:

1. The child reads a familiar story to enhance fluency and experience success.
2. The teacher introduces a new book; the teacher and the student "walk through" the book together, looking at the pictures, and predicting what the book is about.
3. The child reads the new book without assistance from the teacher.
4. The teacher assesses the child using a running record to check the child for types of errors made and comprehension through a retelling.
5. The teacher carries out a lesson that helps the child with word-analysis strategies by looking at the beginning of the word and identifying the word family end of words.

To make the experience more concrete, the teacher engages the child in the use of manipulating letters and word families that are magnetic on a magnetic board. The child is asked to use words learned by writing them on a slate within a sentence. Also, sentences from the book are written on sentence strips for children to put into sequence, and sentences are cut into words for children to identify out of context and to sequence into context. These familiar activities are repeated in different lessons. Reading orally is an important part of this program, as are learning comprehension strategies. The program also requires children to write.

Teachers who participate in Reading Recovery receive special training to help develop their ability to observe and describe the behavior of children when they are engaged in literacy acts. Reading Recovery teacher training emphasizes how to respond to children with appropriate modeling and scaffolding to help them progress. Another feature of the program is the use of authentic literacy experiences balanced with skill development. Reading Recovery has demonstrated increased performance by children at risk. In addition, Reading Recovery strategies have been adapted for small-group guided reading instruction within the classroom.

Although extremely popular at one time, Reading Recovery has lost some popularity. The reason is the cost. The training is expensive, and it involves a one-to-one pairing of child and teacher. Moreover, it is only designed for first grade. Many educators have created their own type of intervention based on Reading Recovery, but with small groups and going up the grades.

Similarly, many schools and publishing companies are creating intervention programs of their own. It is very likely that if a teacher works with a student on a one-to-one basis or in small groups using good strategies, the child should improve regardless of the program used. The extra and personal help children receive is powerful. High-quality instruction, where the teacher selects the intervention program and strategies based on the children's needs, will probably be the most successful intervention plan. In one district, 20 minutes a day was spent with children at risk to supplement their regular instruction. The types of activities in the program were:

1. Directed listening and thinking activities during reading to children (refer to Chapter 9).
2. Retelling of stories read to the children.
3. Repeated readings of storybooks so that children could engage in attempted readings of these stories from hearing them frequently.
4. Active discussions to construct meaning from stories read to the children.
5. Provision for classroom reading and writing centers containing materials that encourage literacy activity (refer to Chapters 4 and 12).
6. Time for children to engage in periods of independent reading and writing to practice skills (Morrow & O'Connor, 1995).

Intervention programs involve work with whole-class, small-group, and one-to-one settings for teachers to discover students' strengths and weaknesses. Basic-skills teachers worked with the classroom teachers during small-group and one-to-one periods of instruction. Students in this program made significant improvement over children also identified as at risk who did not have the advantage of this intervention (Hoover & Patton, 2005; Taylor, Strait, & Medo, 1994).

MyLab Education Application Exercise 4.4

Response to Intervention

Response to Intervention (RTI) was written into U.S. law with the 2004 reauthorization of the Individuals with Disabilities Education Act (IDEA). This law indicates that school districts are no longer required to take into consideration whether a severe discrepancy exists between a student's achievement and his or her intellectual ability in determining eligibility for learning-disability services. Rather, they may use an alternative approach that determines first whether the student responds to "scientific, research-based" classroom instruction and more intensive and targeted interventions. After receiving this more tailored and intensive instruction, students who do not demonstrate adequate progress are then considered for evaluation for special education classification. This approach has come to be known as response to intervention (RTI), although this precise term is not used in the law.

MyLab Education
Video Example 4.4
Response to Intervention
In this video, a first grade teacher describes the RTI process. It is part of a series of videos on RTI. https://www.youtube.com/watch?v=65FkN1BTfhY

In the past, students who were struggling could not receive the special help offered to those who were classified with learning disabilities. The RTI law makes eligible for intervention programs children who are not classified but who are having difficulty with oral expression, listening comprehension, written expression, basic reading skill, reading fluency skills, and reading comprehension. This helps some children get the help they need and avoid classification (Mesmer & Mesmer, 2008).

In a program in a public district in New Jersey, RTI evolved from an extension of its basic skills program. The district's RTI teachers, called *intervention specialists* or *reading specialists*, select or hire the most qualified teachers to work with the most at-risk learners. The district decided not to use a specific program or curriculum since one size does not fit all. Children are evaluated and then programs are designed to meet their needs. The school district has used Reading Recovery with some children, multisensory reading techniques, and teaching of essential strategies. Lessons include pre-teaching concepts, re-teaching a lesson or concept, additional practice of a skill with an alternative method, and making sure that lessons are interesting and relevant. The district has monthly meetings with all those involved in RTI topics. Included in those meetings are reading specialists, coaches, interventionists, administrators, speech pathologists, EL teachers, special education teachers, and classroom teachers. Very detailed formative assessments are done on the child. Then the type of instruction is proposed and implemented, and assessments are conducted on a regular basis to determine progress.

When deciding to implement intervention programs, consider the children involved, the resources you have, and how to best use the talent within your school. Recognizing the need and then taking measures to help is the first step. RTI is a prevention approach based on best practice and includes proactive and reactive features. It is an initiative that interfaces with regular classroom teaching and classification procedures. Early intervention initiatives in math and reading have been found to decrease classification rates.

MyLab Education Self-Check 4.4

Practicing Empathy for Diversity in Literacy Needs

Put yourself in the place of the child. It is difficult for us as adults to understand and appreciate the various processes involved in learning to read and write because, as

Figure 4.4. The Confusabet

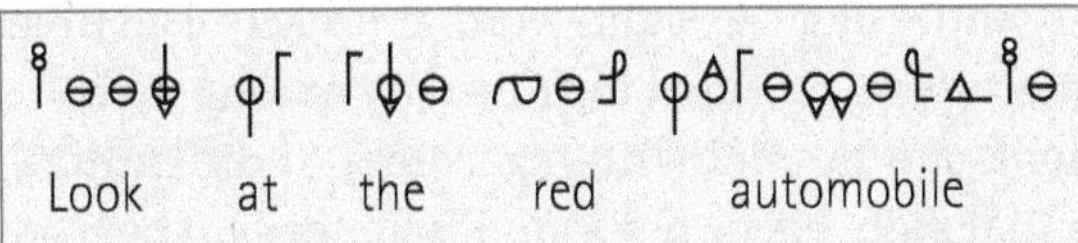
Look at the red automobile

adults, we have been reading and writing for many years. Yet, reading is a complex process, and to the novice, it is overwhelming. For children who have additional problems, such as visual impairments, or those who are English language learners, the process is even more overwhelming. To better understand the nature of learning to read or write, put yourself in the place of the learner.

With a contrived alphabet called the *Confusabet*, I have taken college students and parents back to when they were 5- or 6-years-old and first learning to read and write (refer to Figure 4.4). Whole words are introduced in the unfamiliar alphabet, accompanied by picture and context clues. They are reinforced with worksheets. After being introduced to about 25 words, the students are given a book containing pictures and stories that use these words. They are called on to read just as they were in a reading group in an early childhood classroom. They are also asked to write one sentence about what they read in the Confusabet alphabet.

After the lesson, we discuss how they have just learned to read and write with the Confusabet. Students consistently report similar strategies. They try to relate information they already know about reading and writing. They recognize that Confusabet words have the same number of letters as words written in our regular alphabet, and their knowledge of words in general helps them make sense of Confusabet words. Certain similarities in letter forms help them figure out words. They use context and picture clues as much as possible. Their knowledge of syntax (language structures) and the meanings of words surrounding an unknown word help them determine words. They skip around within a sentence looking for words they might know. Some rely on the first letter of a word to identify it. Many try to memorize words. Most agree that words with unusual shapes or lengths are easy to identify. They acknowledge that to learn, they have to involve themselves actively in the reading process. In short, they guess, make mistakes, and correct themselves.

In addition to the strategies just described, my observations of the students' behavior during this class experience revealed another powerful strategy: the natural tendency to collaborate and cooperate with one another during learning. The students discussed successes and failures with those around them. They wanted to talk about the words they had figured out and share that excitement with others. They expressed frustration when they experienced difficulty, and sought help of others. Some said that they were experiencing such difficulty that they wanted to stop trying and just quit. The room was noisy at times because of the social interaction of the literacy learning experience. At times, two or three of them disagreed about a particular word, finally arriving at consensus. Sometimes problems were solved with one student helping another who was having trouble. They demonstrated a natural curiosity as they flipped eagerly through new materials.

All the students agreed that working together gave them a sense of security, provided easily accessible sources of information, and made the task more fun. They were almost unaware of their socially cooperative behavior until I pointed it out to them. Most found that relying on others while trying to learn the Confusabet seemed to be a natural inclination.

In their descriptions of how they learned to read and write with the Confusabet, the students used problem solving and some behaviorist-type strategies. In all cases, they sought meaning. They approached a printed message looking for visual and auditory clues, and they looked at the total piece, trying to draw on past experience as well as the help of one another. They guessed, predicted, and invented to construct meaning. They also used strategies such as trying to decode words by focusing on the first letter, using context clues, and using the sight–word approach. The diversity of approaches used by the college students reflected the diversity among them.

Younger students are no different; regardless of difficulties, each child is entitled to instruction that suits his or her individual needs. The Confusabet lesson is in Appendix E.

MyLab Education Self-Check 4.5

An Idea from the Classroom

A Cultural Heritage Quilt

I used the following exercise in my classroom on culture appreciation:

A culminating activity involved each child in designing a quilt square [could be done using construction paper, cloth, or any other available materials] that conveyed his or her cultural heritage and that would become part of a classroom community quilt.

The quilt would convey the multiple ways that cultures are represented along with the dynamic nature of culture: cultures intersect, and new cultures evolve from contact as well as conflict.

The children were encouraged to represent themselves pictorially. Laura had a drawing of herself in the center of the square, wearing a T-shirt with a large U.S. flag. Her arms were outstretched and in her hands were flags representing the countries of her heritage: Germany, Poland, Norway, and Ireland. Mia's square had her name in Chinese, pictures of native toys, a drawing of China, coins that were glued on, and a drawing of a bowl of rice, with a broken toothpick representing chopsticks.

This classroom activity had students seriously reflect on culture; through creative reflection children realize that despite differences, universal notions of love, honor, and remembrance unite us all. This unity is symbolically expressed when all the pieces of the quilt come together as one creative piece proudly hung in the classroom. Such creations serve as a constant reminder of the importance of honoring cultural diversity.

Jennifer Del Nero, Literacy Teacher

Summary

4.1 Describe the impact of shifting demographics and cultural diversity on literacy.

By 2030, experts forecast that 40 percent of the school-age population in the United States will be English language learners. Spanish is only one of over 400 different languages reported to be spoken in the United States. Historically, students were expected to ignore their cultural backgrounds, learn English, and assimilate. Although it is critical for English learners to master standard English, it is equally critical for that achievement not to come at the expense of their cultural heritage. To support their students, teachers must be mindful of their own cultural traditions and beliefs as well as develop their understandings of cultural and linguistic differences among their students.

4.2 List ways to help English learners communicate in school.

Children come to school speaking a variety of languages and dialects with different accents and grammars. Teachers need to understand their EL population in terms of the six categories of diverse language ability and recognize that differences don't mean deficits. Showing interest in the students' native culture and language provides a supportive environment in which future literacy learning can flourish. There are four research-supported types of instruction for English language learners: English immersion, EL, bilingual education, and primary language instruction. Because there is no single perfect method of EL instruction, efforts need to be tailored for each student.

4.3 Describe strategies for teaching children with exceptionalities.

Gifted children, students with learning disabilities, at-risk students, and students with physical impairments have widely varying needs that bring diversity to the classroom and that must be addressed. Gifted students need opportunities to expand their knowledge and skills, not just additional basic work. Students with learning disabilities can be easily distracted and have short attention spans, so materials and classroom procedures may need to be modified for them to be successful. Students with moderate physical impairments are often included into the classroom, and the teacher must modify materials and methods to enable them to be successful. If physical impairments are more severe, additional staff will be required. At-risk students may struggle with learning compounded by poverty, homelessness, or other issues and have little if any literacy background experiences.

4.4 Summarize how to address diversity through differentiated instruction.

According to multiple intelligence theory, differentiated instruction is useful for all children because irrespective of ability, all children have unique learning styles: linguistic, logical/mathematical, spatial, bodily/kinesthetic, musical, interpersonal, intrapersonal, or combinations there of. Differentiated instruction occurs on three tiers.

Tier 1 is regular classroom instruction; tier 2 involves small group work or working directly with teachers or peers or independently with materials designed according to interest and achievement level; and tier 3 (response to intervention) involves small-group systematic and explicit instruction to ensure students understand and practice the basic concepts of learning to read and write. Intervention can happen in the classroom or in pull-out programs. One form of preventive differentiated learning is intervention. Early intervention involves proactively working with students to prevent them from falling behind their peers. Reading Recovery is a special intervention for first grade students, and many educators have developed interventions for higher grades. Response to intervention (RTI) allows teachers to use intensive intervention with students who have not been classified as needing special education services.

4.5 Explain the importance of practicing empathy for diversity in the literacy environment.

Because adults have been reading and writing for many years, they may have difficultly remembering the stress and confusion experienced learning to read and write. To cultivate empathy in yourself, your assistants, and your colleagues, you'll need to put yourself in the situation of the learner. The Confusabet, an unfamiliar graphic alphabet, is a useful tool in helping adults recall the feelings associated with learning to read and to witness how learners use various strategies and collaborate to make sense of unfamiliar text.

Activities and Questions

1. In this chapter, the term *diversity* applies to children who are English learners (those who are non-English speaking or have limited English proficiency); children with learning differences (gifted, learning disabilities, ADHD, ADD); children who are at risk; children with physical impairments (visual, hearing, mobility, communication disorders); and children from different cultural backgrounds. Select one of these areas of diversity and describe a theory (from Chapter 2) that you feel has implications for instructional strategies appropriate for a child with that special need. Describe thoroughly one strategy that will be useful for learning for one type of diversity.
2. For each of the students described in Ms. Callihan's second-grade classroom, come up with one Strategy you feel would be successful in helping that student learn to read via differentiation of instruction.
3. Throughout the book strategies, will be presented for teaching literacy learning in classrooms. At all times, have the interest of children with special needs in mind and decide the strategies appropriate for these youngsters. Write them down in a notebook that you create just for special needs children.
4. Enlarge and photocopy the English and Spanish word cards Figure 4.2, color them or copy them on colored paper, laminate them, and cut them out. Hang them on the wall and discuss the words when you put them up and afterwards.

Chapter 5

Early Childhood Language Development: From Birth to Age Two

Photo credit: Patryk Kosmider/123RF

Learning Outcomes

After reading this chapter, you should be able to:

5.1 Understand theories about how language develops.

5.2 Outline the stages of language development from birth to 8.

5.3 Identify strategies to help children develop language from birth to 2.

When I began thinking about this chapter on Language Development, immediately Lewis Carroll's poem *The Walrus and the Carpenter* came to mind it begins:

"The time has come," the Walrus said,

"To talk of many things:

Of shoes and ships and sealing-wax,

Of cabbages and kings"

The beginning of this poem suggests how important talk is and how many things we can talk about. When we talk and listen we learn. From the moment of birth, the infant is surrounded by oral language. The development of language is one of the child's first steps toward becoming literate; it helps make reading and writing possible. Using research methods that involve close observation of children, investigators have been able to describe the strategies by which youngsters learn and use language. Among the many things these researchers have observed is that children are active participants in their learning of language. To learn, children involve themselves in problem solving, first creating hypotheses based on background information that they already have and then interacting with the individuals around them who are generating language. These strategies have implications for initial instruction in early literacy.

From the moment of birth, the infant is surrounded by oral language. The development of language is one of the child's first steps toward becoming literate; it helps make reading and writing possible. Using research methods that involve close observation of children, investigators have been able to describe the strategies by which youngsters learn and use language. Among the many things these researchers have observed is that children are active participants in their learning of language. To learn, children involve themselves in problem solving, first creating hypotheses based on background information that they already have and then interacting with the individuals around them who are generating language. These strategies have implications for initial instruction in early literacy.

A parent of a kindergartener from one of my classes related a conversation she had had with her daughter Melody. Mrs. Tracey said they were outside looking at the sky one evening, and she noticed that the moon was full. She said to her daughter, "Look, Melody, the moon is full tonight." Melody looked up at the moon with a slightly confused expression on her face and said, "Why is it full, Mommy, did the moon eat too much for dinner?" Melody used her background language information to help her understand her mother. Until this time, the word *full* meant filled up with food, and Melody made sense of the discussion with what she knew. Her mother explained what she meant by a full moon and that the same words can have different meanings depending on the situation in which they are used.

Children do not learn language passively; they actually construct—or reconstruct—language as they learn. In another one of my kindergarten classes, we were talking about what the children wanted to be when they grew up. It was Michael's turn. He started by telling us that his dad is a doctor and recently he had taken him to see the operating room where he works. Michael said, "I liked the people and all the machines that my daddy uses and so when I grow up, I want to be an operator, [he meant, *I want to be able to operate on people*] just like my daddy." Michael selected a word for the situation that made sense to him under the circumstances.

VOCABULARY

Neural shearing
Phonemes
Semantics
Syntax
T-unit
Zone of proximal development

Theories About How Language Develops

Although language acquisition is based somewhat on developmental maturity, research has found that children play an active role in their acquisition of language by constructing language. They imitate the language of adults and create their own when

MyLab Education
Video Example 5.1
The Pyramid of Speech and Language Development
In this video, a therapist describes how young children learn and use language.
https://www.youtube.com/watch?v=5Z0rvMbLP2o

they do not have the conventional words they need to communicate their thoughts. Their first words are usually functional words, and they are motivated to continue generating language when their attempts are positively reinforced. Children who are constantly exposed to an environment rich in language and who interact with adults using language in a social context develop larger vocabularies than children lacking these opportunities (Cazden, 2005; Dickinson, McCabe, & Essex, 2006; Gaskins, 2003; Morrow, 2005; Morrow, Kuhn, & Schwanenflugel, 2006).

Children need to learn language processes such as the patterns of language and vocabulary since research has found this is necessary for learning to read. *Reading* has been defined as the use of one's language ability to decode and comprehend text (Roskos, Tabors, & Lenhart, 2009; Vukelich, Christie, & Enz, 2007). Reading is the interaction between the reader and written language. It is the attempt by a reader to figure out the author's message. As readers, we use syntactic and semantic cues of language that enable us to predict what comes next. Our skill in processing semantics (meaning) and syntax (language structure) makes us more adept readers. The reader who encounters unfamiliar language structures and concepts in material to be read has difficulty understanding it. Familiarity with both syntax and semantics enables even very young readers to anticipate the format and content of sentences in print. Our ability to understand what we are reading is based on our construction of the meaning of the printed word. Such understanding is based on our previous experience with the topic, our familiarity with its main concepts, and our general knowledge of how language works.

The relationship between reading and language is evident in studies of children who are early readers. It has been found that early readers score higher on language screening tests than children who were not reading early. Early readers come from homes where rich language and a great deal of oral language are used (Dickinson & Tabors, 2001). When interviewed, parents of early readers revealed that their children tended to use very descriptive language and sophisticated language structures. The youngsters invented words, used humor, and talked a lot. The mother of a 4-year-old early reader reported that while watching the first snowfall of the year, her youngster said, "The snow is swirling down and looks like fluffy marshmallows on the ground." One spring day a few months later, the same child noted, "Look, Mommy, the butterflies are fluttering around. They look like they are dancing with the flowers." Children whose language is not appropriately developed by age 3 because of lack of experiences or exposure to language are already at risk. But with quality preschool that emphasizes language and literacy, these children can catch up.

Early readers have acquired many language skills. They are aware of story language and can retell stories using literacy conventions such as "Once upon a time" and "They lived happily ever after." When telling stories, they tend to use delivery and intonation like those of an adult reading aloud. This "book language" takes children beyond their own language patterns and is characteristic of early readers (Burns, Snow, & Griffin, 1999; Dickinson & Tabors, 2001).

Although we do not have all the answers about language acquisition, many theories help explain how babies learn to speak. Knowing how language is acquired has strong implications for providing environments and strategies that promote language development. Seminal theories in language acquisition are the behaviorist theory, nativist theory, Halliday's theory, Piagetian and Vygotskian theories, and the constructivist theory of language development.

Halliday's Theory of Language Development

Halliday (1975) describes language development as a process by which children gradually "learn how to mean." According to his theory of developmental language, what a child can do during interactions with others has meaning, and meaning can be turned into speech. Children's initial language development is based on function: What can be said reflects what can be done. Language is learned when it is relevant and functional.

Halliday (1975) proposed that there are 7 stages or functions of a child's speech. These are:

Instrumental function—language that is used to fulfill a need, such as to obtain food, drink or comfort. This typically includes concrete nouns, such as "cookie mommy."

Regulatory function—language that is used to influence the behavior of others including persuading, commanding, or requesting. ("Buy me that toy.")

Interactional function—language that is used to develop relationships and ease interaction. This could include phrases like "I love you mummy" or "Thank you."

Personal function—language that expresses personal opinions, attitudes and feelings including a speaker's identity. ("Hi, my name is John.")

Representational/Informative function—language that is used to relay or request information. ("Can you teach me how to ride my two-wheeler bike?)

Heuristic function—language that is used to explore, learn and discover. This could include questions or a running commentary of a child's actions. ("I want to know more about frogs, can you find me a book about them?")

Imaginative function—the use of language to tell stories and create imaginary constructs. This typically accompanies play or leisure activities. ("Let's pretend we are from outer space.")

The Behaviorist Theory

The *behaviorist approach* has influenced our thinking about how language is acquired. Skinner (Skinner, 1992) defined *language* as the observed and produced speech that occurs in the interaction of speaker and listener. *Thinking,* he said, is the internal process of language; both language and thought are initiated through interactions in the environment, such as those between a parent and a child. According to behaviorists, adults provide a language model that children learn through imitation. The child's acquisition of language is enhanced and encouraged by the positive reinforcement of an adult (Cox, 2007).

Early attempts at language are often rewarded, and this reinforcement leads to additional responses by children. These attempts are also *interactive;* that is, the language is mediated by adults through interactions designed to elaborate and extend meaning (Hart & Risley, 1999; Schickedanz & Collins, 2013). When newborns coo or make other verbal sounds, most parents are delighted and respond with gentle words of encouragement. The infant, in turn, responds to the positive reinforcement by repeating the cooing sounds. As babies become able to formulate consonant and vowel sounds, they try them out. It is not uncommon to hear a 10-month-old playing with sounds such as *ba, ba, ba,* or *ma, ma, ma.* The responsive interactive parent perceives such sounds as the child's first words and assumes that the child's *ma-ma* means *mommy.* The delighted adult says more warm and loving things to the baby and adds hugs and kisses. The parent might say, "Come on, now say it again, *ma, ma, ma.*" The baby is pleased with the warm reception and tries to repeat the sounds to receive additional interaction and positive reinforcement.

Unfortunately, the converse is also true. If a baby's babbling is considered annoying, if the parent is aggravated by the sound and responds with negative reinforcement by telling the baby in harsh tones, "Be quiet and stop making so much noise," the child is less likely to continue to explore the use of language.

Children surrounded by rich language begin to use the language they hear. A child can imitate the sounds of the "words" of a familiar song, for instance, with no concern for meaning. A 3-year-old girl sang "My country 'tis of thee" as "My country 'tis a bee." She imitated what she heard and substituted a similar-sounding word that had meaning for her from her own experience, that is, the word *bee* instead of the word *thee*, which she had never heard.

The Nativist Theory

Chomsky (Chomsky, 1965), Lennenberg (Lennenberg, 1967), and McNeil (McNeil, 1970) have described the *nativist theory* of language acquisition. They contend that humans develop language innately. Children figure out how language works by internalizing the rules of grammar, which enables them to produce an infinite number of sentences. They do so even without the practice, reinforcement, and modeling offered by adult language, which are considered necessary by the behaviorists. The ability to learn language must be innate to humans, the nativists believe, because almost all children develop and use language in the first few years of their lives. Language growth depends on maturation: As children mature, their language grows. Children learn new patterns of language and unconsciously generate new rules for new elements of language. The child's rule system increases in complexity as he or she generates more complex language. Lennenberg (Lennenberg, 1967), an extreme nativist, finds nothing in the child's environment to account for language development. Rather, language acquisition is motivated *inside* children; learning language is a natural ability not affected by external factors (Pinker, 2007).

Piagetian and Vygotskian Theories

Piaget's theory of *cognitive development* is built on the principle that children develop through their activities. Children's realization of the world is tied to their actions or their sensory experiences in the environment. According to this theory, children's first words are egocentric, or centered in their own actions. Children talk about themselves and what they do. Their early language and their general development relate to actions, objects, and events they have experienced through touching, hearing, seeing, tasting, and smelling (Piaget & Inhelder, 1969).

Vygotsky's theory of *basic learning* also has implications for language development. According to Vygotsky, children learn higher mental functions by internalizing social relationships. Adults initially provide children with names of things; for instance, they direct youngsters and make suggestions. Then, as children become more competent, the adults around them gradually withdraw the amount of help they need to give. Vygotsky (Vygotsky, 1978) describes a **zone of proximal development**, when the child can perform within a range, but only with adult assistance. Proximal development ends when the child can function independently. The implications for language instruction are clear: To promote language development, adults need to interact with children by encouraging, motivating, and supporting them (Sulzby, 1985b).

As a child builds an oral vocabulary, he/she tries words more frequently. A child will point to a toy and name it. When playing with a ball, a child may say the word *ball* again and again. The attentive parent now interacts with the child by expanding and extending the original language (Burns, Snow, & Griffin, 1999). After the child says *ball*, the parent may say, "Yes, that is a nice, big, round, red ball." Through such expansion and reinforcement of words by the adult, the child acquires new words. The adult extends the baby's words by asking questions, "Now tell me what you can do with that nice red ball?" The extension asks the child to think, talk, understand, and act (Dickinson & Tabors, 2001).

MyLab Education Application Exercise 5.1

The Constructivist Theory

The more contemporary perspective of language acquisition is the *constructivist theory* emerging from the work of Piaget and Vygotsky and described and supported by those who have studied language development (Brown, Cazden, & Bellugi-Klima, 1968; Halliday, 1975). Constructivists describe *children* as the creators of language on the basis of an innate set of rules or underlying concepts. They describe *language* as an active and social process. The child constructs language, often making errors. Making errors is a necessary part of learning how language works. We need to accept language errors in a child's first years.

We have language development charts that show when to expect certain stages of development on average, we do not discipline babies who have not uttered their first words at 8 months or their first complete sentences by 2½-years-old. We respect their individuality and their right to grow at their own pace. Yet, when children enter school, we neglect to recognize developmental differences; we prescribe tasks based on a curriculum, not on the child.

Language acquisition is continuous and interactive in social contexts. Children also learn by playing with language themselves. They try out new words, involve themselves in monologues, and practice what they have learned. The acquisition of language varies from child to child, depending on each child's social and cultural background (Au, 1998). Children's remarks illustrate that they do not *simply* imitate adult language. Children need to express themselves, but may not have sufficient conventional language to draw on, so they create their own based on their backgrounds and their awareness of semantics and syntax. For example, a 3-year-old girl saw a freckled youngster for the first time and said, "Look, Mommy, that little girl has *sprinkles* on her nose." A 4-year-old boy observed an elderly man with deep wrinkles and said, "I wonder why that man has paths all over his face." A father and his 3-year-old daughter were toasting marshmallows; the little girl said, "Mmmm, I can smell the taste of them." After a quick summer rain, a 3-year-old boy observed the sun returning to the sky and the water evaporating all around him. "The sun came out and ate up all the rain," he said. Toward the end of the winter as the snow was melting, a 4-year-old girl noted, "See how the grass is peeking out from under the snow."

MyLab Education Self-Check 5.1

Outlining the Stages of Language Development from Birth to 8

The various theories just discussed explain how language is acquired. Each has something to offer, but none by itself presents a complete picture. We know that children's language grows according to their need to use it, their interests, and the meaning it has for them. Language acquisition is fostered by positive interactions with language between the child and an adult. Children's language is acquired through exploration and invention and is controlled by their own maturity, the development of their brain, the structure of the language, and its conventions. No matter what the language children develop, they use it similarly no matter what country they are from.

MyLab Education
Video Example 5.2
Factors Affecting Language Acquisition

Children's language development is impacted by families, early literacy experiences and the professional knowledge of educators.
https://www.youtube.com/watch?v=c8A38PdipDc

The Role of Brain Development

The study of brain research has made it very apparent that what happens to a child from birth to age 3 can affect his or her language and literacy development. Babies are programmed to learn. Every minute, they search to learn about the environment they are in and to connect with the experiences it has to offer.

When a child is born, he or she has about 100 billion neurons. This is all the neurons or brain cells the person will ever have. For learning to take place, neurons must make brain connections. Brain connections that are repeated and used become permanent; when brain connections are not used, they disintegrate and vanish. This is referred to as **neural shearing**, the loss of brain cells (Shaywitz, 2003). At birth, the baby's billions of neurons or brain cells have already formed 50 trillion connections, or synapses. By 1 month of age, they have formed 1,000 trillion brain cell connections. The brain connections form as a result of experiences the baby has and become permanent when experiences are repeated. The permanent connections mean that learning has occurred (Berk, 2007; Newberger, 1997; Vukelich, Christie, & Enz, 2007). The right experiences must occur for language to develop, and these experiences begin at birth.

There are periods of time when the different areas in the brain are most sensitive for development. For example, the first year of life is the most critical time for language to be learned. At birth, the child has neurons waiting to be connected for every language in the world. Neuron shearing occurs at only 6 months of age, when the baby can no longer recognize sounds of languages never heard. By 1 year, babies are programmed to listen to and learn the language they have heard and are no longer programmed to hear those they have not been exposed to. Those neurons no longer remain (Berk, 2007; Karmiloff & Karmiloff-Smith, 2001; Kuhl, 1994).

What experiences do babies and young children need to create a strong base for language and literacy development so neurons for language and literacy connect and remain permanent? From the time the child is born (and through age 3), family members and child-care providers need to:

- Provide love, food, and clothing
- Talk to them
- Use sophisticated vocabulary
- Use complex sentences
- Respond to cries, smiles, and so on
- Be playful with language, such as using rhymes
- Play with different toys
- Sing songs
- Read books
- Play many different types of music.

MyLab Education
Video Example 5.3
The Linguistic Genius of Babies
Babies have a remarkable ability to discern the sounds of language. Researchers have discovered a critical period of language development.
https://www.youtube.com/watch?v=M-ymanHajN8

Children who don't have these experiences will develop fewer language patterns discussed in the next section and less vocabulary than children who do.

Learning Language Patterns and Rules

Children acquire language through predictable stages. They discover the rules that govern the structure of languages, such as phonology (sound), syntax (grammar), and semantics (meaning).

There are 44 separate sounds, or **phonemes**, in English. With them we produce oral language. Children who grow up in a language-rich environment can learn these sounds very easily. They learn appropriate articulation, pronunciation, and intonation. *Intonation* involves pitch, stress, and juncture. *Pitch* refers to how high or low a voice is when producing a sound; *stress* indicates how loud or soft it is; and *junctures* refer to the pauses or connections between words, phrases, and sentences (Berk, 2007, 2008).

Syntax involves the grammatical rules of how words work together in phrases, clauses, and sentences. Internalizing the syntactic rules of language helps children understand what they hear and what they read. Syntax includes rules for forming basic sentence patterns, and for expanding and combining sentences to make them more complex. The basic sentence patterns are also called t-units or kernels. A **t-unit** is an independent clause with all its dependent clauses attached, assuming it has dependent clauses. It can be a simple or complex sentence. Compound sentences are made up of two t-units. Brief examples follow (Morrow, 1978; Tompkins, 2007).

1. Some Basic Sentence Patterns or t-units
   a. Subject–verb: *The girl ran.*
   b. Subject–verb–object: *The girl ran the show.*
   c. Subject–verb–indirect object–direct object: *Natalie gave James a dime.*
   d. Subject–linking verb–adjective: *Jane is tall.*
2. Some Basic t-units and how they are transformed into other language patterns such as:
   a. Questions
      1. t-unit: *Jim went to the store.*
      2. Transformed into a question: *Did Jim go to the store?*
   b. Negative
      1. t-unit: *Jane is a cheerleader.*
      2. Transformed into a negative: *Jane is not a cheerleader.*
   c. Passive
      1. t-unit: *Jennifer gave Lisa some bubble gum.*
      2. Transformation: *Some bubble gum was given to Lisa by Jennifer.*
3. Some Embeddings (sentence expansion and combination)
   a. Adding modifiers (adjectives, adverbs, and adverbial and adjective phrases)
      1. t-unit: *The boy played with friends.*
      2. Transformed: *The boy in the red shirt played with three friends.*
   b. Compounding (combining words, phrases, or independent clauses to form compound subjects, verbs, etc.)
      1. t-units: *Jane ran. Jane played. Jack ran. Jack played.*
      2. Transformed to be a compound pattern: *Jane and Jack ran and played.*

Semantics deals with the meaning of words that language communicates through content words and function words. It governs vocabulary development. *Content words* carry meaning in themselves. *Function words* have no easily definable meanings in isolation, but they indicate relationships between other words in a sentence. Function words include prepositions and conjunctions, such as *of* and *and* (Fields, Groth, & Spangler, 2007; Pflaum, 1986; Tompkins, 2007).

Specific Stages

Although research has identified stages of language growth, the pace of development may differ from child to child. An individual child's language development also tends to progress and then regress, so the stages of growth are not always exact. However, language development has been studied to the extent that the stages can be described in general.

From Birth to Year 1. In the first few months of infancy, oral language consists of a child's experimenting or playing with sounds. Infants cry when they are uncomfortable and babble, gurgle, or coo when they are happy. Infants learn to communicate specific needs by producing different cries. For example, parents are able to distinguish the cry for hunger from the cry of pain. Infants also communicate nonverbally and by moving their arms and legs to express pleasure or pain.

When babies are about 8- to 10-months-old, their babbling becomes more sophisticated. They are capable of combining a variety of consonant sounds with vowel sounds. They tend to repeat these combinations over and over. It is at this stage that parents sometimes think they are hearing their child's first words. The repeated consonant and vowel sounds, such as *da, da, da* or *ma, ma, ma*, do sound like real words. Most parents reinforce the child's behavior positively at this stage. Repetition of specific sounds and continued reinforcement lead the child to associate the physical mechanics of making a particular sound with the meaning of the word the sound represents.

From 8 to 12 months, children increase their comprehension of language dramatically; their understanding of language far exceeds their ability to produce it. They do, however, tend to speak their first words, usually those most familiar and meaningful to them in their daily lives: *Mommy, Daddy, bye-bye, hi, baby, cookie, milk, juice,* and *no.* As they become experienced with their first words, children use holophrases or one-word utterances that express an entire sentence (Hart & Risley, 1999; Vukelich, Christie, & Enz, 2007). For example, a baby might say "cookie," but mean "I want a cookie," "My cookie is on the floor," or "I'm done with this cookie."

From Age 1 to 2. A child's oral language grows a great deal between the ages of 1 and 2. In addition to holophrases, the child utters many sounds with adult intonation as if speaking in sentences. These utterances are not understandable to adults, however. Children begin to use telegraphic speech from 12 months on, the first evidence of their knowledge of syntax. Telegraphic speech uses content words, such as nouns and verbs, but omits function words, such as conjunctions and articles. In spite of the omissions, words are delivered in correct order, or syntax: "Daddy home" for "Daddy is coming home soon," or "Toy fall" for "My toy fell off the table." Language grows tremendously once the child begins to combine words. By age 18 months, children can pronounce four-fifths of the English phonemes and use 9 to 20 words (Bloom, 1990).

From Age 2 to 3. The year between ages 2 and 3 is probably the most dramatic in terms of language development. Typically, a child's oral vocabulary grows from 300 words to 1000. The child can comprehend, but cannot yet use, 2000 to 3000 additional words. Telegraphic sentences of two or three words continue to be most frequent, but syntactic complexity continues to develop, and the child occasionally uses such functional words as pronouns, conjunctions, prepositions, articles, and possessives. As their language ability grows, children gain confidence. They actively play with language by repeating new words and phrases and making up nonsense words. They enjoy rhyme, patterns of language, and repetition (Bloom, 1990). Consider the following transcription of Jennifer's dialogue with her dog. Jennifer was 2 years, 10 months, at the time. "Nice doggie, my doggie, white doggie, whitey, nicey doggie. Good doggie, my doggie, boggie, poggie. Kiss doggie, kiss me, doggie, good doggie." Jennifer's language is repetitive, playful, and creative, demonstrating characteristics of language production typical for a child her age.

From Age 3 to 4. A child's vocabulary and knowledge of sentence structure continue to develop rapidly during the fourth year. Syntactic structures added to the child's repertoire include plurals and regular verbs. Indeed, children of this age are prone to overgeneralization in using these two structures, mainly because both plural formation and verb inflection are highly irregular in the English language (Jewell & Zintz, 1986; Otto, 2006; Vukelich, Christie, & Enz, 2007). Four-year-old Jesse illustrated both problems when he had an accident in class and came running over very upset. He said, "Ms. Tracey, hurry over, I knocked over the fishbowl and it broked and all the fishes are swimming on the floor." Jesse knew how to form the past tense of a verb by adding *ed,* but he did not know about irregular verbs such as *broke.* He also knew about adding an *s* to form a plural, but again was unaware of irregular plural forms such as *fish.*

As they approach age 4, children *seem* to have acquired all the elements of adult language. They can generate language and apply the basic rules that govern it. However, although their ability with language has grown enormously and they sound almost as if they are using adult speech, children have acquired only the basic foundations. Language continues to grow throughout our lives as we gain new experiences, acquire new vocabulary, and find new ways of putting words together to form sentences. At the age of 3 to 4, children talk about what they do as they are doing it. They often talk to themselves or by themselves as they play. It seems as if they are trying to articulate their actions (Roskos, Tabors, & Lenhart, 2009; Seefeldt & Barbour, 1998; Strickland & Schickedanz, 2009). While painting at an easel, 4-year-old Christopher said to himself, "I'm making a nice picture. I'm making colors all over. I'm painting, pit, pat, pit, pat. I'm going back and forth and up and down. Now I'm jumping as I paint." As he talked and painted, he did exactly what he said, words and actions coinciding.

From Age 5 to 6. Five- and six-year-olds sound very much like adults when they speak. Their vocabularies are always increasing, and so is the syntactic complexity of their language. They have vocabularies of approximately 2500 words, and they are extremely articulate. Many, however, still have difficulty pronouncing some sounds, especially *l, r,* and *sh* at the ends of words. They become aware that a word can have more than one meaning. When they are embarrassed or frustrated at misunderstanding things, they often say something silly. They also tend to be creative in using language. When they do not have a word for a situation, they supply their own. Adults find the language used by children of this age to be delightful and interesting (Krashen, 2003; Seefeldt & Barbour, 1998; Weitzman & Greenberg, 2002):

> *Benjamin ran into school very excited one morning. "Ms. Morrow," he said, "you'll never believe it. My dog grew puppies last night!"*
>
> *My husband and I were going to a formal dance one evening. My 5-year-old daughter had never seen us dressed up like this before. When I walked into the room wearing a long gown and asked Stephanie how I looked, she said, "Mommy, you look soooo pretty. What is Daddy's costume going to be like?"*
>
> *Escorted by her mother, Allison was on her way to her first day of kindergarten. She seemed a little nervous. When her mother asked her if she was okay, Allison replied, "I'm fine, Mommy, but my stomach is very worried."*

There are other characteristics of kindergarteners' language. Kindergartners have discovered bathroom talk and curse words, and they enjoy shocking others by using them. They talk a lot and begin to use language to control situations. Their language reflects their movement from a world of fantasy to that of reality.

From Age 7 to 8. By the time children are 7 years of age, they have developed a grammar that is almost equivalent to that of adults. They do not use the extensive numbers of grammatical transformations found in adult language, nor do they have the extent of vocabulary found in adult speech. Seven- and eight-year-olds are good conversationalists who talk a lot about what they do.

The Effect of Vocabulary Deficits

Language development in children as young as age 3 can predict their success in reading in 11th grade. Those who have delayed vocabulary development are more likely not to be on grade level in reading and many drop out of school. There seems to be a relationship between language development and socioeconomic status (SES). Children on public assistance have a vocabulary of about 500 words at age 3; those who are in working-class families have a vocabulary of about 700 words; and those from homes with parents who are professionals have 1100 words in their vocabulary. Children from families in the professional groups hear almost four times as many words in a day as those in the public assistance group (Hart & Risley, 1995). First-grade children from higher SES backgrounds know about twice as many words than those from low SES groups. High-achieving high school seniors know about four times as many words as their lower-performing classmates (Beck, Perfetti, & McKeown, 1982). With quality preschool, children can catch up. From age 2, children acquire about 10 words a day or about 14,000 words by age 6. Children in the primary grades need to learn about 2500 to 3000 new words per year, which is a rate of seven words every day (Snow, Burns, & Griffin, 1998).

MyLab Education Self-Check 5.2
MyLab Education Application Exercise 5.2

MyLab Education
Video Example 5.4
Skills for Early Literacy-Vocabulary
In this video, a librarian discusses strategies for vocabulary development in young children. This is the first in a series on early literacy.
https://www.youtube.com/watch?v=9DfKlVRYv8E

What Are Strategies to Help Children Develop Language from Birth to 2

"Hi, Natalie. How's my great big girl today? Let's change your diaper now, upsy-daisy. My goodness, you're getting heavy. Now I'll put you down right here on your dressing table and get a nice new diaper for you. Here, want this rubber ducky to hold while I change you? That's a good girl. You really like him. You're really lucky; let's clean you up now. This is the way we clean up Natalie, clean up Natalie, clean up Natalie. This is the way we clean up Natalie, so she'll feel so much better. You like that singing, don't you? I can tell. You're just smiling away, and cooing. Want to do that again? This is the way we clean up Natalie, clean up Natalie, clean up Natalie. This is the way we clean up Natalie, so she'll feel so much better. Wow, you were singing with me that time. That's right, ahhh-ahhh-ahh, now do it again. Mmmmm, doesn't that smell good? The baby lotion is so nice and smooth."

Provide a Rich Language Environment. My grandbaby Natalie was 4-months-old when I had that conversation with her. In print, it reads like a monologue; in reality, Natalie was a very active participant in the conversation. She stared intently at me. She cooed, waved her arms, smiled, and then became serious. I was providing a rich language environment for her. I encouraged her participation in the dialogue and acknowledged her responsiveness in a positive way. I provided her with the environmental stimuli necessary for her language to flourish. I engaged her in this type of conversation during feedings and while changing, bathing, and dressing her. The baby knew that communication was occurring because she responded to the talk with body movements, coos, babbles, and smiles.

Surround Infants with Sounds. Infants need to be surrounded by the sounds of happy language. Whether from mother, father, caregiver at home, or a teacher or aide in a child-care center, sounds and interaction should accompany all activities. Adults responsible for babies from birth through the first year need to know nursery rhymes, chants, finger plays, and songs. It is important for children to hear the *sounds* of language as well as the meanings. Thus, adults can make up their own chants to suit an occasion, as I did when I spontaneously adapted "Here We Go Round the Mulberry

Bush" while changing my granddaughter's diaper. Such experiences make the baby conscious of the sounds of language. Children learn that they can have control over language and that oral language can be a powerful tool as well as fun.

Children should hear different genres of music, including classical, jazz, popular, and so on. Babies need to hear the sounds of "book language," which differs in intonation, pitch, stress, juncture, and even syntax from normal conversation. They need familiarity with language in all its variety so that they can learn to differentiate among its various conventions. Speaking to infants, singing to them, reading to them, and letting them hear the radio and television provide sources of language that help their own language grow. In addition, there are sounds in the immediate environment that need no preparation and are not the sounds of language but that provide practice in auditory discrimination—the doorbell ringing, the teapot hissing, a clock chiming, the vacuum cleaner humming, a dog barking, a bird singing, a car screeching, and so on. Bring them to the baby's attention, give them names, and heighten the child's sensitivity to them.

Surround Infants with Sensory Objects. In addition to hearing a variety of sounds, babies need objects to see, touch, smell, hear, and taste. Objects should be placed in the baby's immediate environment—the crib or playpen. They will stimulate the baby's activity and curiosity and become the meaningful things within the environment from which language evolves. Some of the objects should make sounds or music when pushed or touched. They can have different textures and smells. They should also be easy to grab, push, kick, or pull. The objects can be placed so they are visible and within the child's reach, and at least one item should be suspended overhead: stuffed animals, rubber toys, music boxes made of soft material, mobiles that can be kicked or grasped, mobiles that hang from the ceiling and rotate by themselves, and cardboard or cloth books with smooth edges. Books can be propped open against the side of the crib or playpen when the baby is lying on her or his back or against the headboard. Allow children to play independently with these objects, the adults in charge need to talk about them, name them, discuss their characteristics, and join the child in playing with them occasionally.

From 3 to 12 months, the baby gurgles, coos, babbles, and begins to laugh. Adults or caregivers should recognize an infant's sounds as the beginning of language and reinforce the infant positively with responses aimed at encouraging the sounds. When the baby begins to put consonants and vowels together, again adults should reinforce the behavior, imitating what the baby has uttered and urging repetition. When he or she becomes aware of the ability to repeat sounds and control language output, the baby will do these things. The baby also will begin to understand adult language, so it is important to name objects, carry on conversations, and give the baby directions. At the end of the first year, assuming he or she has experienced both appropriate sounds of language encouragement and pleasant interaction, the baby will be on the verge of extensive language growth during its second year.

Increase Syntactic Complexity. Through the second year of a child's life, the adults in charge need to continue the same kinds of stimulation suggested for developing oral language during the first year. However, because the baby is likely to develop a vocabulary of up to 150 words and to produce two- and possibly three-word sentences during the second year, additional techniques can be used to enhance language growth. These one- and two-word utterances by children at this age usually represent sentences. When a 12-month-old points to a teddy bear and says, "bear," the child probably means "I want my bear." Parents and caregivers at home or in child-care centers can begin to expand and extend the child's language by helping increase the number of words the child is able to use in a sentence or by increasing the syntactic complexity of their own utterances.

Use Scaffolding to Help Language Develop. One method for helping a child develop language ability is a kind of modeling called *scaffolding*. In scaffolding, an adult provides a verbal response for a baby who is not yet capable of making the response itself.

In other words, the adult provides a language model. When the baby says, "bear," for instance, the adult responds, "Do you want your teddy bear?" or "Here is your nice, soft, brown teddy bear." In addition to expanding on the child's language, the adult can extend it by asking the youngster to do something that demonstrates understanding and extends his or her thinking. For example, "Here is your nice, soft, brown teddy bear. Can you hug the teddy? Let me see you hug him." In addition to questions that require action, the adult can ask questions that require answers. Questions and prompts that require answers of more than one word are preferable, for example, "Tell me about the clothes your teddy is wearing." *How, why,* and *tell me* questions encourage the child to give more than a yes or no answer and more than a one-word response. (*What, who, when,* and *where* questions tend to elicit only one-word replies.) As the child's language ability develops, the adult provides fewer and fewer such scaffolds; the child learns to build utterances along similar models (McGee & Richgels, 2008; Otto, 2006; Soderman & Farrell, 2008).

Increase Exposure to New Experiences. Adults should select songs, rhymes, and books for 1- to 2-year-olds that use language they can understand. They are capable of understanding a great deal of language by now, and the selections should help expand and extend their language. Both vocabulary and conceptual understanding are enhanced by experiences. For the 1- to 2-year-old, frequent outings, such as visits to the post office, supermarket, dry cleaners, and park provide experiences to talk about and new concepts to explore. Household tasks taken for granted by adults are new experiences that enrich children's language. Adults should involve toddlers in activities. For example, an 18-month-old can put a piece of laundry into the washing machine or give one stir to the bowl of food being prepared. During such daily routines, adults should surround the activity with language, identifying new objects for the baby and asking for responses related to each activity (Hart & Risley, 1999).

Overgeneralizations. Adults sometimes want to correct children mispronunciations or overgeneralization of grammatical rules. The child who says, "Me feeded fishes," for instance, has simply overgeneralized the rules for the following:

Forming most past tenses (*feeded* for *fed*)

Using pronouns (objective *me* for subjective *I*)

Forming most plurals (*fishes* for *fish*)

Children also can overgeneralize concepts. A child who has learned to associate a bird with the word *bird* might see a butterfly for the first time and call it a bird, thinking that anything that flies is a bird. Correcting such an overgeneralization is best done positively rather than negatively. Instead of saying, "No, that's not a bird," it is better to refer to the butterfly as a *butterfly,* commenting on its beauty, perhaps, and thus expanding the child's verbal repertoire.

Correcting over generalizations is not likely to help young children understand the error or use proper tense and plural forms. Rather, it is likely to inhibit the child from trying to use language. In learning, children need to take risks and make mistakes. Hearing good adult models will eventually enable them to internalize the rules of language and to correct their errors themselves. At least until age 5, children should be allowed to experiment and play with language without direct concern for 100% correctness in syntax and pronunciation. The English language is complex and irregular in many of its rules; in time, children will master these rules in all their complexity, if they have good adult models and plenty of verbal interaction. However, encouraging "baby talk" because it is cute, is likely to inhibit growth because children will use language they believe will please the adults around them.

Provide a Variety of Materials for Language Development. Materials for the 1- to 2-year-old should be varied and more sophisticated than those in the first year. Now that the baby is mobile in the home or child-care center, books need to be easily accessible to the child. Toys should still include items of various textures, such as furry stuffed animals and rubber balls. Other toys should require simple eye–hand coordination. Three- to five-piece puzzles, trucks that can be pushed and pulled, dolls, a child-size set of table and chairs, crayons and large paper, and puppets are examples. Choose objects that require activity, for activity encourages exploration, use of the imagination, creation, and the need to communicate. The number of books in a child's library should be increasing. Those they are allowed to handle and use alone should still be made of cloth or cardboard.

An Idea from a Day Care Center

The population of children in my Day Care Center are mostly from families who came to this country and are speaking a language other than English at home. Many of them want to help their children but don't know how. Some can't read and are embarrassed by that. They all want to know however, "How can I help my child?" I prepare a pamphlet when they first come to our center they are given one the pamphlet says:

- Provide love, food, and clothing.
- Talk to your child when he is playing, when you are changing his diaper, when he is eating.
- Use adult language with your child so they learn difficult words.
- Be playful with language and chant rhymes and sing songs.
- Read books to your child or just talk about the pictures from the time they are born.
- If they watch TV, talk about what they saw.

MyLab Education Self-Check 5.3

Summary

5.1 Understand theories about how language develops.

Reading and language development are related. Reading is the interaction between the reader and written language. It is the attempt by a reader to reconstruct the author's message. The graphic sequences and patterns that appear as print represent the oral sequences of language. Although language acquisition is based somewhat on developmental maturity, it is also dependent on the active engagement of the child and the level of language in the child's environment. Early readers tend to come from homes where rich language and large quantities of oral language are used.

The five main theories of language acquisition are behaviorist, nativist, Piagetian and Vygotskian, constructivist, and Halliday's theory of language development. Behaviorist theory argues children imitate what they hear; they create their own language and use background knowledge to make sense of what they say. Nativist theory contends that language develops innately, and children can figure out language without any external stimulus. Piagetian and Vygotskian theories are developmental theories built respectively on cognitive development and social relationships. Constructivist theory contends that language is an active and social process and that children create language based on an innate set of rules or underlying concepts. Halliday argues language development is a process by which children gradually learn how to make meaning with language and through interactions with others. Halliday identified seven functions of language as instrumental, regulatory, interactional, personal, heuristic, imaginative, and informative.

5.2 Outline the stages of language development from birth to 8.

Brain development is a significant underlying influence on language development in the early years. The richer the experiences a baby has, the more connections the brain's neurons forge and the more flexible and receptive the brain is to language. Children acquire language by moving through predictable stages and along the way learn the structural rules of language such as phonology, syntax, and semantics. Although stages of language development have been identified, each child sets an individual pace of development. The stage from birth to year 1 is characterized by babbling and increased comprehension. The stage from age 1 to 2 is characterized by telegraphic speech. Vocabulary grows dramatically in the stage from age 2 to 3 as well as in the stage from age 3 to 4, at the end of which children have acquired the basic foundations of language. In the stage from age 5 to 6, children sound very much like adults, and in the stage from age 7 to 8, children have developed grammar almost equivalent to what adults use. Socioeconomic status has a significant influence on the vocabulary children have at each stage, with children on public assistance having roughly half the vocabulary of children whose parents are professionals.

5.3 Identify strategies to help children develop language from birth to 2.

From birth to age 2 children need to be in an environment with things to talk about. There should be things to touch, smell, listen to, and see. Children should have new experiences as parents of child care providers talk about them with them.

Materials such as playdough, puppets, simple puzzles, are all appropriate. Adults should scaffold by introducing new language as they talk to the child.

Activities and Questions

1. Record children at play in a daycare center. Identify which characteristics of their language can be described by a particular theory of language acquisition. For example, imitation could be explained by the behaviorist theory.
2. Spend some time in a daycare center for children from birth to 2. Look at the environment. List what is in the center that will help babies develop language and what they need to add.
3. Create a pamphlet for parents about what they can do at each stage of language develop to help their child to acquire appropriate language at this young age.

Chapter 6

Language and Vocabulary Development: Preschool Through Third Grade

Photo credit: Belchonock/123RF

LEARNING OUTCOMES

After reading this chapter, you should be able to:

6.1 Describe strategies to enhance expressive and receptive language.

6.2 Describe a rich literacy classroom environment that will engage children in conversation.

6.3 Describe the Vocabulary Meeting.

6.4 Describe more strategies for developing vocabulary.

6.5 Describe assessment of children's language development.

VOCABULARY

Receptive Language
Expressive Language
Word Consciousness
Aesthetic Talk
Efferent Talk
T-Unit

The last chapter concentrated on how language is acquired, the patterns and structures of language that need to be developed, and some strategies to help develop language from birth through 2 years old. This chapter focuses on developing language patterns and vocabulary in school from age 3 through third grade.

Objectives and Strategies to Enhance Expressive and Receptive Language

A review of theory and research suggests how we can help children acquire and develop language pleasantly, productively, and appropriately. Children acquire **receptive language** first, which involves listening and understanding what is said. Children acquire **expressive language** by emulating adult models, interacting with others when using language, and experiencing positive reinforcement for their efforts. Some language develops naturally as individuals pass through common stages of development, however, they need explicit instruction as well. As children mature, they become capable of generating increasingly complex language structures. They learn language by acting on and within familiar environments. Their first spoken words are those that are meaningful for them within their own experiences. Their earliest language is an expression of needs. They learn language through social interaction with individuals more literate than they, whether adults or older children. Children also create their own language, play with it, and engage in monologues.

Using what we know of language acquisition and developmental stages as guidelines, we can begin to create appropriate materials, activities, and explicit teaching to help children's language development. The following objectives are based on basic standards for children from preschool through third grade.

MyLab Education
Video Example 6.1
Parent–Child Interactions
Parents encourage the development of language beginning at early ages.

Objectives for Receptive Language Development

- Provide children with an atmosphere in which they will hear varied language frequently.
- Allow children to associate the language that they hear with pleasure and enjoyment.
- Give children the opportunity to discriminate and classify sounds heard.
- Expose children to a rich source of new vocabulary on a regular basis.
- Allow children to listen to others and demonstrate that they understand what is said.
- Provide children with opportunities for following directions.
- Provide children with good models of standard English.
- Acknowledge the child's first language and let them hear his or her home language in school.

MyLab Education
Video Example 6.2
Parent–Child Book Sharing
Picture books give parents an opportunity to interact with their children and encourage language development.

Objectives for Expressive Language Development

- Encourage children to pronounce words correctly.
- Help children increase their speaking vocabularies.
- Encourage children to speak in complete sentences.
- Help children to expand their use of syntactic structures, such as adjectives, adverbs, prepositional phrases, dependent clauses, plurals, past tense, possessives, and so forth.
- Encourage children to communicate with others so that they can be understood.
- Give children the opportunity to use language socially and psychologically by interpreting feelings, points of view, and motivation, and by solving problems through generating hypotheses, summarizing events, and predicting outcomes.

- Give children opportunities to develop language from different content areas.
- Provide children with the opportunity to talk in many different settings: in the whole group with the teacher leading the discussion, in teacher-led small groups, in child-directed groups for learning, or in conversation in social settings.
- Give opportunities for children to use their own language freely at any stage of development. This could be a different dialect or mixtures of English, Spanish, or other languages. Their communication should be encouraged, accepted, and respected.

There are tiers for learning vocabulary:

- Tier 1 consists of basic words that are used commonly in informal conversations at home and in play. Examples are *tree, house, food*.
- Tier 2 are academic words. They are words used in school and are not used as frequently as Tier 1 words, therefore they need to be taught. Examples are *impatient, enough, through*.
- Tier 3 words are specialized and are often from content-area subjects. Examples are *divide, chrysalis, isthmus*.

There are additional words called *juicy words*, which happen spontaneously. These are words that just pop up and are extraordinary, such as *proactive* or *ostentatious*. They should be recognized, talked about, and put on a word wall. There are many lists for grade-level words in McKenna and Dougherty-Stahl's (2009) work; also, by using Google and searching the key words *tier 2 and tier 3 vocabulary*, you will find lists for every grade that teachers can use.

Word consciousness needs to be a priority to encourage vocabulary development (Scott & Nagy, 2004). When children are word conscious, they will do the following:

- Use words skillfully by understanding the nuances of word meanings.
- Value learning new words.
- Know there are differences in school language, social language, and language during play.
- Learn the meaning of unknown words. (Blachowicz & Fisher, 2015)

Explicit and Spontaneous Vocabulary Instruction

Research shows that children can learn and must learn a minimum of 5–10 words per week. The role of the teacher is to explicitly teach vocabulary and also allow for a significant amount of spontaneous and embedded vocabulary. This is done by an interesting environment that will create talk.

MyLab Education Self-Check 6.1

A Rich Literacy Classroom Environment That Will Engage Children in Conversation

MyLab Education
Video Example 6.3
Language Development
This video includes information for making a classroom a language-rich environment, with techniques for building vocabulary and inspiring word play.
https://www.youtube.com/watch?v=EB6nSwM1H08

From ages 3 to 8, a great deal of language development occurs. Children should continue to hear good models of language. They need constant opportunities to use language in social situations with adults and other children.Their oral language production must be reinforced positively (Dougherty Stahl & Stahl, 2012; Graves et al., 2014).

To accomplish these continuing goals, early childhood teachers provide an environment in which language will flourish. They organize stations of learning, one for each content area, that include materials for encouraging language use. A science station, for instance, can include class pets such as a pair of gerbils. Gerbils are active, loving animals that are fun to watch and handle. Children surround the cage often and generate talk just from watching them. Gerbils reproduce in 28-day cycles. When litters arrive, the birth process can be observed. The new babies cause much excitement and generate questions, comments, and unlimited conversation.

In my own classroom, our parent gerbils reproduced a second litter 28 days after the first and before the first babies had been weaned. The mother looked tired and thin from feeding and caring for 10 baby gerbils. One morning one of the children noticed that the mother was not in the cage. We could not imagine what had happened to her. A few days later, we found her hiding behind the refrigerator in the teachers' room. We never figured out how she got out of the cage, but we hypothesized all kinds of possibilities, and there was lots of discussion about why she left. No teacher alone could provide a lesson in which language flourished and grew the way it did during that incident, simply because gerbils were part of the classroom.

Teaching English Learners

Tangible objects in stations promote language development for English Learners.

Following are some examples of learning stations and materials in early childhood classrooms that will help generate language and engage children in collaborative discussions.

Learning Stations

Science: aquarium, terrarium, plants, magnifying glass, class pet, magnets, thermometer, compass, prism, shells, rock collections, stethoscope, kaleidoscope, microscope, informational children's literature reflecting topics being studied, and blank journals for recording observations of experiments and scientific projects.

Social Studies: maps, a globe, flags, community figures, traffic signs, current events, artifacts from other countries, informational books and children's literature reflecting topics being studied, and writing materials to make class books about topics being studied.

Art: easels, watercolors, brushes, colored pencils, crayons, felt-tip markers, various kinds of paper, scissors, paste, pipe cleaners, scrap materials (bits of various fabrics, wool, string, etc.), clay, play dough, food and detergent boxes for sculptures, books about famous artists, and books with directions for crafts.

Music: piano, guitar, or other real instruments, CD players, CDs of all types of music, rhythm instruments, songbooks, and photocopies of sheet music for songs sung in class.

Mathematics: scales, rulers, measuring cups, movable clocks, stopwatch, calendar, play money, cash register, calculator, dominoes, abacus, number line, height chart, hourglass, numbers (felt, wood, and magnetic), fraction puzzles, geometric shapes, math workbooks, children's literature about numbers and mathematics, writing materials for creating stories, and books related to mathematics.

Literacy: multiple genres of children's literature, CD players, headsets and stories on CDs, pencils, writing paper, stapler, construction paper, 3 × 5 cards for recording words, hole punch, letter stencils, computer, puppets, a felt board, stationery with envelopes, letters (felt, wood, and magnetic) and letter chunks for building words, sets of pictures for different units (seasons, animals, space exploration, etc.), rhyme games, color games, cards for associating sounds and symbols, alphabet cards, and pictures and words representing out-of-school environmental print. (The literacy station also includes a library corner, a writing center, oral language materials, and language arts manipulatives, described in later chapters.)

Dramatic Play: dolls, dress-ups, telephone, stuffed animals, mirror, food cartons, plates, silverware, newspapers, magazines, books, telephone book, class telephone book, cookbook, notepads, cameras and photo album, table and chairs, broom, dustpan, and child-size kitchen furniture such as refrigerator, sink, ironing board, and storage shelves. (The dramatic-play area can be changed from a kitchen to a grocery store, beauty shop, gas station, business office, restaurant, or the like, with the addition of materials for appropriate themes when they are studied. Include appropriate materials for reading and writing related to the theme of the dramatic-play area (Meacham, Vukelich, Han, & Buell, 2014)).

Block Area: figures of people, animals, toy cars, trucks, items related to themes being studied, paper and pencils to prepare signs and notes, reading materials related to themes, and blocks of many different sizes, shapes, and textures.

Workbench: wood, corrugated cardboard, hammer, scissors, screwdriver, saw, pliers, nails, glue, tape, and work table.

Outdoor Play: sand, water, pails, shovels, rakes, gardening area and gardening tools, climbing equipment, riding toys, crates, playhouse, balls, tires, and ropes.

All stations should have computers.

Children need opportunities to use such areas for interacting with one another and the teacher. They should be given enough time to touch, smell, taste, listen, and talk about what they are doing. Exploring and experimenting with the materials in the centers are creative, imaginative, problem-solving, and decision-making experiences in which children use language. The opportunity to *use* language is one of the key elements in language development.

Some materials remain permanently in the stations; others are replaced or supplemented occasionally so that new items of interest become available. Materials added to the centers are often coordinated with thematic units of instruction. For example, if you are teaching a unit on winter, include winter clothing in the dramatic-play area, a thermometer in the science area, and informational, fiction, and poetry books about winter in the literacy center. The different content-area centers provide sources for language use and development; the literacy center is devoted *primarily* to language development.

MyLab Education Application Exercise 6.1

Themes offer specific language experiences that expand vocabulary and develop syntax, pronunciation, and the ability to understand others and be understood. These experiences should incorporate all content areas and make use of the senses (Antonacci & O'Callaghan, 2003; Combs, 2009; McGee & Morrow, 2005; Spencer & Guillaume, 2006; Tompkins & Koskisson, 2001). The suggestions that follow can be used when a new theme is initiated. They describe activities designed to aid language growth in early childhood classrooms. To illustrate, assume that the topic throughout these suggestions is *winter*.

Teaching English Learners

Since themed units are often of interest to children and utilize real situations and materials, they are useful for children who are English Learners for learning vocabulary.

Discussion: Hold discussions about the unit topic. What is the weather like in winter? What kind of clothing do children need to wear in winter? What fun things can they do in winter that they cannot do at other times of the year? What problems does winter bring? What is winter like in different parts of the country—for example, New York, Florida, and Idaho?

Word Lists: Ask the children to name words that make them think of winter. Your list might include *snow, ice, cold, white, wet, freezing, sleds, snowman, mittens, scarf, hat, slush, skiing, ice skating, snowballs, fireplace,* and *snowflakes*. Classify words on the list into how winter feels, looks, smells, sounds, and tastes or what you can and cannot do in winter. List the words on a chart, and hang the chart in the room. Leave the chart hanging when you go to the next unit. When the wall gets too crowded, compile the charts into a class book.

Pictures: Provide pictures of winter scenes for discussion, each depicting different information about that season. Use actual pictures or digital images projected on a screen.

Sharing Time (Show and Tell): Hold a sharing period during which children bring things from home related to the topic. Give all the children an opportunity to share if they wish, but assign different children for different days, because sharing by more than five or six children in one period can become tedious. Sharing objects from home gives children confidence because they are talking about something from their own environment. Even the shyest children will speak in front of a group if they have the security of sharing something familiar from home. Encourage children to relate the items to the theme if they can. Model speaking in complete sentences, so children will do the same. Let parents know when topics are being discussed so they can help find things to bring to school and share.

Experiments: Carry out a science experiment related to the topic being studied. Involve the children actively. Discuss the purpose and hypothesize what is likely to happen. Encourage children to discuss what they are doing *while* they are doing it. When the experiment is complete, discuss the results with the class. (*Example:* Allow water to freeze, then melt. In warm climates use the freezer for freezing the water.)

Art: Carry out an art activity related to the topic. Allow children to create their own work, rather than making them follow specific directions that yield identical results. Discuss the project and the available materials before the activity. Provide materials that children will want to touch, describe, and compare. While children are creating, encourage conversation about what they are doing. For example, provide blue construction paper, tinfoil, white doilies, cotton, wool, white tissue paper, and chalk for a winter collage. Discuss why these colors and objects were selected. What is there about them that makes people think of winter? Suggest creating a picture that makes one think of winter. Discuss the textures of the materials.

Music: Sing songs about winter, such as "It's a Marshmallow World in the Winter." Music is enjoyable, and lyrics help build vocabulary and sensitivity to the sounds and meanings of words. Listen to music without words, music that creates images concerning the topic. Ask the children for words, sentences, or stories that the music brings to mind.

Food Preparation: Prepare food related to the unit. Make hot soup, flavored snowballs, or popcorn. Discuss food textures, smells, tastes, and appearance. Follow recipe directions, thus learning about sequencing and quantity. Allow children to help prepare the food and enjoy eating it together, encouraging discussion and conversation throughout. Food preparation can be a source of new vocabulary, especially because many of its terms take on special meanings: *stir*, *blend*, *boil*, *measure*, *dice*, and so on.

Dramatic Play: Add items related to the topic to the dramatic-play area—mittens, hats, scarves, boots for dress-up—to encourage role playing and language about winter. Introduce the items by placing each in a separate bag and asking a child to reach in, describe what it feels like, and identify it without peeking. The sense of touch elicits descriptive language.

Outdoor Play: Encourage spontaneous language and frequent problem-solving situations during outdoor play. For example, provide snow shovels, sleds, pails, and cups during playtime in the snow. Discuss outdoor play before going out and again after coming in.

Morning Message: Discuss weather and the calendar in a morning message. Encourage children to share news about themselves; for example, show and describe a new pair of snow boots.

Class Trips: Visit the museum that has displays about the North Pole or show a video about winter. These activities can generate language and encourage its use. Technology can take you on a "virtual trip" to the North Pole.

Read Stories: Read stories about the topic under study. Books such as *The Snowy Day* (Keats, 1996) enhance information and expand vocabulary. Find digital stories to share as well.

Create Stories: Provide the children with a title, such as "The Big Winter Snowstorm," and let them think of a story about it. Figures to create stories are often helpful. Refer to Figure 6.1 for stick puppets for oral language development by creating your own story. Enlarge, photocopy, color, or copy onto firm colored paper. Laminate and cut. Tape a tongue depressor to the back of each figure to create a stick puppet. The teacher will create an original story using the characters provided. The children will be asked to do the same after the activity has been modeled. The teacher can help the student by saying, "You can begin your story with 'Once upon a time there was a girl and a boy. They decided to take a walk in the woods and . . .'" The teacher reminds the children to include a beginning, middle, and end of the story.

Retell Stories: Ask children to retell stories. This activity encourages them to use book language and incorporate it into their own. Retelling is not always an easy task for young children, so props can be helpful—puppets, felt boards and felt characters, and pictures in a book. With these same props, children can make up their own stories.

Very Own Vocabulary Words: In any of these activities, children should be encouraged as often as possible to select their favorite Very Own Words about winter. Favorite Very Own Words can be selected from discussions, art lessons, science experiments, songs, books, poems, cooking experiences, or any other activity. After a particular experience, ask children to name a favorite word. Record children's favorite Very Own Words for

Figure 6.1 Stick Puppets for Oral Language Development

Enlarge, photocopy, color, or copy onto firm colored paper. Laminate and cut. Tape a tongue depressor to the back of each figure to create a stick puppet. The teacher will create an original story using the characters provided. The children will be asked to do the same after the activity has been modeled. The teacher can help the student by saying, "You can begin your story with 'Once upon a time there was a girl and a boy. They decided to take a walk in the woods and . . . '" The teacher reminds the children to include a beginning, middle, and end of the story.

them on 3 × 5 cards and store them in each child's own file box or on a binder ring. When children are capable of recording their own words, assist them with spelling when they ask for help. Favorite Very Own Words enhance vocabulary and are a source for reading and writing development.

Word Walls: As the class learns new words that are especially related to themes, the teacher can place them on a word wall for use. Word walls have many purposes. They are mostly for reading grade-level, high-frequency words. These words should be separated from the new, vocabulary-themed words by color. That is, all high-frequency words may be in red and all new thematic words in blue. The new vocabulary on the word wall is used in different activities, such as alphabetizing words or using them in sentences and stories.

Summary of the Day: Summarize the day's events at the end of the school day, encouraging children to tell what they liked, did not like, and what they want to do the next day in school.

MyLab Education Application Exercise 6.2

Children's Literature and Language Development

Teaching English Learners

Children's literature with its attractive illustrations make books interesting for children who are English Learners and help them with development of their language.

To facilitate language development, select and offer children's literature that represents varieties of languages and experiences. Some children's books, such as the classic *Strega Nona* (dePaola, 1975), feature not only sophisticated, interesting language but also wonderful rhymes that Strega Nona sings throughout the book. The book is excellent for vocabulary development, developing syntactic complexity through the use of adjectives and adverbs, and an emphasis on rhyming words. The book *How Do Dinosaurs Eat Their Food?* (Yolan & Teague, 2005) is composed of questions throughout the book that teach punctuation and sentence structure.

Craft books require children to follow directions. Wordless books encourage them to create their own stories from the pictures. Concept books feature words such as *up, down, in, out, near,* and *far* or involve children in mathematical reasoning. Realistic literature deals with death, divorce, loneliness, fear, and daily problems; discussion of such themes leads to sociopsychological language, interpretation of feelings, sensitivity to others, and problem solving. Books of riddles, puns, jokes, and tongue twisters show children different ways of using language. Poetry introduces children to rhyme, metaphor, simile, and onomatopoeia and encourages them to recite and create poems. (Children's books are listed by these and other categories in Appendix A.) When children hear and discuss the language of books, they internalize what they have heard; the language soon becomes part of their own language. Research studies have found that children who are read to frequently develop more sophisticated language structures and increased vocabulary (Beck & McKeown, 2001; Beck, McKeown, & Kucan, 2013).

Two anecdotes illustrate how children incorporate into their own language the language of books that have been read to them. My kindergarten class was playing on the playground one early spring day. A few birds circled around several times. Melissa ran up to me and said, "Look, Mrs. Morrow, the birds are fluttering and flapping around the playground." Surprised at first by Melissa's descriptive and unusual choice of words, I thought for a moment, then remembered. The words that Melissa was using came directly from a picture storybook we had read shortly before, *Jenny's Hat* (Keats, 1966). In the book, birds *flutter* and *flap* around Jenny's hat. Melissa had internalized the language of the book and was able to use it in her own vocabulary.

One day after a big snowstorm, my daughter asked, "Mommy, can I go out and play? I want to build a smiling snowman." I was surprised and pleased with this sophisticated language being uttered by my 4-year-old. *Smiling snowman* represents a participle in the adjective position, a syntactic structure usually not found in the language of children before the age of 7 or 8. Then I remembered reading the book *The Snowy Day* (Keats, 1996) to Stephanie. In it, Peter goes outside and builds a *smiling snowman.* Stephanie made the book language her own.

MyLab Education Self-Check 6.2

Explicit Strategies for Teaching Vocabulary

MyLab Education
Video Example 6.4
Six Skills for Early Literacy: Vocabulary
In this video, a librarian discusses strategies for vocabulary development in young children.
https://www.youtube.com/watch?v=9DfKlVRYv8E

Explicit instruction is necessary. No matter what the activity, the following steps are needed.

The Vocabulary Meeting

Embedded and spontaneous vocabulary instruction has been discussed thus far. But children need time set aside specifically for vocabulary instruction. We have reading and writing workshops carved into the school day. There must also be a designated time for explicit instruction of vocabulary. I will call that time the *Vocabulary Meeting.* A Vocabulary Meeting can be any time in the school day. If it is carried out early in the day, the new words introduced can be practiced throughout that day. This meeting will be 15–20 minutes daily, and the teacher will prepare a mini-lesson. Many different strategies for teaching vocabulary can be used. I will illustrate one. Using grade-level tier 2 words the teacher has prepared a vocabulary-enriched message containing new words to learn that will have meaning for the children. This vocabulary meeting is early in the day. The lesson is as follows:

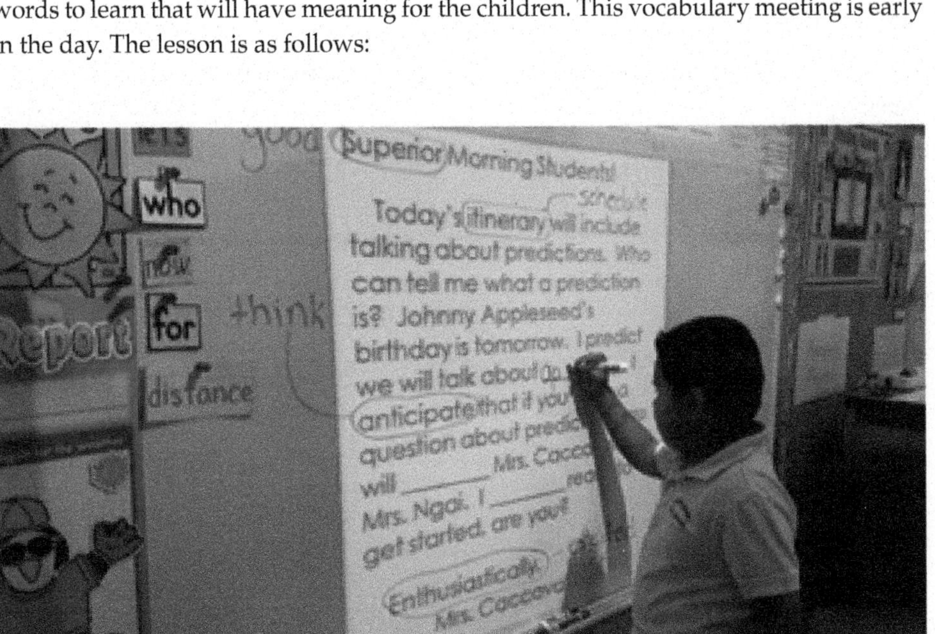

Purpose of the Lesson: To introduce the words *anticipate, itinerary, predictions,* and *superior.*

Materials and Setting: A vocabulary message containing the new vocabulary; the message is projected on to the digital white board. There are markers and index cards with the new works written on them and they are taped to the white board. Each child has a handout with the vocabulary message written on the paper. The vocabulary message is projected onto the digital white board. The new vocabulary is embedded in the message.

Introduction: Ms. Nelson asks the children to follow along on their handout as she reads the vocabulary message to the class.

> Superior Students,
> Superior (good) students. One objective (goal),
> for today is to anticipate (think) about what it means
> to predict (guess). Johnny Appleseed's birthday is tomorrow.
> What fruit do you predict we will talk about?
> Please take time to read the short story about Johnny Appleseed
> at home tonight. I anticipate that tomorrow will be fun eating
> food containing apples.
>
> Sincerely,
> Ms. Nelson

After reading, she asks the children to circle the new vocabulary on their morning message handout. She then asks the children to think of synonyms for the new vocabulary and write them next to the new words on their handout. One child filled in their handout as follows:

> Superior (good) students. One objective (goal) for today is to anticipate (think) about what it means to predict (guess). Johnny Appleseed's birthday is tomorrow. What fruit do you predict (guess) we will talk about?

Guided Practice: The class shares what they wrote and share different synonyms they used.

Independent Practice: Students fill in their four Frayer graphic organizers for vocabulary development with a partner.

Figure 6.2, is another sample Vocabulary Meeting and a lesson for Read Across America Week.

Figure 6.2 Grade Level(s): Kindergarten/First Grade

Reinforced Word Wall Words:	*and, open, of, that, too*
Tier Two Vocabulary Focus:	*magnificent, fond*
Setting a Purpose for Learning: ("Today, we will be learning new vocabulary words based on a text that I have written/chosen based on . . . ")	When we celebrate Read Across America Week, many students are introduced to Dr. Seuss, who was fond of reading for fun. Today I am going to challenge you to decode a text that I have written about the places you will go when you practice reading. See if you can find any unfamiliar vocabulary as you read this text.
Text Type: narrative / riddle poem / informational letter / recipe journal / list song / other	Dear *Magnificent* Readers, Dr. Seuss reminds us that reading can take us to great places and open many doors. Most of all, reading is fun too! You have brains in your head. You have feet in your shoes. Reading will take you any direction you choose! What types of stories are you *fond* of? Sincerely,
Opportunities for Differentiation:	• Vocabulary instruction: *magnificent; fond* • Use of punctuation marks • Rereading for fluency and expression • Follow-up activity: Conduct an interest inventory with the class to learn more about what the students are interested in reading • Read-aloud opportunities: *Miss Malarkey Leaves No Reader Behind* by Judy Finchler and Kevin O'Malley; *How Rocket Learned to Read* by Tad Hills • Sight-word practice • Upper-case and lower-case letters

Morrow, Kunz, and Hall, 2018

More Strategies for Developing Vocabulary

Following are lessons and strategies for vocabulary development that can be introduced when teaching vocabulary explicitly.

Vocabulary Graphic Organizer: There are many types of graphic organizers and they are used to develop many different skills. Figure 6.3 is a graphic organizer to help with vocabulary development. The new word is placed in the middle of the figure. The student is asked to define the word, draw a picture of the word, provide a synonym and antonym for the word, and finally use it in a sentence. This is an explicit activity that helps the child use a new word in many different ways.

Semantic Maps: Semantic maps are diagrams that help children see how words are related to one another (Johnson & Pearson, 1984; Otto, 2006). To enrich vocabulary development and the meaning of words, try the following:

1. Choose a word related to a student's interests or a theme that is being studied.
2. Write a new word on a chalkboard or a piece of experience chart paper.
3. Brainstorm other words that are related to the key word.
4. Create categories for the new words that emerge and classify them into these categories (refer to Figure 6.4).
5. Use the new words in #4 to create a story (Cox, 2007).
6. Use an electronic white board for semantic map vocabulary building.

Context Clues: Using clues from surrounding text is an important way of figuring out word meanings. Leaving blanks in sentences for children to determine the appropriate word is an activity that helps them understand how to use context to find word meanings. Just looking to other words in a sentence to determine meaning is helpful as well. Students need to know that this is one of the best ways to learn new words because they are embedded in meaningful text. The clues they use are other words or phrases in the sentence that tell something about the unknown words. Clues can be before or after the unknown word and are usually close to the word. They could also be in sentences

MyLab Education
Video Example 6.5
Growing Vocabulary: Multiple Meanings

Multimeaning words can be very difficult for young learners. In this video, a second-grade teacher helps her students understand multiple meanings of the word draw.

Figure 6.3 Vocabulary Graphic Organizer

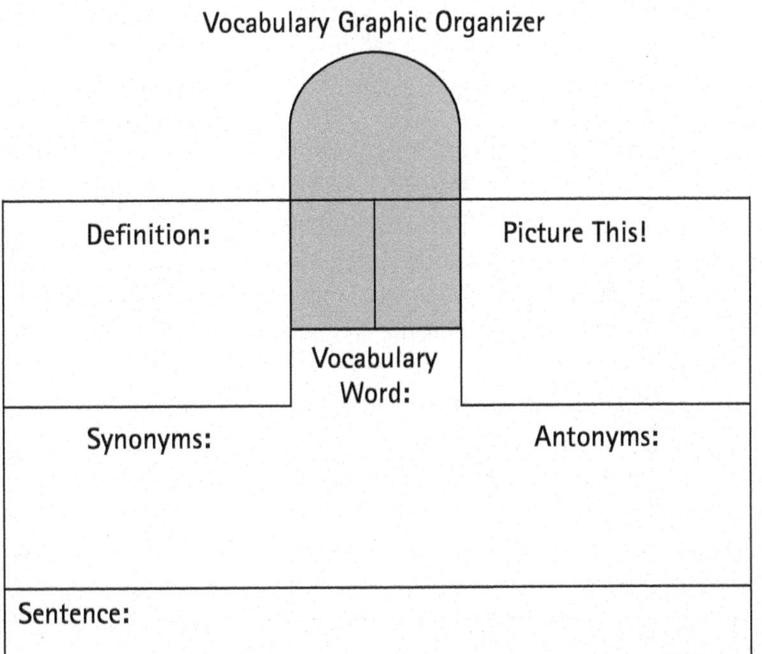

Figure 6.4 Semantic Map about Transportation

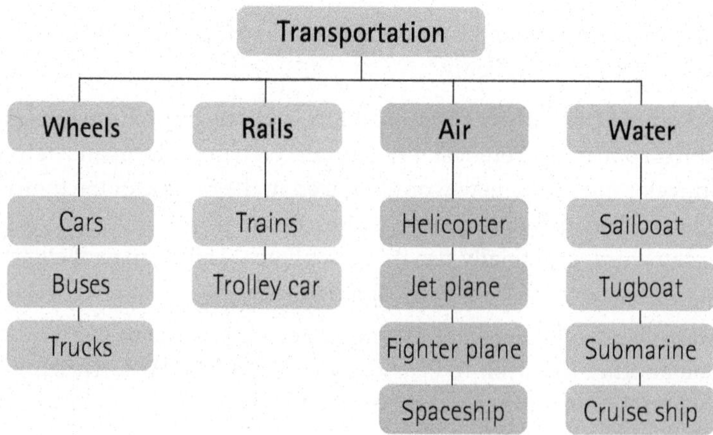

before or after. Have students guess the meaning of the word from the clues and then discuss if the guesses are correct. The following sentence is from the book *Swimmy* (1987) by Leo Lionni. The unusual words that Lionni uses can be grasped from the words surrounding the more difficult ones. *"One bad day a tuna fish fierce, swift, and very hungry came through the waves."*

The teacher left a blank in the sentence for a word that was difficult, but could be figured out. It was for the word *darting*. She read the sentence to the children with the blank and asked what word they thought fit there. They suggested that the word could be *swimming, rushing, shooting out, jumping, pushing*. None said darting, since it was not familiar to them. The teacher praised their choices and put in the word *darting* from the story. She asked the children what they thought it meant. They agreed it meant pushing, shooting out, and maybe rushing, which were words that they had already generated and that defined the unknown word *darting*.

Vocabulary Journals: After learning words post them on a word wall or someplace in the classroom so students can independently reflect on the words and their meanings through the use of vocabulary notebooks or journals. Vocabulary journals provide a space for expanding upon understanding of newly assigned vocabulary words and for jotting down words that students notice and appreciate when reading independently. To maximize time spent on learning, the teacher can create a weekly "vocab list," or short note containing all of the assigned words for the week for students to paste or copy into their notebooks:

Week 1 Vocab List

- afraid
- afternoon
- building
- chatter
- discover
- hidden
- nervous
- plenty

Students should be encouraged to have an open conversation with their peers about their familiarity with the words and possible meanings. Introducing the vocabulary journal at the beginning of the year requires a review of procedures.

Mystery Words: Tape "mystery words" to students' backs and remind students not to peek! Once they are ready to go, students mingle around the classroom and find a partner. Partners then take turns taking the vocabulary words from one another without showing the word.

7-Up Sentences: The teacher can list seven vocabulary words learned recently. Children are to create "7-Up Sentences" for their partners and their partner writes a set for them. They compare sentences (Overturf, Montgomery, & Smith, 2013). 7-Up Sentences can be made for new vocabulary in math, social studies, art, music, health, or science.

The Dictionary and Computer: Using a print or digital dictionary is another way to add to a student's repertoire of strategies to find and check meanings. Students must learn that words have many meanings, and they may all be listed in the dictionary. Therefore, when using the dictionary, they need to select the meaning for the word that makes sense in the context in which it occurs. Dictionaries prepared specifically for young children should be used in the primary grades (Graves, Juel, & Graves, 2006).

Word Parts: Learning word parts is a way for second and third graders to build vocabulary and meaning. Choose word parts that are well-known prefixes and suffixes and commonly used roots of words. With knowledge of a few of these, children can begin to build their own words. Teach children to talk through the use of word parts to get the meaning. For example, when students learn word-part meanings, they can talk through their word building as follows: "I know that the prefix *dis* means 'not,' and I also know that the word *content* means to be happy or pleased. If I add *dis* to the word *content* it would be *discontent*. Now it would mean that someone was not happy."

Word Charades: Children create a charade for a word in small groups. They act it out for the rest of the class to figure out. At times they freeze their charade so the others can look at it for a while. Strategies that involve activity result in vocabulary that is remembered (Overturf et al., 2013).

Books and Games: Vocabulary-rich second- and third-grade classrooms make available a variety of books and word games to enrich language and vocabulary development. The library corner should include riddle books, joke books, and books with puns. There are many genres of children's literature, such as fiction and nonfiction. Word games such as Boggle, Pictionary, Scrabble, and crossword puzzles allow children to experience words in a ludic context and to build and use vocabulary in different ways (Blachowicz & Fisher, 2002).

Vocabulary Rap: Rap is a popular type of music that attracts children's attention. The use of music helps memory. For vocabulary use the sentence "When I say ___________(the vocabulary word), you say ___________ (a synonym for the vocabulary word). This can also be done using antonyms as the second word. Students can create their own vocabulary hip-hop rhymes. Allow children to move as they do to hip-hop music when chanting their rhymes (Overturf et al., 2013).

Vocabulary Board Games: Games such as Bingo and Lotto can be made into vocabulary board games, with definitions and antonyms and synonyms as a way to get Bingo and with matches in Lotto.

Vocabulary Template Games: In Chapter 8, which is about word study strategies, there are several games that children can play to help them with phonics. On page 175 there are puzzle pieces students have to fit together. On these pieces there can be a new vocabulary word and its definition is the puzzle piece that fits. You can also use the vocabulary word and find its synonym match, homonym match, or antonym match. In addition, there is a word wheel template. On the word wheel can be vocabulary words. As you turn the wheel you look for its antonym, synonym, or definition.

Promoting Conversation

By the time children come to school, they have had varied opportunities for talk in their daily lives. Most of the talk is spontaneous and deals with real-life experiences. With their parents, talk has included questions and answers, often with parents directing the discussion. In structured question-and-answer discussions, teachers need to provide open-ended questions that will encourage talk, such as "What would happen if . . . ?" "What would you do if . . . ?" and "Tell us why." The talk is not directed and allows children to play a more active role in creating spontaneous, meaningful language.

Conversations occur best in small-group settings that include three to six children. Any number beyond that becomes a large-group discussion. Conversations can occur in small groups with the teacher or in a formal or informal manner without the teacher.

Small-Group Conversations with the Teacher. For small-group conversations to be productive, guidelines need to be established and followed:

1. Children should listen to others during conversations.
2. Children need to take turns talking.
3. Students should raise hands, if necessary, to ensure everyone gets a turn and individuals do not interrupt each other.
4. Everyone should keep talk relevant to the topic of conversation.
5. Teachers need to help redirect conversation to its stated purpose should it stray.
6. Teacher talk should be kept to a minimum as the teacher becomes a participant.

Teachers should follow the same rules as the children: Listen to others when they are talking, take turns, do not do all the talking, and so on.

Formal Conversations without the Teacher. Another type of structured discussion is a formal conversation without the teacher, such as when children are in charge of their own discussion of a topic. In those situations, a group leader needs to be selected to help direct the conversation and make sure everyone in the group follows the guidelines. The same guidelines for productive conversation when the teacher is present apply when children direct conversations themselves:

1. Children should listen to others during conversations.
2. Children need to take turns talking.
3. Students should raise hands, if necessary.
4. Everyone should keep the talk relevant to the conversation's purpose.

Informal Conversations without the Teacher. In addition to formal opportunities to talk, children need time to talk without leaders or specific outcomes. This type of conversation is likely to occur during free-play periods, center time, or outdoor play. Although classrooms that encourage this type of talk can be noisy, it is important for children to have the opportunity to use language in social settings at school.

Types of Talk. In addition to learning the types of organizational structures in which talk should take place, students need to engage in different types of informal peer-to-peer talk, which includes aesthetic talk, efferent talk, and talk in dramatic activities.

Aesthetic talk typically revolves around children's literature. In this talk, children have the opportunity to interpret what they have read or listened to. Children can participate in aesthetic talk when discussing literature, telling stories, and participating in Reader's Theater. These activities are discussed further in Chapter 9, which deals with using children's literature in the classroom. Involving children in aesthetic talk is easily done. Following is a classroom conversation based on a unit dealing with tolerance and an example of how Ms. Lynn's second graders engaged in discussion about a topic of interest to them.

MyLab Education
Video Example 6.6
3rd Grade Literature Circle Discussions
Children discuss books they are reading in their class using an instructional approach called Literature Circles. https://www.youtube.com/watch?v=tNNQARvoGds

This marking period, the entire school is studying tolerance as a part of a schoolwide character education theme. This topic was introduced during an assembly, which featured a Zumba dance demonstration and excerpts from the book *My Friend with Autism* (Bishop, 2011). At the end of the quarter, the school will hold a Zumba dance-a-thon to raise money for a nonprofit organization that funds research on autism.

Throughout the marking period, teachers moderate discussions and conduct activities on tolerance. Today, Ms. Lynn's second-grade class is listening to a song written and performed by author/educator John Farrell titled, "How Would You Feel?". The students sit in a circle, and each has downloaded a copy of the lyrics from johnfarrell.net.

Ms. Lynn: The song you will hear is based on real-life events—real things that happened to real people. Let's listen carefully and follow along on the page to find out what this song has to do with our tolerance theme.

The students listen and follow on the lyrics page. This helps them focus on the message of the song. Afterward, they hold a discussion recounting key ideas and details from the song. Ms. Lynn begins the discussion.

Ms. Lynn:	Remember, we define *tolerance* as a willingness to accept people who are different than you. Fairness is doing what is right to make sure others are not treated badly. What were some details in the song that match these definitions?
Jervane:	The first part of the song tells the story of a boy getting his candy stolen on Halloween by some big kids. That's for fairness. They are not treating him with fairness.
Brady:	Yeah, they push him over. That's the opposite of "doing what is right to make sure others are not treated badly."
Ms. Lynn:	Yes, you've got that right! What's another detail from the song that matches?
Terra:	Well, in the next line a girl is always picked last for the game. I think she kinda stinks at sports.
Ms. Lynn:	OK, so what does that have to do with our theme?
Connor:	It says with her on the team it's harder to win. So why would they want her? I know it's not fair, but it makes sense why she doesn't get picked.
Terra:	It's not about winning, Connor! They're playing a game to have fun. It's not fun for you *ever* if you aren't wanted. That's not right.
Ms. Lynn:	Great observation, Terra. How about the last example?
Hope:	The last one's a good example for tolerance. The girl dressed differently and talked weird, but they still asked her to be their friend.

From the discussion, Ms. Lynn can tell that the students have a solid understanding of the song. They talked about the most important details and related it to their topic of study.

Efferent talk is used to inform and persuade. Efferent talk occurs in discussion of the themes being studied. It is about facts, details, and information. It also occurs in situations such as show-and-tell, oral reports, conversations about serious things that happen in real life, interviews, and debates. These types of interchanges are more formal than previously discussed and often require preparation on the part of the child.

The following is a discussion from Mr. Hershall's first graders in which efferent talk is used. The children are building concepts of time for their social studies unit, with a focus on the difference between the past and present. For homework, Mr. Hershall has created a VoiceThread for his students to watch and comment on. This online slideshow is a collection of photographs and videos depicting objects used in the past and those used today. VoiceThread is an excellent tool for young learners because users can make video or audio comments in addition to standard written comments. For their homework, the children use the comment feature to record a question on one of the slides. In addition to learning about the past and present, the students are developing an ability to use technology and to ask questions to gain further information or clarify.

Mr. Hershall reviews these comments and responds by posting his own comments. During centers, his students will watch the VoiceThread again and listen to Mr. Hershall's comments. Following is a transcript of audio and video comments from their VoiceThread.

Mr. Hershall:	This is a phonograph. It was invented in the year 1877 by Thomas Edison. It not only played music, but was able to record sound, too!
Video:	[music playing]
Natalie:	Is the flower the speaker?

Mr. Hershall: Yes, the flower is called the "horn," where the sound comes out. This is a laptop. Today people use word-processing programs on their computer, like Microsoft Word, to type.

Jennifer: Is this a MacBook?

Mr. Hershall: No, it is made by HP. Now this is a typewriter. People in the past used it to type. It prints right on a piece of paper as you push the keys.

Video: [someone typing]

John: Did you have one when you were a kid?

Mr. Hershall: No, I always had a computer, but my dad had one I used to play with.

Coleen: How old is it?

Mr. Hershall: This one is from the 1960s.

Jenny: Who invented typewriters?

Mr. Hershall: The first typewriter was made by Henry Mill in 1714. The next typewriter was made for the blind in 1808 by Pellegrino Turri. The first typewriter that had keys in the same place as today's was made in 1878. It was invented by Christopher Latham Sholes and Carlos Glidden.

There are endless ideas for developing vocabulary that are fun, interesting, and will bring enthusiasm to learning new words. There are online sites to develop vocabulary and multiple books such as *Teaching Vocabulary in All Classrooms* (Blachowicz & Fisher, 2015) and *Word Nerds: Teaching All Students to Learn and Love Vocabulary* (Overturf et al., 2013).

MyLab Education Self-Check 6.3
MyLab Education Self-Check 6.4

Assessing Children's Language and Vocabulary Development

It is important to assess children's language to determine if it follows expected stages of development. Assessment also determines how much a child has progressed. The word *assessment* suggests several rather frequent measures by which to judge progress. Assessment should reflect instructional objectives and strategies. It should include evaluation of a wide range of skills used in many contexts. A certain child, for example, may perform better in an interview than on a pencil-and-paper test. Both kinds of evaluation, therefore, should be used. Literacy includes a wide range of skills; it is important to evaluate a child for as many as possible to determine strengths and weaknesses. Unfortunately, many assessment instruments are narrow in scope and frequently do not measure a child's total abilities. Assessments fall into two main categories: informal assessments and standardized language assessments.

Informal Assessments

There are basic concepts to employ when assessing language and vocabulary. Following are some guidelines:

- Use tools that reflect your instruction.
- Incorporate student self-assessment.
- Assess words students need to know.
- Assessment tools for vocabulary should evaluate what it means to know the word.

- Vocabulary assessment should be systematic.
- Assess explicitly taught vocabulary.
- Children should be involved in assessing their vocabulary alone or with other students or the teacher.

There are several ways to measure children's language development in early childhood, which are similar to those used for measuring literacy development, described in Chapter 2.

Checklists are practical because they provide concise outlines for teachers and appropriate slots for individual children. They are most effective if used periodically during the school year (See Figure 6.5). Three to four evaluations during the year can provide sufficient data to determine progress. Program objectives offer criteria to include on checklists.

Anecdotal records are another form of language assessment. They tend to be time-consuming but can reveal rich information. Looseleaf notebooks and file cards offer two means for keeping anecdotal records. These records require no particular format. Rather, the teacher or parent simply writes down incidents or episodes on the days they occur. Samples of a child's language and situations involving language can be recorded. Like checklists, anecdotal samples are necessary periodically to determine growth over a school year.

Audio and *video recording* are another means of evaluating language. The process can take the form of an open interview or a hidden recording. Children who are unaware that they are being audio- or video-recorded are likely to be more spontaneous and uninhibited (Genishi & Dyson, 1984; McGee, 2007; Otto, 2006).

When recording, place the recording device (tape recorder, digital voice recorder, smartphone, or tablet) in such a way as to be able to record language clearly enough to transcribe and analyze. Interviews with children can be more natural when an adult familiar to the child does the interviewing. Or, it is also helpful to allow the tape recorder or tablet to become such a familiar tool in the classroom that the child uses it often in the language arts center. Under such circumstances, the device is not threatening when used in an assessment interview.

To record samples of natural language, discuss the child's experiences. Ask about home, favorite games or toys, favorite TV programs, brothers and sisters, trips taken, or birthday parties recently attended. You should try to collect a corpus of spontaneous language that provides a typical sample of the child's ability with language.

Record audio assessment samples three or four times a year. Let children hear their own recorded voices and enjoy the experience. Then, for assessment purposes, transcribe the recordings. Free transcription software, such as Listen N Write, can reduce

Figure 6.5 Checklist for Assessing Language Development

Child's name: ________________ Date: ________________

	Always	Sometimes	Never	Comments
Makes phoneme sounds				
Speaks in one-word sentences				
Speaks in two-word sentences				
Identifies familiar sounds				
Differentiates similar sounds				
Understands the language of others when spoken				
Follows verbal directions				
Speaks to others freely				
Pronounces words correctly				
Has appropriate vocabulary for level of maturity				
Speaks in complete sentences				
Uses varied syntactic structures				
Can be understood by others				
Teacher Comments:				

the time needed to convert WAV and MP3 files to text and allow you to compile greater quantities of language more easily—and more frequently. Analyze the transcriptions for such items as numbers of words uttered and numbers of words spoken in a single connected utterance (e.g., "Tommy's cookie" or "Me want water"). The lengths of such utterances can be averaged to determine mean length. Length of utterance is considered a measure of complexity. When children begin to speak in conventional sentences, such as "That is my cookie," measure the length of the t-units. A **t-unit** is an independent clause with all its dependent clauses attached, assuming it has dependent clauses. It can be a simple or complex sentence. Compound sentences are made up of two t-units. (Refer back to Chapter 5, page 93.) Length of t-units, like length of utterances, is a measure of language complexity. It typically increases with the user's age and usually the more words per unit, the more complex the unit (Hunt, 1970).

Further analysis of taped utterances and t-units can determine which elements of language a child uses: number of adjectives, adverbs, dependent clauses, negatives, possessives, passives, plurals, and so on. The more complex the embeddings and syntactic elements used, the more complex the language overall (Morrow, 1978). Data from several samples over a year can be most revealing.

The following is a verbatim transcription of a recorded language sample from a 7-year-old boy in the second grade. The child was presented with a picture book and asked to tell a story from the pictures.

> He's getting up in the morning and he's looking out the window with his cat and after he gets out of bed he brushes his teeth then when he gets done brushing his teeth, he eats breakfast and then when he after he eats breakfast he he gets dressed to play some games then in the afternoon he plays with his toys then in the afternoon he plays doctor and early in the day he plays Cowboys and Indians then when it's in the afternoon close to suppertime he plays Cops and Robbers when he's playing in his castle he likes to dream of a magic carpet he's driving his ship on the waves he's uh circus uh ringmaster he's lifting up a fat lady I mean a clown is standing on a horse a clown is on a high wire somebody fell and then hurt their head the cowboy is bringing some ice cream to the hurt man that night he goes in the bathroom and gets washed and then he goes to bed then he dreams I don't know what he's dreaming I will think of what he's dreaming he's dreaming of going to play and he's playing the same things over.

After the sample is transcribed, the language is segmented into t-units. Following is a sample of the segmented t-units (note that utterances such as *aaa* or false starts are not counted):

1. He's getting up in the morning. (6)
2. And he's looking out the window with his cat. (9)
3. And after he gets out of bed he brushes his teeth. (11)
4. Then when he gets done brushing his teeth, he eats. (9)
5. He eats breakfast. (3)
6. And then (when he) after he eats breakfast he (he) gets dressed to play some games. (12)
7. Then in the afternoon he plays with his toys. (9)
8. Then in the afternoon he plays doctor. (7)
9. And early in the day he plays Cowboys and Indians. (10)
10. Then when it's in the afternoon close to suppertime he plays Cops and Robbers. (14)
11. When he's playing in his castle he likes to dream of a magic carpet. (14)
12. He's driving his ship on the waves. (7)
13. He's (uh) circus (uh) ringmaster. (3)
14. He's lifting up a fat lady. (6)

15. I mean a clown is standing on a horse. (9)
16. A clown is on a high wire. (7)
17. Somebody fell and then hurt their head. (7)
18. The cowboy is bringing some ice cream to the hurt man. (11)
19. That night he goes in the bathroom and gets washed. (10)
20. And then he goes to bed. (6)
21. Then he dreams. (3)
22. I don't know what he's dreaming. (6)
23. I will think of what he's dreaming. (7)
24. He's dreaming of going to play. (6)
25. And he's playing the same things over. (7)

Now: (1) Place the number of words per t-unit at the end of each one. (2) Add them. (3) Divide by the number of t-units (this tells you the average length per t-unit). (4) Count the total number of words spoken. (5) Count the number of different words. (6) Count the number of adjectives used in the language sample. (7) Results: The child spoke 129 words and had 5.16 words per t-unit.

Standardized Language Assessment

Assessment for language development thus far has been a discussion of informal measures. There are standardized measures used for different purposes and age levels from preschool through the primary grades. The following are some standardized measures:

- The *Peabody Picture Vocabulary Test, 5th ed. (PPVT™-5)* (Dunn & Dunn, 1997), website: https://www.pearsonclinical.com/language/products/100001984/peabody-picture-vocabulary-test-fifth-edition.html?origsearchtext=100001984

  PPVT is the leading wide-range measure of receptive vocabulary for standard English and a screening test of verbal ability. This individually administered, norm-referenced test has two parallel forms for testing and retesting. Scoring is objective and rapid; administration of the test is 10–15 minutes.

- *Teacher Rating of Oral Language and Literacy* (TROLL), Center for Improvement of Early Reading Achievement (CIERA), University of Michigan, School of Education, Ann Arbor, MI 48109

  TROLL is a rating tool to provide preschool teachers with a way to track the language and literacy development of individual children. TROLL measures language use, reading, and writing. There are 25 items and the test can be administered in 5–10 minutes.

- *Woodcock–Johnson III (WjIII) NU Tests of Achievement*

  The *WjIII NU Tests of Achievement* can be administered in 5 minutes and has two parallel forms. There are tests of oral language, basic skills, and fluency.

Other tests are the *Test of Language Development: Primary, 4 through 8 Years (TOLD)* (Hresko, Reid, & Hammill, 1999) and *Expressive One-Word Picture Vocabulary Test, 2 to 18 Years (EOWPVT)* (Brownell, 2000). These tests provide information for the teacher about children's vocabulary development and their use of complex sentence structure (McGee, 2007).

In today's teaching environment, it is critical to select standard assessment tools that meet your specific needs, assessing students' progress toward meeting the Common Core State Standards in Speaking and Listening and in Language.

MyLab Education Self-Check 6.5

An Idea from the Classroom

Storytelling: The Movie

A favorite activity of first graders is retelling stories using storytelling props, such as felt-board pieces and puppets. This is a great activity to do during shared reading using big books that have been read several times and students know well, and it helps to support comprehension and language development for beginning readers. In my first-grade class, students *love* using felt-board pieces to retell stories such as *Silly Sally*, *The Napping House*, and *Quick as a Cricket*, all by Audrey Wood. After reading the big books aloud several times over the course of a week, students are invited up to add felt-board pieces to the felt board as the story is retold. The entire class chants repeating parts, which helps to build oral language and fluency. After retelling several stories using premade felt-board pieces, students work in partners to select their own story to retell and work together to create their own pieces by drawing on construction paper and gluing felt to the back. After practicing with partners, we film our storytelling performances and invite families in for a storytelling movie, complete with popcorn and VIP seating for our first-grade stars!

Amy Anderson, First-Grade Teacher

Summary

6.1 Describe strategies to enhance expressive and receptive language.

The major objective in language development is to create experiences for children to develop receptive and expressive language. Strategies for developing language from birth to age 2 include providing a rich language environment, surrounding infants with sounds and sensory objects, increasing the complexity of utterances directed at the child, scaffolding language, providing new experiences for the child, and understanding the role of overgeneralizations. As children enter the classroom, strategies to develop language involve creating meaningful experiences through centers, thematic units, and children's literature. In second and third grades, strategies for developing language should focus on expanding vocabulary and word meaning and should include promoting language production through a variety of conversational context, both formal and informal and with and without the teacher.

6.2 Describe a rich literacy environment that will engage children in conversation.

Classrooms are square or rectangular spaces with not much in them. We need to arrange our settings so the environment creates talk. Early childhood rooms should have centers that represent what is being learned. Classrooms need content area materials that will encourage children to describe, manipulate and discuss. There are materials for art, music, math, literacy, social studies, science, and so forth. when studying native Indians, for example, bring books and artifacts representing that culture and children will discuss.

6.3 Describe the Vocabulary Meeting.

Developing vocabulary is one of the most important elements for children in literacy development. If you can decode but don't understand the meaning of the word *decoding*, you can't comprehend. The larger the vocabulary, the better the reader will be. The school day does not designate a time for developing vocabulary as it does with a reading and writing workshop. Therefore, it has been incorporated into the literacy day so that it is not forgotten. At the Vocabulary Meeting, which can happen first thing in the morning, the teacher can feature new vocabulary words from those required in the grade level or those introduced in a theme being studied. Many strategies can be used to teach vocabulary in the Vocabulary Meeting.

6.4 Describe more strategies for developing vocabulary.

There is explicit instruction for learning new vocabulary as well as spontaneous and practice activities. In this section many strategies are introduced to choose from, such as graphic organizers, vocabulary journals, 7-Up sentences, context clues, and more.

6.5 Describe assessment of children's language development.

Formative and summative assessment should be used to identify needs of children as they develop language and vocabulary. Language assessments can be informal or formal. Informal assessments include checklists, anecdotal records, audio and video recording, and t-unit analysis. Formal assessment involves standardized language measures. Prominent standard measures are the Peabody Picture Vocabulary Test (*PPVT*™-5), the Teacher Rating of Language and Literacy (TROLL), and the Woodcock–Johnson III (WJIII) NU Tests of Achievement.

Activities and Questions

1. Select an objective for language development listed in the chapter. Prepare a lesson that will help a child achieve the goal. Identify the theories of language acquisition used in your lesson.
2. Record children at play or working in a group. Identify which characteristics of their language can be described by various theories of language acquisition. For example, imitation could be explained by the behaviorist theory.
3. Begin a thematic unit that you will continue as you read this book. Select a social studies or science topic. Select three objectives for language development, and describe three activities that will satisfy each objective using your theme. An example follows:

   Content Area: Science

   Theme: Creatures That Live in the Sea

   Objective for Language Development: Develop new vocabulary

   Activity: Read *Swimmy* by Leo Lionni. Ask the children to remember two new words they hear in the story. After reading, list words that the children mention on a chart, and discuss their meaning.
4. Observe a preschool, kindergarten, or first- or second-grade class for about 3 hours. Note the amount of time children are given to talk, the amount of time the teacher talks, and the amount of time during which there is no verbal interaction. Compare the three figures. Then classify talk in the classroom into the following categories:

   a. Questions and answers
   b. Whole-class discussion
   c. Small-group discussion led by the teacher
   d. Interactive discussion among children
   e. Interactive discussion between teacher and children
5. Based on the results of this mini-study, determine how often teachers allow children to use language and in how many different contexts or situations.
6. Plan an activity that will elicit aesthetic talk and one that will involve efferent talk. How is the language in each setting the same, and how is it different?
7. Continue the collection of assessment materials for the child for which you began a portfolio in Chapter 2. Collect one language sample from a child age 2–7. Elicit the language by showing a picture to discuss or asking the child to talk about favorite TV shows, pets, friends, family members, or trips. Record the sample and transcribe it.

   a. Check the characteristics of the child's language development according to the descriptions in this chapter and the checklist provided in Figure 6.5 to decide whether the child is above, below, or at a level appropriate for his or her age. Compare with other members of the class who have studied different age groups.
   b. Divide your language sample into t-units and determine the average length per t-unit by counting the number of words per t-unit. Add them and then divide by the number of t-units. Then count the number of different words and types of syntactic elements used.
   c. Collect three additional language samples for the same child at different times in the year. Evaluate the new samples as you did the first time and check for growth.

Chapter 7

Emergent Literacy Skills and Strategies: Helping Children to Figure Out Words

Photo credit: Lord and Leverett/Pearson Education Ltd

Learning Outcomes

After reading this chapter, you should be able to:

7.1 Explain the theory and research relating to figuring out words in early literacy.

7.2 Understand what children need to learn about the concepts of print.

7.3 Identify a variety of methods for teaching the alphabet.

7.4 Describe strategies for figuring out words other than phonics.

7.5 Assess emergent literacy skills.

Word-study skills and knowledge about print involve learning strategies that will help children figure out words and become independent readers. Word-study skills include learning the alphabet and how to use context and syntax to figure out words. The development of a sight vocabulary involves the use of the configuration, or the shape of a word, and structural analysis (attending to different parts of words, such as prefixes, suffixes, or the root). Phonics and phonemic awareness are the best-known word-study strategies and will be discussed in detail in Chapter 8.

VOCABULARY

Big Books
Environmental print
High-frequency words
Language experience approach (LEA)
Morning message
Sight words
Word wall

Figuring Out Words in Early Literacy: Theory and Research

Becoming literate is a process that begins at birth and continues throughout life. Children differ in their rates of literacy achievement; they must not be pressured into accomplishing tasks or placed on a predetermined time schedule. Researchers have found that children learn that print has *functions* as a first step in reading and writing (McGee & Morrow, 2005). The first words a child says, reads, and writes are those with meaning, purpose, and function in his or her life, such as family names, food labels, road signs, and names of fast-food restaurants.

After function, the child becomes interested in the *forms of print*. Details about names, sounds, and configurations of letters and words now serve the child's learning more than simple understanding of how print functions.

A child then learns the *conventions of print*. This process involves recognition that we read and write from left to right, that punctuation serves a purpose in reading and writing, and that spaces demarcate letters and words. Although recognition of the function of print dominates the first stages of reading and writing development, children acquire an interest in and notions about the form and conventions of print at the same time, but to a lesser degree.

Researchers warn that children do not systematically go from one developmental stage to the next in early reading and writing; they can take one step forward and, the next day, one step backward. For example, if you test a child's knowledge of the alphabet and she can identify 15 letters, the next day she may identify only 12.

There are three developmental levels in word recognition: Children first identify words through sight and context, then use letter–sound cues, and finally rely on sounding out words (Cunningham, 2009; McCormick & Mason, 1981). Children's initial questions and comments during story readings are related to the pictures and the meanings of the stories. As they gain experience with story readings, their questions and comments begin to concern the names of letters, the reading of individual words, or attempts to sound out words (Cunningham, 2009; McAfee & Leong, 1997; Neuman & Roskos, 1998). The function of print dominates early responses; the form of print becomes more important in later responses.

Some children have considerable information about reading and writing before they enter school for formal instruction. Some can even read and write before beginning school. Other children come to school with almost no exposure to print and have no books in their home. Children who have had exposure to print and a literacy-rich environment know the difference between drawing and writing, and they associate books with reading. They can read environmental print, and they realize that meaning is a function of reading and writing. Children without this exposure do not have these concepts about books and print.

Early reading and writing is embedded in real-life experience. Many families do things together that involve meaningful literacy. They write each other notes, lists, holiday greetings, and directions. Many children, however, do not have these same opportunities and therefore may not have the same skills developed at the same age (Allington, 2009; Kuhn et al., 2006).

Children are likely to become involved in literacy activities if they view reading and writing as functional, purposeful, and useful. Studies of early reading and writing behaviors clearly illustrate that young children acquire their first information about reading and writing through their functional uses (Cook-Cottone, 2004; McGee & Morrow, 2005). Grocery lists; directions on toys, packages, household equipment, and medicine containers; recipes; telephone messages; school-related notices; religious materials; menus; environmental print inside and outside the home; mail; magazines; newspapers; storybook readings; TV channels; telephone numbers; conversation among family members; letters and their names—these represent just a sample of the functional literacy information with which a child comes in contact daily. Young children are also aware of emails, text messages, and video game directions, and are interested in literacy and technology. Children are familiar with these forms of literacy, they participate in them, they pretend to use them at play, and they understand their purposes. Parents and child-care providers and preschool and kindergarten teachers need to provide experiences with reading similar to experiences children have already had.

In this chapter, we discuss emergent literacy skills to begin the process of understanding what books are for and early strategies for figuring out words. The topics we will discuss include learning concepts about books and print, the alphabet, reading sight words, high-frequency words, language experience approach, environmental print, using context to figure out words and syntax.

MyLab Education Self-Check 7.1

What Do Children Need to Learn about Concepts of Print

When children are very young, teachers discuss how to handle books, the parts of a book, and the difference between pictures and print. Children with early book experience are aware of many of these concepts. The concepts are not innate, they must be taught. Knowledge of concepts about books and print are important steps toward becoming literate. Refer to Figure 7.1, Concepts about Books and Conventions of Print Checklist.

Objectives for Developing Concepts about Books and Print

A child who has a good concept of books:

1. Knows that a book is for reading.
2. Can identify the front, back, top, and bottom of a book.
3. Can turn the pages of a book properly in the right direction.
4. Knows the difference between print and pictures.
5. Knows that pictures on a page are related to what the print says.
6. Knows where to begin reading on a page.
7. Knows what a title is.
8. Knows what an author is.
9. Knows what an illustrator is.
10. Knows that print is read from left to right.
11. Knows that oral language can be written down and then read.
12. Knows what a letter is and can point to it.
13. Knows what a word is and can point one out on a printed page.
14. Knows that there are spaces between words.

Figure 7.1 Concepts about Books and Conventions of Print Checklist

Child's name: ______________________ Date: ________

Directions: The words and phrases in bold are the skills children need to be able to demonstrate. The sentence in italics is the prompt you give a child when assessing his or her knowledge of the conventions of print. This assessment should be administered only after children have had stories read to them where the teacher has labeled the parts of the books and punctuation marks many times. The levels are guidelines that reflect levels of difficulty and may help guide the teacher to the introduction, labeling, and defining of concepts.

Ask the child each of the questions below. If he or she answers correctly, check the C or correct column. If the child answers incorrectly, check the IC column.

Level 1: Concepts about Books	C	IC
Font Cover: *Show me the front of the book.*		
Back cover: *Show me the back of the book.*		
Title: *Show me where the title of the book is.*		
Title Page: *Show me the title page.*		
First Page: *Show me the page we read first.*		

Level 2: Conventions of Print	C	IC
Print Has Meaning: *Show me where it tells the story.*		
Beginning of Text: *Show me where we start to read.*		
Left to Right: *Which way do we read the words?*		
Top to Bottom: *Which way do the words go from there?*		
Return Sweep: *Where do we go at the end of a line?*		

Level 3: Concepts about Words and Letters	C	IC
One-to-One: *Can you point to words as I read?*		
Word Boundaries: *Put your fingers around a word.*		
First Word: *Show me the first word on the page.*		
Last Word: *Show me the last word on the page.*		
Letter Concept: *Put your finger on a letter.*		
Capital Letter: *Put your finger on a capital letter.*		
Lowercase Letter: *Show me a lowercase letter.*		

Level 4: Concepts about Punctuation Marks	C	IC
Period: *Show me a period. What is it for?*		
Question Mark: *Show me a question mark. What is it for?*		
Quotation Mark: *Show me a quotation mark. What is it for?*		
Comma: *Show me a comma. What is it for?*		

The title of the story that I'm going to read is *Harriet, You'll Drive Me Wild* (Fox, 2000). This is the title on the front cover of the book. The author of the book, or the name of the person who wrote the book, is Mem Fox. Here is her name. And the illustrator, the person who drew the pictures, is Marla Franzee. Here is her name on the book. All books have titles and authors, and if they have pictures they also have illustrators. The next time you look at a book, see if you can find the title. It is always on the front cover. And look for the names of the author and illustrator. For some books like this one, *No David*, the person who wrote the book is the author and is also the person who drew the pictures. His name is David Shannon (Shannon, 1998).

Activities to Develop Concepts about Books

We often assume that children know the concepts about books and print just outlined. However, many 2- to 6-year-olds are unfamiliar with these concepts. Ideally, about 1000 books need to be read to a child before he or she enters kindergarten. Exposure to many books helps the child acquire concepts about books and print, so he or she is ready for experiences in reading and writing. To help children learn concepts about books they first must have multiple experiences handling books, be read to often, and have concepts about print explicitly pointed out. You can introduce a story by pointing appropriately as you say: The repetition of such dialogue familiarizes children with the concepts, which they will eventually understand. Similar dialogue helps to explain other concepts. Point to a picture, then point to the print. Identify each, then ask, "Which do we read, the picture or the print?"

As you get ready to read to them, ask children to point out the top and bottom of the book and where you should begin reading on a page. Not only will you give the children the opportunity to learn the concepts, but at the same time you can determine which children understand the concept and which need further instruction.These discussions can be carried out during story readings to small groups or with individual students. The more exposure children have to books, and to concepts about books and print, the more they begin to engage with text in ways that they didn't previously, as the following example illustrates:

> After I read *Knuffle Bunny* (Willems, 2004) to a 4-year-old, she said to me, "Show me, where does Trixie say, 'Aggle Flaggle Klabble'? I want to see it in the book." When I showed her the words, she repeated them while pointing to them and then asked to see them again in another part of the book. She proceeded to search through the book, trying to find the line "Aggle Flaggle Klabble" again. Every time she said them or I said them, she laughed and laughed and laughed.

Big Books Big Books, oversized picture storybooks that measure from 14 × 20 inches up to 24 × 30 inches, are useful tools for teachers to help children develop concepts about books and print. Holdaway (Holdaway, 1979) suggested that the enlarged print and pictures help get children involved with concepts about books, print, and the meaning of text. Big Books are appropriate from preschool through third grade. Active involvement is encouraged when using Big Books in small- and large-group settings. When using a Big Book, the teacher places it on a stand or an easel so that the print and pictures are visible to the children. Class Big Books can be made as well as purchased. When they are made, children become even more aware of book concepts because they are engaged in the books' creation. Figure 7.2 provides directions for making a Big Book.

MyLab Education
Video Example 7.1
Big Books Support Concepts About Print
Teachers use Big Books to reinforce concepts about print including the concept that we read print from left to right and, in English, from top to bottom of pages.
https://www.youtube.com/watch?v=rfcjLS8t7hY

Big Books are effective for developing concepts about books and print mainly because of their size. As the teacher reads the book and tracks the print from left to right across the page, children see that books are for reading, and they see where a person begins to read on a page. They also learn to differentiate the print from the pictures as the teacher asks if the children can point to a letter and a word. The connection is made that the oral language they hear from their teacher is being read from the print on the page in the book. The child learns that the print being read has meaning and that is why it is being read.

In Ms. Win's first grade class, children are always encouraged to read the title of a book and the name of the author and illustrator before starting to read the text. One day during an independent reading and writing period, Damien placed the Big Book *Where Is Everybody? An Animal Alphabet* (Merriam & DeGroat, 1989) on the Big Book stand. He had gathered three children to sit in front of him to read to. He started by saying, "The title of the book I'm going to read is *Where Is Everybody? An Animal Alphabet*." He turned the first page and began reading the text. Patrick popped up and said, "Damien, you

Figure 7.2 Instructions for Making a Big Book

Materials

- 2 pieces of oak tag for the cover (14" × 20" to 20" × 30")
- 10 pieces or more of tagboard or newsprint the same size as the oak tag used for the cover to be used for the pages in the book
- 6 loose-leaf rings (1¼")
- Hole punch

Directions

- Punch three sets of holes in top, middle, and bottom of the cover and paper that is to go inside the book.
- Insert a loose-leaf ring in each hole. The Big Book should have a minimum of 10 pages.
- Print should be 1½ to 2 inches high.

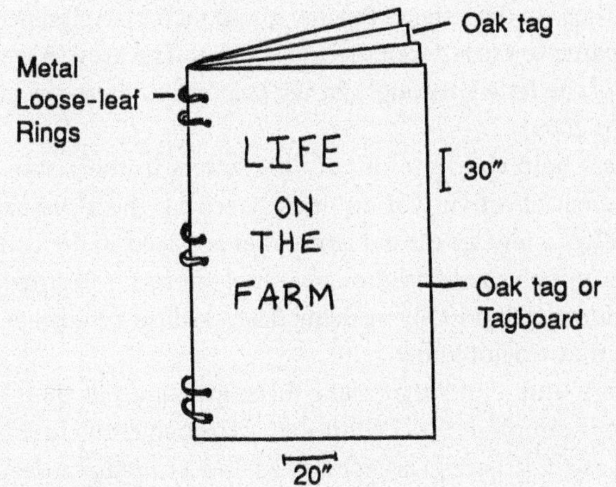

can't read the book yet; you forgot to read who the author and illustrator are." Damien pounded his fist to his forehead, looked somewhat annoyed with himself, and said, "How could I forget that? Let's see, here is the name of the author and the illustrator. Ms. Win can you help? I can't read the names." Ms. Win came over and read, "The author is Eve Merriam, and the illustrator is Diane DeGroat."

MyLab Education Self-Check 7.2
MyLab Education Application Exercise 7.1

Strategies for Teaching the Alphabet

Many young children who cannot yet identify individual letters of the alphabet are able to read. They read words they recognize by sight from print in the environment, such as STOP on STOP signs. They read labels on goods such as Cheerios. They learn other sight words from repeated readings and shared book experiences at home and in school. It is not necessary to be able to identify and name the letters of the alphabet in order to develop an initial sight-reading vocabulary. It is easier for a young child initially to learn whole words already familiar through oral language, rather than learn abstract letters. Familiar words carry meaning for them, whereas isolated letters do not.

Both historically and in standards, educators have long recognized that children need to learn the alphabet to become independently fluent readers and writers. Traditionally, the alphabet has often been the first thing parents try to teach their children at home, and it is usually high on any list of emergent literacy skills in preschool and the kindergarten curricula. It has been demonstrated by research to be a predictor of reading success.

Teaching English Learners

It is particularly important for English learners to be introduced to words that have meaning to them.

How to Introduce Alphabet Letters

Systematic teaching of the alphabet is necessary. One of the most common practices is teaching the alphabet from beginning to end with one letter a week. If the letter of the week is *B*, teachers do many different activities to reinforce that letter. The letter is introduced, and written in both upper- and lowercase. Perhaps the children will do a worksheet that asks them to circle the upper- and lowercase *B*'s on the page. At another time, the class will bake butter cookies in the shape of the letter *B*, and so on. Teaching "the letter of the week" is often criticized when the teaching of the letters occurs in isolation. Additionally, teaching first just one letter per week takes 26 weeks to introduce all the letters of the alphabet. Others have suggested a letter a day or two or three letters a week. This way the alphabet is introduced quickly and you can go back and review each one again (Levin et al., 2006). Reutzel carried out a study about teaching kindergarten children the alphabet with a letter of the week approach and another group with the letter of the day. Those in the letter of the day group increased significantly in their letter recognition compared to the letter of the week group. The growth was attributed to the constant review of the letters throughout the year after letters are initially introduced (Reutzel & Cooter, 2009).

Many teachers help children identify the letters in their own names first. This is probably the most effective way to begin teaching the alphabet. When teaching thematic units, select a few letters to feature that are used in the context of the theme. For example, in a unit on transportation, feature *b* for *boat*, *t* for *train*, *p* for *plane*, and *c* for *car*. Check children individually by using flash cards to determine which letters they know and which they do not know.

Familiar letters, and letters that make the same sound as their name, are learned more quickly—for example, *b*, *p*, *d*. Letters that occur frequently in print are also learned more easily, such as *r*, *t*, *n*. Letters are reinforced and learned at a deeper and more lasting level when children learn to write them concurrently with learning letter names. Letters that don't say their sound, such as *y*, *w*, *h*, and those that do not appear frequently, such as *q*, *x*, *z*, are harder to learn and should be learned after the others. Many letters—those that look similar to each other—such as *m*, *n*, *w*; *p*, *b*, *d*, *q*; *l*, *n*, *h*; *r*, *w*, *m*, *x*, *k*, *y*; and finally *t* and *f*, can be confusing to children (McGee, 2007; Treiman & Kessler, 2003). Letters that are more difficult to learn may need more time spent on teaching them. Different researchers suggest different orders to teaching letters. Some propose beginning with the most frequently used letters first, whereas others feel strongly about children learning the letters of their names first. Some use the thematic meaningful approach. For instance, if you are learning about winter, you teach *w*, *s*, *c*, for *winter*, *snow*, and *cold*. It is probably best to use multiple approaches. Children need multiple exposures to the same letter to really learn it.

Explicit Instruction of the Alphabet

MyLab Education

Video Example 7.2

Phonics to Support Alphabet Learning

In this video, a kindergarten teacher shares a craft idea for teaching the letter K. https://www.youtube.com/watch?v=3-g-Bkl3m2I

Explicit teaching is needed for letter identification. The teacher explains to the children that they will be learning to name, say, and write the upper- and lowercase letter *N*/*n* because learning letters helps them to read and write. The teacher writes an uppercase *N* on the board and says, "This is the letter *N*. What is the letter?" The class answers altogether, "N." Then the teacher writes the lowercase *n*. She says, "This is the lowercase *n*. What is this letter?" The children respond, "Lowercase *n*." She then points to the uppercase *N* and asks the name of the letter and the children respond. Next, she points to each letter in a different order for a response. This is done at least three times. On a daily basis allow children to explore letters explicitly, spontaneously, and in meaningful contexts. Here are multiple items and activities for practicing the alphabet that children can do.

- Alphabet puzzles
- Magnetic upper- and lowercase letters with an accompanying magnetic board
- Sets of wooden upper- and lowercase letters
- Tactile letters made of sandpaper or other textures
- Alphabet board games
- Felt letters and an accompanying felt board
- Letter stencils
- Alphabet flash cards
- Alphabet chart posted along the wall of the classroom at the children's eye level
- A large supply of alphabet books
- Taped songs about the alphabet
- Uppercase letters of the child's first name in a baggie
- Uppercase letters of the child's last name in a baggie
- Lowercase letters of the child's first and last names in baggies as they learn those letters
- Chalk and a chalkboard to write letters
- Markers and a white board to make letters
- Electronic white board for letter games
- Keyboarding letters on the computer
- Software for computer alphabet games
- Finger painting letters
- Painting letters on an easel
- Clay for shaping letters
- Alphabet soup, alphabet cookies, and alphabet pretzels
- Shaping letters with your fingers
- Shaping letters with your body
- Labeling each child's cubbie with her or his name
- Labeling every child's desk with his or her first and last names
- Labeling items in your classroom and at appropriate times mentioning letter names in the labels ("Did you notice that the word *Desk* begins with a *D*? Whose name begins with a *D*?" Daniel and Deborah raised their hands, and then Leonard said, "My name ends with a *D*.")
- Letters in environmental print such as McDonald's, Wendy's, and Burger King.

"An Idea from the Classroom" showcases a technique for teaching the alphabet from kindergarten teacher Ruth Mandel (See the end of the chapter.) Appendix A has a rich list of alphabet books for teachers to use.

Both the International Literacy Association and the National Council of Teachers of English have resources on their websites that contain a wealth of lessons for learning the alphabet. Look for the following books on the NCTE site.

1. *A–Z: Learning about the Alphabet Book Genre*
2. *A Is for Apple: Building Letter Recognition Fluency*
3. *My Amazing ABC Book*

Evaluating Mastery of Alphabet Letters

According to state standards, preschool children are expected to know about half of the alphabet before going to kindergarten. Kindergartners must be able to name and recognize all the letters of the alphabet by the end of that year. Teachers need to check children's knowledge of the alphabet and provide instruction based on the findings. If more explicit instruction is needed to help students, it should be provided one-on-one or in a small group. Students should be exposed to letters of the alphabet on a daily basis and in different settings. Figure 7.3 illustrates how to assess children's letter knowledge.

The teacher points to the first letter and asks the child to name the letter. If the child gives the correct response, put that correct letter in the alphabet response column marked A. If the child's answer is incorrect, put the letter the child said under the heading IR for incorrect response. Some other ways to assess are to ask the children to:

- Identify the first letter in their own names
- Identify all the letters in their names
- Find letters for their names in a random collection of letters
- Identify letters not in their names
- Match letters in their names with letters in names of classmates
- Identify letters in sequence on an alphabet chart or word wall
- Group words that start with the same letter
- Indicate letters from the books that they know
- Match uppercase letters to lowercase
- Sequence uppercase letter cards and identify them by name
- Sequence lowercase letter cards and identify them by name.

MyLab Education Self-Check 7.3
MyLab Education Application Exercise 7.2

Strategies to Figure Out Words Other Than Phonics

Instructional activities designed to help youngsters learn emergent literacy skills and about the function, form, structure, and conventions of print should involve a wide variety of learning experiences. Children need to be socially interactive when they are learning about print; they need direct instruction with models to emulate; and they need to learn through experiences that are meaningful, that are connected with real life, and that incorporate what children already know. If children see a need or usefulness attached to a reading skill, the skill probably will be learned without difficulty.

In the sections that follow, strategies are described to help children learn about print in direct, meaningful, and functional ways. Each strategy is appropriate for youngsters from preschool through third grade; teachers simply adjust the activity to the age groups with which they are working. Learning these skills should be connected to content-area material and functional activities. Activities such as reading to children, pointing out words in the environment, noting their letters and sounds, taking a child's dictation, encouraging children to write in their own way, allowing youngsters to see the print as it is read from a Big Book (an oversized book) and tracked from left to right across the page, and using predictable books that rhyme or have patterned language

Figure 7.3 A Form to Record Children's Letter Knowledge

Letter Identification Score Sheet

Child's name: ______________________ Age: ________ Date: ____________

Recorder: ______________________________ Date of birth: ____________

	A	IR		A	IR
A			a		
F			f		
K			k		
P			p		
W			w		
Z			z		
B			b		
H			h		
O			o		
J			j		
U			u		
C			c		
Y			y		
L			l		
Q			q		
M			m		
D			d		
N			n		
S			s		
X			x		
I			i		
E			e		
G			g		
R			r		
V			v		
T			t		

Confusions:

Letters unknown:

Comments:

A = Alphabet response: (✓); IR = Incorrect response: record what the child says

Test Score: ☐

and that allow children to guess and share in the reading all help youngsters learn about print (Invernizzi, 2003). Through these experiences, children learn that print is read from left to right, that words in a book are oral language that has been written down and can be read, that letters have sounds, that letters make up words, that words have meaning, that pictures hold clues to what the print says, and that words can be predicted based on the meaning of the text. When teaching skills, begin by:

- Telling the child what skill is being taught and what it is used for
- Modeling and scaffolding the skill explicitly to demonstrate what it is and why it is used
- Allowing time for guided practice with the teacher
- Allowing for independent practice
- Reviewing the skill often.

Using Print

Teaching English Learners

Things in the environment are known to children and are excellent sight words for English Learners.

Print materials are essential to helping students recognize letters and begin to figure out words. Environmental print and a morning message are ways to reinforce the meaning and importance of print in a broader context. The **language experience approach (LEA)** helps children convert their oral language to written language and thereby reinforces the integral connection between the two.

Environmental Print. **Environmental print** is familiar print found in the child's surroundings. It includes such print as logos, food labels, and road signs children encounter in the home, outside on the roads, and in restaurants and stores. Several researchers have found that children as young as age 2 can read familiar environmental print (Orellana & Hernandez, 1999; Strickland & Snow, 2002). Others, however, have shown that a child often is reading the sign rather than its print. When the print is separated from its familiar environmental context, the young child sometimes can no longer identify it (Hiebert & Raphael, 1998). Even so, when very young children associate the McDonald's logo with the word *McDonald's* and try to read it, they are learning that a group of letters makes up a word that can be read and thus provides information. The ability to read environmental print also gives the child a sense of accomplishment and usually elicits positive reinforcement of the child's achievement by caring adults.

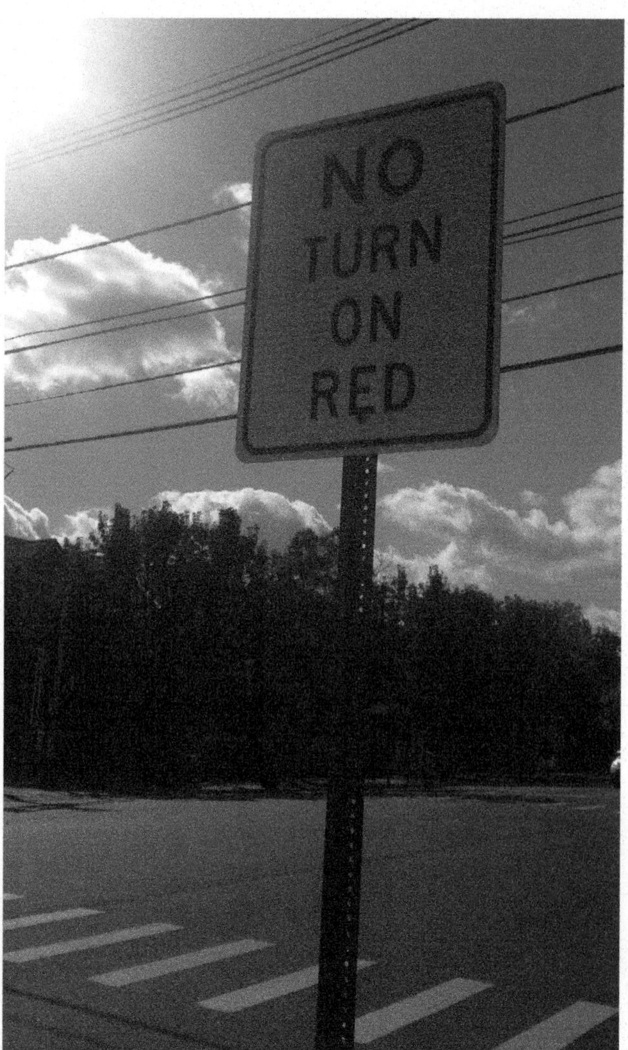

Photo credit: Patricia Taitt

Photograph environmental print in your neighborhood and bring the photos to your classroom. Suggest that children read the words, copy them, and write them in a sentence or a story.

Parents can make children aware of environmental print from the first year of life. During daily routines, parents can point out and read words and labels on food boxes, road signs, stores, and restaurants. The world is filled with environmental print. Early childhood classrooms need to have environmental print brought in from outside, and teachers need to label items in their child-care centers, nursery schools, kindergarten, first- and second- grade classrooms. The print should be traced and copied. This print will become part of a child's sight vocabulary.

The environmental print that children know best appears on food containers for cereal, soup, milk, cookies, detergent, and other items in the home. Among common signs, children recognize fast-food logos, road signs, traffic signals, and names of store chains, supermarkets, and service stations. Collect logos and trade names and make them available in your classroom by posting them on charts, pasting them onto index cards, and creating loose-leaf books of environmental print. Most firms distribute various printed materials free, complete with logos. Photograph environmental print in your neighborhood and bring the photos to your classroom. Suggest that children read the words, copy them, and write them in a sentence or a story (Neumann, Hood, & Ford, 2013).

Start including environmental print in your classroom at the beginning of a school year with only a few signs, such as children's names on their cubbies, and the words *Block Center* to identify that area of the room. Make labels with 5 × 8 index cards and dark felt-tip markers. Begin each word with a capital letter and continue with lowercase script, thus providing youngsters with configuration clues. Hang labels at heights easy for children to see. Point out the labels to the children, and suggest that they read them to friends and copy them. As the school year progresses, label new items that are added to the classroom. Refer to the labels as part of your normal routine so that they are used and will then add to the child's sight vocabulary. Label items because they are of interest to the class and serve a function, such as identifying important classroom materials and learning centers. Use labels for relating messages, such as *Wash your hands before snack.* Refer to the labels often so that the children will identify them as useful and functional.

Also label items related to content-area topics. If you are studying dinosaurs, a popular topic in early childhood, display model dinosaurs and label each with its name. Even long, difficult words—such as brontosaurus and tyrannosaurus—become sight words for many early childhood youngsters. It is common to observe preschool, kindergarten, first-grade, and second-grade children reading labels to themselves or to each other. I observed a kindergarten class after the teacher had posted two new labels in the science center, which featured a lesson involving listening to sounds and identifying them after shaking a canister.

> I watched Jovanna take Juan by the hand and heard her say, "Listen Juan, when I shake this, it sounds like there is sand inside. You try it. See, the word says *Sand*." Juan continued the conversation as he picked up another canister and shook it. "Listen to this one, Jovanna. This sounds like stones. This sign must say *Stones*. Hey look, *Sand* and *Stones* both begin with an *S*," said Juan. The children shook the canisters and pointed to the appropriate label and said *Sand* or *Stone*. They repeated the sequence several times and switched canisters as well.

The Morning Message

Post printed messages and assignments for children daily. Select a permanent spot on the chalkboard or on chart paper. Use rebus or picture writing along with print to help children make sense of the message. Here are a few examples of appropriate messages:

- Today is Tuesday.
- It is raining outside.
- We are learning some more about spiders today.
- I have some new spider books to share.

Teaching English Learners

Because the morning message is often written by the teacher in front of the children, it is easy for children to learn the words on the chart.

This routine will teach children to look at the daily message their teacher has left for them on the message board. From the messages, they will learn that print carries meaning that is interesting and useful. Some teachers refer to this practice as the **morning message** and have formalized it into a lesson when the school day begins (Morrow, 2003).

Morning messages are used at morning meetings, when the class gets together to discuss what will happen in school on that day. Model writing some of the message with the children watching. Use the message to develop various concepts about print. Emphasize specific words or letters, pursue questions about meaning, or let children add sentences to the original message. Have children find letters in their names in the message, or look for similar word endings. For example, in the morning message illustration, the word *day* appears four times at the end of words.

When working with 7-and 8-year-olds, the contents of the morning message and the environmental print displayed in the room will be more sophisticated than when working with younger children. The morning message can be used to point out sound–symbol relationships or phonic generalizations that are appropriate to deal with in first

Today is Tuesday.
We will go to the zoo.
The day after tomorrow
which is Wednesday we
have a guest who will bring
animals to our classroom.

Morning messages emphasize themes being studied as they build vocabulary and word study skills.

and second grade. For example, a morning message such as the following is a perfect opportunity to point out the *sh* digraph:

Shelly is wearing shiny new shoes.

In the next message, there are five examples of the phonic generalization that, in a consonant–vowel–consonant–*e* pattern, the vowel is usually long:

Kate told us that her birthday cake was made in the shape of a kite.

This is an opportunity to observe and discuss this letter–sound pattern.

Teachers use morning messages to teach letter writing by writing some of the messages in the form of a letter and pointing out the elements of the format. Teachers also sometimes purposefully make spelling or punctuation errors in messages and ask the children to be detectives to find the mistakes. Letters of the alphabet can be left out of words to be filled in, or complete words can be left out for children to figure out from the context of the sentence. Some teachers embed the class spelling words or new words into the message. They include words that demonstrate skills being taught, such as words with long or short vowel sounds, or words with digraphs or blends. Children are asked to identify and circle the featured words, vowels, and so on. Messages can be used for vocabulary development as well.

In Mrs. Youseff's kindergarten they had a morning message time daily. The message was similar every day to help learn words, letters, and sounds. Today it said:

Dear Boys and Girls,

Today is Monday January 3.

The weather is cold, and it is raining.

We are learning about reptiles. We talked about

snakes, lizards, and alligators.

Love,

Mrs. Youseff

Since the message is similar every day, the children begin to read it. Soon Mrs. Youseff leaves out a part of a word for the children to identify what is missing, for example:

Today is Tues _ _ _ January 4.

The weather is c _ _ d and it is rai _ i _ g again.

She will leave endings off words such as *day* in the word *today*. She will leave off the year on the date, and so on.

Using the LEA. The LEA helps children associate oral language with written language, teaching them that what is said can be written down and read. It illustrates the left to right progression of our written language. In practice, it demonstrates the formation of letters plus their combination into words, it helps build sight vocabulary, it illustrates meaningful teaching of phoneme–grapheme correspondence, and it is based on the child's interest and experiences. Multiple skills and strategies are used in the LEA.

Many educators have been associated with developing and articulating the language experience approach; among them are R. V. Allen (Allen, 1976), M. A. Hall (Hall, 1976), and J. Veatch and colleagues (Veatch et al., 1973). The LEA is based on the following premises from the learner's point of view:

- What I think is important.
- What I think, I can say.
- What I say can be written down by me or by others.
- What is written down can be read by me and by others.

The interests and experiences on which the LEA builds come from children's lives both at home and at school. The LEA is particularly suited for use with EL students. It is about their lives; the vocabulary comes from them; they make their own books with their own words. In school, the teacher needs to plan experiences—for example, class trips, cooking projects, use of puppets, guest speakers, class pets, holiday events, or the study of topics children enjoy such as dinosaurs, outer space, and other cultures. The language experience lesson is usually carried out with an entire class but can take place with a small group or an individual child. The following is an example of how the LEA functions.

A discussion is usually generated from an interesting or exciting class experience, such as a recent trip to the zoo or the pet gerbil's new litter. To begin the discussion, ask open-ended questions that will encourage descriptive responses rather than *yes* or *no* answers. For example, if the topic is a trip to the zoo, ask children what was your favorite animal? Why was it your favorite animal? What did the animal look like? What did the animal do while you were watching it at the zoo? It is important to accept all the children's responses. Accept nonstandard English without correction, but provide a language model by using standard English to paraphrase what the child has said.

After a discussion has generated several ideas, write them down. With the whole class, write the ideas on a large sheet of lined newsprint paper (approximately 24 × 36 inches)—that becomes an experience chart. It can be taped to the wall or mounted on an easel. Print with a dark felt-tip marker of medium thickness, allowing ample space between words and between lines so that the chart is easy to read. Use manuscript in upper- and lowercase letters, following the conventions of regular print, thus giving configuration to words. Word configuration aids children in word identification.

In recording language on experience charts, teachers should write quickly and legibly, providing good manuscript samples for children to read and copy. As you write what children dictate, use their language unless it is difficult for others to understand. When dictation is difficult to understand, ask a child to restate an idea or, if necessary, help the child restate it. It is important to include the comments of as many children as possible. When creating a new chart, try to remember which children have not contributed in the past and encourage them to contribute to the new chart. It is a good idea to identify who said what. The chart is more interesting to those whose names are included. For example:

> Jacob said, "I liked the gorilla at the zoo. He jumped around and made funny faces."
>
> Jovanna said, "I liked the baby deer. They had big, bright, black eyes, wet black noses, and shiny brown fur."

Try to accompany each sentence with an illustration; this will help children read the charts.

Experience charts dictated by 2- and 3-year-olds can be simply lists of words, such as names of animals with illustrations next to them. Lists of words make appropriate charts for older children as well. They are a quick way to record and reinforce new vocabulary associated with topics being studied. While writing a chart, take the opportunity to point out concepts about print: "Now I am writing the word *gorilla: g-o-r-i-l-l-a.* See, it begins here with a *g* and ends here with an *a.*" Mentally note which letters or sounds interest children. Ask children to point out on the chart where you

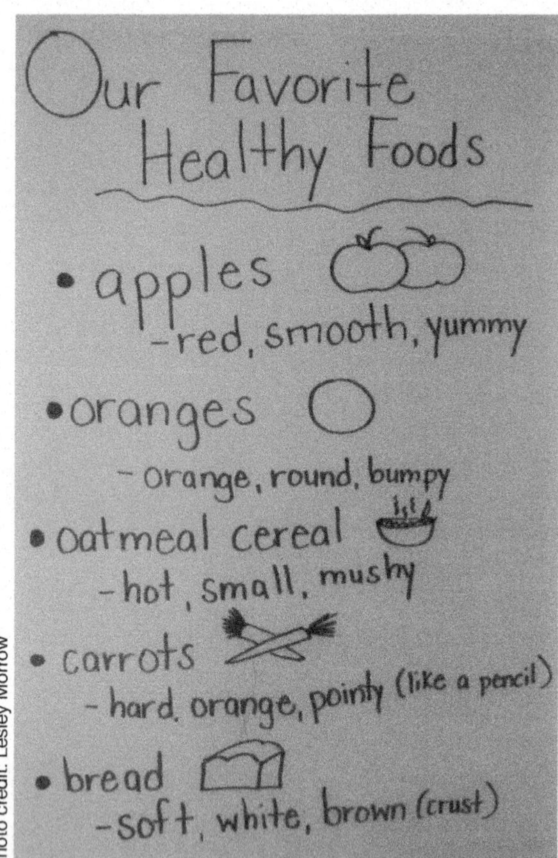

Experience charts, dictated by the children and written by the teacher, develop oral language and encourage reading and writing about what is being studied.

should begin to write. Like directed listening (or reading), thinking activities, and the morning message, the LEA lesson should have a skill objective.

The last step in the LEA lesson is to read the chart to and with the class. Use a pointer to emphasize left to right progression. Let the class read the chart in unison, or ask individual children who contributed different sentences to read them. Leave the chart in a visible spot in the room, and encourage the children to read it and copy parts of it, copy words they like, or add to their Very Own Words collection from the chart. (Very Own Words will be discussed in detail later in the chapter.) Vocabulary charts and experience charts representing different topics discussed in school can be left hanging in the room if space permits and then made into Big Books for children to look at through the school year. If a laminating machine is available, it is wise to preserve charts. Children's dictated stories, books, and class books can be placed in the class library for others to read. Those made by the class often become the most popular books in the room.

Pocket chart activities are associated with the language experience approach. Words associated with experiences the class has had are featured in the chart. Short stories, poems, and songs that students chant can be printed on individual sentence strips. Ask children to copy the charts to practice their writing. In addition, the sentence strips can be scrambled and sequenced into the pocket chart. Sentence strips can be cut up into the individual words for students to work on the word level, to identify and to practice placing them into sentences.

When teaching a unit about animals featuring animal sight words, Ms. Macki selected the anonymous poem "Good Morning" and read it to her kindergarten class to reinforce their ability to read the animal names. The text of the poem is as follows:

Good morning duck
Good morning pig
Good morning to you all
Good morning sheep
Good morning bird
A big hello to you two
Good morning goats
Good morning cows
How are you chickens and hens?

Ms. Macki wrote the words to the poem on chart paper and then on sentence strips. She drew a picture of each animal at the end of each line. She cut a second set of sentence strips into individual words. In this way she provided the children with four activities:

1. Read the poem.
2. Sequence the whole sentences into a story.
3. Build sentences from individual words by using the syntax and semantics of the text.
4. Identify the sight words: *ducks, sheep, goats, hen, chicken, birds,* and *cows.*

Teaching English Learners

Since the Language Experience Approach draws on children's interests and lives, it is an excellent way to build a sight vocabulary.

Pocket chart activities are often used to practice skills during independent center time.

The language experience approach, which is appropriate throughout early childhood and beyond, can be used similarly in the morning message and Very Own Words for noticing phonic generalizations and sound–symbol correspondences. Learning about print in this situation is done with material that is familiar and meaningful. Occasionally, prepare a chart in the language of bilingual children in your class. If necessary, solicit help from bilingual parents or colleagues. This strategy will guide bilingual youngsters in making connections between their language and English.

Materials for the language experience approach are inexpensive and easy to use. They include chart paper, markers, colored construction paper, white paper, index cards, scissors, staplers, pencils, and crayons. With directions from the teacher, these simple classroom materials record the precious words and pictures created by children from their own meaningful, real-life experiences. The LEA should be central, not supplemental, to literacy instruction in early reading programs (Flynn, 2016).

Using Context and Pictures to Figure Out Words

Experiences with literature can lead children to use contextual clues and illustrations to figure out words and recognize that they have meaning. Literature experiences can take place in whole-class, small-group, or one-to-one settings, using directed listening (or reading) and thinking activities, shared book experiences, and repeated readings of stories. For example, select a story that is predictable, in which the text and illustrations are closely related. Ask the children to look at the pictures on a page before reading it to them. Ask what they think the words will say. Then read the page to demonstrate that print and illustration are closely related and that the pictures provide information that can help the children as they read the story.

MyLab Education
Video Example 7.3
Scaffolding Reading Instruction
In this video, a second grade teacher shows her class how to figure out new words in a text. At 6:20, she continues the lesson in small group instruction. https://www.youtube.com/watch?v=lMd-RPnXVKg&list=UU5mN2B-2JYc9XiK1qFQjeSg

The syntax and semantics of a sentence (its grammatical structure and meaning) also help children identify words. Encourage children to use these elements of written language by stopping your oral reading at predictable points in a story and asking them to fill in words. For example, when reading *The Three Little Pigs*, first read the complete repetitive phrases:

> *"Little pig, little pig, let me in," said the wolf. "Not by the hair of my chinny, chin, chin," said the first little pig. "Then I'll huff and I'll puff and I'll blow your house in," said the wolf.*
>
> The second time say, *"Little pig, little _________, let me in." "Not by the hair of my chinny, chin _________." "Then I'll huff and I'll _________ and I'll blow your* _________ in and so on (Brenner, 1972).

This technique is most effective with a Big Book because you can point to the words as the children say them. As the children begin to understand the concept of filling in words, choose more difficult passages for your pauses. Prepare charts and sheets with predictable text, and leave out words to be filled in as you read. Children use their prior knowledge of syntax and context in predicting words. They assimilate and use the strategy when they read themselves.

In addition to these general suggestions, specific experiences to figure out words can be varied so that students have many different strategies for using context. A common way to determine words from context is through the meaning of the text. For example, in the sentence that follows, it is apparent that the missing word is *Queen*. We can show children how to use the meaning of the text to figure out a word that might be unknown to them.

> *The King and _________ lived in the castle together.*

Another context clue exercise involves a series of related words. To help with this exercise or other context clue exercises, the initial consonant can be included. For example:

> *My favorite kinds of fruit are apples, b_________, pears, and oranges.*

A gamelike context clue activity involves the use of scrambled letters, as in the following sentence:

> *I am always on time, but my sister is always _________ (alte).*

When working with context clues, teachers can choose to omit all nouns, verbs, every fourth word, and so on. There are endless ways to use this strategy, and each

MyLab Education
Video Example 7.4
Heart Words to Identify Sight Words
In this video, a kindergarten teacher shares how she asks students to learn sight words.

contributes to helping children figure out unknown words. This approach is referred to as the *cloze procedure.*

Developing Sight Vocabulary

An extremely important skill for beginning readers is to learn sight words. **Sight words** are words immediately recognized by a reader, making word-attack skills unnecessary. There was a time when the most common way to teach children was through sight and repetition of those words. Sight words enable children to read books immediately and then understand what reading is. It is worth repeating that learning as many sight words as possible is very important. There are many children who can learn phonic sounds and rules and are unable to apply them in context.

Using Very Own Words. In the book *Teacher*, Sylvia Ashton-Warner (Ashton-Warner, 1986) described Very Own Words as a method for developing sight vocabulary. Ashton-Warner encouraged children to write their favorite words from a story or content-area lesson on 5 × 8 cards, each word on a separate card. Very Own Words are often from a child's home life: *mommy, daddy, grandpa, grandma, cookie.* They also reflect emotional feelings: *naughty, nice, good, punish.* After Very Own Words are recorded on index cards, they are stored in a child's file box, or in a plastic baggie.

A good way to start Very Own Words collections is through a discussion of favorite things to do at home or favorite pets, toys, friends, and the like. Let children know that after this discussion you will ask them to name their favorite word in the conversation such as:

The teacher held up an index box of her favorite Very Own Words and said:

Teacher: This is my Very Own Words (VOW) box. I collect words about my family, friends, things I like to do, and new words I learn. This one says *bicycle.* I like my bicycle so I made a VOW card for it and now I'll put it into my VOW box. On one side you can see the word; on the other side is the word with a picture of the bicycle. What are your favorite people, things, pets, toys?

Jamal: I love my grandma; I would like to have the word *grandma.*

Kim: I love oatmeal cookies, I want that word.

Amad: I like it when my mom reads books to me. I want the word *book.*

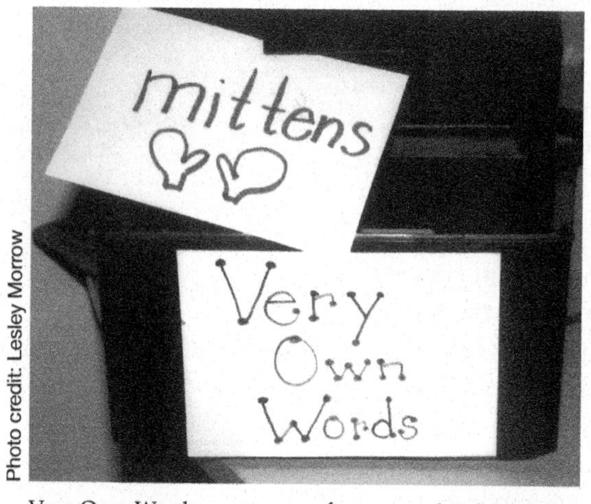

Very Own Words are a source for personal sight vocabulary. Encourage children to copy them, write them, and read them.

Their teacher had cards ready and a marker and wrote *grandma* for Jamal with a picture of a lady's face; on the other side she just wrote *grandma* without a picture. She wrote *oatmeal cookie* for Kim on one side with a picture and on the other, just the words. For Amad she wrote *book* with a picture and on the flip side only the word.

The activity should be a pleasant one that produces interesting language, perhaps about popping corn or making play dough. Children also can choose a favorite word in a storybook or words generated from the study of social studies and science units. Soon children will request their Very Own Words without being asked.

Encourage children to do things with their words—read them to friends or to themselves, copy them, and use them in sentences or stories. Because words are based on a child's expressed interests in situations at home and in school, the collection of Very Own Words is a powerful technique for developing sight vocabulary.

Seven- and eight-year-olds also enjoy and learn from collecting Very Own Words. They should alphabetize them and store them in a file box. Teachers can encourage children to study the letter patterns in their Very Own Words. They can discuss consonant and vowel sounds, blends, digraphs, and structural elements such as prefixes and suffixes, as well as phonic generalizations that may be evident. When a child studies letter patterns in words he or she has selected, it will mean more than doing the same task with words selected by the teacher or found in a textbook.

Teaching English Learners
Very Own Words are those the child chooses to have. When a child wants a Very Own Word it is of interest to them and they are likely to be able to read that word.

Very Own Words are also useful with bilingual children. The index card should include a child's Very Own Word in English and can also have the word written in his or her native language.

Teaching High-Frequency Words as Sight Words

High-frequency words constitute a special group of sight words found frequently in reading materials for young children. These words do not carry meaning on their own, but do when they are in sentences and need to be learned for quick recall. They are often difficult to decode because they have irregular patterns in their spelling. It is helpful for children if they do not have to spend time segmenting these words as they read; they should be able to read them easily because they have been learned by memory or sight.

Sight words should be taught in a systematic and direct manner. The teacher selects several of these words for the children to learn each week. To learn these words, the following activities are used:

- Words are said aloud and used in a sentence.
- The sentence is written on a chalkboard or flip chart and the sight word is underlined.
- Features of each word, such as the letters or its similarity to other words, are discussed. The teacher also points out any regular or irregular patterns the word may have.
- Children are asked to spell the word aloud, spell the word in the air with their fingers, and write the word on paper.
- Children chant the letters as they spell words.
- The teacher has a high-frequency word box. While sitting in a circle, each child has a turn to pick a word, say it, use it in a sentence, and show it to the group.
- The words can be written on index cards similar to Very Own Words and stored with the child's other cards.

Figure 7.4 provides 300 high-frequency words for the early childhood grades (Fry, 1996). The words in the figure can be used for assessing children's knowledge of sight words. These words are used often in reading material and can be difficult to decode, and cannot be figured out from the context of a sentence. Teachers in grades K, 1, 2, and 3 need to make sure these words are learned by sight over this period of time. The following 13 words are 25 percent of the words children find in early literacy texts (Adams, 1990). These should be first on the list to learn:

a, and, for, he (or *she*)*, in, is, it, of, that, the, to, was, you*

To ensure that they are acquiring sight recognition of high-frequency words, children should be tested on their ability to read these words. The teacher should ask children to identify the words with flash cards and find the words in context within passages to read. This testing can be done several times during the school year (Allington & Cunningham, 2007; Cunningham, 2009). There are children who are not able to segment and blend, so they will need hundreds of sight words to become effective readers. Even when children use phonics as beginning readers and later as more fluent readers, learning sight words remains important for students to understand what reading is, to build their confidence, and to build an extensive reading vocabulary.

MyLab Education
Video Example 7.5
Word Study During Shared Reading
In this video, a teacher discusses how she uses a word wall with high-frequency words in her third/fourth grade classroom.
https://www.youtube.com/watch?v=MPTlZPZvuvY

Creating Word Walls. A **word wall** is a bulletin board or other display that showcases high-frequency and challenging words in alphabetical order. Word walls typically have the letters of the alphabet posted across a wall at the children's eye level. As high-frequency words are featured, they are posted under the letter where they belong in alphabetical

Figure 7.4 Fry Sight-Word Inventory of Frequently Used Words

Fry Sight-Word Inventory

This instrument surveys a child's ability to recognize 300 frequently occurring words, as selected by Edward B. Fry (1980). The words are grouped into three sets of 100 by relative difficulty, and each group of 100 words is, in turn, grouped into sets of 25.

Directions for Administration

Place the student version of the First 100 Words in front of the child. There are three blanks for each word, for repeated administrations. You may want to record the date at the top of each column of blanks. Explain that you will be showing the child some words and that you want the child to say them aloud. Use a 3 × 5 index card to make window card as illustrated below so you can reveal the words one at a time. A window card screens the other words and helps the child focus.

For each word, write a plus (+) in the blank next to it if the child correctly pronounces it in less than one second (informally times). If the child takes more time but eventually pronounces the word accurately, write D, for decoded. That is to say, the word was not identified automatically and is therefore not yet a sight word. If the child mispronounces the word, try to spell the response phonetically. If there is no response, write NR. Move the window card to each word in succession while you record the response with your other hand. Proceed through each of the five columns.

Repeat these steps with the Second 100 and the Third 100. Discontinue testing if, in your judgment, the words become too difficult.

If you re-administer the inventory, return only to those words not automatically recognized during previous testing.

Window Card

Scoring and Interpretation

There is no cumulative score. Recognizing each word is actually a separate skill, which means that there is a very direct link between testing and teaching. Any word that is not pronounceable automatically simply requires more practice!

Fry Sight-Word Inventory
First 100 Words

the	or	will	number
of	one	up	no
and	had	other	way
a	by	about	could
to	word	out	people
in	but	many	my

is	not	then	than
you	what	them	first
that	all	these	water
it	were	so	been
he	we	some	call
was	when	her	who
for	your	would	oil
on	can	make	now
are	said	like	find
as	there	him	long
with	use	into	down
his	an	time	day
they	each	has	did
i	which	look	get
at	she	two	come
be	do	more	made
this	how	write	may
have	their	go	part
from	if	see	over

Fry Sight-Word Inventory
Second 100 Words

new	great	put	kind
sound	where	end	hand
take	help	does	picture
only	through	another	again
little	much	well	change
work	before	large	off
know	line	must	play
place	right	big	spell
year	too	even	air
live	mean	such	away
me	old	because	animal
back	any	turn	house
give	same	here	point
most	tell	why	page
very	boy	ask	letter
after	follow	went	mother
thing	came	men	answer
our	went	read	found
just	show	need	study
name	also	land	still

(Continued)

Figure 7.4 Fry Sight-Word Inventory of Frequently Used Words (Continued)

good	around	different	learn
sentence	form	home	should
man	three	us	America
think	small	move	world
say	set	try	high

Fry Sight-Word Inventory
Third 100 Words

every	left	until	idea
near	don't	children	enough
add	few	side	eat
food	while	feet	face
between	along	car	watch
own	might	mile	far
below	close	night	Indian
country	something	walk	real
plant	seem	while	almost
last	next	sea	let
school	hard	began	above
father	open	grow	girl
keep	example	took	sometimes
tree	begin	river	mountain
must	life	four	cut
state	always	carry	young
city	those	state	talk
earth	both	once	soon
eye	paper	book	list
light	together	hear	song
thought	got	stop	leave
head	group	without	family
under	often	second	body
story	run	late	music
saw	important	miss	color

Source: From Edward Fry. Elementary Reading Instruction. Copyright © 1977 Reprinted by permission of Cathy Fry

order. The featured words are ones teachers select as being a priority to learn. Others may be ones that children are having difficulty with reading and spelling. The words are placed on index cards. Children are asked to spell the words out loud, trace them in the air, and copy them. Sometimes words are written and then cut out into the shape of the word, providing visual configuration clues for remembering it. Before putting words up, note their characteristics, such as their pronunciation, spelling, and letter patterns. Suggest to children that the word wall can be used as a dictionary when writing.

The word wall can be used to play word-study games. For example, if the teacher wants to work with substitution of sounds, he or she points to a word such as *went* and says, "This word says *went*. If I take away the *w* and put in a *b*, what does it say?" or "This word rhymes with *look* and begins with a *b*. Can you find it on the word wall?"

Word-wall words can be sorted by word families, rhyming words, words that have the same vowel sounds, and so on. This can be done on paper or on an electronic white board by moving the words around or writing them down on a sheet of paper. Many different lessons for using the wall independently should be provided (Cunningham, 1995; Moustafa, 1997; Xu, 2010).

Although the word wall was designed to teach high-frequency words, teachers use it for new words learned in themes, from books read, and from daily discussions. With very young children, the first words on the word wall will be their *names*. The number of words on the wall with preschoolers is kept limited (O'Kelley Wingate, Rutledge, & Johnston, 2014).

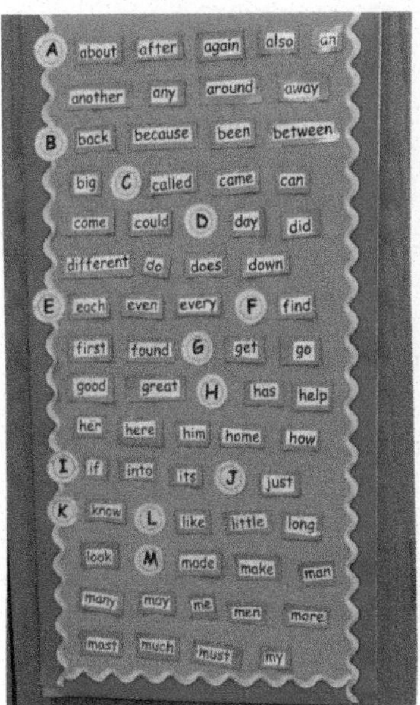

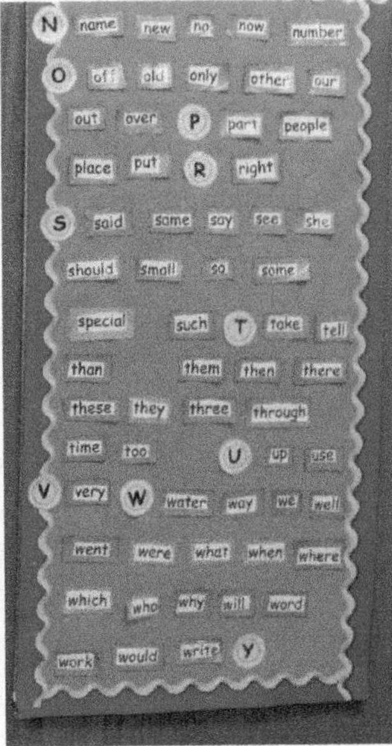

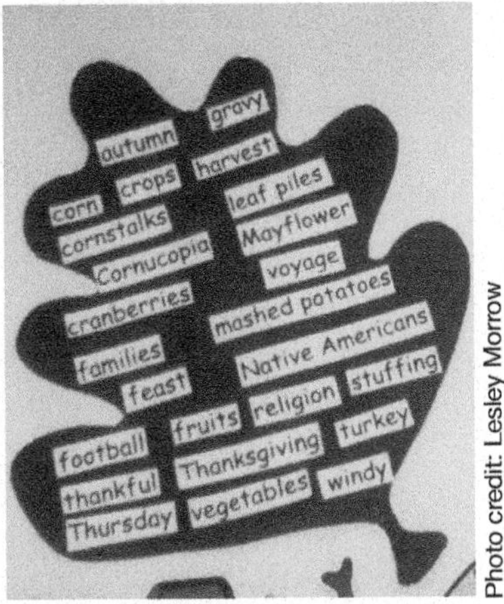

Photo credit: Lesley Morrow

These word walls feature high-frequency words to the left, and theme-related words for autumn to the right and from other units of study in science and social studies.

Some additional word-wall activities that the teacher can lead are as follows:

- Have students sort words by pattern—for example, words with the letters *an* or *at*.
- Classify words into colors, names, animals, and so on.
- The secret word game with the word wall provides the student clues such as:

The secret word has an at *pattern at the end.*

It has three letters.

It is an animal.

It has fur and little pointy ears.

They live in people's houses.

It likes milk. It is a __________ at.

When we read, we use several skills concurrently to decode and derive meaning from the printed page. We therefore need to encourage children to use multiple skills, rather than isolated skills, in their approach to reading. The cloze procedure can also be used to accomplish this goal. Pause, as you read, and leave a "blank" to be filled in by the child. For example, say, "The **b**__________________ flew up to the tree and landed on a branch." Supplying the initial consonant for the word, either by sound or by sight, draws on a child's skills with phonics, context, syntax, and semantics.

Whenever possible, take advantage of spontaneous situations to help children learn about print, as in the following example:

> Christopher, a child in first grade, had just written his name on a picture he drew and exclaimed, "Wow, the word *STOP* is right in the middle of my name. See

Christopher." He pointed to the letters in his name that spelled *STOP*. He continued, "But that doesn't make sense, then I should say my name Chri-*STOP*-her." The teacher immediately seized the opportunity to point out the *ph* digraph and explain to Christopher that the word *STOP* was in his name, but when the letters *p* and *h* come together, they make a new sound as heard in Christopher, like the sound of *f*. She mentioned other words such as *photograph, phone,* and *phantom* that illustrated the *ph* sound.

MyLab Education Self-Check 7.4
MyLab Education Application Exercise 7.3

Assessing Knowledge of Emergent Literacy Skills

Because assessment provides teachers with information to guide instruction, assessment should happen often and take many forms. One of the first assessments done in preschool and kindergarten is to determine a child's concepts about books and print by using Figure 7.1.

To test for knowledge of the alphabet, the teacher can name particular letters and ask a child to circle them on a sheet of paper containing upper- and lowercase letters. Use Figure 7.3 to test a child. Basic sight words can be checked by using Figure 7.4 as high frequency words, environmental print, sight words, language experience approach, word walls, morning messages, Very Own Words, and others. To make sure students are developing the word-study skills they need at an appropriate rate, educators need to assess what students have mastered, what they are working on, and what they are struggling with. In the context of learning to figure out words, formative and summative assessments should be taken frequently, before and after teaching.

MyLab Education Self-Check 7.5
MyLab Education Application Exercise 7.4

An Idea from the Classroom

Teaching the Alphabet

I have a collection of alphabet books. I find them to be very useful for teaching the alphabet with my kindergarten children. I think I have one for every thematic unit I do such as *Animalia* (Base, 1986) when we study animals. I read different books throughout the year, and we do different activities based on the book. One of my favorites is *Chicka Chicka Boom Boom* (Archambault & Martin, 1989). To help my students learn the alphabet, they each make a sign for one letter. They write both the upper- and lowercase letters. The children hang their signs around their necks. When I read the story, each child pops into the story when his or her letter is called. Each letter is mentioned in the story twice. When we read the book again, the children trade signs. I recorded the story as they acted it out, and I put it on the class website for parents and the school community to watch.

Some excellent alphabet books I use with my students and activities to go with them are *The Handmade Alphabet* (Rankin, 1991), *Potluck* (Shelby & Travis, 1991), and *Where Is Everybody?* (Merriam, 1993). *The Handmade Alphabet* (Rankin, 1991) is an alphabet book in which hands are shown signing each letter. When introducing a letter, show the children the sign language hand motion.

Potluck (Shelby & Travis, 1991) is about children going to a picnic and each bringing something. It starts with Acton who appears with asparagus soup, and then Ben who brought bagels. It ends with Yolanda bringing yams and yogurt and Zeke and Zelda zooming in with zucchini casserole. Try to recreate the book naming different food from A to Z.

Where Is Everybody? (Merriam, 1993) is about different animals in different familiar places in the neighborhood doing different familiar things. Act out each page, such as dog at the day-care center.

Ruth Mandel, Kindergarten Teacher

Summary

7.1 Explain the theory and research relating to figuring out words in early literacy.

There are three developmental levels in word recognition: identifying words through context, letter-sound cues, and finally sounding words out. Children are likely to become involved in literacy activities if they view reading and writing as functional, purposeful, and useful. According to the psycholinguistic definition of reading, children rely on three cueing systems when figuring out words. Syntactic cues are those connected to the child's understanding of syntax; semantic cues help children figure out words from potential meaning; and graphophonic cues relate to the visual letters and letter clusters and their associations with corresponding sounds. Emergent literacy skills are a specific category of skills that help students figure out words, including learning the alphabet, how to use context and syntax to figure out words, developing sight vocabulary, and using phonics.

7.2 Understand what children need to learn about concepts of print.

For children who grow up in literate homes that have lots of books things such as knowing what the front of the book is, the top and the bottom, the spine, and the title is learned before schools since parents are reading to their children. Children without much exposure to books will not know things we take for granted such as which is the print and where are the pictures, know how to turn a page, and know how to handle a book with care since it is important.

7.3 Identify a variety of methods for teaching the alphabet.

Learning to identify upper- and lowercase letters in the alphabet is a necessary skill for learning to read. There is a lot of research about teaching the alphabet or identifying the letters. It appears that teaching several letters a week and repeating them throughout the school year is a better way of teaching the alphabet than a letter a week as has been done in the past. The reason for this is that children have the opportunity to meet the letters and practice them multiple times, as they are introduced several times during the year. Letters can be studied when they appear in content themes; for example, pointing out the letter *F* when learning about the fall gives meaning to the letter as does asking children to learn the letters of their names.

7.4 Describe strategies for figuring out words other than phonics.

In addition to using phonics, there are many other ways to figure out words. Teachers must create lessons which incorporate the use concepts about books and print, environmental print, sight words, high-frequency sight words, reading pictures, looking at the shape and length of words, the language experience approach, using context clues, and picture clues. Educators tend to neglect teaching these skills, yet they are extremely helpful especially for readers who have a difficult time decoding, segmenting, and blending.

7.5 Assess emergent literacy skills.

To be sure that students are progressing, educators need to assess what children have mastered, etc. To make sure students are developing the word-study skills they need at an appropriate rate, educators need to assess what students have mastered, what they are working on, and what they are struggling with. In the context of learning to figure out words, formative and summative assessments should be taken frequently, before and after teaching.

Activities and Questions

1. Observe the environmental print in an early childhood classroom. Note what you think could be added to it, both from within the classroom and from the outside world.
2. Write an experience chart dictated to you by children in early childhood. If you do not have access to children, do this exercise in your college class with peers dictating the contents for the chart. Critique the appearance of your chart and note problems you encountered while writing it. Use your self-evaluation for ideas for improvement. Consult Chapter 8 (page) for proper formation of manuscript letters.
3. Select five children from an early childhood classroom in which the students have collected Very Own Words. List all the words in the children's collections. Compare the list with the words you found in basal reading material for the age of the children you selected. How closely do the basal words and the children's Very Own Words match each other? Is one group more or less difficult than the other?

Chapter 8

Phonological Awareness and Phonics Instruction

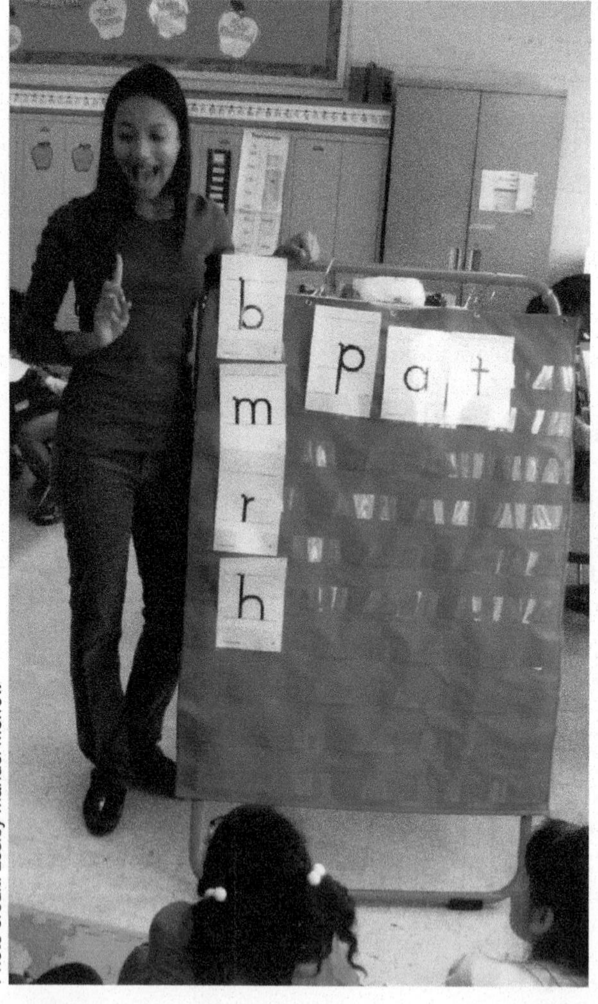

Photo credit: Lesley Mandel Morrow

LEARNING OUTCOMES

After reading this chapter, you should be able to:

8.1 Define phonological and phonemic awareness and identify activities for developing them.

8.2 Define phonics and describe effective strategies for teaching phonics skills.

8.3 Assess knowledge of word study skills.

When parents and others think about teaching reading what comes to mind is learning sound–symbol relationships or phonics. Chapter 5 discussed many other emergent literacy strategies that should be taught either before or along with phonological awareness and phonics. Phonological awareness is a precursor to learning phonics and research has demonstrated the need for children to learn phonics. It is important to be aware that this is one small skill in literacy development, not nearly the whole program. The ultimate goal for literacy development is comprehension. In order to comprehend we must be able to automatically decode words. Additionally, children need to know the meaning of vocabulary in a passage. They won't understand what they are reading unless they know the meaning of the vocabulary.

Teaching phonics and phonological awareness need to be handled carefully. Children might not understand why you are teaching these skills if they are not taught within the context of reading. When children understand what reading is and what it is for, then they will see the purpose of learning phonics. When possible, connect phonics instruction into a meaningful context, such as Mrs. James does in her classroom.

Mrs. James's class was studying nutrition. The dramatic-play area was set up like a supermarket with products displayed separately in food groups: dairy products; breads and cereals; meat, poultry, and fish; and fruits and vegetables. To connect the learning of sound–symbol relationships and letter names with the unit, three letters were featured: *m* for meat, *f* for "fish," and *d* for "dairy." In addition to creating funny stories using the featured letters—such as Fanny the fish was a friendly flounder who liked to flip her flippers as she fluttered through the waves—the children collected things that began with the featured letters and placed them in boxes labeled with the appropriate symbol. These experiences caused them to talk about letters, sounds, and words in spontaneous play. Kathy and Kelly were pretending that they were shopping in the dramatic-play store. Kathy picked up a can of tuna fish and said, "Kelly, let's see how many foods we can find that begin with the letter f." They looked around, and Kathy found a box of Frosted Flakes and some French fries. Kelly found a can of fruit cocktail, Fruit Loops cereal, and a container of frozen yogurt. The girls were excited when each found some food that began with the letter *f*. They said each word with a strong emphasis on the beginning *f* sound. Another activity the children were asked to do was to copy the names of the food that began with *f*. Mrs. James told them to do the same activities for the other featured letters in the unit, *m* for "meat" and *d* for "dairy." Mrs. James does many mini-lessons such as this with the entire class. However, when she works with the children in small groups, she will focus on individual needs based on achievement. Some children will not be ready for sound–symbol correspondence; others will be looking at onsets and rimes in words.

VOCABULARY

Grapheme
Onsets
Phonemes
Phonemic awareness
Phonics
Phonological awareness
Consonants
Vowels
Rimes
Segmenting
Syllabication

MyLab Education
Video Example 8.1
Defining Phonemic Awareness
Learning phonemes or the sounds that letters make is an essential skill for early reading and writing.

Define Phonological and Phonemic Awareness and Identifying Activities for Developing Them

Phonemic awareness and phonological awareness are not phonics, but they are considered to be necessary precursors to learning phonics and are important for achieving successful reading ability. We will discuss phonics in greater detail later in the chapter. We start with **phonological awareness** however since this is an emergent literacy skill needed to figure out phonics. Phonological awareness and phonemic awareness instruction in early literacy lead toward helping students become independent readers. Teaching these skills to children should be done concurrently with other strategies for learning to read, such as acquiring sight words and learning how to use context clues and picture clues.

Figure 8.1 Scope and Sequence of Phonemic Awareness Instruction

Phoneme isolation	What's the first sound in *boat?*
Phoneme identification	What sound is the same in the words: *cake, cup, cook*
Phoneme categorization	Which word doesn't belong: *run, ring, rope, tub*
Phoneme blending	What is this word: /p/-/ă/-/t/
Phoneme segmentation	How many sounds are in the word *pin?* Let's push and say these sounds: /p/-/ĭ-/n/. How many sounds are in the word *pin?*
Phoneme deletion	What is *jeep* without the /j/?
Phoneme addition	What do you have when you add /s/ to the beginning of the word *nap? (snap)*
Phoneme substitution	The word is *kit.* Change the /k/ to /f/. What's the new word? *(fit)*

Phonological and phonemic awareness is one part of a comprehensive program in learning to read (National Reading Panel Report, 2000). It is the concurrent use of several word-study skills that creates a proficient reader (Reutzel & Cooter, 2009). According to the National Reading Panel Report, a total of 18 hours of teaching phonemic and phonological awareness in the kindergarten year is needed for a child to learn the skills. In a 180-day school year, that would be about 6 minutes a day. Figure 8.1 contains a summary of the scope and sequence of phonemic awareness instruction.

Instruction in phonological awareness should be playful as teachers read stories, tell stories, play word games, and use rhymes and riddles. Instruction in the area should be purposeful and planned; we cannot leave it to chance. In the past, this instruction was spontaneous and incidental. Of course, it can still be spontaneous when the moment arises and should be; however, it must be systematically written and follow a sequence addressing every skill in daily plans. Try as much as possible to make your instruction meaningful and with a purpose (Adams, 2001; Cunningham, 2009; Gambrell, Morrow, & Pressley, 2007 Callcott, Hammond, & Hill, 2015).

It is easiest for young children to learn to deal with larger parts of words or whole words first and then smaller parts. **Phonemic awareness** asks children to segment sounds, such as listening for and counting syllables in words. Have children learn about segmenting sounds in words by clapping the sounds in their names. Two difficult phonemic awareness skills are **segmenting** and blending words together using **onsets** and rimes. Work in this area; for example, ask children to listen for the beginning sound in the word "cat," (the onset) which is *c,* and then to put it together with its ending chunk rime *at* to make the whole word "cat" (Yopp & Yopp, 2000; Moats, 2005-6). When teaching activities that help to learn segmenting and blending, we ask children to match sounds, to work with sounds in isolation, and to make sound substitutions and sound deletions. Remember that phonological awareness involves saying sounds and not looking at the letters. They are oral exercises. The following activities ask children to match, isolate, substitute, and delete sounds from words:

Match: When we ask children to match sounds, we say: "Which words have the same sound at the beginning: big and boy? house? go?"

Isolate: When working with individual words, we will say to the children, "What sound do you hear at the beginning of the word 'pen'?" (We are not asking for the letter name; we are asking for the sound.)

Substitute: When we ask children to substitute sounds, we say, "Listen to the word 'bat'; it has a /b/ sound at the beginning. Can you say it, /b/, 'bat'? Now, see if you can make a new word if we say 'mmm' at the beginning of *'at.'* Everyone—'mmmmat.' That was great. What word did we make? 'mat.'"

Delete: When we ask children to delete, we might say, "Tell me what word we have when we say the word 'snowman' without the 'man.'" The answer is snow. In a lesson we can say, "When it is rainy outside, we wear a raincoat. If you take the rain away from the word, what word do you have left?" The children answer "coat." Another deletion could be, "If we take the /p/ away from the word 'pan,' what do we have?" The answer is *an*.

Rhyming is the easiest phonemic awareness task. Early work in this area should be playful. Exposing children to books that contain rhymes, such as *Green Eggs and Ham* (Seuss, 1960) and *Goodnight Moon* (Brown, 1947), helps develop the skill. Teachers can recite rhyming and words that don't rhyme from the books and ask children to differentiate between them. To practice rhymes, have children do the following:

> Can you think of words that rhyme with your name? My name is Ann. Fan rhymes with Ann. Sing songs that rhyme, such as "Hickory Dickory Dock," and separate out the rhyming words. Act out well-known nursery rhymes, such as "Jack and Jill," and identify the rhyming words. Make up new rhymes in a story such as *I Know an Old Lady*. Let the children decide what else she could swallow and what would happen to her if she did. For example, "I know an old lady who swallowed a frog; she began to *jog* when she swallowed a frog."

It is a good idea to have some routine rhymes and songs that the class chants repeatedly. The following chant will allow children to make up rhymes and substitute rhymes:

Let's Make a Rhyme

When it's cold outside,
and you want to play,
Let's make a rhyme,
my teacher would say.
Did you ever see a dog
Pushing a log
On a freezing cold winter's day?
When it's cold outside, and you want to play,
Let's make a rhyme, my teacher would say.
Did you ever see a moose
Pushing a goose
On a freezing cold winter's day?

The next step is for each child to think of an animal to make a rhyme with, for example:

Did you ever see a ____________?
Pushing a ____________?
On a freezing cold winter's day?

Segmenting is an important skill that is more difficult than rhyming for children. It is easier for a child to segment the beginning sound (or onset) and then the ending chunk (or rime). If this is done with the word "man," for example, the child should be guided to say "mmm" for the onset /m/ and then an for the rime /an/.

Play a riddle substitution of onsets game. Say, "I'm thinking of a word that sounds like head, but begins with the /b/ sound," or "I'm thinking of a word that sounds like fat, but has an /mmm/ sound at the beginning."

Syllabication is a way of segmenting words or working on phonological awareness. Children can clap the syllables in their names and in the names of their friends. For example, the name Tim is one clap or one beat, Janet is two, and Carolyn is three.

Syllable Name Chant

If your name has a beat and the beat is one,
Say and clap your name and then run, run, run.
If your name has a beat and the beat is two,
Say and clap your name and hop like a kangaroo.
If your name has a beat and the beat is three,
Say and clap your name, then buzz like a bee.
If your name has a beat and the beat is four,
Say and clap your name and stamp on the floor.

After segmenting words, ask children to blend them back together again. The goal is for children to be able to identify each sound within a word, know the number of sounds heard, and blend the word back together. We can ask them to stretch the word out like a rubber band, which would be asking them to segment and then say it really, really fast as the elastic springs back to blend. The following are some activities that will help children learn to segment and blend:

A good song for segmenting and blending goes to the tune of "This Old Man." You can use the name of the letter featured or use the letter sounds. This song names the letter that we will create words with, but it is an oral activity, not matching a letter seen to the sound it makes.

This Old Man

This old man sings /t/ songs
He sings /t/ songs
He sings /t/ songs all day long
With a Tick, Tack, Takie Tack
He sings his silly song
He wants you to sing along
This old man sings /b/songs
He sings /b/songs all day long
With a Bick, Back, Bakie Back
He sings his silly song
He wants you to sing along
Now make up your own verse with a new sound.

Use Elkonin boxes to engage children in segmentation and blending (see Figure 8.2). Select and write words on a piece of paper. Draw square boxes next to each word. Have chips for students to put into the squares. Say the word on the paper, such as duck, and have the children put the number of chips in the boxes that represent the number of sounds in the word. For the word "duck," children would put three chips into the boxes because the *ck* in the word has one sound (Fitzpatrick, 1997; Invernizzi, 2003; Johns, Lenski, & Elish-Piper, 1999).

MyLab Education Self-Check 8.1

Figure 8.2 Word-Study Game

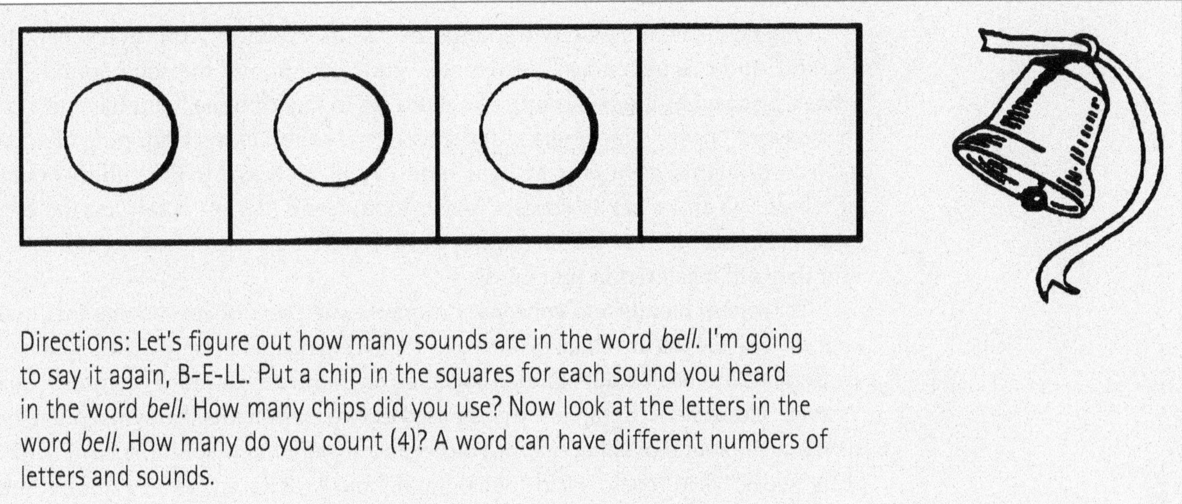

Directions: Let's figure out how many sounds are in the word *bell.* I'm going to say it again, B-E-LL. Put a chip in the squares for each sound you heard in the word *bell.* How many chips did you use? Now look at the letters in the word *bell.* How many do you count (4)? A word can have different numbers of letters and sounds.

Define Phonics and Describe Effective Strategies for Teaching Phonic Skills

Phonics is the connection of sounds and symbols. The use of phonics requires children to learn letter sounds and combinations of sounds (**phonemes**) associated with their corresponding letter symbols called **graphemes.** In the English language there are 26 letters in the alphabet; however, there are at least 44 different sounds. Sound–symbol correspondence is not always consistent in English; there are many irregularities and exceptions to many rules, which are difficult for children to learn. For that reason, phonics should not be the only instructional method used to teach children to decode. In spite of the difficulties with phonics, it is a major source to help children become independent readers (Cunningham, 2015).

There are many approaches to teaching phonics.

1. The *synthetic approach* involves the children in learning the letter sounds one by one. When they approach a word, they decode it by looking at the word one letter at a time and sounding each letter separately (McGeown, & Medford, 2014).
2. The *analytic approach* is more implicit. Each letter is not isolated but taught within the context of an entire word so as not to distort its sound. Words are also looked at to find patterns or chunks so that children can sound out one sound and then a group of letters together to decode a word. Chunking seems to be easier for children than one sound at a time.

Researchers have found that phonics is an important skill for reading success. However, it is the concurrent use of several of the word-study skills mentioned that creates a proficient reader (Bear, Invernizzi, Templeton, & Johnston, 2008; Ehri & Roberts, 2006; Reutzel & Cooter, 2009). Comprehension is the ultimate goal of reading. Phonics only helps to decode. If children don't know the meaning of words decoded, they will not comprehend the text.

MyLab Education
Video Example 8.2
Word Study for Kindergarteners
In this video, a kindergarten teacher uses a word sort to teach beginning consonant sounds.

Consonants

We begin teaching phonics with the most commonly used initial consonant sounds, such as *f, m, s, t,* and *h,* and then use these same sounds in ending word positions. The next set of initial and final consonant sounds usually taught is *l, d, c, n, g, w, p, r, k,* then *j, q, v,* final *x,* initial *y,* and *z.* Most **consonants** are quite regular and represent one sound. Some consonants have two sounds, such as *g* as in the words "go" and "girl," often referred to as the hard *g;* and *g* as in "George," "giraffe", and "gentleman" referred to as the soft *g.*

Other consonants with two sounds are *c* as in "cookie," "cut," and "cost," the hard *c* sound; and *c* as in "circus," "celebrate," and "ceremony," the soft *c* sound. The letter *x* has a *z* sound at the beginning of a word, as in "xylophone," but has the *x* sound as in the word "next." The letters *w* and *y* have one sound at the beginning of a word and act as consonants, as in /w/ in "was" and /y/ in "yellow." In the middle or at the end of a word, *w* and *y* act as vowels, as in "today" and "blow." Learning the consonant sounds begins in preschool in a limited way; more instruction occurs in kindergarten; and they are mastered in first grade.

Consonant blends and consonant digraphs are pairs of consonants that make new sounds. The blends are clusters of two or three consonants in which the sounds of all the consonants are heard, but blended together, as in the words "blue," "true," "flew," and "string." Consonant digraphs are composed of two consonants that when put together do not have the sound of either one, but rather an altogether new sound, such as *th* in "three," *sh* in "shoes," *ch* in "chair," *ph* in "photograph," and *gh* at the end of a word, as in "enough."

Vowels

The next phonic elements we teach are the vowels. We start teaching vowels in kindergarten and continue in first grade. The **vowels** are *a, e, i, o,* and *u.* We teach the short vowels first: *a* as in "cat", *e* as in "bed," *i* as in "hit," *o* as in "hot," and *u* as in "cut." Next we teach the long vowels: *a* as in "hate," *e* as in "feet," *i* as in "kite," *o* as in "boat," and *u* as in "cute." Long vowels have the sound of the name of the letter. As mentioned earlier, *w* and *y* act as vowels in the middle and at the end of words. The letter *y* has the sound of a long *e* when it comes at the end of a word, such as "baby." The *y* has the sound of a long *i* when it is at the end of a one-syllable word, such as "cry" or "try."

Vowels change their sound when they are *r*-controlled. They become neither long nor short, as in "car" and "for."

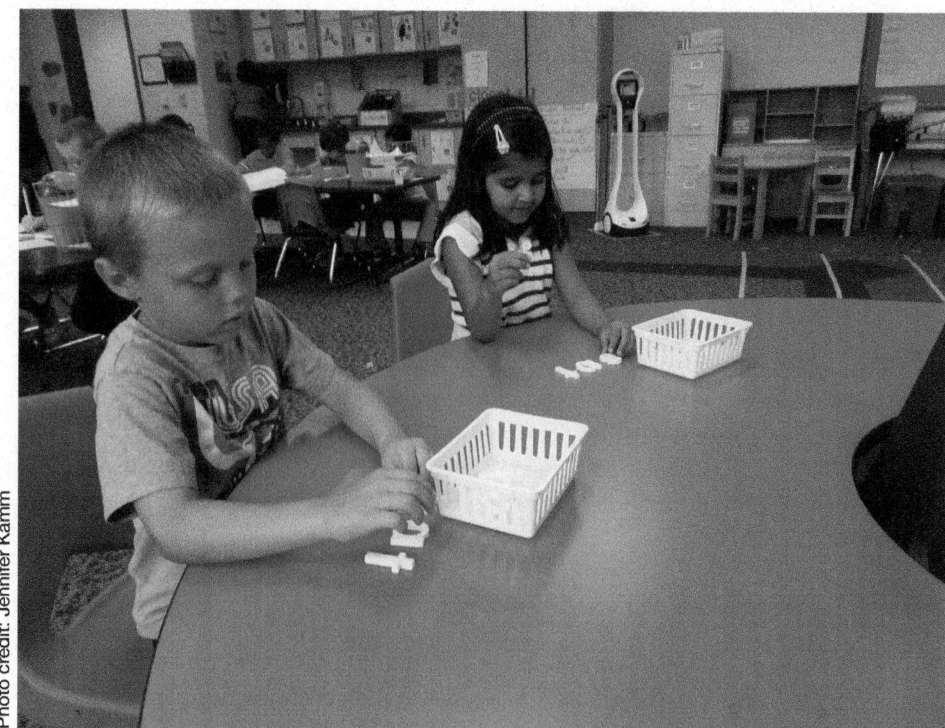

Children sort words and make words with manipulative materials to learn about word patterns.

Photo credit: Jennifer Kamm

Figure 8.3 Common Rimes Used in Early Literacy

ack	al	ain	ake	ale	ame	an	ank	up	ush
at	ate	aw	ay	ell	eat	est	ice	ick	ight
id	ill	in	ine	ing	ink	ip	ir	ock	oke
op	ore	or	uck	ug	ump	unk			

As with consonants, there are vowel pairs that we teach. The first vowel pairs are called *digraphs*. Vowel digraphs include two vowels that have a single sound such as *ai* in "pail" and *ea* in "sea." The next vowel pairs are called *diphthongs*. Diphthongs are composed of two vowels that form a gliding sound as one vowel blends into the other, such as *oy* in "toy" and *oi* in "oil." Vowels can be difficult to learn, since they have many sounds and combinations of sounds that make the sounds change.

At each grade level, teachers should review what has been learned and add on additional work in medial consonants, irregular consonant sounds, and blends. The elements to deal with next include some structural aspects such as compound words, syllabication, contractions, prefixes, and suffixes. Then children will learn about synonyms, antonyms, and homonyms.

Children find it easier to learn about word patterns or chunks rather than individual sounds. Word patterns help in decoding many different words that contain the same patterns, but may have a different beginning or ending sound. Teachers should help students learn familiar word patterns for **rimes**, which are also referred to as *phonograms, word families*, and *chunks*. There are many common rimes. A list is provided in Figure 8.3.

There are many phonic generalizations or rules. Most of them apply to only a few words. I have listed four that are consistent.

1. When a one-syllable word has only one vowel in the middle of the word surrounded by two consonants, the vowel is usually short. Words such as "hot," "cut," and "bet" follow this consonant–vowel–consonant (CVC) word pattern.
2. When there are two vowels in a word with one syllable, and one of them is an *e* at the end of the word, the first vowel is long and the *e* is silent. This is called the consonant–vowel–consonant–*e* (CVCe) pattern or the final *e* rule. Some words that demonstrate the rule include: plate, cute, and bone.
3. When a consonant is followed by a vowel, the vowel is usually long, as in *be, go,* and *because.* This is called the consonant–vowel rule (CV).
4. When two vowels are together, the first is long and the second is silent. This is the consonant–vowel–vowel–consonant (CVVC) rule. Some say, "When two vowels go walking, the first one does the talking," such as in meat, boat, and rain.

MyLab Education Application Exercise 8.1
MyLab Education Application Exercise 8.2

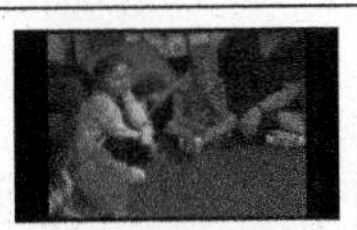

Phonics can be taught synthetically and in meaningful contexts. Students can also use syntax along with graphophonics to decode words. Syntax is the sentence structure and the meaning of the words; graphophonics is the sound-symbol relationships in the letters.

Synthetic Phonics Instruction

Synthetic phonics instruction uses a planned curriculum for teaching phonics. That plan is systematic and follows a scheduled routine for students to learn specific skills throughout the year. A synthetic phonics lesson looks like this:

Phonic Skill: Connecting the symbol *f* with its sound

Materials: Picture cards of a fan, feet, fox, fish, hat, bat

Teacher: Say /f/ and have the children repeat. Explain that face begins with /f/. Tell children to point to their faces and say /f/ each time they hear a word beginning with /f/. Say: The funny fish has fins.

Print *Ff* on the board and identify the uppercase and lowercase letters and remind the children they both say *Ff*. Say the *Ff* sound and have the children repeat it after you. Ask the children to explain what they do with their mouth and lips when they say the *Ff* sound. (You open your mouth a little and put your top teeth on your bottom lip and push out the sound of *Ff*.)

Display the picture cards. Help the children identify the picture on each card. Ask a child to say the word and the sound of *Ff* separately and place the card on the board ledge.

Give each child a workbook page with uppercase and lowercase *Ff* 's to trace. They are to say the sound of the *Ff* as they trace. On the page are pictures in boxes of a fox, fan, bus, cat, fence, fish. Each box has a yellow circle under it, except for the first box. There is a fox in that box and the circle has a smiley face with two eyes and a mouth. The children are to say each picture's name and put eyes and a mouth on the ones that begin with *Ff*. As they make the smiley faces, they should say the sound of *Ff*. The ones that don't begin with *Ff* are left blank.

There is another page for practice and the children are directed to say each word. If the word begins with an *Ff*, they should write an uppercase and lowercase *Ff* in the box; if it does not, they leave that box blank.

Combined Analytic-Synthetic Lesson

Another type of phonics lesson is the combined analytic-synthetic phonics lesson, which looks like this:

Phonic Skill: Connecting the sound of *Ss* with its symbol

Materials: Picture cards of a sun, sand, salad, seal; children's book *The Snowy Day* (Keats, 1996); individual alphabet books; magnetic letters with at least one *Ss* for each child.

The teacher projects the picture cards on the electronic white board. She asks the children to identify each picture as she shows them. First, she projects the sun and the children respond, "That's a sun." She continues with the other words.

She asks, "Is there something the same about each of these words?" Samantha raises her hand and says, "They all begin with an *Ss*. I know because my name does, too. It is Samantha, like *sun, sand, salad*." The teacher responds, "You are right!" She projects an uppercase and lowercase *Ss* on the white board. She asks the children to say the words again and then they talk about what their tongue, teeth, and mouth do when saying *Ss*. Several more pictures are projected on the white board and two children are called to the board to move all the *Ss* words together; the ones that do not begin with an *Ss* make another group.

The teacher asks the children to look around the room to see if they see something that has the *Ss* sound. They get up from their seats and walk around in pairs, and when they find a word that has an *Ss* in it, they stop and stand by their *Ss*. James stands at the word wall since his name has an *Ss* at the end. Everyone looks at his name. Children take turns saying the words they find, such as sink and summer, which is on a poster on the wall. A traffic sign on another poster that says, "stop" and a book called *Swimmy* (Lionni, 1987) are also found. The teacher has the children come to the literacy center rug and she reads the book *The Snowy Day* (Keats, 1996) and asks them to listen for as many *Ss* words as they can hear. When the story is over, the children say words they heard as the teacher writes them on her chart: snow, snowy, snowsuit, snowman, snowballs, stick, and more. The children go back to their seats and turn to the *Ss* page in their alphabet books, which were originally blank notebooks. They write the upper and lowercase *Ss* on the page. Some copy the *Ss* words; some make pictures of a sun, a seal, and snow. Some write sentences with *Ss* words in the sentence. They all add illustrations. At snack time, the children have *sandwich* cookies.

Meaning-Based Phonics Strategies

How can we help children recognize the sound–symbol relationships of consonants and vowels in a meaningful context? Science and social studies themes lend themselves to featuring letters that appear in units. For example, when studying farm, pets, and zoo animals, feature the letter *p*, because it is used frequently with this context. The following types of activities then can follow and be used with other consonants as well:

1. Read *Pet Show* (Keats, 1974) and *The Tale of Peter Rabbit* (Potter, 1902), for example, during the unit, and point out words that begin with the letter *p* in these books.
2. Make word charts using words from the books that begin with the letter *p*.
3. On a field trip, bring peanuts to the zoo to feed the animals.
4. Make lists of animals that begin with the letter *p*, such as peacock, panda, and pig.
5. Read the book *Animalia* (Base, 1986) and point out the *p* page, which is about peacocks.
6. Collect sensory items about animals that begin with the letter *p*, such as Puppy Chow to smell, popcorn to eat, peacock plumes to touch, a purring kitten to listen to, and the book *Petunia* (Duvoisin, 2002) to look at and read.
7. List words from the unit that begin with the letter *p*.
8. Write an experience chart of activities carried out during the unit, and highlight the letter *p* when it appears in the chart.
9. Ask children to add to their Very Own Words collection with favorite words from the unit that begin with the letter *p*.
10. Make a collage of pictures featuring things from the unit, and mark those that begin with the letter *p*.
11. Print the song "Peter Cottontail" on a chart. Sing the song and highlight the letter *p* when it appears.
12. Have children help you make up nonsense rhymes for featured letters and chant them, such as the following:

    My name is Penelope Pig.

    I pick petals off of petunias.

    I play patty-cake

    and eat pretzels with pink punch.

13. Add a page for the letter *p* to a class Big Book entitled, "Our Own Big Book of Letters, Sounds, and Words." Have children draw pictures or paste in pictures of words that begin with the letter *p*. Directions for making a Big Book are in Chapter 7, on pages 126–127.
14. Complete a worksheet for the letter *p* that requires students to trace the letter, write the letter, and circle pictures that begin with the letter *p*, such as pig and popcorn.
15. Encourage children to write about their experiences during the unit, such as their visit to the zoo, the books they read, and the songs they sang.

Teaching English Learners

English learners will have an easier time learning phonics when it is taught in a context that has meaning for children.

In their writing, they will be using the letters emphasized and, although their writing may not be conventional, through the use of their invented spellings, they are indirectly enhancing their phonemic awareness. When children write, they face the problem of mapping spoken language into written language. This process can lead to an understanding of the structure of spoken language. The more children write, the better they become at segmenting sounds in words. This point is demonstrated in Justin's story about the panda bear at the zoo. He wrote,

"I saw a prte panda ber pik up her babi panda at the zooo."

Children's literature is an excellent source for featuring letters attached to themes. Be careful not to abuse the stories by overemphasizing the sounds featured; however, do not pass up the opportunity to feature letters in this natural book setting. For example, in a unit on food, Ms. Fino, a first-grade teacher, featured the letter *b* and read *Blueberries for Sal* (McCloskey, 1948), *Bread and Jam for Frances* (Hoban, 1964), and *The Berenstain Bears and Too Much Birthday* (Berenstain & Berenstain, 1987).

These and similar activities can be carried out for any initial consonant.

Whenever letters being featured in a thematic unit appear in a language experience chart or a piece of children's literature, point them out to the children. Alphabet books generally use sound–symbol relationships as they introduce each letter, as do picture storybooks that use a particular letter prominently. (See Appendix A for children's literature for building sound–symbol relationships.)

When we read, we use several skills concurrently to decode and derive meaning from the printed page. We therefore need to encourage children to use multiple skills, rather than isolated skills, in their approach to reading.

Children should be taught to use context clues and phonic clues simultaneously. One strategy that accomplishes this goal has already been suggested—reading a sentence in which you pause and leave a "blank" to be filled in by the child. For example, say, "The **b**__________ flew up to the tree and landed on a branch."

Supplying the initial consonant for the word, either by sound or by sight, draws on a child's skills with phonics, context, syntax, and semantics.

Evidence-Based Strategies for Teaching Phonics

Children learn as their brains search for patterns. The brain takes what it knows and tries to apply it to the unknown. Patterns such as familiar word endings help children deal with unknowns. Therefore phonics activities that engage children with groups of letters or patterns in words make decoding easier. This type of phonics is often referred to as using onsets and rimes. Some familiar rimes are: ake, an, and it. Rimes often are used in several words. With the onset *b* at the beginning of the words and those three rimes as potential endings to a word, we can make the words "bake," "ban," and "bit." This type of activity helps children learn letter–sound relationships by analyzing the elements in a word or picture and selecting critical features as they place the words or sound pictures in piles. Through sorting, students clarify words and pictures on the basis of sound and spelling and construct an understanding of our spelling system and consequently are able to decode unknown words (Strickland & Snow, 2002; Bear et al., 2008).

The following are hands on activities in which children use onsets and rimes to make words, they sort words, classify words, find little words in big words, blend, segment, and substitute letters to make words. In these activities, children are learning patterns in words via the manipulative nature of the hands-on activities, which is especially appealing to youngsters. When working with manipulatives, it is important for children to write down the words they create so the teacher can assess progress.

Making Words. Many of these activities can be done for a different purpose. The teacher sets the purpose and models the strategy before the child carries it out. All of these activities involve the manipulation of letters and letter patterns.

Children can use magnetic letters, wooden letters, felt letters, letter tiles, or letters written on tag board. In one activity, the teacher asks children to make several two-letter words, three-letter words, and four-letter words from the word "Thanksgiving." The teacher connects the phonics activity to the theme Thanksgiving being discussed in this classroom to give some meaning to the phonics (Gunning, 2003). The children work in pairs, and some create many more words than others, which helps the teacher to see who needs more practice and who doesn't. As the words are made, the children write them down on activity sheets prepared by the teacher. The paper has the word "Thanksgiving" written on the top and then lines for two-, three-, and four-letter words. Some of the words typically created are: an, it, hi; Nat, hat, nag; and thin, than, hang. Children can also make words from a scrambled word; in addition to making little words from the letters, the children must figure out the big word. Another popular type of word-making activity uses onsets and rimes.

With younger children, the teacher provides a few well-known rimes—such as at, an, or in—and asks the children to make as many words with these endings as they can think of by adding different initial consonants or consonant blends to the beginning of the rimes. With the rime "at"—for example, children create the following words: cat, sat, mat, rat, hat, fat, vat, pat, and bat.

Another word-making game provides children with letters. In this lesson they were *a*, *d*, *n*, *s*, and *t*. With these letters children can be asked to make the following words:

Use two letters to make *at*. Add a letter to make *sat*.

Take away a letter to make *at*. Change a letter to make *an*.

Add a letter to make *Dan*. Change a letter to make *tan*. Take away a letter to make *an*. Add a letter to make *and*.

Add a letter to make *sand*. (Cunningham, 2009)

Word Sorts. Word sorts help children learn to decode through patterns. The teacher decides on the purpose of the sort. Sorts can be done over and over for different skills. The activity allows children to practice skills to which they have been exposed. Sorts can be done with pictures or letters and words. Tell children the purpose of the sort by placing a target card at the top of a column.

For example, if you are sorting long and short vowels, the picture and word at the top of one column would be "sock" for short vowels, and the picture at the top of the second column would be "cake" to sort the long vowels.

The activity described when making words from "Thanksgiving" could be turned into a sort. For example, if children make little words from the bigger word "Thanksgiving"—such as thanks, giving, sing, sang, hang, king, thanking, and having—they can be asked to sort the following:

- Words that all have the *-ing* ending
- Words that rhyme
- Words ending with the consonant *g*
- Words beginning with the consonant *s*, and so on.

You can also sort words for blends, digraphs, and numbers of syllables, which are all ways to help students see patterns. Words can be sorted for meaning by categories, such as colors and types of food. Words can also be sorted using rimes. Figure 8.7 provides some well-known rimes. Children can sort words they make using the consonant Tt and the rimes, ap, on, and in (tap, ton, and tin). In the other column, using the same rimes, make words using the onset consonant *Ss* (sap, son, and sin).

Other games to practice decoding skills include: Bingo, Concentration, and Lotto. Just decide the skill and distribute letter cards, blends, digraphs, long or short vowels, beginning sounds, or ending sounds, and play the game.

Classifying Elements in Words. Children will gain a better understanding of the patterns and elements within words they classify or build if they use the study guide shown in Figure 8.4. This word-study classification guide is for young children to use when they are introduced to new vocabulary.

A Station for Word-Study Activities

A station that contains materials for word study is necessary in early childhood classrooms. The activities for making and sorting words discussed earlier can be game like

Figure 8.4 Tell It to Yourself and a Friend Word-Study Guide

- The word is Hat ____________________
- When I say and stretch the word, it sounds like this: ____________________
- The number of letters I see in the word is ____________________
- I hear this number of sounds in the word: ____________________
- The spelling pattern in the word is ____________________
- This is what I know about the vowel in the word:

  ____
- Other words with the same sounds are

  ____
- A sound box for this word looks like this:

  ____

if they are presented with interesting manipulative materials. With onsets and rimes as well as scrambled words, teachers can have children use magnetic letters and a magnetic board for making words. Students can use movable wooden letters, foam rubber letters, or flash cards with letters on them. Flash cards can have word endings on them or initial consonants or consonant blends. All onsets can be written in one color and rimes in another. The flash cards can be used to make words on a table or a pocket chart. To make this activity even more interesting, letter stamps and white slates with magic markers will work for making words. Some teachers use manipulatives such as movable wheels for making words. Board games such as Bingo, Lotto, Concentration, and Candyland and card games can be constructed so that children have to make words within the rules of the game. At the end of the chapter are nine figures for making materials for sorting, making words, classifying parts of words, and so on, for learning phonics. (The directions for making the materials are at the end of the chapter in Figures 8.12 through 8.20.) Games for stations centers can be purchased from stores for teachers and large school-supply companies. Teachers may create numerous word-study activities that children use to reinforce what they know and use independently when teachers are engaged in small-group instruction. Teachers can also seek the help of parents, aides, and upper-grade children to make materials.

Using a Word-Study Station. After children have been introduced to the use of materials, their teacher, Mr. Rosen, is able to assign word-study activities for them to work on while he works with small groups in guided reading instruction. The following explains the activities the children engaged in during station time:

> Four children made as many words from the word *Thanksgiving* as they could. The letters of *Thanksgiving* had been cut up and placed in plastic baggies for each child. In addition to manipulating the letters to create words, the children wrote the words on an activity sheet.
>
> With magnetic letters and their own individual magnetic slates, children created word ladders. They started with one-letter words, then two, then three, and so on. Each child also had a 5 × 8 index card to write his or her word from the bottom of the card up the ladder. A partner checked the words.
>
> Another group of four children worked with ending phonograms or chunks, as Mr. Rosen called them, by creating words with onsets. He had prepared word wheels, which are oak tag circles that have ending phonograms,

with another circle with onsets to create words. Children created words with the word wheels and wrote them down. They also wrote additional words they thought of as well.

Finally, children created sentences with letter and word stamps. The stamps had familiar words for the children to create the sentences.

All these activities were manipulative. They involved children working with words from individual letters, to letter chunks, beginnings and ends of words, and total sentences. They also required children to work together, check each other's work, and collaborate. All the activities had a pencil-and-paper component for recording what was done; for example, the little words made from the big word "Thanksgiving" were written on a sheet of paper provided by the teacher. This way the teacher has a record of work done with manipulatives, and the students are responsible for completing tasks. All children have the opportunity to use every material during this period. Worksheets to be used with the manipulatives are important and provide practice. Often, worksheets are regarded as not very useful; however, as long as children are involved in learning through multiple strategies, an occasional worksheet provides practice and reinforcement. The worksheet is also a form of accountability. In addition to the materials discussed, some quality phonics websites with more teaching ideas are:

- www.starfall.com

  This website has great videos and interactive activities for students. It's broken up by level so you can find exactly what skill you are looking for.
- teacher.scholastic.com/clifford1

  This website has phonics games using *Clifford the Big Red Dog*. The games offer videos, read along, and even options to hear stories in Spanish.
- www.netrover.com/~kingskid/phonics/phonics_main.htm

  This website has an interactive exercise where kids experiment with words. The exercise asks students to spell a word and then gives the sounds of each letter provided.
- www.kizclub.com/phonicsactivities.htm

  This website has various printable activities to teach kids phonics.
- www.kizphonics.com/

  This website has printable activities, videos, and games and is arranged by levels from ages 3 to 8.
- www.turtlediary.com/kids-games/english-topics/phonics-games.html

  This website has both games and printable activities that can help kids learn letter sounds, rhyming words, and many new words.
- Fun Fonix: www.funfonix.com/
- Phonics games, as well as printable worksheets for kids.
- Fun Fonix also includes a program for adult literacy.
- Soft School: www.softschools.com/language_arts/phonics/
- Soft School provides free phonics worksheets, and read aloud flashcards, and games for children
- Reading Bear: www.readingbear.org/
- Reading bear teaches reading through 50 presentations and more than 1,200 vocabulary words that cover fundamental phonic skills.

Flashcards and Phonics lessons Reading A–Z
www.readinga-z.com/phonics/
Reading A–Z provides read along books, phonics lessons and printable flashcards
Reading Rockets: Resources for Teachers and Parents
www.readingrockets.org/teaching/reading-basics/phonics

Phonics guides and research for parent and teacher instruction. Helpful video resources, and help for struggling readers as well as phonics awareness and comprehension.

Teacher Concerns about Phonics

Learning word-study skills helps children become independent, fluent readers. The skills should be mastered by second grade, with attention then shifted mostly to comprehension development. Comprehension skills are also taught in pre-K and kindergarten and throughout the elementary grades. In pre-K through second grade, there is a strong emphasis on learning to decode. Frequent concerns about teaching word study are:

1. When do I teach word study during the school day?
2. How much time do I spend teaching word study?
3. How do I differentiate instruction to meet individual needs in word study?

There should be a daily lesson based on standards and your school curriculum dealing with word study for the entire class. Take advantage of teachable moments when they occur to reinforce the skills being taught. Purposefully integrate whatever skill you are emphasizing into science, social studies, math, play, music, and art. For example, if you are learning the initial consonant *t* and learning about the temperature in different seasons in a science unit, point out the consonant *t* in the word "temperature" and remind the children that they were discussing this in their phonics lesson. Overall, there should be several points over the course of the day during which word-study instruction takes place: a formal time to teach word study to the whole class; informal teaching embedded into content-area teaching; a formal time for small-group instruction to meet individual needs.

How much time to spend teaching word study really depends on the age of the children. Lessons should be shorter for younger children and longer with older ones. Materials selected for instruction should always challenge the children but be easy enough for them to succeed. For example, children who are working with onsets and rimes using magnetic letters and phonograms will make fewer words and more familiar words than those who are moving along more quickly. That will help keep the lesson time the same while simultaneously allowing students to get the most out of the instruction. Small-group instruction with materials that can be used for differentiation of instruction is important for English learners. In some cases, differentiation of instruction may mean that a small group is so advanced or so challenged that the group is working on different skills than the majority of the class.

Differentiating instruction to meet individual needs for word study can be achieved with small groups. Small groups allow you to find out what students have learned and what they need to learn. When differentiating instruction, all children, regardless of their group, have similar goals, but lessons are specifically designed for the students needing more challenging or easier work.

In addition to those practical concerns related to teaching word study, there are other overarching concerns. A major concern about phonics is that so many rules for the English language have exceptions. For example, the sound of *k* in the word "kite" is its usual sound, but when *k* is followed by *n* it becomes silent as in the word "knot." Young children have a limited ability to apply many rules, so teaching fewer rules is more effective than teaching all the rules. Exceptions can be dealt with when they occur in print or treated as sight words when they are uncommon. In early childhood, our main concern should be with sound–symbol relationships and generalizations that rarely have exceptions.

Dialects introduce another challenge with word-study skills and teaching sound–symbol relationships. If a teacher from upstate New York taught in South Carolina or Georgia, he or she would teach long and short vowels with different sounds than those taught by a teacher who was from the South.

English learners may also struggle if a teacher's dialect differs significantly from what they hear in their community or via mass media such as television and radio.

A final challenge with respect to word-study skills involves teaching different types of learners. Auditory learners will process the learning differently than visual learners. A child who is weak in auditory discrimination is not likely to master phonics and is best taught to his or her strength, rather than to a weakness. The skills a child acquires as a result of learning phonics are important for becoming a proficient reader; alternatively, it is just one strategy within the total picture of literacy development, and we need not overemphasize it.

MyLab Education Self-Check 8.2
MyLab Education Application Exercise 8.3

Assessing Knowledge of Word-Study Skills

Numerous word-study skills are discussed in this chapter along with assessment information or tracking guides and checklists. Because assessment provides teachers with information to guide instruction, assessment should happen often and take many forms. One of the first assessments done in preschool, which can also be used in kindergarten, is to determine a child's concepts about books and print by using Figure 8.5.

MyLab Education
Video Example 8.3
Assessing Phonological Awareness
Assessing students ability to blend or segment words is different from assessing sound-symbol relationships. What is the teacher in this video assessing?

Phonemic awareness, considered the precursor to phonics, is important in the literacy development of children. When we test children for knowledge in this area, we try to determine if they can segment phonemes in words, and we ask them to blend words back together again. In tests of phonologic awareness and phonemic awareness, we are interested in the children's ability to hear and say the sounds, not the letters. In addition to segmenting and blending, children need to be able to use a single rime and substitute different onsets to build words. In so doing, they will be substituting one sound for another. *The Phonological Awareness Test 2 (PAT)* assesses a child's phonological abilities as discussed.

The PAT can assess a child's auditory ability in blending, segmenting, and substituting and thus demonstrating phonemic awareness. However, if you present the section on blending, segmenting, isolating, and substituting sounds where children have to look at the letter and respond, then the test would be assessing sound–symbol relationships or phonics. To avoid that, say a word and have the children segment the sounds in the word. Then say the sounds in a word and have them blend it together.

Collect daily performance samples of children's activity sheets and record observations that describe working habits. Checklists (like the one in Figure 8.5) are good for assessing children on word-study skills. Figure 8.6 is an informal phonics inventory to use for a quick assessment of a child's knowledge of the skills. Scoring procedures are included but most important is to find out what a child knows and needs to learn.

MyLab Education Self-Check 8.3

Figure 8.5 A Phonological Awareness Test

As you administer this test, record the child's responses in the space provided. Then, in the farthest column, mark whether the child's responses are correct. Tabulate the final score at the end of the test.

Distinguishing Spoken Words

Play a game with the child using a pencil and paper. Slowly speak the first sentence, making tally marks on the paper as you speak until there are three marks for three words.

1. I like apples.

Once the child understands, ask the student to mark the tallies while you read. Have the child speak the sentence while marking a tally for each word.

		You Read	Child Responds
________	2. Where is the cat?	________	________
________	3 We are all friends	________	________
________	4 Dogs are brown	________	________
________	5. Today I played outside	________	________
________	Total		

Understanding Rhyme

Explain that rhyming words sound the same at the end, giving examples. Then ask the child if two rhyming words rhyme, and if two nonrhyming words rhyme. When the child understands the activity, speak the following word pairs to test his or her understanding. Put an *X* beside each sentence the child tallies correctly.

________ 1. Map, tap ________________
________ 2. Food, yellow ________________
________ 3. Pen, men ________________
________ 4. Book, phone ________________
________ 5. Shelf, mouse ________________
________ Total

Learning to Rhyme

Ask the child to say a word that rhymes with the word you speak. List what the child says even if the child says a nonsense word. The key for this activity is that the word rhyme with the provided word.

________ 1. Dog ________________
________ 2. Light ________________
________ 3. Sad ________________
________ 4. Jump ________________
________ 5. Eat ________________
________ Total

Understanding Syllables

Speak a word while pausing between syllables (e.g., good-bye), and ask the child to identify the word. Write the word the child gives and mark if it is correct.

________ 1. Kit-ten ________________
________ 2. Ta-ble ________________
________ 3. Cell-phone ________________
________ 4. Hap-py ________________
________ 5. Pa-per-clip ________________
________ Total

Figure 8.5 A Phonological Awareness Test (*Continued*)

Deconstructing into Syllables

Say a word normally. Repeat it, this time pausing between syllables and marking a tally for each syllable. Then, have the child speak each word and mark tallies for each syllable as he or she says it. Mark each correct word with an *X*.

_________ 1. Today _________________

_________ 2. Keyboard _________________

_________ 3. Hamburger _________________

_________ 4. Water bottle _________________

_________ 5. Funny _________________

_________ Total

Learning Initial Sounds

Ask the child to tell you the first sound of the word you speak (e.g., "hello" is /h/). Mark down the sound the child hears and if it is correct.

_________ 1. Car _________________

_________ 2. Silly _________________

_________ 3. Chocolate _________________

_________ 4. Fact _________________

_________ 5. Shy _________________

_________ Total

Understanding Phonemes

Say a word while pausing between each sound. Ask the child to identify the word (e.g., "play" is /p/ /l/ /a/ /y/, *time* is /t/ /i/ /m/). Mark down the word the child says and if it is correct.

_________ 1. Crab _________________

_________ 2. Green _________________

_________ 3. Pin _________________

_________ 4. Run _________________

_________ 5. Actor _________________

_________ Total

Counting Phonemes

Ask the child to make a tally mark for each sound in the word you speak. Then have the child speak each word and mark tallies for each sound he or she speaks.

_________ 1. Him _________________

_________ 2. Seven _________________

_________ 3. Blue _________________

_________ 4. Apple _________________

_________ 5. Yes _________________

_________ Total

Switching Phonemes

Ask the child to switch out the first sound of a word with another to make a new word (e.g., pain and /r/ make rain). Write down the word the child says and note if it is correct.

_________ 1. Fan and /r/ _________________

_________ 2. Sit and /p/ _________________

_________ 3. Trip and /g/ _________________

_________ 4. Sew and /b/ _________________

_________ 5. Break and /m/ _________________

_________ Total/45 points

Figure 8.6 Checklist for Assessing Concepts about Print, Strategies to Figure Out Words, Phonological Awareness, and Phonics

Child's name: ______________________ **Date:** ______________________

	Always	Sometimes	Never	Comments
Knows print is read from left to right				
Knows that oral language can be written and then read				
Knows what a letter is and can point one out on a page				
Knows what a word is and can point one out on a printed page				
Knows that there are spaces between words				
Reads environmental print				
Recognizes some words by sight and high-frequency sight words				
Can name and identify rhyming words				
Can identify and name upper and lowercase letters of the alphabet				
Can blend phonemes in words				
Can segment phonemes in words				
Associates consonants and their initial and final sounds (including hard and soft *c* and *g*)				
Associates consonant blends with their sounds (*bl*, *cr*, *dr*, *fl*, *gl*, *pr*, *st*)				
Associates vowels with their corresponding long and short sounds (*a*-acorn, apple; *e*-eagle, egg; *i*-ice, igloo; *o*-oats, octopus; *u*-unicorn, umbrella)				
Knows the consonant digraph sounds (*ch*, *ph*, *sh*, *th*, *wh*)				
Uses context, syntax, and semantics to identify words				
Can count syllables in words				
Attempts reading by attending to picture clues and print				
Guesses and predicts words based on knowledge of sound–symbol correspondence				
Can identify structural elements of words such as prefixes and suffixes, inflectional endings *-ing*, *-ed*, and *-s*, and contractions				
Demonstrates knowledge of the following phonic generalizations: a. In a consonant–vowel–consonant pattern, the vowel sound is usually short b. In a vowel–consonant–e pattern, the vowel is usually long c. When two vowels come together in a word, the first is usually long and the second is silent (train, receive, bean)				
Uses word families often referred to as rimes and phonograms, such as *an*, *at*, *it*, and *ot*, and initial consonants to build words, such as *man*, *can*, *fan*, *ran*				
Teacher Comments:				

Figure 8.7 Informal Phonics Inventory

Directions for Administration

Consonant Sounds

Point to **S.** Say, "What sound does this letter say?" Go from left to right, repeating this question. It is fine if the child reads across a line without prompting. For **C** and **G**, have the child give both sounds. [**Note:** If the child cannot pass this subtest, consider giving an alphabet inventory.]

Consonant Digraphs

Point to **th.** Say, "What sound do these letters say?" Go from left to right, repeating this instruction. It is fine if the child reads all five without prompting.

Beginning Consonant Blends

Point to **bl.** Say, "What sound do these letters say?" Allow child to proceed with or without prompting.

Final Consonant Blends

Point to **bank.** Say, "What is this word?" Allow child to proceed with or without prompting. Listen for the ending sound. Create a word for each beginning consonant using one of the three endings provided.

Short Vowels in CVC Words

Point to **fit.** Say, "What is this word?" Allow child to proceed with or without prompting.

The Rule of Silent e

Point to **cap.** Say, "If this is **cap**, what is this?" Point to **cape** as you say the second part of this sentence. Go from left to right, repeating the question for each pair.

Vowel Digraphs, Diphthongs, and r-Controlled Vowels

Have the child read each word across each line, from left to right.

Context Clues

Ask child to fill in the words.

Scoring

For all subtests and for the total test, use the following criteria:

Mastery	80%+
Needs Review	60–79%
Needs Systematic Instruction Below	60%

The table below gives the number of correct answers that roughly correspond to these percentages.

Subtest	Total possible	Mastery	Review	Systematic instruction
Consonant Sounds	20	16–20	12–15	0–11
Consonant Digraphs	5	4–5	3	0–2
Beginning Consonant Blends	20	16–20	12–15	0–11
Final Consonant Blends	12	10–12	8–9	0–7
Blending and Creating Words	5	5	5	0–5
Short Vowels in CVS Words	10	8–10	6–7	0–5
The Rule of Silent e	4	4	2–3	0–1
Long Vowel Digraphs	10	8–10	6–7	0–5
Diphthongs	6	5–6	4	0–3
r-Controlled Vowels	6	5–6	4	0–3
Context Clues	7	7	7	0–7
Total	**105**	**89–105**	**70–88**	**0–69**

Figure 8.7 Informal Phonics Inventory *(continued)*

Informal Phonics Inventory
Name________
Date________

________/20 *Consonant Sounds*

S	D	F	G	H	J
K	L	Z	P	C	V
B	N	M	Qu	W	R
T	Y				

________/5 *Consonant Digraphs*

th	sh	ch	wh	ph

________/20 *Beginning Consonant Blends*

bl	fl	fr	gl
br	gr	pl	pr
cl	sk	sl	sm
cr	sn	sp	tr
dr	st	str	sw

________/12 *Final Consonant Blends*

bank	apt	limp
band	pact	lilt
bang	lift	lisp
bask	lint	list

________/5 *Blending and Creating Words*

Use B, D, F, M and P with chunks and rimes to create words (an, it, en, etc.)

________/10 *Short Vowels in CVC Words*

fit	led	sup	lap	hug
rot	tin	rag	wet	job

________/4*The Rule of Silent e*

cap	tot	cub	kit
cape	tote	cube	kite

________/10 *Long Vowel Digraphs*

loaf	heat	aim	weed	ray
gain	fee	coal	leaf	due

________/6 *Diphthongs*

town	loud	joy	threw	oil	law

________/6 *r-Controlled Vowels*

tar	hall	sir	port	hurt	fern

________/7 *Context Clues*

The boy r________ down the h________.
The cat drank m________ from a bowl.
The dog p________ a bone in the y________.
The girl p________ with her t________ in the playroom.

*Total:*________/105

Figure 8.8 Initial Consonant Picture Cards for Teaching and Assessment

Directions: To teach with the initial consonant picture cards, make the cards the size that works for you by leaving them as is or enlarging or reducing them on a photocopy machine. Copy on firm colored paper and laminate. Use the cards to alphabetize them, match to words beginning with the same letters, identify initial consonant sounds, or figure out the number of sounds in each word.

To assess with the consonant picture cards, say the word "boat." Ask the child the sound at the beginning of boat. Read the pictures in columns (e.g., boat, girl, lamp, queen, van, zebra, then circle, house, and so on). Do not allow the children to see the pictures or words during this assessment. Record incorrect answers in the box below.

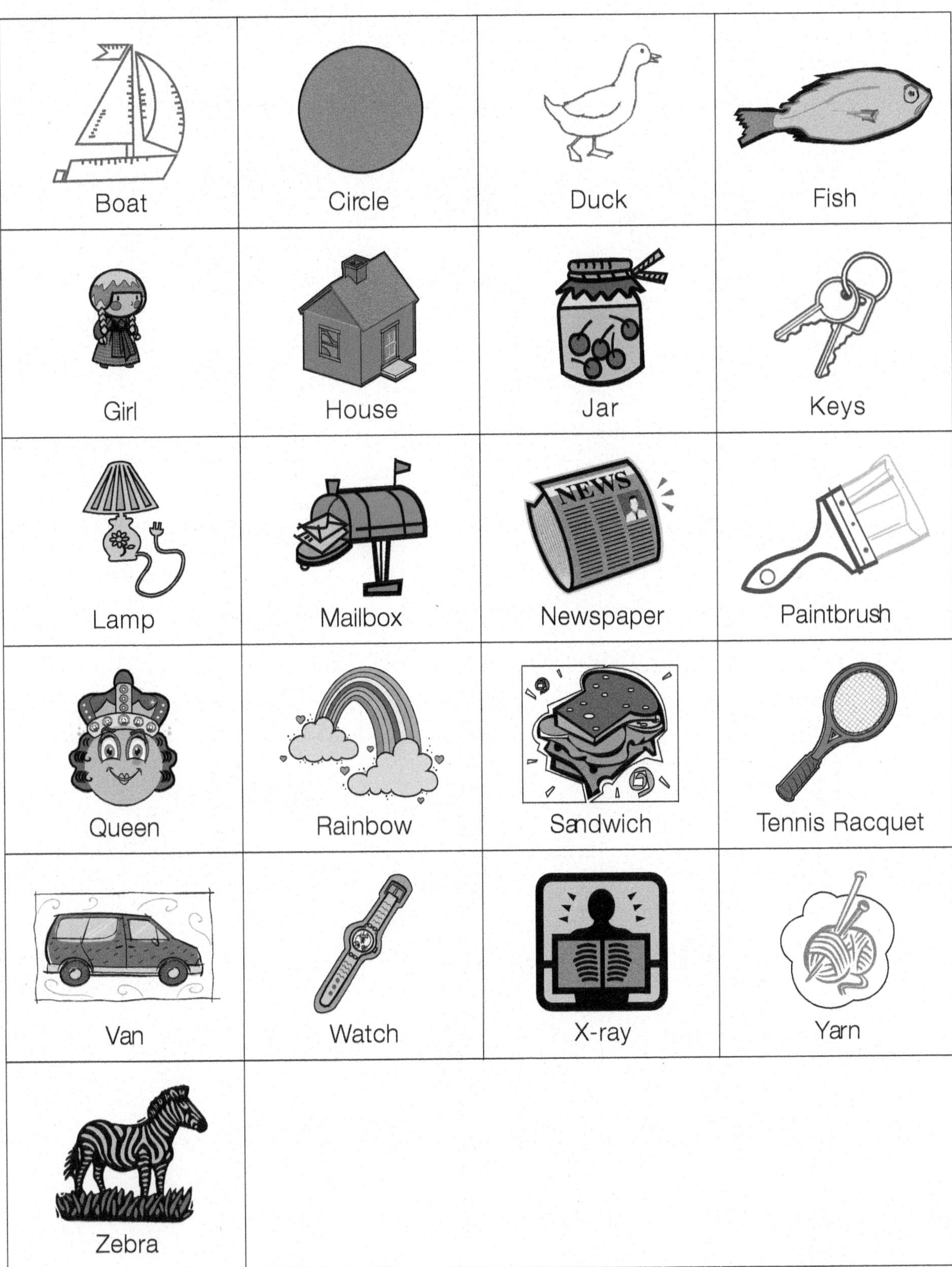

Figure 8.9 Vowel Picture Cards for Teaching and Assessment

Directions: To teach with the vowel picture cards, make the cards the size that works for you by leaving them as is or enlarging or reducing them on a photocopy machine. Copy on firm colored paper and laminate. Use the cards to practice phonemic awareness by figuring out the number of sounds in each word, thinking of a word that rhymes with the words on the page, and segmenting and blending. Identify the vowel and determine if it is long or short. Sort all long-vowel words and all short-vowel words.

To assess with the vowel picture cards, say the word "ape." Ask the child what vowel is in the word. Then ask if the vowel is long or short. Read the pictures in columns (e.g., ape, overalls, apple, octopus, then eagle, unicorn, and so on). Children should not see the pictures and words during this assessment. They need to identify the vowel and then say if it is long or short. Record incorrect answers in the box below.

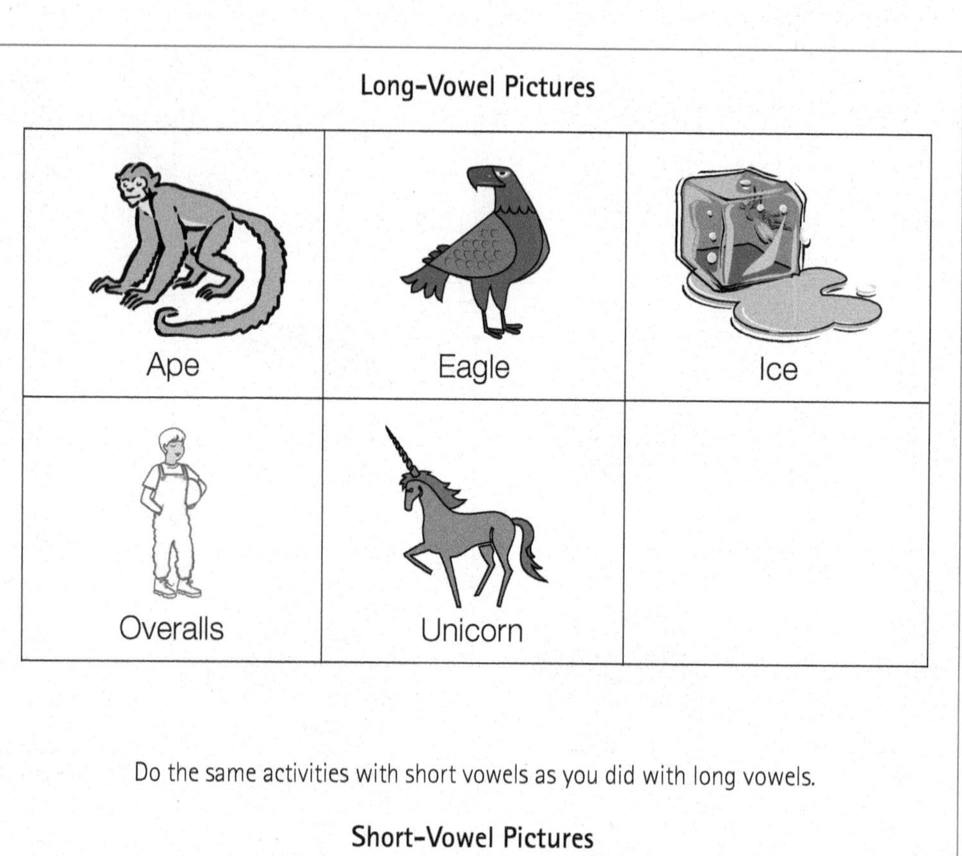

Do the same activities with short vowels as you did with long vowels.

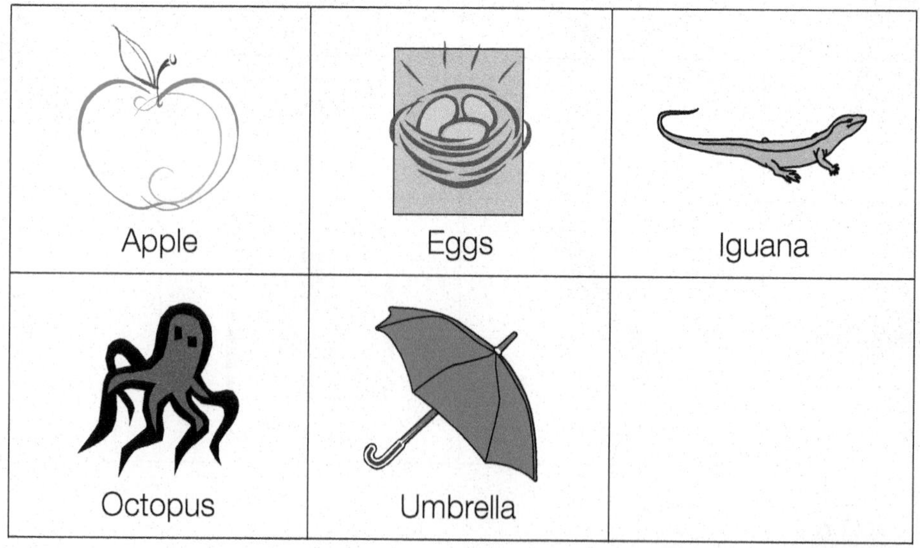

Figure 8.10 Alphabet Cards

Directions: Enlarge if necessary, copy on firm paper, laminate, and cut out. Alphabetize, match uppercase to lowercase, and match letters to picture cards.

Uppercase Letters

A	B	C	D	E	F	G
H	I	J	K	L	M	N
O	P	Q	R	S	T	U
V	W	X	Y	Z		

Lowercase Letters

a	b	c	d	e	f	g
h	i	j	k	l	m	n
o	p	q	r	s	t	u
v	w	x	y	z		

Figure 8.11 Building Words

Onset and Rimes. Enlarge if necessary, copy on firm paper, and laminate.

b	c	d	f	g	h	j
k	l	m	n	p	q	r
s	t	v	w	x	y	z

Rimes

are	ate	ake	ame
ave	ase	ain	ap
ail	ang	ear	eat
ell	end	ent	ive
est	ine	ike	ice
ime	it	ink	ing
ip	ile	in	ot
ock	oke	op	un
unk	ump	ug	uck

Figure 8.12 Sorting Words

Directions: Copy on firm paper, laminate, and cut out. Put key words on the top row of the sorting board. Classify words into their correct pile. * indicates the key word. Make new key words for additional sorts.

Pot*	Kit*	Fat*
Cat	Hot	Sit
Bit	Not	Hit
Sat	Lot	Hat
Cot	Wit	Mat
Fit	Rot	Bat

Figure 8.13 Identifying Digraphs Using Word Wheels

Directions: Enlarge if necessary; copy the two word wheels on firm paper, and laminate. Place the wheel with the onsets at the bottom and the rime at the top. Fill in various digraphs, blends, and chunks. Cut out the square tab. Fasten wheels together with a brass fastener. Rotate the wheel so that new words are made. Write the words you created on the sorting board. Use the word wheel pattern on the next page to make alternative digraphs, blends, and so forth. Students should write the words they create on a piece of paper.

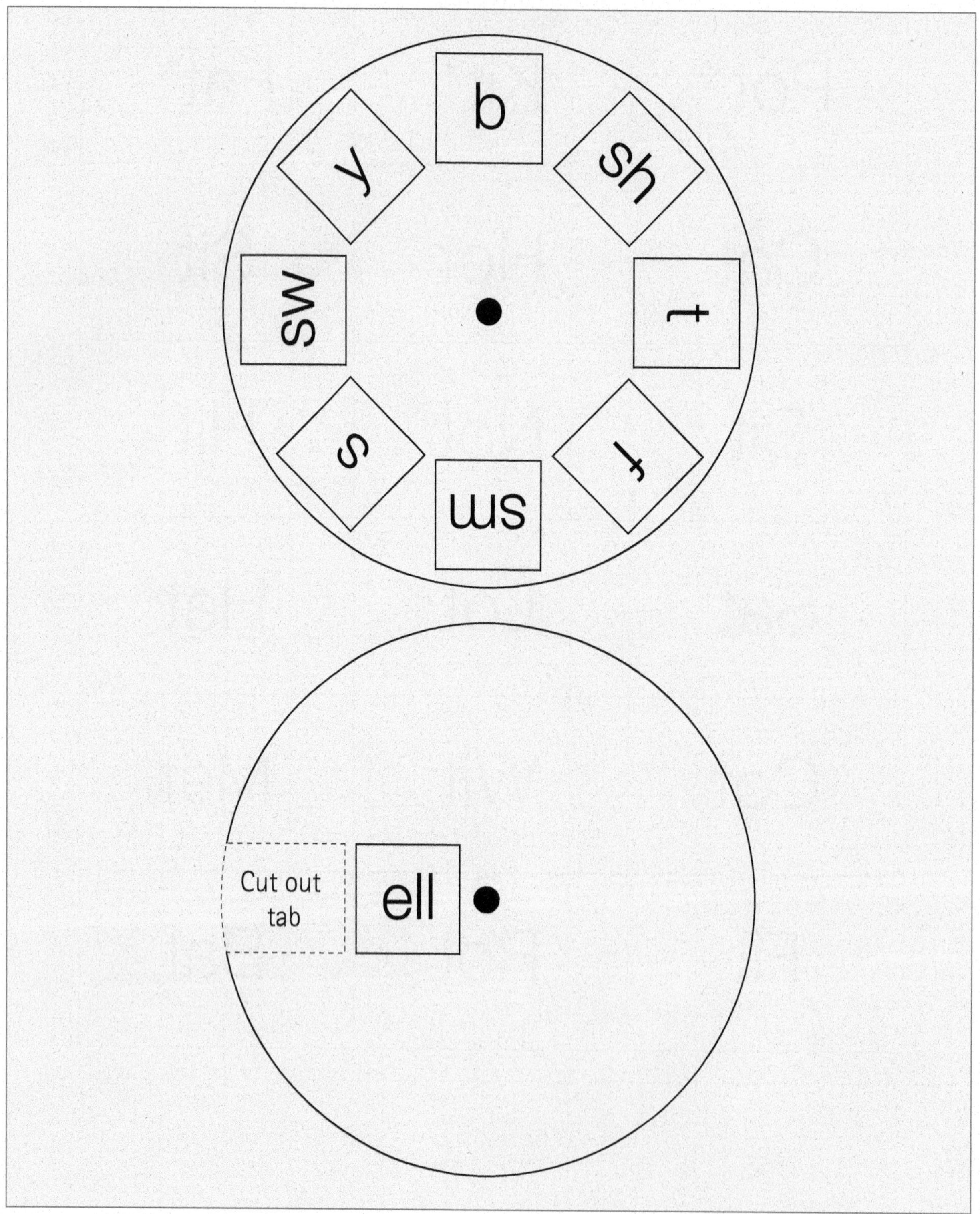

Figure 8.14 Word Wheel Templates

Directions: Enlarge if necessary and fill in phonograms or rimes in the squares of the first word wheel. Put an onset, digraph, consonant, or blend in the second word wheel. Copy the two word wheels on firm paper and laminate. Cut out the square tab. Put that word wheel on top. Fasten the wheels together with a brass fastener.

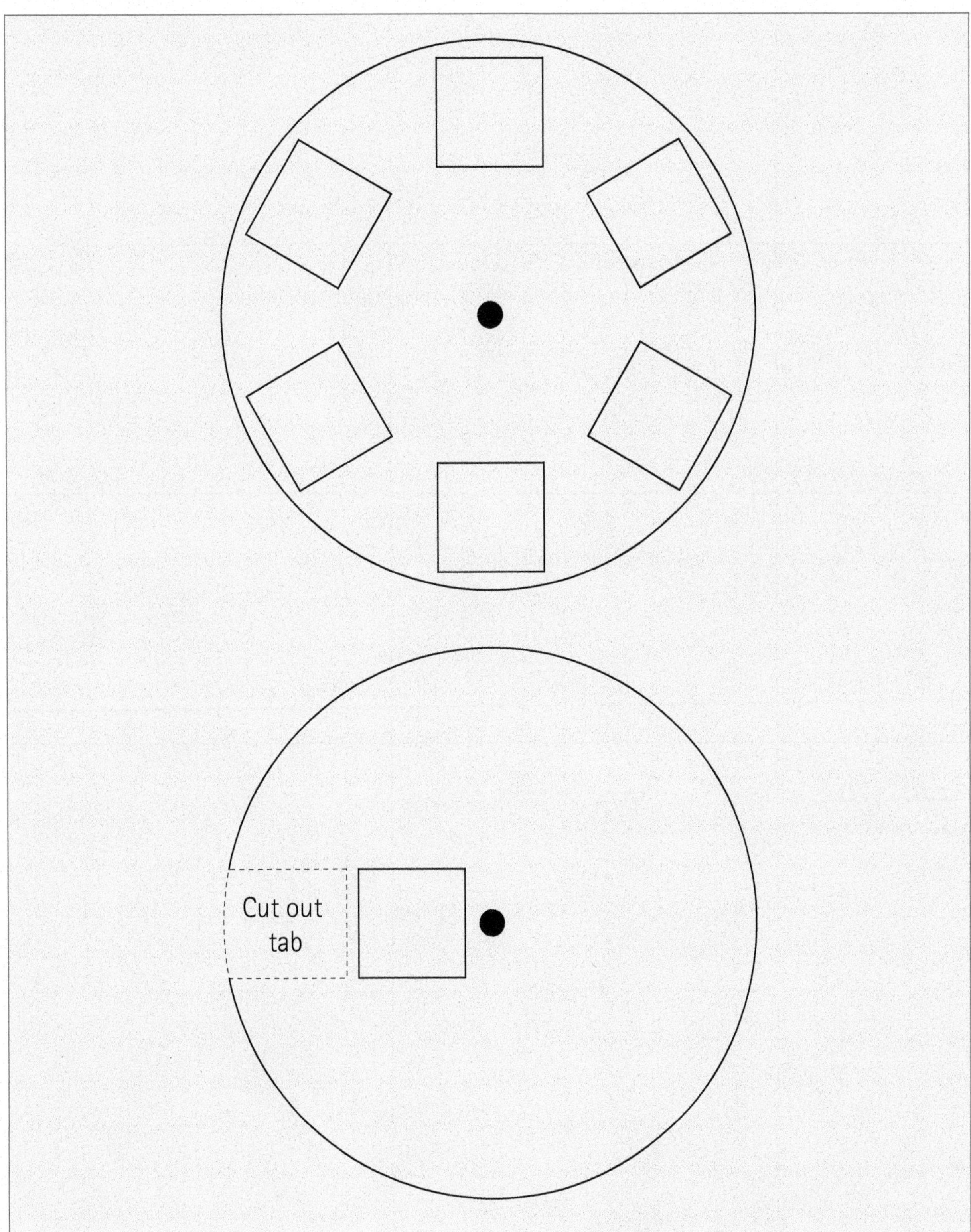

Figure 8.15 Sorting Board

Directions: This board can be used to alphabetize letters, match pictures to letters, build words with onsets and rimes, sort pictures and words by long and short vowels, and so forth. Copy onto firm paper.

Figure 8.16 Puzzle Pieces

Directions: Use the puzzle pieces for matching. Match uppercase to lowercase letters, match rhyming words and pictures to initial sounds. Copy onto firm colored paper and write in the skill or copy letters, rhyming word pictures, and initial sounds from other pages. Laminate and cut.

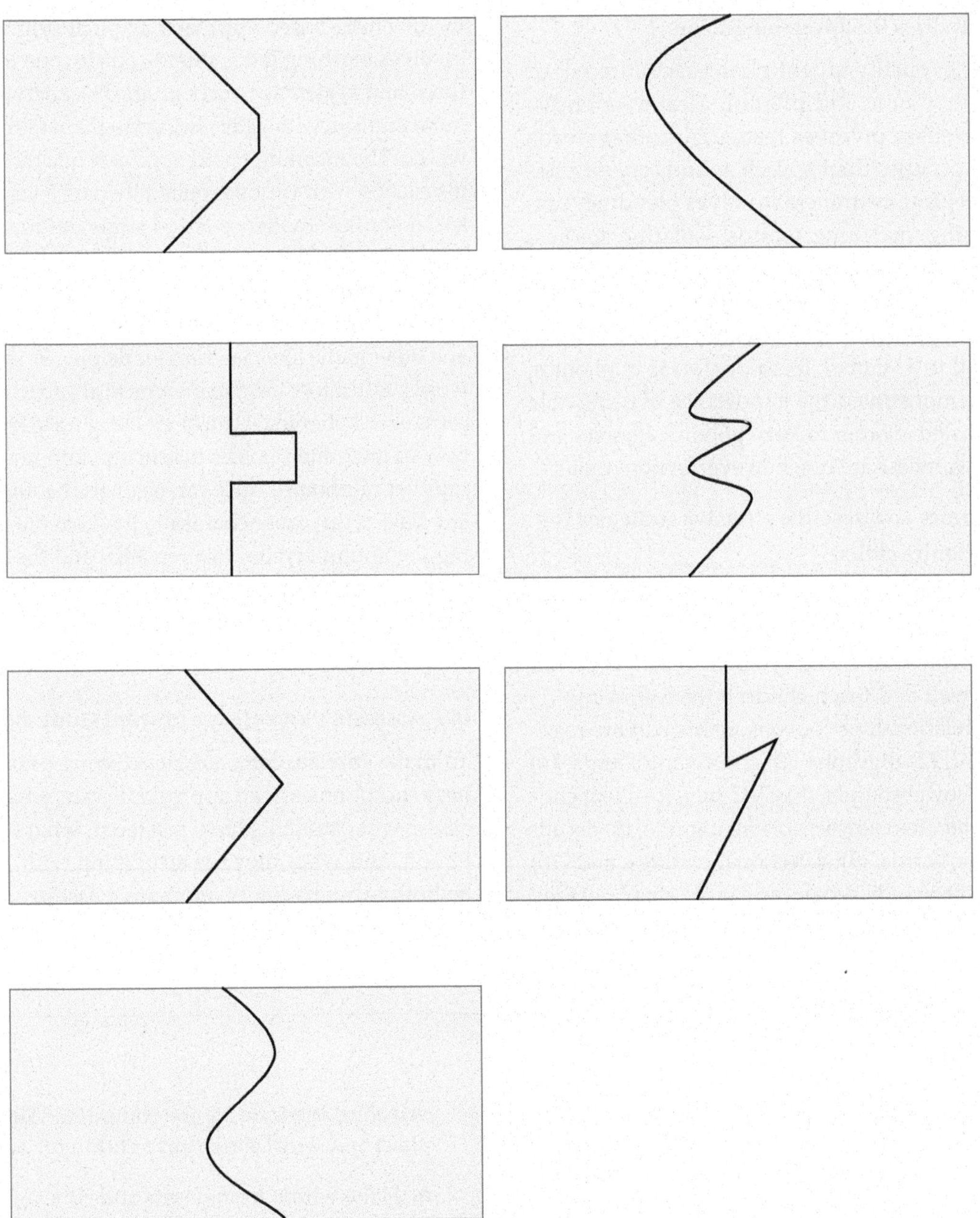

Read Around the Room

After learning a few phonic rules and sounds I assign partners to take their clip board and walk around the room to find words that follow the rules selected for them and to write it down. For example, one partner group was assigned to find words that began with *b*, *d*, and *c*. As they walked they saw *books* and wrote it down, *doors* and wrote it down and *computers*. They walked around several times and found the following words that began with *b*, *d*, and *c*.

boards, boys, boxes
drawings, donuts, desks
coats, colors, closet, candy.

Used with permission from Michelle Hagerty
First Grade Teacher

Summary

8.1 Define phonological and phonemic awareness and identify activities for developing them.

Before they are explicitly taught phonics, children need to be taught phonemic and phonological awareness. Phonemic awareness involves recognizing that words are comprised of individual speech sounds called phonemes. Phonological awareness involves blending, segmenting, rhyming, matching sounds, isolating sounds, deleting sounds, substituting, and identifying the number of sounds or syllables in a word. Phonological awareness can begin in preschool and does not ask the child to attach the sound to a symbol; it is a precursor to phonics. Research has demonstrated the importance of being able to do the tasks listed in order to learn phonics. Phonics and phonological awareness are not, however, synonymous.

8.2 Define phonics and describe effective strategies for teaching phonics skills.

Whereas phonological and phonemic awareness pertain to recognition of sounds and sound groups, phonics is the connection between sounds and symbols. Teachers should know phonics well and teach children the following: (1) sound symbol relationships for consonants that are regular and irregular, (2) digraphs, (3) consonant blends, (4) long and short vowel sounds, (5) CVC rule, (6) silent ending *e* rule, (7) when two vowels go walking rule, (8) decoding multisyllabic words, (9) inflectional endings, and (10) how to create word-study centers and managing how they are used. There are several approaches to teaching phonics, including the synthetic approach, the analytic approach, and the meaning-based approach. Explicit synthetic approach involves teaching letter sounds one by one in a very structured and systematic curriculum. The analytic approach is more implicit, with letters being taught in the context of their words. The meaning-based approach integrates the phonics instruction with various content themes, such as science and social studies. Evidence-based strategies for teaching phonics include making words, sorting words, and classifying the elements in words. Word-study centers should contain materials such as foam letters, flash cards, magnetic letters, and other game like materials for helping students play with words. Educators have many practical and overarching concerns about phonics. It can be challenging to know when and how to integrate phonics instruction into lesson plans. The number of phonics rules can be overwhelming, and different dialects can cause confusion. It is better to teach the most regular sound symbol relationships and the most dependable rules and teach the irregular words by sight. These skills should be taught in grades K, 1, and 2 for the most part, with just a bit more in grade 3.

8.3 Assessing knowledge of word study skills.

To make sure students are developing phonemic awareness and phonics at an appropriate rate, educators need to assess what students have mastered, what they are working on, and what they are struggling with. There should be both formative and summative assessments done frequently throughout the year.

Activities and Questions

1. Select three initial consonants other than *p*. Design classroom experiences that will teach and reinforce the sound–symbol relationships of each. Connect the letters to a thematic topic that is commonly studied in science or social studies in early childhood classrooms. Use traditional and authentic experiences.

2. Create lessons to teach phonics skills using your morning message words. Do another lesson with an electronic white board. Do another lesson by selecting software for the computer. With a pocket chart and word cards, have children:

   a. Make words from onsets and rimes.

   b. Sort words with similar patterns into piles.

   c. Make little words from a big word.

3. There are several pages in this chapter of activities for phonemic awareness and phonics. Select activities children would enjoy, enlarge the pages if necessary, color or copy on colored paper, laminate, and cut. Then practice the activities with children.

Chapter 9

Developing Comprehension of Text and Fluency

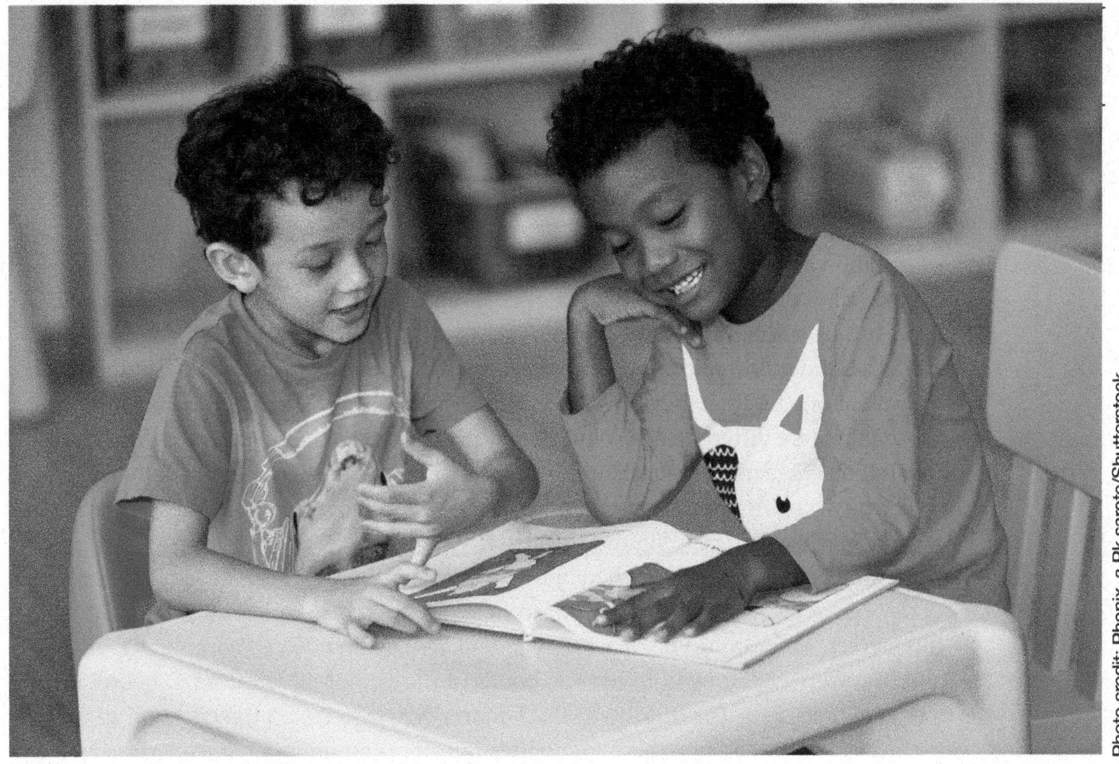

Photo credit: Phonix_a Pk.sarote/Shutterstock

LEARNING OUTCOMES

After reading this chapter, you should be able to:

9.1 Outline recent theory and research about reading comprehension.

9.2 Outline classroom organizational strategies for teaching comprehension.

9.3 Summarize important reading research-based strategies that enhance a child's comprehension of text.

9.4 Discuss the role of fluency in comprehension and strategies to enhance fluency.

9.5 Review and summarize how to assess children's comprehension of text.

VOCABULARY

Antiphonal reading
Buddy reading
Choral reading
Close reading
Comprehension
Directed listening/reading thinking activity
Echo reading
Fluency
Graphic organizers
Informational text
K-W-L
Literature circles
Mapping and webbing
Mental imagery
Metacognition
Narrative literature
Paired reading
Partner reading
Reader's Theater
Reading workshop
Reciprocal teaching
Repeated reading
Think-alouds
Think, pair, share

For several months, Ms. Win has been discussing different authors and illustrators with the children in her first-grade class. She has their favorites on a chart in her classroom. Today Ms. Win asked the children to add names to the list because they had recently read stories by authors and illustrators who were new to them. First, she asked for authors, and the following names were mentioned: Ezra Jack Keats, Tomie dePaola, Leo Lionni, and Arnold Lobel. Next, she asked if they could name some illustrators, and students came up with the following names: Dr. Seuss, Eric Carle, and Maurice Sendak. Jamie raised her hand and said, "Hey, I noticed something weird. All of the authors named are also illustrators and all of the illustrators are all authors too." Christopher raised his hand and said, "That's not so weird. I know a bunch of people who are authors and illustrators. There's me, and Josh, Jennifer, and Patrick . . . " Christopher was looking around the room and naming all the children in the class. When he finished naming his classmates, he continued, "We're all authors and illustrators. We all write books and illustrate them. We publish them and they are in our classroom library. How could we forget that?"

Ms. Win projected two t-charts on the electronic white board (refer to Figure 9.1). One t-chart was labeled "Authors" and the other was labeled "Illustrators." Each chart had "Dr. Seuss" on one side of the t and "Ezra Jack Keats" on the other. Ms. Win explained to the children that the t-chart was a strategy to help organize and understand information read. The t-chart would help them compare and contrast the characteristics of the authors and the illustrators. It would help to find out what they had in common and what characteristics were different. Ms. Win then guided the children by modeling how to use the t-chart. She asked them to think of the characteristics of each author's illustrations first and typed the ideas under each author's name. Then she asked the children to talk about each author's stories as she listed the characteristics they mentioned. When they finished, the class looked for characteristics in common and those that were different. Ms. Win moved the words off the t-chart that described the illustration characteristics and the authors' story characteristics and mixed them up. She selected two pairs of children to move them back onto the t-chart in the proper places.

On another day, Ms. Win did this activity with the whole class again but used two new author–illustrators. She then had pairs of children work on their own t-charts on paper. She walked around the room to help. Finally, the t-chart activity was put into the literacy center to do during independent center time. When completing this task, children were encouraged to use the books of the author–illustrators to help with the characteristics lists, in addition to the t-charts. Ms. Win asked the children to draw a picture or write a sentence about how these authors and illustrators were the same and how they were different.

The steps for instruction included (1) explaining the purpose of the strategy, (2) modeling the use of the strategy, (3) having the students practice the strategy with the teacher's guidance, and (4) using the strategy in a cooperative setting with a partner. Ms. Win gave the children choices to make a decision about summarizing similarities either through illustration or writing.

Figure 9.1. T-charts

Authors		Illustrators	
Dr. Seuss	**Ezra Jack Keats**	**Dr. Seuss**	**Ezra Jack Keats**
Rhymes	No rhymes	Bold colors	Bright colors
Created characters	Real people and animals	Watercolor	Collage
Imaginary	Real-life story	Cartoons	Realistic
Made-up words	Real words		

Theory and Research on Comprehension of Text

Comprehension is necessary for a child to be a successful reader. The ability to decode is necessary for a child to be an independent reader. However, as the reader becomes more sophisticated, he begins to rely less on decoding. Fluent readers who comprehend are successful readers. According to Almasi and Fullerton (2013), readers with good comprehension have the following skills:

- They read materials from the beginning to end.
- They slow down their reading when they come to information that is relevant to what they want to remember.
- They anticipate the content of the text based on prior knowledge about the topic.
- They reflect on ideas in the text by creating summaries about what they have read.
- They refer to the text for important information to clarify issues.
- They use multiple strategies that they intentionally selected because they saw them as those that would help them understand best.
- They can describe to you the strategies they use and why.

Comprehension is an active process in which the reader or listener interprets and constructs meaning about what he or she reads or listens to based on prior knowledge about the topic, thereby making connections between the old and the new (Applegate, Applegate, & Modla, 2009; Pressley & Hilden, 2002). This concept arises from research on schema theory that suggests that we have schemata (background knowledge) for certain information based on prior experience with a given topic. That schema is never complete because more can always be learned about a subject. For example, if someone told us something about a hands-on science museum, we would gain one bit of information; if we saw pictures of this museum, we would have additional information; and if we went to the museum, we would know even more. Then, when we read about this or went to other science museums or listened to a story about them, the new information would expand and refine what we already know. To truly comprehend narrative or expository literature that is read or listened to, a child must integrate his or her prior knowledge concerning a topic with the new text to create new knowledge (Pressley & Hilden, 2002; Hannon, 2012).

Comprehension development is enhanced by children's social interactions with others during reading and writing experiences (Rand Reading Study Group, 2002). For example, children benefit from early experiences with books that are mediated by an adult who provides problem-solving situations. The child is asked to respond, and the adult offers information when necessary. In such situations, children and adults interact to integrate, construct, and make relationships with printed text. Children need to have multiple experiences with a variety of texts and levels of texts on a daily basis to learn to comprehend (Duke & Pearson, 2002).

When children are read to or read independently, their comprehension is determined by:

- The familiarity of the content in the text
- The background knowledge required to understand the text
- The quality of the writing
- How interesting the topic is to the listeners or readers
- The syntactic complexity of the sentences
- The amount and difficulty of vocabulary included
- The length of a selection that is read or listened to (Graves, Juel, & Graves, 1998).

Developing metacognitive abilities is an aid to comprehension. **Metacognition** is one's own awareness of how his or her learning is taking place (Cobb, 2017). When it comes to comprehension, it means that students can articulate how they are able to comprehend something read and what strategies they selected to use and why. These children can also articulate the problems they have comprehended and then discuss how those problems might be solved. When students engage in metacognition, or self-monitoring, they can choose the appropriate comprehened strategy for the text and can regulate, check, and repair their reading processes as they go (Dewitz, Jones, & Leahy, 2009; Gunning, 2003).

In an important and classic piece of research about comprehension, Dolores Durkin (Durknin, 1978–1979) found that comprehension was rarely taught in the primary grades. In early childhood we thought that this was the time we "learn to read" and in the elementary grades we "read to learn." During the 1980s, many investigations about comprehension were carried out by the Center for the Study of Reading at the University of Illinois in Urbana and, as a result of that and other work that followed, more attention has been paid to teaching comprehension in the primary grades. A report entitled *Reading for Understanding: Toward a Research and Development Program in Reading Comprehension*, by the Rand Reading Study Group (2002) and published by the U.S. Office of Educational Research and Improvement in Washington, DC, and a report entitled *National Reading Panel Report* (National Reading Panel Report, 2000) discuss the comprehension strategies that need to be taught to students and how they should be taught. Both reports draw on research about successful comprehension practice. Recently, Almasi and Hart (2011) emphasized that, although we teach children to use strategies, we don't teach them to be strategic readers. Strategic readers can decide which approach is appropriate to use and can employ multiple strategies together.

Objectives and Standards to Develop Comprehension of Narrative and Informational Text

We have many groups that have written standards for comprehension development. The Common Core State Standards had a very strong emphasis on comprehension. The ultimate goal for reading instruction is constructing meaning from text. When getting meaning from text, children are expected to have competence in self-monitoring and self-correcting strategies. When children self-monitor their reading, they are strategic readers. They are able to discuss how they figured out the meaning and what strategies they used (Brown, 2008; Park, 2012). They also raise questions about what the author is saying. Children who demonstrate comprehension can do the following by the end of third grade:

- Comprehend text when reading books that have subplots as well as a main plot.
- Understand nonfiction that contains concepts with different structures presented in complex and compound sentences.
- Grasp meaning from figurative language such as similes and metaphors.
- Compare one text to another text they have read or heard.
- Explain motives of characters (National Center on Education and the Economy and the Learning Research and Development Center at the University of Pittsburgh, 1999). Figure 9.2 lists the generally accepted objectives for teaching comprehension of both narrative and informational text.

Integrating Comprehension into the Curriculum

Comprehension skills are taught from pre-K through college. Each day in school there should be a lesson based on standards and your school curriculum dealing with comprehension. Take advantage of teachable moments when they occur during the day

Figure 9.2 Objectives for Comprehension of Narrative and Expository Literature in Text and Digital Form

1. Attempts to read well-known storybooks that result in the telling of a well-formed story
2. Participates in story reading by saying words and narrating stories as the teacher reads
3. Participates in cooperative learning activities to construct comprehension of text
4. Answers questions and participates in discussions and activities involving:
   a. literal thinking that asks the reader to identify details, such as who, what, when, and where, and to classify, sequence, and find the main idea
   b. inferential and critical thinking that asks the reader to predict with evidence from the text; interpret (for example, how would you feel if you were that character, what would you do); draw from background knowledge; make connections from text to the child's life; make connections from the text to the world; make connections from one text to another; evaluate; compare and contrast; and determine cause and effect with evidence from the text
5. Generates questions, discussions, and activities involving:
   a. literal thinking that asks the reader who, what, when, where to classify and sequence
   b. inferential and critical thinking that asks the reader to predict; interpret (for example, how would you feel if you were that character, what would you do); draw from background knowledge; connect text to life; evaluate; compare and contrast; determine cause and effect; and apply information and problem solve; can answer questions with evidence from the text
6. Uses graphic organizers:
   a. Maps
   b. Webs
   c. K-W-L
   d. t-charts
   e. Venn diagrams
   f. Graphs
   g. Charts
7. Recognizes and understands features of and structures in expository text such as:
   a. Features in expository text
      (1) Table of contents
      (2) Headings
      (3) Glossary
      (4) Index
      (5) Diagrams
   b. Structures to learn in expository text
      (1) *Description:* Gives the reader a picture of the subject based on story observation.
      (2) *Sequence:* Explains the steps that produce a certain product or outcome.
      (3) *Compare and contrast:* These are comparisons that include items with a similar classification that are compared first and then contrasted. Point-by-point comparisons describe similarities and differences alternately.
      (4) *Cause and effect:* Causality tells why something happens.
      (5) *Problem–solution:* A problem is presented, followed by its solution. An understanding of chronology is necessary to comprehend this structure.
      (6) *Exemplification (reason and example):* The main idea is printed with supporting details (Vukelich, Evans, & Albertson, 2003).
8. Recognizes and understands structures of narrative text such as:
   a. *Setting:* beginning, time, place, characters
   b. *Theme:* main character's problem or goal
   c. *Plot episodes:* events leading to solving the main character's problem or reaching his or her goal
   d. *Resolution:* problem solution, goal achievement, ending
9. Engages in summarizing activities
   a. Retelling
   b. Drawing conclusions
10. Engages in mental imagery
11. Can provide evidence from the text
12. Can close read to analyze deep meaning
13. Engages in cooperative activities, such as the following:
    a. Collaborative response groups
    b. Think, pair, share
    c. Think-alouds

Figure 9.2 Objectives for Comprehension of Narrative and Expository Literature in Text and Digital Form (*continued*)

  - **d.** Literature circles
  - **e.** Buddy reading
  - **f.** Partner reading
  - **g.** Reciprocal teaching

14. Uses multiple strategies when needed

15. Monitors his or her comprehension (metacognition)
  - **a.** *Knows* what he or she understands in a passage
  - **b.** *Knows* what he or she doesn't understand in a passage
  - **c.** *Knows* which strategies to use to *help understand what was read*

16. Uses references and study skills that involve the following:
  - **a.** The dictionary
  - **b.** Internet searches
  - **c.** SQ3R: survey, question, read, recite, review

17. Participates in fluency training:
  - **a.** Echo reading
  - **b.** Choral reading
  - **c.** Tape-assisted reading
  - **d.** Antiphonal reading
  - **e.** Paired reading
  - **f.** Reader's Theater
  - **g.** Repeated reading

18. Uses digital literacies for all skills when appropriate

to reinforce the skills being taught. Purposefully integrate as appropriate whatever skill you are emphasizing into science, social studies, math, play, music, and art. For example, if you are reading a book about rain in a theme about weather, let children talk about their own life experiences with rain that were funny or scary or interesting to make text-to-life connections. Then ask about books they have read about weather.

Teaching in small groups helps teachers better determine students' individual needs. Small groups allow you to find out what students have learned and what they need to learn. Small groups also allow you to differentiate instruction by designing lessons for the students needing more challenging or easier work. Strategies should be taught when needed, and children should be encouraged to use multiple strategies simultaneously.

Using Literature Throughout the School Day. Literacy instruction must happen all day long if children are to become fluent readers by the end of third grade. Students who are not reading on grade level by the end of third grade will likely never reach grade level and are at risk of dropping out of school. (Only 10% of students reading below level at the end of third grade ever reach grade level.) There is nothing more important in the primary grades than to teach children to read.

During the time specified for explicit reading instruction, teachers need to use standards as benchmark goals. That is, when teachers are instructing on decoding, comprehension, writing, speaking, listening, and language development, they will rely on standards. These standards and techniques can also be applied to instruction in music, art, math, science, social studies, and physical education. Teachers must connect comprehension standards with their lessons in other content areas. For example, a social studies unit about the meaning of good citizenship and the value of helping others would be enhanced by students knowing the details of a story such as *The Lion and the Rat* (Wildsmith, 1995).

In a science unit about the winter, learning scientific facts can be supported by narrative fiction with themes of the winter and snow, such as *The Mitten* (Brett, 1989). After the children listen to the story, the teacher asks them to recall the animals that went into the mitten to get warm. During art, as a motivation to making winter collages, the teacher can read *The Snowy Day*, by Ezra Jack Keats (Keats, 1996). In all of his books, Keats uses watercolors and collage materials. Children can look through this book to find the collage materials to generate ideas for their snow collages.

Working with narrative text in this way engages the children in practicing skills that will help them with their comprehension of narrative text and enhance their knowledge about the theme they are studying. By integrating reading skills into the theme, the reading skills become relevant and useful to students and motivate them to develop even further.

MyLab Education Self-Check 9.1

Classroom Organizational Strategies for Teaching Comprehension

The Basic Lesson Plan for Teaching Comprehension

When learning strategies, children must play an active role as they respond to literature in different ways. Select narrative and informational literature that is well-structured. **Narrative literature**, contains clearly delineated settings, themes, episodes, and resolutions. Quality informational literature, or **informational text**, presents non-fiction content area information to children in the following structures: description, sequence, compare and contrast, cause and effect, problem solution, and exemplification.

Most comprehension strategies will be useful with both narrative and expository (nonfiction) text. (Throughout the chapter, indications are given as to whether the strategies being discussed are particularly useful with one or the other.) Guided teaching of comprehension strategies has been found to be most effective when using the following techniques:

Photo credit: Annie Fuller/ Pearson Education

Directed listening and thinking activities set a purpose for reading or listening and help focus students' thoughts.

Explanation: The teacher explains what the strategy is, why it is important, and when it is used.

Modeling: The teacher demonstrates the use of the strategy by modeling and scaffolding it for the children.

Guided practice: The teacher provides an opportunity for the students to practice using the strategy. The teacher guides the students in how and when to use the strategy. Guided practice is a good time for students to work together so they can help each other learn.

Independent application: The teacher provides time for students to practice the strategy without guidance so they can carry it out without assistance.

Reflection: The child thinks about how the strategy can be used in other situations. The child thinks about how good he or she is at using the strategy (McLaughlin, 2010).

This basic plan can be used in read alouds, shared reading, in reading workshop, guided reading and most any instructional approach for teaching reading.

Directed Listening/Reading and Thinking Activity

An important structure in promoting comprehension is the **Directed Listening/Reading and Thinking Activity (DLTA/DRTA)**. This strategy is used when a book is being read by the child for the first time or the teacher is reading it to the children.

A key component of the strategy involves setting a purpose for reading and sharing that purpose with the student. Knowing the purpose in advance will help direct students' thoughts and give them a sense of how to approach the reading or listening. The goal is for children to apply the strategy when they read independently and use the structure to aid their comprehension. Teachers who frequently provide a context for reading will have children who internalize the strategy and use it for reading new and unfamiliar material (Morrow, Gambrell, & Freitag, 2009). There are many different objectives for the DRTA or DLTA but the framework is always similar: (1) prepare for reading with some discussion about the book; (2) provide children with the purpose or objective for listening or reading and scaffold that behavior for them; (3) have the children read the story or listen to the teacher read the story to them; and (4) discuss the story after reading with an emphasis on the purpose. This framework offers the reader a strategy for organizing and retrieving information about the text and discussing it.

The DRTA/DLTA strategy can be used to promote different types of comprehension. Following is a lesson that illustrates the application of this strategy with the well-known story of *The Little Red Hen* (Izawa, 1968). The objective or standard for the children is to demonstrate the ability to describe the characters in a story and remember the sequence of events to retell.

Prepare Children to Listen or Read with a Discussion. "Today you will be reading/listening to a story entitled *The Little Red Hen*. Let's look at the pictures to see if you can tell what the story is going to be about." Have the children take a quick *book walk* which is turning the pages of the book and noticing characters, or other things that give clues about the content. This should take no longer than a minute or two. Encourage children to respond as they turn the pages. After they have offered their ideas, say, "The story is about a hen who wants to bake some bread and asks her friends for some help. Have you ever asked people for help? What kind of help? Did they help you? As you listen or read try to remember all the characters in the story. One of the characters is the Little Read Hen. Can you look in the book and tell me another character that is there?" This is repeated so children know what a character is. Then talk about what is first, next and last. By scaffolding for the children, they will better understand what it is you want them to do or learn. Also remember what happened first, next and last. Give evidence from the text about the sequence. That is look back at the book after you have sequenced to see if you are right. "Now that I've told you a little about the story, what do you want to find out when you read it?" Write down the children's questions.

The Children Read the Story. As the children read the story, direct them to look at the pictures to help them understand what they are reading. Allow the children to read the book all the way through. Help them with words if they need assistance.

Discussion After Reading. With the DLTA/DRTA strategy, the objective of the lesson also should be the focus of the discussion. This type of lesson can focus on literal responses such as recall facts and sequencing; inferential responses such as interpreting characters' feelings, predicting outcomes, and relating the story to real-life experiences; and critical responses such as evaluating, problem solving, and making judgments. More concretely, directed narrative reading lessons can focus on identifying elements of story structure and require children to support their answers with evidence from the text under study. Regardless of the objectives, directed narrative reading lessons help youngsters draw meaning from the print. Research has demonstrated that this model can increase the story comprehension of young listeners (Baumann, 1992; Pearson, Roehler, Dole, & Duffy, 1992).

In the example of *The Little Red Hen*, therefore, the post-reading discussion should be guided by the objectives or purpose set for reading: First to list the characters, and then retell the story with what came first, next, and last. At another time with the same book, the goal could be inference and then you might ask the children: What would you have done if you were the little red hen and none of the farm animals would help you? Do you think she did the right thing when she didn't share her bread with the animals? Why or why not? What lesson can we learn from this story?" Were you right when I wrote down for you what you wanted to find out?

Directed Reading and Thinking Activity with Informational Text. When using informational literature, your discussion is likely to be more fact-oriented rather than about feelings. You might be describing the relationship between a series of scientific ideas or concepts and using language that pertains to cause and effect or problem solution.

MyLab Education
Video Example 9.1
Complexities of Comprehension
Danielle Murphy reads an informational text.
www.youtube.com/watch?v=9yZCwEfY7nI

Figure 9.3 contains a vignette of a third-grade lesson for using the informational text *The Red-Eyed Tree Frog* (Cowley & Bishop, 2005). The standard involved is to describe the relationship between the scientific ideas or steps in the text, using language that pertains to time, sequence and cause and effect. Discussing a new piece of informational text is in some ways very similar to discussing a new piece of narrative literature and in other ways very different. When using a directed reading/listening strategy for an informational text:

- Ask the children what they know about the topic.
- Preview the book by looking at the table of contents, pictures, diagrams, and headings.
- Review the headings and prompt children to predict what information they think they will learn. Instruct students to write down their predictions in question form.
- Ask the children to read the text themselves.

Figure 9.3 Example of Expository Directed Reading Lesson

The class had been learning about amphibians and different types of frogs were being discussed. Ms. Erin brought copies of *Red-Eyed Tree Frog* (Croley, 2005) for the students to read on their own. The purpose for the reading was to able to describe the sequence of events in the story and the cause and effect or problem and solution related to the frog in the book. She asked the children to look through the book and jot down some thoughts about the book on sticky notes on the pages that raised issues for them. She told them that when they read the story they were to list the sequence of events and the problem that the frog had and how he solved it. Ms. Erin asked for some predictions about what they were going to read, and Josh said, "Well, it looks like the frog is looking for some animal, or insect, since he seems to be talking with different ones he meets along the way." Elena said, "I think he wants to find his way somewhere and is asking directions." Ms. Erin suggested that they had good ideas but needed to read the book to find out.

She said before they began, "Is there anything about the book itself that you would like to comment on now that you have looked through it but not read it yet?" Zach said, "It is an informational book since it has a table of contents; it also has photographs and in the back is a section called *Did You Know?* It seems like there might be more information there about the frog." "You are right, Zach. Let's read the book now, and when you are done write down the sequence of events and the problem the frog had and how he solved it. When you are done, turn to your partner and discuss this with them before we share with the whole group."

When everyone was finished reading and had some time to turn and talk to a partner, Ms. Erin continued the conversation. "Were any of your predictions correct?" Johanna raised her hand, as did a few other children who had figured out what caused the frog to go from one creature to another. He wasn't looking for directions or information—he was looking for food. Jeremy raised his hand and said, "I understand why the frog didn't eat the iguana and the poisonous caterpillar, but I wonder why he ate a moth but didn't eat an ant or the katydid." Jack raised his hand and said, "I read the end called *Did You Know?* and it said that frogs stay away from ants and caterpillars since ants bite and caterpillars are big for them to swallow and have spines. Their favorite foods are moths, flies, spiders, and small grasshoppers." Mrs. Erin said, "I guess we don't have to look it up now. Please go on to read about other types of frogs and list the interesting things you find out about them."

- Instruct children to review their predictions to see if they were right or wrong.
- Identify the main idea and support their choice with details from the text.
- Sequence the steps that produce a certain product or outcome.
- Think about the cause and effect of actions in the text.
- Identify the problem and discuss the solution (Templeton & Gehsman, 2014; Vukelich, Evans, & Albertson, 2003).

MyLab Education Application Exercise 9.1

The Reading Comprehension Workshop

The **reading comprehension workshop** is an organizational structure that can be used with both expository and narrative text. The workshop begins with

1. A mini lesson to teach comprehension skills.
2. The children practice the skill just learned by reading a book of their choice alone or with a partner
3. The teacher circulates amongst the children or sits at a table and conferences with children discussing the text.
4. There is a share time for children to give book talks about what they read.

To get started, it is important to recognize that the term *workshop* may suggest there is a sequence of activities that occur within a specific amount of time (depending on the teacher's schedule). The components and timing of the workshop are:

1. A high-quality mini lesson to teach a comprehension skill (a sample lesson was just described). The lesson includes a read aloud (30% of the allotted time).
2. Independent/partner reading to practice the comprehension strategy taught (50% of allotted time).
3. The teacher conferences with some of the children during the independent reading to enhance skills (conferencing happens during independent reading, so time is not allotted).
4. The reading comprehension workshop ends with sharing information about what was read and discussing the comprehension skill (20% of the allotted time).

When introducing reading workshop, talk first about where it will be in the classroom. Usually, teachers will conduct the mini lesson with the children sitting on the rug in the literacy center. After they read aloud, the children partner to read independently to practice the skill learned. Similar to musicians, readers need plenty of opportunities to practice. Children need to learn how to read independently read. Teachers need to:

- Ensure that students are engaging in "eyes on the page" reading with a purpose.
- Confer with students during this time to set goals.
- Allow children to choose books to read. They are likely to read if they have some choice.

Children often need help with choosing books. Provide them with this help.

Choosing "Just Right" Books.

- Choose a book that the teacher has read aloud that you liked.
- Choose a book in a series that you are reading and enjoy.

- Look at the cover page and title.
- Look at a few pages.
- Use the "five finger rule."

Open to the middle of the book. Put one hand on the print so that each finger touches a word. Read the five words your fingers are on. If you can read four of the five words, the book is a just right book for you.

Partner Reading. Partner reading is suggested during this independent time. Children will be responsible to each other when working together and consequently produce more. Allow students of different ability levels to work together, however a "just right" partnership is necessary so children support one another. Prior to letting students work together, model a successful partnership with the class looking on, as others model working together. Let children know the accountability for work to complete, partners are accountable to each other and the teacher. Monitor partnerships to ensure that students are working with respect for one another.

Purpose for Conferences. While the children are reading, the teacher will conduct conferences. The purpose of the conference is to:

- Notice students' reading comprehension strengths
- Set goals for reading comprehension
- Encourage worthwhile conversation

Keep conferences brief and confirm that children are on task and completing their work.

What Is the Purpose of Sharing? Sharing creates an environment of respect, rapport, and reinforces a culture for learning. Sharing holds students accountable for staying on task during independent reading. Share time is an opportunity to allow students to discuss their successes, which can include applying a reading strategy, further developing a reading skill, meeting a goal, or overcoming a challenge.

The following is a reading comprehension workshop: The mini lesson begins with the teacher speaking about the purpose for the lesson. The standard objective for this lesson is: *With prompting and support, children can retell the key details of the text in the proper sequence. They will also be able to show evidence from the text based on their responses.*

The teacher will begin with a discussion, then read aloud. There will be more discussion at the end of the story. The discussion will be about the objectives to determine details and the theme of the story. After the lesson, children choose a book and practice thinking about the details and the theme of their chosen book as they read. The following is an example of a reading comprehension workshop mini lesson in a first grade:

> Ms. Monaco said, "Readers, we have been reading informational books and figuring out the details that will lead us to the main idea. We read this informational book called *The Cricket*. What did we find out about crickets?" Jasmine raised her hand and said, "Crickets eat plants." "That's right," said Ms. Monaco. "What else?" Jeremy said, "They also eat garbage and other crickets, and that seems gross to me." "Anyone else?" asked Ms. Monaco. Sarina said, "They eat at night because they are nocturnal." "Very good," said Ms. Monaco. While the children were speaking she wrote down their ideas on chart paper. She read them back and said, "Readers, I'm thinking that the author wants us to know that the main idea is that crickets eat many things including other crickets, and, because they are nocturnal, they eat at night."

The lesson above is based on a first grade standard for informational literature that says: *Children should learn to identify the main topics and retell key details of the text.*

The reading comprehension workshop continues as partners and to discuss the details and main idea with their partner after reading. At share time children report on their findings.

MyLab Education Self-Check 9.2

Summarize Important Reading Research-Based Strategies That Enhance a Child's Comprehension of Text

In addition to receiving formal instruction on skills that foster comprehension, students also need to have multiple types of reading experiences. Individual reading is important, as are collective reading and collaborative reading. Taken together, they convey that reading is a personal as well as social pursuit. Reading experiences should also include opportunities to closely examine texts and to experience the same texts multiple times.

Collective Read Experiences

Collective reading experiences help reinforce techniques and understandings that children have learned in formal instruction and are practicing on their own. It usually involves the entire class or small group instruction. A read aloud, shared book experiences, and small-group readings are important collective reading experiences.

Read Aloud. A read aloud is enjoyed by children at all grade levels. They provide an opportunity for teachers to expose children to fluent reading of both literary and informational text. In a read aloud, the teacher introduces a new book, which can be to use a particular comprehension strategy, new vocabulary, and so on.

Books are often selected because they are related to a theme being studied, such as animals or plants. Often, a read aloud is a selection that is too difficult for children to

Figure 9.4 Guidelines for Teacher Behavior During Storybook Reading

SOURCE: From L. M. Morrow, Young children's responses to one-to-one story readings in school settings, *Reading Research Quarterly*, *23*(1), 89–107. Copyright 1988 by the International Reading Association.

1. Manage
   a. Introduce story.
   b. Provide background information about the book.
   c. Redirect irrelevant discussion back to the story.
2. Prompt Responses with Narrative and Expository Text
   a. Invite children to ask questions or comments about the story when there are natural places to stop.
   b. Scaffold responses for children to model, if no responses are forthcoming. ("Those animals aren't very nice. They won't help the little red hen.")
   c. Relate responses to real-life experiences. ("I needed help when I was preparing a party, and my family shared the work. Did you ever ask for help and couldn't find anyone to give it to you? What happened?")
   d. When children do not respond, ask questions that require answers other than yes or no. ("What would you have done if you were the little red hen and no one helped you bake the bread?")
   e. With expository text, focus on sequencing, description, compare and contrast, and cause and effect.
3. Support and Inform
   a. Answer questions as they are asked.
   b. React to comments.
   c. Relate your responses to real-life experiences.
   d. Provide positive reinforcement for children's responses.

read independently, but is text they can comprehend and one that creates critical discussion. Teachers are often surprised at the deep level of discussion that can be achieved. The format is similar to the directed reading lesson described earlier. (Guidelines for teacher behavior during storybook reading are contained in Figure 9.4.) The following type of approach would be used with a narrative book:

> The read aloud starts with introducing the book using a quick book walk. Ask the children what they think the story will be about. Once reading has commenced, try to sustain it. Stopping to discuss a particular idea is acceptable, but don't interrupt the flow of the reading more than once or twice—save the discussion for after the reading.

Teachers will use a read aloud to nurture comprehension in different ways. With a narrative text, teachers will ask children to make connections to other texts, to the children's lives, or to the world. Children will discuss the traits of characters as well as their feelings and thoughts. Children will also discuss the character's point of view and how the author's use of dialogue, words, and phrases creates a certain style. Conversely, when reading an informational text, teachers will focus less on stylistics and more on developing the new vocabulary in the book. Discussion of this type of text should include descriptions, sequencing of events or steps, identification of causes and related effects, identification of problems and proposed or possible solutions, and comparisons (Santoro, Baker, Fien, Smith, & Chard, 2016).

Shared Book Experiences. Although it may be used in small groups, the shared book experience is usually carried out in a whole-class setting. The format is similar to a read aloud and the directed narrative or informational reading lesson. Whereas those types of lessons are used in conjunction with a new book read to the children, a shared book reading is usually done with a book that has been read to the children in the past. During this activity, children are asked to participate in some way. They may repeat a phrase that is used frequently in the book. Teachers take the opportunity to read with fluency to provide an excellent model.

Often, shared book reading involves reading from a Big Book (described in Chapter 5), so that everyone in the group can see the pictures and the words clearly while the story is being read. When a book is being read for the second (or more) time the text should already be familiar, so immediate participation is encouraged. The teacher uses a pointer during the reading to emphasize left to right progression with younger children and the correspondence of spoken and written words (Morrison & Wlodarczuk, 2009).

Children's participation could include chanting together repeated phrases in the story or having children read key words that are special to the story. Likewise, the teacher could stop at predictable parts and ask the children to fill in words and phrases. Shared book experiences could include echo reading: the teacher reads one line and the children repeat it. After first reading the story with a Big Book, the teacher should make available both the Big Book and regular-size copies of the story to the children.

One way to enhance a shared book reading is to record it and make it available in the listening station. The recording provides a familiar and fluent model for reading with good phrasing and intonation for children to emulate. Shared book experiences by the teacher or on tape provide a participatory and enjoyable read-aloud event. They also enable children to find the key details and listen to a well-structured narrative story that includes the following elements:

1. A setting (a beginning, time, place, and introduction of characters).
2. A theme (the main character's problem or goal).
3. A plot (a series of events in which the main character attempts to solve the problem or achieve the goal).
4. A resolution (the accomplishment of the goal or solving of the problem and an ending).

From hearing many well-formed stories, children can predict what will happen next in an unfamiliar story on the basis of their awareness of its structure. Hearing stories with good plot structures also helps children write and tell their own stories. The language of books is different from oral language and provides a model for their writing and speaking.

Predictable stories are ideal for shared book experiences because they allow children to guess what will happen next, thereby encouraging participation. Predictability takes many forms. I have purposefully selected well-known favorites as samples to learn about these types of texts. The use of catch phrases, such as "'Not I,' said the dog," "'Not I,' said the cat," and so on, in *The Little Red Hen* (Izawa, 1968) encourages children to chant along. Predictable rhyme enables children to fill in words, as in *Green Eggs and Ham* (Seuss, 1960). Cumulative patterns contribute to predictability. For example, new events are added with each episode and then repeated in the next, as in *Are You My Mother?* (Eastman, 1960). This book repeats phrases and episode patterns, as its central character, a baby bird, searches for its mother by approaching different animals and asking the same question, "Are you my mother?"

Conversation can contribute to predictability, as in *The Three Billy Goats Gruff* (Brown, 1957) or *The Three Little Pigs* (Brenner, 1972). All books become predictable as children become familiar with them, so repeating stories builds a repertoire for shared book experiences. Books that carry familiar sequences, such as days of the week, months of the year, letters, and numbers, are predictable. *The Very Hungry Caterpillar* (Carle, 1969) is a good example. Books gain predictability through good plot structures and topics familiar to children. Books in which pictures match text page by page tend to be predictable to children, especially if everyone in the group can see the pictures as the story is being read.

Predictable books are excellent for emergent and conventional readers in shared book experiences as well as in independent reading. They allow the child's first experience with reading to be enjoyable and successful with minimal effort. Such immediate success encourages the child to continue efforts at reading.

We often stop reading to children as they begin to read themselves. But, it is crucial to continue reading to them as they get older. Reading to them in a shared book setting enhances skills already learned and motivates interest in the books featured in the classroom.

Research indicates that shared book reading benefits the acquisition of reading and writing. It enhances background information, gives a sense of story structure, and familiarizes children with the language of books (Beauchat, Blamey, & Walpole, 2009; Bus, 2001; Morrow, 1985). Both informational and narrative literature can be used in shared book reading.

Small-Group and One-to-One Story Readings. The importance and benefits of reading to small groups and to individuals must not be overlooked as collective reading experiences. Too often considered impractical in school settings, one-to-one and small-group readings yield such tremendous benefits that they must be incorporated into school programs. The most striking benefit of one-to-one story readings at home, often called the *lap technique,* is the interactive behavior it involves, along with the immediate access children have to information. It also provides the adult with insight into what the child already knows and wants to know. Very young children participate best in small-group and one-on-one readings, since they need the attention that this setting offers.

Through observations and investigations (Morrow, 1988), it has been determined that one-to-one readings in a school setting had positive results with at-risk preschoolers even though they had little previous experience with storybook reading or interacting with adults during this time. Teachers introduced stories by providing substantive background information before reading and used interactive behaviors during reading (Meller, Ricardson, & Hatch, 2009). Frequent readings by teachers who followed the guidelines outlined in Figure 9.4 increased the number and complexity of the children's responses. The youngsters offered many questions and comments that focused on meaning. Initially, they labeled illustrations. Later, they gave increased attention to details, their comments and questions became interpretive and predictive, and they drew from their own experiences. They also began narrating: "reading" or mouthing the story along with the teacher. As the program continued, some children focused on structural elements, remarking on titles, settings, characters, and story events. After many readings, the children began to focus on print, reading words and naming letters and sounds (Barone & Morrow, 2003; Morrow, 1987; Xu & Rutledge, 2003). Compared with one-to-one reading, reading to small groups of children seems to encourage more participation and engagement. Children tend to repeat one another's remarks, and they are motivated to respond to and elaborate on what their peers have said. Research concerning small group and one-on-one readings of informational text reveal that children react in a similar fashion as they do with narrative text (Duke, 2004).

The following segments from transcriptions of small-group story readings illustrate the various questions and comments children make when they are involved in the activity and the wealth of knowledge and information they receive from the responding adult. The transcriptions also illustrate what the children already know and what their interests are, which helps teachers design instruction. Finally, the excerpts also show how small-group and one-on-one story readings help students meet many required standards such as, using key ideas and details, understanding craft and structure, integrating knowledge and ideas, experiencing a range of reading and level of complexity, and working with word study. The also demonstrate understanding of the text structure and concepts about print.

Story: *The Very Hungry Caterpillar* (Carle, 1969) (The child asks questions about book concepts.)

Jerry: Pointing to the picture on the front of the book he says, "Why does it have a picture on it?"

Teacher: The cover of the book has a picture on it, so you will know what the story is about. Look at the picture. Can you tell me what the book is about?

Jerry: Ummm, I think that's a caterpillar. Is it about a caterpillar?

Teacher: You're right, very good. The book is about a caterpillar, and the name of the story is *The Very Hungry Caterpillar*. When you look at the pictures in a book, they help you find out what the words say.

In this segment, the child asks and answers questions about unknown words in a text.

Story: *Caps for Sale* (Slobodkina, 1947) (The child asks for a definition.)

Teacher: I'm going to read a story today called *Caps for Sale*.

Jamie: What are caps?

Teacher: A cap is a little hat that you put on your head. See, there is a cap in the picture.

Jamie: I never knew that before. I knew about hats, but I never heard about caps.

In this segment, the child asks and answer questions about unknown words in a text.

Story: *Chicken Soup with Rice* (Sendak, 1962) (The child attends to the print.)

Chris: Wait, stop reading. Let me see this again. (He turns back to the page about the month of June.) How come they're the same? (He refers to the words *June* and *July*.)

Teacher: What do you mean?

Chris: Look at the letters, J–U, J–U. They look alike.

Teacher: Look more closely at the ends of the words. Are they the same?

Chris: Ohh, nooo, just the front part.

In this discussion, the child is given prompting and support, asks and answers questions about key details in a text.

Story: *Caps for Sale* (Slobodkina, 1947) (The child predicts.)

Colleen: I wonder why those monkeys took the caps?

Teacher: I don't know. Can you think why?

Colleen: Well, the peddler was sleeping and those monkeys looked at the caps, and maybe they think they're for them. Or, I know! Maybe they're cold so they want a cap.

Teacher: Those are good ideas, Colleen.

In this segment, the child compares and contrasts the adventures and experiences of characters in familiar stories.

Story: *Madeline's Rescue* (Bemelmans, 1953) (The child relates the text to real-life experience.)

Jamie: What's the policeman going to do?

Teacher: He's going to help Madeline. Policemen are nice; they always help us.

Jamie: Policemans aren't nice. See, my daddy beat up Dominic and the policeman came and took him away and put him in jail for no reason. And my daddy cried. I don't like policemans. I don't think they are nice.

The children's comments and questions relate to literal meanings, raise interpretive and critical issues by associating the story with their own lives, make predictions of what will happen next in a story, or express judgments about characters' actions. In these examples, the children's comments and questions relate to matters of print, such as names of letters, words, and sounds. The same types of questions and comments occur when small groups of children read together without the presence of a teacher. Recording and then analyzing one-to-one and small-group story readings reveal what children know and want to know (Morrow, 1987). The coding sheet in Figure 9.5 aids such analysis.

It is difficult to provide one-to-one and small-group readings in school because of time limitations and the number of children. Asking aides, volunteers, and older children to help in the classroom and with storybook reading one-to-one or in small groups can solve the problem.

Photo credit: Emese/Shutterstock

Children practice comprehension during partner reading.

Collaborative Reading

Collective reading experiences—such as read alouds, shared book experiences, and small-group story readings—all put the teacher in the role of director. However, in collaborative reading students participate with one another, independently of the teacher.

The National Reading Panel suggested that collaboration is an important strategy for developing comprehension (National Reading Panel, 2000). These strategies are often referred to as **response groups** because they enable children to engage in productive and personal conversations about the text. Response groups allow students to exchange ideas, listen to each other, refine ideas, and think critically about issues related to what they listened to or read. Because young children need the

Figure 9.5 Coding Children's Responses During Story Readings

Child's name: ______________________ **Date:** ________

Name of story: ______________________

Read one story to one child or a small group of children. Encourage the children to respond with questions and comments. Tape-record the session. Transcribe or listen to the tape, noting each child's responses by placing checks in the appropriate categories. A category may receive more than one check, and a single response may be credited to more than one category. Total the number of checks in each category.

1. Focus on story structure ______
   a. Setting (time, place) ______
   b. Characters ______
   c. Theme (problem or goal) ______
   d. Plot episodes (events leading toward problem solution or goal attainment) ______
   e. Resolution ______
2. Focus on meaning ______
   a. Labeling ______
   b. Detail ______
   c. Interpreting (associations, elaborations) ______
   d. Predicting ______
   e. Drawing from one's experience ______
   f. Seeking definitions of words ______
   g. Using narrational behavior (reciting parts of the book along with the teacher) ______
3. Focus on print ______
   a. Questions or comments about letters ______
   b. Questions or comments about sounds ______
   c. Questions or comments about words ______
   d. Reads words ______
   e. Reads sentences ______
4. Focus on illustrations ______
   a. Responses and questions that are related to illustrations ______

Total ______

teacher to model behavior for response groups before they participate in them with peers, the groups are first introduced in teacher-directed settings. Common types of response groups include literature circles, reciprocal teaching, buddy reading, and partner reading. Think, pair, share and visualizing are two additional collaborative reading strategies.

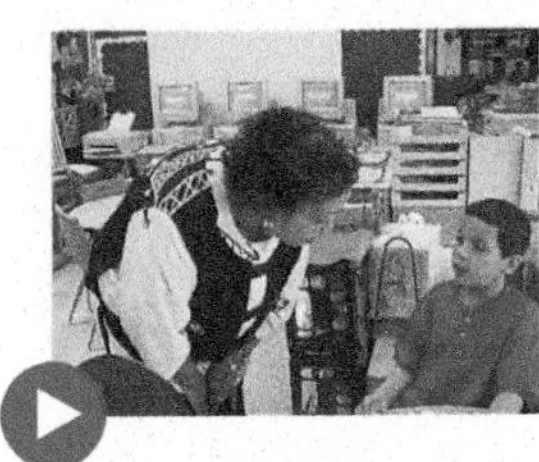

MyLab Education
Video Example 9.2
Literature Circles

This video shows an example of a literature circle among students.

Literature Circles. **Literature circles** consist of a group of children who have read the same book and discuss the book independently of the teacher. Teachers need to model literature circle activities so that children can carry them out independently. Literature circles are organized as follows:

1. Small groups are formed by the teacher. Each group selects one book from the list provided by the teacher and reads and discusses the book.
2. The teacher helps the students with discussion by using prompts similar to those reviewed in previous sections dealing with promoting conversations about books.
3. The students are given jobs within the group. Common jobs include the following:
    a. The *discussion director* is responsible for the opening and closing remarks, reminding members to refer to their books to find support for their comments, and ensuring that everyone participates. The discussion director asks questions that the group will discuss.
    b. The *word finder* selects words that are important to the book. He or she lists the words, and they are discussed.
    c. The *illustrator* draws something related to the reading.
    d. The *creative connector* finds the connection between the book being read and the outside world. The connections can be to themselves, a student in the class, a friend, a family member, or other books.
    e. The *summarizer* writes a summary of the reading. It should be short and to the point (Daniels, 1994).

Children can place sticky notes on pages to remember issues to discuss. They ask the group to turn to the page as they refer to it. Children can comment on an issue, ask a question of others, or ask for clarification to help them understand. This activity requires guidance from the teacher and practice on the part of children. There can be jobs other than those discussed, such as *passage picker*, who would select a few funny, sad, or interesting passages to read to the group. Figures 9.6 through 9.9 are some examples of worksheets that can be used with the different roles in a literature circle.

Literature circles can also be used with young children in kindergarten and first grade. The teacher will, however, need to lead the literature circles, act as discussion director, and ask the following questions:

- Which parts of your book did you like?
- What information in the book was most interesting to you?
- Which parts of the book did you not like?
- How would you end the story if you were the author?

Reciprocal Teaching of Comprehension. **Reciprocal teaching** is a guided comprehension strategy done in a collaborative setting. Children are assigned roles, and, after they learn the strategy, they will carry it out independently. First, the teacher explains the procedure and what the four strategies are (predict, question, clarify, summarize), why they are important, and how they help to comprehend what is read. Next, the teacher models the strategies using a piece of literature. Finally, the teacher involves the children in the strategies as a whole class. The children are divided into groups of four. Each person in the group is given one of the four reciprocal strategies to focus on. Each group has reading material appropriate for its reading level (Pilonieta & Medina, 2009; Pratt & Urbanowski, 2016). The reciprocal strategies are (McLaughlin, 2003):

1. Predicting prompts prior to ending:
   I think the book is about . . .
   I bet the book is about . . .
   I wonder if the book is about . . .
   I imagine the book is about . . .

Figure 9.6 Literature Circle Discussion Director

Discussion Director

You will be in charge of directing the discussion in your book club. List below who you will ask to speak first, second, and so on. Be prepared to introduce the topics with each of your members' roles.

1. ____________________

2. ____________________

3. ____________________

4. ____________________

5. ____________________

6. ____________________

7. ____________________

Figure 9.7 Literature Circle Word Finder

Word Finder

The word finder selects interesting and challenging words from the text and defines them for the group.

Word: ______________________________

Definition: ______________________________

____

____

Word: ______________________________

Definition: ______________________________

____

____

Word: ______________________________

Definition: ______________________________

____

____

Word: ______________________________

Definition: ______________________________

____

____

Figure 9.8 Literature Circle Illustrator

Illustrator

Illustrate a part of the book you like a lot. Discuss with your book club members. Write a few sentences that describe what is happening in your illustration.

Figure 9.9 Literature Circle Summarizer

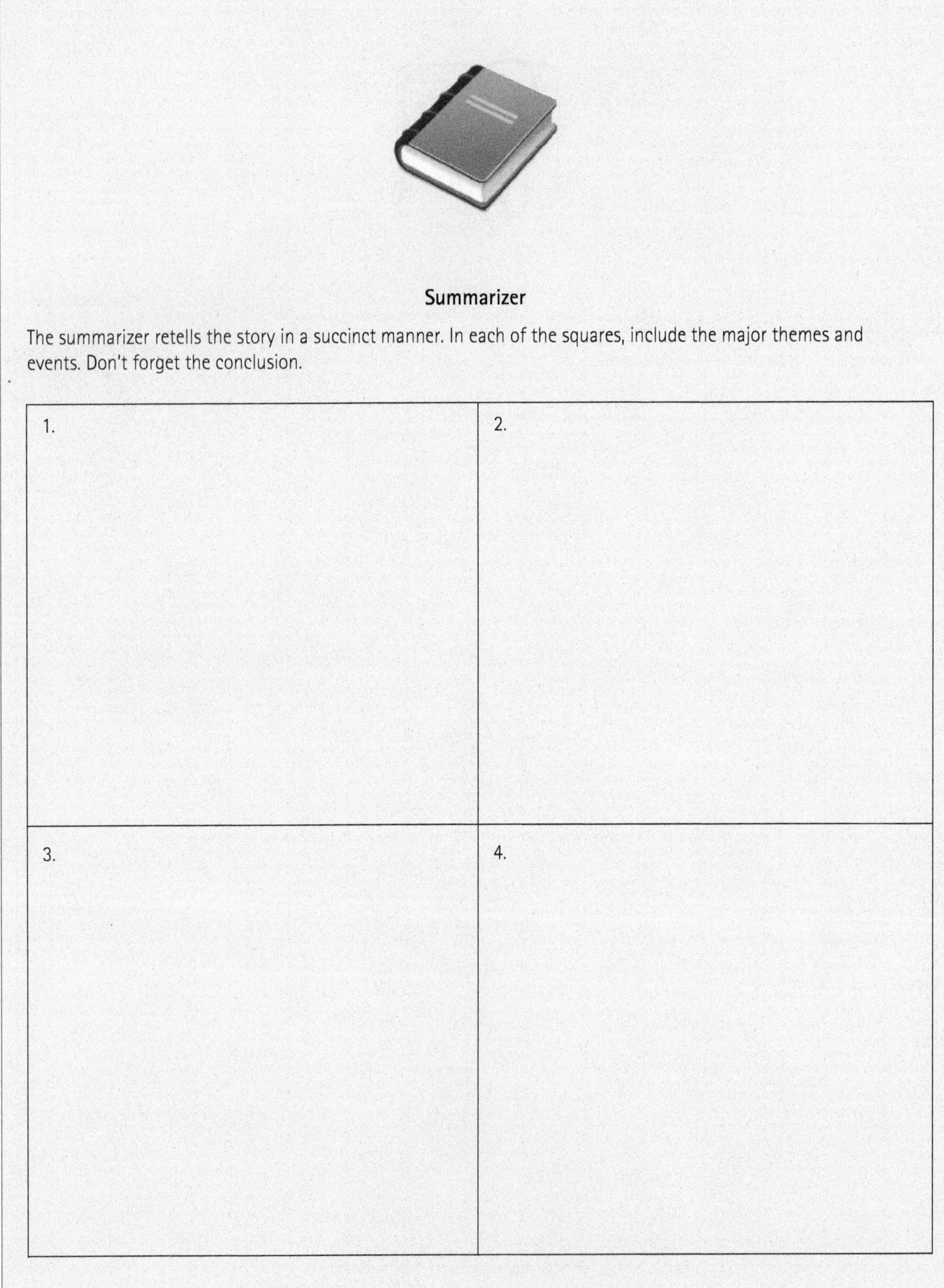

Summarizer

The summarizer retells the story in a succinct manner. In each of the squares, include the major themes and events. Don't forget the conclusion.

1.	2.
3.	4.

2. Question yourself after reading:
   Who? Where? When? What? How?
   What if?
   I wonder how? Why did?
   What is your opinion and why?
3. Clarify what you don't understand:
   I didn't understand the part where . . .
   I need to know more about . . .
   This changes what I thought about . . .
4. Summarize:
   This part is about . . .
   The most important ideas in what I read are . . .
   New facts I learned were . . .

Buddy Reading. **Buddy reading** is usually a situation in which a child from an upper grade is paired with a child in kindergarten or first or second grade. The child in the upper grade is instructed how to read to children. At specified times during the school week, buddies get together for storybook reading and discussions (Christ, Chiu, & Wang, 2014).

Partner Reading. **Partner reading** involves peers reading together. This may simply mean that the children take turns reading to each other, or that they read sitting side by side. Teachers can structure partner reading similar to literature circles with topics posed for partners to discuss after reading to each other.

Think, Pair, Share. The **think, pair, share** strategy involves teacher-posed questions, which students are asked to think about before answering. Students are then paired with peers to discuss their answers to the questions. They return to a larger group to share the answers they have discussed (Gambrell & Almasi, 1994).

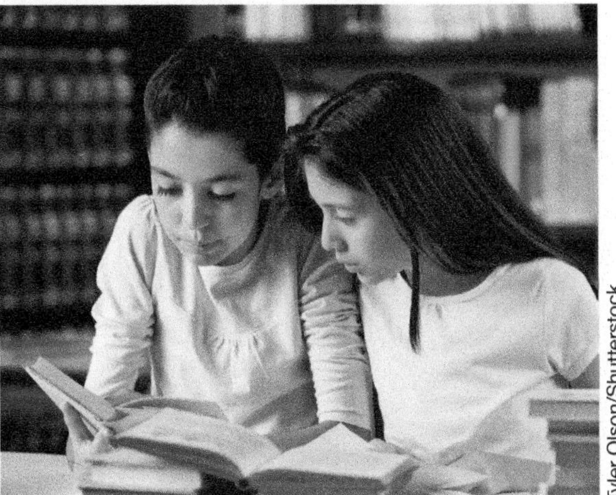

Tyler Olson/Shutterstock

Cooperative strategies (when children read together as in partner reading and think, pair, share) enhance comprehension.

Think Alouds

Visualizing. Mental imagery and think-alouds involve children in several strategies, alone, together, and with and without the teacher. **Mental imagery** asks children to visualize what they see after they have been read to or have read a passage themselves. We ask children to "Make a picture in your minds to help you remember and understand what you read or what was read to you." After the mental imagery, we ask children to **think aloud** and talk about their images to peers or to the teacher. We also ask children to predict what will happen next in the story. We tell children to ask themselves questions about the story and to reread when they need to clarify ideas or remember forgotten details. We also ask them to personalize the text by asking them if they have ever been in a similar situation and what they did. Visualizing ideas and relating those visualizations orally help clarify information and increase understanding (Gambrell & Koskinen, 2002; Seglem & Witte, 2009).

Close Reading

Close reading involves selecting short text passages for close reading or careful analysis. This detailed examination of the text helps students practice critical reading skills. understand what critical reading is. Close reading should not be a daily activity; once a week is a reasonable amount of time to spend in second and third grades.

Although more appropriate for, second, third, and fourth grades, close reading can also be used in kindergarten and first grade with a great deal of scaffolding. Close reading helps the child to understand that some difficult reading must be done very slowly. Close reading helps you learn how to analyze text. A close reading passage is read three times. It is read first by the teacher with the children following. The next reading can be done with partners, and a third reading alone. Close reading can help children understand what they can comprehend and need help with by using a sheet such as the one in the box called Readers Annotate to Show Their Thinking during the close read.

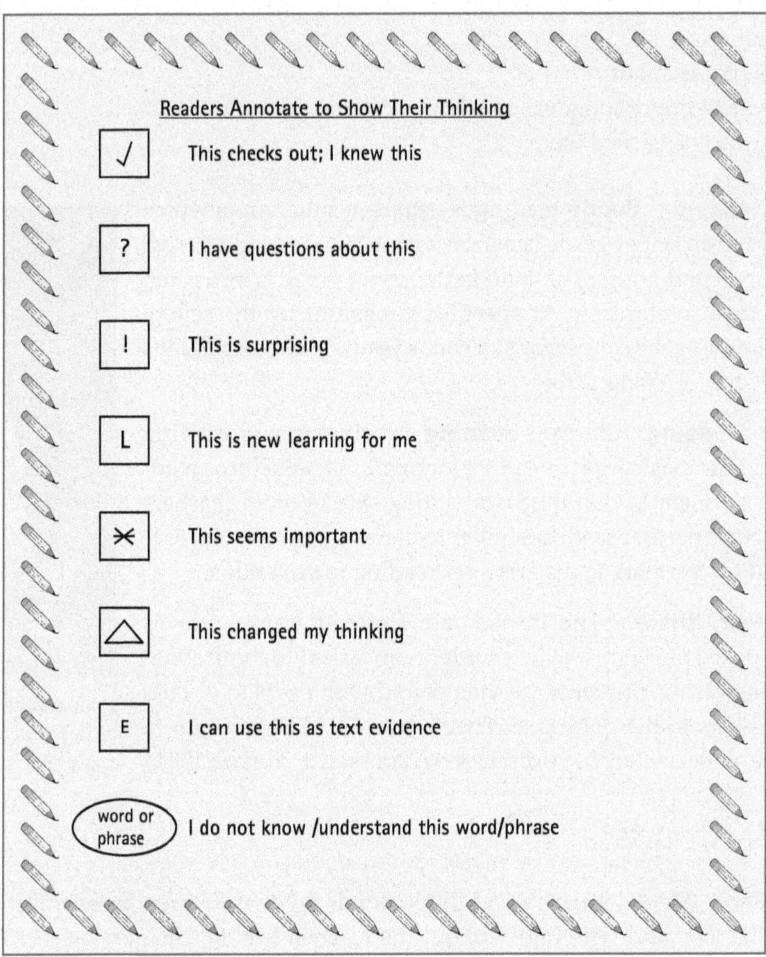

The following vignette illustrates a first-grade class doing a close read with careful guidance from the teacher.

Mr. Kent sat on a chair in front of his first graders, who were on the carpet. He explained to them that they would be doing a close reading lesson. The title of the book from which they would read a short passage was "Helping Out a Friend." He connected it to another book they read which was similarly about friendship. He told the students that he chose the text because it was a challenging expository text. He asked the children, "Do you remember how we defined expository?" The children responded together rhythmically, and pointing to their head said, "Expository text is about real information." The teacher said, "I bet you all know about kidney beans and they are shaped like this." He drew one on the white board. "But this kidney is inside of you." Then, he touched one of his thumbs to the other and did the same with his pointer fingers to create a kidney sign to use to remember the word "kidney."

"Kidneys are the part of your body that cleans the blood." He made the kidney sign and, placing hands near his own kidneys, said again, "Kidneys are the part of the body that cleans the blood." He asked the children to repeat what he said, and they did so with the sign. "Let's choral read the purpose for the reading today, 'Children will be able to ask clarifying questions to learn about the meaning of unknown words.'"

Each child was given a copy of the passage to echo read with the teacher, who told the children not to worry about vocabulary questions until after they finished reading the passage twice. The students read with him; some dropped out when they reach a word they didn't know. Students followed along with their finger or their pencil. Children circled the words they didn't know.

The teacher told the children to read the passage again and then to turn to their partners and discuss the definitions of their circled words. They were to help each other clarify meanings of words. The teacher instructed the children to raise their hands if they were having trouble with any words, so he could help them. After a few minutes he asked for a volunteer to tell the definition for a new word they learned. Joshua stood and stated the definition of a word. Students who disagreed raised their hands, stood up, and said, "I respectfully disagree with you," and explained why.

The teacher then asked the students to return to their partners and discuss more of the vocabulary they needed clarified. The teacher checked with each pair to see what words were circled for clarification and offered help as needed. After the children discussed in pairs for a few minutes, they came back together as a whole group for additional clarification.

Before reading the passage again, the teacher asked if the students had any questions. Jose asked, "How do you give other people your kidneys?"

"That is a great clarifying question. Let's read again and find out." After the first couple of sentences, the teacher stopped. Charlie and Nina raised their hands, and Charlie asked, "Could you clarify *transplant*?" The teacher instructed everyone to circle *transplant* and write it on the vocabulary sheet. The teacher then told the students to read to see if the passage contained any clues to help them figure out the meaning of *transplant*. The class read through some sentences but didn't find the meaning.

"Where else can I look?" the teacher asked.

The class shouted, "The dictionary!"

Roger said, "You can find a dictionary or glossary at the end of an expository text, sometimes." The students turned to the glossary and found the meaning of the word *transplant*. The teacher instructed the children to point once more to the word in the story and then write the meaning on their vocabulary sheet. They kept reading, and *transplant* appeared again. The teacher stopped the students and directed them to turn to their partners and tell them again what *transplant* means.

After the final close read, the students asked any lingering clarifying questions about unknown vocabulary words. To wrap up the close reading, students volunteered to tell the class what words they learned during that lesson. The teacher had them say the word and read the definition.

Repeated Reading

Children enjoy repetition. Being familiar with an experience is comfortable, like singing a well-known song. Besides offering the pleasure of familiarity, a repeated story helps develop concepts about words, print, and books. Furthermore, repeated readings of the same text increase the number, kind, and complexity of the children's responses to the text. A group of 4-year-olds, for example, read the same story three times. After each reading, there was a discussion. Their responses became more interpretive, and they began to predict outcomes and make associations, judgments, and elaborative comments (Morrow, 1987; Sipe, 2008). They also began to narrate stories as the teacher read (their first attempts at reading) and to focus on elements of print, for example, by asking names of letters and words. Even children who were considered to be struggling with comprehension seemed to make more responses with repeated readings than with a single reading (Ivey, 2002; Beauchat, Blamey, & Walpole, 2010).

Repeated readings are important to youngsters because they can engage in the activity on their own. Children who are able to read themselves or participate in pretend reading behaviors will often select the same book to look at or read over and over again. Teachers should repeat readings of stories to children and encourage youngsters to read stories more than once. They should carry out discussions about books that have been read and discussed previously.

The following dialogue is from a transcription of a child's responses to a third reading of *The Little Red Hen.* This excerpt primarily includes the child's comments and questions and the teacher's responses; most of the story text has been omitted.

Teacher: Today I'm going to read the story *The Little Red Hen.* It is about a hen who wanted some help when she baked some bread. (The teacher begins to read the story.) Who will help me to cut this wheat?

Melony: "Not I," said the cat. "Not I," said the dog. "Not I," said the mouse.

Teacher: That was good, Melony. You are reading. (The teacher continues reading.) Who will take this wheat to the mill to be ground into flour?

Melony: "Not I," said the cat. "Not I," said the dog. "Not I," said the mouse with the whiskers.

Teacher: Very nice, Melony. (The teacher continues to read.)

Melony: I want to read that part, but I don't know how.

Teacher: Go ahead and try. I bet you can. I'll help you: The cat smelled it.

Melony: The cat smelled it and she said umm, that smells good, and the mouse smelled it, and it smelled good.

Teacher: (The teacher continues reading.) Who will eat this bread?

Melony: The mouse, the doggy, the kitty!

Teacher: You're right again, Melony. (The teacher reads to the end of the story.) Did you want to say anything else about the story?

Melony: He was bad so he couldn't have no bread. (Melony searches through the pages.) That's the wrong part.

Teacher: Show me the part you are talking about.

Melony: There it is, almost at the end. She's going to make bread and she'll say who's going to bake this bread for me? And the cat says, "Not I," the dog says, "Not I," the mouse says, "Not I." And then when she's cooking it, they smell a good thing and then they wanted some, too, but they didn't have any, 'cause they didn't plant the wheat.

Teacher: You're right. They didn't help do the work, so they didn't get to eat the bread.

Melony: Where does it say, "Not I"? Show me the words in the book.

Teacher: Here it is. Can you find it again?

Melony: (She flips through the pages.) I'm looking for where she bakes the bread. Here it is. Yeah. And he smelled it. And he smelled it. And the mouse smelled it. (She turns pages.) They're going in the kitchen. And she said, "All by myself, I cut the wheat. All by myself, I took it to the mill to get it into flour. All by myself I baked the bread. All by myself I'm going to eat it."

Teacher: That's terrific, Melony. That's what the hen said.

Melony: (She points to the dog.) The dog was not happy. Where does it say dog?

Teacher: You're right. He doesn't look happy. Here is where it says dog (pointing).

Melony: There's the word, dog, dog, dog. How does that dog look?

Teacher: He looks hungry and mad because he can't have any bread.

Melony: You're right. But it's his fault. He didn't help. And that's the end (Morrow, 1987).

This type of sophisticated response can happen only when a child has heard a story that has been repeated many times.

Adults often tire of the repetition, but children enjoy hearing the same book read to them over and over again. That's why repetition has great value in early reading development. There should be a repertoire of books considered favorite stories that are read repeatedly to children at home and in school. To study emergent reading behaviors, Sulzby (1985a) observed children from ages 2 to 6 attempting to read favorite storybooks. They could participate in the activity because they knew the stories so well. Although they were not yet readers in the conventional sense, the children were asked, "Read me your book." Sulzby found that, in their "reading," the children produced speech that could indeed be categorized as a first act of reading; that the speech they used as they "read" was clearly different in structure and intonation from their typical conversation; and that different developmental levels could be observed in these "oral readings."

From children's attempts at storybook reading, we can then develop and determine particular characteristics of reading behavior. Since the activity is developmental and leads to literacy, teachers should ask children to participate in it to encourage their emergent literacy behaviors and to evaluate it as well (refer to Figure 9.10). This test is for 3-, 4-, 5-, and 6-year-olds who may not yet be reading.

Full comprehension is not the result of simply reading; students need to engage actively with the text in productive ways that deepen their understanding of the material and their engagement with the text. Interactive discussions, building graphic organizers, and summarizing the text are ways to actively work with texts to enhance comprehension.

Figure 9.10 Sulzby's Classification Scheme for Children's Emergent Reading of Favorite Storybooks

SOURCE: Children's emergent reading of favorite storybooks: A developmental study. *Reading Research Quarterly, 20*(4), 458–481, by Elizabeth Sulzby. Copyright (c) 1985. Reprinted with permission of John Wiley & Sons, Inc.

Check elements that best represent the child's reading behavior.

1. *Attending to pictures but not forming stories.* The child "reads" by labeling and commenting on the pictures in the book but does not "weave a story" across the pages.

   yes ☐ no ☐

2. *Attending to pictures and forming oral stories.* The child "reads" by following the pictures but weaves a story across the pages through wording and intonation like those of someone telling a story. Often, however, the listener too must see the pictures in order to understand the story the child is "reading."

   yes ☐ no ☐

3. *Attending to a mix of pictures, reading, and storytelling.* The child "reads" by looking at the pictures. The majority of the child's "reading" fluctuates between the oral intonation of a storyteller and that of a reader.

   yes ☐ no ☐

4. *Attending to pictures but forming stories (written language-like).* The child "reads" by looking at the pictures. The child's speech sounds like reading, both in wording and intonation. The listener rarely needs to see the pictures in order to understand the story. With his or her eyes closed, the listener would think the child was reading print. The "reading" is similar to the story in print and sometimes follows it verbatim. There is some attention to print.

   yes ☐ no ☐

5. *Attending to print.* This category has two divisions:

   a. The child reads the story mostly by attending to print but occasionally refers to pictures and reverts to storytelling.

   b. The child reads in a conventional manner.

   a. ☐ b. ☐

Interactive Discussions

Studies carried out in school settings illustrate that active participation in literacy experiences enhances comprehension of and sense of text structure (Morrow, 1985; Pellegrini & Galda, 1982).

As children discuss text with others, they are first interested in the illustrations and will label the items pictured or repeat the words said by the adult who is reading (Bowman, Donovan, & Burns, 2000). Such interactive behavior leads children to respond with questions and comments, which become more complex over time and demonstrate more sophisticated thinking about printed material. Eventually, children's remarks about the content of the text demonstrate their ability to interpret, associate, predict information, and elaborate. Their remarks focus sometimes on title, setting, characters, and story events (Morrow, 1988; Roskos, Christie, & Richgels, 2003) and at other times on print characteristics, including names of letters, words, and sounds. Teachers help students to discuss and thus respond to text by:

- Prompting children to respond before they do on their own.
- Scaffolding responses for children to model when they are not responding themselves.
- Relating responses to real-life experiences.
- Answering students' questions.
- Asking questions.
- Offering positive reinforcement for children's responses.

Generating Questions. Productive discussions result from good questions. Discussion questions should reflect children's interests and have many appropriate responses, rather than just one correct answer. Discussions prompted by questions must generate more than a few words by participants. To that end, asking different types of questions produces richer, more varied discussion. Teachers should mix the use of literal questions, inferential and critical questions, aesthetic questions, and efferent questions depending on the topic and book being discussed. Teachers should also be sure to ask questions that prompt students to clarify, explain, predict, and justify.

Literal questions identify who, what, when, and where details and so are great starting points to use as a warm-up to start discussion. Literal questions are those that require students to:

- classify ideas
- sequence text
- find the main idea.

Once a foundation has been established with literal questions, the students will be better prepared to answer *inferential and critical questions* that ask them to:

- draw information from their background knowledge
- make text-to-life, text-to-world, and text-to-other-text connections
- predict outcomes (what do you think will happen next?)
- interpret text (put yourself in the place of the characters.)
- make comparisons
- determine cause and effect
- apply information
- problem solve
- answer questions by showing evidence from the text.

Figure 9.11 is a quick comprehension test of questions dealing with literal and inferential comprehension.

Some questions should stimulate discussion and elicit responses that reflect what children think and feel about what has been read. That is, the teacher should also ask *aesthetic questions* that require children to synthesize ideas, sensations, feelings, and images. Not only do aesthetic questions broaden the scope of a discussion, but they also promote students making comparisons with other, similar texts and with their own life experiences. (Note how the last two questions listed deal with text-to-world and text-to-text connections.)

Figure 9.11 Comprehension of Literal and Inferential Thinking After Being Read to or After Reading a Narrative or Expository Text

Child's name: ____________________

Name of story: ____________________

Date: ____________________

After reading a text to a child or after a child reads a text, make up the following types of questions for the narrative or expository text. Ask only questions appropriate for the text. Some are narrative questions, and some are for expository text only. Ask the questions and record the answers next to each question.

Literal questions identify who, what, when, and where details. Ask children to answer:

1. Literal questions ______
   a. Who, what, when, and where. ______
   b. Classify ideas. ______
   c. Sequence text. ______
   d. Find the main idea of the theme. ______
2. Inferential and critical questions ask students to do the following:
   a. Draw information from the child's background knowledge. ______
   b. Make text-to-life, text-to-world, and text-to-other-text connections. ______
   c. Predict outcomes. (What do you think will happen next?) ______
   d. Interpret text. (If you were the main character how would you feel? What would you have done?) ______
   e. Compare and contrast. (What in your life is like the story you just read? What in your life is not like the story?) ______
   f. Determine cause and effect. ______
   g. What questions do you have about the book? ______
   h. What did you learn from what you read? ______
   i. What ideas did you find most interesting? ______
   j. If you could speak with the author, what would you like to ask him or her? ______
   k. Have you read other books similar to this one? Name the books. ______

To elicit an aesthetic response from children and encourage an aesthetic discussion, ask the following types of questions:

- How did you feel about the story?
- What did this story mean to you?
- Do you agree with what the characters did in the story? Why? Why not?
- What in your life is like the story you just read?
- Have you read other books that are similar to the one you just read?
- Describe how (Gambrell & Almasi, 1994).

Finally, the *efferent stance* is a questioning protocol used with both expository and narrative text and dealing with content information. Questions that ask for an efferent response require students to remember and analyze details and descriptions, sequences, and cause and effect.

Some questions and prompts to elicit efferent responses (Gunning, 2003; Rosenblatt, 1988) include the following:

- What questions do you have about the book?
- List the most important things you learned.
- How will the information in the book be useful to you?
- Can you put the facts in sequential order?
- Provide details about the book.
- What is the cause, and what is its effect?
- What is the main thing that the author is trying to tell you?
- What did you find most interesting?
- How you could find more information about the topic?
- If you could speak with the author, what would you ask him/her?

We need to help students know where to find answers that are explicit—that is, answers that are clearly and explicitly stated in the text. Students also need to be able to find implicit answers to questions when the answer is not exactly stated but can be found within a few sentences in the text. Students must be able to give evidence to support their assertions about both types of answers—implicit and explicit. The same is true when students are asked aesthetic or efferent questions. Children must be able to cite textual evidence in support of their assertions, be they aesthetic or empirical. Not only is the ability to provide evidence proof of greater comprehension, but it is also encoded in the Common Core State Standards.

Graphic Organizers

Graphic organizers are visual illustrations or representations of text information that help readers see relationships between concepts or events in a narrative or expository writing. They can help teach many elements needed for comprehension, such as vocabulary, cause and effect, problem solving, and so on. Teachers and children like graphic organizers since they make the act of reading visible. They are however, used too much. Use them appropriately and don't over use. Following are descriptions of well-known types of graphic organizers and examples of the same.

Mapping and Webbing. Maps and webs are graphic representations, or diagrams, for categorizing and structuring information. They help students see how words and ideas are related to one another. Webs tend to be drawn using a spiderlike effect, and maps may have boxes with labels in them that connect in different places. **Mapping** and **webbing** strategies build on children's prior knowledge. They help the child retrieve what is known about a topic and use the information in reading and listening to text. Research has demonstrated that the use of webbing and mapping strategies develops vocabulary and comprehension. Mapping and webbing helps struggling readers, children from diverse backgrounds, and English learners as well (Pittelman, Heimlich, Benglund, & French, 1991).

When webbing or mapping is used to develop vocabulary concepts and definitions related to a word, the word is written on the board or chart paper. Children are asked to brainstorm ideas related to the word. For example, after reading *The Snowy Day* (Keats, 1996), the teacher asks the children to provide words that describe what snow is like. The word *snow* is written in the center of the chart or board, and the words given by the children are attached to it. A sample of a snow web by kindergartners is shown in Figure 9.12.

Another web about the same story could be used to expand ideas about activities to do in the snow. In Figure 9.13, a first-grade class generated the things that Peter did in the snow in the story and then other things that they can do in the snow.

A map provides a different format for graphically presenting materials before and after listening to or reading a book. Maps deal with more complex representations; therefore, boxes for different categories are needed to present the ideas graphically. Story structures can be mapped to help children learn about the structural elements in the text. Sequences of events or studies of individual characters can be mapped also. Figure 9.14 is a map of the story *Mr. Rabbit and the Lovely Present* created by a second-grade class. The map illustrates the structural elements in the story.

K-W-L. K-W-L is a cognitive strategy to enhance comprehension. It is used mainly with expository text. K-W-L stands for What We *Know,* What We *Want* to Know, and What We *Learned* (Ogle, 1986). With this technique, students use prior knowledge to create interest about what is to be read. It helps set a purpose for reading to direct thinking, and it encourages sharing of ideas. The K-W-L chart (refer to Figure 9.15), which lists items generated in a K-W-L discussion, is particularly useful when reading material for thematic instruction (Sampson, 2002). The following are the steps involved in putting the strategy into practice:

1. Before reading expository text, children brainstorm what they think they know about a topic. For example, if the book they are going to read is *Volcanoes* (Branley, 1985), the class would list What We *Know* about volcanoes.
2. Children list questions about What We *Want to* Know about volcanoes before reading the book.
3. After reading the text, children make a list of What We *Learned* about volcanoes.

After reading the book, children can compare information learned from the text with what they already knew before reading the book. They can determine what they learned as a result of reading the text and, finally, what is still on the list of what they would like to learn because it was not included in the book.

Figure 9.12 A Web for Expanding Vocabulary

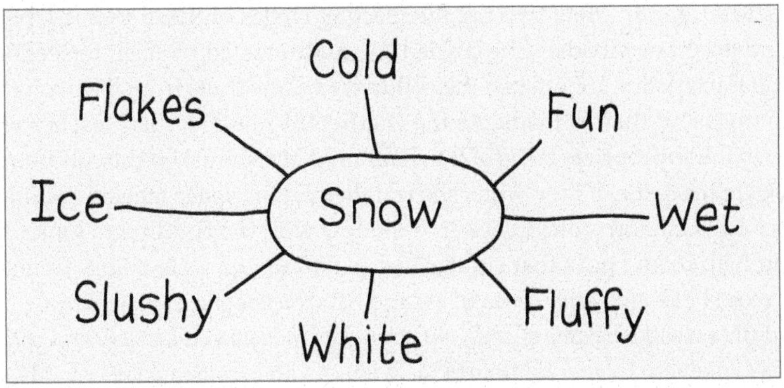

Figure 9.13 A Web for Expanding Ideas

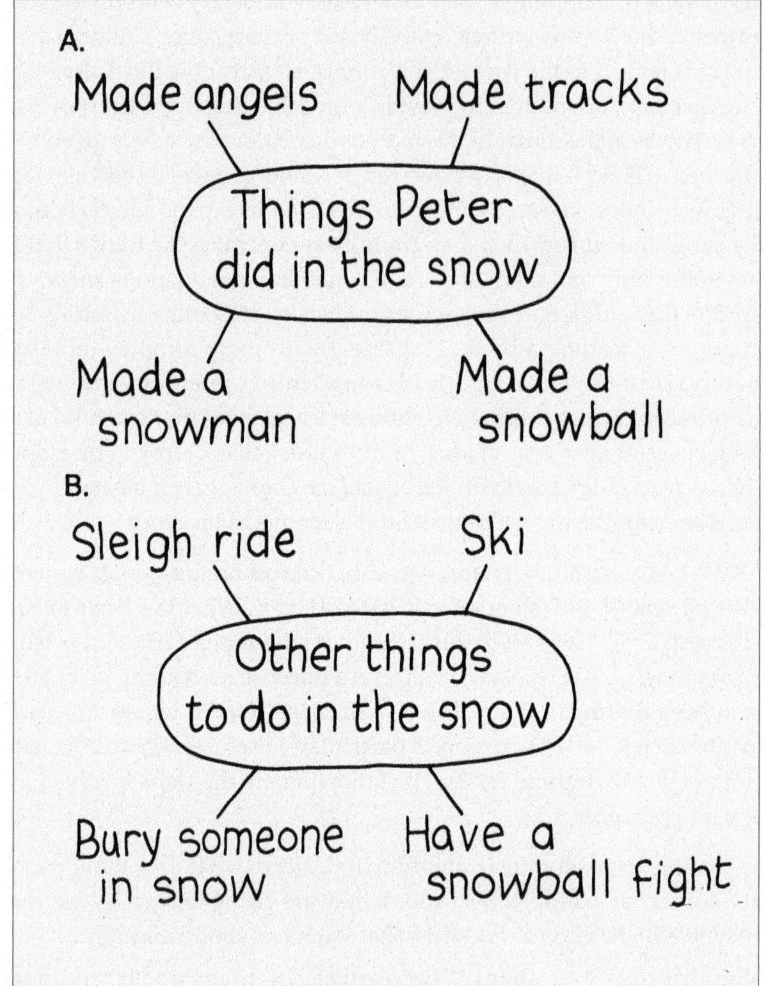

Venn Diagrams. A *Venn diagram* is a graphic organizer that uses two overlapping circles to show relationships between ideas. The Venn diagram helps compare two or three concepts in a text (Nagy, 1988). When comparing two concepts, list the main characteristics of each in the outer circles and place common characteristics in the intersecting space. With expository text, a comparison can be made between a book about polar bears and one about black bears. The Venn diagram can be used with expository or narrative text (refer to Figure 9.16).

Ms. Cannon read the book *Frogs and Toads and Tadpoles, Too!* (Fowler, 1992) to her class. This informational story highlights the similarities and differences between frogs and toads. Ms. Cannon drew two big intersecting circles on chart paper, labeling one "Frogs" and the other "Toads." She labeled the space created by the intersecting circles "Similar Characteristics." She asked the children to name traits from the book that were specific to frogs and then to toads. As the children responded, their teacher wrote the comments in the appropriate areas of the diagram. Then she asked the children if any of the traits were the same. If they were, she put them in the space labeled "Similar Characteristics." Ms. Cannon looked back into the text with the children to look for words that would help them know that similarities or differences were being discussed. For example, words like *similarly, likewise, as,* and *nevertheless* indicate sameness, whereas words and phrases like *in spite of, still, but, even though, however, instead,* and *yet* indicate differences (Vukelich, Evans, & Albertson, 2003). As an extension activity, Ms. Cannon

Figure 9.14 A Story Structure Map

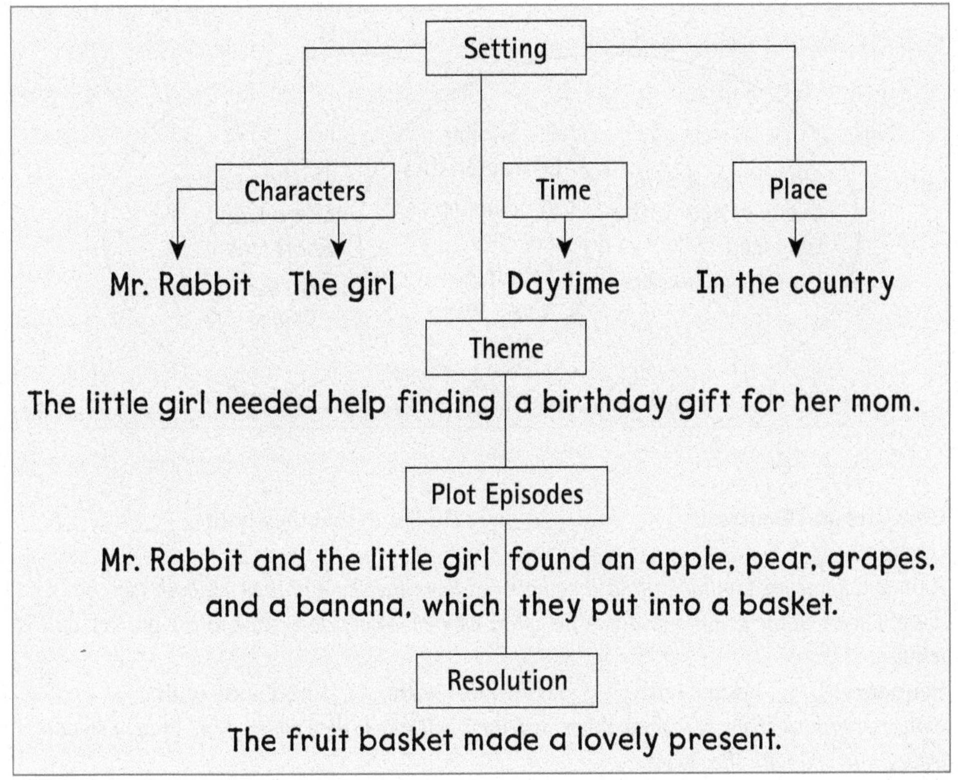

had the students work with partners to create Venn diagrams using another expository text that included ideas to compare and contrast.

Graphic Organizers for Informational Text. Graphic organizers can help children learn the structural elements characteristic of expository text. Although not fully graphic, the following series of sentences provide a hybrid of text and graphic that can help students with expository text structure. Each sentence represents a particular and common type of expository text structure, and the series of sentence prompts can be used over and over again with different topics.

Description: A(n) _____ is a kind of _____ that _____
An apple is a kind of fruit that is red and juicy and sweet.

Figure 9.15 K-W-L Chart

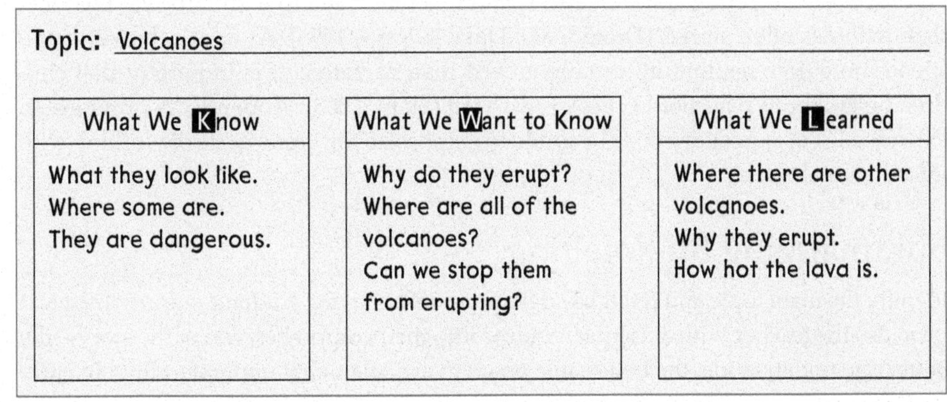

Figure 9.16 A Venn Diagram

Copyright Pearson Education

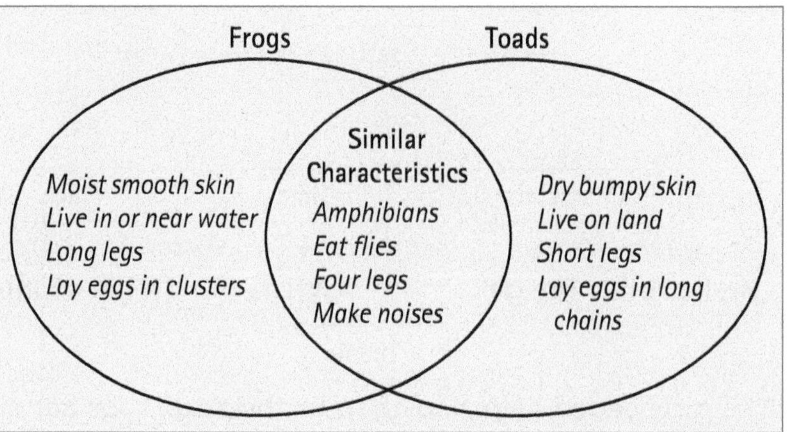

Compare and Contrast: __X__ and __Y__ are similar in that they both _____, but __X__, whereas __Y__

Rain and snow are similar in that they both fall from the sky and they are both wet, but rain doesn't stick to the ground and has no color, whereas snow does stick to the ground and is white.

Sequence: _____ begins with _____, continues with _____, and ends with

Flowers begin as seeds, we water them, and they will grow; they continue to grow a stem and leaves, and end with the flower.

Problem–Solution: _____ wanted _____, but _____, so _____

The children wanted to play outside but couldn't because of the rain, so they played in the school gym instead.

Cause and Effect: _____ happens because _____

The car got stuck and wouldn't go because it was out of gasoline.

The following informational text phrases and words are associated with the previous text structure and should be taught to children:

Description: for example, for instance, most important
Compare and Contrast: however, on the other hand, either . . . or, although, unless
Sequence: before, after, when, first, second . . . , next
Problem–Solution and Cause and Effect: therefore, because, as a result, if . . . then

From those sentences, fully graphic organizers can be built. For example, Figures 9.17 and 9.18 provide graphic organizer outlines for sequence-of-events and cause-and-effect structures in expository text.

Research shows that early childhood classrooms have fewer nonfiction texts than narrative stories. Young children also spend less time dealing with informational text than with narrative stories (Duke, 2000; Duke & Kays, 1998). As adults, however, we spend more time reading informational text than narrative. It is important that children be taught to read both types of text well (Stahl, 2008). Appendix A provides an extended list of expository texts by grade to emphasize the importance of working with informational books.

MyLab Education
Video Example 9.3
Summarizing

A second-grade teacher teaches her students how to summarize text. What elements of effective comprehension instruction does she use?

Summarizing by Retelling

Identify the main topic and retell key details of a text. Having students summarize a text provides the teacher with a unique window into their comprehension of the story—the better one understands, the better able one is to articulate that understanding. In early

Figure 9.17 Graphic Organizer for Sequence of Events

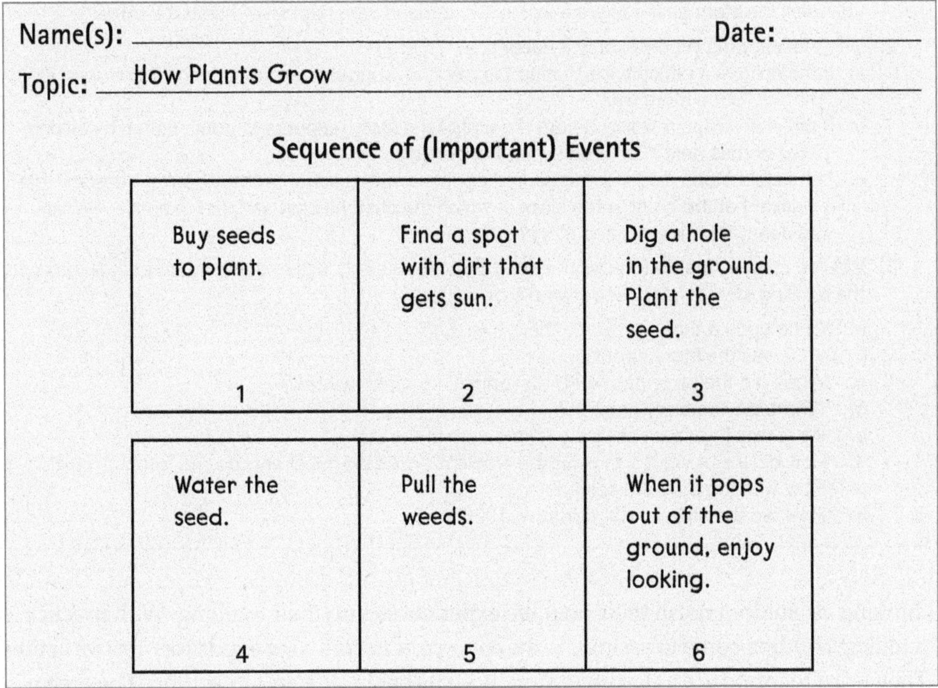

childhood classrooms, a simple and effective way to have students summarize texts is to ask them to retell the story.

Name(s):
Date:
Topic: How Plants Grow
Sequence of (Important) Events
Buy seeds to plant.
1
Find a spot with dirt that gets sun.
2
Dig a hole in the ground. Plant the seed.
3
Water the seed.
4
Pull the weeds.
5
When it pops out of the ground, enjoy looking.
6

Encouraging a listener or reader to retell or rewrite a story offers active participation in a literacy experience that helps develop language structures, comprehension, and sense of story structure (Paris & Paris, 2007). Retelling, whether it is oral or written, engages children in holistic comprehension and organization of thought. It also allows for original

Figure 9.18 Graphic Organizer for Cause and Effect

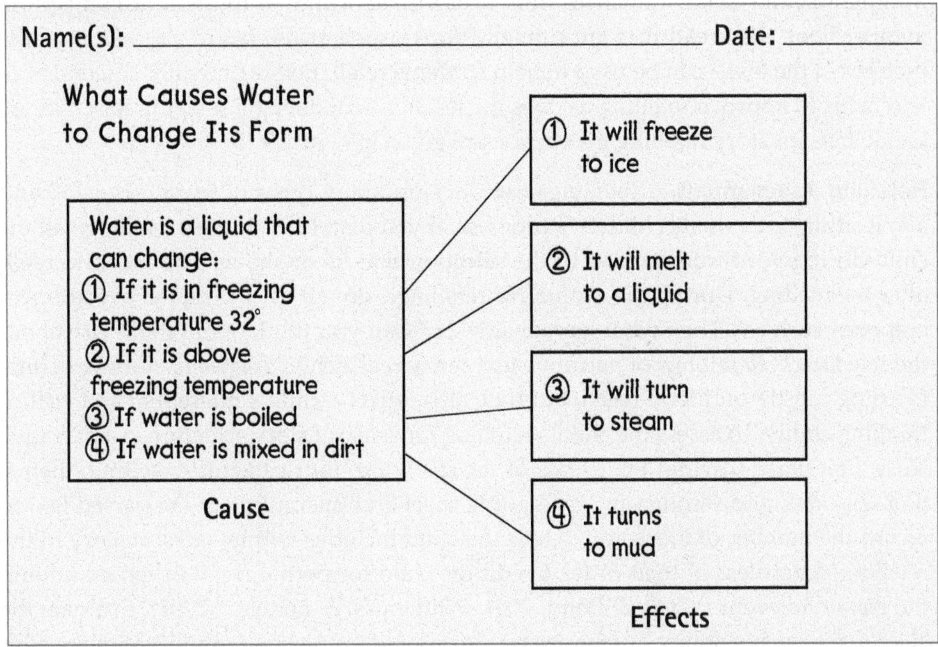

Figure 9.19 Guidelines for Story Retelling Instruction

1. Ask the child to retell the story. "A little while ago, I read the story [name the story]. Would you retell the story as if you were telling it to a friend who has never heard it before?"
2. Use the following prompts only if needed:
   a. If the child has difficulty beginning the retelling, suggest beginning with "Once upon a time" or "Once there was . . . "
   b. If the child stops retelling before the end of the story, encourage continuation by asking "What comes next?" or "Then what happened?"
   c. If the child stops retelling and cannot continue with general prompts, ask a question that is relevant at the point in the story at which the child has paused. For example, "What was Jenny's problem in the story?"
3. When a child is unable to retell the story or if the retelling lacks sequence and detail, prompt the retelling step by step. For example:
   a. "Once upon a time" or "Once there was . . . "
   b. "Who was the story about?"
   c. "When did the story happen?" (day, night, summer, winter?)
   d. "Where did the story happen?"
   e. "What was [the main character's] problem in the story?"
   f. "How did [he or she] try to solve the problem? What did [he or she] do first [second, next]?"
   g. "How was the problem solved?"
   h. "How did the story end?" (Morrow, 1996)

thinking as children mesh their own life experiences into their retelling. With practice in retelling, children come to assimilate the concept of narrative or expository text structure. They learn to introduce a narrative story with its beginning and its setting. They recount its theme, plot episodes, and resolution. In retelling stories, children demonstrate their comprehension of story details and sequence, organizing them coherently. They also infer and interpret the sounds and expressions of characters' voices. In retelling expository text, children review what they have learned, sequence events, describe new concepts, and recall cause and effect. In short, they explain what they know and how they know it.

Retelling is not an easy task for children, but they improve quickly with practice. To help children develop the practice of retelling, let them know before they read or listen to a text or story that they will be asked to retell or rewrite it (Morrow, 1996). Further guidance depends on the teacher's specific purpose in the retelling. If the immediate intent is to teach or test sequence—for instance, instruct children to concentrate on what happened first, second, and so on. If the goal is to teach or assess the ability to integrate information and make inferences from text, instruct children to think of things from another book they read that are similar. Props—such as felt board characters or the pictures in the text—can be used to help students retell. Before and after discussion of text helps to improve retelling as does the teacher's modeling a retelling for children. Guidelines for story retelling instruction are given in Figure 9.19.

Retelling Assessment. Retellings can develop many types of comprehension and allow adults to evaluate children's progress. If you plan to evaluate a retelling, tell the child during your introduction of the selection that he or she will be asked to retell after the reading. During the evaluative retellings, do not offer prompts beyond general ones such as "Then what happened?" or "Can you think of anything else about the selection?" Retellings of narrative text can reveal a child's sense of story structure, focusing mostly on literal recall, but they also reflect a child's inferential and critical thinking ability. To assess the child's retelling for sense of story structure in a narrative story, first parse (divide) the events of the story into four categories: setting, theme, plot episodes, and resolution. Use a guide sheet and the outline of the parsed text to record the number of ideas and details the child includes within each category in the retelling, regardless of their order. Credit the child for partial recall or for recounting the gist of an event (Wasik & Bond, 2001; Whitehurst & Lonigan, 2001). Evaluate the child's sequencing ability by comparing the order of events in the child's retelling with the proper order of setting, theme, plot episodes, and resolution. The analysis indicates which elements the child includes or omits, how well the child sequences, and thus where instruction might be focused. Comparing retellings over a year will indicate the child's progress.

Parsed stories and verbatim transcriptions are two tools educators can use to evaluate how well children comprehend a story or reading. The following example uses a parsed outline of the narrative story *Jenny Learns a Lesson* (Fujikawa, 1980). The parsed outline is accompanied by transcriptions of a child's retelling of the story. The retelling guide sheet in Figure 9.20 illustrates a quantitative analysis of the first transcription told by a child named Beth (Morrow, 1996).

Figure 9.20 Evaluation Guide Sheet for a Quantitative Analysis of Story Retelling and Rewriting

SOURCE: From L. M. Morrow, Story Retelling: A Discussion Strategy to Develop and Assess Comprehension. In *Lively Discussions!: Fostering Engaged Reading*, ed. L. B. Gambrell & J. F. Almasi, pp. 265–285. Reprinted by permission of Linda B. Gambrell.

Child's name: Beth Age: 5

Title of story: Jenny Learns a Lesson Date: ______

Directions: Give 1 point for each element included as well as for gist. Give 1 point for each character named as well as for such words as *boy, girl,* or *dog.* Credit plurals (*friends,* for instance) with 2 points under characters.

Sense of Story Structure

Setting

a. Begins story with an introduction		1
b. Names main character		1
c. Number of other characters named	2	
d. Actual number of other characters	4	
e. Score for "other characters" (c/d):		.5
f. Includes statement about time or place		1

Theme

Refers to main character's primary goal or problem to be solved	1

Plot Episodes

a. Number of episodes recalled	4	
b. Number of episodes in story	5	
c. Score for "plot episodes" (a/b)		.8

Resolution

a. Names problem solution/goal attainment	1
b. Ends story	1

Sequence

Retells story in structural order: setting, theme, plot episodes, resolution. (Score 2 for proper, 1 for partial, 0 for no sequence evident.)	1

Highest score possible: 10 Child's score: 8.3

Parsed Story

Setting

1. Once upon a time there was a girl who liked to play pretend.
2. *Characters:* Jenny (main character), Nicholas, Sam, Mei Su, and Shags, the dog.

Theme

Every time Jenny played with her friends, she bossed them.

Plot Episodes

First episode: Jenny decided to pretend to be a queen. She called her friends. They came to play. Jenny told them all what to do and was bossy. The friends became angry and left.

Second episode: Jenny decided to play dancer. She called her friends and they came to play. Jenny told them all what to do. The friends became angry and left.

Third episode: Jenny decided to play pirate. She called her friends and they came to play. Jenny told them all what to do. The friends became angry and left.

Fourth episode: Jenny decided to play duchess. She called her friends and they came to play. Jenny told them all what to do. The friends became angry and left.

Fifth episode: Jenny's friends refused to play with her because she was so bossy. Jenny became lonely and apologized to them for being bossy.

Resolution

1. The friends all played together, and each person did what he or she wanted to do.
2. They all had a wonderful day and were so tired that they fell asleep.

Parsed stories give children a foothold on the trajectory of the text. To determine how well the students have really understood the essence of the story, ask them to retell the story while you take a verbatim transcription of their rendition. The following retelling by 5-year-old Beth was transcribed when she was in the first part of her kindergarten year.

> Once upon a time there's a girl named Jenny and she called her friends over and they played queen and went to the palace. They had to do what she said and they didn't like it, so then they went home and said that was boring. It's not fun playing queen and doing what she says you have to. So, they didn't play with her for seven days and she had an idea that she was being selfish, so she went to find her friends and said, I'm sorry I was so mean. And said, let's play pirate, and they played pirate and they went onto the ropes. Then they played that she was a fancy lady playing house. And they have tea. And they played what they wanted and they were happy. The end.

To demonstrate how retellings can become more sophisticated and improve with practice and time, have children do another retelling at the end of their kindergarten year. In the second part of her kindergarten year, Beth retold the story *Under the Lemon Tree* (Hurd, 1980). The story is about a donkey who lives under a lemon tree on the farm and watches out for all the other animals. A fox comes in the night and steals a chicken or duck and the donkey hee-haws loudly to protect them. He scares the fox away, but wakes the farmer and his wife who never see the fox. This happens frequently until the farmer can no longer take the noise and moves the donkey to a tree far from the farmhouse. The donkey is very unhappy there. The fox comes back and steals the farmer's prize red rooster. The other animals quack and cluck and finally wake up the farmer who chases after the fox. When the fox passes him, the donkey makes his loud noises again, frightening the fox, who drops the red rooster. The farmer realizes that the donkey has been protecting his animals and moves him back to the lemon tree where he is happy again.

As you read 5-year-old Beth's retelling of *Under the Lemon Tree* from April, recall her retelling of *Jenny Learns a Lesson* from earlier that same year in September. Note her progress:

> Once upon a time there was a donkey, and he was in a farm. He lived under a lemon tree close to the animals on the farm. In the morning all the bees buzzed in the flowers under the lemon tree. He was next to the ducks, the chickens, and the roosters. It was night time. The red fox came into the farm to get something to eat. The donkey went "hee-haw, hee-haw" and then the chickens went "cluck, cluck" and the ducks went "quack-quack." Then the farmer and his wife waked up and looked out the window and saw nothing. They didn't know what came into their farm that night. They said, "What a noisy donkey we have. When it gets dark we will bring him far away." So, when it get darker and darker they brang the donkey over to a fig tree. And he had to stay there. He couldn't go to sleep alone. That night the red fox came into the farm again to try and get something to eat. All the ducks went "quack-quack" and the turkeys went "gobble-gobble." The farmer and his wife woke up and said, "Is that noisy donkey back again?" They rushed to the window and saw the fox with their red rooster in his mouth and yelled, "Stop thief, come back." The fox passed the donkey and he shouted "hee-haw, hee-haw." The red fox heard it and dropped the rooster and ran away. The farmer and his wife said, "Aren't we lucky to have the noisiest donkey in the whole world?" And they picked up the rooster and put one hand around the donkey and they all went home together and tied the donkey under the lemon tree.

Retellings can be evaluated for many different comprehension tasks. The directions to students prior to retelling and the method of analysis should match the goal. Figure 9.21 provides a qualitative analysis form for evaluating oral and written narrative retellings in which checks are used instead of numbers for a general sense of the elements a child includes and to determine progress over time. Also provided in the form is a qualitative evaluation of interpretive and critical responses. Using Figure 9.21, a child could engage in self-evaluation (with help from the teacher) by changing the words to: I began the story with an introduction, I named the main character, I was able to list other characters, and so on.

MyLab Education Self-Check 9.3

Fluency as a Path to Comprehension

There are many standards or goals for fluent readers, for example:
Read with sufficient accuracy and fluency to support comprehension.

- **a.** Read on-level with purpose and understanding.
- **b.** Read on-level orally with accuracy. Appropriate rate and expression on successive readings.
- **c.** Use context to confirm or self-correct word recognition and understanding, rereading as necessary.

MyLab Education
Video Example 9.4
The Importance of Fluency
In this video, Dr. Tim Shanahan tells about the importance of fluency and how to effectively teach it.

A skill that needs more emphasis in literacy instruction is fluency. According to the National Reading Panel Report (2000), helping children become fluent readers is crucial for literacy development.

Fluency is a combination of accuracy, automaticity, and prosody when reading. More simply, a child who reads fluently is able to decode text automatically and accurately. He or she does not have to labor over every sound. In addition, the child reads with the appropriate pace and expression. This aspect of language is referred to as

Figure 9.21 Evaluation Guide Sheet for a Qualitative Analysis of Story Retelling and Rewriting

Child's name: ______________________ **Date:** ________

Name of story: ______________________

Setting	**Yes**	**No**
a. Begins story with an introduction	☐	☐
b. Names main character	☐	☐
c. List other characters named here: ____________ ____________		
d. Includes statement about time and place	☐	☐
Theme		
a. Refers to main character's primary goal or problem to be solved	☐	☐
Plot Episodes		
a. Episodes are recalled	☐	☐
b. List episodes recalled	☐	☐
Resolution		
a. Includes the solution to the problem or the attainment of the goal	☐	☐
b. Puts an ending on the story	☐	☐
Sequence		
a. Story is told in sequential order	☐	☐

Interpretive and Critical Comments: Read through the retelling or rewriting and list comments made or written by students that are of an interpretive or critical nature.

prosody. Prosody suggests that the student is comprehending the text because he or she is reading with appropriate expression and rate (Kuhn & Stahl, 2003; Kuhn, Schwanenflugel, & Meisinger, 2010). The ultimate goal for reading instruction is that students become fluent readers.

To reach that goal, children should participate in fluent reading activities daily. They are easy to do, they don't take much time, and they are fun. Fluency can be worked on as early as preschool. Preschoolers can participate in all the fluency activities, but as listening activities rather than reading. They are exposed to the rhythm, pace, and expression involved in fluent reading. Preschoolers can echo speak instead of echo read. The teacher recites, and they repeat. Choral speaking can be done with memorized pieces of poetry. They can be involved in paired listening with an older child, listening to excellent models of storybook reading on tape, and repeated readings.

Methods for Practicing Fluency

Research has shown that several strategies are useful in helping to develop fluency, including echo reading, choral reading, paired reading, Reader's Theater, and antiphonal, tape-assisted, and repeated reading.

Echo Reading. **Echo reading** is when the teacher or a more able reader reads one line of text, and the child then reads the same line. The number of lines read is increased as the child's reading improves. When reading, be sure to model with appropriate accuracy, pace, and expression and Additionally, be sure the children are looking at the words and reading the words, not simply listening and repeating. Ask them to look at and follow the print on the page with their fingers. Try to echo read a few times a week.

MyLab Education
Video Example 9.5
Echo Reading
A teacher demonstrates the use of echo reading in the classroom.
http://youtu.be/exHfkO07_wc

Choral Reading. When **choral reading**, the entire class or a small group of children reads an entire passage together along with the teacher. The teacher ensures that he or she provides a model for pace and expression. Short passages and poetry are good for choral reading. When choral reading, the child "feels" the correct pace and expression necessary in reading fluently. Try to choral read a few times a week.

Paired Reading. **Paired reading** involves a more able reader in the same classroom or from another classroom as a model of fluent reading for less fluent readers. When they read together, the more able reader acts as the tutor. The children should read material that is easy for the child who is less fluent. The readers should take turns; for example, the tutor can read a page and then the less fluent reader repeats the same page. They can alternate reading page by page. The tutor helps the less able reader with accuracy, rate, and expression.

Reader's Theater. **Reader's Theater** is the oral reading of a short play. The children have assigned parts and practice the parts for the presentation. This provides a model of what fluent reading. sounds like. Invite parents to school to hear the class perform a Reader's Theater piece and take the opportunity to introduce them to the concept of fluency. Teach them some of the strategies by having them participate with you and their children. A Reader's Theater script is provided for you in Figures 9.22 and 9.23. There are also face puppets with directions for carrying out the activity (Young & Rasinski, 2009).

Antiphonal Reading. **Antiphonal reading** is a choral reading in which parts are taken by groups. Poetry with conversation works well with this activity. Divide your class into two, three, or four groups. Assign each group a different part to read. Practice each part and then read together (Johns & Berglund, 2002). Sometimes antiphonal choral readings can be judged as to which group had best expression and pace.

Tape-Assisted Reading. Listening to fluent reading samples on CDs while following the written text provides an excellent model for children. These CDs can be purchased or made by teachers, parents, and other students who present fluent models for reading.

Repeated Reading. Read the same story three or four times in one week. When a story is repeated, it offers the opportunity for fluent reading because of its familiarity. When children can read a text well, they will understand what fluent reading is. Select a short story, and on the first day, read the text to the children as they follow along. On the second day, do an echo reading. On the third day, do a choral reading, and on the fourth, do a partner reading. Help support the reading of the text and use challenging books with rich vocabulary.

Materials for Fluency Training

Reading materials for reading instruction, such as basal selections or leveled books, are good for fluency training. They can be read using echo and choral reading as part of the instructional routine when new text is introduced. Books with dialogue, such as fables, are good for Reader's Theater, since the characters provide parts for children to read. Short pieces of text and poems are best for choral, echo, repeated, and paired reading. A book of poems by Mary Ann Hoberman called *You Read to Me, I'll Read to You* (2001) has delightful poems with at least two characters talking to each other in

Figure 9.22 Little Red Hen: Reader's Theater for Fluency

The teacher assigns parts for the Reader's Theater for the children to practice. During the delivery of the play, five other children assume the roles of the animals, using the face puppets (refer to Figure 9.24).

Characters: Narrator, Little Red Hen, Cow, Pig, Dog

Narrator: Little Red Hen found a sack of wheat seed and rushed to tell her friends. Perhaps they will help her plant the seeds.

Little Red Hen: Cow, will you help me plant my seeds?

Cow: Not I, not I. It is too hot to do such work.

Little Red Hen: Pig, will you help me plant my seeds?

Pig: Not I, not I. it is too hot to do such work.

Little Red Hen: Dog, will you help me plant my seeds.

Dog: Not I, not I. It is too hot to do such work.

Narrator: So Little Red Hen planted the seeds all by herself. Several weeks went by and the seeds began to grow. Little Red Hen decided to ask her friends to help her tend and weed the garden.

Little Red Hen: Cow, will you help me weed the garden?

Cow: Not I, not I. The shade is too cool to leave.

Little Red Hen: Pig, will you help me weed the garden?

Pig: Not I, not I. The mud is too cool to leave.

Little Red Hen: Dog, will you help me weed the garden?

Dog: Not I, not I. The doghouse is too cool to leave.

Narrator: So Little Red Hen weeded and tended the garden all by herself. As the weeks went by, the sun ripened the wheat until it was ready to harvest. Little Red Hen decided to ask her friends to help her harvest the wheat.

Little Red Hen: Cow, will you help me harvest the wheat?

Cow: Not I, not I. It is too hot today.

Little Red Hen: Pig, will you help me harvest the wheat?

Pig: Not I, not I. It is too hot today.

Little Red Hen: Dog, will you help me harvest the wheat?

Dog: Not I, not I. It is too hot today.

Narrator: Once again Little Red Hen had to do all the work herself. She harvested the wheat. When she had finished, she asked her friends to help her grind the wheat into flour.

Little Red Hen: Cow, will you help me grind the wheat into flour?

Cow: Not I, not I. It is too close to milking time.

Little Red Hen: Pig, will you help me grind the wheat into flour?

Pig: Not I, not I. It is too close to supper time.

Figure 9.22 Little Red Hen: Reader's Theater for Fluency (*continued*)

Little Red Hen: Dog, will you help me grind the wheat into flour?

Dog: Not I, not I. It is too close to supper time.

Narrator: So Little Red Hen ground the wheat into flour all by herself. Then Little Red Hen decided to bake her flour into bread. She decided to give her friends another chance to help her.

Little Red Hen: Cow, will you help me bake this flour into bread?

Cow: Not I, not I. It is too hot to bake.

Little Red Hen: Pig, will you help me bake this flour into bread?

Pig: Not I, not I. It is too hot to bake.

Little Red Hen: Dog, will you help me bake this flour into bread?

Dog: Not I, not I. It is too hot to bake.

Narrator: Little Red Hen baked the bread all by herself. When it was done, she let it cool for awhile. Before she knew it, the time came to cut and eat the bread. Looking around, she didn't see anyone.

Little Red Hen: Hum, I wonder who will help me eat this bread?

Cow: (rushing up) I will!

Pig: (rushing up) I will!

Dog: (rushing up) I will!

Little Red Hen: No. You didn't help me plant the seeds. You didn't help me water the seeds. You didn't help me hoe the weeds, thresh the wheat, nor bake the bread. Now you may not help me eat the bread. I will do it myself.

Narrator: And she did!

every poem. The poems are in different colored print for the different characters. It is perfect for Reader's Theater and echo, choral, antiphonal, paired, and repeated reading. A portion of one poem entitled "I Like" is colored in purple for one character and pink for another, and blue represents reading all together, represented here by regular, italicized, and boldface print.

Evaluating Fluency

Listen to a child's reading of a passage that is at his or her instructional level. The child can read it to you, or you can tape-record the passage and evaluate it later.

1. Check the number of words read per minute in comparison with expectations at the child's grade level.
2. Do a running record to determine the types of errors made that disrupt fluency.
3. Use an informal fluency tool that describes the reading, such as:
   a. Reading is word by word.
   b. There are long pauses between words.
   c. Many words are missed.
   d. The reading is in a monotone voice with little evidence of use of punctuation or sense that the text is understood.
   e. The rate is slow and laborious.

Figure 9.23 Little Red Hen Face Masks

Directions: Enlarge the figures or copy on firm colored paper. Tape on a tongue depressor for children to hold when using.

The following are appropriate reading rates for first, second, and third graders:

The mean number of words read per minute for first graders in December is 54, in February is 66, and in May is 79.
The mean number of words typically read by second graders is 53 in the fall, 78 in the winter, and 94 in the spring.
For third graders, the mean number of words read in a minute is 79 in the fall, 93 in the winter, and 114 in the spring.

MyLab Education Application Exercise 9.2

Have students evaluate their own fluency about four times a year. They can listen to the taped reading and evaluate their reading as follows:

Okay: Reading is word by word, slow, and choppy with some words missed and not enough expression to show an understanding of the text.

Good: The pace of the reading is slow but not choppy. Most words are pronounced properly with enough expression to show some understanding of the text.

Fluent: Reading flows smoothly at a good pace. All words are decoded properly and expression demonstrates an understanding of what is being read.

MyLab Education Self-Check 9.4

Assessment of Comprehension of Text

The techniques described in this chapter are designed to develop concepts about books and comprehension of story through the use of expository and narrative text. The skills listed in the checklist in Figure 9.24 can be developed and assessed by a broad range of strategies used in various contexts. To determine how much children know about books--such as their front, back, top, and bottom; which part is print and which parts are pictures; how pages are turned; where reading begins; and what titles, authors, and illustrators are--one can observe regularly how youngsters handle books; hold one-to-one interviews with children; question and encourage response in whole-group, small group, or individual interaction; or use any of the several other techniques described in this chapter. Children's responses can be literal, interpretive, or critical. They can reflect simple recall, detail, sequence, association, prediction, judgment, and evaluation. Children's comprehension of story can be demonstrated and evaluated through their story retelling, story rewriting, attempted reading of favorite storybooks, role-playing, picture sequencing, use of puppets or felt boards to reenact stories, and questions and comments during storybook reading. When possible, keep periodic performance samples of activities, such as a story rewriting and audio or videotapes of retellings.

Throughout this chapter, assessment tools for evaluating strategies have been provided. These materials should be placed in a child's portfolio to evaluate his or her concepts about books and comprehension of text. Baseline data from children should be collected early in the school year with assessment measures repeated every 6 to 8 weeks.

MyLab Education Self-Check 9.5

Figure 9.24 Checklist for Assessing Concepts about Books and Comprehension of Text

Child's name: ______________________ **Date:** ______________________

Concepts about Books	**Always**	**Sometimes**	**Never**	**Comments**
Knows a book is for reading				
Can identify the front, back, top, and bottom of a book				
Can turn the pages properly				
Knows the difference between the print and the pictures				
Knows that pictures on a page are related to what the print says				
Knows where to begin reading				
Knows what a title is				
Knows what an author is				
Knows what an illustrator is				
Comprehension of Text				
Attempts to read storybooks resulting in well-formed stories				
Participates in story reading by narrating as the teacher reads				
Retells stories				
Includes narrative story structure elements in story retellings:				
Setting				
Theme				
Plot episodes				
Resolution				
Responds to text after reading or listening with literal comments or questions				
Can summarize what is read				
Responds to text after reading or listening with interpretive comments or questions				
Responds to text after reading or listening with critical comments or questions				
Generates questions that are literal, intentional, and critical				
Can answer question showing evidence from the text				
Can close read to unpack the meaning				

Figure 9.24 Checklist for Assessing Concepts about Books and Comprehension of Text (*continued*)

Participates and Responds During

Use of graphic organizers

Partner reading

Buddy reading

Literature circles

Mental imagery

Think-alouds

Discussions

Think, pair, share

Vocabulary Development

Learns new words daily in oral language

Uses new words in writing

Recognizes and understands features of expository text:

- Table of contents
- Glossary
- Index
- Diagrams, charts

Expository structures such as description, sequence, comparison and contrast, cause and effect, exemplification

Teacher Comments:

An Idea from the Classroom

Visualizing Mental Images

Visualizing helps my third-grade children to comprehend by creating mental images. I choose a passage of either narrative or expository text that contains vivid descriptions. I start the lesson by writing the word *visualizing* on the board. I ask students what they know about visualizing and write down their responses. I explain that visualizing involves making mental images or pictures in your mind that connect to the words you hear or read. I describe a situation in which I used visualization to understand and remember something, and ask the students to provide their own examples. Next, I read the chosen text, but do not show any of the pictures. I ask the students to listen carefully and to make a picture in their minds that helps them remember the story. They can close their eyes if it helps them. After the read aloud, I have the students return to their seats and illustrate the "pictures they made in their minds," or their interpretation of the text and write about it. The students can share their illustrations with their classmates and explain their individual interpretations. Finally, I lead a discussion of the similarities and differences in the students' ideas and compare student illustrations with those in the text.

Used with permission from *Heather Casey, Third-Grade Teacher*

Summary

9.1 Outline recent theory and research about reading comprehension.

Comprehension is the ultimate goal for reading instruction. It is an active process that involves making connections between prior knowledge, the topic under study, and the words being read. It is the ability to understand what we read. It is not only about who the characters are or what the facts are; comprehension includes the ability to infer about what happened even though it might not be written in the text, analyze the words on the written page, and come to conclusions. Social interactions enhance comprehension, as does the level of a student's metacognition. Although children in early grades are regularly taught strategies for decoding and reading, they are rarely taught techniques for enhancing their comprehension. Encouraging the integration of reading and comprehension techniques into other curricular areas allows children to practice their skills throughout the school day in the context of the many disciplines they study.

9.2 Outline classroom organizational strategies for teaching comprehension.

Students must learn to comprehend narrative (literature) and expository (informational) text. Formal strategies for teaching comprehension skills include reading workshop and directed reading lessons. Reading workshop combines a read aloud with a mini lesson, silent reading, and sharing time. Directed listening/reading thinking activities, which can be used with narrative and expository text, follow a framework of preparing for reading (creating the context), reading, and discussing the story after reading it.

9.3 Summarize important reading research-based strategies that enhance a child's comprehension of text.

Collective, collaborative, close, and repetitive reading experiences enhance student comprehension. Collective reading occurs in groups and is directed by the teacher. A teacher is able to introduce a new book to the students by using a read aloud. In narrative text, a read aloud should focus on stylistics and informational text should focus on developing new vocabulary. Shared book experiences involve reading a book that students have previously read. Teachers often use Big Books for shared book experiences and may record a reading so that students may experience it in another modality. Small group and one-on-one reading are also critical collective reading experiences that allows students to connect more intimately with the text. Collaborative reading experiences are peer-to-peer and occur independently of the teacher. Literature circles, reciprocal teaching, and buddy and partner reading are types of collaborative reading experiences. Think, pair, share and visualizing are two other collaborative strategies. Even though collaborative reading occurs independently of the teacher, nonetheless the teacher should model behavior for response groups. Close reading involves selecting short text passages and reading and analyzing them in a detailed fashion. Although more appropriate for older grades, close reading can be used in lower grades as well. Repetition of reading in all of these experiences helps students build comprehension because the texts are familiar.

Interactive discussions, building graphic organizers, and summarizing the text are ways to actively work with texts to enhance comprehension. Interactive discussions allow children to engage with each other and the text. Generative questions are key to sparking discussion. Questions should have more than one answer and relate to students' interests. Teachers should ask literal, inferential and critical, and aesthetic questions to generate deeper, multifaceted discussions about the text. Graphic organizers help students see relationships between concepts or events in a text. Maps, webs, K-W-L, and Venn diagrams are common types of graphic organizers. Maps and webs are graphic representations for categorizing information. K-W-L charts organize what children know, want to know, and learned about a text. Venn diagrams show areas of commonality between two or more concepts or texts. Graphic organizers for expository texts help students understand the text through description, comparison, sequencing, and identification of problem and solution and of cause and effect. Summarizing by retelling is another strategy for actively working with texts. By practicing retelling stories and expository material, students gain skills in synthesizing concepts and events into a cohesive summary.

9.4 Discuss the role of fluency in comprehension and strategies to enhance fluency.

Children who read fluently are able to decode text automatically and accurately, so fluency is an indicator of comprehension. Children should practice fluency every day. Echo reading, choral reading, paired reading, Reader's Theater, antiphonal reading, tape-assisted reading, and repeated reading are all ways to practice fluency. Leveled books are good for echo and choral reading; fables and books with dialogue are good for antiphonal reading and Reader's Theater. Short passages and poems work well with echo, choral, paired, and repeated reading.

In addition to teachers evaluating their students' fluency, the students themselves should evaluate their own fluency several times a year.

9.5 Review and summarize how to assess children's comprehension of text.

Comprehension skills can be assessed by a broad range of strategies in a variety of contexts. Children's responses to assessment can be literal, interpretive, or critical and can involve simple recall, detail, sequence, association, prediction, judgment, and evaluation. Teachers should keep periodic performance samples of activities, such as a story rewriting and audio or videotapes of retellings. Assessments should be collected at the beginning of the year and then every 6 to 8 weeks until the end of the academic year.

Activities and Questions

1. Meet several times with one child between the ages of 4 and 8 years. Each time you meet, let the child practice retelling a story. Record and transcribe each session. Using the forms provided in Figures 9.2 and 9.3, analyze the recordings for the elements of story structure, details, and sequence. Discuss if and how the child improved from the first time to the third retelling.
2. Select a piece of informational text and narrative text. Prepare a directed informational reading lesson that will involve children in literal, interpretive, and critical thinking. Then change these questions into activities (such as role-playing stories or felt stories) that enable children to demonstrate their comprehension of the story.
3. Using another comprehension strategy, such as graphic organizers, create a lesson to teach the strategy with both expository and narrative texts.
4. Select a strategy to enhance fluency and create a lesson to teach the strategy. Identify selections you will use for reading.
5. Use the assessment checklist in Figure 9.23 as you observe a child interacting with books and reading. Write a plan to help the child develop areas of weakness.
6. Try the Reader's Theater activity in your class or in a practicum.
7. The following passages describe a guided reading lesson in a small group taught by three different first-grade teachers. Each use strategies to promote comprehension. While reading these passages, think about the following questions:

   a. Do the questions posed by the teachers foster factual or interpretive thought?
   b. Is there an emphasis on specifics or an understanding of issues raised?
   c. Is the plan flexible or predetermined?
   d. Is there time for problem solving in an interactive manner with peers?
   e. Is the atmosphere constricted, controlled, supportive, warm, or rewarding?
   f. Can children raise questions?
   g. Are students asked to predict and analyze?
   h. Is there an emphasis on higher-order thinking or literal levels of thought?
   i. Is there concern for individual differences?

Read passages "Teacher A" and "Teacher B" and then answer the questions. If you had to select just one of these teachers, which one would you choose to be and why? After answering the questions, read Teacher C and then go back and answer all the questions again.

Teacher A

Teacher A begins her lesson by introducing the entire class to the story they will be reading, Goldilocks and the Three Bears *(Daley & Russell, 1999). The teacher guides the children through a book walk, looking at the pictures and discussing what is happening on each page, to become familiar with the story in advance of reading. Before reading the story, she tells the children she will want them to remember the important details of the story, such as the main characters; where the story takes place; what happened first, second, and so on; and how the story ends. She writes this information on an experience chart.*

The teacher asks the children to read the story orally together in very quiet voices. To check their comprehension, the teacher asks factual questions about the text, such as "Who are the main characters in the story?" and "What did Goldilocks do first when she got to the bears' house?" She asks similar questions all the way through the passage.

After the discussion, the children are given a worksheet to complete. The worksheet is designed to reinforce the details of the story. It includes questions that require the children to circle the correct answer. When the children are finished with the worksheet, the lesson is over.

Teacher B

Teacher B begins her small group reading lesson by asking the students to share things they have done that they knew were wrong. After the children describe their experiences, the teacher asks why they did these things. She then introduces the children to the story they will read, Goldilocks and the Three Bears. *Before reading, she has the children take a book walk by looking at the pictures in the book. She asks the children to predict what they think is happening on the different pages and what the story might be about. The teacher asks the class to think about who does things they shouldn't in the story while they read. The class then reads the story orally together from beginning to end. Afterward, the teacher asks questions designed to elicit information about the students' comprehension of the story theme by asking, "What are the main events in the story? Who does things that they shouldn't do? Why was it wrong? Was it okay for Goldilocks to go in the bears' house uninvited? Why yes or why no?" Children are asked to discuss favorite parts of the story and read these parts to the class.*

The teacher offers the children three choices for extended activities related to the story—for example, draw a picture about the story, act out the story, or make a felt story and tell it. The children decide to draw pictures about the story and make a class book. Different parts of the story are given to each child. They write what is happening on their page. The book is put together for the class to read.

Reminder: Answer the questions posed at the beginning of the case study activity and then read

Teacher C

Teacher C begins his small-group reading lesson by asking the students if they have any special things at home that they like very much. He asks how they might feel if someone came and took or used their special things without asking and ruined them. He introduces the story Goldilocks and the Three Bears *and has the children do a book walk, looking for how the bears' special things were used and ruined. Before reading, Teacher C asks the children to think about what special things were used and ruined. They read the book aloud together. The teacher asks the class to discuss how they think the bears felt when they got home and found someone had been in their house. All suggestions are accepted as the teacher explains that there can be many correct answers. The teacher asks the children to create an entirely new story about Goldilocks. The teacher allows the children to decide which students they would like to work with. In pairs they brainstorm and create their new story with illustrations and text. When they complete their work, they share their stories.*

Now answer the questions at the beginning of this case study activity for Teacher C and decide which teacher you would like to be now that you have read Teachers A, B, and C. Support your answer.

Chapter 10

Writing, Spelling, and Literacy Development

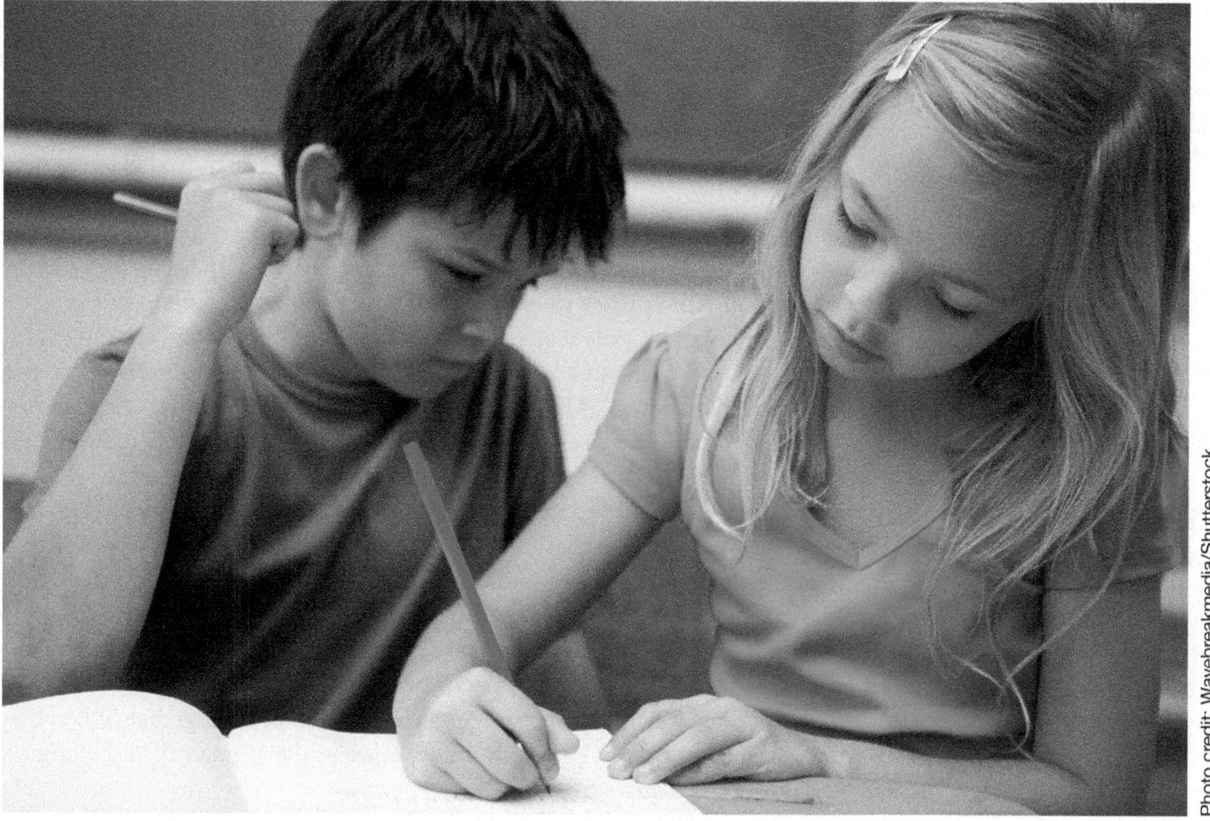

Photo credit: Wavebreakmedia/Shutterstock

Learning Outcomes

After reading this chapter, you should be able to:

10.1 Explain the theories underpinning early writing development.

10.2 Describe strategies used to help children from birth to pre-K develop writing.

10.3 Describe strategies to be used for developing writing in kindergarten through third grade.

10.4 Discuss the types of writing most appropriate for early childhood and give examples of how to develop each.

10.5 Demonstrate the important mechanical aspects of writing that children must learn.

10.6 Assess student writing.

VOCABULARY

Descriptive writing
Informational writing
Formative feedback
Functional writing
Invented spelling
Journal writing
Narrative writing
Persuasive writing
Poetry writing
Process approach to writing
Rubrics
Summative feedback
Writing workshop

According to Donald Graves (1983), children learn to write before they read. "Children want to write. They want to write the first day they attend school. This is no accident. Before they went to school they marked up walls, pavements, newspapers with crayons, chalk, pens or pencils, anything that makes a mark. The child's marks say, 'I am'."

As we look into Mrs. Brice's classroom, she is doing an interactive writing lesson. She is using the story *I Know an Old Lady*. It is a nonsense tale that is read and sung. A number of versions are available in picture-book form. The story is composed of rhymes and each segment is repeated to make it predictable. The purpose of the lesson is for children to engage in open-ended, problem-solving, to develop vocabulary, and to use rhyme. The style of the writing makes the story perfect as a mentor text. It demonstrates a type of patterned writing that children can use in their own writing.

After the story, Mrs. Brice asked her second-grade children to think of other things the old lady might swallow and what she would do or say as a result. Tasha said, "I got one. I know an old lady who swallowed a snake, ummm, ummm, she got a big ache when she swallowed the snake." Mrs. Brice suggested she come up to the flip chart to write her idea down on the chart paper. Jason added, "I think it might sound better if we said what a mistake to swallow a snake." Mrs. Brice asked if they wanted to make any other changes. Tasha said, "I know an old lady who swallowed a snake what a mistake to swallow a snake because the snake made her stomach ache." The class agreed with Tasha's suggestion. The teacher gave Tasha the white correction tape to put over the sentence so that she could write it again the way the class wanted it.

Christopher raised his hand and said, "I know an old lady who swallowed a frog, what a hog to swallow a frog." Molly said, "We can't do that, because in the real story when she swallows a dog, they say what a hog to swallow a dog." Christopher thought and said, "I know—I know an old lady who swallowed a frog, she started to jog when she swallowed a frog." "That's great," said Molly. Mrs. Brice asked Christopher to come up and write his rhyme on the chart paper.

MyLab Education
Video Example 10.1
There Was an Old Lady
A video of the song "There Was an Old Lady Who Swallowed a Fly. www.youtube.com/watch?v=8a13-JbxC98

Many of the children had ideas that were written down. Several of the ideas were improved by the group. Numerous new words popped up, and there were discussions about how to spell them and their meanings. The class agreed on 10 lines for their story and it would be done. Each child had paper on a clipboard to copy their interactive story. When the chart was complete, the class chanted the poem together. When they were done, Michael said, "You know, I think what we wrote is better than the original one." Everyone nodded and agreed.

Different Theories of Writing Development

Many researchers have explored the manners in which children develop competencies in written language. They have discovered a tight connection between reading and writing and that the development of written language occurs in discernable stages.

Relationships Between Reading and Writing

The purposes for reading and writing are similar. We read and write to construct meaning. Readers deal with meaning by responding to what has been read. Writers deal with meaning by constructing text (Bromley, 2011). When reading and writing, children engage in similar activities. Readers and writers:

- Generate ideas
- Organize ideas
- Monitor their thoughts
- Problem solve
- Revise how to think about their ideas.

Children learn about reading and writing in similar ways. They experiment and pretend at reading and writing and engage in trial and error as they practice literacy skills they have learned. Children are inventive when learning to read and write—they decorate letters, symbols, and words; they mix drawing and writing; and they invent messages in various forms and shapes (refer to Figure 10.1). Similarly, when children read they guess at what the text may say by reading pictures, they create character's voices and predict story outcomes. We teach children phonics skills, so they can decode text independently. When children write, they need to use the same phonics skills to create written work. It is important to realize how similar reading and writing are and to engage children in both daily. When children read, they strengthen writing skills, and when children write, they strengthen reading skills.

MyLab Education Application Exercise 10.1

Early Writing Acquisition

Children's early literacy experiences are embedded in the familiar situations and real-life experiences of the family and community (Ritchie, James-Szanton, & Howes, 2003). Many things family members do on a regular basis involve literacy. They write each other notes, make to-do lists, send greeting cards, write directions, draw pictures, and so on (Schickedanz & Casbergue, 2009; Soderman & Farrell, 2008).

Early writing development is characterized by children's moving from playfully making marks on paper, to communicating messages on paper, to creating texts. Children are initially unconcerned about the products of their "writing"; they lose interest in it almost immediately. However, once they begin to understand that the marks made can be meaningful and fun to produce, they are determined to learn how to write (Tompkins, 2000).

Figure 10.1 Writing Sample

In this writing sample, a 4-year-old uses writing as a part of the drawing.

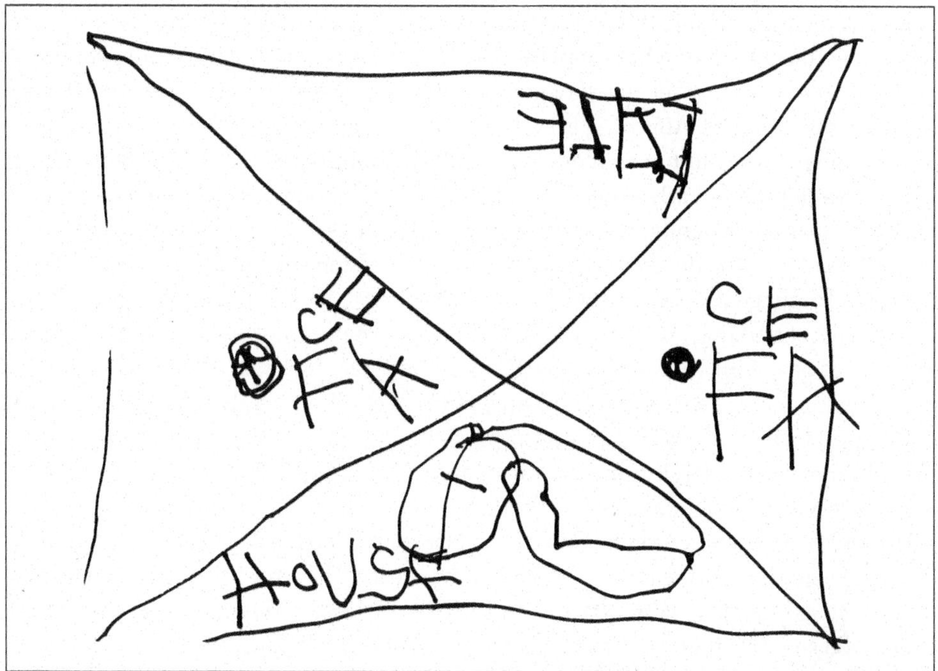

Figure 10.2 Functional Writing

A 5-year-old attempts functional writing in a letter to his friend.

Children learn the uses of written language before they learn the forms (Bromley, 2007; Gundlach, McLane, Scott, & McNamee, 1985). In observing children scribbling and inventing primitive "texts," researchers have noted that children seem to know what writing is for prior to knowing much about how to write in a conventional manner. The letters to friends or relatives, greeting cards, and signs they produce are not conventional forms of writing. Yet, the children seem impelled by an understanding of the function of written texts (Refer to Figure 10.2).

Drawing should play an integral role in early childhood literacy practices not only because it represents a crucial step in emergent literacy, but also because it affords the artist creativity, voice, and the ability to grapple with both the real and imaginary. Wright (2010) frames the importance of this research within the broader contexts of recent studies on multimodality, or multiple modes of communication, and new literacies. As such, studies have raised debates of what counts as a "text." By viewing drawings as texts unto themselves, the notion of what counts as a literacy act expands. Most children naturally enjoy the act of drawing. Yet, in today's early childhood classrooms, drawing is becoming less and less privileged. Affording early childhood students ample time for drawing acts as a stepping-stone into future literacy practices and supports students in their visual literacy development. Early childhood teachers should pay attention to what children draw and their metacognition—or what children are thinking aloud while drawing.

Children's writing develops through constant invention and reinvention of the forms of written language (Calkins, 1994; Dyson, 1986; Graves, 1994; Spandel, 2008). Children invent ways of making letters, words, and texts, moving from primitive forms to closer approximations of conventional forms (Hansen, 1987; Jalongo, 2007). Parents and teachers of preschool children need to show an interest in children's early writing and accept and support their youngsters' primitive productions. Children invent writing forms from their observations of environmental print, as well as from observing, modeling, and interacting with more literate individuals who write in the children's presence.

Students learn about writing through explicit instruction from teachers, by observing others more skilled than themselves, and through practice. They must be guided and taught about writing by supportive adults, and they need to observe adults participate in writing. People who are more proficient writers play an important modeling role in children's writing development (Jalongo, 2007; Temple, Nathan, Burris, & Temple, 1988; Tompkins, 2007).

Figure 10.3 Repetition of Similar Letter Patterns

Mia (age 3½) practices writing through the repetition of similar letter patterns from left to right across the page.

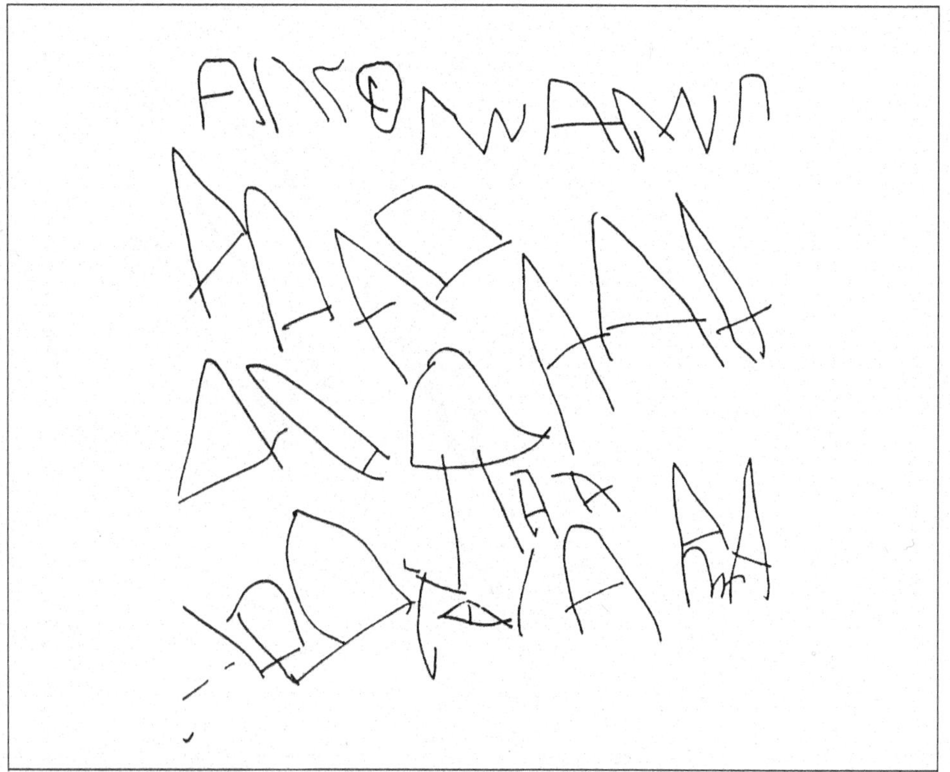

When children write independently, they are involved in practicing aspects of writing—letter formation, similarities or differences between drawing and writing, spelling, punctuation, and so forth. When children engage in independent writing, they try new writing they haven't done before. They become more conscious of what they know. (Refer to Figures 10.3 and 10.4.) Independent writing also allows children to experiment with writing words that have meaning and with recording their thoughts on paper.

Children need to write in social settings to learn. When children write with each other, with a teacher, or with a more literate other, they talk about what they write, they share each other's writing, and they imitate the more literate other. Social interaction is crucial in learning to write.

Writing development is part of a child's journey to literacy development. Literacy learning starts with drawing, then writing, and then reading (Vygotsky, 1978). Children's main resource for literacy learning is their knowledge of ways to symbolize experiences and to communicate through those symbols. This theoretical framework can be summarized as follows:

1. Literacy development encompasses the development of reading, writing, listening, speaking, and viewing.
2. Literacy development involves learning to use the symbols involved in reading, writing, listening, speaking, and viewing.
3. Literacy development in reading, writing, listening, and viewing engages the child in gaining information and being involved in social and cultural meanings.

For most children, the process for writing development occurs as a continuum. Under normal circumstances, children's early literacy development begins first with learning to communicate nonverbally, then by talking, next with symbolic play, and finally by drawing. Each new phase is rooted in earlier phases and forms a new network of communication resources.

Figure 10.4 Writing versus Drawing

Robert (age 4) separates his writing from his drawing by enclosing each in a circle during self-initiated practices.

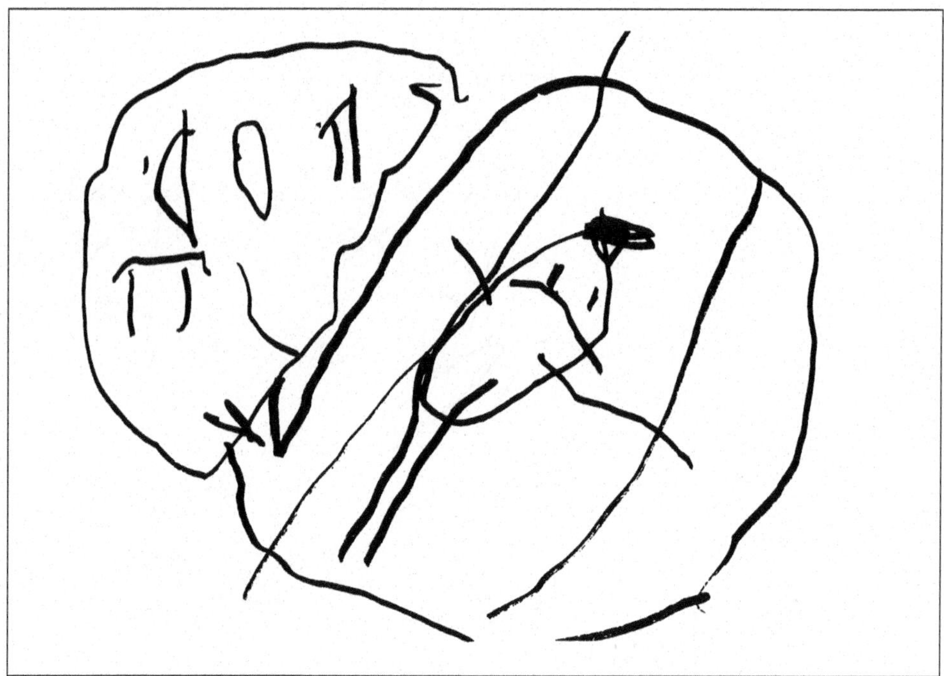

As children move from playing with written language to using it to communicate, they invent and reinvent forms. When children first begin making marks on paper, most do so with no knowledge of the alphabetic nature of the written language's symbol system. Shortly thereafter, they view letters as referring to actual people or things. It is quite a bit later when children realize that writing represents language (Spandel, 2001).

The Development of Writing Ability

Children learn a lot about literacy through play, especially in literate societies where they imitate adult models by making their own pretend play marks on paper. Soon the marks become written messages from which children achieve a sense of identity in their own eyes and in the eyes of others. The continuum from playing with drawing and writing, to communicating through written messages, to writing narrative and expository text reflects the basic theories of early literacy development (Dyson, 1993; Schickedanz & Casbergue, 2009; Turbill & Bean, 2006).

Researchers have recorded varied descriptions of the developmental stages of writing in early childhood (Dyson, 1985; Soderman & Farrell, 2008; Sulzby, 1985b; Tompkins, 2007). Most agree that if there are stages, they are not well-defined or necessarily sequential. Dyson (1986) describes children's writing development as having two broad phases. From birth to about age 3, children begin to explore the form of writing by scribbling. Then, as children progress from age 3 to 6, their controlled scribbling gradually develops into recognizable objects that they name, and similarly, the scribbling gradually acquires the characteristics of print, including linearity, horizontal orientation, and the arrangement of letter-like forms.

Sulzby (1985a) identified six broad categories of writing in kindergartners, cautioning that these should not be considered a reflection of developmental ordering. They do, however, describe children's early attempts at writing.

1. **Writing via Drawing:** The child will use drawing as a stand-in for writing. Then the child begins working out the relationship between drawing and writing, ceasing

to confuse the two. He or she sees drawing–writing as communication of a specific and purposeful message. Children who participate in writing via drawing will read their drawings as if there is writing on them (Li-Yuan, 2009). (refer to Figure 10.5.)

2. **Writing via Scribbling:** The child scribbles, but intends it as writing. Often, the child appears to be writing and scribbles from left to right. She or he moves the pencil as an adult does, and the pencil makes writing-like sounds. The scribble resembles writing. (refer to Figure 10.6.)

Figure 10.5 Writing via Drawing

When asked to write something, Eli (age 4) drew a picture and included a few letters. He told the teacher that it said "Daddy and me."

Figure 10.6 Writing via Scribbling

When asked to write, Natalie (age 3) scribbled randomly. She eventually progressed to a left-to-right scribble and then purposeful marks that could be periods to end the sentence.

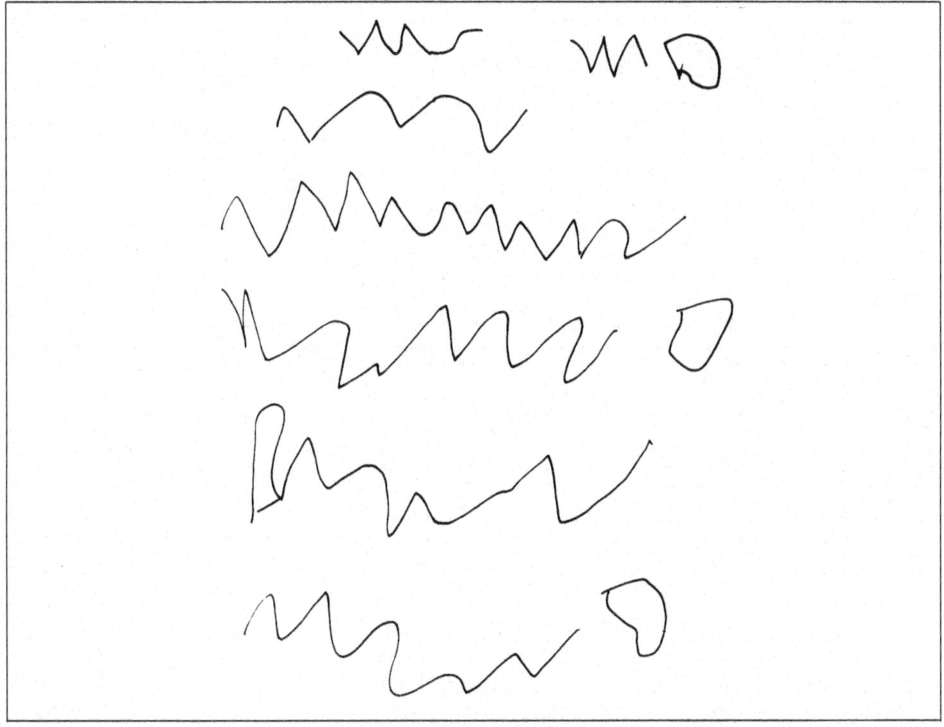

3. **Making Letter-like Forms:** At a glance, shapes in the child's writing resemble letters. Closer inspection reveals the shapes are not even poorly formed letters, but a series of letter-like creations. (refer to Figure 10.7.)
4. **Writing via Reproducing Well-learned Units or Letter Strings:** The child uses letter sequences learned from sources such as his or her own name. The child sometimes changes the order of the letters, writing the same ones many different ways, or reproduces letters in long strings or in random order. (refer to Figure 10.8.)

Figure 10.7 Writing via Making Letter-like Forms

James (age 4) wrote letter-like forms from left to right.

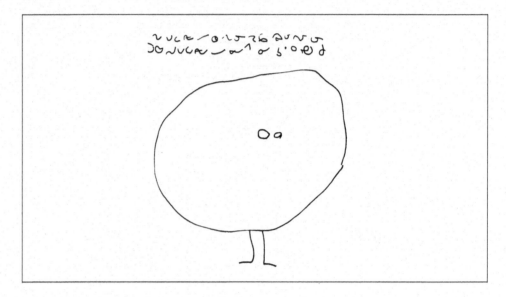

Figure 10.8 Writing via Reproducing Well-learned Units or Letter Strings

Written by Brian (age 4), these letters go from left to right across the page.

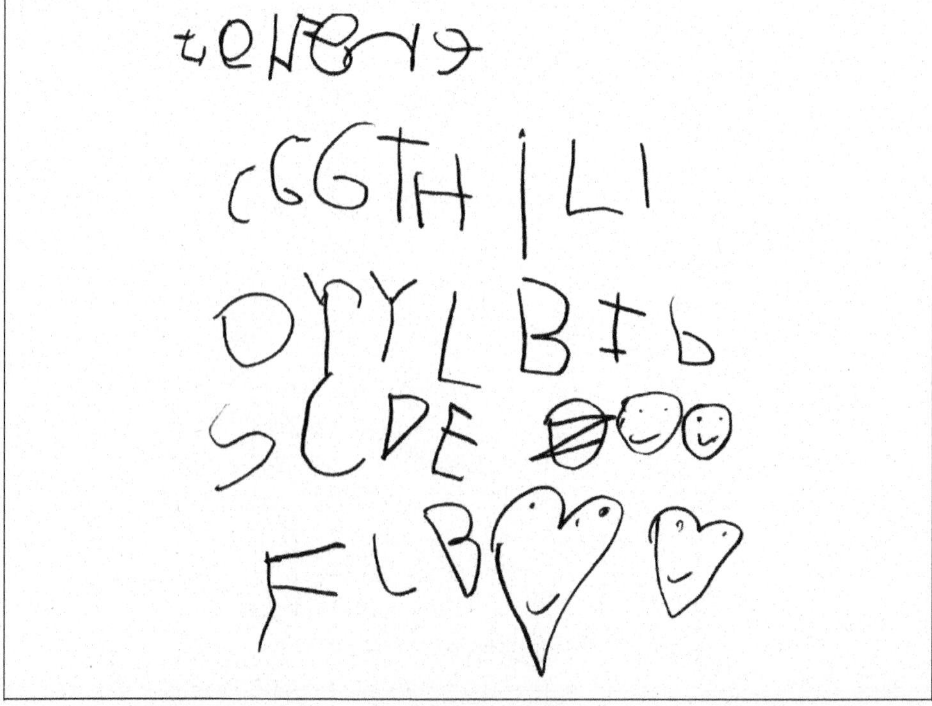

5. **Writing via Invented Spelling:** Children use many varieties and levels of **invented spelling** refers to when children create their own spelling for words when they do not know the conventional spellings. Using invented spelling, one letter may represent an entire word, and words sometimes overlap or are not properly spaced. As the child's writing matures, the words appear more like conventional writing, with perhaps only one letter invented or left out.
6. **Writing via Conventional Spelling:** The child's writing resembles adult writing. (refer to Figure 10.9.)

This general description of early writing is helpful for teachers and parents when they are observing and describing children's writing. These categories are not necessarily sequential. Some children skip a category or go back and forth with the categories (Hullinger-Sirken & Staley, 2016).

Objectives and Standards for Writing

Thinking about writing development changed enormously in the 1970s. We always encouraged children to use crayons and paper to develop motor coordination in preparation for writing, but we never thought of writing to convey meaning as being an integral part of an early literacy program for children as young as age 2. We now integrate strategies for writing into the daily routines of babies, toddlers, preschoolers, kindergartners, and first graders. We consider even the youngest child's marks on paper as early attempts at writing, rather than as random marks. This perception is necessary in programs for early literacy development (Horn & Giacobbe, 2007).

Generally, the best way to assist young children in language and literacy development is to provide explicit instruction and create situations that are meaningful. This principle applies equally in the home, child-care center, preschool, kindergarten, first,

Figure 10.9 Conventional Spelling

This story was written by a third grader.

Little Red Riding hood

Once upon a time there
was a little girl named
little red riding hood.
No one knew why she always
walked, she should be riding
something. The next morning
Mrs. Shobert asked little Red
riding hood why are you always
walking? Then she walked
away and she was thinking
"hmm" that gave her an idea
to buy something. She went to
a toyota deler, she didn't like
anything. Then she went to
a bike place and said, "I
think I like that one." Now
Red riding hood rides.

second, or third grade. The following objectives for promoting writing development derive from the perspective that children learn language, including writing and reading, by using it purposefully in many situations (for example, in playing or communicating).

Objectives for Writing Development

1. Children will be provided with an environment in which they are regularly exposed to many kinds of print.
2. Children will experience print as a source of pleasure and enjoyment.
3. Children will regularly observe adults writing for work and leisure purposes.
4. Children will be given opportunities and materials for writing.
5. Children's attempts at writing, whatever the form, will be responded to as meaningful communication (e.g., drawings, scribble writing, letter-like forms, random letters, invented spelling).
6. Students will write daily in pre-K through grade 3 to develop the desire and need to write regularly.
7. Children will be able to select their own topics and experiment with writing.
8. Children will be instructed in and encouraged to use writing for a wide range of purposes, such as creating stories, informational text, persuasive writing, descriptive writing, journal writing, and functional writing, such as lists, letters, signs, narratives, and announcements.
9. The use of writing will be integrated throughout the curriculum.
10. Children will experience constructivist activities prepared for them when writing in school and explicit instruction on skills in writing.
11. Children will be taught manuscript and cursive writing.
12. Children will learn keyboarding, so they can do their writing on the computer.
13. Teachers will take the opportunity through children's writing to point out sound–symbol correspondences as the spoken word is transformed into the written.
14. Children will be exposed to and taught the use of some aspects of punctuation: periods, commas, and quotation marks.
15. Children's invented spelling will be accepted as working toward conventional writing.
16. Teachers will provide instruction in spelling.
17. Children will be given the opportunity to write collaboratively.
18. Children will be able to read peers' work and provide feedback.
19. Children will receive a balance of both **formative feedback** (feedback while creating) and **summative feedback** (feedback at the end of an assignment).
20. Children will be granted regular opportunities to share their writings with other school members, their families, and the community.
21. With teacher assistance, young learners will be exposed to and be able to partake in digital writing practices, such as posting a response on a class wiki or website and completing a journal entry for a story on a blog. (Digital literacies are described in more in Chapter 12.)

Your state standards will include grade-by-grade writing standards from kindergarten through grade 3. They are very specific and explicit, overlapping at many points with the previously listed objectives. In addition, writing standards encourage children to have experiences with the following:

- A variety of types and purposes for writing
- Writing opinion and persuasive pieces with reasons

- Writing dialogue
- Providing concluding statements for writing
- Writing informative and narrative text
- Using mentor texts that are good examples of different types of writing on which children can model their own writing
- Demonstrating the ability to sequence events in writing, including details
- Guidance from adults, collaboration, and use of digital tools in the production and distribution of writing
- Doing research and writing with guidance to build and present knowledge.

MyLab Education Self-Check 10.1

Strategies for Early Writing Development

Techniques for helping children develop writing skills vary depending on age. Therefore, strategies for writing development from birth to age 2 must address needs different from those that occur in pre-K classrooms.

Strategies for Writing Development from Birth to Age 2

In earlier chapters, we described strategies that parents and day-care providers can use to help children with oral language development and early reading. It is crucial to remember that speaking, reading, and writing are dynamically linked in children's development. When we help children with oral language, we also contribute indirectly to their literacy development by increasing their language experiences. Similarly, reading development contributes to speaking and writing, and writing to speaking and reading. This understanding forms the basis for an integrated language arts approach.

Teaching English Learners
Inform parents about early writing so they will encourage their children to participate in the activities discussed for children from birth to age 2.

Children's early attempts at writing should be supported. While some children may make their first such attempts between 18 and 24 months old, others may not begin until they are age 2½ or 3. When children begin scribbling (some at age 18 months), they bang on the paper with their writing implements. As they become more familiar with writing, they will begin using smoother, more deliberate and coordinated movements to make their marks. When children are in their first, primitive stages of scribbling, we can show them how to hold markers or crayons. We can guide their hands to paper, not making marks for them, but helping them to understand that the paper is the place for writing. Most important is to sit next to them and model writing behavior by doing your own writing and drawing.

Our responses to children's early scribbling are important. It is better not to urge children to write particular things. They should make marks spontaneously and decide for themselves when these marks are intended to represent something. It is important not to press them to tell us what their marks mean or represent. It is better to say, "I like that," than to ask, "What are you drawing?" Another helpful response is, "Can you write some more?" Do not, however, insist if the child doesn't wish to respond. Expressing genuine pleasure in children's early markings, whether they resemble writing or not, and seeing them as an important step in a long developmental process are positive responses that will encourage children to continue. By continuing their "writing," they will incorporate in it what they are learning about print from daily literacy events.

We can also model writing for youngsters by allowing them to see us writing letters, lists, emails, text messages, notes, and filling out forms and encouraging them to interact with us while we do. For example, you might say, "I'm writing a letter to invite your parents to school. Do you have ideas of what I should say? Do you want to write something on the paper to them?" When writing, invite the youngsters to sit with you, watch you, ask questions, and try their own hand at writing. This gives children opportunities to see how to go about writing and to begin to understand that the marks we make convey meaning.

An important way that we can support children's writing development is to provide experiences with environmental print they see on food cans and boxes and road signs. Talk with children about their experiences with environmental print by commenting, asking questions, and encouraging them to identify and remember signs, letters, and bits of print out of their normal contexts (for instance, an *M* used somewhere other than in a McDonald's sign).

Children enjoy writing or making marks on flyers, brochures, ads, announcements, and forms. They will write over the print and in the blank spaces. The print gives them the model and inspiration to make their own marks.

Repeating rhymes and singing songs also contributes to children's early writing, as can using hand puppets and playing with toys and games, such as puzzles that can be taken apart and put back together. Manipulative toys that require dexterity help with the fine motor development needed to shape letters. Playing with play dough, finger painting, using chalkboards, and painting on easels help build motor coordination as well. Children should have access to keyboards in preschool since use of digital tools is now an integral part of their lives. Of course, reading to children not only develops oral language and promotes early reading attempts, as discussed earlier, but it also can motivate children to emulate the writing or to make their own books, no matter how crude the first attempts. Parents and caregivers in child-care centers can display children's early writings on walls, doors, and appliances, to be enjoyed and not judged or corrected (Rowe & Neitzel, 2010; Schickedanz & Casbergue, 2009).

Writing in Pre-K Classrooms

Like younger children, preschoolers take more pleasure in the process of writing than in its products. The act of writing is their center of interest, although they gradually develop concern for the products. When they play waiter or waitress, for example, and take an "order," they may be concerned that others can "read" it. The same thing might happen with notes or greeting cards sent to relatives or friends. Children begin to express concern that recipients are able to read their messages—perhaps so they can write back. Children who have had little experience pretending to write might be reluctant to make marks on paper (even by kindergarten age), possibly because they have become aware that their marks are not conventional writing and thus might not be accepted. It is important to let them know that unconventional writing will be accepted. Some children may request conventional spellings and will not write unless they know it is correct. They should be given the help they want.

MyLab Education
Video Example 10.2
Beginning Writing

Knowing a number of sight words and being able to create a sentence are skills that help beginning writers have success.

Learning to write involves learning to compose texts that convey meaning. As children gain experience with writing, they will learn the skills and mechanics of writing through practice and instruction. Learning to write uppercase and lowercase letters is appropriate for pre-K classrooms as is discussing punctuation.

Although they must begin learning the mechanics, young children should be free to write in unconventional ways, such as using invented spellings as pictured earlier. In doing so, they are enhancing phonemic awareness and establishing preliminary understandings of phonics. When children write, they have to transform the spoken word into written language. This process fosters understanding of the structure of spoken language and how it is related to written language. The more children write, the better they become at segmenting sounds and blending them into words, which develops not only their ability to write but also their ability to read independently (Horn & Giacobbe, 2007).

Young children choose to write if a situation has meaning for them. If we impose on them our selection of what they should write about all the time, we are not likely to see positive results. Children express themselves differently in early literacy, and it is important to attempt to understand their approaches (Zecker, 1999). Knowing this, we can create strategies and appropriate environments for helping children write. One such strategy is taking dictation.

Taking Dictation. Many children in pre-K and kindergarten have a lot to say, and because they cannot yet write well enough, we often take dictation. Taking dictation from children was a common Language Experience Approach (LEA) strategy that was used before we realized that young children could and should write in their own unconventional ways. Taking dictation, however, does play an important role in writing development. We model reading for children by reading to them before they read conventionally; we should also model writing for them by taking dictation some of the time. When teachers take dictation, children have the opportunity to grow more in their writing ability, as they watch an adult model for them the process (Shannahan, 2006). The following ideas are important when teachers take dictation (Morrow, 2007):

Teaching English Learners

Encourage children to write about their own experiences. This is particularly important for English Learners.

1. Begin with discussion to encourage ideas
2. Write exactly what the child says, using standard spelling
3. Make sure the child can see you write
4. Write legibly
5. Read the dictation back to the child when finished, tracking the print from left to right as you read it
6. Encourage children to read the dictation by themselves, to another child, or to an adult.

Encouraging children to write on their own, even if it is one letter, is important. Although we do take dictation from children as they are beginning to show an interest in writing, too much dictation makes them dependent on the teacher, aide, or parent.

MyLab Education Self-Check 10.2

Strategies for Writing in Kindergarten Through Grade 3

The strategies we have discussed thus far are mostly for pre-K, but should be used in kindergarten through third grade as well. Teachers often want to know how children move from one level of writing ability to another or from unconventional writing to conventional. It is somewhat individual for every child, but trends do emerge. It is imperative to provide an atmosphere in which children will write.

For that reason, writing programs in early childhood should be initiated at the beginning of the school year. Teachers should refer to children as authors and writers so that they perceive themselves as such. Teachers may model writing through messages on the message board, notes to parents, thank-you notes to children, and experience charts dictated by the class. This modeling can motivate children to want to write.

Similarly, interesting experiences can spark children's interest in writing. A second-grade teacher talked about how nature motivated her children to write. She took her children outside to observe nature in the fall. Learning to be a good observer is the first step in becoming a good writer. While walking outside, a gust of fall wind blew and the leaves swirled around them. The children and their teacher spontaneously started to swirl, mimicking the leaves. They did leaps, dives, twirls, and lunges. The children started a chant, which they yelled in between gusts: "Come on wind, come on wind, blow on me!" The excitement built as the wind picked up, and the leaves fell all around them. The yard was filled with shrieks of joy (Freedman, 2007). This experience served as a vehicle for authentic, meaningful writing. When they got back to the classroom, their teacher led them in an interactive writing of a poem, which ended up saying: "Come on wind, come on trees, drop some leaves, down on me!" Children wrote and read aloud their interpretations of what happened. A pair of students danced like the leaves as they read what they wrote. The reading was expressive and meaningful because the students were able to choose how they responded to an exciting event they experienced.

Not all children are excited at the prospect of writing. Teachers, therefore, must be particularly supportive when working with young reluctant writers by encouraging them to write (Bromley, 2003; Martinez & Teale, 1987; Sulzby, 1985b). Youngsters need to know that their work does not have to look like adult writing. Showing them samples of other children's writing, including drawings, scribble writing, random letters, and invented spelling helps reluctant children see that they can do the same thing. Adults need to facilitate young writers' attempts by taking dictation if children cannot or will not write for themselves. Spell words they need, show children how to form letters when asked, and answer questions that arise during writing. Like other areas of literacy, writing requires social interaction, which promotes development. Teachers need to give young writers feedback, encouragement, and positive reinforcement.

> Jamie was a resistant writer, but when given choices of writing topics and genres that were meaningful to him, and when he was given the chance to talk with peers and the teacher about his interests, his writing motivation increased. After hearing Jamie repeatedly remark that writing was "stupid," Jamie's teacher devised "The Stupid List" (Lassonde, 2006). His teacher hoped that if he began to write down his negative feelings rather than blurting out comments that distracted everyone, he could preserve his thoughts to talk about at a later date. His teacher wrote "Stupid List" right on top of the paper in big letters and told him that every time he thought of something about writing that disturbed him, he should write it down on his list and talk about it later with her. Allowing Jamie to vent his negativity toward writing provided the necessary motivation for him to write. Jamie was able to write his thoughts and share them with the teacher. This activity paved the way for Jamie to become more open to writing activities. Thus, for struggling or resistant writers, teachers must tap into their interests and opinions, and tailor writing activities to match these components. Not surprisingly, Jamie's Stupid List on writing became smaller and smaller as time progressed. Eventually, he had this to say to a peer in regard to writing: "Writing is really good because you can write everything on the paper you are thinking even if it isn't nice because it's private and it's your feelings and no one can see it"
>
> (—Lassonde, 2006, p. 5)

We foster acceptance so that children will attempt writing. As youngsters learn more about phoneme–grapheme correspondence, they begin to realize that their invented spelling is not conventional spelling. At this point, they begin to ask for correct spelling as they move into the conventional stage of writing. It may seem as if they are taking a step backward, because suddenly they will not be writing as much or as spontaneously as they did in the past. Their concern for writing correctly has this effect on their performance. This regression, however, will last for a short time. As their spelling vocabulary increases, students both learn to use the dictionary and seek help from friends and the teacher. Conventional writing is a gradual process in which a child often goes back and forth from conventional to unconventional writing until sufficient proficiency is gained for the writing to be considered completely conventional.

Although children in grades 1 through 3 need experiences in writing similar to those in pre-K and kindergarten, older children also need more explicit and goal-oriented instruction. For these grades, it is important to understand writing as formulating an idea and composing it into text that has meaning and purpose, in a context that can be easily understood by others when read. Writing is most often created for others to read, thereby establishing it as a social activity. The following list will help teachers understand what they need to teach to help children become good writers. It will also help children understand what they need to learn. Good writers:

- Write things they know
- Write about what they are interested in
- Ask them to write to people out of school
- Write using a specified point of view
- Write with a specific purpose in mind
- Write fewer rather than more words
- Use interesting and varied vocabulary and sentence structures
- Use sensory details and figurative language, such as similes
- Write paragraphs that flow from one to the next
- Write pieces that have a logical sequence of events
- Write pieces that have a beginning, a middle, and an end to their work
- Make the reader believe what they have written
- Revise and edit their work
- Edit important pieces with good spelling, punctuation, grammar, and handwriting.

Children will demonstrate the qualities of good writers through multiple experiences that are explicitly taught, modeled, and provided by the teacher including guided, shared, interactive, and independent writing. (Kissel, 2008). These strategies are introduced in the following sections.

MyLab Education
Video Example 10.3
Writing Workshop
Teachers provide mini lessons to teach skills such as writing paragraphs.

Create a Writing Center to Provide a Writing Environment

Homes, child-care centers, and classrooms should provide rich environments for writing. A literacy area at home or in the classroom should also include a place designated for writing. It should be easily accessible, attractive, and inviting. This area can be a part of the library corner. It should be furnished with a table and chairs, and a rug for youngsters who want to stretch out on the floor to write. Materials should consistently be stored in the place provided for writing so that the children will learn how to select materials and put them away independently. The writing center should contain writing implements and supplies, materials for making books, anchor charts, and message boards.

Writing Implements and Supplies. Writing implements should include plenty of colored felt-tip markers, large and small crayons, large and small pencils (both regular and colored), a regular whiteboard and an electronic whiteboard, and small individual whiteboards for children to write with. Various types of paper should be available, lined and unlined, plain white or newsprint, ranging from 8 × 11 inches to 24 × 36 inches. The writing center should be equipped with computers for word processing and the creation of websites, blogs, and so on (Sylvester & Greenidge, 2009–2010). Index cards for recording "Very Own Words" (discussed in Chapter 7) should be stored in the writing area, as should the children's collections of Very Own Words. Each child should have a writing folder to collect samples of his or her written work during the school year.

Photo credit: Pearson Education

Caitlin works on her page for the class book during writing workshop.

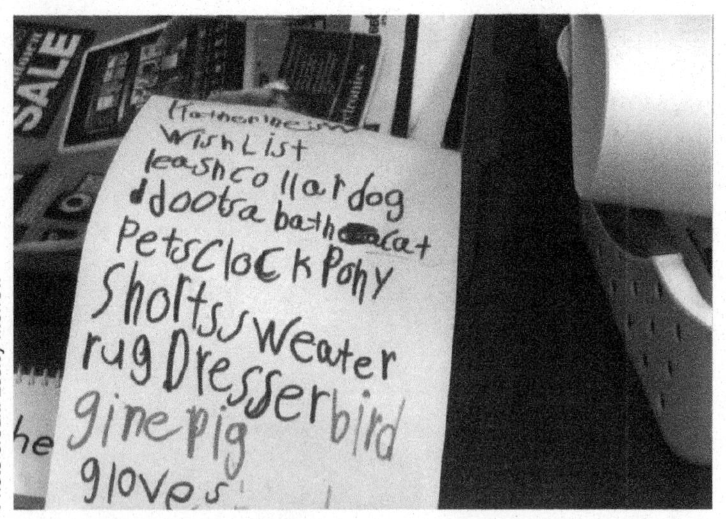

Photo credit: Lesley Morrow

Natalie writes a functional piece—a holiday wish list.

An alphabet chart in easy view helps children identify and shape letters they may need while writing. Plastic, magnetic, wooden, and felt letters should be among the language arts manipulatives. Using them helps children develop eye–hand coordination and helps them recognize and form letters. Small white slates are good for practicing new words and writing sentences that feature these words. A bulletin board should be available for children to display their own writing, with a space for posting notices or sending and receiving private messages. "Mailboxes" for youngsters' incoming and outgoing "mail" can be placed in the writing center. (The mailboxes for a pen pal program are discussed later in this chapter.) The writing center should be labeled with a sign that says "Author's Spot" or with a name selected by the children. A word wall with thematic words and grade-level sight words helps with spelling.

In addition to having writing implements and supplies in the writing center, some writing supplies should be stocked in other learning centers around the room. The accessibility of these materials will encourage writing (Bromley, 2003). A child might want to record the outside temperature on a chart in the science center, protect a construction of blocks with a "Do not touch" sign, or copy a Very Own Word in the social studies or science area. A group might decide to turn the dramatic-play corner into a dentist's office and so would need writing materials such as an appointment book for recording dates, times, and clients' names; appointment cards; clients' records; and a prescription pad for medications.

Book-Making and Publishing Materials. Having book-making materials in the writing station allows children to publish their work. "Why publish?" almost answers the question "Why write?" According to Graves, "Writing is a public act, meant to be shared with many audiences" (1983, p. 54). When children know their work will be published, they write for an authentic purpose, which increases motivation. Work slated for publication becomes special and is given greater care and detail by a child.

Children can publish their work in many ways. The most popular is to bind writings into books, which are placed in the literacy center and featured on open bookshelves for others to read. Materials for binding books should be in the literacy center. (Three ways of making a blank book are illustrated in Figures 10.10, 10.11, and 10.12.) Other means of publishing include creating felt-board stories or roll movies, telling stories to classmates, role-playing what has been written, and presenting the story in a puppet show.

Figure 10.10 Stapled Book

Cut colored construction paper and white writing paper into a desired shape. Staple at the side.

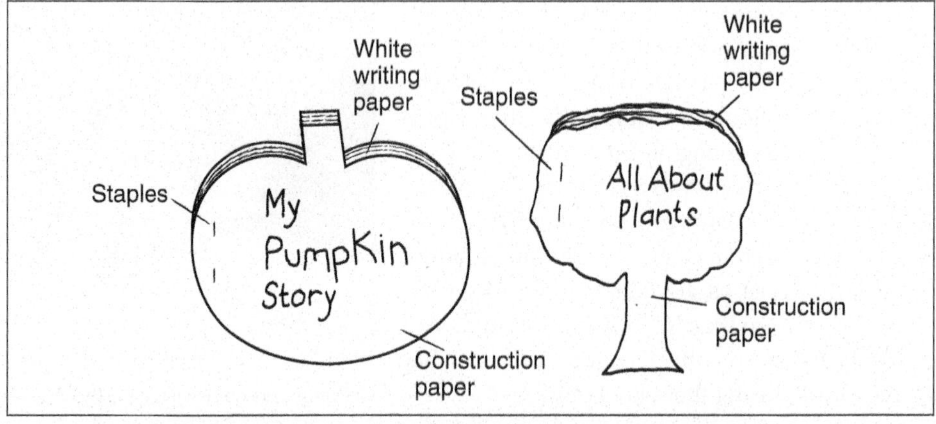

Figure 10.11 Folded, Stitched, and Glued Book

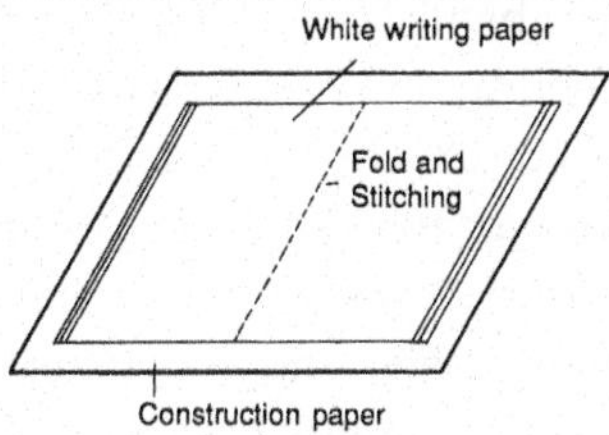

a. Sew a running stitch down the center of eight to ten sheets of 8½ x 11 plain white writing paper backed with a piece of 9 x 12 colored construction paper.

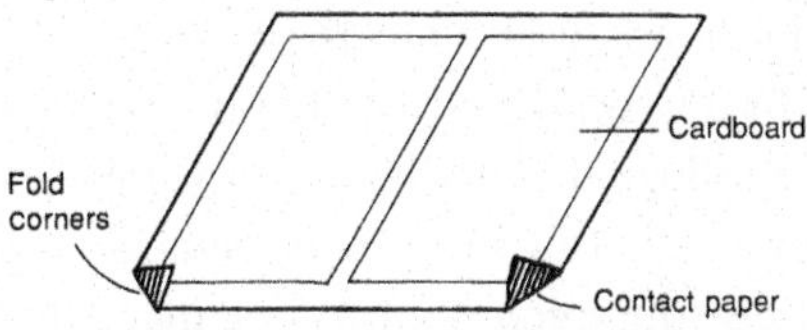

b. Place an 11 x 14 piece of contact paper or wallpaper face down. Paste two pieces of 6 x 9 oak tag or cardboard on the peeled contact paper a quarter inch apart, leaving about a 1-inch border. Fold each corner of the contact paper onto the oak tag to form a triangle (glue if using wallpaper).

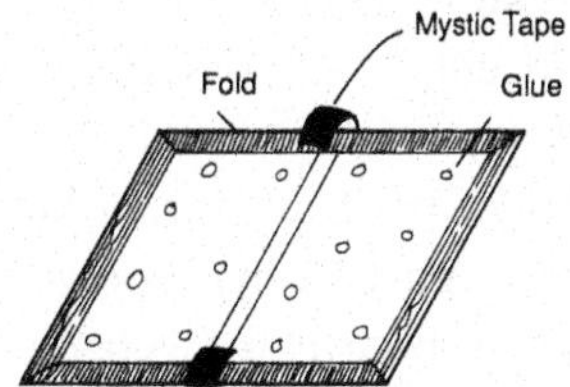

c. Fold the edges of the contact paper onto the oak tag (paste down if using wallpaper). Place a 12-inch piece of Mystic Tape down the center of the contact paper and over its edges. Put glue on the two exposed pieces of oak tag and on the quarter-inch space between them.

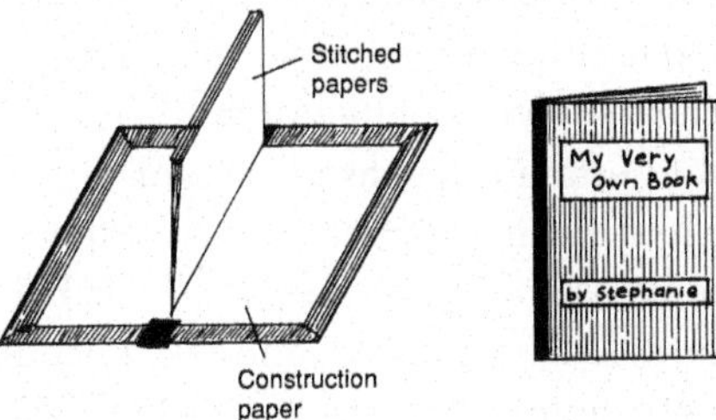

d. Place the folded and stitched edge of the construction paper and plain white paper in the quarter-inch glued space. Paste the construction paper onto the oak tag and over the contact-paper border to make the inside covers.

Figure 10.12 Sewn Book

Punch holes into oak tag and writing paper. Sew together with yarn.

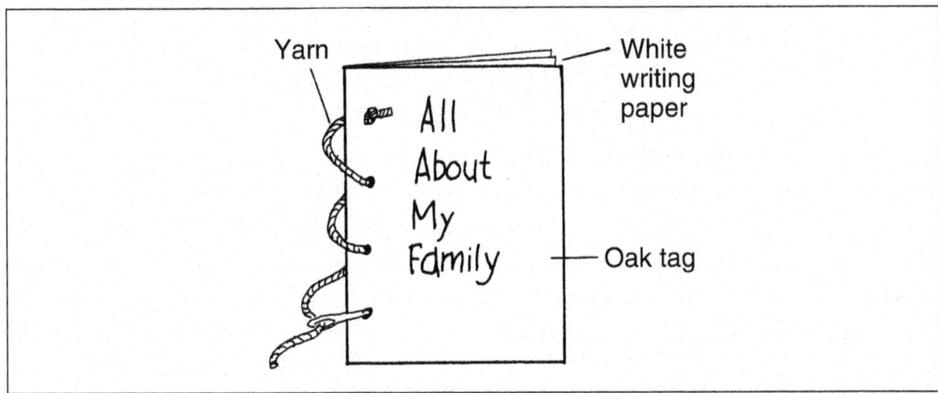

Photo credit: Lesley Morrow

Stephanie puts the finishing touches on the cover of a book she has written.

Colored construction paper for book covers, plain white paper for inside pages, a stapler, and scissors should be available for students to make books. Teachers can prepare blank books for all types of writing, and keyed to special occasions, for children to use. For example, a blank book shaped like a snowman, made of construction paper with five or six sheets of plain white paper stapled inside, provides inviting space where children can write a story, poem, experience, or greeting to a family member about winter. Bookbinding tools are inexpensive and easy to use, including a plastic coil binding. Stock bare books (books with hard covers but no print inside) for special projects and blue books used for examinations are perfect for young children's writing. They can be purchased inexpensively from school supply companies. They come with 12 or 16 pages, which is usually just right for an original story by a young child. Try to purchase blue books with the name of a university or college that is close to your school or select a university well known to your students. Children feel special writing in these books. Keep a supply of interesting pictures, posters, magazines, and newspapers; these can stimulate, decorate, or illustrate children's writing.

In addition to paper book-making supplies, computer programs allow students and teachers to create books that look as if they were professionally produced by a publisher. Students can digitally enhance their writing using a storybook program that allows them to integrate pictures and even a musical background if desired (Miller, 2010). Shutterfly is a well-known program for making books. In addition to using computers to create and print more polished books, children can also use them to digitally publish their writing on their class website or blog. Just having access to word-processing programs familiarizes students with a primary tool of modern writing and book production.

Anchor Charts. Include various anchor charts in the writing center, for example, one to remind students to use their five senses when writing. (The chart has an obvious symbol for each of the five senses.) Suggest that, before starting to write, children make a list of senses that pertain to the topic on which they are preparing to write. For example, prompt a child writing about a summer experience at a park to consider the senses chart and then close her eyes, pretend she is back at the park, and think about what she saw, heard, smelled, tasted, and felt. Encourage her to use sensorial words in her writing. For example, prompt her to think about the color of the sand. How did it feel under her toes? Have books about the beach available to help with the writing (Blau, Elbow, Killgallon, & Caplan, 1998). Provide her a prompt, such as starting each sentence with "At the beach. . . ." Here are samples of two children's writing:

> At the beach there is sand all around. The sand was soft, tan, and squished through my toes. When you put water on the sand it changed color from light to dark tan, from being soft to almost muddy and could be shaped like clay.
>
> At the beach I saw the ocean. The ocean was dark blue, almost black. There were big and small waves that curled up to the shore making a splashing sound. The water was cold and tasted salty. Under the water you could see shells, and seaweed. The air smells fishy and salty at the ocean.

Other anchor charts can be used to enhance the use of figurative language in writing, for example, a chart that says "is like." Sketch household objects such as a key, rubber band, pencil, paper clip, and toothbrush on a piece of chart paper, and place the actual items into a container by the chart. After introducing the chart to the children, pass around one of the items for them to manipulate and touch. While holding the item, each student shares what he or she thinks the object "is like." For example, when passing around a paper clip, one student might say, "It is like spaghetti because it is twisty." This activity helps young students experiment with figurative language such as similes.

Create additional anchor charts to encourage other associations, for example, *as cold as, as bright as, as hard as*, and so on. As students explore and develop figurative language, they will inevitably start with clichés and overused images, for example, "as cold as ice." Students will, however, eventually develop more creative similes such as "as cold as a scary-looking person" and "as cold as an igloo in the North Pole."

Notice Board. The writing center should have a notice board for exchanging messages (McGee & Morrow, 2005; Newman, 1984). Children can tack (or tape) pictures for each other as beginning messages. The teacher needs to provide a model by leaving messages for individuals and for the entire class. Notices about school or class events are appropriate. Draw attention to the board when posting a class message or when leaving messages for individuals so that children will get into the habit of looking for messages and leaving them for others. A place for private messages should also be created. For example, private messages can be posted on the notice board in an envelope or in student mailboxes. Some teachers have taped brown bags to each child's desk for students to receive private messages. Occasionally, the teacher should check the messages to see what the children are writing. One teacher found the note in Figure 10.13, written by Asia, a first-grade girl, to Andre, a first-grade boy.

Figure 10.13 A Private Message Sent by a First-Grade Girl to a First-Grade Boy

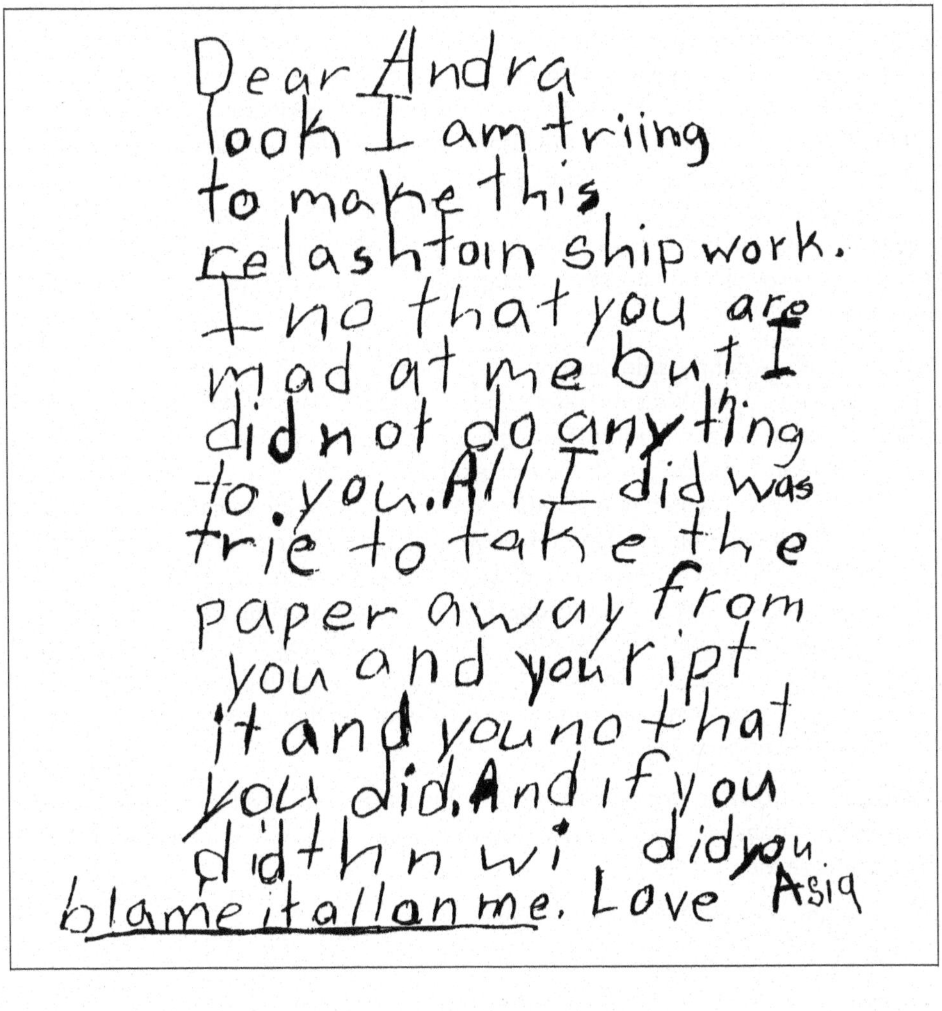

Dear Andra
look I am triing
to make this
relashtoin ship work.
I no that you are
mad at me but I
did not do any thing
to you. All I did was
trie to take the
paper away from
you and you ript
it and you no that
you did. And if you
didthn wi did you
blame it all on me. Love Asia

MyLab Education
Video Example 10.4
Pattern Books

In this video, first grade teacher Amy Monaco teaches a Writer's Workshop mini lesson on patterns. At 2:30, she introduces a mentor text and at 6:20 students reflect on the author's use of patterns. https://www.youtube.com/watch?v=SqHIQ8X3mJw

The Writing Workshop

The **writing workshop** is a period of time set aside for explicit writing instruction of any kind, such writing opinions, informational text, journal writing, or independent writing. In the writing workshop, a purpose for the workshop is set. The teacher then teaches a writing skill in a mini lesson and children are given time to use the skill taught in the mini lesson. The teacher conferences with children providing input on their writing and then children take time to share their writing. In the writing workshop, 30% of the time is spent on the mini lesson, 50% is spent on writing, and 20% on share time. Conferences happen during the writing time.

Purpose. Each writing workshop needs to have an established purpose and audience for the writing that will be done. The purpose should be meaningful and relevant for the children. Teachers should share with students sample texts, which model the type of writing children should emulate. For example, if you would like the students to write about their family, share published work about families, and other children's work for another year. Students are inspired by the writings of children their own age, so samples of past student writing are great texts to share. Children also enjoy their teachers' own writings. When teachers share their writing, and sincerely identify with students in terms of writing joys and challenges, it illustrates that the teacher is a fellow writer and fosters a sense of a writing community within the classroom.

Mini Lesson. After articulating the purpose of the workshop, the teacher delivers a short lesson on a particular type of writing skill, such as letter writing, writing informational text, editorial (persuasive) writing, or patterned writing modeled after a book read. The lesson should include sample texts—an exemplar, a piece by the teacher, a piece by a student, or all of the above—that illustrate the type of writing that is the goal. Doing so prepares the children to practice writing with the new skill. There should also be samples of the type of writing sought, written by children or the teacher. One way to structure the lesson is as a shared interactive writing experience between the teacher and the students. The mini lesson can also be referred to as *guided writing*, since it is an explicit lesson about a specific writing skill.

These mini lessons can be delivered to the whole class or to small groups. When teaching a writing skill specified by the curriculum, opt for a whole-class lesson. Small-group mini lessons should cover a writing skill to address the specific needs of a few children.

Writing Time. After the mini lesson, allow students about 30 minutes to write independently, with a peer. While the children are writing, the teacher should offer informal guidance and meeting with individual children or pairs of children to discuss the writing they are doing and help with the new skill they are practicing. The meetings with the teacher are called conferences. Conferences are discussed more in the following text.

If children are working collaboratively, encourage them to discuss with each other what they think they will write or actually write together. Providing the opportunity for peer feedback is critical. Peer feedback is helpful for all children, including those with emotional and behavioral disorders. When students are given time to collaborate in drafting and revising their work, their writing is more creative and descriptive. Students are often more open to accepting and incorporating their peers' suggestions than the teacher's (Kindzierski, 2009).

Conferences. During independent writing the teacher can meet with some children to answer questions they may have, to read their work and provide some feedback that might improve their process.

- Begin conferences with a compliment
- Ask the writer to explain what they have been working on
- Discuss the child's goals for the writing they are doing

- Track the writer to determine if
    - The child has the stamina to focus for the time needed to write for a period of time
    - Help the child focus on the most important parts of the writing. Determine next steps for instruction.

Revise. After conferences, each child should go back and revise his or her work based on peer and teacher input. Often the piece of writing will not be finished during the writing workshop; the children will need to continue revising for a few days. Some writing workshops produce finished work, and others do not. This flexibility emphasizes that writing is a process and that even when a piece is "done," it can still be improved.

Teachers may hold writing workshops with small groups of children based on a need for the development of different writing skills. This type of arrangement is similar to the guided reading lessons described in Chapter 13.

Share. When students complete a writing assignment, it is important that they share their finished work with a partner, a small group, or the whole class. Students can share feedback such as "I really like the way you described that horse in your story—I could actually picture him in my mind" or constructive comments, such as "You did a good job of describing the size of the horse and his parts. Could you add something about his color that would help me visualize him better?" All comments should relate to the skill that was emphasized in the mini lesson. (In this case, it was descriptive language.) Whenever possible, invite school community members and family members to share in the joy of the students' writing. An authentic audience serves to heighten writing motivation. Some classrooms have an author's chair where children sit when sharing their work with others. In Chapter 9 the Reading Comprehension Workshop is described. The components of the Reading Comprehension Workshop are very similar to those in the Writing Workshop defined in this chapter. Activities such as the mini lesson, independent writing, partnering, conferencing and share time are well-defined.

The Process Approach to Writing in Early Childhood

The **process approach to writing** makes children realize that writing involves thinking, organizing, and rewriting before a piece is complete. They become aware that a first draft rarely constitutes a finished product. Typical steps in this approach include prewriting or brainstorming, drafting, conferencing, revising, editing, and publishing (Calkins, 1986; Fletcher & Portalupi, 2001; Tompkins, 2007; Turbill & Bean, 2006).

Students should be taught at an early age that sometimes the steps in this progression are repeated or that writers may even return to an earlier step. For example, a student may complete multiple prewriting attempts and/or drafts. Another student might be drafting and decide to temporarily stop writing to create an observation chart of an important moment that she or he wants to make more vivid in the draft. Students should be taught that the writing process is fluid and flexible. Each writer approaches it with his or her own perspective, and the process may change with different assignments (Blanch, Forsythe, Roberts, & Van Allen, 2017).

All the strategies that follow could be taught first as writing workshop mini lessons to a whole group or in a guided writing lesson to a small group (Fletcher & Portalupi, 2001).

Prewriting. Prewriting is sometimes referred to as brainstorming or planning. Prewriting helps students select a topic to write about, figure out the purpose of the piece, and decide for whom the piece is being written. While prewriting, students need to decide what form the writing will take, such as a poem, letter, or narrative. Prewriting also involves collecting the information needed to write and creating the organizational structure for the writing (Tompkins, 2003). Frequently, prewriting involves brainstorming ideas related to the topic and organizing those ideas using a graphic organizer, observation charts, lists, or outlines (Blau et al., 1998). Prewriting can take place with the entire class, a friend, the teacher, or independently. Some writing ideas that appeal to children are topics related to family life, friends, vacations, pets, holidays, pictures, milestones, sporting events, extracurricular activities, hobbies, movies, television, pop culture/media, video games, current events, special possessions, and school events.

Drafting. In this second part in the process, the author makes a first attempt at writing the piece by getting the words down, either on paper or in a word-processing file on the computer. The prewriting done earlier serves as a guide during the drafting stage. At this point in the process, getting the ideas written down is more important than spelling, punctuation, correct grammar, or handwriting.

Conferencing. Conferencing is done with a teacher or, sometimes, a student partner. Conferencing is a time to reflect on what has been written and determine if changes are needed. The discussion has mostly to do with content changes. The teacher or peer can use many statements or questions to get the conference going, for example:

- Tell me how your writing is coming along.
- Can you read a bit of it to me?
- What will you write next in this piece?
- Is there another way of describing the characters in your story?
- Do you have questions that I can help you with?

Children should be taught to reflect on their own work and the work of their peers. We can teach them to use some of these questions with each other.

Revising. This is the process of making substantive changes in ideas and finding ways to make the piece more descriptive or informative. Revising may involve activities such as rewriting the introduction, adding or deleting a sentence, and so on. At this stage, the focus is on revising the information and how it's presented, not on the mechanics of the writing. The goal is to produce a coherent and cohesive flow to the writing.

Editing. The last part of the process approach is editing, which has to do with the mechanics of writing—punctuation, grammatical corrections, spelling, and handwriting. Students often confuse the terms *revising* and *editing*, so it is important to differentiate between the two. We must teach students early on that meaningful writing revision is not about finding surface errors. Self-planning sheets for prewriting and revising are helpful for students in late first grade and beyond (refer to Figures 10.14 and 10.15).

Figure 10.14 Prewriting Guidance Sheet

SOURCE: Gunning, *Creating Literacy Instruction for All Children*, 4th edition. © 2003. Adapted by permission of Pearson Education.

Author:________________________________

Who am I writing this for?

Why am I writing this?

What is being explained?

What happens:

- First
- Second
- Third
- Then
- Finally

Figure 10.15 Revising Guidance Sheet

SOURCE: Gunning, *Creating Literacy Instruction for All Children*, 4th edition. © 2003. Adapted by permission of Pearson Education.

Author: ______________________________

What do I like about my writing?

- Why?

Did I:

- Tell what was being explained?
- Change the parts that needed changing?

What are the changes made?

- Make a list.

Sharing or Publishing. Children need to share their writing with an audience. When they know they will be sharing their work, they will write for that audience and have a greater purpose for writing. Sharing means a written piece is put on a class website for many others to read or is read aloud to another child, the teacher, or the class (Tompkins, 2007). At a designated time during the day, usually at the end when the class gets together to review the day's happenings, a child can be selected as Author of the Day to share something that he or she has written (Graves & Hansen, 1983; Rog, 2007; Routman, 2005). More than one child can be Author of the Day. Those authors who read their writings in a particular week should display them on a bulletin board in the writing center along with photographs of themselves. When sharing work, the child can sit in a chair marked Author's Chair. Classmates should be encouraged to make constructive comments about their friends' work with such statements as "I like what you wrote" or "I fell and cut my knee once, too." The children may not comment readily at first, so the teacher will need to model comments for the audience, whose young members will soon emulate the behavior (McElveen & Dierking, 2001). A sample of sharing follows:

> It was Steven's turn in the Author's Chair. He sat down, organized his materials, and said, "I've been working on a series of stories. They are all about the same character, and in each one he has another adventure. It is patterned after *Clifford the Big Red Dog* books. My stories are about a cat, and the first one is called *The Cat Named Buster.* I call that Part I; I already have Part II and Part III. Part II is called *Buster Meets Pretzel.* Pretzel is a dog. Part III is called *Buster Gets Lost.* I'll read Part I to you.
>
> After Steven read Part I of his series of stories, Philip said, "Can I read one?" Steven replied, "Sure, but you should read all of them. They go together." Philip continued, "I just want to read the second one about "Buster meeting Pretzel the dog." Steven said, "OK, but you don't know what you're missing if you don't read them all."

MyLab Education
Video Example 10.5
Author's Chair

In this video, two kindergarten students present their picture stories from the Author's Chair.

Students should also be given the opportunity to publish their work in a more formal manner. The following vignette from the classroom provides an example of how children can publish their work using digital tools. Experiences with writing should be focused on meeting standards from your state or curriculum. In this vignette, the standard to meet is that *with guidance and support from the teacher, students will use a variety of digital tools to produce and publish writing, in collaboration with peers.*

The students in Ms. Sano's first-grade class sat in a row of chairs at the front of the room, looking out onto a sea of family members. The students had participated in many writing celebrations over the course of the school year, but today was the culmination of how far the first graders had come as writers since September, and students were each publishing a final piece of writing for the year. They had worked for several weeks on a study of weather and seasons in science and had developed a final piece of writing that provided information about each student's favorite season, activities that take place during this time of year, and facts about the weather in this season. The students had worked with Ms. Sano to revise, edit, and type their informational writing on the classroom's computers. After each student had completed this process, Ms. Sano had transferred the collective typed work into the website StoryJumper.com and, through a grant, was able to purchase hardback books of the class book, titled *Wild About Weather*, for each student to take home. The students had practiced reading their section aloud fluently and were ready to share them with their families.

During the family writing event, Ms. Sano used the StoryJumper website to display the class book of weather information, and as she clicked to each student's portion of the book, its first-grade author stood up, walked over to a microphone set up at the front of the room, and read his or her writing aloud to a smiling audience.

Leah: My favorite season is winter. In winter, you can go sledding, drink hot chocolate, and have a snowball fight. In winter there is a lot of snow, and snowflakes are made of ice crystals.

Julia: My favorite season is fall. In fall, you can go pumpkin picking, and I love to go trick or treating on Halloween. A fact about fall is that leaves change color and fall off the trees, and another name for fall is autumn.

Jason: My favorite season is summer. I like to go in the pool, go to the beach, and even go in the ocean. I learned that in summer the days are longer and the nights are shorter. The temperature is higher than in the other seasons.

After all the students had shared their work, Ms. Sano passed out a hardback book to the students, who then dispersed through the crowd to share the class book with their guests. Throughout the classroom, parents and their children sat together, reading aloud each classmate's writing and chatting with family members about what it felt like to be a "real published author." After students had an opportunity to share their books, Ms. Sano used a projector to display a slideshow of the students working on the creation of *Wild About Weather* in the classroom, so that parents had a glimpse into the process of writing and digitally publishing their stories.

Concerns about the Process Approach. The process approach just outlined (prewriting, drafting, conferencing, revising, editing, and sharing or publishing) should be used cautiously and only occasionally with children in early childhood. The prewriting phase may be accomplished through discussion and word lists with very young children and throughout the grades. Prewriting can be done often and involves the selection of a topic on which to write. We want to allow the children themselves to select topics as often as possible. Many children just cannot seem to make such choices. Having a purpose for a writing activity is helpful when trying to select a topic. For example, the writing activity should have a particular form, such as writing an acrostic poem, or a particular focus, such as learning about writing a well-formed expository piece. It can be easier to select a topic once the type of writing is identified. If students are struggling to come up with a topic, consider associating the writing activity to a general topic studied previously in class, such as the rain forest. Children can then select their particular topic more easily. With this type of support, students will eventually become more capable of selecting topics on their own.

Drafting can also be done by very young children and throughout the grades, but the products of drafting will be different depending on the development of the child. A draft could be an entire story or a series of letter strings. Conferencing, when the teacher asks children to discuss their work, can also be done at all ages and stages. Older children can be asked how they think they can change their work to make improvements. Most younger children should not be asked to revise every piece they write. Depending on age, level, and ability, editing might also be too tedious. The teacher should be mindful and understanding of the developmental level of the children with whom he or she is working. Some children may be frustrated by revising and editing, particularly having to copy over their work. Be selective in choosing students with whom to use the process approach. Involve only those who seem capable of handling it. Try only one or two of the steps in the process. As children increase their skills, more of the steps can be used. Not all writing, however, needs to be revised or edited.

Writing conferences between a teacher and a child are times to discuss what the child has written, to encourage the child in writing, and to assess progress by observing and reviewing the writing products gathered in the child's folder. During the conference, the teacher can take dictation or help the child with a word, caption, picture, or publishing activity. This is an especially good time to work with students who are capable of dealing with any of the steps in process writing and to encourage reluctant writers.

MyLab Education
Video Example 10.6
A Writing Conference
Teachers meet one-on-one with students to review their writing and offer praise and ways to improve their writing.

Teaching English Learners
Social interaction promotes engagement. Interactive writing is particularly important for English Learners.

Interactive Writing

Interactive writing provides a model for children, so they will know what to do when writing on their own. The teacher guides the lesson and writes on large chart paper in a whole- or small-group setting. Sometimes the children are writing as the text is being created on personal whiteboards or on large oversized chart paper. Whiteboards can work well for interactive writing activities because the many edits that typically occur during the process can be easily made.

Any type of writing can be done in the interactive setting, such as writing a letter, a narrative piece, or an informational piece (McCarrier, Pinnell, & Fountas, 2000). The purpose of interactive writing is to support instruction, so the goal is to produce a well-written text in content and form. The teacher often determines the topic for the writing with some input from the class. It is beneficial to select writing that has a purpose for the class and that includes a part of the writing curriculum. If the class is studying water, for example, it might want to summarize the unit by making a list of the uses of water. In addition to recording what they learned, the children will also learn about writing lists.

During the interactive writing process, ideas suggested by students are written down by the teacher. The teacher then guides students almost word by word as they record their ideas. The entire class can contribute to the conversation to improve the writing. White correction tape is used to conceal any errors made during interactive writing. Instead of crossing out a misspelling or incorrect form of a word, the teacher just covers errors with the white tape. When a child notices an error in the writing, he or she can use the tape as well. Using the tape, allows for editing to occur and for the students to have a clean, error-free copy of the final collective product.

The Vignette below is an example of interactive writing in Mrs. Jenkins's class.

Mrs. Jenkins's objective for this lesson is for children to be able to demonstrate command of the conventions of standard English such as capitalization, punctuation, and spelling when they are writing.

Mrs. Jenkins decided to teach her first-grade students about being courteous and writing thank-you notes. She wanted to teach them about the content of thank-you notes and the format. She concentrated on punctuation, and correct spelling. As part of their study of good health habits, a mother in the class, who was a nurse, was invited to be a guest speaker. Mrs. Jenkins used this talk as the reason for writing a thank-you note to the nurse. She presented the lesson to the entire class in an interactive writing experience. While writing the letter, there was a discussion about the indentation of the first word in the paragraph. They discussed other things to say in a thank-you note besides thanking the person. They decided they could say what they liked about the presentation, and they thought they could ask her if she might come again. They discussed different ways to end the letter, such as using the word *love* or *sincerely*, and when to use one or the other. The activity accomplished three tasks: the need to teach courteous behavior and the need to learn about the content and format for thank-you notes.

Independent Writing and Reading

During independent reading and writing, children can select activities based on several options, and they may choose to work alone or in collaboration with others. Independent writing allows children to practice whatever writing they might prefer. When children are given the time to engage in independent reading and writing, it is often a cooperative effort. During this period, children have the opportunity to select from a list of literacy activities, such as the following:

Teaching English Learners

Children's literature with its attractive illustrations make books interesting for English learners and help them with development of their language.

- Read a book, magazine, or newspaper alone or with a friend
- Use the Internet to explore digital literacies such as reading digital stories, looking up news events, browsing websites for information on a writing topic, and so on
- Listen to an audio story at the listening station
- Read or tell a story using a felt board and story characters
- Read or tell a story using puppets
- Listen to an audio story recorded of the teacher reading a book as a model for children
- Write a story alone or with a friend
- Write a story and make it into a felt-board story
- Write a story and record it for the listening station
- Write a story and perform it as a puppet show
- Present a play based on a story they wrote or read
- Bind a story wrote into a book and place it in the library corner for others to read
- Participate in content-area activities that involve reading and writing
- Use computer software programs available for literacy games and activities.

The following anecdotes from independent reading and writing periods in a second-grade classroom illustrate how closely reading and writing are linked. Many of the things children chose to do were motivated by what they had read or what was read to them. When writing, they often looked for additional information by reading more in other sources.

In this vignette concerning independent writing, the teacher is interested in having her children write for a short and an extended time for different disciplines, purposes, and audiences.

After listening to the teacher read *My Cat, the Silliest Cat in the World* (Bachelet, 2006), Stephanie, Jason, Kevin, and Nicky decided to make an advertisement poster for the book that showed key pictures with captions. The children called their poster "Scenes from *My Cat, the Silliest Cat in the World*." They drew episodes from the story and wrote their own captions for the pictures. After a few days, the poster was complete, and the children presented their work to the class. Stephanie and Jason held the poster, and Kevin and Nicky were the spokespersons. Kevin explained how the group wanted to illustrate the story in an unusual way and decided on a poster. Kevin and Nicky took turns pointing to the pictures they had all drawn and reading the captions they had written for each. Television shows, rock stars, and current events also motivated three girls to create three biographies for each member of a well-known singing group. They used very descriptive language that they had learned about in writing workshop.

Current events and books that children have read motivated writing. Joey was reading a book about the U.S. Civil War. He asked the teacher to read it to the class, which she did. Joey decided to write his own book about the Civil War, and Christopher joined him. Christopher called the book "U.S. Saratoga." As they were drawing pictures, they made bombing sounds. Suddenly Joey said, "Wait a minute, this is weird. We're making airplane carriers fighting in the Civil War." The two boys changed their minds and decided to do a book about a war that could be happening now. These boys were sorting out, collecting, and organizing their ideas, which are skills they learned about writing informational text.

Julia and Katie wrote a script for a play they were going to have some children act out. It was a wedding ceremony, and their text is reproduced in Figure 10.16. Conversation is another skill being practiced here, which the students have been taught about during journal writing and narrative writing.

Figure 10.16 A Play Written by Julia and Katie During an Independent Writing Period

> We are gathered here today to join these two wonderful people in holy matrimony. Silvia do you take Jim to be your lawful wedded husband? "I do". "Jim do you take Sylvia to be your lawful wedded wife?" "I do". "May we have the rings. Sylvia put this ring on Jim's finger. Jim put this ring on Sylvia's finger. I now pronounce you man and wife. You may now kiss the bride.

These episodes during independent reading and writing reveal the wide variety of topics that appeal to and excite children. We would probably never think to ask children to write about some of them. The children have enthusiasm because they selected the topics themselves. We also don't know all the interests of students. Some of the topics they might select to write about are very sophisticated. Children have original ideas that they can draw on from their varied and rich life experiences. The topics they select have meaning and function for them, and therefore they write freely and enthusiastically about them.

Independent writing activities can be adapted for children with special needs. Children can write to other youngsters who may share their problems. As many teachers know, there is something for everyone during independent reading and writing—the gifted, the child who attends basic skills classes, and the youngsters who are English learners.

Journal Writing

Teaching English Learners

Allow children to write in their primary language if they can.

Another successful strategy for developing writing in early childhood classrooms is **journal writing**, with entries made daily or at least several times a week. Journals can be written in notebooks, on pages stapled together to create a book, or electronically. Children are encouraged to write freely in their journals at times and to write at their own developmental levels. Thus, some children's journals might include pictures and no writing, scribble writing, random letters, or invented spelling. The teacher models journal writing, perhaps with a personal message, such as "I'm very excited today. My daughter is going to be in a play tonight, and I'm going to watch her." Through example, children are given an idea about the kinds of entries that are appropriate. Some children draw or write stories in their journals, others write about personal experiences, and still others write about information they learned. Journal entries can be related to topics studied, such as recording the growth of a seed that was planted, charting daily temperatures, or reacting to a story that was read. From time to time, the journal can also take dialogue form, with the teacher responding to a child's journal entry with a comment. If the child writes, "I had a picnic," the teacher might respond, "That sounds like fun. What did you eat?" The quality of journal entries improves when the activity is continued regularly throughout a school year (Gunning, 2003).

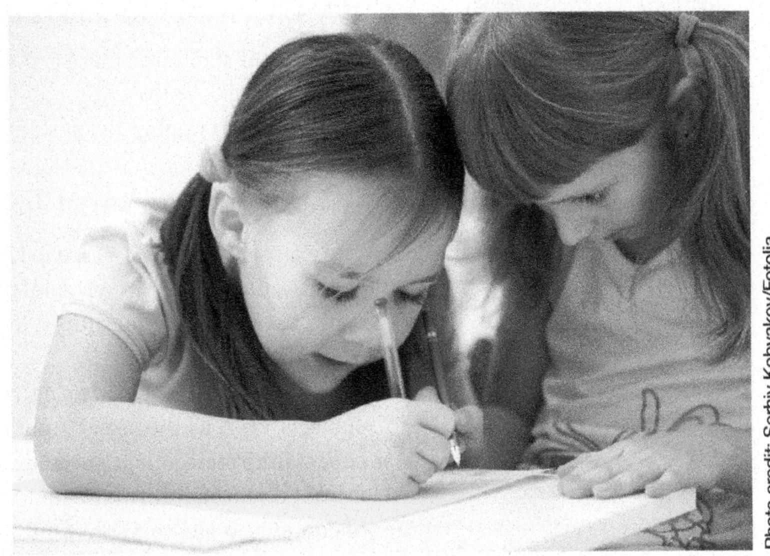

Photo credit: Serhiy Kobyakov/Fotolia

Journal writing helps students become more fluent writers.

Because there are different names for journals, it often becomes confusing as to which one should be used. It is the concept of journal writing that is important—that is, putting one's thoughts and early

Photo credit: Y Photo Studio/Shutterstock

Teachers encourage student writing when they take time to respond to students in dialogue journals.

writing attempts down on paper without concern for the mechanics of writing. Journals can take many forms: personal journals, dialogue journals, reading-response journals, and learning logs are some of the more prevalent types.

Personal journals are private journals in which children write about their lives or topics of special interest to them. These are shared only if a child chooses to do so. These are never subject to correction for spelling or punctuation or grading for mechanics or form.

Dialogue journals can be written about any topic, but they are shared with teachers or peers. The journal is similar to a conversation, except that the conversation is done in writing instead of speaking. A dialogue journal could be shared with the teacher or a peer responding to a journal entry that is written. It can also be an actual conversation between two people in which one is writing to the other and a response is expected.

Reading-response journals are those in which children respond to narrative or informational text read. They write their feelings concerning responses to the story or information. Teachers do review reading-response journals.

Learning logs usually involve content areas, such as social studies or science. Children record information being learned, such as charting the progress of a setting. The more children learn about content-area subjects, the more they will have to write. The writing can take many forms, such as charting or summarizing information.

Journal writing helps students become more fluent writers, choose topics to develop, learn the mechanics of writing, and reflect on and articulate ideas. Regardless of what the journals are called, students should have regular opportunities to engage in the four main journaling types described previously.

MyLab Education Self-Check 10.3

Types of Writing

Most recent standards place a strong emphasis on writing in various forms and for various purposes. At the early childhood level, the primary text types are informational, narrative, and poetry. Let's examine those types in greater detail.

MyLab Education
Video Example 10.7
A Classrooom Writing Project
In this video, Michelle Kern's first-grade students write chapters for a book they are creating about deserts. Note how she supports the young writers as they think about the parts of the informational mentor text and include them in their writing.

Informational and Explanatory Texts and Writing

The examples that follow are to help children accomplish the following standards. Children should be able to write informative/explanatory texts in which they introduce a topic, use facts and definitions to develop points, and provide a concluding statement or section.

Informational writing is nonfiction and uses information from content-area subjects, such as the social studies or science. In this type of writing, children need to collect information and summarize it. The writing does not include personal views; it is built on facts. Informational text has features different from narrative such as a table of contents, a glossary, photographs instead of drawings, charts, graphs, and so on.

When we ask children to engage in expository writing, we might ask them to write up an interview with someone, prepare a report about an informational text, or summarize a unit of study (Read, 2005). Expository text structures that are required to teach to and practice by children in writing are:

- **Description:** This structure gives the reader a picture of the subject of the written piece based on observation.
- **Sequence:** This explains the steps that produce a certain product or outcome.
- **Comparison:** This can include comparisons of items with similar classification that are compared first and then contrasted. Point-by-point comparisons describe similarities and differences alternately.
- **Cause and Effect:** Causality tells why something happens.
- **Problem Solving:** A problem is presented, followed by its solution. An understanding of chronology is necessary to understand this structure.
- **Exemplification:** This can also be called *reason and example.* The main idea is presented with supporting details (Vukelich, Evans, & Albertson, 2003).

Graphic organizers can help children read, understand, and write expository text. For example, a K-W-L chart (discussed in Chapter 9) encourages children who are going to write a report on spiders. The first section gives students the opportunity to write what they already know about spiders. The next section deals with what they want to know and gives them guidelines about what they need to research in books or on the Internet. As they find that information, they write it down. When the children have the first two columns of the chart written, they have information to draft their piece about spiders. The last part of the chart says, "What did you learn?" Here, the children summarize the most important points they feel they ascertained. A Venn diagram can help with identifying contrasts and commonalities. If studying bears, children could compare polar bears and black bears for characteristics that are similar and different. And in the overlapping space they could identify characteristics the two types of bears have in common. For example, they both have fur, but the color of their fur is different. Refer to Figures 9.13, 9.14, 9.15, 9.16, and 9.17 in Chapter 9 for sample graphic organizers that help students understand the information by organizing text that is read to them. A strong structure in the lesson guides children in their first experiences (Bromley, 2006).

Functional writing could be considered informational text. It is writing that serves clear, real-life purposes. Class writing projects that are particularly purposeful include greeting cards for birthdays, holidays, and other occasions for parents, grandparents, sisters, brothers, friends, and relatives. Another example of functional writing is thank-you notes to guest speakers who come to class, to adults who help on class trips, to the director of the zoo you visited, or to the librarian who spent time with the class at the public library. Also, you may prepare lists of things to remember to do in preparing a party, a special program, or a class trip; make address and telephone books with entries from class members; and write notes to parents about activities in school.

Some preschools and kindergartens, as well as elementary classrooms, have established mail service and pen pal programs (Edwards, Maloy, & Verock-O'Loughlin, 2003; Teale & Gambrell, 2007). Children are offered pen pals to write to regularly (once a month is reasonable). Teachers or aides may have to help children write their letters or may have to take dictation. Encourage children to use the writing capabilities that they have, even if they cannot produce conventional writing. Teachers also may have to read the incoming letters to students who cannot yet read conventionally. The use of email for pen pals (called *key-pals*) is another way for children to communicate with others for functional reasons. Email gives children the opportunity to write to others around the world, and the sending and receiving of messages is almost immediate (Pole, 2015).

Another form of informational writing is "how-to," that is, writing out information about how to perform a task or procedure. "How-to" writing can apply to recipes, riding a bike, taking care of a dog, swimming, and so on. It can also figure as part of a larger expository or informational writing assignment. Ms. Kelly is teaching her children how to write "How-to Books," using graphic organizers. The children worked in groups of four, and each group had four pages for the book. Ms. Kelly would scaffold how to do a page, let the children imitate making that page, and then have the children make the next page on their own.

The first page was called "Different Kinds of Dogs." There were four rectangles on the page with two lines under each. The children came up with four types of dogs, and then one person in the group wrote a type of dog under each rectangle and then drew a picture of that dog. The second page was called "Parts of a Dog." On this page was a picture of a dog. The children discussed the parts of the dog, and it was one child's job to fill in the words identifying the parts of a dog. The third page was called "How to Care for a Dog." On this page, there were four rectangles with lines next to them. The children generated ideas for this page, and one child wrote the text and drew pictures for the topic. The last page was called "How to Walk a Dog." The children once again generated ideas together. The child in charge of this page wrote the text on the lines provided next to a rectangle and drew the pictures. The teacher prepared a table of contents for the book. The children produced the following robust piece of informational writing:

All About Dogs

Table of Contents

Chapter 1: Different Kinds of Dogs
Chapter 2: Parts of a Dog
Chapter 3: How to Care for a Dog
Chapter 4: How to Walk a Dog

Chapter 1: Different Kinds of Dogs

The different kinds of dogs we know about are poodles that have curly hair, terriers that have short, rough hair, a Dalmatian that has black and white spots, and a mutt that is more than one kind of dog.

Chapter 2: Parts of a Dog

A dog has the following parts. A dog has a head, ears, eyes, a nose, teeth, lips, legs, toes, feet, hips, a tail, and a back.

Chapter 3: How to Care for a Dog

If you want a healthy dog, you need to take care of him. You should have fresh water at all times for the dog. You should have a nice cozy bed for your dog to sleep in. Select good dog food for your dog to eat and don't give him candy. Take him for regular checkups.

Chapter 4: How to Walk a Dog

Dogs need to be walked. The best way to walk a dog is to attach the leash to the dog's collar. Put a coat on your dog if it is cold outside. Take the dog outside and let him do his business. Give your dog a treat after the walk.

Creating "how-to" booklets is a simple way to engage students with informational text. Allow the child to select what she or he will write about. The children's book about dogs included two "how-to" chapters. We will use "How to Walk a Dog" as an example, but nearly any topic in any content area could be used. The first page lists materials needed to walk a dog. The next page has a sequence of about four steps involved in walking a dog. The third page has a picture with labels, such as how to walk a dog. Draw a picture of dog with a person holding the dog's leash illustrated by the child. The last page is a glossary with words from the book and definitions. The child can go back and put in a table of contents after the book is written. This structured format helps children succeed. Figure 10.17 provides a guide for writing how-to books.

Figure 10.17 How to Make a Booklet

Directions: Write about how to make something, such as a fruit salad or a craft project. List the materials on page 3 and the steps to make it on page 4. Draw a picture of what you are making on page 5. Write a glossary of new words on page 6. Then come back to page 2 and fill in the table of contents. Enlarge if necessary.

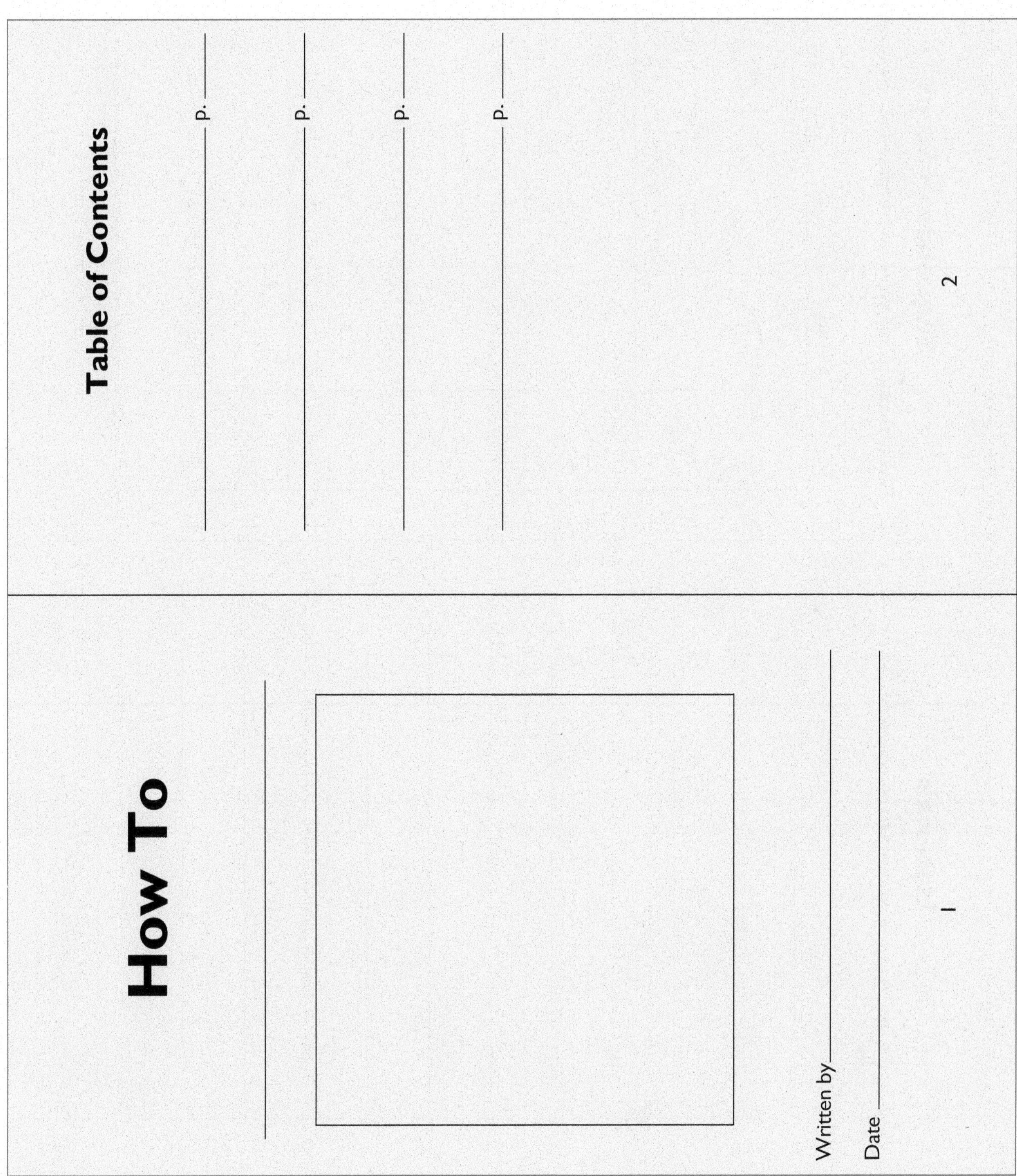

Figure 10.17 How to Make a Booklet (*Continued*)

Materials

List the materials you will need to complete this how-to activity.

____

____

____

____

____

____

____

____

____

____

____

____

3

Sequence of Steps

Write the steps and details to complete this how-to activity

Step	Details

4

Figure 10.17 How to Make a Booklet (*Continued*)

Picture

Draw a picture of your topic in the box below. Label your picture with words.

5

Glossary

Word: __________

Definition: __________

____

Word: __________

Definition: __________

____

Word: __________

Definition: __________

____

Word: __________

Definition: __________

____

Word: __________

Definition: __________

____

Word: __________

Definition: __________

____

6

Teachers can make other books like this for different informational formats to help children structure their writing. For example, when teaching how to write expository text, provide the children with a structured lesson in a similar format to the one just described (Calkins, 1994). After the guided lesson, the students will be able to do it alone. The following vignette from the classroom is another writing activity with informational text.

Children need to be able to write informative and explanatory texts in which they introduce a topic, use facts and definitions to develop points, and provide a concluding statement or section. To fulfill this standard in Ms. Tucker's second-grade class, the students were seated in a circle in the classroom meeting spot with several informational books in the center of the carpet. They had been studying conventions of nonfiction texts and were planning to use what they had learned to create their own informational texts. Ms. Tucker had a diagram of a flower with parts labeled, such as the petals, pistil, and stamen. One of the children picked up the book *From Seed to Plant*, showing the class that there was a similar diagram in the book he had read. The children had been exploring information texts and their teacher asked them to look at the different elements in these books such as diagrams.

Angelina said: I found the table of contents in Baby Dolphin's Tale! And all of the headings match the names in the book!

Ryan, grabbing Rescue Dogs from the carpet: Are these captions?

Another student confirmed that they were, and Ms. Tucker nodded in agreement.

The second graders were exploring these texts with the intention to write informa-tive texts, in which they would introduce a topic, use facts and definitions to develop points, and provide a concluding statement or section. Students were permitted to self-select topics of interest, and subjects ranged from dogs to flowers to football. Ms. Tucker collected books from the classroom and checked out books from the school library on each student's topics, and students researched carefully to be sure to include a variety of information in their completed texts. Students were also provided with various writing templates, which helped them to include several nonfiction conventions in their texts, such as a table of contents, how-to writing, interesting facts, a diagram, a glossary, and so on. As students worked, Ms. Tucker met with a small group of students who needed assistance with adding an *Interesting Facts* page to their books.

Ms. Tucker: Brianna, you're writing about horses. Let's think of some fun facts that you can add about your topic.

Brianna: Um, I know that a baby horse has a special name, but I can't think of it.

Nadia: Brianna, I know. It's called a foal.

Ms. Tucker: That sounds like an interesting fact to use. Here's a copy of the book *Horse Life Cycle* from our True Animal Books bin. Look through it and see if it helps you to find any interesting facts. Nadia, I see you have an interesting fact about a tennis racket. What else are you planning to add?

Nadia: My mom told me that Venus Williams is a great tennis player. I want to add that, but what else can I say about her?

Ms. Tucker: Let's see if we can find some information online and I'll print it out for you.

In addition to the interesting facts, the children listed words they met while reading these books and put them in the glossary of their books:

Glossary of Words to Know

- **Whiskers:** The little lines coming out from the fur
- **Fences:** A fence is like a gate. It could be made out of wood
- **Pet:** An animal you keep
- **Claw:** A claw is sharp. Some pets have claws
- **Cage:** A pet cage is used for taking a pet out to the vet
- **Love:** Love is something you like, and love is needed to take care of a pet.

When students' informational texts were completed, they used the classroom laptops to design and print book covers, including a title, a graphic to represent their topic, and, of course, a byline listing themselves as the authors. Ms. Tucker laminated the covers of the students' books and bound them. At the writing celebration, families were invited to share in reading or the completed books.

Narrative Texts and Writing

In addition to understanding and working with informational and expository text, students need to be comfortable with narrative text. Narrative text can be complex, and mentor books can help children with models for writing narrative texts. Children's literature makes for perfect mentor texts because it is as natural a medium for encouraging writing as it is for encouraging oral language and reading (Tompkins, 2000; Vukelich, Evans, & Albertson, 2003). Reading several books by the same author or illustrator helps children identify different styles and helps them with their writing and illustrations. Old favorites and series books—those that use the same character in several different books, such as *Madeline* (Bemelmans, 2000), *Curious George* (Rey, 1941), and *Harold and the Purple Crayon* (Johnson, 1981)—can motivate children to write their own books or a class book about the character. Books such as *Swimmy* (Lionni, 1964) and *Alexander and the Terrible, Horrible, No Good, Very Bad Day* (Viorst, 1972) involve the main character in a series of adventures or incidents as the story proceeds. Children can be asked to write still another episode or adventure for the character. Such stories lend themselves to writing about personal experiences. (Figure 10.18 illustrates one child's response to this task.) (Shubitz, 2016).

Teaching English Learners

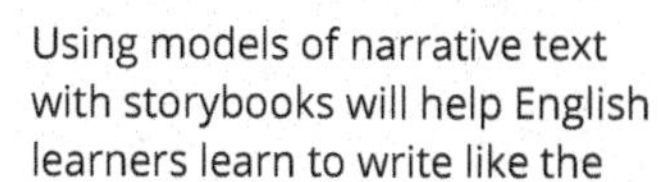

Using models of narrative text with storybooks will help English learners learn to write like the authors.

Shared book experiences and small-group story readings (described in Chapter 9) all can lead to writing experiences. Predictable books provide patterns that children can imitate in their own writing through cumulative patterns, as in *I Know an Old Lady* (Hoberman, M.A., 2006); repetitive language, as in *Are You My Mother?* (Eastman, 2005); familiar sequences, as in *The Very Hungry Caterpillar* (Carle, 2007); or catch phrases, as in *What Cried Granny: An Almost Bedtime Story* (Lum & Johnson, 2002). (Refer to Appendix A for a list of such books.)

There are standards for narrative literature as well as informational literature we just discussed. The general writing standards for text types and purposes is: Children should be able to "Write narratives in which they recount a well-elaborated event or short sequence of events, include details to describe actions, thoughts, and feelings, use temporal words to signal event order, and provide a sense of closure."

Narrative writing involves writing original stories that are typically fiction or retelling a story that was read to the children or that the children read themselves. Good narrative stories have a beginning, middle, and end. They follow a basic story structure with:

- A setting at the beginning that introduces the characters, time, and place
- A theme, which is the problem or goal of the main character
- Plot episodes, or the events that help the main character solve his problem or accomplish his or her goal
- A resolution that deals with solving the problem or the accomplishing the goal and an ending to the story.

Activities that provide practice in narrative writing include the following:

1. Give the children graphic organizers for help with story structure. Have them fill in these forms prior to writing an original story. When the story is complete, the children check to see that all the elements are included. (Refer to the story structure graphic organizer map in Figure 9.15 in Chapter 9.)
2. Instruct the children to rewrite a story that was read to them or that they read independently.

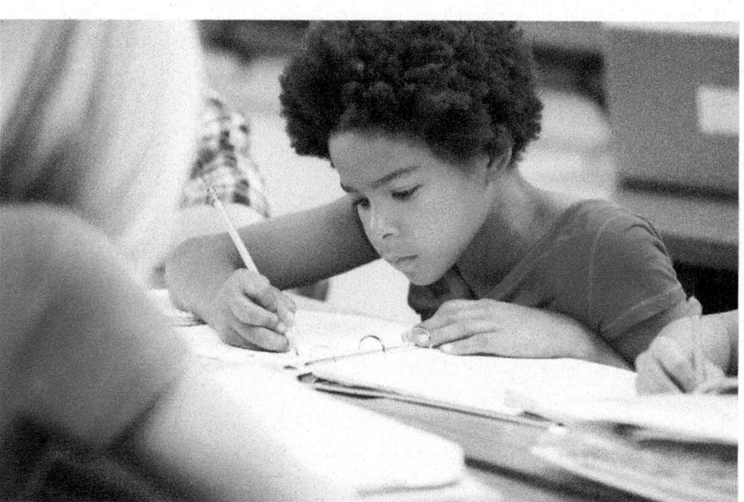

Photo credit: Monkey Business Images/Shutterstock

When children write with a partner, they help each other.

Have the children check that all the story structure elements are included in their rewrite.

3. Have the children discuss and then write a story together. When the ideas are complete, each child takes another part of the story structure to develop completely. The story is shared and then students give constructive feedback for improvement.
4. Have the children create a new structure element for a well-known story, such as another setting, theme, episode, or resolution.

Descriptive writing involves writing with language that describes precisely. When we help children describe, we ask them to be involved in using their senses: listening, seeing, smelling, touching, and tasting. We practice using many different words to tell about the same thing. Asking children to describe a flower, compare two things, or to use their five senses when writing about a specific topic will help them with descriptive writing.

Persuasive writing involves trying to get the reader to adopt the author's point of view on a given topic. Examples of persuasive writing activities include a book review, in which the author is trying to persuade someone to read a book. Other activities include creating a poster or advertisement for a product or writing a movie review. Students like discovering that, in the act of creative writing, they can take on another point of view. The opportunities are infinite, and children become excited when they realize they can "pretend" to be something they are not through writing, whether it is a dog, a tree, or even an inanimate object, such as a rug.

To help children understand and experiment with point of view, have them read mentor texts with unique points of view. One example is *The True Story of the Three Little Pigs* (Scieszka, 1996), told from the point of view of "the big bad wolf." After reading the texts, have students write the story of *The Three Little Pigs* from another point of view, or select a different nursery rhyme, fairy tale, or commonly known story. Children have written about *That Terrible Cinderella, Grow Up, Peter Pan,* and *Nasty Little Red Riding Hood.*

Figure 10.18 An Example of Writing Motivated by Children's Literature

Writing a narrative story with a quality structure is an important goal. Children can learn to do this by using a patterned mentor text that has definitive characters, a setting, an important theme, and a resolution. For example, Ms. Evans used *Franklin in the Dark* (Bourgeois, 1986) as a mentor text for an assignment to write a story that has a good story structure with the elements previously mentioned. *Franklin in the Dark* is about a turtle that is afraid to go into his shell because it is too dark. His mother suggests that he explore the world to help solve his problem. He meets a bird that is afraid to fly and uses a parachute, a duck that is afraid to swim and uses water wings, and a lion that is afraid of his roar and wears earmuffs. When he returns home, he tells his mother about his adventures, and they put a night-light in his shell to solve the problem.

After discussing the structure of narrative text and the pattern of the mentor text, Ms. Evans and her first-grade class discussed multiple writing topics. She gave her students a graphic organizer to outline a setting, a theme, episodes, and a resolution. Children worked in groups of three. The teacher left out patterned books to which children could refer for help with their style of writing. Ms. Evans wanted the children to write something that dealt with the theme they were studying—good health and nutrition. Jana and Iram decided to write a story about the characters in *Frog and Toad Are Friends* (Lobel, 1974). Frog and Toad would be planning a birthday party for a friend. They wanted to have birthday cake and ice cream but thought they should have some healthy foods as well. They went to one store and could only find candy; they went to another store and could only find cookies. Finally, they found a fruit and vegetable market. Here they found delicious blueberries, raspberries, peaches, and sweet cherries. In another part of the store, they found carrots, sweet snap peas, and fresh broccoli, and finally they found flavored yogurts and almonds. They added these to the birthday cake and ice cream. When the frogs and toads in the village came to the party, they mentioned what a wonderful menu they had selected with delicious healthy foods and sweet treats.

Using Mentor Texts to Inform Writing Style. One of the best ways to learn is when something is modeled for us. Rather than telling a child about a particular writing style, we have begun to use the work of good authors for children to learn from. The hope is that it will show them many styles of writing and use them as a part of their writing. Certain books are better mentor texts than others since the style is very evident. In a social studies unit about great cities in the United States, children got to select cities to write about. They were to include in the reports, things that the city were known for. The teacher provided a mentor text to provide the children with a writing style for their reports. The mentor text was *Brown Bear Brown Bear What Do You See* (Carle, 2009.) The book continues, I see a red bird looking at me. Following this model, here is part of one child's report on New Your city.

> New York, New York what do you see?
> I see the Statue of Liberty looking at me
> Lady Liberty what do you see?
> I see Broadway looking at me (etc.).

Writing Poetry

Another form of writing enjoyed by young children is poetry. With very young children, the class can enjoy **poetry writing** together in a shared writing experience on chart paper. Poetry that rhymes is probably the most well-known type; however, poetry doesn't have to rhyme. Many types of *formula poetry* are enjoyed by children. Some educators feel that formula poetry is an exercise in following directions and that the children think more about getting it written the correct way rather than about the meaning. Formula poetry, however, does seem to motivate children, and it provides a good introduction to writing poetry. *Acrostic poems* are very popular. They begin with a topic word that is written vertically on the page. The word could be a child's name, a season, a place, or a thing. The poem uses the letters of the topic being written about. You can use just a word, a phrase, or a sentence. For example, here is an acrostic poem I wrote about my grandson James:

James

Jolly
Adorable
Magnificent
Enthusiastic
So sweet, so silly, so special

Triangle poems follow a specific formula. The first line has one word, which is a noun, the second line is made of two adjectives, the next line has two "ing" words, and the fourth and last line is a sentence. Here is a triangle poem about spring:

Spring
New, pretty
Dancing, playing
It's so nice to be outdoors.

A *cinquain* is a poem of five lines following the pattern of (1, 2, 3, 4, and 1) in each line. The first line is the title; the second line is an adjective description of the title; the third line is the action of the title; the fourth line is a statement or feeling; and the fifth line is a synonym for the first line. Because of its strict rules and few words, the cinquain is appealing to young poets. It serves as an excellent means for teaching parts of speech. This cinquain is about vacations.

Vacation
Fun, relaxing
Laughing, playing, talking
Great time for all
Retreat

A *diamante* is a poem that is shaped like a diamond that conveys a contrast between opposite things. This poetic form would be most appropriate for older students or would need teacher assistance in the younger grades. Line one is the first topic; line two contains two adjectives describing the first topic; line three contains three "ing" verbs describing the first topic; the fourth line gives four nouns describing the second, contrasting topic; the fifth line contains three "ing" verbs describing the second topic; and the sixth and final line is the name of the second topic. Here is a season diamante.

Summer
Hot, sticky
Swimming, sunbathing, skateboarding
Snow, hot chocolate, mittens, hats
Shoveling, bundling, shivering
Winter

Poetry activities can also help students develop vocabulary and syntax. Select a topic about something you are studying—for example, the rain. Make that the topic word in the poem. Brainstorm what rain is like and what it does, and then write down the ideas. Next, take it further by putting the word *rain* after each word and chant the poem.

Rain	**Rain**
Heavy, Light	*Heavy rain*
Cold, Warm	*Light rain*
Falling, Blowing	*Cold rain*
	Warm rain
	Falling rain
	Blowing rain

TIPS FOR READING AND WRITING POETRY WITH YOUNG CHILDREN. Asking even very young children to write poetry may seem like a daunting task, but it can be quite achievable with these guidelines:

- Choose poems to read that might be familiar to children
- Choose poems to read that you like
- Don't choose overly abstract poetry
- Select poems with repetition and predictability
- Read some rhyming poems and some poems that do not rhyme
- Discuss the poem before reading; point out new vocabulary, and ask guided questions for students to consider as you read
- Have a copy of the poem on an easel written in large print
- Give the children a copy of the poem
- Have the children keep a poetry folder of the poems you give them
- Illustrate the poem
- Read the poem again on another day
- Discuss the poem after it is read
- Feature a poem a week
- Stock your class library with poetry books
- Make poetry bookmarks and greeting cards
- Send poetry postcards
- Have a poetry podcast
- Have a class poetry website
- Have a poetry reading afternoon with tea and cookies and invite an audience.

MyLab Education Self-Check 10.4

The Mechanics of Writing

This chapter has emphasized the importance of promoting children's interest in writing and giving them enjoyable opportunities to write. The writing talked about is created by the child. This section deals with another part of writing—that is, the mechanics of writing. According to most standards that deal with writing in early childhood, children should be able to demonstrate command of the conventions of standard English capitalization, punctuation, and spelling when writing.

MyLab Education
Video Example 10.8
Practicing Letters with Concrete Materials
In this video, a five year old practices writing the letters in her name using the "Wet-Dry-Try" method.
https://www.youtube.com/watch?v=Jukn9cEeXek

Handwriting

Writing requires dexterity. Preschoolers and kindergarteners need to play with puzzles, crayons, and sewing cards to strengthen their fine motor coordination. When they have the appropriate motor coordination, they can be taught letter formation. In the earlier discussion of the literacy center, other materials that help with writing and identifying letters were mentioned, including magnetic letters, letter forms to trace and copy, and whiteboard slates to practice writing letters, words, and sentences. The letters of the alphabet should be displayed at eye level for children, and the teacher can model the correct formation of upper- and lowercase manuscript (Refer to Figure 10.19).

Legibility needs to be the main goal for handwriting. Learning about spaces between words is important so that words will not run into each other. There are only a few lines and shapes to learn when writing manuscript. They include a vertical line, a horizontal line, diagonal lines, a half circle with the opening on the left, right, top, or bottom, and a

Figure 10.19 Forming the Letters of the Alphabet

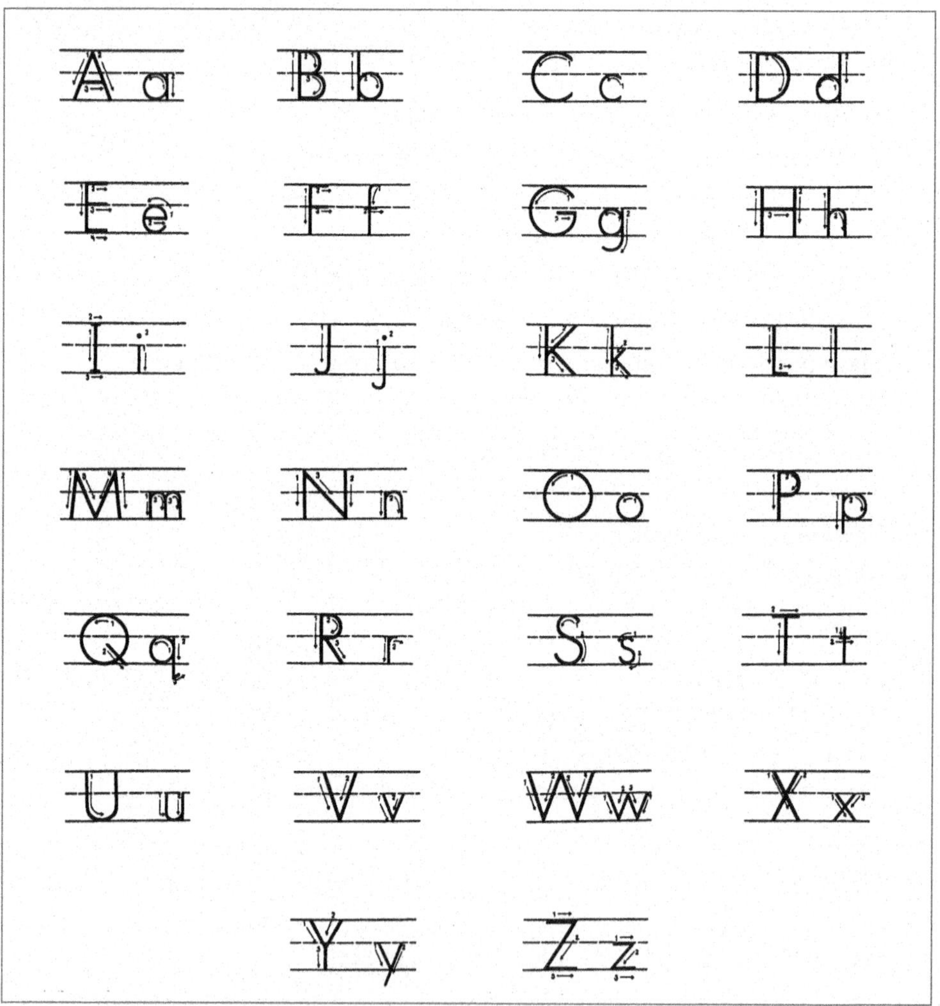

Figure 10.20 Manuscript Forms

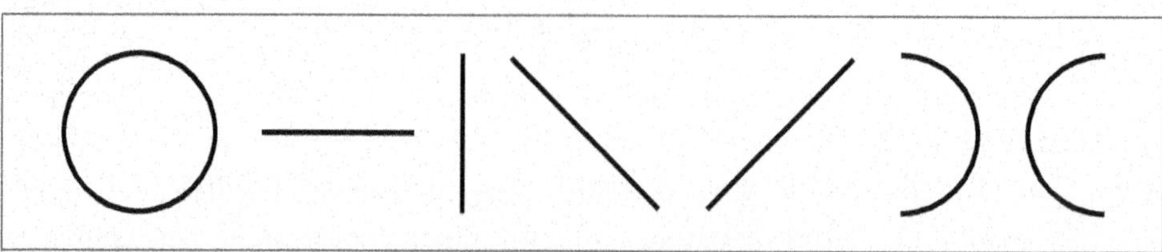

full circle (Refer to Figure 10.20). The straight lines in manuscript are called *sticks.* All lines are written from the top to the bottom. All circles and half circles are written from the top to the bottom. The letters *h, m, n, r,* and *u* are written without lifting the pencil off the page beginning with the stick. To make the *h,* you start at the top of the stick and go down to the line and go back up half of the stick to make the half circle with the opening on the bottom. The letters *b, d, g, p,* and *q* are made with a circle first and then the stick is attached.

Teach children about putting spaces between letters and words. A good rule is that one finger space will help separate words. Children can and will develop their own handwriting style, but they need to learn that, whatever their style, neat handwriting is a form of courtesy for those who will be reading what they write. Neat handwriting also ensures that the message they are communicating can be deciphered by the reader. Initially, writing will be on unlined paper. When children have developed sufficient dexterity, they can begin to use lined paper. This level will be reached at the end of kindergarten and into first grade (Shubitz, 2016).

Children in preschool and kindergarten need to explore and experiment with keyboards as well. Children may have already had the opportunity to do so before school, however they will use computers in the early childhood grades and must learn to keyboard early. If they don't learn in kindergarten or first grade they will teach themselves by hunting and pecking which is an inefficient way of typing and difficult to change.

Spelling and Punctuation

Spelling and punctuation should be taught when the need arises and also in a systematic fashion during mini lessons. Opportunities for dealing with commas, question marks, periods, and capital letters occur when reading a morning message, for example, and then the mechanics of writing are being discussed in a natural setting. Spelling and punctuation have become areas of concern. Many teachers are not sure when to begin formal teaching of spelling, punctuation, and correcting invented forms. Children should be encouraged to write in any way that they can in their first attempts. However, they need to know that it is "a child's way of writing and not grown-up writing." When children are comfortable writing and do so freely in their own style, teachers should begin to point out elements of spelling and punctuation that will help them make the transition from invented spelling and punctuation to conventional forms (Moats, 2005–2006). Figure 10.21 outlines stages of spelling development.

Some suggestions follow for encouraging conventional forms of spelling and punctuation. When you take dictation from a child, you can comment on the spelling of some unusual words and appropriate punctuation. When children use certain consistent invented forms of spelling and punctuation in their writing, put the correct form on a 3 × 5 Very Own Words card for them to copy the next time they use that word or punctuation. When children ask how to spell certain words, get them into the habit of writing those correctly spelled words on index cards to help them develop their own spelling word list. Point out punctuation and spelling when using Big Books.

Use the morning message for teaching spelling and punctuation. Write new spelling words in the message for children to copy in their writing. Leave blanks for children to fill in words from a choice of the new spelling words for the week. You also can use incorrect spelling and punctuation, so children can act as detectives to correct the errors. Or, a message can be written in all lowercase letters for children to correct with appropriate capitals put in the right place. Use incorrect spacing between words and sentences to provide for conversation about these mechanics of writing. This activity leads to an opportunity to help children with spacing in their own writing by telling them how one finger space is used between words and two finger spaces between sentences. Simply allowing children to use a word-processing program will aid in spelling, as the misspelled words will be highlighted for the children, and they can click to find

Figure 10.21 Stages of Spelling Development

SOURCE: Based on J. Johns, S. D. Lenski, and L. Elish-Piper, *Early Literacy Assessments and Teaching Strategies*, pp. 139–140. Copyright © 1990, Kendall/Hunt.

Precommunicative Spelling

- Children use scribbles.
- Children are developing a sense of directionality with scribbles.
- Children write some letters.
- Children write random strings of letters and numbers mixed with no association of the letters, marks, or numbers to sounds (e.g., *L4TZMP* for *house*).

Semiphonetic Spelling

- Consonants begin to represent words and are related to the sounds of the words (e.g., *TIMGTAK—Today I am going to the park.*).
- Beginning and ending consonant sounds may be included (*bg* for *bug*; *bd* for *bed*).
- One or two sounds may be correct in a word.

Phonetic Spelling

- Children spell words as they sound (e.g., *sokar* for *soccer*).

Transitional Spelling

- Children use a high percentage of correctly spelled words, and the remaining words are spelled using some type of spelling generalization (e.g.,*afternewn* for *afternoon*).

Conventional Spelling

- Children apply the basic rules of English to spelling and correctly spell 90 percent of the words they write.

the appropriate spelling. Encourage children to do free writing, which will result in improved spelling and punctuation.

Phonics lessons, which teach about word families and sound–symbol relationships, will help with spelling. Make children aware that they should be using their knowledge of sound–symbol relationships when they spell words, and that phonograms, chunks, and digraphs such as *ch* and *sh* are spelling patterns to learn.

In writing conferences with children, take the opportunity to make them aware of editing, which includes correct spelling. Here are some additional suggestions:

- Make children aware of spelling resources, such as the dictionary.
- Teach the children how to use spell- and grammar-check tools on the computer.
- Use word lists of common difficult words to spell, such as *the, this,* and *but*, for children to memorize. Several words a week should be part of a spelling list to learn. The older the children, the more words they will be able to be responsible for per week. (Figure 7.3 is a list of high-frequency words.)
- Have children keep their own spelling dictionary of words. As they learn new ones, they put them into their spelling notebook, which they can use as a reference over and over.
- Add words from theme units to spelling lists.
- Encourage children to help each other with spelling words and punctuation.

It is vital to free children to write their thoughts on paper without concern for the mechanics of writing. When they are ready, it is also important for children to become aware of writing that is mechanically correct. There are times for free writing and times for edited pieces; in other words, children should not have to turn all writing activities into finished products. Children should know that each type of writing is acceptable, but each occurs in different settings. The discussion in Chapter 8 about phonics provides activities that will help with spelling through word building. The following are some spelling games that are easy to use in the classroom to reinforce spelling words being taught (Rosencrans, 1998):

- **Letter Box:** Put five or six letters that make up the week's spelling words in a box. Students will arrange letters to make spelling words.
- **Mixed-Up Scrambled Words:** Write spelling words with the letters mixed up, and ask children to write each word correctly.
- **Spelling Collage:** Ask children to write their spelling words randomly on a 9×12 paper, covering as much of an area as possible with the words. With markers and crayons, have the students trace over the spelling words in different colors in a decorative manner. Display the spelling collages on a bulletin board.
- **Spelling Detectives:** In various communications such as on word walls, morning messages, center activity directions, or job descriptions, make errors in spelling words. It is the children's job to find the errors daily.
- **Word Hunt:** Have students look regularly for spelling words that appear in all that they do at school and at home—for example, in a math book, a science book, the newspaper, a book they are reading for pleasure, food lists at home, and so on.
- **Trace a Word:** Have students "write" spelling words on a partner's back using their pointer finger. The partner has to guess the word.
- **Hidden Words:** Prepare a list of spelling words that are surrounded by other letters.
- Have students find and then circle or color the spelling words embedded within (for example: *ovisrm mxtheuv qrbutzi*).

In the following vignette, the classroom will help children demonstrate command of standard English conventions, such as capitalization, punctuation, and spelling when writing.

The second graders in Ms. Richards's class had been working on writing informational texts to correspond with a social studies unit on American symbols. Students were at various stages of completing their texts, and during this social studies block, several students sat with laptops to research information using the website Brain Pop Jr., while a small group sat at a round table reading over *O, Say Can You See?*, a book Ms. Richards had read aloud several days before. Other students worked independently on their writing, while Ms. Richards met with students individually. Ms. Levitt, a special education teacher in the classroom, worked with a small group of students at a table near the literacy center. They had completed their writing and were ready to edit their informational texts.

Ms. Levitt: Last night, I took your books home with me to read, and wow! You really included lots of great information about the American symbols we've been studying. It seems like you're all ready to do some editing. Who can remember something we should check when we're editing our writing?

Luke: We need to have spaces between our words and make sure we've spelled the words on our word wall the right way.

Ms. Levitt: You're absolutely right! What else?

Kory: Um, we need capitals?

Anthony: Oh, and periods and question marks!

Ms. Levitt: You got it! We need to make sure our writing has capitals at the beginning of our sentences and punctuation at the end. Let's do some work with punctuation today. I'm going to read my writing aloud without punctuation. Your job is to listen carefully to help me decide where the punctuation should go. Listen to spots where my voice pauses.

She began to read aloud from a copy of her writing projected onto the interactive whiteboard: "The Statue of Liberty is an important American symbol it can be found in New York City the statue holds a torch in one hand."

Ms. Levitt: It's hard to understand my writing without punctuation, isn't it? Does anyone notice a spot that needs some punctuation?

Anthony: I think after "symbol." Before the part about it being in New York City.

Ms. Levitt: Great noticing. Don't forget that the first letter in the next word will need to be a capital for the beginning of a new sentence.

Anthony took the interactive whiteboard marker, added the punctuation in the correct spot, and changed the "i" in "it" to a capital letter. The group continued in this way until all of the missing punctuation and capitalization was added.

Ms. Levitt: Great work everyone. Now let's try the same thing with your writing. Please read it aloud to yourself and listen for spots where your voice pauses for the end of the sentence. That's the spot that you'll need to add punctuation. You'll need to work independently, but I'll be listening in to help you while you work.

At the end of the social studies block, the second graders returned their informational texts to their social studies folders to work on later in the week. They would soon be creating models or posters of the American symbol they selected to present with their writing at the school cultural fair later that month.

MyLab Education Self-Check 10.5

Assessment of Children's Writing

As in other areas of literacy, assessment of a child's writing should take place throughout the school year. That way, the teacher can determine a child's level of development, monitor progress, and plan programs accordingly. Quantitative and qualitative assessment measures for narrative story rewriting after reading or listening to a story read are found in Figures 10.21 and 10.22. Figure 10.22 provides another means of evaluating children's written original stories. Read through an orally-taped story and the written original story and record comments and responses that demonstrate interpretive and critical thought. An assessment for evaluating children's informational writing is found in Figure 10.23.

The assessment checklist in Figure 10.24 is used to analyze individual writing samples collected all year for the specific characteristics outlined in the measure. The checklist in Figure 10.25 provides a resource the teacher can use to evaluate the classroom writing environment.

The measures for evaluating writing and the checklists in this chapter provide the teacher with information about the language the child uses, the concepts included in the writing, the purpose for writing, and the writing mechanics used. The checklists provide information about the conventions of writing. They will indicate the stage of writing or spelling that a student is demonstrating, as well as the mechanics of writing used, such as capitalization and punctuation. The measures for story rewriting and writing of original stories will determine how well the child uses meaning and structure in his or her writing. All these assessment tools will help determine appropriate instruction and practice a child needs in order to progress in writing development (Bromley, 2007).

Teachers should maintain a portfolio of materials related to a child's writing development, such as observation notes as the child writes, samples of the child's writing over a period of time, notes from conferences with the child, notes from conferences with the child's parents, and completed checklists. The portfolio should include the best of the child's work as well as samples showing need for improvement. The portfolio can be used during parent conferences and can accompany a child to his or her next teacher. Children should have their own writing folders in which they keep samples of their writing throughout the year.

Figure 10.22 Evaluating Oral and Written Original Stories

Child's name:________________________________ **Date:**________

Name of story:____

Setting	**Yes**	**No**
a. The story begins with an introduction.	☐	☐
b. One or more main characters emerge.	☐	☐
c. Other main characters are talked about.	☐	☐
d. The time of the story is mentioned.	☐	☐
e. Where the story takes place is mentioned.	☐	☐
Theme		
a. A beginning event occurs that causes a problem for the main character or for the goal to be achieved.	☐	☐
b. The main character reacts to the problem.	☐	☐
Plot Episodes		
An event or series of events is mentioned that relates to the main character solving the problem or attaining the goal.	☐	☐
Resolution		
a. The main character solves the problem or achieves the goal.	☐	☐
b. The story ends with a closing statement.	☐	☐
Sequence		
The four categories of story structure are presented in typical sequential order (setting, theme, plot episodes, resolution).	☐	☐

Interpretive and Critical Comments: Read through the orally-taped story and the written original story and record comments and responses that demonstrate interpretive and critical thought.

Figure 10.23 Evaluating Informational Text

The expository text includes some of these characteristics:	**Yes**	**No**
1. **Comparing and contrasting** Noting similarities and differences	☐	☐
2. **Sequencing** Listing factual information that happened in proper sequential order	☐	☐
3. **Cause and effect** Describing how something happened and why	☐	☐
4. **Exemplification** Providing a reason and an example	☐	☐
5. **Description** Giving a good picture of what specific information looks like	☐	☐

Figure 10.24 Checklist for Assessing Writing Development

Child's name: ____________________ **Date:** ____________________

Teacher fills out the checklist for each child	**Always**	**Sometimes**	**Never**	**Comments**
Explores with writing materials				
Dictates stories, sentences, or words he or she wants written down				
Copies letters and words				
Independently attempts writing to convey meaning, regardless of writing level				
Can write his or her name				
Check (✓) the level or levels at which the child is writing				
_____ Uses drawing for writing and drawing				
_____ Differentiates between writing and drawing				
_____ Uses scribble writing for writing				
_____ Uses letter-like forms for writing				
_____ Uses learned letters in random fashion for writing				
_____ Uses invented spelling for writing				
_____ Writes conventionally with conventional spelling				
Collaborates with others in writing experience				
Writes in varied genres:				
narrative (stories)				
expository (personal and informational reports)				
Writes for functional purposes				
Stays on topic				
Thinks about the audience				
Makes opinions clear				
Teacher fills out the checklist for each child				
Gives details and examples				
Puts things in order or sequence				
Includes a beginning, middle, and end				
Uses a variety of words and sentences				

Figure 10.24 Checklist for Assessing Writing Development (*continued*)

Mechanics for Writing	**Always**	**Sometimes**	**Never**	**Comments**
Forms uppercase letters legibly				
Forms lowercase letters legibly				
Writes from left to right				
Leaves spaces between words				
Uses capital letters when necessary				
Uses punctuation correctly				

Spelling Development

Check (✓) the level or levels at which the child is spelling

_____ precommunicative spelling				
_____ semiphonetic spelling				
_____ phonetic spelling				
_____ transitional spelling				
_____ conventional spelling				

Teacher Comments:

Figure 10.25 Checklist for Assessing the Classroom Writing Environment

	Yes	**No**
Space provided for a writing center		
Tables and chairs included in center		
Writing posters and bulletin boards for children to display their writing themselves		
Writing utensils (pens, pencils, crayons, magic markers, colored pencils, etc.)		
Typewriter and/or computer		
Writing materials (many varieties of paper in all sizes, booklets, pads)		
A message board or private message area for children to leave messages for the teacher and other members of the class		
A place to store Very Own Words		
Folders in which children place samples of their writing		
Materials to make books		

Figure 10.26 Self-Assessment Evaluation for Writers

Name: ______________________________ **Date:** ______________

The good things about this writing are:

Parts I should take out are:

I could make this writing better if I:

I used correct spelling:

I used my best handwriting:

Is writing hard or easy for me?

For me writing is (a) fun, (b) not so much fun.

Writing could be better if:

Next time I write something, I will try to do the following things to make it better:

Children also should be involved in the assessment process by participating in parent-teacher conferences and in conferences with the teacher alone. Figure 10.26 provides a general way for children to assess their own writing interest and ability. For kindergartners and young children, something simpler can be used for self-evaluation. The children can evaluate with a friend or the teacher whether their work is *Wow, Good,* or *Okay*. The teacher says *Wow* with a very enthusiastic voice; *Good* is much more toned down; and *Okay* is said just that way, okay. When they evaluate, they discuss why the writing was *Wow, Good,* or just *Okay*. The evaluation is based on the child's achievement level as well. When evaluating together, check to see whether the children took time with their illustrations. Was their writing done to the best of their ability?

All these suggestions support the purpose of assessment to (1) enhance the teacher's understanding of children's writing ability, (2) aid in program planning, and (3) help children and parents understand a child's progress and the processes involved to help gain more competence in writing.

MyLab Education
Video Example 10.9
Portfolios and Self-Assessment

Portfolios provide children a way for them to see their own literacy growth over time.

The evaluation of writing is not only done in the classroom, but it is also based on standards set by different states. To evaluate children's writing, states often create rubrics. **Rubrics** are scoring guides and are useful tools for students and teachers to get a sense of what students should strive for in their writing. It is helpful for students to see writing samples that have excellent rubric evaluations to help them with their own work. In preparation for state standards tests in writing, teachers must begin in pre-K. A standards test may provide a child with a picture and a prompt to complete a writing task in 30 minutes. The prompt may simply say, "Create a story about what is happening in the picture and persuade the audience about your point of view based on what you write." The writing is evaluated on a rubric that might look like the one in Figure 10.27.

Figure 10.27 Early Childhood Writing Rubric

	Inadequate 1	Limited 2	Partial 3	Adequate 4	Strong 5	Superior 6	Score
Was the prompt responded to clearly and appropriately?							
Was the writing supported with appropriate details?							
Is there an introduction?							
Are there appropriate transitions?							
Is there a conclusion?							
Was varied sentence structure used?							
Was varied vocabulary used?							
Were print mechanics (spelling, punctuation, capitalization) used properly?							

Figure 10.28 Checklist for Self-Assessment of Writing

Did you remember to

_____ Stick to the topic?

_____ Think about your audience?

_____ Give details and examples?

_____ Put things in order?

_____ Include an opening and a closing?

_____ Use a variety of words and sentences?

_____ State your opinion clearly?

_____ Use capitals and punctuation correctly?

_____ Write neatly?

The rubric in Figure 10.27 is adapted from the New Jersey Registered Holistic Scoring Rubric. Each of the items on the rubric rates children on a scale of 1 to 6. Children receive a score of 1 if their work is evaluated as inadequate, 2 if their writing is considered limited, 3 for writing that shows partial command on items being evaluated, 4 for adequate writing, 5 for a strong command of their writing, and 6 for superior writing. Therefore, if a sample is evaluated on how clearly and appropriately the student responded to the prompts, he or she could receive anywhere from a 1 to 6 from the evaluator.

MyLab Education Application Exercise 10.2

One way to help young writers ensure that they are working to the best of their ability is to provide them with a checklist for checking their work, such as the one shown in Figure 10.28 (New Jersey State Department of Education, 1998). These assessment strategies aid in children's self-reflection and will get them used to rubrics that will be used to assess their writing, all of which will nurture future writing success.

Another helpful tool for developing writers is to evaluate each other's writing. This relieves the teacher of doing all the assessments, and it teaches children how to work both together and independently. Figure 10.29 offers a form for students to evaluate each other's writing.

An Idea from the Classroom

First-Grade and Preschool Pen Pals

Children from a nearby preschool wrote to my first graders to find out what the elementary school was like. We wrote a class letter back answering their questions and included our pictures. One week later, we received a response. Now we had established a letter-writing routine. The children in my class took turns writing parts of each letter on chart paper. We went through the writing process steps of brainstorming, revising, editing, and rewriting for our new audience. Three children acted as scribes, while the rest of the class developed the letter. Later, three new children were chosen to revise and edit. Finally, three more children rewrote the letter. We also used email to send messages that needed quick responses to pen pals. Being pen pals became a part of our writing curriculum. We invited the preschoolers for a snack and a paired-reading session and to our end-of-the-year play. In turn, the preschoolers invited our class for a picnic at the preschool. We developed a friendship with the younger students, and our first-grade class learned the purposeful and very rewarding skill of letter writing. In addition, the preschoolers became familiar with our school, which most of them would be entering soon.

Used with permission from *Donna M. Ngai, First-Grade Teacher*

Figure 10.29 Evaluating Each Other's Writing

Name of Writer: ______________________________ Date: __________

Name of Editor: ______________________________ Date: __________

Peer Evaluation

(1) Exchange your first draft with another student. Read over each other's paper. As you read, think about what you like, consider suggestions, and list any questions you might have. Record your evaluation here.

(2) Use this form for practicing **comprehension** for a story you read by answering: What I really liked about this story was. . . . I think the story would be better if the author. . . . Here are some things I wasn't sure about when I read. . . .

Praise

I really like the way you______________________________

____

____

____

____

____

Suggestion

I think your writing would be better if you______________________________

____

____

____

____

____

Questions

Here are some things I wasn't sure about when I read your story.

____

____

____

____

____

MyLab Education Self-Check 10.6

Summary

10.1 Explain the theories underpinning early writing development.

A tight connection exists between reading and writing, and the development of written language occurs in discernable stages. Children learn about reading and writing in similar ways. Early writing development is characterized by children's moving from playfully making marks on paper, to communicating messages on paper, to creating texts. Students learn about writing through explicit instruction from teachers, by observing others more skilled than themselves, and through practice. They progress from scribbling, to drawing for writing, to writing via making letter-like forms, to writing via reproducing well-learned units or letter strings, to writing via invented spelling, and then finally to conventional writing. Key to developing literacy is providing children with meaningful opportunities to write.

10.2 Describe strategies used to help children from birth to pre-K develop writing.

Strategies for writing development from birth to age 2 address needs different from those that occur in pre-K classrooms. From birth to age 2, children should be encouraged to make spontaneous markings and not be urged to write particular things. Adults should express pleasure in early markings, model writing for children, invite children to participate in meaningful writing experiences, and give children ample opportunities to interact with print.

In the classroom, children should begin learning to compose text that conveys meaning, but they should be free to write in unconventional ways. For example, teachers in pre-K classrooms can model writing is by taking student dictation.

10.3 Describe strategies to be used for developing writing in kindergarten through third grade.

During this period, students should evolve from unconventional writing to conventional writing. Strategies for developing writing in this stage include creating a writing center, using writing workshops, incorporating a process approach to writing, and incorporating time for interactive writing, independent reading and writing, and journal writing. The classroom atmosphere needs to encourage writing and provide support, feedback, and encouragement to reluctant writers. Older children need more explicit and goal-oriented instruction. A writing center stocked with multiple writing implements, papers, bookmaking materials, anchor charts, notice boards, and other supplies provides a contextual environment for writing. The writing workshop is a time for explicit instruction on the forms and facets of writing. After the purpose of the workshop is set, there is a mini lesson followed by time to write independently and then time to share writing. The process approach to writing provides a framework for students to follow and helps them realize that advance planning and thinking are needed before writing. The process approach generally includes the following steps: prewriting or brainstorming, drafting, conferencing, revising, editing, and publishing. Although intuitive, the process approach should be used judiciously with young children, and teachers should adjust each step according to realistic expectations based on the children's developmental stage and ability. Interactive writing is a joint effort as the teacher and the children create the writing together (collaborative). Independent reading and writing allow children to engage in the activities of their choice, which they often do with other children (cooperative). Journal writing can occur in personal, dialogue, reading-response, or learning-log journals. Regardless of the format, journals are a private for students' own individual writing (personal).

10.4 Discuss the types of writing most appropriate for early childhood and give examples of how to develop each.

At the early childhood level, the primary text types are informational (expository), narrative, and poetry. Informational (expository) writing is nonfiction and uses information from content-area subjects. Children collect information and summarize it. The writing does not include personal views; it is built on facts. Informational text has features different from narrative such as a table of contents, a glossary, photographs instead of drawings, charts, and graphs. Expository structures include description, sequence, comparison, cause and effect, problem solving, and exemplification. Functional writing—writing that serves a clear, real-life purpose—is a subset of expository writing. Narrative texts and writing are fictional accounts and are often complex and difficult to distill linearly. Mentor texts help children identify different styles and the components of original stories: setting, theme, plot episodes, and resolution. Common narrative structures are descriptive writing and persuasive writing. Poetry is a form of writing that involves playing with structures and concepts. Although criticized by some, different types of formula poetry, such as acrostic, triangle, cinquain, and diamante, make poetry accessible to young children.

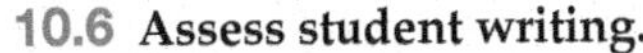

10.5 Demonstrate the important mechanical aspects of writing that children must learn.

In addition to the ideas produced in writing, young children need to learn about the mechanics of writing. They must learn how to write manuscript and how to use punctuation and proper spelling. A key element in the mechanics of writing is a student's actual handwriting, which requires dexterity to create the legible letters that are the source of meaning. Punctuation and spelling should be taught in mini lessons in a systematic fashion. Children need to realize that a child's way of writing (using unconventional spelling and shapes) is not adult writing—it's just a step on their journey to become writers. Mechanics can be incorporated into the morning message, into shared reading, with cloze exercises, through direct phonics instruction, and even through games and puzzles.

10.6 Assess student writing.

Assessment of a child's writing should take place throughout the school year. Teachers should maintain a portfolio of materials related to a child's writing development, such as observation notes as the child writes, samples of the child's writing over a period of time, notes from conferences with the child, notes from conferences with the child's parents, and completed checklists. The portfolio should include the best of the child's work as well as samples showing need for improvement. Teachers should evaluate students' progress in writing expository and narrative text and allow students to evaluate their own work. Peer review, in which students evaluate each other's work, is also a valuable form of assessment. Rubrics help ensure that assessments are performed consistently from student to student and regardless of when they are conducted.

Activities and Questions

1. Ask three children of different ages—for example, ages 3, 5, and 7—to write about their favorite food, television show, storybook, or game. Take notes on their behavior during writing, and analyze the sample of their writing to determine each child's writing developmental level.
2. Many functional and meaningful writing experiences are related in this chapter. Try to think of writing experiences not dealt with in the chapter that you could suggest for which children to participate.
3. Think of several dramatic-play themes that you could create in an early childhood classroom, such as a restaurant or a travel agency. For each theme, think of the writing materials you could provide for that play area for children to use.
4. Continue the portfolio assessment for the child you selected to assess for language development in Chapter 6. Observe the child using the assessment checklists provided in this chapter and the rubric in Figure 10.27 concerning the evaluation of writing development. Collect writing samples from the child over the course of several months. Evaluate them to determine the child's development in writing over time.
5. Continue the thematic unit that you began in Chapter 6. Select three objectives in the area of writing development and describe three activities that will satisfy each objective using your theme. Be sure that your activities reflect functional and meaningful writing tasks.
6. Create an activity to enhance spelling and punctuation for young children.
7. Use pages in the chapter with a child in your class or at your student teaching placement. Try making webs as a precursor to writing; try K-W-L, Venn diagrams, writing expository text, and so on. Explanations for these graphic organizers are in Chapter 9.
8. Think of a writing assignment or mini lesson that engages students in the use of digital literacies that you could use in your early childhood classroom.

Chapter 11

Using Children's Literature in the Classroom

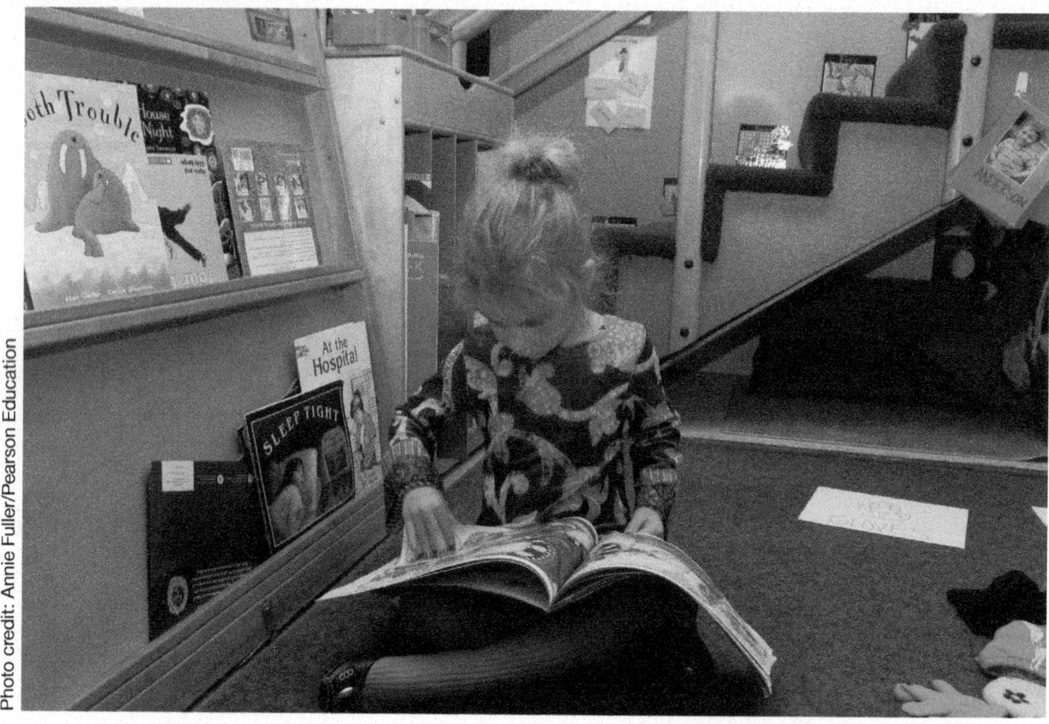

Photo credit: Annie Fuller/Pearson Education

Learning Outcomes

After reading this chapter, you should be able to:

11.1 Identify the features of a well-designed literacy station.

11.2 Discuss types of children's literature to have in your classroom.

11.3 Identify activities that can be done with children's literature.

11.4 Describe storytelling techniques and encourage independent reading.

11.5 Assess children's attitudes toward books.

Russell Stauffer (1980) said it best:

> *Love of reading and writing is not taught, it is created. Love of reading and writing is not required, it is inspired.*
>
> *Love of reading and writing is not demanded, it is exemplified. Love of reading and writing is not exacted, it is quickened.*
>
> *Love of reading and writing is not solicited, it is activated.*
>
> —Russell Stauffer, 1980.*

VOCABULARY

Biography
Library corner
Literacy station
Picture concept books
Picture storybooks
Traditional literature
Wordless books

We want children to love reading. We hope chilldren will find reading and writing joyful. Creating a literacy station in your classroom provides a place to store children's literature and motivate children to read. The hope is that children will complete their elementary grades wanting to read for pleasure and to read to seek information.

During a period of independent reading and writing, second graders Trisha and Jessica chose a story to tell using stick puppets for the book *Are You My Mother?* (Eastman, 1960). The following transpired as they worked together reading the story and manipulating the puppets:

Jessica: Can I read the story?

Trisha: OK.

Jessica: (She begins reading with enthusiasm as Trisha works the stick puppets.) The baby bird asks the cow, "Are you my mother?"

Trisha: (Trisha has the baby bird stick puppet in one hand and the cow stick puppet in the other.)

Jessica: Moooooooo. (Jessica continues to read the book.)

Trisha: Look at this picture. (She points to the baby bird. Both start to giggle.)

Jessica: Here I am, Mother! (She reads in a high-pitched voice.) Mother, Mother, here I am?

Trisha: I like it when he says to the tractor, "You are my mother, snort, snort."

Jessica: Snort, snort! I thought I had a mother. (She puts her hand to her head as she says this, using a baby bird voice and swaying back and forth pretending she is crying.)

Trisha: (She imitates Jessica by putting her hands on her head.) I thought I had a mother!

Jessica: (She points to the puppets.) Can I do this now and you read? (They trade places, and Trisha starts reading. She speaks in dramatic and different voices for the Mama bird and the baby bird. Trisha is reading too fast.

Jessica: Wait, wait. Will you wait a minute, Trisha? (She picks up the dog stick puppet, and Trisha continues.) Wait, wait, wait! (She picks up the mother bird)

This dialogue illustrates two second-grade students' engagement while reading independently in their classroom literacy station. The children were practicing literacy skills in an atmosphere that promotes the desire to read and write using motivating literacy materials.

Create A Literacy Station: Establish Good Reading and Writing Habits

Cultivating good reading and writing habits is also a critical element to fostering a literacy friendly atmosphere. The National Center on Education and the Economy and the Learning Research and Development Center at the University of Pittsburgh (1999)

* Russell Stauffer, 1980. Adapted from Wilson Library Bulletin. © 1980. Used with permission of EBSCO Information Services, Ipswich, M.

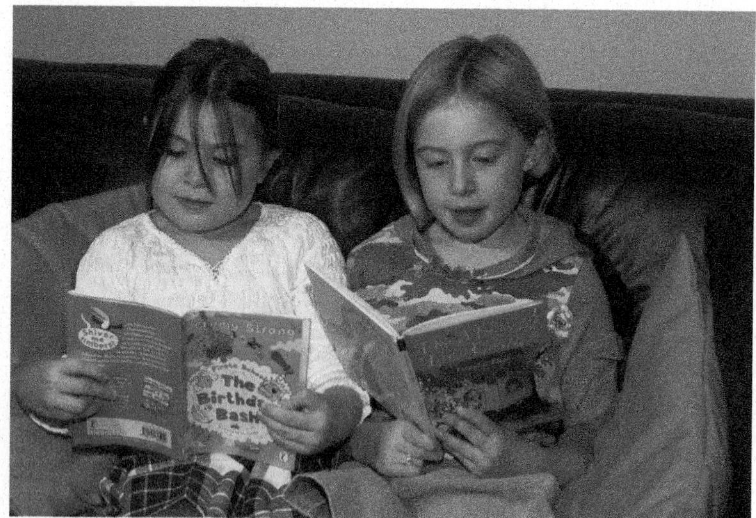

Photo credit: Annie Fuller/Pearson Education

Children participate in independent partner reading.

has articulated standard practices that help kindergartners through third graders establish good reading and writing habits.

Good reading habits are established when children have frequent opportunities to read choice texts independently. Children should be read books that are of high literary quality and interest, represent multiple genres, and are at a greater difficulty level than children could read on their own. Children can comprehend and discuss when listening to more difficult text than they can read, and also can learn new vocabulary. In the early childhood grades, children must be given the following opportunities to develop strong reading habits:

a. Read a wide range of genres in literature, such as poems and stories, digital texts, functional text (e.g., signs, messages, and labels), and narrative and expository texts.

b. Have the opportunity to read for pleasure for at least 20 minutes a day at school.

c. Read books daily at school and discuss them with text-to-life connections. Listen to and read books with parents.

d. Good writing habits are established when children have frequent opportunities to write independently about choice topics.

e. Children should listen to recitations of each other's writing.

f. Many different forms of writing should be practiced, such as functional, informational, and narrative writing.

To develop good writing habits and enhance writing motivation, children in the early grades should:

a. Write often and listen to what others write.

b. Write independently and in collaboration.

c. Write in a wide range of genres, such as poems and stories, functional text (signs, messages, and labels), digital texts, narrative texts, and informational texts.

d. Share writing with peers and discuss each other's work.

e. Write at home.

Much like establishing good personal hygiene habits early in life is critical to maintaining good health, establishing good reading and writing habits early is critical to building a solid foundation for literacy (Short, Lynch-Brown, & Tomlinson, 2018).

The Literacy Station Creates a Rich Literacy Environment

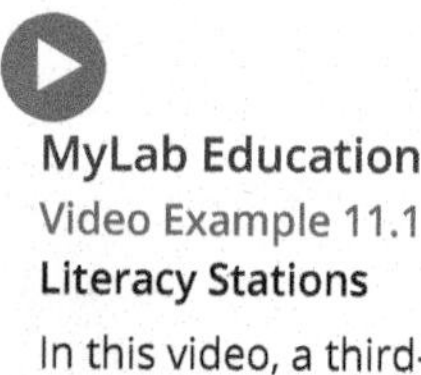

MyLab Education
Video Example 11.1
Literacy Stations

In this video, a third-grade teacher provides a virtual tour of 10 different literacy station activities.
https://www.youtube.com/watch?v=xe5clH7CSc0

To create a literacy rich environment that supports students' motivation to read, teachers can create classrooms with spaces that foster an interest in reading and writing. In fact, classrooms need multiple stations for children to practice skills independently. A classroom **literacy station** is comprised of a library corner and a writing area. In literacy stations children have choices, they collaborate, and they face challenging tasks and help each other to succeed with them. The literacy station will be described in this chapter. The writing station was discussed in Chapter 10.

A classroom literacy station is essential for children's immediate access to literature. Children in classrooms with literature collections read and look at books 50%

more often than children in classrooms without such collections. The efforts spent in creating an inviting atmosphere for a classroom literacy station are rewarded by increased interest in books (Guthrie, 2002). Morrow (1987) found that well-designed classroom literacy stations significantly increased the number of children who chose to participate in literature activities during free-choice periods. Conversely, poorly designed literacy centers were among the least popular areas at free-choice periods in early childhood rooms (Morrow, 1982; Short, Lynch-Brown, & Tomlinson, 2018). Therefore, the physical features of a classroom literacy station play an important role in motivating children to use the area.

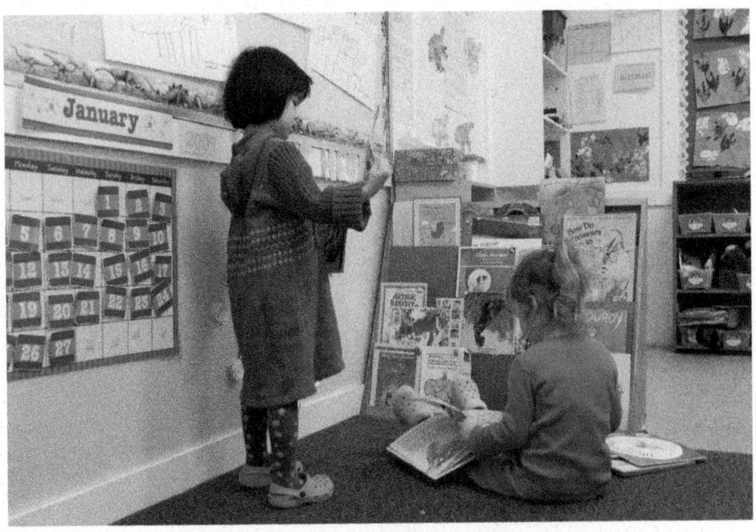

Photo credit: Jennifer Kamm

A well-designed literacy station is a popular choice during students' free time.

Features of Well-Designed Literacy Station

This area, should be immediately visible and inviting to anyone entering the classroom. To provide privacy and physical definition, it should be partitioned on two or three sides with bookshelves, a piano, or file cabinets. The dimensions of the literacy station will vary with the size of the classroom. Generally, it should be large enough to accommodate five or six children comfortably. The literacy station (refer to Figure 11.1) should be furnished with the following:

- A rug
- Pillows or beanbag chairs
- A small table and chairs
- Headsets and audio stories
- A rocking chair called the "Literacy Chair of Honor" (for teachers to read to children, for children to read to classmates, and for invited guests to read to the class)
- Elements of softness such as stuffed animals
- Books related to stuffed animals when possible, such as a stuffed rabbit next to *The Tale of Peter Rabbit* (Potter, 1902)
- A felt board with figures of story characters or a magnetic board with figures with magnets on the back
- Puppets (hand puppets, stick puppets, and finger puppets)
- Posters from the Children's Book Council (12 West 37th Street, 2nd Floor, New York, NY 10018; www.cbcbooks.org) and from the American Library Association (50 East Huron Street, Chicago, IL 60611; www.ala.org).
- An "author's spot," or writing station (described thoroughly in Chapter 10)

Children have little privacy in school, and many have none at home. Many children relish being alone and sometimes read in coat closets and under shelves. Because it is partially partitioned from the rest of the room, the literacy station should offer readers some privacy. Listening to stories on headsets is another way for readers to have privacy, and an oversized carton, painted or covered with contact paper, makes a cozy separate reading room.

The "author's spot" is an integral part of the literacy center. It usually consists of:

- A table and chairs
- Colored markers, pencils and crayons

Figure 11.1 A Classroom Literacy Center

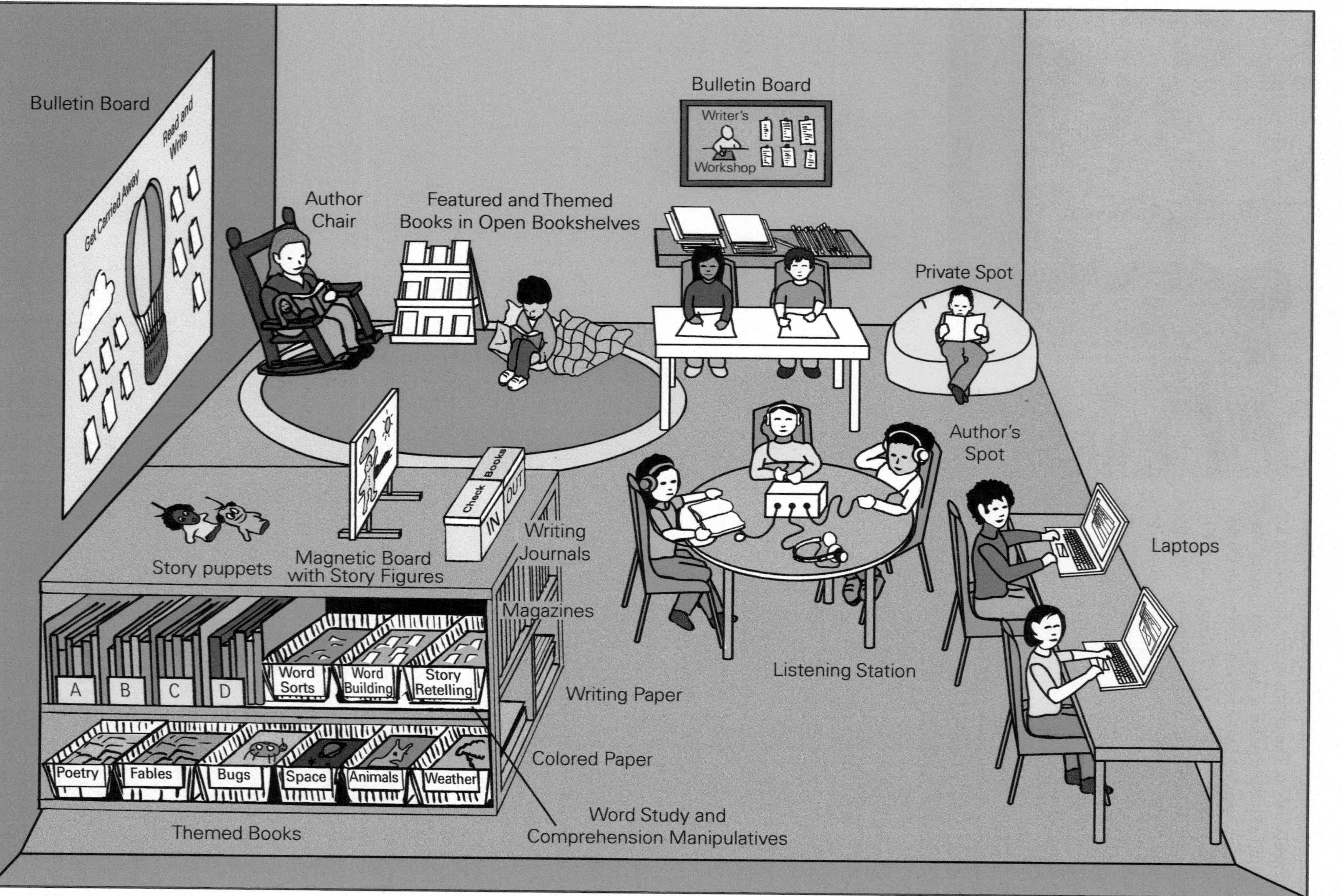

- Lined white paper and unlined paper in a range of sizes
- Several computers
- Book-making materials
- Colored construction paper
- A stapler and scissors

Children should be involved in the planning and design of a literacy station. They can develop rules for its use, be in charge of keeping it neat, and select a name for it, such as "The Book Nook."

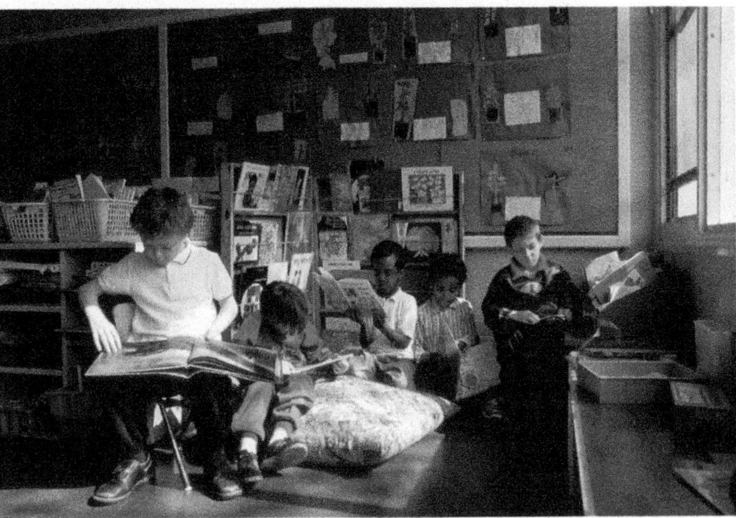

Photo credit: Annie Fuller/Pearson Education

A classroom literacy center is crucial for children's immediate access to books.

The Library Corner. The **library corner** is probably the most important part of the literacy station used for storing books. There are several ways to do so. A common practice is books shelved with the spines facing out. Another type is open-faced shelves, allowing the covers of the books to be seen; this method is important for calling attention to special books. Featured books should be changed regularly and placed on the open-faced shelves or circular wire racks commonly seen in bookstores for easy access. These racks and open-faced shelves should highlight books with themes being studied. Baskets are very popular for storing books.

Teaching English Learners

As with other children a writing station and library corner are visual statements that say reading and writing are important.

Books in the collection should be shelved by category. They can be color coded according to the type of book. Identify all animal books, for example, by placing a blue dot on their spines and clustering them on a shelf marked "Animals," with a blue dot next to the label.

A popular method is to store genres in plastic baskets, with labels on the front naming the types of books in the container.

A classroom library should have five to eight books per child, covering a range of three to four grade levels. Books should include narrative and informational literature. Half of the books should be informational texts and the other half narrative stories (Moss, Leone, & Dipillo, 1997; Marinak, Gambrell, & Mazzoni, 2012).

Books are not difficult to accumulate. They can be purchased inexpensively at yard sales or flea markets. Teachers can borrow up to 20 books a month from most public libraries, ask for book donations from parents, and hold fundraisers for book purchases. In addition, children's paperback book clubs offer inexpensive books and free bonus books for bulk purchases. Children's magazines and newspapers also belong in the classroom library, even if they are not current. For the cost of shipping, some publishers and local magazine agencies will donate outdated periodicals to schools. Collect other written materials for your classroom library, such as advertisements, menus, airplane and train tickets, brochures for businesses, organizations, and anything else that you believe would be of interest to them.

In addition to printed books, incorporate digital books for children to read and experience. Several companies provide sites where students can read books across multiple genres and levels. Scholastic (www.scholastic.com/home/) is one such service. Some subscription plans allow books to appear on all digital tools in a school building at the same time. Digital books offer interactive features, such as reading a book aloud to a child (audio narration). A common feature of digital books formatted for use on touchscreen devices is a highlighting tool. As a child reads and uses their finger to slide over the print on the screen, the text is highlighted simultaneously. This capability allows children to read books that might be too difficult for them.

To ensure continued interest, the teacher must introduce new books and materials and recirculate others in the library corner. Approximately 25 new books should be introduced every 3 weeks, replacing 25 that have been there previously. In this way,

Figure 11.2 Loose-Leaf Notebook Page for Checking Out Books

Name: Tamika Jones

Name of book	Date out	Date in
Green Eggs and Ham	Feb 10	Feb 17
Carrot Seed	Feb 20	Feb 26
Curious George	March 3	March 9
Where the Wild Things Are	March 15	March 21

"old" books will be greeted as new friends a few months later. Recirculation also compensates for limited budgets.

Books from the library corner should be available for students to check out and take home for a week at a time. The checkout system should be simple. Young children should have specified times to choose and bring books they want to borrow to the teacher, who notes the date, child's name, and book title. Preschool and kindergarten children can be taught to check out books themselves by copying titles and recording dates on 5 × 8 cards filed under their own names. Other youngsters enjoy keeping track of books borrowed and read by recording titles and dates on index cards held together with a key ring. Another method for checking out books is a loose-leaf notebook with a page for every child to record books taken out and returned. Figure 11.2 provides a sample checkout notebook page.

MyLab Education Self-Check 11.1

Children's Literature in Your Classroom

Books and other materials selected for the library corner should appeal to a variety of interests and span a range of grade levels. It is advisable to stock multiple copies of popular books. Children sometimes enjoy reading a book because a friend is reading it (Morrow, 2002; Pressley, Allington, Wharton-McDonald, Block, & Morrow, 2001; Roskos, Tabors, & Lenhart, 2009). Be sure to have several types of children's literature.

Picture storybooks are the most familiar type of children's literature. Their texts are closely associated with their illustrations. Picture storybooks are available on a wide range of topics, and many are known for their excellence. The Caldecott Medal is awarded annually to the illustrator of an outstanding picture storybook. Many of these books have become classics and their authors are renowned—Dr. Seuss, Ezra Jack Keats, Tomie dePaola, Jon Scieszka, Maurice Sendak, and Jan Brett, to name just a few. Every child should have the benefit of hearing some of these books read aloud. However, emergent readers will often find the vocabulary and syntax too sophisticated to read on their own. Quality picture storybooks will include a setting, a well-defined theme, episodes closely tied to the theme, and a resolution of the story.

Informational books offer nonfiction for readers. For a while, educators included very little informational or expository text in classroom libraries, thinking that young children preferred narratives. There also wasn't a lot of informational text appropriate for young children. As adults, we read material that is mostly nonfiction; therefore, we need a lot of exposure to this type of text. Informational text can be about the solar system, other countries, famous people, dinosaurs, and so on. These texts broaden children's knowledge, help them explore new ideas, introduce them to new vocabulary, and often stimulate a deep interest in a particular topic. There is a great deal of excellent informational literature today. Quality informational text will have a definitive structure. Good structures found in expository texts include description, sequence, compare and contrast, cause and effect, problem and solution, and exemplification. Children should be exposed to narrative text 50% of the time and to informational text 50% of the time.

Picture concept books are appropriate for the very young child. Most don't have story lines, but they often have themes, such as animals, colors, numbers, or the alphabet. Each page usually has a single picture identified by a printed word. Many picture books are made of cardboard, cloth, or vinyl to withstand rigorous handling.

Traditional literature includes nursery rhymes and fairy tales, familiar stories that are part of our heritage and that originated in the oral tradition of storytelling. We assume that children are familiar with *Goldilocks and the Three Bears* (Daley & Russell, 1999) and *The Three Little Pigs* (Zemach, 1991), yet many youngsters have not been exposed to these traditional stories. Traditional literature also includes *fables* and *folktales*. Many of these stories are from other countries and cultures and broaden a child's experience and knowledge base.

Realistic literature is a category within picture storybooks that deals with real-life problems. *Tight Times* (1983) by Barbara Hazen, for example, describes how a family handles the problems that arise when the father loses his job. He tries to explain the situation to his son so he will understand when he calls it "tight times." Books in this category deal with issues that many children face, such as bedtime fears or problems that arise when a new baby comes into the family. These books touch on very sensitive issues, such as divorce, drugs, alcohol, and death. Some can be read to the entire class if they address issues that all share. Teachers should use discretion as to what is read to the whole class. Specific titles can be recommended to families of children who face difficult issues.

Wordless books have a definite story line within pictures, but there are no words. They are not appropriate for very young children since they have an intricate story line. These books are good for children who are age 5 and older. The child creates a story by reading the pictures.

Poetry is often forgotten in collections of children's literature. There are many themed poetry anthologies for young children; they are an important part of the library corner.

Novels are longer books with chapters. We can begin reading novels to young children to expose them to the genre. Youngsters are attracted to them because they know they are for older children. Children call novels *chapter books*.

MyLab Education
Video Example 11.2
Culturally Responsive Literature

Teachers can use culturally responsive literature to engage children in familiar stories (like an African tale for Cinderella) as they are told in other cultural settings.

Biography is another genre appropriate for young children. There are simple biographies of historical figures, popular figures in sports, television performers, and many more.

Digital texts include any text that students read on the computer, an e-reader, or a tablet. These might include digital stories, emails, websites, and computer games. Since digital and global texts are now being used as well as print and paper-based books, it is critical that we introduce and incorporate digital texts in the early childhood classroom.

Graphic novels are popular with older children. The book is written with equal amounts of print and pictures to grasp children's attention. Graphic novels can be lengthy and quite sophisticated with in-depth plots.

Leveled books can be in the literacy center. Leveled book are those that come from commercial publishers and have been selected or written based on grade level such as appropriate for grades K, 1, 2, 3, and so on. Levels are determined by numbers of different words, length of sentences, syntax, syllables in words, and so on. Leveled books are mostly for instructional purposes in guided reading groups and will be discussed in depth in Chapter 12. Children can select leveled books to read if they wish during independent reading and when they are given a choice to read. It is encouraged that children not worry about a book's level during this time. These are times when we want children to choose literature that is of interest to them regardless of difficulty.

In addition to these categories of books, young children enjoy age-appropriate nontraditional texts, such as joke and riddle books, craft books, graphic novels, comic books, cookbooks, participation books (which involve them in touching, smelling, and manipulating), books in a series built around a single character, and books related to television programs and pop culture appropriate for their age. Magazines and newspapers should also be choices for reading in the library corner. They provide a nonthreatening format, different topics, and reading matter for diverse ability levels. Because new issues arrive regularly, the periodical material in a library corner refreshes itself. Menus, directions, and maps can be read as well.

Children enjoy literature that is predictable because it helps them to understand the story. It also enables them to read along. Predictable literature contains rhyme, repetition, catch phrases, conversation, familiar sequences (such as days of the week or numbers), cumulative patterns (where events are repeated or added on as the story continues), stories about familiar topics, uncluttered illustrations that match the text, and stories that have well developed story structures.

Photo credit: Lesley Mandel Morrow

Children's literature is stored by categories in baskets that are labeled for access.

Listings of children's literature in several categories, including books for children with special needs and multicultural books, are in Appendix A. A special emphasis is placed on informational books in the appendix, since we have neglected this type of text in the past. There is also a list of websites for locating children's books in Appendix D.

Children's book awards are given annually. Two important awards are the Caldecott Medal, given by the American Library Association for outstanding illustrations, typically in a picture storybook, and the Newbery Medal, also given by the American Library Association, for an outstanding story in a book or novel.

Other Materials in the Literacy Station. The literacy station needs to contain language arts materials for skill development. Manipulatives that help children learn letters of the alphabet, rhymes, and sound–symbol relationships of consonants, digraphs, and long and short vowels should be included in a special section of the center. These manipulatives come in the form of magnetic letters, puzzles, bingo games, and board games, to name a few. Teacher-made materials can also be used. (These types of materials are described more fully in Chapter 8, which covers decoding.) Materials to enhance comprehension must also be available in the literacy center. Techniques described later in this chapter, such as using a felt board and story characters for storytelling and organizing puppet presentations, engage children in demonstrating knowledge of story sequence, structure, classifying details, predicting outcomes, and interpreting text. These activities enhance comprehension while simultaneously motivating students.

Headsets with audio stories are also popular materials in the literacy center. Children can listen to the audio story while reading along. This technique is especially helpful with English learners because it provides a model for correct English. Audio stories are also good for struggling readers who can follow along in the text while listening to a fluent reader. Audio books are available for purchase, or you can have parents, older students, the principal, teachers, the nurse, the superintendent, and others record stories for the listening center. In addition, there are programs that download hundreds of books on all digital tools in school buildings that will read the text, highlight the text, or just provide the text for reading.

MyLab Education Self-Check 11.2

Activities That Can Be Done with Children's Literature

The literacy station is an important part of the classroom that acts as a source for motivating reading and writing. Children read books, write stories, and engage in projects, such as creating puppet presentations for pieces they have written or read. Most activities are done in groups of two or three and involve peer cooperation and peer tutoring. The groups are composed of single and mixed genders. Children take charge of their learning and demonstrate the use of oral reading, silent reading, and writing, and demonstrate their comprehension of text in literal and inferential discussions (Morrow, Sharkey, & Firestone, 1994). Literacy station activities expose children to reading and writing in many forms and give them the opportunity to make choices. These activities constitute a positive approach toward activating interest in reading and writing and provide a time to practice and learn skills.

The materials are designed so they are suitable for all children regardless of their achievement level and therefore can be used by everyone: gifted, average, and children with special needs. Children with language differences are welcomed as members of groups doing puppet shows and felt stories and are given roles they can participate in.

I work with teachers regularly to implement programs similar to those described here. Mrs. Lynch had a second-grade class in an urban district that I had been working with for an entire school year. I visited her room on the last day of school to say goodbye to the children. Mrs. Lynch and I shared a sense of pride while observing the children during literacy center time. We saw some children curled up on a rug or leaning on pillows in the literacy center with books they had selected themselves. Louis and Ramon were squeezed tightly into a rocking chair, sharing a book. Marcel, Patrick, and Roseangela snuggled under a shelf—a "private spot" filled with stuffed animals. They took turns reading.

Tesha and Tiffany were on the floor with a felt board and character cutouts from *The Gingerbread Boy* (Galdone, 1983), alternately reading and manipulating the figures: "Run, run as fast as you can! You can't catch me, I'm the Gingerbread Man!"

Four children listened to an audiotape of Maurice Sendak's *Pierre* (1991), each child holding a copy of the book and chanting along with the narrator, "I don't care, I don't care."

Tyrone had a Big Book and gave several other children copies of the same story in smaller format. Role-playing a teacher, he read to the others, occasionally stopping to ask who would like to read.

MyLab Education Application Exercise 11.1

Literature Activities Initiated by the Teacher

Literature activities need to be modeled and initiated by teachers to encourage children's interests. The following series of lists enumerates several motivating suggestions to use on a regular basis:

Carry Out on a Daily Basis

1. Read or tell narrative and informational stories to children.
2. Discuss literal and interpretive issues in stories read.

3. Allow children to check books out of the classroom library.
4. Have children keep track of the books they have read.
5. Have children keep the library corner neat and organized.
6. Make digital literacies an integral part of the literacy classroom experience.

Do Several of the Following Each Week

1. Have the principal, custodian, nurse, secretary, or a parent read to the children at school.
2. Discuss authors and illustrators.
3. Have older children read to younger children.
4. Have children read to each other.
5. Show DVDs of stories and have headsets and the DVDs in a center for children to use.
6. Use literature across the curriculum in content-area lessons.
7. Use art to respond to books (e.g., draw a mural of a story using art techniques modeled after a particular illustrator).
8. Sing songs that have been made into books and have the book on hand (e.g., *I Know an Old Lady*).
9. Have children tell stories.
10. Have children act out stories.
11. Prepare recipes related to stories (e.g., make stone soup after reading stone soup).
12. Read TV-related stories, such as *Clifford the Big Red Dog*.
13. Make class books and individual books; bind them and store them in the library corner.
14. Tell stories using creative techniques such as the felt board.
15. Make bulletin boards related to books.
16. Have children write advertisements for books they have read.
17. Discuss proper ways to care for and handle books.
18. Read, recite, and write poetry.
19. Have a 10- to 20-minute independent reading period a few times a week.
20. Use pop culture, sports, digital material, and current events to create authentic and relevant reading experience.
21. Discuss and integrate what students are reading outside of school, including nontraditional texts such as graphic novels, comic books, and so on.

Carry Out on a Regular Basis

1. Feature and introduce new books on the open-faced bookshelves.
2. Introduce new books added to the library corner.
3. Circulate 25 new books into the library corner every 3 weeks.
4. Have a bookstore in the school where children can buy books regularly.

Carry Out a Few Times a Year If Possible

1. Give bookmarks to children.
2. Give each child a book as a gift.
3. Have a young authors' conference (share books children have written; bind books; invite authors, illustrators, storytellers, poets).
4. Have a book fair for children to purchase books.

5. Have a book celebration day (e.g., dress up as book characters, tell stories to each other).
6. Have children order books from a book club.
7. Invite an author or illustrator to speak to the children about her or his work.
8. Collaborate with the art teacher, IT teacher, music teacher, and others to make literary themes cross-curricular and multimodal.

Reacting to Literacy Station Activities

Much of the information about literacy centers represents the results of studies that involved classroom observation and intervention in kindergarten through second grade. Children in these classrooms participated in literacy programs that included activities described in this chapter.

As part of these programs, teachers and children were interviewed to determine their attitudes toward literacy center activities. Teachers commented that children learned a lot in literacy centers and that children liked the centers because:

- They could select books they chose to read.
- They could work with manipulatives, such as puppets and felt stories.
- They could work together and cooperate with each other or work alone.
- They could be independent and make decisions.
- They learned about narrative and informational story structures.
- They learned new vocabulary.
- They had a better understanding of what they read or what was read to them.
- They developed an appreciation for books and knowledge of different genres of literature.
- They learned that peers were willing to teach and help them.
- They learned that engaging in literacy station activities created a social family atmosphere that was conducive to learning.
- They learned that the station has something for everyone. Most materials were for both advanced and slower children.

In student interviews, children were asked what they learned in the literacy station, and they answered:

- You learn to read and write better because you read a lot.
- You learn to understand what you are reading, and you learn a lot of new words.
- You get to learn how to read better because kids who know how to read well help you.
- You learn about authors and illustrators and that they are people like you, and you think that you could be one (Morrow, 1992).
- You learn that reading can be fun.

Students in these literacy programs scored significantly better on tests of reading comprehension. Specifically, their ability to retell and rewrite stories, and their ability to create original oral and written stories by including elements of story structure was scored higher than children in classrooms that did not participate in the program. Children in the treatment group showed significant improvement in use of vocabulary and language complexity (Morrow, 1990, 1992; Morrow, O'Connor, & Smith, 1990). Most importantly, the children were intrinsically motivated to participate in these literacy activities, as they were enjoyable and meaningful to the students. These children are well on their way to becoming lifelong readers and writers.

The Role of the Teacher in Motivating Literacy Interest

The teacher plays a critical role in influencing children's attitudes toward literacy reading and their voluntary reading. One of the clear points to emerge from research into reading failure is that there was no association between reading and pleasure. The role of teachers in stimulating voluntary reading among children and young people is potentially the most powerful of all adult influences upon the young (Irving, 1980, p. 7).

Programs that incorporate pleasurable literary experiences create interest in and enthusiasm for books, which increases children's voluntary use of books (McKenna, 2001; Marinak, Gambrell, & Mazzoni, 2012). Teachers should read or tell stories to children daily. Interest heightens when stories are discussed both before and after being read, especially if they are related to issues that reflect children's real life experiences or current school topics. Literal and inferential discussions can be introduced even at the preschool level. The following example describes a discussion about *Goldilocks and the Three Bears* in which inferential and critical comprehension is being developed with 4-year-olds.

After reading *Goldilocks and the Three Bears*, I asked which characters were good in the story and which were not as good. Hands waved in the air, and Jennifer answered, "Goldilocks was good and the bears were bad." When I asked Jennifer why she thought that, she said, "Well, the bears scared Goldilocks."

Another hand went up and Tim said, "No, that's not right. The bears are good and Goldilocks is bad. Goldilocks went into the bears' house when they weren't home. She ate their food without asking."

"That's right," said Megan, "and she broke their chair and went to sleep in their bed and didn't even ask if it was okay."

Chris chimed in, "Yeah, Goldilocks was really bad. She did a lot of bad things because she didn't ask if she could."

"Would you go into a stranger's house and do the things she did?" I asked. The whole group called out in unison "Nooooo." I asked why not. Sara answered, "Because that is bad. It's like stealing. She was bad. If the cops found out, they would arrest her."

Discussion about authors and illustrators also arouses interest. Reading different stories by the same author or a series of books about the same character, such as *Frog and Toad Are Friends* (Lobel, 1979) or *Amelia Bedelia* (Parrish, 1970), increases interest as well. Read different kinds of literature to the class; when possible, coordinate stories with class themes. Recruit older children, the principal, the custodian, the librarian, parents, and grandparents to read to different classes, small groups, and individuals.

Many popular folk songs have been adapted into picture storybooks, such as *Old MacDonald Had a Farm* (Quackenbush, 1972). These books are particularly good to read to children because they are likely to be familiar with the words and want to read or pretend to read the books themselves. Cooking is another pleasurable activity that can be related to literature. Many picture storybooks feature food, such as *Bread and Jam for Frances* (Hoban, 1964). After reading the story, the class can make bread and jam or whatever food is appropriate. Art activities also can be motivated by story readings. After reading *The Snowy Day* (Keats, 1996), have children create a winter collage from blue construction paper, white cotton, wool, doilies, chalk, and silver foil.

After reading *Where the Wild Things Are* (Sendak, 1963), ask kindergartners and first-graders to think of a wild thing and draw a picture of it. Gather their pictures into a class book.

Making Story Reading Pleasurable

The warmth that accompanies storybook reading by a caring adult lasts beyond the experience. It involves ritual, sharing, and mutual good feelings. Certain books take on special meanings between an adult and child since they are read over and over and become favorites or have a special meaning to the teacher and children or parent and child. My daughter and I have a special relationship with the book *Alexander and the Terrible, Horrible, No Good, Very Bad Day* (Viorst, 1972). I first read it to Stephanie when she was 4 years old, and whenever things seemed to go wrong for her, I found myself saying, "I guess you're having a terrible, horrible, no good, very bad day." Soon, when things were not going well for me, she would say the same thing to me. When Stephanie was in the seventh grade, she came home from school one day wearing only one sneaker and looking quite distraught. "What's the problem?" I asked. She replied, "Someone stole one of my sneakers, I got yelled at for talking when my friend asked me a question in class and I answered her, I have tons of homework, and I lost my assignment notebook." "I guess you're having a terrible, horrible, no good, very bad day," I said. She smiled and said, "You're right, so I think I'll move to Australia." "Some days are like that, even in Australia," I replied.

We both laughed.

A more recent ritual started with my grandson James and the book *What Cried Granny: An Almost Bedtime Story* (Lum & Johnson, 2002). In the book, Patrick is sleeping overnight at his Granny's house for the first time. She says it is bedtime, but he has no bed, so Granny cuts down trees and makes him a bed. This same scenario continues; he has no pillow, so Granny collects feathers from the hens in the hen house, and so on. Each time Granny says it is bedtime, Patrick finds something that is missing, such as, "But Granny, I have no blanket." "What!" cried Granny. Consequently, before a sleepover, James (my grandson) says as I am tucking him in to go to sleep, "Oh Granny, you forgot to give me socks to sleep in; it is cold tonight." So I take out my knitting needles and pretend to be knitting a pair of socks and in no time, they are made. James giggles and giggles. Good feelings gained in story readings transfer to the act of reading itself (Dickinson, De Temple, Hirschler, & Smith, 1992; International Reading Association, 2006).

The word *story* refers to the use of both narrative and informational text. A *story* is the reading, telling, or reporting of an event or series of events. For quite a while, narrative stories have been used almost exclusively with young children, with little exposure to informational text. The concept has been that children must learn to read narrative text in the early grades before reading to learn information in expository text in the later grades. This unilateral separation has caused difficulties for students when the focus shifts to expository text in the fourth grade and children are unfamiliar with the genre. This separation also reflects the misconception that 3 to 8-year-olds are too young to understand and enjoy informational books.

To make story reading as enjoyable and pleasurable as possible, select good pieces of narrative literature that include the following:

- A **setting** with well-delineated characters, a time, and a place.
- A well-designed **theme** concerning the problem or goal of the main character.
- **Episodes**, which are a series of plot related events that help the main character solve his or her problem or achieve a goal.
- A **resolution**, which is the solution to the problem, or the achievement of the goal.

Quality expository text also should be selected for reading as often as narrative and include a definitive structure. The types of informational text that children should be exposed to include the following:

- **Description:** Gives the reader a picture of the subject based on story observation.
- **Sequence:** This explains the steps that produce a certain product or outcome.
- **Compare and contrast:** Comparisons are usually made in two ways. In block comparisons, two items (with a similar classification) are compared and then

contrasted. In point-by-point comparisons, similarities and differences are compared alternately.

- **Cause and effect:** Causality tells why something happens.
- **Problem solution:** A problem is presented, followed by its solution. An understanding of chronology is necessary to comprehend this structure.
- **Exemplification (reason and example):** The main idea is presented with supporting details (Vukelich, Evans, & Albertson, 2003).

A teacher should read to youngsters in a relaxed atmosphere in a location designated for such readings. Each day, let a different child sit close to you while you are reading, with the other children in a single or double semicircle. If you have a rocking chair, use it as the place where you sit when you read. Because children enjoy seeing illustrations in books during story reading, hold the book so it faces the group or turn the book at appropriate pauses so its pictures can be seen. Before reading a story to a group, practice reading it aloud to yourself. Be expressive in your reading, change your voice and facial expressions when a different character speaks, and highlight special events. A story reading is like a dramatic presentation. Read slowly and with a great deal of animation. Record or videotape your readings so that you can evaluate and improve your technique. Begin a story with an introduction like the following:

Today I'm going to read a story about a little girl who wants to get a birthday present for her mother. She asks a rabbit to help her since she can't think of anything. The title of the story is *Mr. Rabbit and the Lovely Present* (Zolotow, 1977). The author's name is Charlotte Zolotow, and the illustrator is Maurice Sendak. While I read, I would like you to think about what you like most about the present.

After the story is read, I begin a discussion with a question. I ask, "Who would like to tell me which part of the present you like best?" Taking time to ask such evaluative questions will provide some sense of students' comprehension.

MyLab Education Self-Check 11.3

Storytelling and Independent Reading

Storytelling strongly attracts children to books (Ritchie, James-Szanton, & Howes, 2003). To strengthen that attraction, the storyteller should be free to use creative techniques. Doing so keeps the storyteller close to the audience. Telling a story produces an immediate response from the audience. Long pieces of literature can be trimmed so that even very young children can hear whole stories in one sitting. Considered an art, storytelling can be mastered by most people. Storytelling is an extremely important technique for classrooms filled with children from diverse backgrounds. Many of these children come from cultures where storytelling, as opposed to storybook reading, is more the norm. This strategy will make these students feel at home in the classroom, while serving as a pleasurable experience for all.

It is not necessary to memorize a story but be sure you know it well. Use all the catch phrases and quotes that are important to the story. Use expression in your presentation, but do not let your dramatic techniques overshadow the story itself. Look directly at your audience and take their attention into consideration. Storytelling allows you to shorten stories if children's attention spans seem to be short. It is important to have the original book at hand when you have finished telling a story so that the children can see it and enjoy it again through its pictures and printed text.

Creative techniques help storytelling come alive. They excite the imagination, involve the listeners, and motivate children to try storytelling themselves and create their own techniques. Take clues for creative techniques from the story. Some stories lend themselves to the use of puppets, others are perfect for the felt board, and still others can be worked up as chalk talks. Informational books can be retold using these techniques as well.

Photo credit: Mark Bassett/Pearson Education

Children act out a story with face masks.

Puppets are used with stories rich in dialogue. There are many kinds of puppets, including finger, hand, stick, and face puppets. Shy children often feel secure telling stories with puppets. Such stories as *The Gingerbread Boy* (Galdone, 1983) and *The Little Red Hen* (Pinkey, 2006) are appropriately told with puppets because they are short, have few characters, and repeat dialogue.

Sound–story techniques allow both audience and storyteller to provide sound effects when they are called for in a book. The sounds can be made with voices, rhythm instruments, or music. When preparing to tell such a story, first select those parts of the story for which sound effects will be used. Then decide on each sound to be made and who will make it. As the story is told, students and the storyteller chime in with their assigned sounds. Record the presentation, and then leave the CD in the literacy center with the original book. Among books that adapt easily to sound–story techniques are *Too Much Noise* (McGovern, 1992) and *Mr. Brown Can Moo! Can You?* (Seuss, 1998).

Prop stories are easy to develop. Simply collect stuffed animals, toys, and other articles that represent characters and objects in a story. Display the props at appropriate times during the storytelling. Three stuffed bears and a yellow-haired doll aid in telling *Goldilocks and the Three Bears* (Daley & Russell, 1999). Several toy trains help to tell *The Little Engine That Could* (Piper, 1990).

Chalk talks are another technique that attracts listeners. The storyteller draws the story while telling it. Chalk talks are most effective when done with a large chalkboard so that the story can keep going in sequence from beginning to end. The same technique can be carried out on mural paper hung across a wall; the storyteller simply uses crayons or felt-tip markers instead of chalk. The chalk-talk technique can also be adapted to easel and chart paper or an overhead projector. Choose a story with simple illustrations. Draw only a select few pictures as you tell the story.

Some stories have been written as chalk talks, including the entire *Harold and the Purple Crayon* (Johnson, 1981) series. In the *Harold* books, Harold, draws the story as it occurs.

MyLab Education

Video Example 11.3

Using Puppets to Tell Stories

Clever teachers can lead children to use puppets to tell familiar stories, helping students understand settings, characters, the plot, and other narrative story elements.

https://www.youtube.com/watch?v=mWwbXRA_g8

Felt boards and magnetic boards with story characters are popular and important tools in a classroom. You can make characters or purchase them. Prepare your own characters with construction paper covered with clear contact paper or laminate them. Attach strips of felt or sandpaper to the backs of the cutouts so they cling to the felt board. Narrative and expository texts that lend themselves to felt board retelling are those with a limited number of ideas or a limited number of characters who appear throughout the story. (In the An Idea from the Classroom, the teacher created a felt board storytelling experience for her children.)

Digital techniques enhance story experiences. When children are videoed during a dramatic retelling of a story, they enjoy viewing themselves. There are many ways to video children acting out a story. It can be done with a cell phone and transferred onto a computer to watch. Children and teachers can also scan a book and make it into a PowerPoint presentation and add sound or music. These can be shared with the class and be made available for their parents on your class website. Useful sites for recording stories include Voice Thread (http://voicethread.com) and Animoto (http://animoto.com) (Kesler, Gibson, & Turansky, 2016).

This is by no means an exhaustive list of storytelling techniques. The teacher should, however, model all of the techniques mentioned to motivate children to become storytellers themselves. After modeling, children can do the following:

- Tell the story that the teacher modeled with one of the techniques the teacher used.
- Create a technique for presenting a piece of literature they know well that has been selected by the teacher.
- Present the completed project to the class.
- Write an original story and create a technique for presentation. When it is complete, the children can present it to the class and then place it in the literacy center for others to use.

Storytelling activities involve children in literal comprehension because they must know the sequence, details, and elements of the story. They must problem solve as they create the materials, deciding what parts of the story to include or delete. They interpret voices of characters as they make a presentation of their project to the class.

The teaching of specific skills can be embedded into teacher presentations of storytelling techniques. For example, if you need to teach letter-writing skills, the story *A Letter to Amy* (Keats, 1998) is an excellent selection. The story is about a boy who wants to invite a girl to his birthday party, but he worries that his friends might laugh. He sends her an invitation and wonders if she will come and what will happen. The book contains a lot of discussion about the invitation. This is a perfect opportunity to teach about writing invitations. Tell the story using a felt board with characters for *A Letter to Amy*. One of the items in the story is an envelope with a well-written invitation letter. Included in the letter is the appropriate heading, format, and so on. Children can use this model to write letters of invitation to others.

Encouraging Independent Reading

Research has shown that the amount of free reading done by children, both in and out of school, correlates with reading motivation and achievement. In a large-scale investigation of elementary school children, it was found that students who reported reading 2 minutes a day outside of school scored at the 30th percentile on standardized reading tests. Children who read 5 minutes a day scored at the 50th percentile. Those who read 10 minutes a day scored at the 70th percentile, and children who read 20 minutes a day scored at the 90th percentile (Anderson, Fielding, & Wilson, 1988; Taylor, Frye, & Maruyama, 1990). Children who read voluntarily develop lifelong, positive attitudes toward reading.

The teacher plays an important role maximizing independent reading time and genuinely encouraging children to read for pleasure. To be more productive, an independent reading period can be done with a partner or alone. It can focus on a content-area theme that is being studied in the classroom, an author or illustrator, or a particular genre of children's literature. For example, if children are learning about animals, the teacher can explain that their book selection for independent reading can only be about this topic. The teacher should separate these books from others on the shelf. There can be a special spot or basket for independent reading books. Limiting the number of books helps make the selection task easier and quicker for the child (Ritchie, James-Szanton, & Howes, 2003).

For the purposes of accountability to help keep children stay on task, the teacher can require children to keep a log of the number of pages read during independent reading, write one sentence about what they read, or copy a sentence from the book they liked. Keep the task very simple and one that will take very little time. With simple tasks, children are more likely to concentrate on independent reading rather than have their minds wander. Teachers need to set rules similar to the ones shown here and review them before independent reading begins:

- Select your book quickly.
- Read only one book in a period.
- Record the name of the book and the date it was read in your log.
- Write a one-sentence note to the author about what you liked about the book. There can be different tasks on different days.

MyLab Education Application Exercise 11.2

Story Reading and Storytelling Vignettes

Teachers who read and tell stories to children regularly share many important comments.

"The children enjoy being read to, and they never grow tired of this activity. I thought that in second grade, reading to youngsters wasn't that important anymore; however, the benefits of read-aloud sessions became quite evident as I involved my children in them more and more. The stories generated sophisticated discussion; we'd relate them to the students' own life experiences. We discussed authors, illustrations, and elements of story structure." Through these story readings and discussions, I found that my students seemed to appreciate literature more, they became more aware of the different genres of children's literature that exist, and vocabulary and comprehension were enhanced as well. I realized how important it was for me to model reading to children and in many different ways. I read using felt characters and chalk talks. I learned how to make reading more appealing for the children. Consequently, I saw an increased desire in my children to read as they modeled my behavior in reading stories I had read to them and used the storytelling props.

A discussion in one second grade was as follows: Tamika said, "Well, in *Peter's Chair* the illustrations look like a painting. They are made like they are real. I think Ezra Jack Keats is a very good drawer. I like the colors he uses."

Ms. Payton explained that not only does Mr. Keats paint his pictures but he also uses collage as a technique. When you look closely at his illustrations, you see bits of wallpaper, newspaper, doilies, and so on, blended into his pictures.

Ms. Payton asked if someone would like to describe the style of the other book. Marcel raised his hand. He said, "Dr. Seuss is very different from Keats; he uses lots of lines and sort of fantasy little shapes. He uses colors on people and things that aren't what we usually expect. His drawings look like cartoons, and the other ones look like real things."

When you read more difficult text to children, they learn the vocabulary, have in-depth discussions, and are motivated to want to read difficult book themselves.

MyLab Education Self-Check 11.4

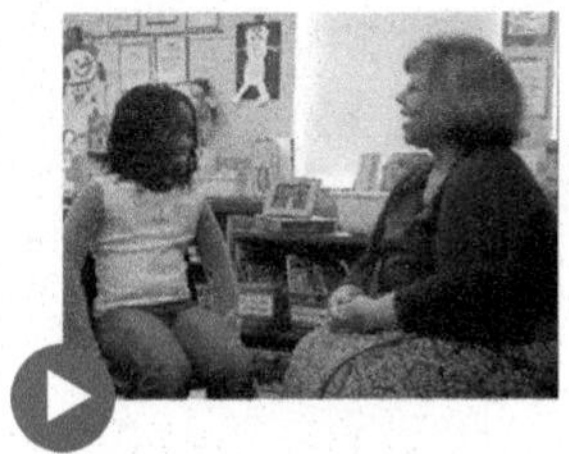

MyLab Education
Video Example 11.4
Reading Motivation Interview
Interviewing children about their reading can reveal their motivation to read and help teachers steer students to literature that encourages them to read more.

Assessing Children's Attitudes Toward Books

Directly observing children's behavior while they are listening to stories, reading silently, or looking at books is an effective method for assessing their attitudes toward books. How much attention do they give to the books they are looking at or reading? Do they simply browse? Do they flip through the pages quickly, paying little attention to print or pictures? Do they demonstrate sustained attention to pictures and print throughout (Martinez & Teale, 1988)? You should also note how frequently children choose to look at books when offered other options. In occasional interviews with individual children, asking what they like to do best in school and at home might reveal interest in reading. During conferences, ask parents if their children voluntarily look at books or pay close attention when they are read to. At the same time, ask parents how often they read to their children. Gather facts about the home literacy environment that will help you understand the child's attitude toward books.

A checklist for assessing attitudes toward reading and writing is provided in Figure 11.3. A form for assessing motivation for reading is shown in Figure 11.4. These materials can be used for a child's portfolio.

Figure 11.3 Checklist for Assessing Attitudes toward Reading and Writing and Amount of Voluntary Reading and Writing

Child's name: ______________________ **Date:** ______________

Teacher evaluates child.	**Always**	**Sometimes**	**Never**	**Comments**
Voluntarily looks at or reads books at school				
Asks to be read to				
Listens attentively while being read to				
Responds during book discussions with questions and comments on stories read to him or her				
Takes books home to read voluntarily				
Writes voluntarily at home				
Writes voluntarily at school				

Teacher Comments:

Figure 11.4 Motivation Interview

SOURCE: Assessing motivation to read. *The Reading Teacher, 49*(7), 518–533, by Gambrell, Linda B., Palmer, Barbara Martin, Coding, Rose Marie, and Mazzoni, Susan Anders.

Directions: Tell the child that you would like to find out more about what kids like to do and how they feel about reading and writing. Ask each question in the interview and read the multiple-choice responses.

1. How often would you like your teacher to read to the class?
   (2) every day (1) almost every day (0) not often
2. Do you like to read books by yourself?
   (2) yes (1) it's okay (0) no
3. Which would you most like to have?
   (2) a new book (1) a new game (0) new clothes
4. Do you tell your friends about books and stories you read?
   (2) a lot (1) sometimes (0) never
5. How do you feel when you read out loud to someone?
   (2) good (1) okay (0) bad
6. Do you like to read during your free time?
   (2) yes (1) it's okay (0) I don't read in my free time
7. If someone gave you a book for a present, how would you feel?
   (2) happy (1) okay (0) not very happy, disappointed
8. Do you take storybooks home from school to read?
   (2) almost every day (1) sometimes (0) not often
9. Do you read books out loud to someone in your family?
   (2) almost every day (1) sometimes (0) not often
10. What kind of reader are you?
    (2) I'm a very good reader (1) I'm okay (0) I'm not very good
11. Learning to read is
    (2) easy (1) a little hard (0) really hard
12. Do you like to write?
    (2) yes (1) it's okay (0) I'd rather do something else
13. Do you write in your free time?
    (2) a lot (1) a little (0) not at all
14. What do you like to read best?
    (2) books and magazines (1) schoolwork (0) nothing

MyLab Education Self-Check 11.5
MyLab Education Application Exercise 11.3

An Idea from the Classroom

A Felt Board or White Board Story Lesson

I wanted to introduce my students to the use of the felt board as a means for retelling stories and creating their own original stories. I selected a story that was easy to illustrate and a theme that would generate interpretive conversation, and I encouraged the opportunity to write additional episodes for it. The name of the story is "A Bunny Called Nat," an anonymous tale. The story is about "a bunny named Nat, who was sassy and fat, and he could change his color, just like that." This rhyme is repeated several times throughout the story. At the end of the rhyme, fingers are snapped when you say, "just like that." The bunny in the story is a gray bunny who does not like his color because it is so plain. He is able to change his color, but each time he does, he has an unpleasant adventure. Finally, at the end of the story, he realizes that as a gray bunny, things are just fine and so he decides it's not so bad being just the way you are, and that's the way he stays. The story can be used with very young children just for identifying colors and classifying colors with episodes. With older children the idea of self-esteem is an appropriate conversation.

When I introduced the story to the children, I asked them to listen for the different colors that Nat becomes and the problems he faces each time. I then told the story, and at the appropriate time placed a different colored bunny character on the felt board. When the story was over, we discussed Nat and his different colors. We also discussed the ending of the story and its meaning, trying to relate it to the experiences of the children. We discussed whether they ever wanted to be anyone other than themselves and why, who that might be, and what it would be like. We also discussed if they thought it would be better than being themselves.

After the discussion, I asked the children to think of another color that Nat could become with an adventure attached to it as in the real story. I then asked them to write their story and draw and color a bunny to add to the felt story we already had. The bunnies were made of construction paper, and felt strips were glued onto the back to make them stick to the felt board. Instead of felt you can put pieces of magnets on the back of the bunnies which will attach to a white board.

Seven-year-old Lindsey wrote the following:

> "I'm a bunny named Nat, I'm sassy and fat, and I can change my color just like that." And Nat became a red bunny. He was red like an apple, red like a cherry, and red like a fire truck. All of a sudden, a group of bees was coming. They saw Nat in the red color and they were thinking that Nat was an apple. The group of bees was going where Nat was sitting, they wanted to eat him. Then Nat saw the bees. He ran and ran but the bees followed him. So he said as he ran, "Being red is not so good, but I'm a bunny called Nat, I am sassy and fat, and I can change my color, just like that." Nat changed to brown and was saved from the bees.

In this activity, children are involved in the discussion and creation of a story. The theme of the story, concerning self-image, is an important topic for conversation and can help children understand each other's strengths, weaknesses, and needs. Following is the story, "A Bunny Called Nat," and a pattern for the bunny (refer to Figure 11.5).

Sample Felt Board or White Magnetic Board Story

"A Bunny Called Nat" (adapted version of an anonymous tale)

As the story is being told, hold up and then place a new colored bunny on the felt board as each bunny is named.

Figure 11.5 Felt Figure for "A Bunny Called Nat"

Materials

Five bunny characters drawn identically, but in the following colors: gray, blue, green, yellow, and orange. The bunny pattern is found in Figure 11.5 The characters could also have magnets on the back instead of felt to use on a magnetic board.

Once upon a time there was a little gray rabbit and his name was Nat. One day he looked around and saw that all his brothers and sisters, cousins and friends were gray, too. He thought he would like to be different from them. So he said:

I'm a bunny

called Nat, I'm sassy and fat,

And I can change my color

Just like that. (Snap your fingers.)

And suddenly Nat was a blue bunny. He was blue like the sky and blue like the sea. He was blue like the twilight and blue like the dawn. It felt nice and cool to be blue. He decided to take a look at himself in the pond. He hurried to the edge and admired his reflection in the water. He leaned over so far and SPLASH! He fell into the pond. Nat fell deep into the blue water and he couldn't swim. He was frightened. He called for help. His friends heard him, but when they came to the pond they couldn't see him because he was blue just like the water. Fortunately, a turtle swam by and helped Nat get safely to shore. He decided that he didn't like being blue. So he said:

I'm a bunny

called Nat, I'm sassy and fat,

And I can change my color

Just like that. (Snap your fingers.)

And this time, he changed himself to yellow. He was yellow like the sun, yellow like daffodils, and yellow like a canary bird. Yellow seemed like such a happy color to be. He was very proud of his new color, and he decided to take a walk through the jungle. Who do you think he met in the jungle? He met a lion and the tiger. The lion and the tiger looked at Nat's yellow fur and said, "What are you doing in that yellow coat? We are the only animals in this jungle that are supposed to be yellow." And they growled so fiercely that Nat the bunny was frightened and he ran all the way home. He said:

(Repeat poem.)

And this time what did he change his color to? He became green. He was green like the grass and green like the leaves of the trees. He was green like a grasshopper and green like the meadow. As a green bunny, Nat thought he'd be the envy of all the other bunnies. He wanted to play with his other bunny friends in the meadow. Since he was the color of the grass in the meadow, he could not be seen and his friends just ran and jumped over and around him not seeing him at all. So Nat the bunny had no one to play with while he was green. Being green wasn't much fun. So he said:

(Repeat poem.)

And what color was he then? He turned himself into orange. He was orange like a carrot, orange like a sunset, orange like a pumpkin—he was the brightest color of all. He decided he would go out and play with all his brothers and sisters and friends. But what do you suppose happened? When his friends saw him, they all stopped playing and started to laugh. They said, "Who ever heard of an orange bunny?" No one wanted to play with him. He didn't want to be orange anymore. He didn't want to be a blue bunny because if he fell into the pond no one could see him to save him. He didn't want to be a yellow bunny and be frightened by the lion and the tiger. He didn't want to be green because then he was just like the meadow and none of his friends could see him. And so he said:

(Repeat poem.)

Do you know what color Nat the bunny changed himself into this time? Yes, you're right. He changed himself back to gray. And now that he was gray all his friends played with him. No one growled or laughed at him. He was gray like a rain cloud, gray like an elephant, gray like pussy willows. It felt warm and comfortable being gray. From that time on, Nat the bunny was always happy being a gray bunny, and he decided that it's really best being just what you are and that's the way he stayed.

Used with permission from *Stephanie Bushell, Second Grade Teacher*

Summary

11.1 Identify the features of a well-designed literacy station.

A literacy station combines a library corner with a writing center. The physical design of literacy station can motivate children to go to this area of the classroom and engage in reading and writing. Stations should be colorful and attractive and have a small rug, a rocking chair, soft pillows, tools for writing, and lots of books. In the library corner, books can be stored on bookshelves with spines outward or open-faced with covers showing. Books can be sorted into categories by genre or theme and stored in baskets labeled accordingly. Many types of books—narrative and informational as well as print and digital—should be available in the literacy station.

11.2 Discuss types of children's literature to have in your classroom.

Classroom libraries should have 5 to 8 books per child at three to four different grade levels. Multiple genres should be represented such as informational books, biography, picture story books, concept picture books, novels, narrative books, wordless books, series books, magazines, newspapers, books for the theme being studied, and any other material that children would enjoy reading.

11.3 Identify activities that can be done with children's literature.

There are an endless number of activities to do with children's literature. Teachers should use as many techniques as possible. Read aloud to children and focus on a particular element of the story to discuss after the book is read. Allow children to partner read. Let children choose books they would like to read. Make a poster to advertise a book. Do author studies to compare and contrast style of writing, book illustrations, and so on.

11.4 Describe storytelling techniques and encourage independent reading.

The teacher plays a critical role in influencing children's attitudes toward literacy and their voluntary reading. Teachers can motivate literacy interest by making story reading pleasurable and by using creative storytelling techniques that engage the students. Puppets, sound stories, prop stories, chalk talks, felt and magnetic boards, and digital techniques are all ways to enliven storytelling. Teachers also motivate literacy interest by encouraging independent reading on a regular basis and providing structure (and accountability) for independent reading time: students must select books quickly, read only one book during the time frame, keep a record of what they've read, and be accountable to writing a quick summary statement about their reading. Various literature activities need to be conducted on a daily, weekly, regular, and intermittent basis. Some activities should also involve parents.

11.5 Assess children's attitudes toward books.

To understand the extent to which students are motivated to read and write, teachers need to assess their attitudes toward books. One way to measure those attitudes is with a periodic motivational interview that elicits students' thoughts and feelings about books and reading, both individually and collectively. Another way to measure attitude is with a checklist that notes the amount of reading children do voluntarily and identifies attributes of their reading behavior.

Activities and Questions

1. Select a literacy skill to teach that is grade appropriate for you. Then choose a piece of children's literature that provides an example of that skill and a creative storytelling technique that seems appropriate for the story and skill (e.g., felt characters, chalk talk, sound story). Create materials for the story and tell it to a group of children or to your peers. Evaluate your performance according to the criteria for storytelling discussed in the chapter and request feedback for how well the skill was taught.
2. Observe an early childhood classroom on three different occasions. List all the literacy activities carried out by the teacher that you believe contribute to developing positive attitudes toward reading and writing.
3. Continue your portfolio assessment for the child you selected to assess. Observe the child using Figure 11.3 concerning the evaluation of his or her attitudes toward writing and reading. Interview the child using the motivation survey (Figure 11.4).
4. Draw a diagram of a literacy station you would like to have in your classroom. Assume that money is not object.

Chapter 12

Creating a Motivating Environment for Literacy Development: Positive Mindset, Technology, Integration, and Play

Photo credit: Monkey Business Images/ Shutterstock, Inc

LEARNING OUTCOMES

After reading this chapter, you should be able to:

12.1 Create a literacy friendly classroom.

12.2 Strategize for motivating readers and writers.

12.3 Create a positive growth mindset in your classroom.

12.4 Integrate technology into reading and writing activities.

12.5 Explain how dramatic play can engage children in reading and writing.

12.6 Integrate literacy learning into thematic units and project-based instruction.

VOCABULARY

Blog
Extrinsic motivation
Intrinsic motivation
Motivation
New literacies
Podcast
Padlet
Scaffolding
Wiki

Ms. Hagerty set up her classroom like a veterinarian's office. I watched as the children were engaged in dramatic play and literacy and heard and saw the following.

> Christopher came into the veterinarian's office with his teddy bear. He told Preston, the doctor, that his teddy bear was very sick. Preston, the doctor, examined Christopher's teddy bear and wrote out a report in the patient's folder. He read his scribble writing out loud and said, "This teddy bear's blood pressure is 29 points. He should take 62 pills an hour until he is better and keep warm and go to bed." While he read, he showed Christopher what he had written so that he would understand what to do. He asked his nurse to type the notes into the computer and print them out for Christopher.

Increasing Motivation in the Classroom

A survey of classroom teachers concerning priorities for research indicated that motivating children to want to read and write was ranked high on the list of suggestions (O'Flahavan, Gambrell, Guthrie, Stahl, & Alverman, 1992; Melekoglu & Wilkerson, 2013). This is a critical topic—without the motivation or desire to read, it is unlikely that a child will learn to read well. Children need to know why they are learning to read and the benefits they will have in later life as a result of being able to read. To help with motivation is creating a positive mindset to promote an attitude of "*I can*" in a classroom that learns to be a community.

Motivation is defined as initiating and sustaining a particular activity. It is considered the tendency to return to and continue working on a task with sustained engagement (Brophy, 2008; Gambrell, Palmer, Codling, & Mazzoni, 1996; Guthrie, 2004; Wentzel, 2009). Motivation is typically divided into two domains: extrinsic and intrinsic.

Extrinsic motivation represents the domain where individuals engage in an activity as a means to an end; its emphasis surrounds external rewards such as prestige, praise, or good grades. Giving children extrinsic rewards, such as stickers or pencils for a job well done, is okay some of the time. However, it only takes a short time for rewards to lose their appeal.

The real emphasis, however, must be placed on nurturing **intrinsic motivation**, which is the desire to engage in behaviors for enjoyment, challenge, pleasure, or interest. The level of intrinsic motivation a child has for literacy can help or hinder achievement (Lepper, Corpus, & Iyengar, 2005).

We must work at not only developing readers to gain information or because of obligation, but children who want to read by choice for pleasure as well. In other words, educators must work to develop children's intrinsic motivation for reading and writing. The following techniques can be applied in that regard:

1. Immerse children in a literacy-rich environment with choices of literacy materials that are challenging.
2. Model literacy behaviors for children to emulate.
3. Provide opportunities collaborative and independent reading and writing activities.
4. Provide children with choice when selecting literacy activities.
5. Read to children in a pleasant and relaxed atmosphere.
6. Provide time for responses to stories read through discussion, role-playing the use of puppets, and retelling.
7. Allow children to take books home from your classroom library corner.
8. Provide varied experiences with multiple genres of children's literature.
9. Use technology as a source of motivation in reading and writing.
10. Provide literacy in all content areas such as play, math, science, social studies, art, and music. This can be done through the use of thematic units.

11. Create positive mindset of "*I can*" in your classroom and make it a classroom with a community of children who wish to learn.
12. Provide activities that are relevant, of interest to your children, and have a real purpose such as improving the school library, being pen pals to people in are armed services, and so on.

MyLab Education Self-Check 12.1

Strategies for Motivating Readers and Writers

Literacy activities that provide children a real purpose for reading and writing will motivate them. Researchers have found that experiences that offer choice, challenge, relevance, authenticity, social collaboration, and success will intensify a child's motivation to want to read and write (Guthrie, 2004).

Choice

Choice instills intrinsic motivation, as it allows children to play an active role in their educational experience, as well as explore topics of personal interest (Gaskins, 2003; Guthrie, 2002, 2011). Encouraging children to make choices about literacy tasks and selecting materials they will read and write gives them responsibility, control over the situation, and a sense of confidence. Choice needs to involve multiple modalities for learning literacy skills such as combining traditional activities that use pencil and paper with modalities that use technology, drama, or graphic arts. Only provide a few choices at a time; otherwise, the child will likely become overwhelmed and unable to make decisions.

Challenge

Students must perceive that there is some challenge to an activity but that it is one they can accomplish. Tasks should be regarded as not too hard but not too easy. When tasks are viewed as too easy, children aren't interested. If tasks are too difficult, they become frustrated (McKenna, 2001; Stahl, 2003). Literacy activities must be differentiated so that they fit this criterion for all students.

To minimize frustration, teachers need to engage in **scaffolding**, a strategy in which teachers provide modeling and support to help their students acquire a new skill. When teachers use scaffolding appropriately, then challenge is energizing rather than frustrating. Therefore, teachers need to provide explicit instruction and guidance when new material is presented and gradually move into the background as the child begins to master the new concept and carry out the task independently. This gradual release of responsibility, as mastery and self-esteem build in the child, nurtures motivation. Students are more dedicated to completing the task if they believe they can meet the challenge (Brophy, 2004; Guthrie, 2011; Marinak, Gambrell, & Mazzoni, 2012).

Relevance and Authenticity

Relevance and authenticity are similar and have characteristics that motivate. Research illustrates that when children do not understand the relevance for a given lesson, motivation declines (Brophy, 2008; Marinak, Gambrell, & Mazzoni, 2012). Literacy lessons should serve to enhance the literacy abilities of students outside the classroom. Children need to know why they are learning a particular skill and how it will be useful to them in real life. For example, bring in menus to discuss ordering food or newspaper articles that children can read and relate to their own lives.

Similarly, as often as possible, children should read and write for authentic purposes. For instance, engaging students in reading about a current event that they can relate to, followed by a discussion, is an authentic reading experience. Reading directions to bake cookies and then actually baking and eating them is an authentic literary experience. So is following directions to construct a toy and then building it. And, whenever possible, the children's audience should go beyond that of the teacher as an evaluator. Children should have the opportunity to share their literacy creations with classmates and members of the school community. That way, children will see learning as more than just achieving a grade; they will come to understand that it is much more encompassing (Gignoux & Wilde, 2005).

Often, children see little relevance or authenticity to what they are learning because connections between students' in and out-of-school literacy experiences are not made explicit. Children need to see reading and writing for a variety of reasons. They should see their parents writing thank-you notes and business letters (Wilson, 2008). When they see that reading and writing serve a purpose beyond the classroom, motivation increases.

Social Collaboration

Learning involves social collaboration, which increases motivation. When observing children at play, it is obvious how they learn from one another through their dialogue and interactions. When children have the opportunity to learn in social situations involving collaboration with the teacher or peers, they are likely to get more done than they could do alone. Learning becomes a collective process; thus, the responsibility for learning is shared among students, which lessens fear of failure. Like adults, children enjoy social interaction and opportunities to learn from each other (Guthrie, 2002; Marinak, 2012). In this type of environment children learn to respect each other, empathize with each other and help each other.

Success

When students complete a task they must consider it a success (Ritchie, James-Szanton, & Howes, 2003). When a child has met with some (but not total) success, such as spelling the word *read* as *reed,* he or she should be acknowledged for the part of the spelling that is correct. After all, three of the four letters are right. The child's success should be noted. However, at the same time, he or she needs help with the correct spelling of the word. Success for one child is getting from step two in the project and for others it is completing the task. If you don't feel some success and get some positive reinforcement, it often feels like you would rather not go forward, and just quit.

MyLab Education Self-Check 12.2
MyLab Education Application Exercise 12.1

Creating a Positive Growth Mindset in Your Classroom

Creating a positive growth mindset will help to motivate children. Before thinking about what to teach, it is important to consider the culture within which learning takes place. Classroom cultures that encourage children to take risks and overcome challenges are vital to development. Develop a context in which the teacher and children collaborate, help each other, and share a warm and supportive relationship. The way in which you interact with students affects what they will learn about themselves, about others, and about literacy.

MyLab Education
Video Example 12.1
Positive Classroom Culture
Teachers can motivate children from the tone of voice they use and the positive comments they make. https://www.youtube.com/watch?v=ZEZBBFUqJws

The language we use with children and the manner in which it is delivered will set the tone of the classroom. First, remember that your tone of voice is very important. The same statement can feel like positive reinforcement or sarcasm. For example "Wow, you chose a great book there," can make a child feel good about the book chosen or really bad, depending on how it is said. Sarcasm and criticism are hurtful, especially for young children, and, therefore, should always be avoided. It is also important to give children your attention, despite the many demands for your attention. Match your body language and your verbal language. If a child is talking to you about a problem he or she is having, focus your attention and eyes on the youngster. Also, positive reinforcement of desired behaviors and redirection of off-task or undesired behaviors is much more effective and creates a much more pleasant environment than negative reinforcement.

Language that positively reinforces desired behaviors is best when focused on the class as a group, rather than calling out specific children. For example, rather than saying, "I love how Tiffany and Damon are cleaning up the library corner," say "Many of you are remembering the rules about cleaning up the library." Similarly, use language that specifically points out the desired behaviors. For example, instead of saying, "Good job," name the task saying instead, "You did a really good job of listening to the story today." Asking questions that prompt children to think about the effects of particular behaviors provides them with a feeling of ownership and pride. For example, you might say, "The Authors Spot looks great. I see that you remembered to put paper, pencils, markers, back neatly where they belong. Why is this important?"

As you interact with children for instructional purposes use techniques that give all children a voice and an opportunity to participate. When you ask a question be sure to employ sufficient wait time (approximately 5 seconds) before selecting a student to answer. Doing so allows for greater participation and provides children with an opportunity to think before answering. Also, avoid asking questions that reward only children who have knowledge of something that you haven't yet taught. For example, don't begin a study of the rainforest by asking, "What do we call a forest that is very warm and wet?" This question may be appropriate on day 3 or 4 of learning about rainforests, but not on day 1. When you ask a question that has a specific answer, be sure to provide verbal reinforcement that explains why the response is correct; don't simply repeat the correct answer. Use words that extend the child's answer when appropriate. We want to balance our use of teacher directed discussions with opportunities for children to talk and explain their thinking without trying to supply a specific correct answer. For example, after watching a video clip of a species of monkey that lives in the rainforest, you might ask the children to think about how the animal uses different body parts to help it move around from tree to tree. Give the children a chance to talk to one another about the parts of a monkey's body that help it move well in the trees (e.g., "Turn to a friend and tell her what you notice . . . "). Afterward, you might return to a whole class discussion and ask the children to share their discussions. For example, you say, "As you were talking, I heard several groups talking about the monkey's tail. José, can you tell everyone what you and Michael were saying about how the monkey was using its tail?"

Recently, the work of psychologist Carol Dweck (2007), who wrote the influential book *Mindset*, has influenced thinking about the qualities of the learning environments that most benefit young learners. We have come to recognize that the teaching of skills and the modeling of learning strategies—while essential—should be accompanied by messages that help children develop a mindset of "*I can succeed*." We want young children to view learning through a lens of growth through effort (e.g., working hard to overcome challenges), rather than what is called a *fixed mindset* (e.g., believing that people are either naturally good or bad at something). As teachers, we can use language that helps children adopt a *growth mindset*. We can explicitly talk about responses to tasks that are hard, encourage children to keep trying, and to notice their improvements over time (Carol Dweck, 2006). Examples of language that will promote growth mindset:

- I was watching you gather all of the materials for your report on the red-eyed tree frog. You worked hard to find books and to find pictures online. What do you think will be the hardest part about writing the report? What will be the easiest part?
- Last week you remembered how to make the first letter in your name. Today you remembered how to make the first three letters! Pretty soon you are going to be able to write all five letters.
- I knew you could beat yesterday's time for sitting and reading at your book. You are within reach of your goal.
- I noticed that you haven't finished your project yet and see that you are pretty frustrated. Can you tell me what is hard? Can we come up with some things you could do to help you get going again?

During literacy instruction, teachers can simultaneously work toward building growth mindset and developing students' strategies—for decoding new words, for comprehending, for learning new vocabulary, and for writing. This can be accomplished by talking directly about the challenges students face during literacy-related tasks and by encouraging students to talk about how they approached various challenges and then overcame them. For example, students are taught a range of strategies for decoding words they don't automatically recognize. As teachers share each of the strategies with young readers and provide them with opportunities to practice using them, they can also talk directly about the challenges posed by new words in texts and invite students to decide which strategies work best for them and how they used these strategies with success. At the end of a guided reading lesson, a teacher might say, "Emily, I noticed that you figured out the word *careful* after a few tries. I was so glad you kept at it and didn't give up. A few months ago, I think you would have stopped after one try. Do you agree? Can you tell us what strategy you used to figure out the word *careful*?" By both focusing on the strategies used for decoding and on the students' increasing confidence and willingness to employ strategies, the teacher encourages a growth mindset among her young readers. When classroom environments are supportive and encourage risk-taking and when teachers help children acquire a growth mindset, opportunities to learn literacy skills and strategies are maximized.

MyLab Education Self-Check 12.3

Integrating Technology into Reading and Writing

Teaching English Learners

Children are attracted to digital tools. The fact that they can control their smart phone or computer may play a significant role in their digital literacy.

Technological advances are changing the way students learn literacy. We are in the midst of a dramatic transition from relying exclusively on print on paper or in a book to relying on both print and digital materials. In the not-so-distant past, educators used computers as an addition to literacy instruction; today, computers and digital devices are an integral part of literacy instruction. That shift has created new demands on teachers and students (McKenna, Labbo, Conradi, & Baxter, 2010).

Literacy research now includes the notion of multimodalities, or alternative modes for learning, communicating, and making meaning. For example, when a young child plays educational video games on a cell phone, a tablet, an e-reader, or a computer, the text uses visuals for understanding. In addition, the child is required to click on items, push or swipe with his or her finger, listen to the sounds of voices and letters, and enter a variety of texts. Each mode of interacting with the device (and the content of the game or text) elicits different responses that require different skills (Rowsell & Lapp, 2010).

In order for academic literacy to remain relevant, authentic, and motivating, literacy classrooms must embrace these transitions and alter their educational practices to reflect them. Teachers are typically most comfortable teaching in the way in which they learned, but that way is not necessarily the same way young children learn today. Redesigning instruction to reflect **new literacies** first involves acknowledging that the acquisition of literacy can take place in multiple venues, including print, art, music, and technology. That is, technology and technological modalities can be leveraged for the purpose of literacy instruction and making changes to reflect the new influences and opportunities made available through technology takes time and courage.

Teachers must keep an open mind when integrating new literacies or new technologies and realize that not succeeding is part of the learning process (Sheridan & Rowsell, 2010). What a wonderful lesson for students to learn from their teachers! In addition, many school districts and teacher evaluation models factor the use of technology into their observation protocols; and, while technology does not replace intentional instruction, teachers are encouraged to consider how the use of such tools might enhance the teaching of literacy strategies and skills.

It is important to note that students are often more comfortable with these new literacies than their teachers. Students are digital natives, but their teachers may very well be digital immigrants (Prensky, 2001). In other words, the youngsters "have spent their entire lives surrounded by and using computers, video games, digital music players, video cams, cell phones, and all the other toys and tools of the digital age"; these technologies are a natural and integral part of their lives (Prensky, 2001, p. 1). Today's children think and process information differently than children of past cohorts and generations. Those of us who were not born into this digital age, but attempt to utilize and integrate technology into practice, have to consciously choose to embed the technologies in our lives and instruction (Prensky, 2001).

We must effectively integrate technology into classroom pedagogy. Computer-related activities must be woven into daily classroom routines through planned activities such as (1) teacher interactive demonstration and (2) collaboration among students and teachers (McKenna et al., 2010). To help teachers incorporate technology into their literacy instruction, practical ideas and tools for using technology in teacher-directed lessons and student projects will be discussed.

Photo credit: Terrie L. Zeller/Shutterstock

During literacy station time, children may choose to listen to a book on a DVD.

We must also be intentional about integrating technology into the classroom. For example, because children are using digital literacy tools on a regular basis, teachers must be proactive in teaching them keyboarding. Many children teach themselves to hunt and peck for letters before learning how to touch-type in school. Once they learn to hunt and peck, it is difficult to change that habit to touch typing. It is wise, therefore, to teach touch typing in first and second grade. A common way that teachers use computers with children is through the use of Internet programs. When allowing students to use the Internet as a learning tool, these general rules should be followed (Wepner & Ray, 2000).

Instructions for children are concise, clear, and easy to follow. The activities are engaging, promote active participation, and will hold the attention and interest of children.

- The content matches and expands on what children are learning within their school curriculum.
- The program provides practice for concepts being learned.
- The text is narrated and highlighted for children to be able to deal with the activities independently.
- There is information for the teacher to provide guidance for the site.
- Assessment is provided.

Quality websites are available for every type of literacy skill, such as the development of phonemic awareness, phonics, comprehension, writing, and vocabulary. According to Wepner and Ray (2000), the following criteria should be used to select quality programs to develop reading skills such as phonics and phonemic awareness: (1) skills are introduced in a predictable sequence, (2) feedback is focused and immediate, (3) there is opportunity for repetitious feedback, and (4) children are engaged in an active manner.

Electronic books of children's literature present stories to children in a variety of ways. Images move on the screen, books are read aloud, and the text is clearly shown. Because these stories can be animated, they are motivating to children. Another advantage to electronic books is embedded in the book there are skill development techniques such as K-W-L, emphasis on development of story structure, and the use of a directed reading and thinking activity format (Wepner & Ray, 2000). Some electronic books are available now at websites, such as starfall.com and PBSkids.org, free of charge or for a small fee (McKenna et al., 2010). Another well-known resource includes learningally.org, an auditory tool designed to help students with dyslexia and students with learning disabilities. Regardless of the preferred tool, many of these electronic books can be downloaded on several or all of the school's digital tools at the same time. Electronic books have been found to motivate children to read and enhance their achievement in analyzing words, recalling details of stories, and acquiring a sense of story structure (Kinzer & McKenna, 1999; Labbo & Ash, 1998; Stine, 1993; Siegle, 2012).

The Internet has become a regular classroom tool that affords endless possibilities. Pen pals correspond instantly all over the world using email. The Internet is an unlimited resource for information related to whatever children are studying. For example, when the class is learning about outer space, the teacher can get a collection of titles of fiction and nonfiction books from the Internet and instructions on where to locate them for her classroom. These books might be in electronic format, which will allow children to read or listen to them on the Internet. The teacher should help the children locate an appropriate website as a source of information about outer space, for example, the NASA website, which provides reading and interactive opportunities for children. Using trusted sources, teachers can teach students to analyze articles and one-page wonders through the use of annotation and close reading strategies. Because of the plethora of information available, teachers should consult their curriculum guides and thematic units to develop text sets, or collections of text related to the same topic. Using such approaches deepens students' understanding of complex topics and content presented across the curriculum.

In addition to developing comprehension and piquing students' interests through wonder, the Internet provides opportunities to experience writing in interactive ways. Pbskids.org has a writing contest for young story writers. The online tools allow students either to upload illustrations and text for a story they've already written or to create one using stock illustrations and drawing tools embedded into the site.

In addition to having access to commercial and organizational websites, schools and classrooms can create their own websites for various reasons. Children's work can be posted on websites, electronic newsletters can be sent home to parents, and websites can provide a space for discussion out of school about what is being studied.

Similarly, many teachers are also creating blogs for their classes. A **blog** is an Internet forum where individuals post thoughts and feelings and/or respond to a topic. A blog is similar to a journal or diary, only it is made public by the author and available on the Internet. Blogs are personal responses to topics of interest to the individual blogger. A blog is an excellent alternative to a pencil-and-paper journal for reading responses, or in response to a current event. A free user-friendly site for creating a blog is www.blogger.com, which is now part of Google's suite of online tools and functionalities.

Christina Hughs, a literacy teacher who uses digital literacies in numerous ways in her classroom, suggests the following ideas for using technology on a classroom website in a section for blogs in early literacy. Tabs for storing different class activities such as the following can be made:

- Book reviews
- Videotaped skits about sections of a book
- Theme-related activities on video clips
- Classroom news blogs
- Reflection blogs
- Parent updates/communication
- Story sharing (post student stories through text or audio)
- Poetry.

The following blogging websites show different ways blogging can be used as a tool to support literacy instruction:

- Third-grade teacher blog: http://yollisclassblog.blogspot.com
- EL teacher blog: http://rosenglish.blogspot.com
- Teacher showcase blog: http://creativevoicepbs.blogspot.com

Websites need to be an integral part of every classroom. A **wiki** can be your class website, as it is an online space to record classroom activities and engage in activities. Students can post comments on the wiki. What makes wikis particularly useful is that they can be created without cost or any particular software. Teachers who have programs for building websites can use those. Through websites or wikis, students can respond to discussion questions or activities posted by teachers or each other. Visuals, podcasts, and links to websites can be added to a wiki. A user-friendly site for setting up a wiki is www.wikispaces.com. Anyone can create their own space with no cost involved or special program installed. More ideas for using websites or wiki spaces in early childhood literacy classroom include posting:

- Collaborative writing
- Class stories
- Brainstorming ideas for a project

- Videos, images, and links about a topic
- A student showcase (each student gets her or his own page to upload content)
- Discussion about classroom topics
- A resources library to share with other classes.

Padlet, (http://padlet.com) can also be added to a wiki, is an online notice-board ideal for making announcements, sending good wishes to people, keeping notes, and so on. Think of it as an online bulletin board to which students can "stick" digital Post-it notes. For example, the teacher could create a board for the word of the day and then require each student to post a sentence containing the word to the board.

Many teachers are also turning to the use of *SeeSaw*, a digital app that allows the teacher to be in control of what is posted and how it is shared. For example, a teacher might engage the students in a strategy lesson during reading workshop and later ask students to take a snapshot of their best annotations. Using a class code, students can log in, share their work, and comment on one another's inner conversations and tracked thinking. The opportunities are endless for digital collaboration, and all students have a voice. Bulletin board displays related to student work can also be used. SeeSaw allows parents to scan a QR code using their smartphones so that they are immediately taken to their child's work. While many basic features of the digital resource are free, more complex uses for the tool, including the creation of digital literacy portfolios, can be accessed by purchasing additional program features.

Another popular technology for the classroom is the **podcast**, a digital media file containing audio and/or visual recordings that can be uploaded to the Internet. Podcasts can be posted to a class website as well. For example, if a teacher created a class wiki website, he or she could upload a podcast on the opening page of the wiki. Students could then click on the podcast and hear and/or see their teacher talking to them. What a wonderful way to welcome students to a new and exciting year! Additionally, because the podcast can be viewed on any computer, family members could click on the podcast and become acquainted with the teacher. A relationship is immediately established with students as well as families through the use of introductory podcasts. They are an excellent venue for effective and exciting communication with students and their families. This use of technology can also be used to further develop students' reading fluency through repeated readings. Knowing that their work will be made public, students are motivated and encouraged to reread in order to show off their most expressive and fluent reading abilities.

After seeing their teacher model a successful podcast, students can also (with teacher assistance) create podcasts for class projects and activities. These digital files can be uploaded on the class website and made available for parents to watch at home. Audacity is a free open-source program for audio podcasting that can be downloaded and used by educators. For video podcasting, teachers can use external webcams (if the computer does not have one already built in). Corresponding computer programs, such as iMovie for Mac users or Windows Movie Maker for Windows users, assist in recording, editing, and saving videos. The following websites provide more information about podcasts:

- Student-recorded interviews: www.podkids.com.au
- iPod flashcards: www.mrcoley.com/flashcards/index.htm
- Thousands of education-related podcasts: http://tinyurl.com/66grdx
- Forty-three interesting ways to use your pocket video camera in the classroom: http://tinyurl.com/234bdqf
- Podomatic.com.

Blogs and wikis are both online, collaborative communities that can foster literacy motivation. Both formats are critically reliant on social discourse, which is one of the factors that increase motivation (Boling, Castek, Zawilinski, Barton, & Nierlich, 2008; Morgan & Smith, 2008). These spaces are also relevant and authentic, as many older students are already using digital collaborative technologies in their leisure time, and younger children are likely to have been exposed to them by their older siblings, parents, and other relatives and in school. Students who may be less likely to communicate in class may be more comfortable communicating in an online forum. Some of the latest forms of this discourse include the use of Google classroom, where students are able to collaborate, receive feedback from their peers and the teacher, and submit assignments digitally. By keeping a digital record of completed work through Google Docs, students can be guided to stop throughout key points of the school year (perhaps each quarter) to reflect on how they have grown as readers and writers. Reflecting on student work can also guide more meaningful reading and writing conferences with the teacher, who can lead students to selecting additional goals to work on throughout the year. Monitoring such goals through the use of digital learning environments fosters a growth mindset, where students can carry out learning plans with a positive attitude likely to result in experiencing new successes.

However, teachers must also be aware of the school district's policy for Internet use, particularly for young children. Teachers should also obtain permission from parents for students to join online communities, such as blogs and wikis. Teachers must invest the time to explicitly instruct students on how to find, navigate, and use various websites. Teachers must explain the rules, responsibilities, and expectations for using digital materials.

Teachers can also introduce children to the educational uses of informative websites. It is the teacher's responsibility to help students find websites that will be useful for them and to help them learn how to find others on their own. For safety reasons, teachers must always actively monitor students while they are on the Internet and encourage parents to do the same at home. A helpful reference book is *1001 Best Web Sites for Kids* (Kelly, 2004). When selecting websites for children, Wepner & Ray (2000) advise the following considerations:

- The website loads quickly.
- The title page presents a thorough overview of the contents.
- The content of the website fits with your purpose.
- There are icons that link to pages on the site needed and possibly to other relevant sites.
- The graphics are attractive and enhance the concepts.
- The narration is clear and enhances the concepts to be learned.
- Check the urls for sites you recommend before sharing them with parents to ensure they are still available and safe.

Teachers may also integrate new literacies into their lesson to enhance literacy motivation. They can show video clips from YouTube (www.youtube.com) that correspond with the curriculum. Discovery Education (streaming.discovereducation.com) contains educational video clips organized by topic and grade level. YouTube is free to access, whereas Discovery Education requires a subscription. Other well-known resources for videos to enhance learning include watchknowlearn.org, ted.com/talks, and brainpop.com. Looking to give your students a brain break

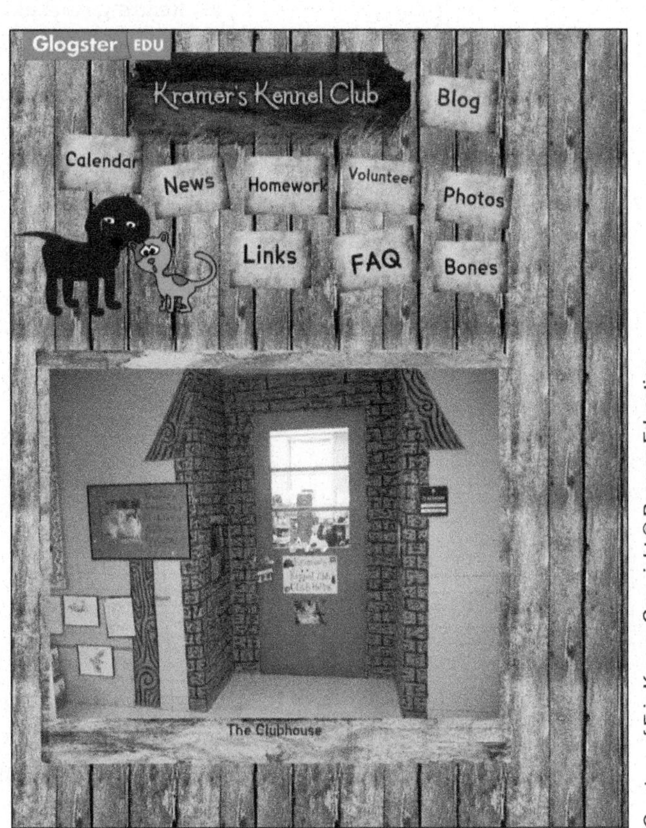

A website created by a first-grade teacher.

and an opportunity to stretch and shake out some energy? Check out gonoodle.com. Regardless of where clips reside, teachers should always preview clips in their entirety to ensure relevance and appropriateness for student viewers.

PowerPoint presentations and Google Slide presentations also provide an alternative to lessons and sharing information. These types of activities can include sound, motion, color, and visuals to enhance the material being learned. Prezi (www.prezi.com) is another digital presentation tool that can enhance the dynamic presentation of classroom lessons.

It is easy, particularly for new teachers, to feel overwhelmed by all of the technological possibilities to use in the classroom, and the resources discussed in this chapter are just a sampling of the many new literacies that continue to evolve. By the time you are holding this book (or downloading a digital version), even more resources would have become available for enhancing instruction. Regardless, teachers should not let fear keep them from attempting to use them. Some educators select one technology to learn over an extended period of time. If possible, teachers should collaborate with colleagues who are also interested in learning the same technology. Teachers might want to seek professional development opportunities on new literacies that they wish to master.

New literacy materials—with all their capabilities for creativity, correspondence, and retrieval of information—must be included in daily routines for learning. Children will need to function with these technologies on a daily basis. Appendix D provides a list of software and websites designated for the development of children's literacy skills. These also include ideas for teachers for almost any activity or lesson plan they would like to do. A short list of excellent websites that include almost any idea a teacher might need for any grade level is given below.

- Annenberg Learner
- Read, Write, Think
- Reading Rockets
- Read Works
- Teaching Channel
- Thinkfinity
- Doug Fisher and Nance Frey's YouTube Teaching Channel

Technology changes daily. Those that exist today may be replaced tomorrow by something capable of doing other activities. Once you step into this territory, you will continue to learn more and it will continue to become easier. This is just a glimpse into the world of new literacies—new ideas, new materials, and new possibilities. What we thought was a possibility is already a reality. In some schools children are not using textbooks and carrying backpacks that are bursting at the seams. Instead they are carrying tablets and e-readers to download whatever texts they need in science, social studies, math, reading, and more. Districts will also save on the cost of materials by only purchasing online access to texts. As a teacher, it will be important to assess the digital landscape of where you teach and use this as a starting point for setting goals related to the use of instructional technology.

Digital Tools

In today's educational environment, educators and students are faced not only with incorporating a plethora of new technology and websites into the instructional day, but also with a continuously growing and varied collection of devices to use in conjunction with those soft technologies. Personal computers and laptops, the bulwark of classroom technology for nearly two decades, are now joined by cell phones, tablets, and digital whiteboards, all of which have unique capabilities, as well as some overlapping ones. Tablets allow for individual and more personal digital experiences, and digital whiteboards support more collective digital literacy experiences.

Tablets. Tablets have become a part of modern classrooms, and there are numerous educational applications (apps) available for each tablet platform. As tablet types and operating systems proliferate, however, it is important that teachers consider the availability of the apps they want to use in the classroom on those platforms. This is a particularly thorny consideration when dominant platforms begin to have serious competition, for example, when Apple's iPad lost market share to tablets using Google's Android platform. Educational apps may only be available in one or two platforms; before requiring students to use apps, be sure they have access to them from the device they are using. For classrooms that have multiple device platforms available, this is especially important so that all students are able to engage with the material.

Interactive Whiteboards. An electronic/interactive whiteboard is a display board that includes software that can transform it into a large-scale type of tablet. Because of the technological capabilities of the display, the technology of a digital whiteboard can greatly enhance teaching when used correctly. All you have to do is plug it into your computer and hook up an LCD projector and you have everything you need. The board has touch-screen capabilities for writing, clicking, dragging, and highlighting pertinent information.

In terms of literacy instruction, interactive whiteboards have numerous applications. For example, students can use the board to touch and sort spelling words. They can use context clues on the board to guess concealed mystery vocabulary words (the technology activates the reveal). Lessons can be saved, revisited, and printed out. Because the electronic whiteboard connects to the Internet, teachers can easily incorporate one of several interactive multimedia websites into whole-group and small-group instruction. The board can also be used to display PowerPoint slides and to connect to TeacherTube and YouTube. In Mrs. Bernero's classroom, students are inspired by the *American Idol* TV show, so they create and play their own version of *Fluency Idol* to practice their reading skills. In Mrs. Tapia's classroom, complex texts are uploaded onto the interactive whiteboard so that students can collectively close read and annotate information as a class. Although the interactive whiteboard provides a logical mounted space for whole group instruction, the teacher may also choose to later utilize the tool for small group instruction or independent practice.

Virtual Field Trips. As educators, we wish we could take all of our students around the world to give them firsthand experience with places and things being studied in the classroom. With technology, we can. Virtual field trips allow students to explore museums, monuments, national parks, and other places through interactive videos. Google Maps/Street View and Google Earth allow students to feel like they are visiting foreign cities and walking along the streets. Use this link to search through various free field trips to share with your students: www.internet4classrooms.com/vft.htm.

A preschool teacher took her children on a trip to Israel. They dramatized being on the airplane and being the pilot and the crew. They read signs, observed safety rules, and enjoyed the flight. When they arrived—via the Internet—they visited the Wailing Wall and left messages for loved ones. Using the Internet, they virtually climbed the Masada and were told the story about what happened there thousands of years ago. The children drew pictures about their trip and were able to print pictures off the Internet. Parents were greatly impressed with the children's knowledge and descriptions of their experience. Many commented on how vivid the experience must have been and how much their child had discussed it at home. I asked one of the children about the trip and he answered, "Oh we aren't home yet, I can tell you about it when we finally arrive."

MyLab Education
Video Example 12.2
Integrating Technology into Literacy
In this video, the second grade teacher provides 10 tips for using digital storytelling in the classroom.
https://www.youtube.com/watch?v=ywOlXTq_Yfo

Digital Storytelling. Digital stories provide students with the opportunity to share personal stories or retell favorite stories using a combination of audio, video, and still images. These stories can be published on a class website in the form of blogs in order to be shared among students. The following link provides resources, examples, and ideas for using digital storytelling with students: www.techteachers.com/digitalstorytelling.htm.

Leveraging the Unique Capabilities of Technology

When using technology to motivate interest in literacy learning, it is important to leverage its unique capabilities. Using technology to the fullest will maximize the student experience and generate interest in the content and the tools used to present it.

MyLab Education Self-Check 12.4

How Dramatic Play Can Engage Children in Reading and Writing

Teaching English Learners
Children can participate in dramatic play which will give them a sense of belonging

A curriculum area we must continue to implement is motivating literacy learning through play. In play settings, children interact and collaborate in small groups. When designed to promote literacy behaviors, the dramatic-play area is coordinated with a social studies or science theme that is being studied to bring meaning to the experience. Materials for reading and writing are provided to support the play theme, and during play, children read, write, speak, and listen to one another using literacy in functional ways.

Although early childhood educators have realized the value of play for social, emotional, and physical development, in the past play has not been viewed as a means to motivate literacy. More recently, play has gained greater importance as a medium for practicing literacy behaviors because it provides repeated, meaningful, and functional social settings. During observations of children playing, one can see the functional uses of literacy that children incorporate into their play themes. Children engage in attempted and conventional reading and writing in collaboration with others (Morrow, 1990; Neuman & Roskos, 1992; Roskos & Christie, 2000; Cavanaugh, Clemence, Teale, Rule, & Montgomery, 2016).

Objectives for Play Experiences

Dramatic play provides endless possibilities for literacy development through the use of oral and written language and reading. The materials and activities typical of dramatic-play areas stimulate considerable language, and the addition of new props and materials provides the opportunity for continued growth. Dramatic play provides realistic settings and functional reasons for using print. New units in social studies and science trigger opportunities to add print materials that stimulate reading, writing, and oral language. A unit on community helpers, a topic familiar to early childhood teachers, invariably leads to a discussion of firefighters, police officers, supermarket clerks, doctors, nurses, mail carriers, and office workers. The mention of any of these community helpers is an opportunity to add literacy materials to the dramatic-play area.

Role-playing supermarket is aided by the addition of food and detergent containers, a toy cash register, play money, notepads, a telephone and directory, store signs, a schedule of hours, advertisements, and posters for food and other products. Teachers or aides might visit a nearby supermarket to note the print that is there and to pick up outdated signs and posters. Store managers readily give away such materials when they no longer need them.

Among the materials for dramatic play about supermarkets should definitely be a bookshelf full of magazines and books "for sale." All these materials help children engage in conversation as they role-play a store manager, clerk, or shopper. They read posters, books, signs, and magazines and write shopping lists, orders, and new signs when they are needed.

Many topics lend themselves to dramatic play and incorporating literacy materials. A study of health-care personnel can lead to the creation of a doctor's office. A waiting room can be set up with magazines and pamphlets about good health for the patients to read. There can be a no smoking sign, a notice displaying the doctor's hours, and posters on the wall concerning good health habits. There should be an appointment book for the nurse, a pad for writing appointment reminders for patients to take with them, a pad for writing prescriptions, patient folders containing forms to be filled out, and a patient address and phone book.

When studying transportation, the class can create a travel agency. Here there would be maps, travel posters, pamphlets about places to visit, tickets to be issued for planes and trains, and perhaps even mock passport application forms for travel to foreign destinations.

Children enjoy role-playing in these situations because the activity includes meaningful experiences. In dramatic play, children are voluntarily participating in reading and writing. Dramatic play is considered appropriate in preschools and kindergartens; however, we seldom leave time for it in first and second grade or think of it as an area in which learning can take place. In classrooms that integrate content themes into dramatic play with 6- to 8-year-olds, extremely sophisticated productions of reading, writing, and oral language result. It is suggested that first- and second-grade teachers incorporate play into their curriculum. In early childhood, play experiences include providing opportunities for:

1. Problem solving
2. Role-playing real-life experiences
3. Coping with situations that require sharing and cooperating
4. Developing language and literacy through play.

Technology has made it more acceptable to engage in dramatic play with second and third graders as they search the Internet for train and plane routes when role-play is about travel or information for other themes (Manning, Manning, & Long, 1994; McGee & Morrow, 2005; Purcell-Gates, Duke, & Martineau, 2007; Walmsley, 1994).

MyLab Education Application Exercise 12.2

Observations of Literacy Behavior During Dramatic Play

To demonstrate the importance of the social, collaborative, and interactive nature of literacy development, let us visit a classroom where Ms. Hart, the teacher, has designed a veterinarian's office to go along with an animal theme. The dramatic-play area was designed with a waiting room; chairs; a table filled with magazines, books, and pamphlets about pet care; posters about pets; office hour notices; a no-smoking sign; and a sign advising visitors to "Check in with the nurse when arriving." A nurse's desk holds patient forms on clipboards, a telephone, an address and telephone book, appointment cards, a calendar, and a computer for recording appointments and patient records. The office contains patient folders, prescription pads, white coats, masks, gloves, cotton swabs, a toy doctor's kit, and stuffed animals to serve as patients.

Ms. Hart guides students in the use of the materials in the veterinarian's office—for example, she reminds the children to read to pets in waiting areas, fill out forms with prescriptions or appointment times, or fill out forms with information about an animal's condition and treatment. In addition to giving directions, Ms. Hart also models behaviors by participating in play with the children when the materials are first introduced.

The following anecdotes relate the type of behavior that was witnessed in this setting. There were books and writing materials. The teacher modeled reading and writing that children observed. There were also opportunities to practice literacy in real-life situations that had meaning and function. Children were collaborating and reading and writing with peers.

> Jessica was waiting to see the doctor. She told her stuffed animal dog Sam not to worry, and that the doctor wouldn't hurt him. She asked Jenny, who was waiting with her stuffed animal cat Muffin, what the cat's problem was. The girls agonized over the ailments of their pets.
>
> After a while, they stopped talking and Jessica picked up a book from the table and read *Are You My Mother?* to her pet dog, Sam. Jessica showed Sam the pictures as she read.
>
> Jennie ran into the doctor's office, shouting, "My dog got runned over by a car!" The doctor bandaged the dog's leg; then the two children decided that the incident must be reported to the police. They went to the computer to google local police and got the phone number. Then they googled the spot where the dog had been hit. They called the police on the toy phone to report the incident.
>
> Another patient came in with his owner. It was Christopher with his teddy bear. Preston, the doctor, examined Christopher's teddy bear and wrote out a report in the patient's folder. He read his scribble writing out loud and said, "This teddy bear's blood pressure is 29 points. He should take 62 pills an hour until he is better and keep warm and go to bed." While he read, he showed Christopher what he had written so that he would understand what to do. He asked his nurse to type the notes into the computer. (refer to Figure 12.1) shows forms that may be used in the dramatic-play center when it is designed as a veterinarian's office during a unit on animals.

This type of play sets the stage for opportunities for EL students and those from diverse backgrounds. They will learn about functioning in real settings with other children. With the props and the informal nature of the experiences, they will feel comfortable participating. Additional play settings that encourage reading and writing at different grade levels follow:

1. **Newspaper office:** Includes telephones, directories, maps, computers, paper, pencils, and areas that focus on sports, travel, general news, and weather.
2. **Supermarket or local grocery store:** Can include labeled shelves and sections, food containers with their labels left on, a cash register, a telephone, computers, receipts, checkbooks, coupons, and promotional flyers.
3. **Post office:** Can be used for mailing the children's letters and needs to include paper, envelopes, address books, pens, pencils, stamps, cash registers, computers, and mailboxes. A mail carrier's hat and bag are important for delivering the mail by reading names and addresses.
4. **Airport:** Can be created with signs posting arrivals and departures, tickets, boarding passes, luggage tags, magazines and books for the waiting area, safety messages on the plane, and name tags for the flight attendants. A computer is used to get onto the Internet to make plane reservations and check when a plane is arriving.

Figure 12.1 Forms to Use for the Veterinarian's Office in the Dramatic-Play Center

Appointment Card

Name: ______________________

Has an appointment on ______________

☐ Mon. ☐ Tues. ☐ Wed. ☐ Thurs. ☐ Fri. ☐ Sat.

Date __________ at ______ a.m. p.m.

Prescription

Patient's Name:

Prescription:

Refills: Instructions:

Franklin A. Morrow, D.V.M.

Patient Record Form

Patient's Name: ______________ Type of Animal: ______________

Owner's Name: ______________ Date of Visit: ______________

Address: ______________ Telephone Number: ______________

History and Physical Findings: Treatment:

5. **Gas station and car repair shop:** Can be designed in the block area. Toy cars and trucks can be used for props. There can be receipts for sales, a cash register, a computer, road maps to help with directions to different destinations, auto repair manuals for fixing cars and trucks, posters that advertise automobile equipment, and empty cans of different products that are sold in stations (Morrow, 2007).
6. **Restaurant:** Can be set up near the kitchen area and table and chairs. Props might include a tablecloth, tableware, menus, ordering pad and pencil, plastic food items, open and closed signs. (See Figure 12.2 for useful illustrations. Enlarge, color, or copy them onto firm colored paper and laminate. Write the name of the restaurant you are creating—for example, Our Japanese Restaurant, Our Mexican Restaurant, Our Jewish Deli, and so on).
   (1 to 6: From Promoting Literacy during Play by Designing Early Childhood Classroom Environments,Lesley Mandel Morrow and Muriel K. Rand, The Reading Teacher Vol. 44, No. 6 (Feb., 1991), pp. 396–402. Reproduced with permission from John Wiley & Sons,Inc.)

For literacy materials to be used to their fullest potential, they must be natural and from the children's environment and serve a real function. Ensure the dramatic-play area matches a theme being studied. Change the area when you begin to study a new theme. Initially, teachers need to provide a model of how to use the materials in the play area (Barone, Mallette, & Xu, 2004; Neuman & Roskos, 1997).

The materials in dramatic-play areas should be accessible. All levels of literacy development should be accepted and reading or writing attempts should be recognized as legitimate literacy behaviors. Teachers might find it useful to record anecdotes about literacy activities engaged in by children.

MyLab Education Self-Check 12.5

Figure 12.2 Creating a Classroom Restaurant

Welcome To

Our ______________________

Restaurant

Figure 12.2 Creating a Classroom Restaurant (Continued)

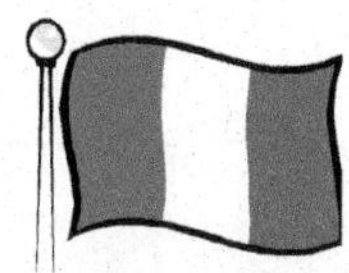

Italian Garden Menu

Drinks	Main Course	Desserts
Milk $1.00	Spaghetti $10.00	Italian Cookies $3.00
Water FREE	Pizza $2.00	Cheesecake $3.00

Mexican Restaurant Menu

Drinks	Main Course	Desserts
Milk $1.00	Bean Burrito $5.00	Ice Cream $2.00
Juice $1.00	Chicken Quesadilla $5.00	Rice Pudding $2.00

Figure 12.2 Creating a Classroom Restaurant (Continued)

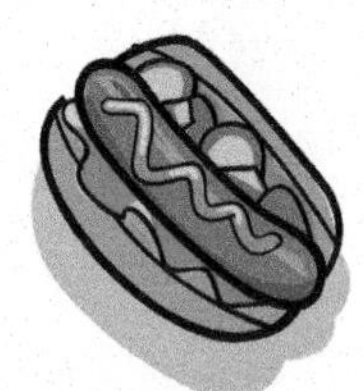

Bob's Barbeque Menu

Beverages	**Main Entrees**	**Desserts**
Juice $1.00	Hamburger $3.00	Oatmeal Cookie $1.00
Water FREE	Hot Dog $2.00	Ice Cream $1.00

Create a menu for a different restaurant. Draw pictures and write in the words.

____

Beverages	**Main Entrees**	**Desserts**

Figure 12.2 Creating a Classroom Restaurant (Continued)

Restaurant: ____________________

Restaurant Order Form and Bill for Table ________

Drinks: ____________ $ ______
____________ $ ______

Main Course: ____________ $ ______
____________ $ ______

Desserts: ____________ $ ______
____________ $ ______

Total: $ ______

Thank You for Coming to

____________________ Restaurant

Total: $:____________

Come Back Again!

The waiter or waitress fills in the Thank You form (top).
The customer completes the Survey (bottom).

Restaurant Survey

How did you like your food? ☺ ☹

How friendly was your server? ☺ ☹

How fast was the service? ☺ ☹

Integrating Literacy Learning into Thematic Units and Project-Based Learning

In this book, the discussion has been about how to develop skills to read automatically and fluently with comprehension. During the school day, explicit skill instruction typically occurs in the morning. This alloted time is often called the *language arts block.* The time spent on explicit instruction is about 1½ to 3 hours. This work time is crucial. Do not forget that to motivate children they need to read and write about things that are relevant and authentic to them with activities that will create interest.

Primary grade teachers need to purposefully teach reading all day long. The explicit part of this instruction has been discussed. Small group-differentiated instruction usually occurs early in the day, and for the rest of the day, teachers must embed literacy skills intentionally in content area subjects. Literacy will come alive and have meaning and purpose with these activities, and children will become involved in experiences where they choose to read. Children will become engaged in reading and writing with content-area themes in social studies and science about topics such as different cultures, famous citizens, bugs, dinosaurs, animals, and so on. Teachers should plan projects that involve experiments and exploration.

John Guthrie (2004) created a motivational approach to supplement the teaching of reading called *Concept-Oriented Reading Instruction (CORI).* The purpose of CORI is to provide literacy development by activating motivation through the use of science. His evidenced-based research demonstrates that students in his CORI program scored better than other students in activating background knowledge with new knowledge and learning how to question and search for information to answer questions than students who were not in a CORI program. CORI students were able to organize and summarize materials. Most importantly, students in the CORI program were more engaged or motivated to want to participate by providing hands-on activities related to reading, providing students with choices in the learning process, using interesting literature for instruction, and creating projects that required collaboration (Guthrie, 2004).

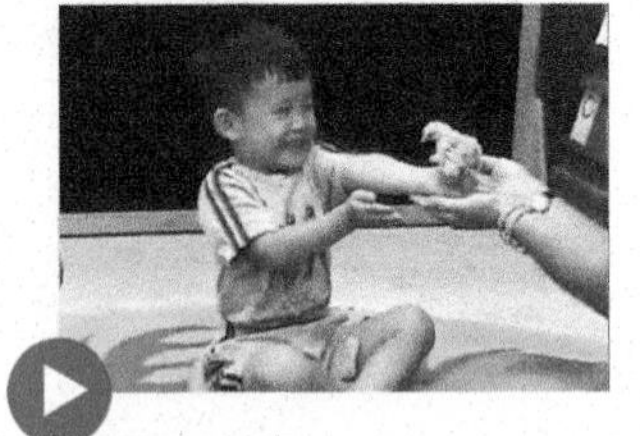

MyLab Education
Video Example 12.3
Birds: An Integrated Unit Study
A preschool in Hawaii engaged children in a thematic study of Birds. This motivating unit engaged children in literacy, art, and science activities.

The CORI program consists of several science units. During the unit, children are asked to observe information about a topic such as birds. Some observation activities include taking a walk with the class and observing and discussing birds seen in their neighborhood. What do they look like, what do they eat, and where do they sleep? The class may visit a museum and a local zoo that has an aviary or a bird section to observe and describe many different species. Have a guest speaker from the zoo talk about the birds. This can be done at the zoo or in school with live birds. Next, children discuss questions they have about birds and do some hands-on activities such as creating several bird feeders outside the school, having a bird in their classroom as a pet, or dissecting owl pellets. These hands-on activities prompt students to have—and teachers to ask—questions. Children decide which ones they would like to answer and find others interested in the same questions. They are encouraged to work together. To find the answers to the questions, they read books that are provided at all reading levels that include narrative and informational literature. They search the Internet for information, watch online videos, and contact places that work with birds. Along with providing a written summary, children can summarize their findings using art, music, an experiment, or a PowerPoint or Prezi presentation.

Dewey (1966) was largely responsible for bringing the concept of an interdisciplinary approach to teaching to educators' attention. This approach, which is referred to as the *integrated school day*, teaches skills from all content areas within the theme being studied. The themes that are studied at school derive from children's real-life experiences and topics in which they demonstrate an interest. Learning experiences are socially interactive and process oriented, giving children time to explore and experiment with varied materials. If, for example, a class is studying dinosaurs, the students talk, read, and write about them; do art projects related to dinosaurs; and sing songs related to the theme. According to Dewey, when children are taught this way they develop skills in literacy and content areas (in this case, about dinosaurs).

Literacy activities can be integrated into the study of themes and into all content areas throughout the school day (Morrow, 2004; Pappas, Kiefer, & Levstik, 1995).

Important work in interdisciplinary learning and embedding literacy into content areas is project-based instruction (PBI). Different than having many themes during the school year, PBI may focus on just one or two topics. Often the children select the project-based topics based on what is happening in the news, in their town, in the country. Similar to themes children work together and use informational text in content areas. They also read and write and have a motivating culminating activity. PBI is different than themes since the topics deal with real problems that need to be solved, not just in school but in the outside world as well. In PBI children work for a long period of time to build something, to create something, to solve a real problem, or to address a real need (Duke, 2004).

Ms. Nelson's third-grade class had been investigating what their PBI topic would be this year. James heard a commercial on television about hunger in America and specifically children. He was really surprised to hear about this and shared the information. The commercial suggested if you wanted to help you could be in touch with FeedingAmerica.Org. James said to the class, " I can't believe there are children who don't have enough food in this country. Wherever I go there is food and usually a lot left over. The cafeteria has food left over at lunch, we throw away some food after dinner since there is left over. When we have a school party, there is food left over. How can we help these children and where are they." The class and teacher agreed that this would be an excellent topic for this year's project. They made a list of what they think they would like to do to help with this problem. They came up with the following:

Search the Internet to find out where there are children who don't have enough food. Find out what FeedingAmerica.org does, speak to someone at FeedingAmerica.org.

Make a pamphlet to distribute to parents and businesses in their town with information about Feeding America.org and the numbers of hungry children in this country and where they are. They thought they could start their own vegetable garden and when harvested, they could give the food to a local food pantry. The children could create a guidebook on how not to waste food and they can help. The project was for the school but the entire town as well. Children were anxious to begin right away and had to decide what to do first and how to divide responsibilities.

Over the course of the project, their teacher taught informational reading and writing skills as well as content. The skills were taught intentionally although the children were not aware. For example, the teacher taught students how to organize the information they gathered and plan their writing using a planning map. The teacher knew that this strategy helped address some standards for third-graders to "group related information together" when writing, but the students focused on learning the strategy to help serve the project in which they were engaged (Duke, 2016).

MyLab Education
Video Example 12.4
Project-Based Literacy Learning
In this video, kindergarten students investigate, plan, and build a butterfly garden as part of a project-based learning unit. https://www.youtube.com/watch?v=dsyusb5FdUI

Children learn content about the topic of their Project. Projects often involve a great deal of reading and writing, for instance, they could be writing surveys; reading, analyzing, and writing up the survey results; reading and synthesizing documents, recording observations; and writing up results. Students usually must communicate, both orally and in writing, with people outside of the classroom. Within the classroom, considerable speaking and listening are typically required as students work together to achieve the project goals. Students will be using twenty-first-century skills such as technology, creativity, critical thinking, collaboration, and learning to be active good citizen (Duke, 2000).

Research suggests that reading and writing for specific purposes, beyond just acquiring basic skills and meeting certain school requirements, is associated with stronger reading and writing growth. PBI involves writing for different audiences beyond members of the classroom. Research suggests that students actually write better under such circumstances. With projects that children choose and activities they plan to achieve they will read and write because there is a real world problem to solve. Children are more likely to do homework related to the project since it helps them get closer to the goal. Students may choose to read more since they want to know more about the topic. Because a good bit of the work will be read by those in the school and town, they will revise and edit their work and they are enthusiastic about sharing what they have learned.

Literacy Skills Embedded into Content Area Disciplines

Art Activities and Literacy Development

Art experiences allow children to explore and experiment with interesting materials, such as finger paints, watercolors, printing, string painting, sponge painting, colored pencils, felt-tip markers, crayons, colored construction paper, tissue paper, foil, transparent wrap, paste, scissors, yarn, fabric scraps, pipe cleaners, clay, and play dough. If children are encouraged to discuss such materials as they use them, language development flourishes. Children immersed in finger painting—for instance, use such words: mushy, slushy, gushy, and squiggle. Playing with dough or clay elicits the words: pound, squeeze, roll, press, and fold. Watercolors stimulate such comments as "Oooh, it's drippy," "The paint is running down the page like a stream of water," "Look how the colors all run together," "The red is making the blue turn purple," and "My picture looks like a rainbow of colors across the sky." The teacher can take the opportunity to make word lists from the language generated in art activities and to encourage the children to share and talk about what they are doing. The words that individual children generate are a source of Very Own Words.

Children are often eager to exhibit their creations. This practice is likely to result in children's asking each other how they made their projects. The resulting description provides an excellent opportunity for literacy development. Children sometimes ask to dictate or write sentences and stories about their artwork or write about it themselves. Individual works of art on similar subjects can be bound together in books that include captions, titles, or stories. Art activities also can highlight concepts such as the letter *p*—for example, through the use of purple and pink paint, paper, and play dough.

In early childhood, art experience should offer children the following:

1. Being exposed to varied art materials
2. Exploring and experimenting with these materials
3. Expressing feelings through art
4. Gaining an appreciation for varied art forms
5. Naming and discussing the content of art: line, color, texture, and shape

6. Learning new vocabulary with the use of different art projects and materials
7. Experiencing literacy learning in art activities: Reading books about art being studied, learning vocabulary specific to art being studied, doing reflective journals about art.

Music Experiences and Literacy Development

Music provides ample means for literacy development. Children find new words in songs, thus increasing vocabulary. Songs emphasize word patterns and syllabic patterns, which should be brought to the children's attention. Songs can be written on charts and sung, the teacher pointing to the individual words while tracking the print from left to right across the page. Picture storybooks adapted from songs, such as *Old MacDonald Had a Farm* (Quackenbush, 1972), provide predictable reading material for young children. Listening to classical music often creates images and is a rich source for descriptive language. Children can create stories about the music, describe their feelings, or describe the sounds of various instruments.

In early childhood, music experiences should include:

1. Having intense involvement in and responding to music and expressing feelings
2. Being exposed to different forms of music (instruments, singing, types of music), being able to discriminate among them, and developing an appreciation for varied forms
3. Having music experiences that involve listening, singing, moving, playing, and creating
4. Experiencing literacy learning in music activities: reading books about the type of music being sung or about the composer, discussion music vocabulary, and so on.

Social Studies and Science Experiences and Literacy Development

Social studies and science themes for the most part provide the meaning and function for learning literacy. Themes provide a reason to read and write about topics of interest. Skills are learned within a context, rather than in isolated lessons for skill development.

In early childhood, social studies experiences should include:

1. Learning social skills for functioning, such as sharing, cooperating, and communicating with others
2. Recognizing and respecting similarities and differences in others
3. Increasing knowledge of other culture, ethnic, and racial groups
4. Using social studies to promote literacy development as a result of reading, writing, listening, viewing and speaking about the content through comparing and contrasting, describing, summarizing, and so on.

In early childhood, science experiences should include activities that involve:

1. Observing, hypothesizing, recording data, analyzing, and drawing conclusions
2. Increasing understanding in
   a. Biological science, the study of living things
   b. Physical science
   c. Earth/Space science

Using the content of science to promote reading, writing, listening, viewing and speaking science and social studies are probably the two content areas that provide the greatest opportunities for literacy development. Their contents typically generate enthusiasm, meaning, and a purpose for using literacy strategies. A unit about farms can lead to oral language development through discussions about farm work, different types of farms, and farm animals. Word lists of farm animals, crops, and jobs on the farm can be made. Pictures of farm scenes, a trip to a farm, or a visit by a farmer all generate discussion, reading, and writing (Kesler, Gibson, & Turansky, 2016).

To encourage positive attitudes toward books, the teacher can carefully select good pieces of children's literature about farms to read to the class. The *Petunia* series (Duvoisin, 2002) deals with a delightful goose that lives on a farm. *The Little Red Hen* (Pinkney, 2006), *The Tale of Peter Rabbit* (Potter, 1902), *Barnyard Banter* (Fleming, 2001), and *Chicken or the Egg?* (Fowler, 1993) are just a few examples of good children's literature that relate to the farm. The teacher should select some multicultural trade books as well. These books will motivate youngsters to pick up the books on their own, retell them, role-play them, and share them with each other. A farm visit can be retold in stories or drawings, bound into class books, recaptured in a language experience chart, or reflected in Very Own Words. The teacher can associate letters and sounds in farm words with those in children's names or in environmental print.

Science experiments and food preparation are opportunities for discussion and an exchange of interesting vocabulary. The block center can stimulate literacy activities. For instance, when introducing a unit on transportation, the teacher can add toy trucks, trains, cars, boats, and airplanes to the block corner, along with travel tickets, luggage and freight tags, maps, tour brochures, travel posters, and signs common to airports, train stations, and bus depots, such as gate numbers, names of carriers, and arrivals and departure signs (Kersten, 2017).

Math Experiences and Literacy

Math is a specialized area that needs more attention than can be dealt with in a content-area unit. Still, many activities can bring meaning to mathematics through unit topics and include literacy as well. Stories related to numbers can be read, children can count wrapped cookies for snack time to make sure there are enough for the class, and children can be in charge of collecting and counting milk money. When studying weather, a chart of daily temperatures can be graphed to observe the variability from day to day.

Early childhood mathematics activities should involve:

1. Dealing with mathematical materials and ideas
2. Moving from dependence on the concrete to abstract ideas
3. Being able to classify, compare, seriate, measure, graph, count, identify, write numbers, and perform operations on numbers
4. Using mathematical vocabulary
5. Reading math problems that are written as word problems rather than just number calculations.

Preparing a Thematic Unit

Unit themes can be selected by the teacher and the children. Giving students choices concerning what they will learn is important. When a topic is selected, allow the children time to brainstorm what they would like to know about. You might begin by suggesting categories to focus on and letting them fill in subheadings (Katz & Chard,

2000; Rand, 1993; Tompkins, 2003). In preparation for a unit on nutrition, I asked a class of kindergarten children to help decide what they might like to learn. I created a web with nutrition as the theme. I wrote down the four categories of focus (Why is food important? What foods are good for you? Where do we get food from? and How are different foods prepared to eat?) and invited children to share their ideas, which I added to our chart. The web in Figure 12.3 illustrates the children's responses and the content to be studied for the unit.

In planning a unit, the teacher needs to pay attention to integrating the content throughout the day by using a variety of activities. The following is a mini-unit written by Ms. Ngai, a first-grade teacher. As you will see, she integrates content-area activities throughout the day that focus on the theme.

Thematic Instruction: Good Food

An interesting theme can make learning come alive for children. With food as our theme and popcorn as our weeklong focus, things were really "popping" in our first-grade classroom!

Here are some exciting ways to make learning about popcorn fun, while tying in content-area instruction.

The Friday before: We planted popcorn kernels in baking tins lined with paper towels. We spread popcorn in the pans, watered the seeds, and covered the pans with plastic wrap. In a few days, the roots began to sprout *(science).*

Monday: Using a log, we recorded the growth of the seedlings over the weekend. We read *The Popcorn Book* by Tomie DePaulo (1978). We discussed that the Native Americans introduced popcorn to the colonists. We used the compound word "popcorn" to trigger a list of other food compound words, such as "cupcake" and "milkshake" that we wrote on a chart. Any time a student thought of or came across a compound word, he or she would write it down on the chart. By the end of the week, the chart paper was full (science, language arts, social studies).

Tuesday: We set up an experiment chart for making popcorn. We asked ourselves, "What do I want to find out?" (How does a corn kernel change to popcorn?) "What do I think will happen?" "How will I find out?" "What actually happened?" and "What did I learn?" We answered the first two questions. We used an air popper to pop the corn and then completed the experiment chart, answering the remaining questions. We also enjoyed the popcorn for our snack. We planted our seedlings in paper cups filled with soil (science).

Figure 12.3 Curriculum Web for a Thematic Unit on Nutrition

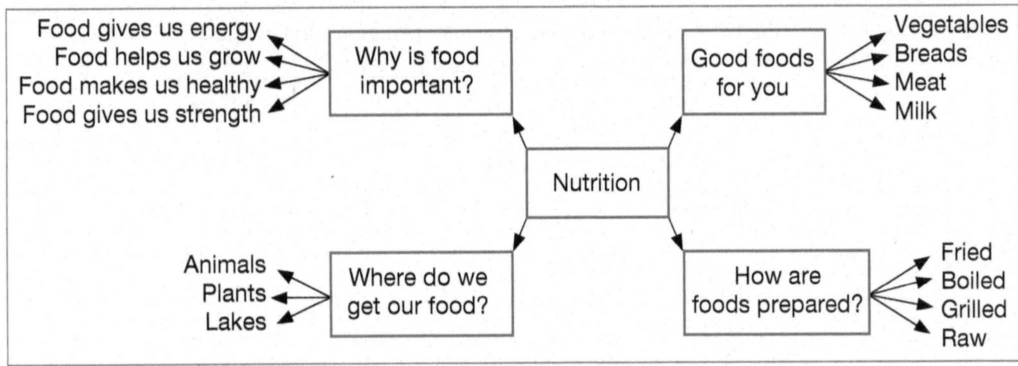

Wednesday: We made more popcorn to create an estimation lesson for math. Each child grabbed a handful of popcorn from a large bowl and guessed how many kernels were in his or her hand. Then we used a simple record sheet to log estimations. We then counted to find the actual number. We tried it a second time to see if we arrived at a more accurate estimation (mathematics).

Thursday: One way Native Americans popped corn was to put an ear of dried corn on a stick and hold it over a fire until the kernels popped. Another way was to throw kernels into the fire until they popped out all over the place. Still another way was to use clay pots filled with hot sand, in which the kernels were mixed until they eventually popped to the top of the pot. We illustrated the method we thought was the best and wrote a few sentences as to why we felt that way. We discussed how the Native Americans made necklaces out of popcorn. Using the popcorn from Wednesday (Stringing popcorn is easier if it is not fresh.), we gave it a try. We used large, blunt needles and heavy thread and created necklaces (writing, art, social studies).

Friday: As a culminating lesson, we had parent volunteers come into our classroom to make popcorn balls (We popped more corn.). We checked for any growth of our corn plants and recorded the information in our science logs (science, cooking). See Appendix B for a complete integrated language arts unit entitled Healthy Bodies, Healthy Minds for use in the classroom.

MyLab Education Self-Check 12.6

Project-Based Instruction: An Idea from the Classroom

When studying animals as one of our thematic units we incorporated a project-based activity. When the children had visited the zoo as part of the unit they noticed that there were many parts in poor condition that needed to be repaired. They decided to raise money to send to the zoo to fix specific things such as a bigger space for the lions, some things for the animals to play with that we know they would enjoy, fixing some of the cages that looked like they could be painted and to purchase new bars for some of the cages. The list was a long one.

The children decided to create an animal fair for parents and children to attend. There would be an admission fee to come to the fair which would be sent to the zoo for the repairs mentioned above. They thought about activities to have at the fair and decided they should use an animal theme. They created posters and flyers to advertise the fair. Children were responsible for different activities at the fair as follows.

Three students put on a puppet show about a favorite animal story.

The class made a literacy station with all types of animal books for people to read. They prepared animal games such as Go Fish, Horseshow Ring Toss, Pin the Tail on the Donkey, Leap Frog, and others. The children also had an animal art table with directions for creating an animal collage on long brown paper that many people could work on at the same time.

They played music with animal songs and set up a table with snacks that included animal crackers, goldfish crackers, and a cake in the shape of an animal. To end the fair they had a piñata in the shape of a donkey and people took turns hitting it with a stick. It finally broke and lots of candies shaped like animals came out for the guests.

Summary

12.1 Create a literacy friendly classroom.

The first step to fostering a literacy-friendly atmosphere is to increase student motivation to engage in literacy activity. Extrinsic motivation involves rewards or consequences; intrinsic motivation involves wanting to do an activity for its own sake. Experiences that offer choice, challenge, relevance and authenticity, social collaboration, and success work to intensify a child's motivation to want to read and write. Establishing good reading and writing habits becomes an important element in maintaining and enhancing children's motivation to engage in literacy activities.

12.2 Strategize for motivating readers and writers.

Many strategies can motivate children. Strategies should offer children choices, challenges, social collaboration and successful experiences. Very important to these elements is that activities have relevance for the child and meaning for their lives.

12.3 Create a positive growth mindset in your classroom.

Creating a positive growth mindset will help to motivate children. Before thinking about *what* to teach, it is important to consider the culture within which learning takes place. Classroom cultures that encourage children to take risks and overcome challenges are vital to development. Develop a context in which the teacher and children collaborate, help each other, and share a warm and supportive relationship. The way in which you interact with students affects what they will learn about themselves, about others, and about literacy. The language teachers use with children and the manner in which it is delivered will set the tone of the classroom. First, remember that your tone of voice is very important. Sarcasm and criticism are hurtful, especially for young children, and, therefore, should always be avoided.

12.4 Integrate technology into reading and writing activities.

Technology has changed literacy instruction dramatically in a short period of time. Literacy acquisition can take place in multiple venues, including technology. Because students have grown up surrounded by technology, they may be more comfortable using it than teachers are. Teachers, therefore, need to be proactive in using different types of technology on a regular basis. Computer software and the Internet provide ways for students to interact with content in a multimedia context. Teachers and students can create websites, wikis, and blogs for sharing literacy experiences and developing skills. New devices, such as tablets and digital whiteboards, offer both individual and collective opportunities for digital experiences. It is critical for teachers to leverage the unique capabilities of digital technologies in their literacy instruction. Two ways to do this are through virtual field trips and digital storytelling.

12.5 Explain how dramatic play can engage children in reading and writing.

Although play has been often been overlooked, it must be considered an important activity in early childhood classrooms. Dramatic play settings can be linked to themes being studied and include purposeful use of reading and writing. For example, when studying transportation, having a travel agency in your classroom will allow children to study tour guides, look at maps to see where different places are, purchase tickets, and write out a plan for a trip. Although mostly appropriate for younger children, dramatic play is also useful for integrating content themes with 6- to 8-year-olds. Play provides opportunities to solve problems, role play real-life experiences, work through situations requiring cooperation, and develop language and literacy.

12.6 Integrate literacy learning into thematic units and project-based instruction.

Teachers can integrate literacy instruction in content areas as a way to have literacy instruction occurring throughout the day. Concept-Oriented Reading Instruction (CORI) is one method to develop literacy by activating motivation in science. Other areas through which literacy instruction can be delivered and enhanced include art, music, social studies, and mathematics. Applying literacy learning techniques in the context of content-based instruction deepens the students, understanding of and interest in the content while providing additional practice in literacy skills.

When preparing a thematic unit, teachers should work with the students to select a topic of study, identify questions the students have about the topic, and then identify how to incorporate various literacy techniques. Project-based instruction and themes have similarities. The main difference is that project-based instruction topics will last over a longer period of time. They will also accomplish something real in the life of the children, such as help to clean up after a storm, collect money to improve the playground, etc.

Activities and Questions

1. Create a play experience for second and third graders that will develop literacy.
2. Briefly research a new literacy that you are unfamiliar with (wikis, blogs, podcasts, etc.). Create a lesson that utilizes this new literacy.
3. Write a lesson plan that requires children to use the Internet to find information. Be sure that children are using literacy skills in the assignment.
4. Continue the thematic unit that you began in Chapter 6.
5. Select three objectives for building positive attitudes toward reading. Describe three activities using your theme that will satisfy each objective.
6. Use Figure 12.2 to create a restaurant in your classroom or where you are student teaching. Real-life literacy will occur.

Chapter 13
Organizing and Managing Literacy Instruction

Photo credit: Erin Kramer

LEARNING OUTCOMES

After reading this chapter, you should be able to:

13.1 Explain how to help children manage their behavior in school.

13.2 Organize a literacy-rich physical environment.

13.3 Organize for differentiated instruction.

13.4 Organize for guided reading: Small-group explicit instruction of skills.

13.5 Explain how to organize and manage daily literacy schedules.

VOCABULARY

Differentiated instruction
Guided reading
One-to-one instruction
Small-group instruction
Whole-group instruction

What is honored in a country will be cultivated there.

Plato

Applied to literacy instruction, teachers should note that children will succeed if they know the expectations, rules, and structure about how the classroom works. If a teacher puts special emphasis on the value of literacy instruction, the children will recognize how important learning to read and write is. For example, in the first several weeks of school, Ms. Johnson models organization and management strategies for her second-grade children to use in different settings. Then, she has her children practice them.

When center time is over, the children know to get ready for math because Ms. Johnson claps three times and then pauses. The children clean up and sit at their desks with their math books on top. The teacher continues to clap three times and pause. The children who are ready participate in the clapping until everyone is in their seats. Often, Ms. Johnson checks how long it takes, records the time on the whiteboard at the front of the room, and the class competes against itself the next day to see if it can beat its fastest time.

When it is clean-up time, Ms. Johnson announces that the timer is set for 3 minutes and she expects that the children will be in their seats ready for their next activity when the bell on the timer goes off.

When her children line up at the door Ms. Johnson chants and the children chime in: "1, get ready; 2, stand up; 3, push your chair in; and 4, line up."

When it is circle time on the rug, Ms. Johnson does this rap: "Everybody tip toe, everybody tip toe, everybody tip toe to the rug, rug, rug." They use the same rap for lining up, walking on tip toes on a bright yellow mystic tape path she put on the floor. Children are told to walk on marshmallow feet, and when they sit on the floor they say, "Crisscross applesauce" (i.e., sit with your legs crossed). Different children are in charge of observing behaviors of their fellow students. They put a "popsicle" stick (craft stick) in an individual's pocket on the good citizen chart when they see good transitioning and listening.

Ms. Johnson uses praise to point out positive behavior, such as "I can see that most of you are all sitting in your crisscross position, that is great." Ms. Johnson has many different chants, raps, songs, and poems with rules and routines for station time, guided reading, and so on. She sings to the tune of "Happy Birthday to You," to help children remember to put their names on their papers. "Put your name on your paper, put your name on your paper, put your name on your paper before you hand it in." When an organizational routine stops working, she changes it.

How Can We Help Children Manage Their Behavior in School

The success of your literacy program depends, to a large extent, on how it is organized, designed, and managed. Even creative and knowledgeable teachers struggle unless they carefully plan and prepare the environment, organize lessons, and manage daily routines. This chapter provides models for successful implementation of a comprehensive literacy program. Throughout this book, the emphasis has been on how to teach skills while simultaneously motivating children to want to read and write. It is crucial to know how to organize the instruction of skills into an exemplary day that involves explicit instruction that meets the needs of all children. This exemplary day will also weave together literacy instruction and interesting science and social studies topics that motivate children. The result is that literacy will be taught all day. A list of suggestions follows to help achieve this goal.

1. Teach management routines, so children know how to transition from one activity to another.

2. Teach children how to care for materials.
3. Be sure that children know where to go when.
4. Work on self-regulation of behavior appropriate for school.
5. Prepare the physical environment, including selection of materials and their placement in the classroom.
6. Integrate literacy activities throughout the school day in all content areas.
7. Meet with small groups to differentiate instruction for individual needs.
8. Provide rules and routines for behavior expectations during instruction in whole groups and small groups, as well as in centers.

For a classroom to work well, teachers need different strategies to help children regulate their behavior. For example, when children work at stations independent of the teacher, they need to learn to move around the room without bothering others. At the beginning of the school year, teachers should spend a good deal of time on management skills, so that learning can transpire. When children can follow the organization and management routines, optimum learning can occur (Morrow, Reutzel, & Casey, 2006).

An early childhood classroom should be a busy active place. The teacher needs techniques for getting attention. It is best practice to develop a repertoire of attention-getting techniques. Having several techniques will allow you to switch to a new method if one used previously is no longer effective. A few of the attention-getting techniques that we've observed work well are:

- Ringing a bell
- Using a clapping rhythm
- Holding up a hand with fingers extended and putting one finger down at a time during a count down from five.
- Using a catchy phrase such as "Hocus, Pocus, it's time to focus" or "1, 2, 3, eyes on me" (to which children respond "1, 2, eyes on you.")

MyLab Education Self-Check 13.1

Preparing Literacy-Rich Physical Environments

Historically, theorists and philosophers who studied early childhood development emphasized the importance of the physical environment in learning and literacy development. "Pestalozzi" (Rusk & Scotland, 1979) and Froebel (1974) described real-life environments in which young children's learning could flourish. Both described the preparation of manipulative materials that would foster literacy development. Montessori (1965) depicted a carefully prepared classroom environment intended to promote independent learning, and she recommended that every material in the environment have a specific learning objective.

Piaget and Inhelder (1969) found that children acquire knowledge by interacting with the world or the environment around them. Ideal settings are oriented to real-life situations, and materials are chosen to provide opportunities for children to explore and experiment. Dewey (1966) believed in an interdisciplinary approach where learning takes place through the integration of content areas. He said that storing materials in subject-area stations encouraged interest and learning.

Based on these discussions, any classroom designed to provide a literacy-rich environment and optimum literacy development will offer an abundant supply of materials for reading, writing, and oral language. These materials will be housed in a literacy station. Literacy development will be integrated with content-area teaching reflected in materials provided in content-area learning centers. Materials and settings throughout the classroom will be designed to emulate real-life experiences and make literacy meaningful to children. They will be based on information children already possess and will be functional so that children see a need and purpose for using literacy. Careful attention to a classroom's visual and physical design contributes to the success of an instructional program.

Preparing a classroom's physical environment is often overlooked in planning instruction, however. Teachers and curriculum developers tend to concentrate on pedagogical and interpersonal factors and give little consideration to the visual and spatial context in which teaching and learning occur. They direct their energies toward varying teaching strategies, yet the environment remains unchanged. The environment needs to be arranged to coordinate, otherwise instruction will not be as successful as it could be (Weinstein & Mignano, 2003).

When teachers purposefully arrange the classroom environment, they acknowledge the physical setting as an active and pervasive influence on their own activities and attitudes, as well as on those of the children in their classroom. Appropriate physical arrangement of furniture, selection of materials, and the visual aesthetic quality of a room contribute to teaching and learning (McGee & Morrow, 2005, 1990; Morrow & Tracey, 1997; Morrow & Weinstein, 1986; Tompkins, 2003, 2007). For example, design of spatial arrangements alone affects children's behavior in the classroom. Rooms partitioned into smaller spaces facilitate verbal interaction among peers, fantasy, and cooperative play, more than rooms with large open spaces. Children in carefully arranged rooms show more productivity and greater use of language-related activities than do children in randomly arranged rooms (Moore, 1986; Reutzel & Cooter, 2009).

Studies that investigated the role of literacy-enriched, dramatic-play areas based on themes being used in the classroom, found that those areas increased language and literacy activity and also enhanced literacy skills (Morrow, 1990; Neuman & Roskos, 1993, 1997). These researchers also have found that dramatic play with story props improves story production and comprehension, including recall of details and ability to sequence and interpret.

The physical design of a classroom has been found to affect the choices children make among activities (Jalongo, 2007; Morrow & Tracey, 1997; Morrow & Weinstein, 1986; Otto, 2006). The design of the room should accommodate the organization and strategies of the teaching that occurs there. Programs that nourish early literacy require a literacy-rich environment, an interdisciplinary approach to the development of literacy, and recognition of individual differences and levels of development.

Research investigations have found the physical design of classrooms strongly suggests that, by purposefully arranging the space and materials, teachers can create physical environments that exert an active, positive, and pervasive influence on instruction. Educators must think of their classrooms as places to project a visual atmosphere that communicates a definitive message. The following sections describe the visual presentation of a literacy-rich physical environment to motivate reading and writing based on the research discussed in previous chapters.

Print in Your Classroom

Literacy-rich classrooms are filled with functional print that can be seen easily. There are labels on classroom items and signs communicating functional information and directions, such as *Quiet please* and *Please put materials away after using them.* There are charts labeled *Helpers, Daily Routines, Attendance,* and *Calendar,* to name a few (McGee & Morrow, 2005). Labels identify learning centers and each child's cubby. When the class has children from diverse backgrounds, it is a good idea to label in more than one language.

A notice board placed prominently in the room can be used to communicate with the children in writing. Experience charts and morning messages are used to display new words generated from themes, recipes used in the classroom, and science experiments conducted. Word walls display high-frequency words learned, new spelling words, sight words, and words that feature phonics elements being taught.

Word walls were mentioned earlier. Multiple word walls need to be present in the classroom. Each wall serves a different purpose. Children can use the word wall for finding new words they don't know how to spell. The teacher must use the word wall in lessons, otherwise it won't be used by students. To ensure classroom print is being noticed teachers should discuss and use the print in the classroom with the children. Children are encouraged to read and to use words from the print in their writing (Axelrod, Hall, & McNair, 2015; Ritchie, James-Szanton, & Howes, 2003).

Classroom Stations

Stations in classrooms play an important role. It was discussed in other chapters, but it is important to talk about using the materials in the stations. Stations contain one or many activities that children can do alone or with others. A station can simply be a folder with directions for a particular activity, a shelf containing a few activities, or a chart with directions for a task. Station activities relate to skills being learned in the classroom and have been introduced by the teacher before they are used.

1. Activities in stations are used to engage children in productive literacy work as soon as they arrive at school.
2. When children finish their work early, the stations are areas with activities that keep students productively engaged in learning.
3. Stations free teachers to work with small groups of students in differentiated reading instruction, one-on-one teaching, and assessment.
4. Stations allow students to select and enjoy literacy activities in a social setting during periods set aside to read and write for pleasure and information. The purpose of these activities is to develop lifelong voluntary readers and writers.

All stations need materials that can serve the achievement level and interests of all children in a given grade. Therefore, in the library corner there are books of three or four reading levels about multiple topics and varied genres of literature. In this way, the teacher is attending to differentiating instruction, so that all children can participate in the same activities and be successful. In a word-study center, for example, let's assume there are materials for making little words from big words. With this material, the struggling readers may only be able to figure out two-and three-letter words, whereas a more advanced child would be able to find more words and longer words. Therefore, if the class is studying animals in the jungle and the big word is *elephant*, the following words can be found depending on the child: *at, ant, hat, let, pet, tape, pant, heap, heat, heal*, and more. All center materials must provide for differentiation of instruction in this manner so that all children can participate and enjoy the same activities, improve, and be successful.

The following example shows children participating in functional literacy activities in a classroom environment prepared with materials and space that stimulated reading and writing.

> Mrs. Shafer's kindergarten class is learning about workers in the community. While discussing news reporters, the children decided they would like to have a news office in the dramatic-play area where they could publish their own newspaper. Their teacher helped create the station where they placed writing paper, telephones, phone directories, a typewriter, and a computer. There were pamphlets, maps, and other appropriate reading materials for the different sections of the newspaper, such as sports, travel, weather, and general daily news. The class completed its first newspaper, and Yassin was in charge of delivering the paper the first month. He had a newspaper delivery bag, and each paper had the name of a child on it. As the delivery person, Yassin had to match the names on the papers to the names on the children's cubbies. He also delivered the papers to the principal, the nurse, the secretary, the custodian, and all the teachers in the school. Later, when the kindergartners read their newspapers,

they shared them with great enthusiasm. Each child had contributed something to the paper—for example, a drawing, a story, or a group poem. The newspapers went home to be shared with parents.

The Literacy Station. As discussed in Chapter 11, the literacy station consists of a library corner and a writing corner and should be the focal point in a classroom. Children's immediate access to literature and writing materials increases the number of children who participate in literacy activities during the school day. Both the reading and writing areas in the literacy center need to be obvious and inviting, but they also should afford privacy and be clearly defined. The areas should accommodate four to five children comfortably. The station says to children that as teachers we value literacy by making it an important part of our classroom. The materials range in difficulty to meet individual needs and the different developmental levels of the children. Each set of materials has its own place and is to be respected. The literacy station includes materials for reading, writing, oral language development, listening, and developing word-study skills. The different parts of the center have already been discussed in other chapters (the library corner in Chapter 11, the writing station in Chapter 10, oral language station materials in Chapter 6, and materials to develop word study in Chapter 8).

The library corner in the literacy station should be comfortably furnished to encourage children to linger and relax with books and be decorated with posters that celebrate reading. Children should be allowed to check out books to take home, and materials for active involvement in storybook reading and storytelling should be made available. Multiple copies of some favorite books encourages working with others.

The **writing station** requires a table and chairs, plus all manner of writing implements and papers. Index cards should be available for Very Own Words, and each child should have an individual writing folder. Computers, book-making materials, and blank books should also be included in the writing corner. Display children's writing on a bulletin board. Equally valuable are notice boards—on which messages can be exchanged with classmates or the teacher. Involve children in designing and managing the literacy station. They can help develop rules for its use and keep it neat and orderly.

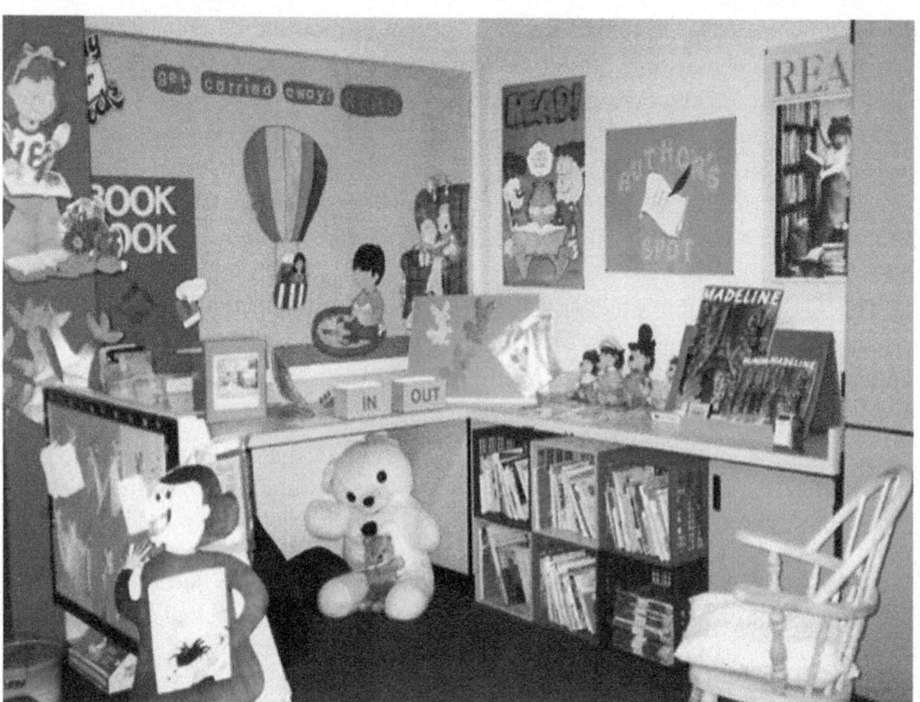

Photo credit: Lesley Mandel Morrow

The literacy center should be the focal point in a classroom.

Literacy Station Activities

Library Corner

1. Read a book, magazine, or newspaper. Write why a friend should read what you read.
2. Partner read. Write what you discussed.

Listening and Reading Comprehension Center

1. Listen to a taped story and follow the words in the book. Draw a picture about the story
2. Create figures for a felt board depicting a story you read or wrote to show comprehension.
3. Draw a picture about a story you read.
4. Create a PowerPoint show about the story

Writing Corner

1. Write a story.
2. Make a book for a story you wrote.
3. Write a puppet show and perform it for friends.
4. Write a letter to a pen pal.
5. Write a recipe.
6. Write a joke or riddle.
7. Use Animoto to make a video and act out the story you wrote.
8. Write an advertisement for a story you wrote telling why others should read your story.

Word Study Center

1. Use a word-study game for learning the alphabet. Write the letters you worked on.
2. Build words with onset and rhyme tiles. Write the words you made on a piece of paper.
3. Make little words from big words. Write them on a piece of paper.
4. Do word sorts for different words.

Interdisciplinary Stations in Your Classroom

Programs that motivate early literacy development require literacy-rich environments that recognize the need for an integrated approach to literacy learning and awareness of individual differences and developmental levels. These classrooms are arranged in centers designed for particular content areas. Stations contain materials specific to topics currently under study and general supplies and resources. The materials are usually manipulative and activity-oriented. They are also designed, so that children use them independently or in small groups. Stations are partially separated from each other by furniture that houses their materials. Stations should be labeled and their materials stored on tables or shelves, in boxes, or on a bulletin board. Each piece of equipment in a station should have its own designated spot so that teachers can direct children to it and children can find and return things easily. Early in the school year, a station should have only a small number of items. New materials are gradually added as the year progresses. The teacher should introduce the purpose, use, and placement of each new item added.

Content-area stations can be created for social studies, science, art, music, math, literacy, dramatic play, and block play. Stations contain materials pertinent to the content area, and materials are added that are specific to themes being studied, such as nutrition or animals. Each subject-specific center includes literacy materials as well: things to read, materials with which to write, things to listen to, and things to talk about. These materials create interest, new vocabulary, and a reason for participating in literacy activities. With each new theme studied, additional books, posters, artifacts, music, art projects, dramatic-play materials, and scientific objects can be added to create new interest. Chapter 6 describes general materials for each content-area station and then discusses additions made for the study of particular themes. The classroom floor plans in Figures 13.1 and 13.2 illustrate learning environments from preschool through fifth grade that will support an exemplary program.

Notice in Figure 13.1, in the preschool through first-grade floor plan, that the art center is placed by the sink for easy access to water. Located in this same area are children's cubbies for storing individual work. Because the working needs of early childhood classrooms are better met by table surfaces than by desks, children should be provided with these storage areas to remedy the storage limitations of tables. In addition to all the materials available in the stations, it is important that each has books and writing materials. The music station, for example, can include picture storybooks adapted from songs, such as *Chicken Soup with Rice* (Sendak,1962).

Figure 13.1 Classroom Floor Plan for Prekindergarten through First Grade

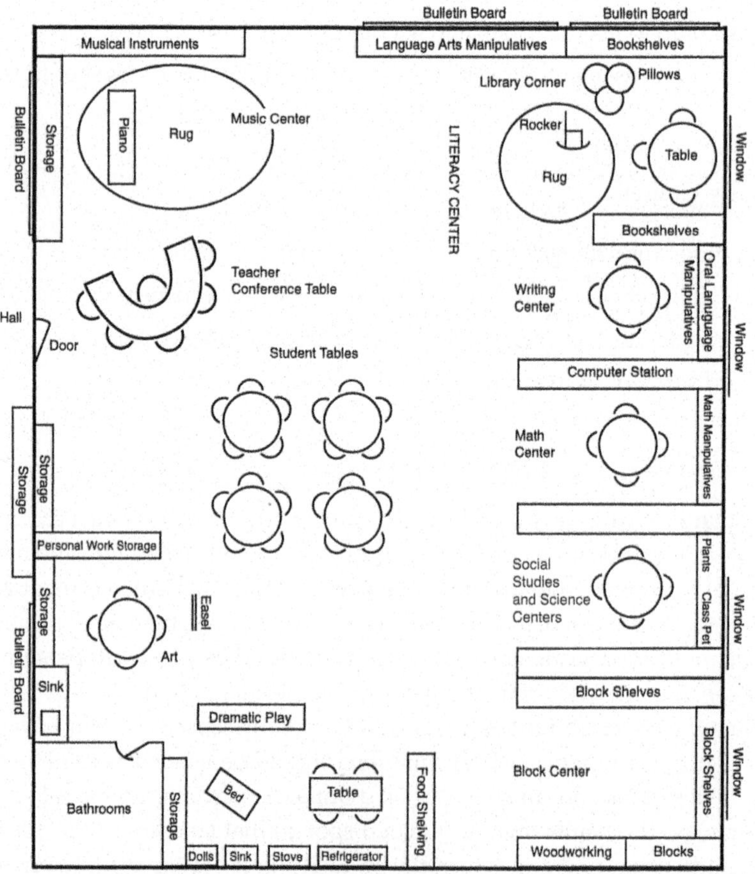

Figure 13.2 Classroom Floor Plan for Second through Fifth Grades

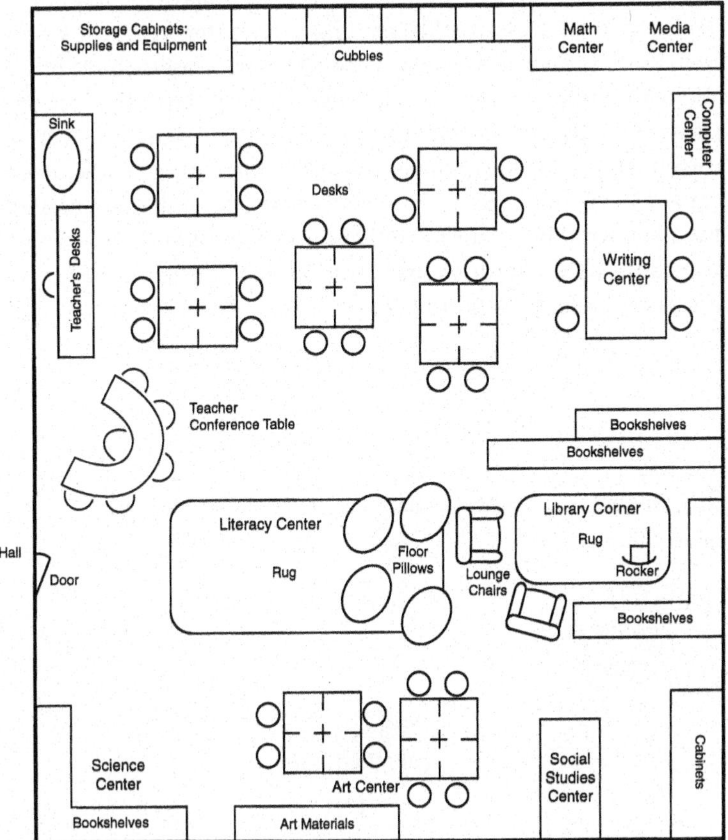

In addition to looking at the book, children may choose to copy words from the story. Certainly, social studies and science centers should hold informational books and children's literature that relate to topics being studied. The art station might have books with craft ideas, including directions and diagrams. Books are also appropriate in the dramatic-play area. If the class is discussing outer space, the area should have books about space and space stories for pretend caregivers to read to their "children." The block station can contain books that help develop ideas for building. Books that contain maps or plans of communities might motivate children to create such communities in their block play.

In addition to generating a rich literacy atmosphere and an interdisciplinary approach, the room is designed to cater to different teaching methods, organizational strategies, and grouping procedures so that the differences among the children can be readily accommodated. The stations provide space for independent or social learning, exploration, and self-direction. The tables illustrated in the classroom floor plan (Figure 13.1) provide a place for whole-class instruction, as does the open area in the music center with the rug on which children can sit. The teacher's conference table is a place for individual learning or small-group lessons. All furniture is, of course, movable so that any other teaching arrangement can be accommodated as needed. The stations are located to create both quiet, relatively academic areas and places for more active play. The literacy station, for example, which houses the library corner and the writing and oral language areas, is next to the math station. Because these areas generally house activities that require relative quiet, they are in close proximity. Alternatively, dramatic play, woodworking, and block play tend to be noisier activities, so they are placed at the opposite end of the room from the quiet areas. The art station can also be a noisy area and is set aside from the quieter sections of the room. The teacher's conference table for small-group explicit reading and writing instruction is situated in a quiet area, yet allows the teacher a view of the rest of the classroom. While the teacher is involved in small-group or individualized instruction at the conference table, the rest of the class is working independently. The table's location allows the teacher to see all the children even while working with just a few. The plan for the physical environment shown in Figure 13.1 is used in many nursery schools and kindergartens and some first and second grades, with the assumption that the design plan is for younger children. Teachers in first and second grade should consider these designs because they encourage literacy learning (refer to Figure 13.2).

Figure 13.3 General Center Materials and Center Theme Materials

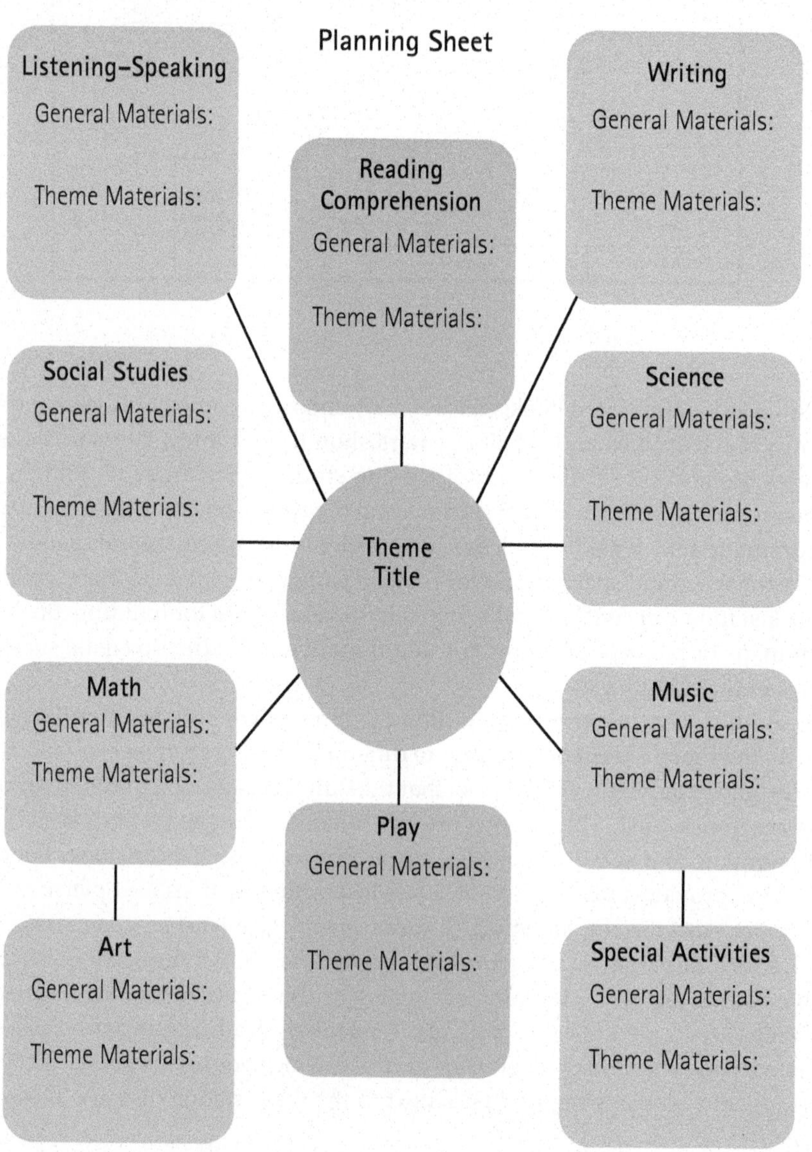

Figure 13.3 is a planning sheet for you to fill in the general materials for your stations and the materials to add that are specific to a particular theme. The checklist in Figure 13.4 is an evaluation form for assessing your stations and the richness of your literacy environment (Worthy et al., 2015).

Figure 13.4 Checklist for Evaluating and Improving the Literacy Environment

Teacher uses the checklist to evaluate his/her classroom

The Literacy Center	**Yes**	**No**
Children participate in designing the center (e.g., develop rules, select a name for center, develop materials).		
Area is placed in a quiet section of the room.		
Area is visually and physically accessible, yet partitioned from the rest of the room.		
There are a rug, throw pillows, rocking chair, beanbag chair, and stuffed animals.		
There is a private spot in the corner, such as a box to crawl into and read.		
The center uses about 10 percent of the classroom space and fits five to six children.		
The Library Corner		
Bookshelves for storing books with spines facing outward		
Organizational system for shelving books		
a. books shelved by genre	a.	
b. books shelved by reading level	b.	
Open-faced bookshelves for featured books		
Five to eight books per child		
Books represent three to four grade levels of the following types: (a) picture books, (b) picture storybooks, (c) traditional literature, (d) poetry, (e) realistic literature, (f) informational books, (g) biographies, (h) chapter books,(I) easy to read books, (j) riddle and joke books, (k) participation books, (i) series books, (m) textless books, (n) TV-related books, (o) brochures, (p) magazines, (q) newspapers.		
Twenty new books circulated every 2 weeks		
Check-out/check-in system for children to take books out daily		
Headsets and taped stories		
Felt-board and story characters with related books		
Materials for constructing felt stories		
Other story manipulatives (e.g., roll movie, puppets, with related books)		
System for recording books read		
Multiple copies of the same book		
The Writing Center (The Author's Spot)		
Tables and chairs		
Writing posters and bulletin board for children to display their writing themselves		
Writing utensils (e.g., pens, pencils, crayons, magic markers, colored pencils)		
Writing materials (many varieties of paper in all sizes, booklets, pads)		
Computers		
Materials for writing stories and making them into books		
A message board for children to post messages for the teacher and students		
A place to store Very Own Words		
Folders in which children place samples of their writing		
A place for children to send private messages to each other		
Literacy-Rich Environment for the Rest of the Classroom		
The classroom should include literacy materials in all centers. Materials should be changed often to reflect the unit being studied; for example, in the science center there should be books on the unit topic, and in the music area, there should be posters of songs related to themes. Play areas should reflect units with themed play and literacy materials. All centers should contain the following:		

Figure 13.4 Checklist for Evaluating and Improving the Literacy Environment (*continued*)

Teacher uses the checklist to evaluate his/her classroom		
Environmental print, such as signs related to themes studied, directions, rules, and functional messages		
A calendar		
A current events board		
Appropriate books, magazines, and newspapers		
Writing utensils		
Varied types of paper		
A place for children to display their literacy work		
A place for teachers and children to leave messages for each other		
A word wall		
Print representative of multicultural groups present in the classroom		
Content-area centers present are: ☐ music ☐ art ☐ science ☐ social studies ☐ math ☐ dramatic play		

MyLab Education Self-Check 13.2

Organizing For Differentiated Instruction

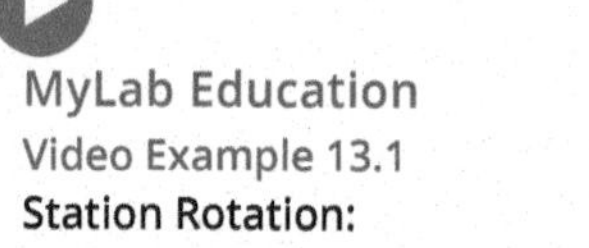

MyLab Education
Video Example 13.1
Station Rotation: Differentiating Instruction to Reach All Students
In this video, first-grade teacher Valerie Gallagher describes using stations to support differentiated instruction.
https://www.youtube.com/watch?v=Kg38A1ggYiE

Teachers need to use a variety of strategies for organizing classroom space and strategies to meet individual needs through **differentiated instruction**. With our diverse population, the "one size fits all" curriculum will not meet the needs of all children (Walpole & McKenna, 2007). For teachers to provide instruction that is attending to the needs of all children, they must assess their students' achievement and then implement instruction tailored to the different needs.

Differentiation can be achieved through individual or small-group instruction and even with the whole class. For group work, children can be placed in homogeneous or heterogeneous groups based on achievement and interests. Using a variety of organizational strategies is important because some children benefit more in one setting than in another. Similarly, creating several different grouping schemes within the same classroom also tends to eliminate the stigmas attached to a single grouping system. Variable grouping ensures that children will interact with everyone at some time in one group or another.

Whole-Group, Small-Group, and One-to-One Learning

Whole-group instruction, introducing information to the whole class together, is rarely used in preschool, as very young children have difficulty sitting and concentrating for periods of time. Whole-group lessons, sometimes referred to as *shared experiences*, are appropriate when information needs to be introduced to all the children, and the presentation can be understood by all. Whole-group instruction provides and builds a sense of community in the classroom. In early childhood literacy development, storybook readings by an adult, singing songs, and short class discussion are appropriate whole-group activities. For the teaching of skills, small groups must be used.

Small-group instruction involves close interaction between the teacher and a few children for explicit instruction (based on needs and interests) and for assessment. Small groups also are used for collaborative projects with children working independently of the teacher. Teachers should use many types of small-group formations, such as reading groups, for explicit instruction of skills. Groups can be based on friendships or interests and academic achievement. In the description of the language arts block at the end of

Photo credit: (left) Jules Selmes/Pearson Education; (right) Annie Pickert Fuller/Pearson Education

Whole-group and small-group settings are used for different approaches to literacy instruction.

this chapter, many types of grouping configurations are included. Teachers need to plan for many types of groups so that children experience working with different peers, which also avoids the stigma or classification of ability often associated with grouping. When using groups, not only do group members need to rotate, but group placements need to change from time to time.

Researchers have found that teachers are better able to retain students' attention in small-group instruction. The small group offers the opportunity for more student participation (Combs, 2009; Lou et al., 1996; Slavin, 1987; Sorenson & Hallinan, 1986). In addition, teachers can change instructional methods and materials to meet the needs of each student in the small group. When groups are homogeneous, teachers are able to provide more individualized instruction at the appropriate level (Jalongo, 2007; Slavin, 1987). In small groups, instruction can be planned for children's achievement level and teaching styles can be modified to meet different learning styles (Combs, 2009; Hallinan & Sorenson, 1983).

There are, however, some disadvantages of grouping. For example, if groups are inflexible, once a student is tracked in a particular group, that placement may never change throughout his or her school career. This practice affects self-esteem and the type of instruction a student receives (Antonacci & O'Callaghan, 2003; Slavin, 1987). Another disadvantage of grouping is that frequently only one measure determines a child's group placement. Often there is a set number of groups, such as three, in which all children must fit. In addition, teachers sometimes have low expectations for students in the lower-level groups, which can lead to continued low performance for these students (Gambrell & Gillis, 2007; Hallinan & Sorenson, 1983).

Finally, working with students one-on-one is a way to increase differentiation. Working with children on a one-to-one basis and allowing them to work independently are forms of individualized instruction. Although children need to work in collaboration with peers and adults, they also need to problem solve and accomplish tasks on their own. **One-to-one instruction** is individualized instruction. As such, it provides an opportunity for the teacher to offer personal attention and to learn a lot about a child. When a teacher works with a child alone, for example, he or she can take running records and do story retelling instruction and assessment. These individualized conferences can determine the type of instruction needed and provide it for the child. One-to-one meetings are usually short, and a great deal of work gets done (Porath, 2014).

MyLab Education Self-Check 13.3
MyLab Education Application Exercise 13.1

MyLab Education
Video Example 13.2
Differentiated Small Groups
In this video the teacher discusses how explicit teaching classroom procedures helps her manage guided reading time effectively.

Organizing for Guided Reading: Small Group Explicit Instruction of Skills

Guided reading is a form of explicit instruction that takes place in small groups that are led by the teacher.

> In guided reading a teacher works with a small group. Children in the group are similar in their literacy development with similar skill needs. Groups have children in them whose instructional reading levels are also similar. The emphasis is on improving skills and reading levels. Children are grouped and regrouped based on continuous observation and assessment (Fountas & Pinnell, 1996, p. 4).

Furthermore, The overall purpose of guided reading instruction is a way to meet individual needs. Guided reading instruction is systematic instruction with a scope of skills and objectives to accomplish. Activities are designed to meet the objectives. Skill instruction is not left to chance; it is assured. Although there is a systematic plan, guided reading instruction should allow for spontaneous instruction when needed.

Literacy instruction is viewed in tiers of achievement levels with regard to the response-Omit this to-intervention (RTI) model. Tier 1 instruction is at grade level and usually done with the whole class. Tier 2, the guided reading tier, attends to individual differences with small-group instruction led by the teacher to meet the student's achievement level. Tier 3 instruction is for those students who are struggling with reading or writing and need more intensive instruction. Within this model, struggling readers often receive instruction in reading three times a day.

For most youngsters, teachers must provide explicit instruction designed to meet their individual needs. This is best accomplished with an introduction to the whole class followed by explicit instruction delivered in small groups or on a one-to-one basis. Without explicit literacy instruction, some children will miss learning many important skills. It is crucial that teachers be aware of the individual needs of their students and accommodates those needs with an appropriate balance of instructional strategies, both explicit and open ended.

Selecting Children for Guided Reading Groups. Small groups for explicit instruction for teaching of reading and writing skills are formed based on similar needs and achievement. These groups are selected by the teacher. When we differentiate instruction, we create groups to be taught with different materials and activities best suited to meet them.

Many pieces of information should be used to determine students' needs and abilities for explicit guided reading and writing group selection. Throughout this book, I have discussed several types of assessment that should form a composite picture of the child to help determine group placement. One of the most important pieces of information is teacher judgment. Other types of assessment that will help to establish group placement include the following:

- Running records to determine text reading level, types of strengths and weaknesses in word analysis, comprehension, fluency, and self-monitoring (refer to Chapter 3)
- Letter-recognition tests (refer to Chapter 8)
- High-frequency word tests (refer to Chapter 7)
- Comprehension evaluations (refer to Chapter 9)
- Standardized test scores (refer to Chapter 3)
- Informal reading inventories (refer to Chapter 3).

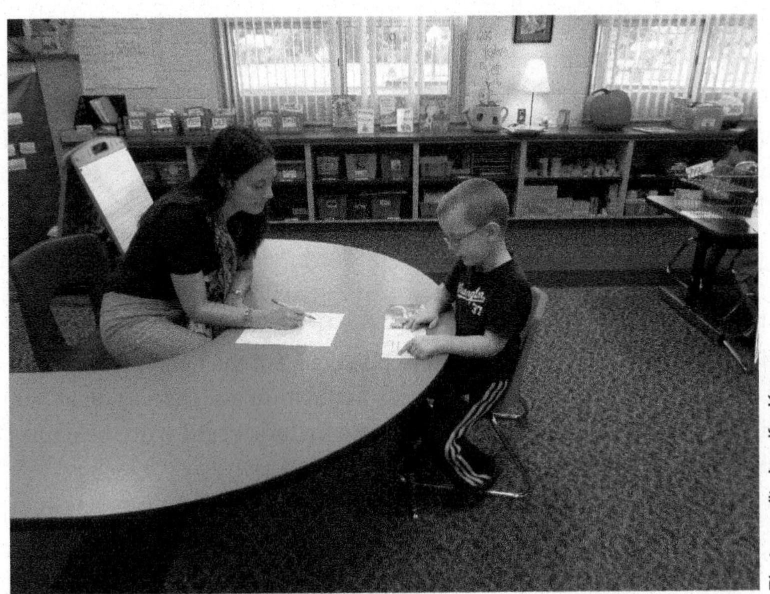
Photo credit: Jennifer Kamm

During one-to-one instruction the teacher does frequent running records to determine a child's strengths, needs, and reading level.

Teachers often use alternate rank ordering as a way to assign children to groups. This method is mainly based on teacher judgment. As the teacher, list all the children in your class, with the child you rank as having the highest literacy ability at the top and the others following, to the last child, whom you rank with the lowest ability. To assign groups, select the top and the bottom child to start two different groups. Place the next child from the top into the group with the top child, and place the next child from the bottom into the group with the child with the lowest ability. Continue this procedure, each time asking yourself if these children are enough alike in their reading achievement to be in the same group. When the answer to that question is no, then start a new group. You should end up with four to six groups for your class, with about five children per group. After several meetings, if the groups do not seem to be right for certain children, change their placement. As children are evaluated on a regular basis, their grouping placement could change. For guided reading in early childhood, children are often grouped based on their instructional level and all reading the same leveled book. Sometimes, the teacher will have strategy groups and they are for children having the same difficulty such as the need for more word study skills.

Managing Small-Group Work During Guided Reading. When the teacher is working with a guided reading group, the rest of the children are working independently at stations. Therefore, children need to learn to work independently and in social settings with peers. It is a time for children to practice skills already learned. When first learning to work in stations, the teacher acts as a facilitator by answering questions and helping children stay on task if necessary. During guided reading and writing, the teacher is occupied with small-group instruction and cannot be disturbed; therefore, the children in stations need to know exactly what to do, when to do it, and where.

To illustrate how teachers manage this time, we will discuss Ms. Shea's classroom. The activities that Ms. Shea models for her class for independent work are often skill and theme related. In the beginning of the school year, she spends time introducing children to the stations in the room and the types of activities they include. She has her class practice working on the different activities. At this time, Ms. Shea does not work with small groups during station time; rather, she helps the children so that they eventually will be able to work independently. The children are assigned tasks and, in some cases, have choices when they complete required activities. The tasks engage the children in reading and writing to help with skill development. Children should never run out of work to do at center time. There should always be something else to participate in, such as select another book to read or write in their journals. Their center groups are heterogeneous; the children move to new activities when Ms. Shea rings the bell. In the following example, all children will do activities 1, 2, 3, and 4.

1. For partner reading, children pair off and read the same book together. One will read one page and then the other the next page. They also may read separate books and then tell each other about the story they read. Because the class is studying animals, children are to select books from the open-faced bookshelves that include stories and expository texts about animals. Discussion about what is read is encouraged. Each child must fill out an index card with the name of the book read and one sentence about the story.
2. The writing activity requires the children to rewrite the story called *Ugly Fish* (LaReau & Magoon, 2006) that Ms. Shea read at the morning meeting. In their rewritings, children are to include story elements discussed, such as setting, theme, plot episodes, and the resolution. They may consult copies of the book in the classroom if necessary. Each day there is a different writing activity related to the story read.
3. The working with words activity asks children to create new words by adding prefixes to word cards. They write the words on a sheet of paper so the teacher can check their work.
4. The listening center has taped stories about animals. For each story, there is a sheet of paper with a question to answer about the story. Two titles on tape are *Is Your Mama a Llama?* (Kellogg, 1989) and *Arthur's Pet Business* (Brown, 1990). Answers require students to give evidence from the text and say what the author wanted us to know was the main idea. Children are to create a piece of informational text about an animal of their choice and include a photo of the animal and music in the background.
5. If all station work is complete, children can go to the art center, which has magazines with many pictures of animals that can be used to create animal collages. This should be followed with the students creating a list of the animals in the collage.

Ms. Shea has an organizational chart that she uses for children to see their station assignments. Just before starting small-group instruction, she makes sure that everyone at the stations knows what to do and is engaged in the work. Then she can begin her guided reading with a small group. When Ms. Shea is finished with her first group, she rings a bell and the children move to the next center, and she calls the next group of children for guided reading. This rotation coincides with her small-group meetings. Children are moving every 15 or 20 minutes which is how long guided reading groups meet for. Every station requires a finished product to be handed in. There is a basket for completed work. The management of station time is crucial for its success. Students must know the rules designated (refer to Figure 13.5).

For stations to work well, the teacher models the use of the literacy activities before they are ever put into the stations so children know what to do. The teacher helps children to get activities started and offers guidance when they need assistance.

Putting effort into helping children become independent when using the literacy center will reap benefits later when the teacher wants to work with small groups for guided reading instruction. The children in stations need to be productively involved in independent literacy activities, without seeking the help of the teacher. To ensure that she can teach the small group without being interrupted, she appoints some children in the room to answer questions and says: "Ask 1, 2, 3 and then me." One teacher had an anchor chart that said, "During guided reading, do not interrupt me unless: The school is on fire, you are bleeding or throwing up, or if it is an emergency of any kind."

Photo credit: Amanda Baker

Children work independently in productive activities.

A major concern during literacy station time is helping children who are not on task. Typically about 90% of a class will work well independently. When teaching the whole group, teachers can't really tell who is listening or not. During station time, it's much easier to see who is on or off task. Be sure those who tend to wander off task understand

Figure 13.5 Rules for Cooperating in Groups during Literacy Center Time

1. The teacher will assign you to an activity.
2. When the teacher is with a small group in a guided reading lesson and you need help, use the "Ask Three and Then Me" rule. This means ask three designated students for help. If you still need help after asking the students, you can ask the teacher.
3. Return materials to their designated place.
4. Speak in soft voices.
5. Share materials.
6. Help others if they need it.
7. Be ready to share completed activities.
8. Record completed tasks on sheets provided (refer to Figure 9.9 on page 396).
9. Keep the center materials in good condition by handling them carefully.
10. Put your completed work in the center basket.

what to do throughout station time. Consider pairing them with a buddy to guide them. Be sure activities have a task to complete to give to the teacher for accountability.

Teachers record anecdotes of activities and collect work samples. They can record the groups at work and also record their completed tasks. Include children in evaluating literacy station time. Children and teachers discuss how to collaborate and the how to complete tasks at stations. Ask students for suggestions for improving station activities.

Teachers often move centers from one area of the room to another, because they find a space that is bigger, brighter, or quieter. They add books and manipulatives to provide more choices for children. Be sure you model how to use materials in stations before putting them out for the children to use. Children should only have about five choices or less during station time.

There are multiple ways that teachers designate what station children will go to. The stations chart in Figure 13.6 is one. The chart provides several choices for three or four different heterogeneously grouped children. You can use a pocket chart to put in figures representing center activities. At the top of each row is a place to put names of children. The figures are movable, as are the name cards (Reutzel & Cooter, 2009; Fontas & Pinnell, 1996). Additional station activities with illustrations for teachers to use are shown in Figure 13.7. This rule means that children with questions should seek out other children in the classroom who may have the answers to their concerns. If they ask three other students and still haven't solved their problem, then the teacher can be asked.

Rather than have students go to a station, the teacher will bring materials to students. This is done when teachers have children sitting in pods, which are four desks pushed together to form a large surface. Occasionally teachers will have an informal station time when they aren't teaching small groups, and children can select whatever station they would like to go to. Using necklaces is another way for a teacher to organize station time. Necklaces are made of a heavy yarn and a star or circle made of laminated construction paper. At each center the necklaces are a different color. There are five necklaces at each station (refer to Figure 13.8). There is also an activity log (refer to Figure 13.9) to fill out when station time ends for children to check off completed tasks.

Putting a Guided Reading Lesson into Practice

Once children are working independently (and with confidence) in stations the teacher can implement guided reading lessons in small groups that reflect the reading level of the group and the skills they need help with. Small-group lessons should focus on a systematic sequence of skills (Reutzel & Cooter, 2009).

Small-group reading instruction in classrooms today is characterized by the following:

1. Children are assessed regularly so that their group placement is in tandem with changes to their reading ability; students are not fixed in one group forever.
2. The teacher purposely uses other types of groups for instruction throughout the day so that students never associate themselves only with their guided reading group. There can be groups for writing, interests, and so on.
3. There is no ideal number of groups; the number of groups is determined by the number of different ability levels represented in a given classroom. Typically, there are four to six.
4. Books selected for instruction allow for differentiation by meeting the needs of the students regardless of their grade level.
5. Small-group instruction is designed to provide children with strategies to become independent fluent readers.

Figure 13.6 Center Chart

Source: Reprinted with permission from *Guided Reading: Good First Teaching for All Children* by Irene C. Fountas and Gay Su Pinnell. Copyright © 1996 by Irene C. Fountas and Gay Su Pinnell. Published by Heinemann, Portsmouth, NH. Reprinted by permission of the Publisher. All Rights Reserved

All figures and name cards are removable and can be changed around.

Figure 13.7 Center Cards

Independent Reading

Listening Center

Science

Math

Figure 13.7 Center Cards (*continued*)

Writing
Center

Poetry
Center

Literature
Circles

Figure 13.8 Station Necklace

Directions: Use yarn or string threaded through a hole at the top to create center necklaces.

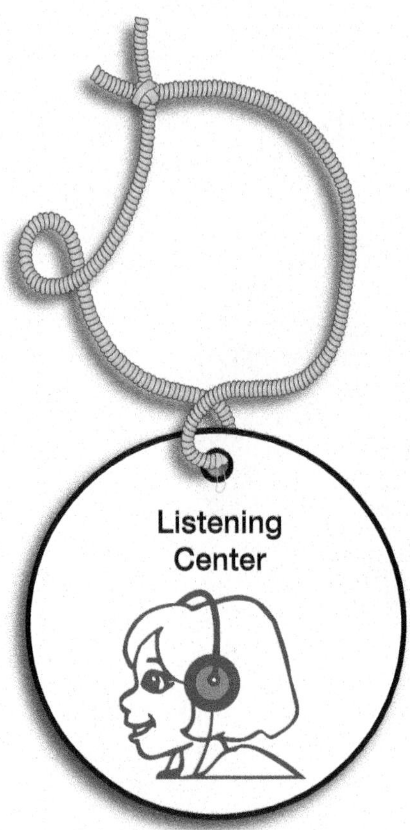

6. Activities provided for children who are not in guided reading groups are often in stations. Children are actively engaged in interesting, productive, active work practicing skills that have been taught. Teachers can use some workbook pages for independent work, but hands-on manipulatives are more engaging.
7. Station activities attend to differences in children achievement, as they can be completed in a more or less complex manner appropriate for advanced or struggling readers.
8. Guided reading lesson last no more than 15 to 20 minutes each.

A guided reading lesson should be carefully planned and deal with skills needed by the children in a particular group.

These components are as follows:

1. The lesson begins with children reading something that is both easy and familiar. This creates fluent, smooth, oral reading with good pronunciation, intonation, and flow.
2. The teacher introduces a new book to children by taking a "walk through the book" that lasts only a minute or two to build some background knowledge about it before it is read. This helps generate children's prior knowledge about the book's topic, which should help them comprehend what is read (Anderson & Pearson, 1984; Jalongo, 2007; Tompkins, 2007). As they walk through the book the teacher can do the following:
   a. Ask the children to predict what they think might happen in the story and the teacher writes down their ideas.

Figure 13.9 Activity Log

The child puts a star (*) in the rectangle designating what he or she will do and a check (√) in the Done box when the activity is completed.

Activity Log

Activities I Will Do and Activities I Completed at Center Time

Name____________________ Date__________

Things to Do	Specific Activity	Done
	Partner Reading	
	Writing Prompts	
	Oral Language	
	Word-Study Manipulatives	
	Comprehension	
	Computer	
	Reading Fluency	
	Independent Reading	
	Other Activity	

   b. The teacher introduced new vocabulary and has the children look at the words in the book before reading.
   c. The teacher introduces new patterns in words.

3. Kindergarten and first-grade children whisper read the book, second and third graders can read silently. Be sure to listen to all your children read out loud often regardless of grade.
4. While the children read, the teacher listens to provide guidance or scaffolding when a child cannot figure out a word. The teacher also takes notes about the children's reading strengths and weaknesses.
5. The teacher may have a different child from each group sit next to him or her during the lesson. This is the student the teacher will take the most notes about, which makes record keeping easier. The next day a different focus child will sit next to the teacher during guided reading.

6. The teacher often writes notes to parents during the guided reading lesson for children to take home. The note suggests homework for the child and how parents can help.
7. A running record, as described in Chapter 3, is usually done on an individual basis. an individual basis. A child is asked to stay after the lesson and read a passage to administer the assessment. Teachers should do a running record with children at least three to five times a year.
8. Children who are struggling should meet daily for guided reading. Children who are on grade level should meet three to four times a week and children who are achieving well need guided reading also and they should be seen once a week.

Each time there is a guided reading lesson, the teacher should select a different child to sit next to him or her. The teacher can take a running record (refer to Chapter 3) as that child reads along with the group. The teacher should also collect frequent writing samples for the child's portfolio and take observation notes about reading behaviors.

Teachers should also use the checklists provided in each chapter in this book that deal with different aspects of literacy development.

MyLab Education
Video Example 13.3
Guided Reading with English Learners

In this video, a first grade teacher models guided reading with a small group of students who are English language learners. https://www.youtube.com/watch?v=7_jXuw_KncO

The Guided Reading Lesson

Mrs. Mede is ready for a guided reading lesson. First she engages her children with independent work. When students are working well on their own, she calls on her first group for guided reading instruction. She begins her small-group reading lesson with a familiar text that each child has in his or her baggie. She calls this "a book in a bag," and every day the children bring it to reading group. She uses a familiar text for fluency, which helps create a feeling of success. The children enjoy the ease with which they can read this old friend.

Guided reading lessons must be carefully planned. The components of a guided reading lesson are as follows:

Before Reading (3–5 minutes). The teacher names the objective or skill to be learned during the lesson. The teacher sets a purpose for reading related to the mini-lesson skill. A warm-up activity is used to review skills and strategies previously taught.

Photo credit: Jules Selmes/Pearson Education Ltd

Teachers meet with guided reading groups three to five times a week for direct instruction of skills. The teacher arranges her guided reading groups based on achievement level and selects the books for the children to read based on their reading level.

During Reading (10 minutes). The children whisper read the book in the primary grades. This is not round-robin reading when children take turns reading aloud, nor is it choral reading. When children whisper read they read at their own pace in soft voices. Older children should be encouraged to read silently. While the children read, the teacher listens to provide guidance or scaffolding when a child cannot figure out a word. The teacher takes notes about the children's reading strengths and weaknesses. The teacher has a focus child in the group sitting next to him or her and takes more careful notes on that one student. The next day a different focus child will sit next to the teacher during guided reading. Teachers who choose to listen to more than one student should limit anecdotal note taking to no more than two students, as quality is more important than quantity.

After Reading (5 minutes). Revisit the purpose for reading or the objective. Students should have an opportunity to discuss the comprehension focus question. Engage students in a brief activity using the skill or strategy taught during previous whole group lessons. Help students refine their practice with that skill or strategy. Be sure to ask students how today's instruction helps them as readers.

Following is a guided-reading lesson from Ms. Keefe's first grade classroom:

> Ms.Keefe believes strongly in the need for small-group instruction to find out what individual children know and what they need to learn. She has organized the class into five groups of four to five children (each who have similar reading needs and are reading at about the same level). She moves children from one group to another based on her assessment of their progress. A typical lesson could be about any literacy skill, such as (1) repeated reading to develop fluency, (2) working on a word analysis skill, (3) developing comprehension strategies, or (4) reading a new book with teacher support.

Ms.Keefe calls her first group for guided-reading instruction. She follows the outline for a guided reading lesson.

Before Reading. Ms.Keefe discusses her objective for the lesson which is to learn four new vocabulary words for a new book they will begin to read. She writes four sentences on the whiteboard, leaving one word blank in each. She asks the children to predict what word might make sense in the blank. She then asks them to write the words on their white boards. They discuss the new words and how they figured out their meaning from the context of the sentences. Ms. Keefe introduces a new book about animals selected from her leveled books and asks the children to whisper read and look for the new vocabulary. When they find them they write them on a sticky note, and when they finish reading they copy the words into their Very Own Dictionaries. She also poses a focus comprehension question to the group related to one of the words, carefully making sure that she can assess students' understanding of the text.

During Reading. Ms. Keefe reads the first page of the book to the children and then asks the group to whisper read the story at their own rate. She listens carefully to support those in need of help. She selects a focus child for the day for which she takes a running record as she listens to her read. The next time she meets with this group, another child will sit by her side to be assessed.

After Reading. The children and teacher discuss the story. Ms. Keefe asks questions that relate to the new vocabulary and to ensure that students were able to comprehend the text. Ms. Keefe prepared another practice sheet with four more sentences that have the new vocabulary words missing. She asks the children to fill in the missing words. A strategy is introduced to help students better use context clues when reading. As the lesson ends, Ms. Keefe writes a short note to one of the parents of the children she sees in a group about his or her progress, what they were learning, what they needed help with, and what their homework is.

MyLab Education
Video Example 13.4
Before Reading
Pre-reading strategies can aid students' in their comprehension.

Guided reading is about instruction in a child's instructional level. However another form of guided reading deals with teaching a specific strategy that children are having trouble with. The following lesson highlights what a strategy group might look like. Strategy groups can be used at any grade level. There is a difference in what happens during the before/during/after structure between guided reading and strategy group instruction.

Before Reading. Set clear objectives and precedence for what the group will work on. Mrs. Mede starts her lesson as follows:

> We have been working on inference questions and answers. Let's review what an inference is and how we might find them. Inferences are clues that the author gives us, but doesn't just say it outright. For example, let's look at this picture (hold up a picture of a child that has fallen off of a bike in a park setting). What can you tell me about how this child is feeling right now?

The children raise their hands and suggest he is feeling "sad" or "upset." Mrs. Medea asks, "How do you know that the child is feeling this way?" One student observes that he/she has fallen off their bike. Whereas another child notices that the illustrator shows tears on the child's face. However, when a child says, "Mad, because their parents weren't watching them," Mrs. Medea draws the group in to say, "It is possible that his parents weren't watching him, but we cannot infer that based on the clues in the pictures or the text therefore we don't have enough information to draw that conclusion."

"Let's try this again with another picture, what clues in the picture can we find to tell us about something this little boy is hoping for?" Mrs. Mede holds up the image. Again, she has the children make inferences based on the picture.

She then begins to read two to three sentences excerpted from various books. Here is an example of how this could be done:

> Mrs. Mede says, "Now let's read some sentences without pictures to see if there are any clues here. This is different than a picture where we can see the clues. This time, we will have to use words to help us. Let's look at this example. Close your eyes and visualize what I am reading. I will read it two times:
>
> 'Where's Papa going with that ax?' said Fern to her mother as they were setting the table for breakfast. 'Out to the hog house' replied Mrs. Mede. 'Some pigs were born last night.'"
>
> She pauses and asks, "How do you think Fern is feeling?" "What information in the text suggests that Fern is feeling upset, but doesn't tell you in words or show you with pictures?"

The teacher should follow with questions that are inference-based. For example, after reading more to give the students additional context and content of Fern's character, Mrs. Medea asks "If Fern were given three wishes, what would they be? What evidence in the book do we have to make these conclusions?"

This would command the students to use text-evidence to support their claims as well as explore character development qualities that the author has put into place without simply stating it to the reader. This 5-minute mini-lesson paves the way for learning about inference.

During Reading. Mrs. Mede says, "We are going to begin reading this book, and you will notice that there is a sticky note on this page. This is where I'd like you to stop reading. If you finish before the rest of your team, you can reread the section again or look at the pictures. Since we are acting like detectives today, you may find clues in the pictures or when you reread the pages." Place the sticky notes at a designated stopping place and include an inference question on the sticky note. This will prepare the children for a later discussion.

After Reading. As the facilitator of the discussion, Mrs. Mede keeps the conversation about inference going as long as needed. She has the children make up inference questions to ask each other and asks the children to describe what an inference means and how making inferences help the students as readers.

Mrs. Mede often sends notes home to the parents about what is happening in school. When the group finishes its work for the day, all members put their books in their plastic baggies with their homework notes. They place their materials in their own box, which sits on the windowsill, until it is time to go home.

The discussion concerning the instruction described above includes practices suggested by Snow, Burns, and Griffin in their edited book *Preventing Reading Difficulties in Young Children* (1998). The guided-reading lesson is changed depending on the achievement level of the children involved providing for differentiation of instruction or meeting their individual needs.

MyLab Education
Video Example 13.5
After Reading Strategies
Using after-reading strategies allow teachers to determine if students are using the strategies they have been taught to comprehend what they read.

MyLab Education Application Exercise 13.2

Leveled Books for Guided Reading

When we discuss explicit instruction and differentiation, it is natural to talk about published materials for reading instruction. Published materials, such as basal readers, anthologies, supplementary materials, workbooks, and so on, have been available for many years and continue to play an important role in literacy instruction. Today, those materials come in a multitude of formats, from print to e-book to software to cloud based.

Teachers select the materials for small-group reading instruction based on meeting the skill needs of the children. There are many texts to choose from, such as those from a reading program or children's literature. Leveled reading books, often called *little books,* are materials used for small-group explicit instruction based on needs. These books have been leveled for difficulty, making it easy for teachers to select appropriate items for particular groups. The texts should be at the child's instructional reading level. (Review Chapter 3 for information on determining how difficult a particular text is for a student.)

Standards have suggested that children be exposed to more complex text that is above their instructional level to stretch their reading ability. This can be done with modeling and scaffolding the text for the children. Teachers can read the story to the children, echo read with them, and allow them to partner read before they read alone.

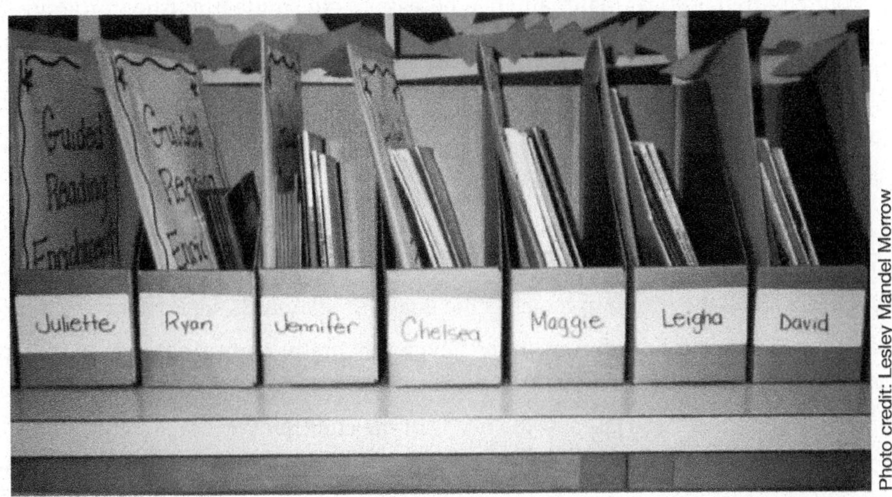

Photo credit: Lesley Mandel Morrow

Books stored in boxes or pocket charts are an ideal way of storing children's literature.

Teachers can read difficult text and discuss it in pre-K through grade 3, but complex text should not be given to children to read until second grade, as their reading is not fluent enough. Reading of complex text is not done daily.

Exposing the children a few times a week is sufficient. Publishers' materials, often referred to as basal readers, have always had grade designations. One problem with grade designations, however, is that, although the material is probably appropriate for instructing most of the children, every classroom has students reading above the level of their designated grade and students reading below. Leveled books take the grade designation out of the assessment. By disregarding the grade assignment, a truer reading level can be determined for each child and appropriate books selected for instruction. For instruction to be useful, the level of the material is critical.

Commercially published leveled books are typically little paperbacks with difficulty levels designated by A, B, and C; by color; or by 1, 2, and 3. Using Lexile frameworks provides a way to evaluate the readers and texts being used together. Lexiles for difficulty are based on multiple criteria. There are quantitative, qualitative, reader, and task considerations (Morrison & Wilcox, 2013: Fountas & Pinnell, 1996). Some quantitative measures include:

- The length of a book, including number of pages and words
- Word length and frequency of use
- Number of different words
- Number of syllables in words

The size and layout of the print qualitative measures include:

- Levels of meaning or purpose
- Structure of text and genres
- Language conventionality and clarity
- Syntactic complexity
- Abstract concepts
- How well illustrations support the text
- Reader and task considerations (Morrison & Wilcox, 2013).

Each teacher needs to make critical decisions about the use of materials in his or her instructional program. The teacher should be in control of published materials and not allow the materials to dictate the teacher. For example, select sequences to use from the material that seem most appropriate. You need not start at the beginning of a book and follow it page by page to the end. Eliminate sections that you feel are inappropriate for your children. Repeat material when necessary. No single published program will determine the success or failure of literacy development with all young children. It is how you use the materials that will make the difference.

Published programs are used by most school districts since they provide an instructional plan along with the materials. Some general rules should be applied to the selection and use of commercial materials:

1. Study the objectives for the published program and determine if they incorporate the latest findings on strategies for nurturing early literacy.
2. Determine if the program matches the goals for standards set forth by the district.
3. Determine if the program includes developmentally appropriate practice as you view it in your district.
4. Ensure that the materials suit the needs of the children you teach.
5. Urban and rural children may need materials different from children in suburban settings. Are there materials suited for children who speak English as a second language?

6. Examine the materials for clarity, appeal to children, and durability.
7. Analyze the teacher's editions for clarity of objectives, descriptions of plans, suitability of lesson content, and flexibility for teachers in using the material. The program should put the teacher in charge of the materials; the materials should not dictate to the teacher.
8. Are there ample leveled books at all grades to meet the different needs of all children? In addition, ask the following questions about the published materials:

    1. Are technology components available?
    2. Are there practice materials?
    3. Do the books have adequate multicultural representation?
    4. Are a variety of genres, including ample expository and narrative texts, fables, folktales, poetry, and so on, presented in the books?
    5. Do the stories link to other content areas?
    6. Are there manipulative and independent activities for centers and independent work?
    7. Does the assessment component meet district needs?
    8. Are there plans for organizing and managing the delivery of the program?
    9. Does the teacher have to follow a script or can he or she use the materials to meet the needs of his or her class?
    10. Is there an intervention program for struggling readers?
    11. Does the publishing company provide adequate professional development with the program?

Answering those questions thoughtfully will help you determine if a publisher's program is right for your classroom.

Remember that a publisher's program is never the entire literacy program. Children need to read a great deal of literature aside from what is included in basal readers and practice phonics with more than a published workbook. Children need to read multiple genres and at multiple levels. Children need to make choices about what they read. Without published programs teachers may feel there isn't enough direction for them when teaching reading. Such programs often feel too prescriptive. Teachers need to find the appropriate balance for successful literacy development.

MyLab Education Self-Check 13.4

Organizing And Managing Daily Literacy Schedules

Scheduling the daily routine in nursery school, kindergarten, and first, second, and third grades must take into account the social, emotional, physical, and intellectual levels of the children. It must also reflect the best from theorists' models of early childhood education, including those of Piaget, Froebel, Dewey, Montessori, and Vygotsky. The environment should be prepared so that learning can take place naturally but with the guidance and instruction that will help children achieve their fullest potential.

Young children cannot sit for long periods, so their schedule needs to vary. Whole-class lessons that require sitting and listening must be few and short. Children need large blocks of time for exploring environments. They need play situations, manipulative materials, learning stations, and outdoor areas. Activities that require sitting and listening need to be followed by ones that allow movement. Quiet times must be followed by noisier times. To nurture literacy, the teacher must allow for rich literacy experiences throughout the day—experiences in using and enjoying language in all its forms and functions.

When scheduling literacy instruction, keep in mind that children should participate in whole group, small-group, and independent reading and writing. They need to engage in interactive reading and writing, independent, and guided reading and writing. They must read out loud and read silently. Teachers should prepare lessons that include explicit instruction and give children the opportunity for self-directed activities. From time to time, children should have choices about what they read and be allowed to do their work in social, collaborative settings. Being successful in some of these activities is important. Occasionally, children can perform reading and writing in front of their peers. Not all of these experiences may be able to happen daily, but most should occur frequently throughout the week.

Children in preschool through grade 3 should participate in skill development in the following areas: (1) work in phonological awareness, (2) phonics, (3) vocabulary, (4) comprehension, and (5) fluency instruction (National Reading Panel Report, 2000). In addition to workshops for reading skills, there needs to be a writing workshop. The federal government stipulates that at least 90 minutes a day or more should be spent on developing language arts and literacy in kindergarten through third grades. Children cannot be pulled out for specials during this time. The amount of time spent in each skill depends on the grade and the needs of the children. Sometimes skills blend together and are taught simultaneously. In preschool and kindergarten, time spent on lessons is going to be shorter than in grades 1, 2, and 3. Because an hour and a half is suggested teachers do not have to stop there. The most important thing you can learn in early childhood is to read fluently. Literacy instruction must happen all day long.

Standards advocate the integration of literacy into social studies, science, art, music, play, and math. Teachers must intentionally plan to integrate the language arts into these content areas by selecting appropriate literature, writing projects, and discussion topics. In the early childhood grades, the teaching of reading should happen all day long, with explicit teaching of skills occurring in one part of the day, followed by embedding those skills into more meaningful situations in other parts of the day.

Oral language development for example should also happen all day long, but during the morning meeting is a good time to have specific oral language development lessons planned. During the morning meeting, engage in discussion about the weather, happenings in families, current events, or the theme being studied. Use the morning message to encourage discussion and converse before and after reading a story. It should also be a time to introduce new vocabulary. At least 15 minutes should be devoted to oral language at this point in the day. Furthermore, teachers need to have a vocabulary meeting daily since without a large meaningful vocabulary children will not be able to comprehend.

Stories read during the morning meeting should stress comprehension development during reading comprehension workshop by asking the children to retell or sequence events. Build fluency by asking children to listen to the expression used by the teacher when reading. Have the children choral read and imitate what the teacher sounded like.

There should be about 20 minutes of decoding or working with words. There can be a mini-lesson dealing with decoding—for example, and practice afterwards with manipulatives.

Small-group guided reading generally about 5 to 15 minutes per group. For guided reading, the teacher plans lessons that could include word work, comprehension skill development, vocabulary instruction, fluency, or writing. While this is happening in small groups, children are in stations engaging in activities to practice skills in decoding, vocabulary, comprehension, writing, and fluency. Children participate in about three of these stations a day.

Although sometimes there is interactive writing during the morning meeting or writing activities in stations, the teacher will set aside 40 minutes daily for writing workshop. Begin with a mini-lesson to teach a writing skill such as writing thank-you notes.

The sample schedules that follow illustrate where and when specific opportunities to promote literacy can occur. The schedules provide a routine or structure for the day that seem to make children comfortable. Keep in mind that there is not one schedule for all classrooms. All of the skill areas need to be attended to but you will not necessarily do all every day and if the order of the skill development does not work for you, it can be changed. The schedules and descriptions found in the next section were created as a result of classroom observations. They are presented in the following order:

1. Programs for kindergarten through grade 3
2. Full-day program for preschool (ages 3 and 4)
3. Full-day program for kindergarten
4. Half-day program for preschool (ages 3 and 4)
5. Half-day program for kindergarten
6. Child-care centers: full-day program for infants and toddlers

MyLab Education Self-Check 13.5

An Idea from the Classroom

Programs for Kindergarten through Grade 3

The following is a description of a model for organizing and managing an early literacy language arts block, from a study of exemplary first-grade teachers from the Center for English Language Arts and Achievement at the State University of New York at Albany (Morrow & Asbury, 2003). The teachers in the study were identified by their supervisors as exemplary based on observations of their teaching. The exemplary nature of their teaching also was confirmed by other teachers, parents, students, and the children's scores on literacy tests. The teacher in the description (given the pseudonym Ms. Tracey) is a composite of many we observed when trying to discover a model for exemplary teaching. This description includes many theories and strategies discussed throughout the book.

8:30–8:45: Do now

As soon as the children entered Ms. Tracey's class, they began to engage in literacy activities. Each child located his or her name and photograph on the attendance chart and turned the picture face up to indicate his or her attendance. Children who were buying lunch signed their names under their choices on the lunch chart. The children then focused their attention on the daily jobs chart, on which Ms. Tracey changed the children's names every day after school. Those with morning jobs quickly got busy. Damien watered the plants while Angel fed the rabbit. Patty and Ashley worked together to write the date on the calendar and complete the days of the week charts. Kelly was responsible for completing the weather graph and asked Dalton to help her. Stephanie and James were the reporters whose job it was to write one or two sentences of daily news, such as what was going to happen during the school day.

Aside from doing their jobs, the "do now" task was buddy reading. The "Do now" tasks alternated between buddy reading and journal writing. Darren began reading a book about winter, which was the content-area theme being studied.

At 8:45, Ms. Tracey clapped a rhythm that indicated to the students they had 3 minutes to clean up and join her on the rug for their morning meeting. They were to write a sentence in their journal about what they read.

8:50–9:10: Vocabulary meeting

Discussion began with new words learned in the winter thematic unit, which were *glaciers* and *thermal* in reference to clothing.

Morning meetings include messages about what will be done today. It is also the time that Ms. Tracey teaches vocabulary and the children discuss the theme they are learning about—including *frost-bite*, *eastern standard Time*, 32 degrees *fahrenheit*, *avalanche*, and other words related to the topic of winter. Ms. Tracey discussed the words and showed illustrations that helped define them. The children wrote each word on a separate page in their own dictionaries. They wrote the definition of the word. They made up sentences for each word. They drew pictures that illustrated the word and tried to think of a synonym for the word. Ms. Tracey put the new words on their thematic word wall.

8:50–9:40: Reading comprehension workshop

Ms. Tracey then read a theme-related piece of children's literature, called *The Mitten* (Brett, 1989), about what happens to a mitten lost by a child who walked through the woods. She asked the children to discuss experiences they had had in the snow.

(Continued)

She showed the children some of the pictures in the book and they discussed them. She set a purpose for reading by asking the children to think about the story structure—that is, the setting, theme, episodes, and resolution.

After the story, the class talked about the elements of story structure in the book. Ms. Tracey wrote them down on a graphic organizer map for displaying the structure of a well-written piece of narrative. Children filled in the graphic organizer for each structural element.

After the story and discussion children were able to choose a book about winter with a partner and read the book. As they read they are to think about the plot structure and discuss it with each other. Ms. Tracey had collected lots of books about winter that all had good plot structure with a setting, a theme, episodes, and a resolution. She allowed children to select one from the pile with a partner and to use it as a mentor text. She asked the children to read the book together and look for the setting, theme, episodes, and resolution and write their findings in their own graphic organizers that she had given to them. Children were to work as partners. As the children read, the teacher walked around and sat next to a pair and discussed their reading and ideas. When they were done, the class discussed the parts of the story again.

9:40–10:20: Stations and small-group guided reading
Ms. Tracey explained and modeled center activities for the children to participate in while she met with small groups for guided reading instruction. The following station activities were available to the children:

Reading alone or buddy reading: Children selected a book about the theme being studied. After reading alone or with a buddy, they made written recommendations about the book on 5×8 cards for others to read.

Writing corner: In the writing corner, children wrote their responses to the shared book reading of *The Wild Toboggan Ride* (Reid & Fernandes, 1992). The graphic organizers that were previously modeled were in the center to help the children sequence their stories. The children collaborated with a partner while writing. They conferenced after completing the organizer to check if their stories were clearly sequenced and if their use of sequencing words was appropriate.

Listening center: In the listening center, the children listened on headsets to tape-recorded stories. Ms. Tracey had placed several theme-based books of assorted genres in this area. Titles included *The Hat* (Brett, 1997), *Rabbit's Wish for Snow: A Native American Legend* (Tchin, 1997), *When Winter Comes* (Maass, 1993), and *Manatee Winter* (Zoehfeld, 1994). She also made available two digital recorders for the students to record and listen to their own reading of favorite stories and poems. She found this to be a motivating way for the children to develop fluency and expression. After listening to their audio reading, the children wrote evaluations of their reading.

Word study: A copy of the winter words list was kept in the word-study area. Today, Ms. Tracey asked the children to write the words down and identify whether the vowels in the words are long or short and explain why. For example, "frost" has a short *o* since it is surrounded by a consonant blend and a consonant ending. "Bite" has a long *i* since there are two vowels in the word and the last one is an *e* at the end so the first vowel is long. Completed recording sheets were placed in the center basket.

Computer station: Two computers were used throughout the day. This morning, two children were copying winter poems, which had been learned earlier that week. Ms. Tracey frequently used poems along with children's books in her themed literacy instruction. She found poetry to be a rich context for teaching word chunks, high-frequency words, phonics, and rhyming. She also highly valued the joy of poetry. Many of the children had started their own books called *My Favorite Poems*. They often used the computers to write and illustrate the poems they wanted to include in their collections.

Science station: Ms. Tracey was planning to conduct an experiment with the class later in the day. The children would be timing how long it took different frozen items to melt. She wanted the children to think about, write, and explain their estimations before carrying out the experiment. A recording sheet was provided. Their predictions would be tallied and graphed prior to the experiment and confirmed and discussed after the experiment.

Art station: Materials for making puppets were available to the children in this area. Ms. Tracey had chosen three winter stories with well-defined, sequenced plot episodes for use during shared reading: *The Wild Toboggan Ride* (Reid & Fernandes, 1992), *Do Like Kyla* (Johnson, 1990), and *The Mitten* (Brett, 1989). The children selected characters from the stories to make as puppets, which could be used in retellings of the stories. The class was going to work on the puppet shows and perform them for the kindergarten classes at the end of their winter unit.

The children were reminded that they were required to do two of the activities: read alone or with a buddy and complete the writing response. They had to spend at least 20 minutes on each. They then could choose which center area they wanted to work in for the remainder of small-group instruction. Because the science experiment was to be done that afternoon, Ms. Tracey reminded those who had not yet made their predictions to do so.

9:50–11:15: Guided reading
While the children engaged in the self-directed activities, Ms. Tracey met with small groups of students for guided reading instruction. She had organized her class into five groups of four to five children who had similar reading behaviors, had control of similar reading strategies, and were reading on the same level. It was common for the children to move frequently from group

to group based on Ms. Tracey's ongoing assessment of the children's progress. She met with each group three or four times a week for 20 to 30 minutes. After each group, she selected one child to focus on and assessed reading development by taking a running record and listening to a story retelling.

This morning's first guided reading group began with a mini-lesson about attending to print. Ms. Tracey had observed that these children were attending only to the first letter of an unknown word, rather than gleaning all the information found in the print. She also wanted these children to learn to cross-check printed information by checking to see if the word they used made sense in the sentence. She wrote a sentence on a small white board but left one word blank. She asked the children to predict what word might make sense in the blank. She then asked them to predict what the word would look like by writing it onto their small writing boards. They then worked together to fill in the missing word of the sentence correctly. After doing three sentences this way, the children discussed with Ms. Tracey how this might help them when they are reading.

Then a new book was introduced to the group. All of the children in the group are reading at the same instructional reading level. Each child had his or her own copy of the story *The Crazy Quilt* (Avery & McPhail, 1993). Ms. Tracey used a set of leveled books for most of her guided reading instruction (Hastings, 2016). She did, however, use a rubric to level some of her easier to read classroom books about winter. She used the books she leveled for guided-reading instruction whenever appropriate. She did a short book walk with the children and discussed necessary background information and vocabulary so that the children could read and comprehend the book independently. Following the book walk, she directed the children to begin reading. The were to whisper read so Ms. Tracey could hear them and they wouldn't bother each other. Ms. Tracey listened in as they read and guided children when necessary.

After the children read the story, Ms. Tracey praised the use of good reading strategies that she had observed in their reading. She particularly reinforced cross-checking behaviors and attending fully to print. The children then composed a sentence that modeled the repetitive pattern of the story. The sentence was cut apart and reassembled word by word. Ms. Tracey then selected two words from the sentence to be cut apart and reassembled, again emphasizing the need to attend to all the graphophonemic information in a word. As the group was dismissed, each child placed a book into his or her book basket to be read later during independent or buddy reading time. Ms. Tracey kept records regarding the children's performance during the guided reading group on a clipboard. She wrote brief anecdotal notes during and after the group meeting. She also wrote a note to each parent, letting her or him know what had been accomplished in the guided reading lesson, homework the child had to do, and how the parent could help. This all went in the child's baggie to take home. Guided reading ended at 11:15.

11:15–11:30: Cleanup, bathroom

11:30–12:20: Lunch and recess

12:20–12:30: Read Aloud

When the children returned from recess, Ms. Tracey read aloud from *Little Polar Bear, Take Me Home!* (DeBeer, 1996). They did some choral reading to learn about expression modeled by the teacher.

12:30–1:15: Writing workshop

Ms. Tracey started the workshop with a 10-minute mini-lesson about the use of capital letters and punctuation. She noticed during her writing conferences with the students, that they needed review about when to use capitals. Although most students were using periods and quotation marks regularly, she wanted them to use question marks and exclamation points consistently.

She had written a paragraph from *Little Polar Bear, Take Me Home!* (DeBeer, 1996) on the white board. She omitted capitals and punctuation from the paragraph. As a class, the children discussed where and why capitals and punctuation needed to be inserted as they edited the paragraph. The children were then dismissed to get their writing folders. Ms. Tracey gave each child a blank graphic organizer to brainstorm a story about winter that had a good plot structure since it had been something they had been working on. They talked about it first and worked for the remaining 35 minutes. Their mentor books were those they had read earlier as well as *The Mitten* (Brett, 1989).

Children wrote as partners. Throughout the workshop, Ms. Tracey conferenced with some students individually to discuss their progress and to help them plan the next step in their writing process. Because Ms. Tracey's mini-lessons often focused on how to partner together, the children were productively engaged with one another. At the end of writing workshop the class shared a bit about what they had written.

1:15–2:00: Science Lesson

After writing workshop, Ms. Tracey conducted the whole-group science lesson on freezing and melting and freezing again. She had some information books that discussed the process. Each child had a cup to put water in and place outside where the temperature was below freezing. The next day, they would write about how their water turned to ice, what it looked like, and what it felt like.

2:00–2:45: MATH

The science lesson was followed by a 45-minute math workshop.

In math, the children were working on math problems and simple subtraction. As part of their work, they were to write a subtraction problem that included something about winter.

2:45–3:00: Wrap Up

The day concluded with a 10-minute whole-class meeting. They reviewed the day and things they needed to work on for the next day. They sang a winter song called "It's a Marshmallow World in the Winter." Ms. Tracey then gave last-minute reminders about homework and returning permission slips. She asked the children three things they remembered most about reading and writing today and they wrote it on a sticky note to take home. Children packed their things for dismissal.

An Idea from the Classroom

Child-Care Centers: Full-Day Program for Infants and Toddlers

6:45–7:45: Arrival, caring for infants' needs (diapering and feeding)

When involved in these routine activities, caregivers talk to babies, sing nursery rhymes, recite poems, and reinforce babies' responses.

Activity period should consist of play (in small groups or one to one) with blocks, manipulative toys, books, or paper and crayons. Teachers and aides provide language models by identifying materials and talking about their use, as well as providing positive reinforcement for such literacy activities as attempting oral language, looking at books, and using crayons on sheets of paper.

7:45–8:30: Breakfast for toddlers, accompanied by song or poetry

Infants are fed whenever necessary.

8:30–9:00: Free play

9:00–9:15: Cleanup

Washing, diapering, caring for babies' needs. Adults interact with children verbally through conversation, songs, or rhymes.

9:15–9:30: Morning snack

9:30–10:30: Exploration time at learning centers

This time may include a brief whole-group lesson.

10:30–11:00: Outside play

11:00–11:45: Lunch

Conversation involves the taste, smell, and texture of the food.

11:45–12:00: Bathroom and wash up

Babies are readied for nap time with washing and diapering.

12:00–12:15: Storybook reading

12:15–2:15: Nap time or quiet time

Naps are begun with a song and carried through with quiet background music.

2:15–2:30: As children wake, their needs are taken care of again, and a small snack is provided.

2:30–3:40: Indoor and outdoor play

In either setting, adults work with small groups, reading stories, encouraging responses from children, and pointing out print.

3:40–4:00: Group session

The teacher attempts a group session involving singing a song or reading a book aloud. The last 10 minutes of the day are spent preparing the children to leave—toileting, diapering, and general care.

As noted in the introduction to this chapter, child-care centers need to emulate as much as possible homes with rich literacy environments if they are to ensure the natural development of literacy in infants and toddlers.

An Idea from the Classroom

Half-Day Program for Preschool (Ages 3 and 4)

Some preschool children cannot sit very long for whole-group lessons. During these times, provisions need to be made for those unable to participate with the help of the aide in the classroom. As the year progresses, there should be a greater expectation for participation in whole groups, especially for 4-year-olds. Include a theme.

8:00–8:30: Arrival at school and greeting, storage of outdoor clothing
Quiet activities and short circle time to explain new centers and activities for the day.

8:30–9:30: Exploration time with learning stations and special daily activities
9:30–9:40: Cleanup and hand washing
9:40–10:00: Whole-group music, movement, and dramatic play
10:00–10:20: Snack
10:20–10:50: Small-group guided literacy lessons
The rest of the class works at literacy station or on special projects.

10:50–11:40: Free play or outdoor play
11:40–12:00: Whole-group storybook reading using various strategies, including shared book experiences, role-playing, creative storytelling. Summary of the day.

An Idea from the Classroom

Half-Day Program for Kindergarten

8:30–8:50: So Now
Arrival at school, storage of outdoor clothing.
Quiet activities.

8:50–9:20: Whole-group Meeting
Discussion of unit topic new vocabulary, songs or musical movement activities related to unit topic, daily news, planning for the school day.

9:20–9:40: Whole-class lesson
Language arts, mathematics, social studies, or science, varying from day to day, with an assignment to complete that flows into the next period.

9:40–10:00: Small group guided-reading lessons
The rest of the class completes work from the whole-class lesson; children work on individual contracts in small groups or at designated stations (literacy, social studies, science, or mathematics).

10:00–10:35: Station time
All centers open, including art, music, blocks, dramatic play, literacy, science, and social studies. Special projects may be set up at different stations, such as art or science. Children work alone or in small groups independently of the teacher.

10:35–10:50: Cleanup and snack

10:50–11:10: Literacy station time
Children use materials from the literacy center (library corner, oral language area, writing area).

11:10–11:30: Outdoor play
If weather permits, or large motor games in the gymnasium.

11:30–12:00: Whole-group storybook reading
Use various strategies, including shared book experiences, role-playing, creative storytelling. Summary of the school day. Dismissal.

An Idea from the Classroom

Full-Day Program for Preschool (Ages 3 and 4)

Some preschool children cannot sit very long for whole-group lessons. During these times, provisions need to be made for those unable to participate with the help of the aide in the classroom. As the year progresses, there should be a greater expectation for participation in whole groups, especially for 4-year-olds. There should always be a theme being studied.

8:00–8:30: Do Now
Arrival at school and greeting, storage of outdoor clothing. Quiet activities and short circle time to explain new stations and activities for the day.

8:30–9:30: Exploration time
Children use learning stations and special daily activities.

9:30–9:40: Cleanup and hand washing.

9:40–10:10: Whole-group music,
There are movement activities, and dramatic play.

10:10–10:30: Morning snack.

10:30–11:00: Small-group guided literacy instruction.
The rest of the class works at on special projects with the aid helping.

11:00–11:30: Free choice
Play at stations or go outdoors for play if weather permits.

11:30–11:40: Cleanup and preparation for lunch.

11:40–12:15: Lunch and outdoor play or other activities to develop large motor skills.

12:15–12:45: Shared storybook reading
Involve children in creative storytelling, repeated story readings, roleplaying, shared book readings, use of Big Books.

12:45–1:45: Rest time with music.

1:45–2:20: Play at centers.

2:20–2:45: Circle time. Summary of the day's activities, planning for the next day, sharing items brought from home that are related to a theme being studied, songs, story.

2:45–2:55: Cleanup and preparation for dismissal.

An Idea from the Classroom

Full-Day Program for Kindergarten

It should be noted that full-day schedules allow for larger blocks of time and more time for learning through exploration and manipulation of materials. There should be a theme being studied.

8:30–9:00: Do Now
Arrival at school, storage of outdoor clothing. Quiet activities.

9:00–9:30: Vocabulary Meeting
The eeting, opening exercises, morning message, discussion of unit topic and new vocabulary, songs and musical movement activity related to the unit topic, daily news, and planning for the school day.

9:30–9:50: Reading Comprehension Workshop
The teacher reads a story based on the theme being studied and includes a comprehension strategy. The children choose books to read to reinforce the skill and learn more about the theme. The teacher meets with individuals to discuss the readings. The class comes together to reinforce the skill and information gained from reading.

9:50–10:15: Small-group guided reading instruction
The rest of the class completes work from the whole-class lesson or works on individual contracts from small groups or at stations designated for use during this quiet period (literacy center, math, social studies, science).

10:15–10:45: Play with themes activities included
All centers open, including dramatic play, blocks, and woodworking. Special art or food-preparation projects are set up in the art center once each week for small groups independent of the teacher.

10:45–11:00: Cleanup and snack.
11:00–11:30: Shared storybook reading. The teacher uses different modalities for reading stories and engaging children in creative storytelling, repeated story readings, shared book readings, and the use of Big Books.

11:30–12:15: Literacy station time
Children use materials in the literacy station (library corner, writing area, oral language area, and language arts manipulatives), including Very Own Words.

12:15–1:15: Lunch and outdoor play
Outdoor play when weather permits or large motor activities in the gymnasium.

1:15–1:45: Whole-group lesson in science or social studies
A Whole group lesson in science or social studies incorporating language arts, music, or art.

1:45–2:15: Center time (literacy, mathematics, science, and social studies)
Special projects can be set up in any of these for small groups to rotate through in a given week. The teacher meets with small groups for instruction in math or literacy skills.

2:15–2:50: Whole-group circle time, Summary of the day
Summarizing activities that day planning for the next day, sharing of items brought from home that are related to study units, performance of work created by children, songs, and adult story reading.

2:50–3:00: Preparation for dismissal. Dismissal.

Summary

13.1 Explain how to help children manage their behavior in school.

In the first several weeks of school, the teachers must work with children on routines, tasks, rules, use of materials so they can function as a group and independently in small groups.

Children need when to listen and when they can communicate with each other. They need to learn signals for attention, where materials belong, and make rules for themselves. With the regulations set at the beginning of the year, children will have a hard time learning.

13.2 Organize a literacy-rich physical environment.

Historically, theorists and philosophers who studied early childhood development emphasized the importance of the physical environment in learning and literacy development.

Classrooms designed to provide a literacy-rich environment for optimum literacy development have an abundant supply of materials for reading, writing, and oral language. Materials and settings throughout the classroom should be designed to emulate real-life experiences and make literacy meaningful to children. Appropriate physical arrangement of furniture, selection of materials, and the visual aesthetic quality of a room contribute to teaching and learning. Dividing the room into smaller, intimate spaces encourages verbal interaction, fantasy, and cooperative play.

13.3 Organize for differentiated instruction.

The organization of today's classrooms must allow for differentiated instruction. Students can be taught as a whole class, in small groups, or on a one-to-one basis. Whole-group instruction is appropriate when all the children need to be introduced to the same information. Small groups should be used for teaching skills and can be based on friendship, interests, or academic achievement. Students should rotate into different small groups throughout the year. One-to-one instruction is for individualized instruction and assessment.

13.4 Organize for guided reading: Small-group explicit instruction of skills.

Groups for explicit instruction should be tailored to meet students' needs. These groups are called *guided reading*. Guided reading is a technique that allows for explicit instruction in the context of small groups. It also allows for regular assessment and differentiation of materials. Students not participating in the guided reading work independently at centers and stay on task with the help of center charts, cards, and necklaces. Instructional materials should also be differentiated.

13.5 Explain how to organize and manage daily literacy schedules.

Scheduling the daily routine in nursery school, kindergarten, and first, second, and third grades must take into account the social, emotional, physical, and intellectual levels of the children. In the early childhood classroom, activities that require sitting and listening need to be followed by ones that allow movement, and quiet times must be followed by noisier times. Explicit instruction should be delivered in (1) phonological awareness, (2) phonics, (3) vocabulary, (4) comprehension, and (5) fluency. Oral language development should happen all day; approximately 20 minutes should be spent on story time in the morning meeting; approximately 30 minutes should be spent decoding words; approximately 30 minutes should be spent on writing workshop and similar time on reading workshop. Finally, approximately 5 to 15 minutes should be spent daily with each guided reading groups, allowing children to visit at least three centers per day.

Activities and Questions

1. Plan a school day with an interdisciplinary approach to literacy instruction. Select a grade level of your choice from pre-K to third grade.
   a. Prepare the environment to provide rich literacy materials and to accommodate the thematic unit studied.
   b. Prepare a letter to send home to parents concerning the activities happening in class and inviting them to participate. (Chapter 14 shows a sample letter.)
   c. Include guided-reading instruction and independent center activities during guided reading.
2. Observe an early childhood classroom to evaluate the literacy environment. Use the "Evaluating and Improving the Literacy Environment" checklist in Figure 13.4.
3. Review the sample materials you have collected in the assessment portfolio you began for a child at the beginning of the year. Write a summary concerning the child's literacy development at this time and the progress he or she has made in the months you have been collecting the materials; include suggestions you have for his or her program of instruction.
4. Imagine you have been assigned to teach kindergarten in the room illustrated in Figure 13.10. Create a floor plan that reflects the needs of your new class and justify your choices.

Figure 13.10 Room Assignment

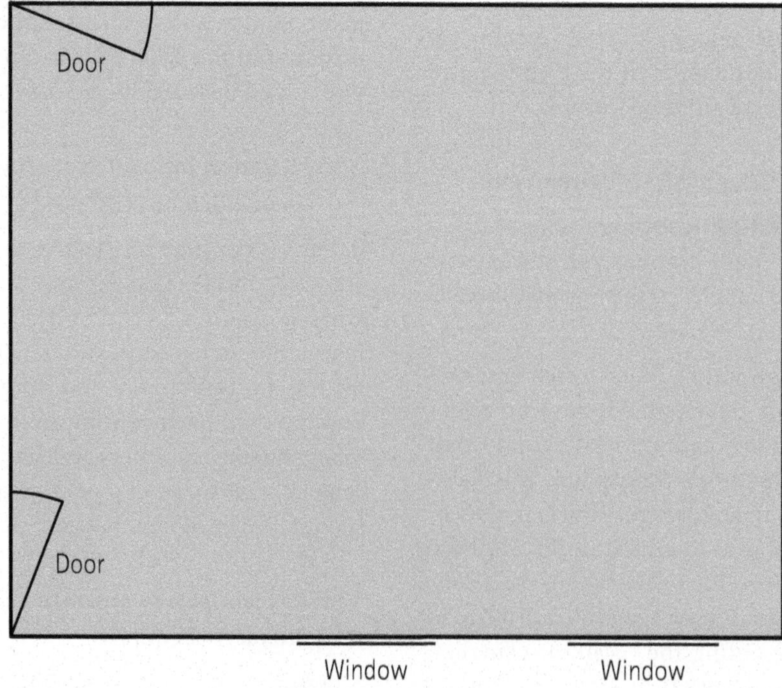

Chapter 14
Family Literacy Partnerships
Home and School Working Together

Photo credit: Lesley Morrow

Learning Outcomes

After reading this chapter, you should be able to:

14.1 Discuss the role of families in developing literacy.

14.2 Describe a framework for involving parents in literacy instruction.

14.3 Identify materials and activities for creating a rich family literacy environment.

14.4 Explain cultural issues that influence family involvement and literacy.

14.5 List methods to cultivate family involvement in literacy instruction.

VOCABULARY

Family literacy
Intergenerational literacy initiatives
Parent-involvement framework

Strickland Gillilan wrote these well-known words:

> *You may have tangible wealth untold:*
> *Caskets of jewels and coffers of gold.*
> *Richer than I you can never be—*
> *I had a Mother who read to me.*
>
> —Strickland Gillilan, "The Reading Mother" from *Best Loved Poems of the American People*

This chapter focuses on how the school and home can work together to enhance literacy development. Teachers have children for about 30 hours a week or 15% of their daily lives. Families have their children for the other 138 hours or 85% of the time. What happens in families outside of school plays a big role in the success a child will have in learning to read. All children need families that talk to them, read to them, provide experiences that build their vocabularies and are aware of the important role they play in helping their children to read. Mrs. Waters is one of those family members that knows exactly what to do.

> Mrs. Waters spread the newspaper on the floor as her two grandchildren, Tiara, 6, and Anias, 4, placed their play dough on the paper. She always used newspaper to protect the floor when the girls did something messy. As she spread the paper, she said, "Now let's see what section of the newspaper we have out on the floor today." "Oh look," said Tiara "It's the food section. It is showing healthy food for the summer." Mrs. Waters read, "Fruits and vegetables are at their best in the summer and we need several portions of each a day." Mrs. Waters always had the girls look at the contents of the newspaper on the floor. The children often would continue to investigate the newspaper and almost forget their play dough or paint. Sometimes they would make figures about what they had just read. Mrs. Waters was taking advantage of the print in her environment that was a familiar part of the children's lives and was making it a pleasurable experience that would enrich their literacy knowledge.

Rianna, a student in one of my graduate courses, shared this family story:

> I don't remember being read to when I was young. What I do remember is storytelling. I remember listening to personal stories told over and over by my parents, grandparents, and relatives that had to do with funny, sad, but all real-life happenings about the family. Everyone took a part in telling the stories, adding parts they felt were missing. This was a special and favorite family tradition that took place every Sunday after church as we sat around the table having lunch in my grandmother's kitchen. I remember looking forward to it. The stories were often the same, but I wanted to hear them again and again.

Family Literacy

Family literacy is the different ways family members use literacy in their daily lives. Family literacy is complex. Here are some descriptions of family literacy based on several sources (Donahue, Finnegan, Lutkus, Allen, & Campbell, 2001; Dunsmore & Fisher, 2010; Melzi, Paratore, & Krol-Sinclair, 2000; Morrow, Paratore, & Tracey, 1994).

1. Family literacy encompasses the ways families, children, and extended family members use literacy at home and in their community.
2. Family literacy occurs naturally during the routines of daily living, such as a "to do" list, and helps adults and children "get things done."
3. Examples of family literacy might include using drawings or writing to share ideas, composing notes or letters to communicate messages, keeping records, making lists, following written directions, or sharing stories and ideas through conversation, reading, and writing.

4. Family literacy may be initiated purposefully by a family member, or it may occur spontaneously as families and children go about the business of their daily lives.
5. Family literacy activities also reflect the ethnic, racial, or cultural heritage of the families involved.
6. Family literacy activities may be initiated by the school. These activities are intended to support the acquisition and development of school literacy for children and families. These activities could include storybook reading, writing, and helping with homework assignments.
7. Family literacy involves parents coming to school for back-to-school night, conferences, and programs children participate in.
8. Family literacy involves parents coming to their child's classroom to observe; to read to the children; to share artifacts, hobbies, and their professions; and to help with center time.
9. Family literacy involves parents in workshops at school to help them learn about and understand what they can do at home to help their children.

Why Family Literacy Is Important

Family members who care for children are children's first teachers. They are also children's teachers for the longest time. Beginning at birth, children's experiences affect their success in becoming literate. The success of the school literacy program frequently depends on the literacy environment at home. Studies carried out in homes have been a major catalyst for new early literacy strategies. Because some children come to school already reading and writing, apparently without formal instruction, investigators began to study the characteristics of those children and their homes.

MyLab Education
Video Example 14.1
Family Literacy
A mother asks a teacher for advice on some reading strategies she can use with her child at home.
https://www.youtube.com/watch?v=PYPLALi4nKQ

This line of investigation has been extremely helpful from two points of view. First, the findings reveal home practices that could be successful in school settings. Second, they provide information on the crucial role a family plays in the development of children's literacy and on how they can help.

I can attest to the vital role of the home in the development of early literacy. From the day my grandson James and granddaughter Natalie were born, their parents and grandparents read to them on a daily basis while the children sat on someone's lap or on the same comfortable couch. They were given the opportunity to look at books. The pictures were talked about and stories read. By age 5 months, James and Natalie would listen as we read to them. We chose mostly cardboard (Publishers call them Board Books) picture storybooks with only a few words on each page. From time to time, their eyes focused intently on the brightly colored pictures. They might be serious or have a wonderful smile. Sometimes they reached out to tap the book or put it in their mouths. They made pleasant sounds that seemed like attempts to imitate our reading voices. Because the experience was daily and positive, they became familiar with story readings and welcomed them.

As James and Natalie got older, their responses to the readings increased. Before they could talk, they pointed to pictures and made sounds as if naming objects or characters. As they acquired expressive language, they labeled things in the book as we read to them. We always responded with pleasure, reinforcing their attention and understanding of the concepts. We often explained things beyond the words in the book. Book sharing was looked forward to; it was relaxing, warm, and pleasurable.

Photo credit: Noam Armonn/Shutterstock

The interactive behavior between parents, grandparents, and children during storybook reading involves constructing meaning related to print.

By the time each of them was about 14 months old, they often sat on the floor reading a book—that is, reading as a 14-month-old child can. He or she knew how to hold the book right side up, knew which was the beginning of the book and which was the end, and knew how to turn the pages. They looked at the pictures and chanted in tones similar to the sound of reading. Except for a few words, little of their language was understandable. From a distance, however, one might think that they were reading. Actually, they were—not in the conventional manner, but by demonstrating emergent literacy behavior. They had favorite books that they looked at over and over again. They asked that the preferred books be read to them frequently.

On the other hand, Joseph has six siblings, both parents work, and there are no children's books in the house. Furthermore, his parents do not speak English fluently, and they had very little education and limited literacy in their first language. Joseph had never had a story read to him when he came to preschool. He didn't know the purpose of books, he didn't know the front, the back, the top or the bottom. He didn't know what print was for. Clearly, children will enter school with completely different literacy backgrounds. My grandchildren will be eager to learn to read when they enter preschool, while Joseph will have little readiness for school.

MyLab Education Application Exercise 14.1

Homes That Promote Literacy

In homes that promote literacy, books are everywhere around the house. They are on accessible shelves in a child's room or in crates alongside the toys. Books are in the kitchen, bathroom, and even in the car. Children in these homes see their parents' books and so encounter both recreational reading materials, such as novels, magazines, and newspapers, and work-related reading materials. Children see their family members reading frequently and at times join them with their own books. The family may use a Kindle, Nook, Surface, iPad, or computer for reading.

In addition to books, these children live in literacy-rich environments where they have access to pencils, crayons, markers, and a supply of different kinds of paper. By age 2, it is natural for these children to pick up a crayon and a sheet of paper, draw a picture, and "scribble write" about it. Adults probably won't be able to identify what the toddlers drew, but they talk about it together. These children are aware of the difference between drawing and writing, and their squiggles of "print" look different from their scribble drawings. Although not capable of either drawing or writing in the conventional sense, they attempt to do both and differentiate between them.

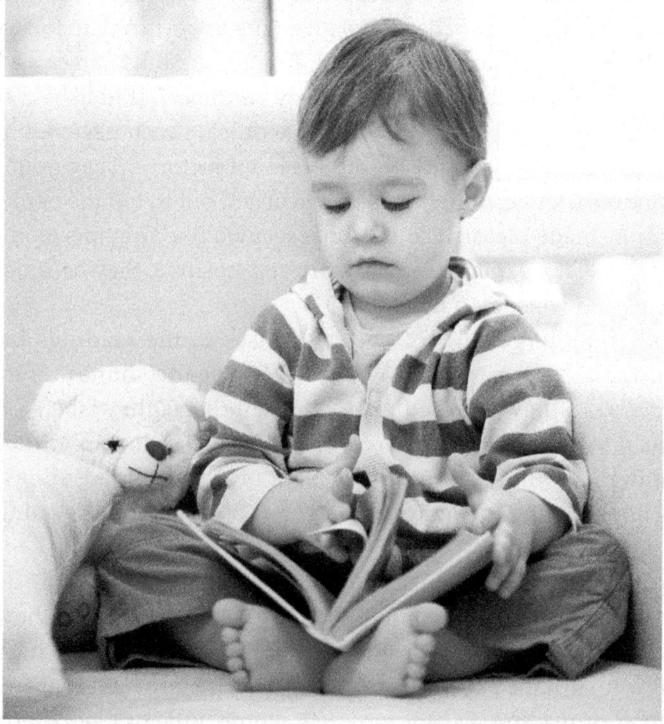

Photo credit: Serhiy Kobyakov/Shutterstock

Books should be available to children from birth on in beds, cribs and play areas. There are waterproof books for bathtubs.

In the house and on trips to the supermarket or post office, environmental print surrounds families. Cognizant of its importance in early literacy development, parents point out stop signs at street corners and ask their children to read as many signs as they can as they drive along. At home, parents read cereal boxes, directions for assembling new toys, letters that come in the mail, and email. As a result, the children's awareness of the print around them and of its functions is heightened. The children ask what labels say and look to print for information. These parents play with language with their children all the time (e.g., "What rhymes with *car*?" or "What other words do you know that have an *S* in them like *snowman*?"). Environmental print is a natural source of reading material which provides literacy experiences with items familiar to children (Clay, 2000; Neuman & Roskos, 1997; Vukelich & Christi, 2009). Families focused on literacy point out the environmental print that is meaningful to children and encourage them to do the same.

By age 3, children from this type of environment have very interactive story times. The child will begin to ask questions and make comments about pictures and episodes. The questions are answered and comments are made by the adult that will expand the language in the discussion. Children will begin to narrate familiar stories as adults read. Occasionally, children will ask what certain words say as their attention focuses more and more on print as well as on pictures.

In this type of home, children will suddenly pick up a book and begin reading words. I experienced this wonderful moment with my daughter Stephanie. One day while driving home from the library, I heard Stephanie reading a book we had selected. It was a story called *Ten Apples up on Top* (LeSieg, 1961). The book used a limited number of words, repetitive vocabulary, and rhyme. The attractive illustrations reflected the text. As she read, I first assumed that the book was one we had read together before. Suddenly I realized it was not. I pulled to the side of the road and with great excitement confirmed what I thought was true. Stephanie was reading on her own! She had made the transition from part-reading, part-narrating stories to reading each word. Stephanie had reached this point in her literacy development gradually. The family offered some informal instruction. Because of her constant exposure to books and print from birth, she developed a large sight vocabulary and a number of reading skills. Her ability to read did not just happen; it developed within an environment that fostered literacy through the guidance and encouragement of supportive adults. (Hindin, Steiner, & Dougherty, 2017).

The Role of Responsive Adults

The family members of early readers answer their children's questions about books and print, offer information, provide experiences that enhance literacy development, and praise children for engaging in literacy behaviors. This support system in the home encourages the development of reading. Durkin (1966) found that families who attempted to teach children explicitly, however, were not as successful as families who simply responded to children's requests for information about reading.

Responsiveness between family members and children should begin early and be cultivated. Language provides an opportunity for developing responsiveness. Responsive adults answer questions and initiate activities that promote literacy. While dressing, diapering, or feeding an infant, a family member should talk to the child, sing, recite nursery rhymes, and tell stories. The baby responds by smiling and cooing, thus encouraging the parent to continue, and a mutual responsiveness develops.

Teaching English Learners

The next two paragraphs discuss home practices that are good for all children, especially English learners.

Family members who provide rich literacy environments provide varied experiences for their children. They take them to libraries and bookstores. They talk to them a great deal, a habit that builds the children's vocabulary. Trips to zoos, fire stations, airports, and parks all foster literacy growth if they are accompanied by oral language and positive social interactions. It should be emphasized that a trip not only broadens a child's experience, but also allows verbal interactions between a family member and child before, during, and after. These interactions include providing the child with background information about the place to be visited and the things to be seen, answering questions about the experience, offering information, reading stories related to the experience, and discussing the trip afterward so that new ideas are absorbed. Children can record their experiences by drawing a picture about them and dictating a story for a family member to write. This will expand literacy growth.

In a series of informal interviews with family members whose children were early readers, it became apparent that literacy was embedded in daily activities that were meaningful, functional, and part of the mainstream of their lives. Various print materials were visible in the homes. Language was used interactively and frequently, and the home had a positive environment.

There was praise for children who participated in literacy activities. In these homes, literacy had functions, such as keeping the house running smoothly. Many of the experiences had social objectives to promote personal relationships and to teach responsibility and manners. Here are some ideas related by these parents:

> To encourage writing and make it a special event, I purchased stationery for my children to write thank you notes and letters to their grandparents who live a good distance away. Writing becomes special when the children do it on their own note cards.
>
> —Lisa Mullin

> I started a baby book for each of my children from the day they were born, with information about their weight and height, and I included pictures. I reported major events, such as first words, first steps, and events of interest to me. I looked at the book frequently, and my toddler would snuggle beside me showing great interest. I've continued the books, which now have become their own journals where they record things that happen to them.
>
> —Used with permission from Stephanie Bushell

> As a grandfather I don't get to see my grandchildren as frequently as I would like. In order to keep close contact, I often send them things through the mail. I'll enclose games cut from the children's section of the newspaper, which I'll ask them to complete. I send them pictures of famous people and ask them to call and tell me who they think they are. This keeps us in close contact.
>
> —Milton Mandel

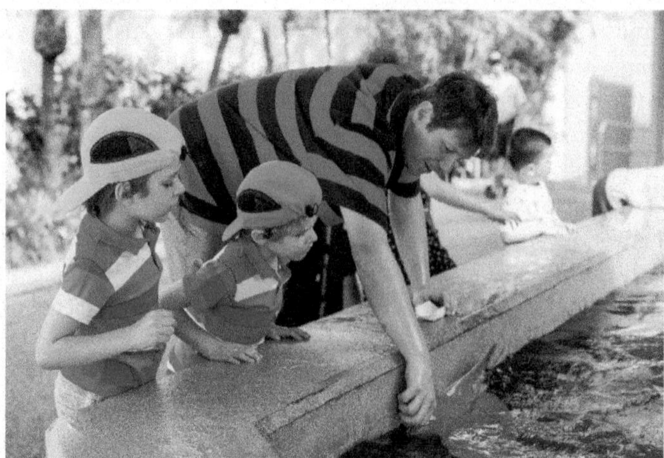

Photo credit: Irina Schmidt/123RF

Trips to interesting places foster literacy growth that is accompanied by oral language and positive social interactions.

I started leaving notes for my children in surprise places before they could read. Somehow they managed to find out what the notes said, even at the pre-reading stage. Now I put messages in their lunch boxes. The notes often just say "hello." Sometimes I'll write a riddle or a joke, and sometimes the note may require an answer. This has become a family tradition, and lately I find surprise notes addressed to me left in the most unusual places.

—Used with permission from Heather Casey

The amount of TV viewing by our 3-and 4-year-old children was a source of aggravation to us. To make the experience more meaningful, we read the television program guide to decide on what programs to watch and to limit the number of selections in one day.

—Used with permission from Michelle Rosen

I've always kept a journal recording my daily experiences. My 4-year-old found me writing in it one day and asked about what I was doing. She wanted to do the same thing, so we started a joint journal. I'd write things that happened to me during the day, and she'd tell me what to write for her. Soon she was able to do her own writing. Sometimes I'd ask her questions about what she'd written. I did this by writing in the journal.

—Used with permission from Kelly Dunston

Challenges in Developing Family Literacy

The pictures painted in the preceding section is the ideal situation for children to grow up in, yet, unfortunately, this type of environment is not always the norm. Today, in about 75% of families, both parents work. That leaves little time to think about literacy. Many children are being raised in single-parent families, leaving the one remaining parent, with so many responsibilities, that time for reading, writing, and talking to each other sounds like a luxury. The number of different cultures in our country is constantly increasing. Many parents speak different languages but don't speak English fluently. There are significant cultural differences in how we educate our children in the United States and how other cultures approach literacy, which makes it difficult for those children and their parents to understand our system. We also have significant numbers of family members who are not literate and therefore feel as if they don't know what to do about engaging their children in literacy-rich experiences. Since many working families are so concerned about feeding and clothing their family members, paying the rent and the rest of the bills, literacy often doesn't rank high on their list. They may not see the relevance or the importance. Some who live in poverty might not think about buying books, going to the library, or even having space for a box of books in their home (Hart & Risley, 1995).

MyLab Education
Video Example 14.2
What Is Family Literacy?
This video discusses challenges for promoting Family Literacy in the homes of English learners. https://www.youtube.com/watch?v=EK8SgpyaGtU

Dealing with poverty in our multicultural society is not easy when it comes to literacy development. However, it is the job of the school and teachers to put forth the effort. What we can do is try to help parents understand how important they are in supporting the literacy development that occurs in the school and how important it is for their children to become literate to get jobs and live healthy lives. There are many things these parents can do to help, even if they themselves cannot read or speak the language fluently.

Differences in language and perceptions about literacy are sources of extreme frustration for both parents and teachers. We plan parent events at school, but few attend. We make suggestions that aren't followed and feel defeated. But if we reach three parents, we have helped three families and then another and another and another. Even little successes must be appreciated for their great significance and potential future impact (Hoover-Dempsey & Whitaker, 2010; Lonigan & Whitehurst, 1998).

MyLab Education Self-Check 14.1

A Parent/Guardian Involvement Framework

MyLab Education
Video Example 14.3
Literacy and Family Engagement
In this video, you will hear different perspectives about the importance of family involvement in schools. How might you involve families in your literacy program?
https://www.youtube.com/watch?v=e_r7urslMIQ

To overcome the challenges educators face in cultivating family literacy, teachers need to create a workable **parent-involvement framework**, or a network of programs designed to involve and inform parents about activities that will promote their children's literacy development in school. The information that follows is a parent-involvement framework that suggests a general mainstream approach to family literacy. However, the constructs are appropriate for all homes. The purpose is not to discourage what is already happening related to different cultures and literacy, but to also include these school-like literacy activities in their homes. This approach can be used with family members who have the literacy and language ability to share the experiences discussed; it also is appropriate for use in the primary language of any family. After this discussion of family-involvement literacy practices, which include basic ideas and strategies, a broader perspective will be discussed to take into consideration families who have limited literacy ability and speak different languages. The ultimate goals are for all parents to be able to carry out the suggestions in this section and to help them understand the value of literacy.

Various researchers have studied homes, in which children read and write early without direct instruction (Leseman & de Jong, 1998). The results have consistently established that certain characteristics are common to these homes. Early readers have family members who read to them and readily help them with writing and reading. These family members read a variety of material, including novels, magazines, newspapers, and work-related information. They own or borrow books, for both themselves and their children. Reading and writing materials can be found throughout their homes. Family members in these homes often take their children to libraries and bookstores (Morrow, 1983; Morrow & Young, 1997). The homes hold ample supplies of books and writing materials, and reading and writing are generally valued as important activities. Books are associated with pleasure, and literary activities are rewarded. The homes are well-organized, with scheduled daily activities, clear rules, and designated responsibilities for family members. They provide a setting where interactions between adults and children are socially, emotionally, and intellectually conducive to literacy interest and growth (Anderson, Hiebert, Scott, & Wilkinson, 1985).

Children with an early interest in reading and writing are from homes where reading and writing materials are accessible. During play, they will be writing and drawing with paper and crayons or looking at books. Family members in these homes enforce rules for selecting and limiting television viewing. Family members talk to each other often and want to know what children are doing in school. These children are rated by their teachers as higher than average in social and emotional maturity, work habits, and general school achievement (Anderson, Anderson, Friedrich, & Ji Eun, 2010).

The following elements affect the quality of the literacy environment in the home: (1) the physical environment or literacy materials in the home; (2) interactions that occur during literacy experiences shared by children, family members, and other individuals in the home; and (3) positive and supportive attitudes about literacy and family aspirations for literacy achievement (Zeece & Wallace, 2009).

Schools and other community agencies need to get information into homes about the need for rich literacy environments even before children enter school. Information can be disseminated at a special meeting for expectant parents, in hospital maternity wards, in obstetricians' and pediatricians' offices, and through churches, synagogues, mosques, and community agencies. A succinct handout such as the guidelines listed in Figure 14.1, Guidelines for Promoting Early Literacy at Home, will be a helpful start and should be printed in languages found in the community in which you live. It is provided here in Spanish and English.

Figure 14.1 Guidelines for Promoting Early Literacy at Home.

This checklist is to be filled out by parents.

Your child's ability to read and write depends a lot on the things you do at home from the time he or she is born. The following list suggests materials, activities, and attitudes that are important in helping your child learn to read and write. Check off the things you already do. Try to do something on the list that you have not done before.

Materials

❑ 1. Have a space at home for books and magazines for your child.

❑ 2. If you can, subscribe to a magazine for your child.

❑ 3. Place some of your child's and some of your books, magazines, and newspapers in different parts of your home.

❑ 4. Provide materials that will encourage children to tell or create their own stories, such as puppets, dolls, and story tapes.

❑ 5. Provide materials for writing, such as crayons, markers, pencils, and paper in different sizes.

Activities

❑ 1. Read or look at books, magazines, or the newspaper with your child. Talk about what you looked at or read.

❑ 2. Visit the library and take out books and magazines to read at home.

❑ 3. Tell stories together about books, your family, and things that you do.

❑ 4. Look at and talk about written material you have, such as catalogs, advertisements, work-related materials, and mail.

❑ 5. Provide a model for your child by reading and writing at a time when your child can see you.

❑ 6. Point to print outside, such as road signs and names of stores.

❑ 7. Write with your child and talk about what you write.

❑ 8. Point out print in your home, such as words on food boxes or recipes, directions on medicine, or instructions on things that require assembly.

❑ 9. Visit the post office, supermarket, and zoo. Talk about what you saw and read. When you get home, draw and write about it.

❑ 10. Use print to talk to your child. Leave notes for each other. Make lists to do things, such as food lists, lists of errands, and lists for holiday shopping.

Foster Positive Attitudes toward Reading and Writing

❑ 1. Reward your child's attempts at reading and writing, even if they are not perfect, by offering praise. Say kind words like: "What nice work you do." "I'm happy to see you are reading." "I'm happy to see you are writing. Can I help you?"

❑ 2. Answer your child's questions about reading and writing.

❑ 3. Be sure that reading and writing are enjoyable experiences.

❑ 4. Display your child's work in your home.

❑ 5. Visit school when your child asks. Volunteer to help at school, and attend programs in which your child is participating, parent conferences, and parent meetings. This lets your child know you care about him or her and school.

Visit School and Speak to Your Child's Teacher

❑ 1. If you want to volunteer or help in any way.

❑ 2. If you want to visit your child's class during school hours.

❑ 3. If you have concerns about your child's reading and writing.

❑ 4. If you feel your child has problems with vision, hearing, or other things.

❑ 5. If you need help because the language you speak at home is not English.

❑ 6. If you need help with reading and writing yourself.

❑ 7. If you would like to know more about how you can help your child at home.

❑ 8. If you want to know more about what your child is learning at school.

Figure 14.1 Guidelines for Promoting Early Literacy at Home. *(continued)*

Fomentar en el hogar el desarrollo temprano de la capacidad de leer y de escribir

La capacidad de su jovencito de leer y de escribir depende mucho de las cosas que hacen en casa desde el momento de su nacimiento. Usted puede hacer muchas cosas que no ocuparán mucho de su tiempo. La lista siguiente sugiere materiales, actividades, y actitudes que son importantes en ayudar a su hijo(a) a aprender, a leer y a escribir. Ponga una marca al lado de la sugerencia que usted ya practica en su casa. Procure hacer algo de la lista que no ha hecho antes.

Materiales

- ❑ 1. Prepare un lugar en su casa para poner libros y revistas para su hijo(a).
- ❑ 2. Si es posible, subscríbase a una revista para su hijo(a).
- ❑ 3. Coloque algunos de los libros de su hijo(a) y algunos de los suyos, incluyendo revistas y periódicos, en diferentes lugares en su casa.
- ❑ 4. Provea materiales, tales como títeres, muñecos, y cuentos grabados, que animarán a los niños a contar o a crear sus propios cuentos.
- ❑ 5. Provea materiales para escribir, tales como creyones, marcadores, lápices, y papel de various tamaños.

Actividades

- ❑ 1. Junto con su hijo(a), lean u hojeen libros, revistas o el periódico. Hablen sobre lo que hayan hojeado o leído.
- ❑ 2. Visiten la biblioteca y saquen algunos libros y algunas revistas para leer en casa.
- ❑ 3. Juntos, cuenten cuentos sobre libros, sobre su familia, y sobre las cosas que hacen.
- ❑ 4. Hojeen y hablen sobre el material escrito que tengan en su casa, tal como catálogos, anuncios, material relacionado con su trabajo, correo.
- ❑ 5. Sea un modelo para su hijo(a) leyendo y escribiendo en los momentos cuando él o ella le pueda observar.
- ❑ 6. Llame a la atención de su hijo(a) cosas impresas afuera, tales como letreros en la carretera y nombres de tiendas.
- ❑ 7. Escriba con su hijo(a) y hablen sobre lo que hayan escrito.
- ❑ 8. Indique palabras impresas en su casa, tales como las que están en cajas de comida, en recetas, en las instrucciones para medicinas, o en objetos que hay que armar.
- ❑ 9. Visiten la oficina de correos, el supermercado, el jardín zoológico. Hablen sobre lo que hayan visto y leído. Cuando regresen a su casa, hagan dibujos y escriban sobre estas experiencias.
- ❑ 10. Use la escritura para hablar con su hijo(a). Déjense notas el uno para el otro, hagan listas de cosas que hacer, tales como listas de comida para la compra, listas de tareas que hacer, listas de cosas que comprar para los días de fiesta.

Fomente Actitudes Positivas Hacia la Lectura y la Escritura

- ❑ 1. Recompense con elogios los intentos de su hijo(a) por leer o escribir, aun cuando sus esfuerzos no sean perfectos. Use palabras bondadosas, tales como: "¡Qué trabajo más bueno haces! Estoy muy contento(a) de ver que estás leyendo. Estoy muy contento(a) de ver que estás escribiendo. ¿Te puedo ayudar en algo?"
- ❑ 2. Responda a las preguntas de su hijo(a) sobre la lectura y la escritura.
- ❑ 3. Procure que el leer y el escribir sean experiencias agradables.
- ❑ 4. Exhiban el trabajo de sus hijos en la casa.
- ❑ 5. Visite la escuela cuando su hijo(a) se lo pida. Ofrezca su ayuda en la escuela, asista a los programas en los cuales su hijo(a) esté participando, asista a las conferencias y reuniones de padres. Esto permite que su hijo(a) se dé cuenta de que usted se interesa por él o por ella y por la escuela.

Visite la Escuela y Hable con el Maestro o la Maestra de su Hijo(a)

- ❑ 1. Si usted quiere ayudar de alguna manera.
- ❑ 2. Si usted quiere visitar la clase de su hijo(a) durante las horas cuando la escuela está en sesión.

Figure 14.1 Guidelines for Promoting Early Literacy at Home. *(continued)*

- ❑ 3. Si usted tiene dudas acerca del desarrollo do la lectura y la escritura en su hijo(a).
- ❑ 4. Si usted cree que su hijo(a) tiene problemas especiales con su visión, con su oído, o con cualquier otra cosa.
- ❑ 5. Si usted necesita ayuda porque el idioma que habla en casa no es el inglés.
- ❑ 6. Si usted necesita ayuda con sus propias habilidades de lectura y de escritura.
- ❑ 7. Si a usted le gustaría saber más sobre cómo puede ayudar a su hijo(a) en el hogar.
- ❑ 8. Si a usted le gustaría saber más y comprender mejor lo que su hijo(a) está aprendiendo en la escuela.

MyLab Education Self-Check 14.2

Materials and Activities for a Rich Family Literacy Environment

Books need to be readily accessible to children at home (Soderman, Gregory, & McCarty, 2005). Family members can create little library areas for their children by placing books in a cardboard box or plastic crate serving as a bookshelf. Books should be in the kitchen, bedrooms, play area, bathrooms, and family car because children spend considerable time in these places. Every room can hold books that are visible and accessible. Before babies are crawling or walking, books can be brought to them in cribs and playpens. Waterproof books are available for bathtubs.

A variety of books should be selected for the home. For babies up to 18 months, brightly colored concept books with cardboard, plastic, or cloth pages are appropriate. They must be safe, with rounded edges, and sturdy enough to withstand chewing and other rough treatment. As the child becomes a toddler, preschooler, and kindergartner, parents should make available picture storybooks, nursery rhymes, fairy tales, folktales, realistic literature, informational books, alphabet books, number books, poetry, books related to favorite television programs, and easy-to-read books (those with limited vocabularies, large print, and pictures closely associated with the text). Children's magazines offer attractive print material and are a special treat if they come in the mail. In addition to children's literature, print material for adults—including books, magazines, newspapers, and work-related material—should be obvious in the home. Some type of digital material for reading and writing is a necessity, as digital formats are a critical part of our lives.

Storytelling is an important practice that parents should consider using to supplement the basic reading of storybooks. Have discussions about stories told in religious books particular to a family's culture. Have books from the culture represented in the home and in the primary language of the home (Carter, Chard, & Pool, 2009).

Research indicates that children who are read to regularly by parents, siblings, or other individuals in the home and who have family members who read themselves become early readers and show a natural interest in books and digital reading materials (Educational Research Service, 1997). This is not surprising. Through frequent story readings, children become familiar with book language and realize the function of written language. Story readings are almost always pleasurable, and that pleasure builds a desire for and interest in reading (Cullinan, 1992; Huck, 1992). Continued exposure to books develops children's vocabularies and sense of story structure, both of which help them learn to read.

It is clear that verbal interaction between adult and child during story readings has a major influence on literacy development (Cochran-Smith, 1984; Vukelich & Christie, 2009). Such interaction offers a direct channel of information for the child and, thus, enhances literacy development (Heath, 1982; Morrow, 1987). Interaction leads children to respond to story readings with questions and comments. These responses become more complex over time and demonstrate more sophisticated thinking about printed material. Research on home storybook readings has identified a number of interactive behaviors that affect the quality of read-aloud activities. These behaviors include questioning, scaffolding (modeling dialogue and responses), praising, offering information, directing discussion, sharing personal reactions, and relating concepts to life experiences (Edwards, 1995; King & McMaster, 2000; Roser, 2010).

The following transcription from the beginning of a story reading between a mother and her 4-year-old son Ian illustrates how the adult invites and scaffolds responses, answers questions, offers positive reinforcement, and responds supportively to the child's questions and comments. As a result of the prompts, information, and support, Ian pursues his questions and receives additional information.

Mother: Are you ready for our story today, Ian? This is a new book. I've never read it to you before. It's about a mother and her baby bird.

Ian: (points to the title on the front cover) Hey, what's this for?

Mother: That's called a title. It says, *"Are You My Mother?"* That's the name of the book. See, it's right here, too: *"Are You My Mother?"*

Ian: (long pause, then points to the words) *"Are You My Mother?"*

Mother: Right, you read it. See, you know how to read.

Ian: It says, *"Are You My Mother?"* (points again with finger)

Mother: You read it again. Wow, you really know how to read!

Ian: Um, now read the book and I'll read it, too (Morrow, 1986).

Ian's mother read the story. Each time they came to the words "Are You My Mother?," she paused and looked at Ian, pointed to the words, and exaggerated her reading of the sentence. After two such episodes, Ian no longer needed prompting and simply read along each time they came to the phrase.

Research findings suggest that teachers should encourage family members to read to their children daily. Reading can begin the day a child is born. However, an infant's ability to listen attentively is generally limited and varies from one reading to the next. An infant may prefer to chew on the book or pound it rather than listen to it. However, babies who have been read to from birth begin to be attentive in storyreading situations sooner than others not read to.

One of my graduate students shared this story in his class journal about his first literacy experience with his new baby. She was born during the semester he was taking a course with me.

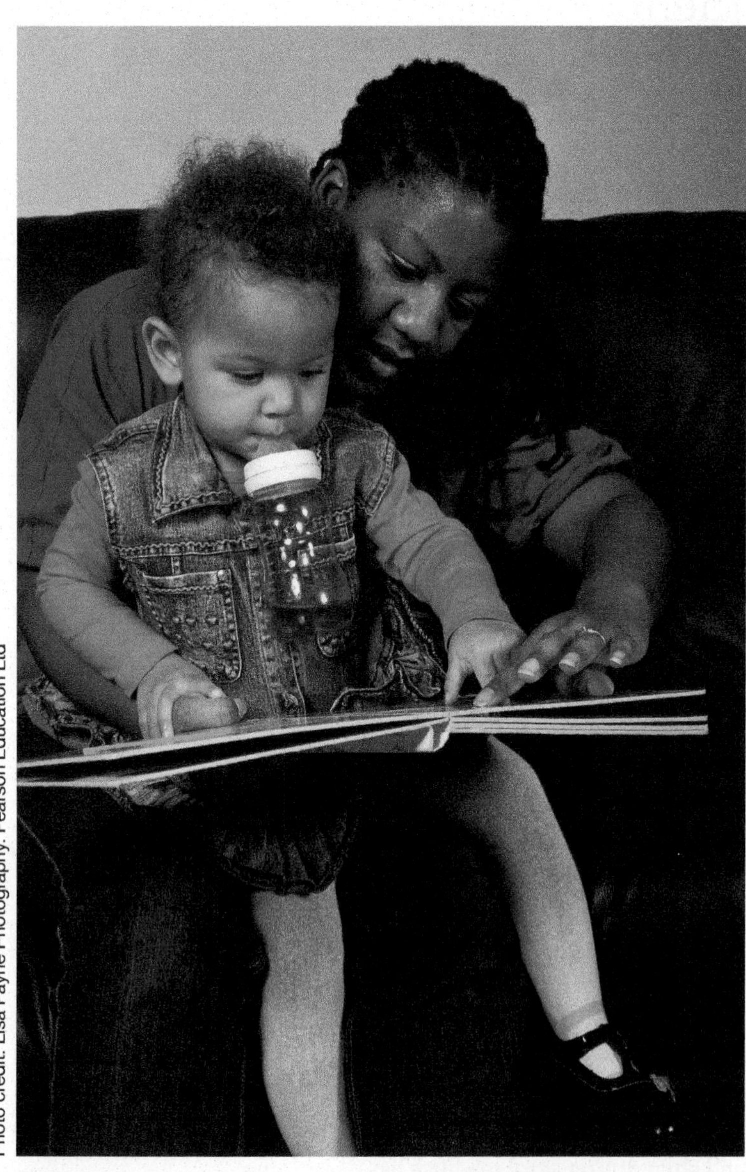

Children who are read to very early in life often take a leadership role in turning pages, sounding as if they are reading, and they become very involved in shared reading.

Our First Literacy Experience by John T. Shea

When my wife and I packed for the trip to the hospital on the night before her scheduled caesarean procedure, one of the items that I included in my travel bag was my childhood copy of *The Real Mother Goose*, a book my mother had given back to me when she learned that she was going to be a grandmother. My first literacy experience with Casey came much sooner than I had expected.

After she was born, Casey was taken to the nursery and placed under a heat device designed to help her body adjust to the change in temperature she experienced at birth. There were some chairs set up next to the heat devices for new fathers. As I sat beside my daughter and marveled at her beauty, it suddenly occurred to me that I could read to her at that very moment. I asked the nurse if I could take a book into the nursery to read to my baby. The nurse smiled and said, "You're the first father in my 20 years as a maternity nurse to make such a request. I guess it's okay."

I was with Casey for the first hours of her life in the nursery, sitting by her side, listening to her breathe, and reading selections to her from *The Real Mother Goose* book. Prior to my reading she had been a bit fussy and crying, on and off. When I started reading, she became very quiet and hardly stirred.

Reading to Children at Home from Birth to Age 8

From birth to 3 months, a child's attention to book reading is erratic. The baby who stares at the pictures and seems content and quiet can be considered receptive. If the baby wiggles, shows discomfort, or cries, the adult might just as well stop reading until the next time.

From 3 to 6 months, babies become more obviously involved in book readings. They begin to focus on pictures and to listen. Often, they will grab for a book, pound it, and try to put it in their mouths. As long as they seem content, they are probably involved with the reading.

MyLab Education
Video Example 14.4
How to Read with Your Child
In this video, the Atlanta Speech School presents four important steps for parents to take every time they read to their children. https://www.youtube.com/watch?v=WTMheEhQq_8

Six- to nine-month-olds can be purposefully involved in story readings. They might try to turn pages. They might respond to changes in the reader's intonation or make sounds and movements to demonstrate involvement and pleasure. They sometimes begin to show preferences for books that have been read to them before.

One-year-old babies will show strong involvement in being read to. They might take a leadership role in turning pages or babble along in tones that sound like reading. They actively look in the book for familiar things that they remember from other readings.

By 15 months, babies who have been read to can tell which is the front and which is the back of a book and if the book is right side up. They begin to identify and name characters in the book. They read along with the adult, including verbalizing (Burns, Snow, & Griffin, 1999; Schickedanz & Collins, 2013). They show book preferences at this age when they have been read to.

Fathers, mothers, grandparents, babysitters, and older siblings should all read to younger children. Let reading become a ritual, done at the same time and in the same place each day. Bedtime is a favorite time, and bedtime stories are a good reading habit to establish. Both child and family members look forward to it as a time to share at the end of the day. Reading before children go to sleep has a calming effect; it establishes a routine for the children, who will eventually read by themselves before going to bed.

Spontaneous readings are encouraged as well, and if a family member finds it easier to read at different times of the day, it is certainly more desirable to do this than not to read at all. Reading to babies requires that the infant be held in the family member's arms. When the youngster is able to sit up alone, the family member and the child

Photo credit: Cathy Yeulet/123RF

Fathers, mothers, siblings, grandparents, and great-grandparents should read together with young children.

should be close to each other, preferably with the child on the adult's lap. The book with its pictures and print must be visible to the child. Children should be considered active participants in the story reading. Their comments and questions should be encouraged and acknowledged. Family members should relate comments about the story to life experiences whenever possible and question children about familiar things in a relaxed manner to encourage their involvement.

Reading to children does not end when they begin to read themselves. This is a crucial time to continue to support and guide them in this activity. When children are able to read, the bedtime story tradition can change to the child's reading to the family member. Or it can continue with the family's reading books above the reading level of the child. Six- to eight-year-olds are often interested in books with chapters, but are not yet ready to read them themselves. Family members can take this opportunity to share more grown-up pieces of literature with these youngsters to encourage their interest. Another important parent motivation is making sure that children have new material to read that is always accessible and of interest to them. Sometimes families must continually put new books right in their hands, even as they grow older and seem to have the reading habit established. Be sure to let them help select books to read. It shouldn't always be a narrative story. Informational books are very interesting to children, and newspaper or magazine articles are a good idea too. They encourage a great deal of conversation and provide information.

In addition to reading to their children and reading themselves, families should provide time to sit around the kitchen table together, or in any place comfortable in their home, and read. Each person reads his or her own book. Talking about what family members are reading is an important experience as well.

MyLab Education Application Exercise 14.2

Materials for Writing in the Home

Teaching English Learners

Families of English learners may know less about how to encourage emergent writing. Be prepared to suggest ways EL families can support writing development.

Some researchers have suggested that writing develops before reading. Many children invent writing systems of their own that seem to have meaning for them. Whether reading comes before writing or writing before reading is an unsettled issue. What is known, however, is that learning to read is enhanced by concurrent experiences with writing and that the development of writing is facilitated by experiences with reading (McGee & Richgels, 2008; Schickedanz & Casbergue, 2009).

One implication of these findings is that writing materials should be made available for children at home. Unlined white paper in various sizes is preferable, especially for babies. As children become preschoolers, smaller sheets can be added to the household supply. A child in kindergarten might like lined paper. Pencils, crayons, colored pencils, a chalkboard and chalk, and white slates and markers are appropriate home writing tools. Manipulatives such as magnetic, felt, or wooden letters are also useful. Children should have access to them early. In addition, home computers encourage writing and are appropriate for preschoolers. There are many websites for children that promote reading and writing (see Appendix C).

As with book reading, youngsters need to see their families involved in writing activities. Family members should communicate with their children through writing as often as possible. When children begin preschool, notes can be placed in lunch boxes that say simply "Hi! Love, Mommy and Daddy." Notes on pillows can say "Good night" or "Good morning."

Make writing a family event whenever possible. Families can write thank-you notes and letters together. They can fill out school forms with children or make up the family grocery list together. Children will emulate family members who communicate through writing.

Technology Ideas

Television is part of our lives. To make the most of TV viewing, families should watch some programs with their youngsters, posing questions, raising critical issues, and changing passive viewing into responsive interaction. They should also choose programs that celebrate books, such as *Sesame Street* or *Clifford*. When stories are scheduled on television, such as *The Grinch Who Stole Christmas* (Seuss, 1957a), families can purchase, download, or borrow the book from the library before viewing.

Computers, iPads, iPhones, Kindles, Nooks, Surfaces, and others tablet devices allow children to experience books in a multimedia context. Those same digital devices, however, offer opportunities to play online computer and video games which, if not monitored, can become the primary activity on the device. Adults should carefully review and select the games and then play them with their children. Time spent watching television and viewing and playing DVDs and video games should be limited.

A strong way to integrate technology and literacy is to create a family website and have everyone contribute something to it every week. At the end of the week, review what has been contributed to the site. Use a free program called Padlet to post notes to each other that call for a response or that are clues to family scavenger-hunt games. (Marsh, Hannon, Lewis, & Ritchie, 2017).

Literacy Activities to Do at Home

Every year at back-to-school night, I hand out a sheet to parents, reproduced as Figure 14.2, called "Top 10 Things to Do with Your Child at Home." I tell them that doing about three of the ten activities a week and reading to your child daily is as important as them coming to school. If parents engage children at home with these activities, children will improve and succeed at school. In addition, children leave a hand-made bookmark for their family. Plans for making the bookmark are shown in Figure 14.3.

Figure 14.2 Top 10 Things to Do with Your Child at Home

Top 10 Things to Do with Your Child at Home

Here are fun and easy ways you can promote reading and writing at home.

Read to and with your child. Talk about books or other reading material with your child.

Leave a note in child's lunchbox.

Help your child with homework.

Talk about your day or share stories at mealtime.

Discuss or retell plots from television programs.

Keep a parent and child journal. Share writing.

Keep a chart of chores. Keep lists, such as grocery lists.

Create a library in your home and visit a library.

Cook with your family following a recipe.

Record family trips.

Figure 14.3 Bookmarks for the Family

Directions: Copy on colored paper. Paste the poem on the front and "Choosing a Just-Right Book" on the back. Laminate. Give them to parents and children as gifts.

Before you go to sleep tonight, read a book, then turn out the light.

Choosing a Just-Right Book

1. Look at the cover.
2. Read the title and the author.
3. Read the blurb on the back cover. (Does the book interest you?)
4. Flip through the book.
5. Read the first page and use the Five Finger Rule.

If you come across a word that you don't know, put a finger down. Determine if this book is good for you:

0–1 finger - Too Easy

2–3 fingers - Just Right

4–5 fingers - Too Hard

MyLab Education Self-Check 14.3

Multicultural Perspectives on Family Involvement and Family Literacy

In this chapter, family literacy has been approached from the perspective of family members helping children to support their reading and writing development on their own or as a result of involvement in literacy activities at school. Many families in our country, however, do not speak English and so are unable to help their children in the ways that schools may suggest. In addition, many families have limited literacy ability and, although eager to help, cannot do so with the suggestions that might typically come from school. In some cases, the parent is a teenager who has dropped out of school. Therefore, when we speak of family literacy, in many situations we need to recognize that it must be an intergenerational matter in which environments are created to enable adult learners to enhance their own literacy and at the same time promote the literacy of their children.

Teaching English Learners

Be aware that many families don't speak English and that the adults are English learners as well as the children.

There is evidence that many low-income, minority, and immigrant families cultivate rich contexts for literacy development. Their efforts are different from the school model to which we are accustomed. We must learn from and respect families and children from cultures in which books are not readily available, although evidence of literacy activity, such as storytelling, singing, and reading and discussing the Bible and other religious materials, exists (Schrodt, Fain, & Hasty, 2015; Morrow, 1995).

Research shows that the types and forms of literacy practiced in some homes are different from those that children encounter in school (Heath, 1983; Paratore, Melzi, & Krol-Sinclair, 2003). Although literacy activity is present in one form or another in most families, the particular kinds of events that some family members or caregivers share with children may have a great deal of influence on school success. Conversely, the kinds of literacy practiced in classrooms may not be meaningful for some children outside of school (Auerbach, 1989; Bryant & Maxwell, 1997). Family literacy must be approached to avoid cultural bias, and intervention must be supportive rather than intrusive. (Salinas, Pérez-Granados, Feldman, & Huffman, 2017).

Researchers are interested in advancing an understanding of the ways in which literacy is used within families. In these studies, emphasis is placed on the richness of one's heritage and experiences, rather than on perceived educational deficits. In some cases, researchers are exploring literacy events that occur naturally within diverse families. In other cases, researchers are describing the effects family literacy has on children's developing concepts about reading and writing. With the knowledge gained from such studies, educators can better understand the literacies that exist in diverse families and can help make literacy instruction in school more meaningful for both family members and children.

Delgado-Gaitan (1992) carried out a study to determine the attitudes of Mexican American families toward the education of their children and the roles played by these families. A major goal was to observe and describe the physical surroundings, emotional and motivational climates, and interpersonal interactions between parent and child. Results of the study demonstrated that the Mexican American parents provided special areas for study for their children, in spite of space limitations. The parents wanted their children to succeed in school. Parents sought the help of friends, relatives, and others to assist them or their children with school-related matters. Parents punished their children for poor grades and rewarded them for doing well. All parents believed that a person cannot be considered well educated through "book learning" alone, but also must learn to be respectful, well-mannered, and helpful to others. Family stories about life in Mexico guided the children's moral learning.

From the findings about these families, it seems that schools need to respond in the curriculum to Latinos' concerns that children learn good manners and respect. The schools need to be aware of and help with language problems that families encounter when they want to help their children. They also need to incorporate oral history and storytelling into the curriculum, because it is an important aspect of the Latino culture familiar to both parents and children (Paratore et al., 1995; Rodriguez-Brown, 2010).

African American children from low-income families represent a group with a large achievement gap. Research regarding these families, where parents placed value on education and helped as much as they could, indicated that children succeeded in spite of the fact that they were economically disadvantaged. The skills parents taught their children and the role they played in their children's education were responsible for successful literacy outcomes—for example:

- Parents were involved in their children's literacy development at home and in school.
- Parents were aware of the child's progress in school.
- Parents were optimistic about how they could help and that their children could succeed.
- Parents had high but realistic expectations for their children's success.
- Parents set goals for their children to achieve.
- Parents had positive parent–child relations.

On the other hand, if underachieving African American students had parents who felt hopeless and helpless, they had low expectations for their children, and were not involved in their children's education (Edwards, 2010).

MyLab Education Self-Check 14.4

Cultivating Family Involvement

Family involvement requires more than just parents to engage in creating an environment that supports literacy learning. In this section, when I speak about parents, I am referring to any adult or older sibling who is involved with a child at home. Teachers need to view parents as partners in the development of literacy and be intentional about connecting the family to both the classroom and to additional opportunities to develop the family's collective literacy.

Connecting the Classroom to the Family

Every teacher has the responsibility to inform families on a regular basis about what is happening in school and how they can help their child. Teachers need to involve family members in activities at home and in school and make them feel like partners in the education of their child. They should be given the opportunity to offer input about what they would like their child to learn, to express how they feel about what happens in school, and to offer suggestions. They also need to feel safe enough to let the teacher know if they feel that their literacy ability is such that they can't read to their child, or that if they don't speak English fluently, they may ask for help, perhaps with an interpreter. Teachers must have the support of the home for children to succeed. Following are some suggestions about ways to make families an integral part of the school. All materials that are sent should be in English. However, if a there are a large number of Latino parents, for example, it is good to send notes home in both English and Spanish.

Teaching English Learners

Make family members feel comfortable in school, especially those who are EL's. Parents in immigrant families, where English is not the first language, may be reticent to trust the authority schools and school personnel represent. Find ways to communicate, potentially in the family's first language, to make them feel comfortable and begin to build a trusting partnership.

1. At the beginning of the school year, send home the goals to be achieved for literacy development for the grade level you teach in a format that can be understood by all.
2. With each new unit of instruction or concept being taught in literacy, send a newsletter to let family members know what you are studying and what they can do to help.

3. Invite family members to school for informational workshops, family meetings about curriculum decisions, conferences, and school programs.
4. Invite families to help with literacy activities in the classroom, such as reading to children, helping with bookbinding, taking written dictation of stories, and supervising independent activities while teachers work with small groups and individual children.
5. Invite parents to the classroom simply to watch.
6. Send home activities for parents and children to do together, and require feedback about working together. Include activities such as writing in journals together, reading together, visiting the library, reading print they see in the environment, writing notes to each other, cooking together and following recipes, putting toys or household items together that require following directions, and watching and talking about programs on television. Participating in homework assignments is extremely important.
7. Invite families to school to talk about their cultural heritage, hobbies, jobs, and the like.
8. Send home notes when a child is doing well. Don't wait to send notes just for problems.
9. Provide lists of literature for family members to share with their children. Appendix A provides suggested books.
10. Family members should be invited to school to participate with their children in literacy activities. During center time, for example, parents can read and write with their children, see what the literacy environment is like at school, and become a more integral part of the child's literacy development.
11. Be in touch with families often through phone calls, messages sent, and conferences. Try to focus on happy news, not only bad news.
12. Include family members in helping to assess their child's progress. Provide forms, such as the one in Figure 14.4, for them to fill out about their child's literacy activities and things they do with their child at home. Have them contribute information about their child's progress at parent conferences.

Figure 14.4 Checklist for Observing Child's Literacy Growth

Child's name: ____________________ **Date:** ____________________

To be filled out by parents	**Always**	**Sometimes**	**Never**	**Comments**
1. My child asks to be read to.				
2. My child will read or look at a book alone.				
3. My child understands what is read to him/her, or what he/she reads to himself/herself.				
4. My child handles a book properly, knows how to turn pages, and knows that print is read from left to right.				
5. My child will pretend to read or read to me.				
6. My child participates in the reading of a story, with rhymes and repeated phrases.				
7. My child will write with me.				
8. My child will write alone.				
9. My child will talk about what he/she has written.				
10. My child reads print in the environment such as signs and labels.				
11. My child likes school.				

Comments about Your Child:

Establishing Successful Programs and Activities

Because no two communities are the same, family literacy programs need to be tailored to the needs of the individuals they serve. Here are some tested guidelines to follow that will help programs be successful.

Objectives for Family Literacy Programs

1. Respect and understand the diversity of the families you serve.
2. Build on literacy behaviors already present in families. Although they may be different from conventional school-like literacy, most families use literacy in the routine of their daily lives. These behaviors should be identified, acknowledged, respected, preserved, and used in family literacy programs.
3. Be aware of the home languages used within the community so that materials can be translated and understood.
4. Do not take a "fix the family" attitude. Rather, view families as a supplement to the interactions available to family literacy programs that already exist.
5. Hold meetings at various times of the day and days of the week to accommodate all schedules.
6. Hold meetings in accessible locations that are friendly and nonthreatening. Transportation needs to be provided if no public transportation is available or if family members do not have a way of getting to meetings. Provide child care at meetings.
7. Provide food and refreshments at meetings.
8. Follow sound educational practices appropriate for literacy development of children and adults. Use varied strategies for literacy learning. Include writing together, reading together, and sharing materials that are fun and interesting for all.
9. Work with family members alone and with parents and children together. There should be sharing times when parents and children work together.
10. Offer support groups for family members to encourage talk about helping their children and to find out what they want to know.
11. Use family literacy programs to not only help with literacy development but also to improve interactions between parents and children.
12. Provide family members with ideas and materials to use at home.
13. Recognize that good programs provide easy-to-carry-out functional literacy activities that families consider useful, such as talking and reading about child-rearing concerns, community life problems, housing, and applying for jobs and keeping them.
14. Understand that programs should include the opportunity for family members' participation in school activities during school hours.
15. Ensure that portions of school and home programs should parallel each other. Activities done in school should be the same as those sent home for family members to do with children. When this occurs, family members can participate in their children's learning.

MyLab Education
Video Example 14.5
Engaging Families in Children's Literacy Development
This video illustrates ways families can support early literacy development. Try making a list of what is shown and compare it to what you learn in this chapter. https://www.youtube.com/watch?v=tw_B3pKSOsI

Family Involvement Initiatives

Family involvement initiatives include programs that are designed to involve and inform families about activities that will promote their children's literacy learning in school. Such programs involve families as agents in supporting their child's literacy development and may originate from the school, library, or other community agencies. Often, they are collaborative efforts among these agencies. A basic premise of parent-involvement programs is to enlist the help of families to increase the reading achievement of their children. The programs I will discuss have been used in the past, and some of them are still active at this time. I selected them because they have sound principles and the elements they utilize are easy for others to incorporate.

Reading Is Fundamental. The purpose of Reading Is Fundamental (RIF) (www.rif.org) is to get books into the hands of young children in need, and it usually involves a parental component. One of its family literacy programs is *Running Start (RS).* This school-based project, created by RIF, is designed to get books into the hands of first-grade children and to encourage and support family literacy. The goals of RS are (1) to increase first-graders' motivation to read so that they eagerly turn to books for both pleasure and information, (2) to involve families in their children's literacy development, and (3) to support schools and teachers in their efforts to help children become successful readers. Participating classroom teachers are provided with funds to select and purchase high-quality fiction and informational books for their classroom libraries. Children are challenged to read (or have someone read to them) 21 books during the 10-week program. A Reading Rally is held to involve the community in supporting literacy development, and families are encouraged to support their child in meeting the 21-book challenge by sharing books and stories with their children in a variety of ways. When a child meets the 21-book goal, he or she gets to select a book for his or her own personal library. Studies have demonstrated that both first-graders' reading motivation and family members' literacy activities in the home significantly increased in families that participated in the program (Gambrell, Almasi, Xie, & Heland, 1995).

Parents and Children Together. Parents and Children Together (PACT) is a nationwide intergenerational family literacy program established by the National Center for Family Literacy (NCFL) (www.familieslearning.org) in Louisville, Kentucky. Parents who lack a high school diploma and their 3- and 4-year-old children attend school together three to five days a week. An early childhood program is provided for the children, while the parents attend an adult education program to learn reading, math, and parenting skills.

In the adult education portion of the program, parents work on improving their reading and math skills and are taught to set goals and collaborate with other parents in the program. Parent Time is a component of the program during which the adults discuss a variety of topics, ranging from discipline to self-esteem. The last component of the program is Parent and Child Together Time. During this hour, families play together. The activities are led by the children. Parents find they can learn both with and from their children (National Center for Family Literacy, 1993).

Intergenerational literacy initiatives, such as PACT, are specifically designed to improve the literacy development of both adults and children. These programs view family members and children as co-learners and are generally characterized by planned and systematic instruction for both adults and children. Instruction may occur when family members and children work in either collaborative or parallel settings. The instruction for adults is intended to improve their own literacy skills, while simultaneously teaching the adults how to work with their children to aid their development (Wasik, Dobbins, & Herrmann, 2001).

The Belle Project. The BELLE Project (Bellevue Project for Early Literacy, Language and Education) is a community program initiated by pediatricians from New York University School of Medicine (http://pediatrics.med.nyu.edu/developmental/research/the-belle-project).

This program includes ongoing research with a large randomized controlled study to test the outcomes. The goal of this research is and has been to determine the impact of mother–child relationship interventions on parenting, language, literacy, and child development to enhance school readiness. Interventions occurred during primary pediatric care appointments at an urban public hospital that serves ethnically diverse, at-risk families.

This project builds on the Reach Out and Read (ROR) model. In ROR, during primary care visits which begin at birth, volunteers read to babies and children in the waiting room. During the visit, the doctor makes an effort to find out about the language and literacy development of the baby and what the mothers are doing to help at home. Suggestions for helping are made by the physician. Each parent–child pair receives a book to take home. This part of the program is called ROR, for which a large number of studies have documented a positive impact on a child's language development, based on parent–child shared read alouds. The participants in the program are babies who get their pediatric care at the Bellevue Hospital Clinic.

In addition to the ROR part of the program, a Video Interaction Project (VIP) was added to the pediatric primary care setting. In VIP, mother and child met with a Child Development Specialist (CDS) at each well-child visit for about 30 to 45 minutes. The first visit takes place within one or two weeks of discharge from the nursery, and subsequent visits were at one-to-three-month intervals. The CDS works with the mother to promote interactions and interactive play that facilitate language, literacy, and child development (Hart & Risley, 1995; Morrow, Mendelsohn, & Kuhn, 2010; Tamis-LeMonda, Bornstein, & Baumwell, 2001).

The core component of VIP involves videotaping the mother and child for five to seven minutes; the videotape is watched by the mother and the CDS to identify strengths and promote other positive interactions. The CDS gives each parent a toy, a children's book, and a booklet about early language, literacy, and child development activities. Research documents the efficacy of VIP with mothers who have limited education. Parents involved in VIP demonstrated helpful language and literacy play interactions with their child that were significantly better than parents who were not involved in the program (Mendelsohn et al., 2007). This program was piloted in a preschool setting and was extremely successful in improving the interactive language between parent and child during storybook reading and play (Mendelsohn, Huberman, Berkule, Brockmeyer, Morrow, & Dreyer, 2011).

***Highlights for Children* Parent Involvement Program.** Family literacy programs should promote parent–child interaction in a wide range of literacy events. Programs must view participating families from the perspective of the richness of their experiences and heritage, rather than from the perspective of their deficits and dilemmas. Home–school programs need to be easy to use. Materials sent home should first be introduced to children in school. The content should be nonthreatening and culturally diverse, and the activities need to be fun. For example, I created a Highlights for Children Family Involvement program in a school district I worked in. The *Highlights for Children* magazine was the home-school connection material.

Teachers featured articles in the magazine at school, and each child had a school copy. Another copy was sent home with activities for family members and children to do together that were similar to what was being done in school. The program was successful because children knew what to do with the materials. In addition, the magazine provided the following features that should be present in any home–school connection material: (1) multiple options from which families could select activities, (2) a nonthreatening format that is not school-like, (3) activities appropriate for many age levels and abilities, (4) culturally diverse content, (5) some activities that do not require the ability to read, and (6) activities that are fun and therefore engage families and children in literacy together (Morrow, Scoblionko, & Shafer, 1995; Morrow & Young, 1997).

Educators are recognizing that the family is one of the important keys to successful literacy development. Policymakers from a wide range of agencies and enterprises need to collaborate and form partnerships in their efforts to create and support effective family literacy programs. Literacy programs in school will be more successful if they have home support; therefore, family literacy programs are crucial (Crosby, Rasinski, Padak, & Yildirim, 2015).

Appendix A provides a bibliography of children's literature about families for teachers and families to share with children. The books are representative of diverse cultural backgrounds. Each book illustrates some special relationship between family and extended family members. It could be parents, grandparents, an aunt or uncle, sisters or brothers, or a person who becomes like family although he or she is not actually related.

Frequent Contact with Parents: Conferences, Phone Calls, and More. Formal programs are not the only tool for increasing family involvement. Simply being in touch with parents often will make them feel welcome and a part of the school, going a long way toward connecting the classroom and the family. There are many ways to reach out to parents and families, including:

- **Invitations.** Invite parents to school frequently. By doing so, parents will begin to feel more comfortable about being there and will understand better what you do in school. Make the times different so that those who work can arrange their schedules so that they can come a few times during the year (refer to Figures 14.5 and 14.6).
- **Newsletters.** When beginning a particular topic, be sure to send a newsletter to let parents know what it is about and how they can help. Figure 14.7 is an example.
- **Call parents on the phone.** In the past if a teacher called a parent, it was often because something really bad happened in school, such as the child misbehaved or was ill. However, if parents are called when good things happen, the teacher and family can build a relationship that will help everyone. Call to remind parents about a school event that is about to happen and how much you hope they can be there. Call a parent when a child has made important gains in their school work, and demonstrate how excited you are about it and hope the parent will practice with the child at home. If you call for good things, then it will also be fine to call with concerns.
- **Conferences.** Conferences to discuss progress are regularly scheduled in schools. Prior to the conference ask the parent to fill out a form such as the checklist in Figure 14.4, "Observing Child's Literacy Growth." This way, the parent comes with some expectations of what will happen in the conference, and it can be a two-way conversation; that is, both the teacher and parent will contribute. In addition, the teacher can send home a note in advance to say that the two of you will discuss how his or her child is doing socially, emotionally, physically, and with schoolwork. Be sure to start your conference with many positive comments about his or her child. Some lovely anecdote about something that happened in school would be a nice touch as well. Let the parent give you information from the checklist in Figure 14.4, then it is your turn as the teacher to share information about the child's progress. Touch on how children get along with others in the class, and discuss their work in all areas, with an emphasis on literacy development. Document comments with samples of the child's work. Give suggestions to the parents on how they can help support what is happening in school. At the end of the conference, review what happened at the meeting and ask if they have any questions.

  More than one conference a year is important, one after a few months of school and one toward the end. Of course, a conference may be arranged if necessary at any time during the year.
- **Occasional notes.** Similar to phone calls, sending regular notes provides an important point of contact between the parent and teacher. Send notes about positive behavior and growth on the part of the children and how the parent can help at home. Notes do not need to be long to be remembered and appreciated (Vukelich, Christie, & Enz, 2007).
- **VIP certificates.** So parents can feel good about their involvement, provide a certificate for them called the VIP Certificate for a Very Important Parent (refer to Figure 14.8).

Figure 14.5 Invitation for Family Participation in English

Family Members Wanted
to Visit Your Child's Class

Dear Family Members,

Please come to school and be a part of our reading and writing time. On the form below list the types of things you can do when you visit. There is a space for you to let us know the time of day and dates that you can attend. We are flexible and will arrange our time when it is convenient for you. All family members are welcome—brothers and sisters, babies, grandparents, and of course parents. Please come and get involved in your child's education and help us form a true home and school partnership.

Sincerely,
Mrs. Gallagher's second-grade class

Please fill out the following form and send it back to school with your child:

Your name: ______________________________

Your child's name: ______________________________

The days I can come during the week are: ______________________________

The time of day I can come to school is: ______________________________

When I come to school I would like to do the following:

☐ 1. Watch what the children are doing.
☐ 2. Participate with the children.
☐ 3. Read to a small group of children.
☐ 4. Read to the whole class.
☐ 5. I am from another country and I would like to tell the children about my country and show them clothing, pictures, and books from there.
☐ 6. I have a hobby and would like to share it with the class.
My hobby is: ______________________________
☐ 7. I have a talent and would like to share it with the class.
My talent is: ______________________________
☐ 8. I'd like to tell the children about my job.
My job is: ______________________________
☐ 9. Other ideas you would like to share: ______________________________
☐ 10. Give children who need it some extra help.
☐ 11. I'd like some help in deciding what to do.
☐ 12. I would like to come on a regular basis to help.
I can come at the following times: ______________________________

Figure 14.6 Invitation for Family Participation in Spanish

Se Buscan Miembros de Familia

Para Visitar la Clase de su Niño

Ayudenos Aprender—

Comparta sus Talentos y Envuélvase con Nuestra Clase:

Observe la clase y su niño

Cuente historias

Hable de su cultura

Lea libros

Comparta su pasatiempo favorito

Traiga su bebé o animal mimado

Explique su trabajo

Cocine o traiga dulces para la clase

Venga a cantarle a los niños

Comparta con nuestras actividades de "Highlights"

Por favor ponga los días, o día, que pueda venir a la clase:

Mes: Dia(s): Horas:

____

- -

Devuelva este papel a la maestra de su niño.

Nombre: ____.

Visitaré la clase en esta fecha _______________ y a esta hora _______________.

Me gustaría compartir: ____.

Figure 14.7 Newsletter to Parents about Our "Healthy Bodies, Healthy Minds" Unit of Study (See Appendix B.)

Dear Parents:

Your child will be participating in a unit that explores what it means to be healthy in body and mind. This unit will include study of why we should eat healthy foods, the five food groups, exercise, rest, cleanliness, and the importance of self-esteem.

The good health unit will cover all subject areas—play, art, music, social studies, science, math, and literacy (reading, writing, listening, and oral language), which will be incorporated in the theme. Some of the exciting activities we do here at school may also be carried out at home with your child.

At School and at Home

Art: Your child will refine eye–hand coordination and visual discrimination skills and explore and experiment with different art materials. At school we will be creating food collages and abstract bean mosaics. At home you can encourage your child to use his or her imagination by providing these and other food-related materials for art activities. Remember that art is for exploring what can be done with different materials, rather than copying an adult model.

Science: We will be making applesauce, which will give the children an opportunity to listen, follow directions, and learn where apples come from and how they are grown, as well as how food changes as it is cooked. Making healthy snacks at home, such as a fruit or lettuce salad, and involving your child in the preparation by using simple recipes will help to extend listening skills.

Literacy: Please assist at home by labeling healthy food items with the letters ***h, f,*** and ***b*** (associated with ***health, food,*** and ***body***) or pointing out words that have these and other beginning sounds. Read signs and point out these letters when you are outside the home as well.

Please read to your child stories, poems, informational books, cookbooks, exercise magazines, and other literature related to our theme of good health. Some books that will be featured in the unit include:

Achoo! by P. Demuth, 1997

Children around the World by D. Montanari, 2001

Gregory, the Terrible Eater by M. Sharmat, 1984

No More Baths by B. Cole, 1989

Mooncake by F. Asch, 1983

We Need Your Help

We would like your assistance with our multicultural food of the week or your favorite food at home. If you are able to prepare a snack one day and discuss it, please sign your name and indicate what type of snack you would like to prepare on the attached sheet.

If you can come in and read your child's favorite bedtime story to the class, please sign your name and indicate what date you are available on the attached sheet.

If you have any other materials at home related to our theme, such as empty food containers, seeds, nuts, beans, or exercise or yoga magazines that we may use in our dramatic-play area, please send them in with your child.

Figure 14.7 Newsletter to Parents about Our "Healthy Bodies, Healthy Minds" Unit of Study (*Continued*)

Other Activities to Do with Your Child

Go to the supermarket with your child. Prepare a list beforehand of the food you need to purchase. Have your child check the things off as you put them in the cart. Try to purchase food from each food group.

Plant watermelon, avocado, or carrot seeds at home. Keep a diary or record of their growth, making comparisons between them.

Make simple, nutritious recipes at home, such as fruit salad, mixed green salad, butter, or peanut butter to help our lessons carry over from class to home.

Take the time to engage in some exercise with your child each day. A brisk walk or bike ride will help your child learn that exercise is fun and should be done often. It is an activity your family will enjoy together.

Remind your child at bedtime that rest is important for our bodies. Share a special bedtime story each night with your child.

Child's Corner

Ask your child to write or draw something he or she did in school related to our theme.

Help your child keep a journal of what foods he or she eats each day. Keep track of any exercises your child does. Keep track of how many hours of sleep your child gets, writing the number in the journal. Graph the numbers. The journal can be written in a notebook, on a pad, or on pieces of paper stapled together like a book.

If you have any questions about the unit or any additional ideas, please contact me. If you are in a profession that is related to our theme, such as a nutritionist or any fitness-related career, please consider coming into class and talking to us.

Sincerely,
Lisa Lozak

I would like to prepare the following snack for your healthy bodies, healthy minds unit:

Snack: ______________________ Parent's Name: ______________________

I am able to come in on the following date for a story reading: ______________

Book: ______________________ Parent's Name: ______________________

Resources for Teachers and Families

Agencies, associations, and organizations that deal with family literacy can be contacted for further information on ways to establish, administer, and evaluate family literacy programs. There are general resources as well as resources specifically for families.

About Family Literacy. The following organizations provide general information and resources about family literacy:

- The Barbara Bush Foundation for Family Literacy, 516 N. Adams Street, Tallahassee, FL 32301, www.barbarabush.org.
- International Literacy Association, 800 Barksdale Road, PO Box 8139, Newark, DE 19714-8139, www.literacyworldwide.org.

Figure 14.8 Very Important Parent (VIP) Award

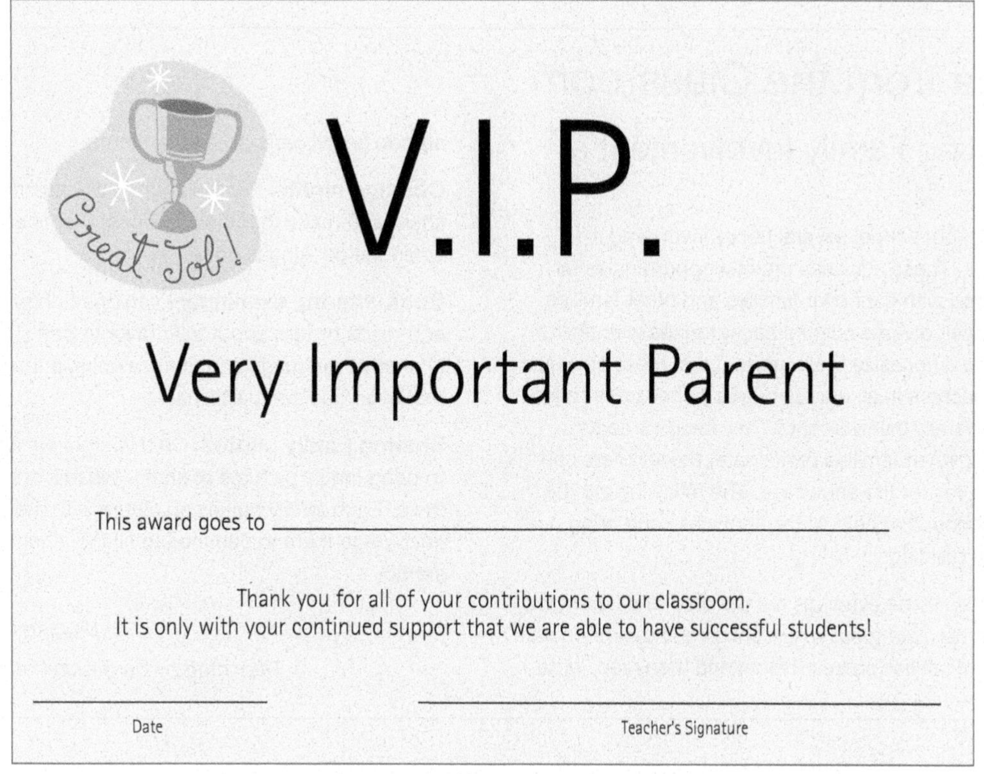

- National Center for Family Literacy, 325 West Main Street, Suite 300, Louisville, KY 40202-4251, www.familieslearning.org.
- Reading Is Fundamental (RIF), P.O. Box 33728, Washington, DC 20033, www.rif.org.

Resources For Families. Resources include the following:

- *Raising a Reader, Raising a Writer: How Parents Can Help* (Brochure available from the National Association for the Education of Young Children, 1313 L St. NW, Suite 500, Washington, DC 20005, www.naeyc.org)
- Brandt, D. (2001). *Literacy in American Lives.* New York: Cambridge University Press.
- Lipson, E. R. (2000). *New York Times Parent's Guide to the Best Books for Children.* New York: Crown Publishing Group.
- Stillman, P. R. (1998). *Families Writing* (2nd ed.). Portland, ME: Calendar Islands Publishers.
- Trealease, J. (2013). *The Read-Aloud Handbook* (7th ed.). New York: Penguin Books.

Resources for Parents for Activities to Do with Their Children

Growing Book by Book, growingbookbybook.com/9-family-literacy-activities/
Get Ready to Read, www.getreadytoread.org
PBS, www.pbs.org/parents/education/reading-language/reading-activities/

MyLab Education Self-Check 14.5

An Idea from the Classroom

Highlighting Family Involvement at School

Every month in our school several family involvement activities occur. These activities provide opportunities for children to bond with their own families and other families and to share their diverse cultural backgrounds with their classmates. To emphasize the importance of these activities and others, teachers in all grades began a showcase called "Highlighting Family Involvement." They keep cameras in school so that, when families participate, the teachers can take their pictures for the showcase. The following are the activities at school that help fill the showcase and bring families to the building:

Theme nights: These evenings are devoted to different topics, such as other countries, where children and families can learn together. Families share artifacts and then read, write, and do art projects about the theme.

Cooking nights: Families bring easy favorite recipes to share and make together. The best part is eating the goodies when the cooking is done.

Book-sharing evenings: Everyone brings a favorite book and reads or tells about their favorite part. The book can be in another language and, if necessary, a translator is used so that everyone can participate.

Sharing family photos: On this night we ask everyone to bring family pictures to share. We talk and write about them. Each family makes an album with the photos, and we encourage them to continue to fill the album they started at school.

Margaret Youssef, Teacher

Reprinted by permission of Margaret Youssef

Summary

14.1 Discuss the role of families in developing literacy.

Families are the first teachers children have, and the ones they have for the longest period of time. Families influence how well children will do in school based on the experiences they offer their children, the model they provide by reading and writing themselves, and how they articulate the importance of learning to read and write. Parents who come to school for meetings and programs, who sit with their child when they do homework, and who value literacy themselves will have children who will succeed.

14.2 Describe a framework for involving parents in literacy instruction.

There is a basic framework in families that promote literacy. Family members read to their children and readily help them with writing and reading. These family members read a variety of material, including novels, magazines, newspapers, and work-related information. They own or borrow books, for both themselves and their children. Reading and writing materials can be found throughout their homes, and reading and writing are generally valued as important activities. Family members in these homes often take their children to libraries and bookstores. Books are associated with pleasure, and literary activities are rewarded. The homes are well organized, with scheduled daily activities and rules and designated responsibilities for family members. They provide a setting where interactions between adults and children are socially, emotionally, and intellectually conducive to literacy interest and growth.

14.3 Identify materials and activities for creating a rich family literacy environment.

In addition to having physical reminders of the importance of literacy (ample reading and writing materials), creating a literacy-rich environment involves reading to children consistently from an early age, making available writing materials throughout the home, co-opting technology in the service of literacy education, and intentionally integrating literacy activities into family routines and entertainment. Reading and writing with children at home should be a ritual that starts at birth. As children grow, encourage them to participate in reading by asking questions, repeating phrases, and asking for them to read certain words. Provide many and varied writing implements and papers, and involve children in writing for a variety of purposes. Relate any technology usage, including television and movie viewing, back to literacy activities, such as reading storybooks upon which media are based, writing notes to the characters in shows or movies, or extending the themes of shows, games, or movies into storybooks and reading time.

14.4 Explain cultural issues that influence family involvement and literacy.

Different cultures deal with literacy in different ways. Some homes do not have books nor can some parents read, so storytelling becomes the main form of literacy. Sometimes religion provides the literacy framework in the home, for example, when the Bible is the only book the family owns. Educators must value the different manner in which literacy is practiced as well as try to enhance literacy levels.

14.5 List methods to cultivate family involvement in literacy instruction.

Parents are partners in the development of literacy, and cultivating family involvement in literacy instruction rests on the teacher's ability to connect families to the classroom. This can be achieved through formal programs such as Reading Is Fundamental (RIF), Parents and Children Together (PACT), or the BELLE Project. It can also be achieved through informal yet structured programs such as the *Highlights for Children* program, or simply through being intentional about reaching out to parents on a regular basis. Parents should be informed about happenings at school, have the opportunity to participate in the classroom, be asked for input, and be encouraged to express their feelings about school and offer suggestions. Successful outreach to parents involves regular invitations to come to school, sending regular newsletters, holding conferences, sending notes about positive aspects of the children's performance, making phone calls to invite and update, and recognizing parental involvement. Many outside groups provide support for literacy involvement, including the International Reading Association (IRA), the Barbara Bush Foundation for Family Literacy, the National Center for Family Literacy, and Reading Is Fundamental.

Activities and Questions

1. Interview members of your family or friends who are parents. Ask them to relate specific activities they have done with their children to promote literacy with natural events that arose from daily living. Collect ideas from all members of the class, and put them together in a newsletter or pamphlet format to distribute to family members of early childhood youngsters.
2. Using the memories of your own home when you were a young child or the home of a friend or family member who is a parent of a young child, observe the physical characteristics and record activities done with children that promote literacy development. Determine elements that could improve the richness of the literacy environment you analyzed.
3. Select a child and his or her family to begin a portfolio of assessment materials to collect throughout the semester. Start a portfolio that you will keep in a folder for the child, and provide a folder for the family. Make copies of Figure 14.1, Guidelines for Promoting Early Literacy at Home, for yourself and one for the family with whom you will be working. Ask a family member to fill out the form for himself or herself and a copy for you. Provide the family member with two copies of Figure 14.4, Checklist for Observing Child's Literacy Growth. Have him or her fill it out at the beginning of the semester and at the end. Be sure to get a copy for your folder as well.
4. Create a family literacy program for a familiar community. If it is a community in which families have literacy and English skills, you will probably want to develop a family involvement program; if it is in a community where families speak other languages or have limited literacy ability, you may need to engage in an intergenerational program that involves development of literacy skills for families and training them to help their children. Be sure that whichever program you design, portions of the home and school activities are similar to each other.
5. Provide parents with a list of literacy activities (refer to Figure 14.2) to participate in, and ask them to record what they do. Give parents a VIP (Very Important Parent) award (refer to Figure 14.8) for participating in and out of school with literacy help for their child. Create bookmarks for parents and children (refer to Figure 14.3).

Afterword

This book has presented a theory- and research-based program for developing literacy in early childhood. It has emphasized the importance of literacy-rich environments, social interaction, peer collaboration, and whole-class, small-group, and individual learning with explicit instruction and problem-solving experiences. The activities suggested meet current literacy standards and underscore the concurrent teaching of listening, speaking, reading, writing, and viewing. The book has outlined education that is functional and related to real-life experiences and is therefore meaningful and interesting to the child. It has provided for the integration of literacy activities into content areas through the use of themes that add enthusiasm, motivation, and meaning. This book is also about project-based instruction, which provides real life experiences using reading and writing. In addition, the book has suggested careful monitoring of individual growth through explicit instruction and frequent assessment using multiple measures and allowing ample space for children to learn through play, manipulation, and exploration. The book also promotes the necessity for creating a positive growth mindset of "I can" in the classroom. It is also concerned with social justice and equity for all of our children.

New information about learning is constantly being generated; subsequently, we often need to change the strategies we use to help children learn. Teachers must stay abreast of the constant stream of available literature after they complete their formal education. They must engage in multiple forms of professional development and stay up to date with the latest research, theory, policy, and practice. There are many ways in which professional development can take place.

Teachers can continue their education and receive a master's or doctoral degree or additional teaching certifications. They can also take courses to strengthen their knowledge in a particular area of concern as they update their certification. It is also important for teachers to join professional organizations, such as those listed in Appendix D. Professional organizations have local, state, and national conferences. They publish both practical and research journals with the most current information available. Some professional organizations also publish books. Through these organizations, teachers connect with others and have the opportunity to talk and reflect. In addition to these individual initiatives taken by teachers, all teachers need to work on a professional development plan with their schools. The plan can involve the entire school or focus on a certain grade level. It can be a one-year plan that can continue annually. The professional development plan should be based on what teachers and administrators believe they need to work on in literacy. It should be revised as needed and, if necessary, new goals and new experiences should be created frequently. Collaborative models involve individuals from various perspectives working together to bring new ideas to the classroom. Current professional development models are called Study Groups (SGs) and Professional Learning Communities (PLCs). While these are completely different models, they also have a lot in common; commonalities include:

- Collaborative models involve individuals from various perspectives working together to improve classroom practice and student performance.
- Collaborative procedures provide for teacher input.
- Collaborative models provide support and direction from other colleagues, administrators, and/or researchers.

The following are the goals for a professional development program in a school:

- Change classroom practices when necessary to improve.
- Change teacher attitudes toward professional development.
- Create a school that is composed of a community of learners.

How can this be done?

- Focus on changing classroom practices.
- When teachers can observe changes in student learning as a result of changing classroom practice, changes in teacher beliefs and attitudes will follow.
- Bring in experts to model the teaching practice you wish to implement.

Study Groups are composed of a group of teachers at any grade level who have an interest in making the same changes in their classrooms. The group selects a topic of mutual concern and similar reading material. Readings are done outside of the study group and discuss new methods introduced in the readings when in study groups. Teachers then try some of these methods in their classrooms. When they next meet in their study groups, the teachers discuss how they implemented the new practices and how the outcomes might be improved. When they are ready, the teachers move on to another topic, read about it, try it out, reflect on it, and refine it.

Professional Learning Communities consist of teachers at the same worked based on grade level. They meet to assess student performance in a particular area, such as comprehension. They decide on actions to take to improve student performance in this area. They may also read material to enrich their knowledge. The teachers try the practices they discussed and, when they meet later, determine how well the new practices worked and if they improved student performance.

Components of Good Professional Development

Good professional development programs include:

- administrative support for the project prior to beginning
- professional development workshops to provide information about new strategies from motivating and knowledgeable consultants
- goals set by teachers with administrators
- a coach in the school to model new strategies in the classroom and to support teachers
- accessible materials
- classroom observations by other teachers in their building, the coach, and others to determine progress
- teacher discussion groups to foster collaboration and reflection with reading materials to provide new ideas, and
- time to change.

Teachers' Comments About Participating in a Good Professional Development Model

Teacher 1: The professional development program helped me try new ideas. Sometimes the district asks you to do new things without allowing time to learn about them and without the help needed for implementation. The best way to foster change in teachers is to introduce ideas by having a motivating and competent consultant demonstrate strategies. We had excellent support to help us understand the new ideas and implement them. We were given lesson plans that were very helpful. I also found that visiting other teachers' classrooms to see my peers using the new strategies was extremely valuable. It is very important to realize that change happens slowly. We were not rushed. I liked our discussion groups because we needed to talk to each other about our progress, exchange ideas, and get advice from the consultant.

Teacher 2: The thing that influenced me to change the most was the realization that my students' needs were not being met and therefore the students were not reaching their full potential. Soon after I started to change my instruction, I began to see a change in student behavior. The students were now capable of what was being asked of them.

Teacher 3: I felt as though I had a lot to learn about teaching reading through small-group reading instruction, and I learned a lot in the professional development program. I intend to remain active in professional development to keep learning. I will definitely participate in meetings with the consultant and my peers. I will also be happy to help other teachers who may want to begin guided reading in their classrooms!

The Teacher–Researcher

Another area of professional development involves the teacher acting as a researcher by reflecting on his or her own teaching. This can be done to discover strengths and weaknesses and to develop questions of concern to the teacher about teaching students. To be a teacher–researcher requires formulating questions about teaching strategies, child development, classroom environment, curriculum development, or other relevant topics that will clarify issues to help generate new information. Questions should be generated from daily experiences in the classroom and be of personal interest to the teacher. When teachers are researchers, they increase their knowledge and skill.

When an area of inquiry is decided on, the teacher should focus on collecting data that will help answer questions posed or clarify issues. Data can be collected in the following ways: Observe and record anecdotes of classroom experiences that are relevant to the question being asked; videotape classroom segments; collect samples of children's daily work over a period of time; interview children, teachers, and parents; administer formal and informal tests; and try new techniques.

By becoming a teacher–researcher, you will always be on the cutting edge of what is current and appropriate, and you will always find your teaching interesting because you will be learning about new things on a daily basis. You will enjoy your work more because you'll have extended your role to include additional professional activities. And you will be practicing both the art and science of teaching. The science involves inquiry, reading, observing, and collecting data. The art involves reflecting on findings and making appropriate changes. As a teacher–researcher, you will become empowered to be a decision-maker and catalyst for making change in your school. As you study questions for which you have tangible data, you are more likely to be heard when you propose new ideas or recommend changes. Rather than having change mandated based on the research by individuals outside your school district or by administrative personnel, you will confidently take responsibility for the changes that will occur because you have researched the issues yourself. Each year you teach, you can select another area of inquiry to study. When appropriate, collaborate with your colleagues on research projects. Collaboration with adults, as well as with children, results in projects you might not have been able to do alone. The learning theory that has been adopted over the years in early literacy development is due to research by college professors and classroom teachers. It must continue.

The literacy program described in this book is meant to be motivating for teachers and children. Motivation allows teachers to work with vigor and enthusiasm. Motivation allows children to associate literacy with a school environment that is pleasurable, positive, and designed to help them succeed. One of the most important elements in learning to read and write is a teacher who can encourage children to *want* to read and write. Wanting to read and write motivates a desire to learn the skills necessary to become proficient in literacy. With those skills develops a lifelong interest in refining and using literacy skills. The program portrayed in this book is designed to help us "reignite our romance with the written word" (Spielberg, 1987).

Appendix A

Children's Literature for the Classroom: Multigenre and Multimedia for 21st Century Learners

Books for Babies

Cardboard Concept Books

Boynton, S. (1984). *Doggies.* New York: Little Simon.

Boynton, S. (2012). *Tickle time!* New York: Workman Publishing Co.

DK Board Books. (2004). *My first farm board book.* New York: DK.

Kubler, A. (2002). *Head, shoulders, knees and toes.* New York: Children's Play International.

Kubler, A. (2003). *Ten little fingers.* New York: Children's Play International.

McDonald, J. (2017). *Hello, World! Backyard Bugs.* Doubleday Books for Young Readers.

Seuss, Dr. (1996). *Mr. brown can moo! Can you?* New York: Random House Children's Books.

Cloth Books

Golden Books. (2003). *Sleep bunny.* New York: Random House Children's Books.

Katz, K. (2007). *Baby's day.* New York: Little Simon.

Magsamen, S. (2007). *Messages from the heart: Good night, little one: Huggable, lovable, snuggable books.* New York: Little, Brown & Co. Books for Young Readers.

Meyer, M. *Dazzle Dots and the Missing Spots.* Taggies Soft Books.

Priddy, R. (2003). *Fuzzy bee and friends.* New York: Priddy Books.

Priddy, R. (2003). *Squishy turtle and friends.* New York: Priddy Books.

Plastic Books

Aigner-Clark, J. (2003). *Baby Einstein: Water, water everywhere.* New York: Hyperion Books for Children.

Boynton, S. (2007). *Bath time.* New York: Workman Publishing.

Davis, C. (2009). *Animals on the farm: My first noisy bath book.* Hauppauge, NY: Barron's Educational Series.

Priddy, R. (2013). *Hello baby: Bathtime bath book.* New York: Priddy Books.

Romendik, I. (2002). *The musical Mary had a little lamb (rub-a-dub book).* Westport, CT: Straight Edge Press.

Small World Creations ltd. (2017). *Splish Splash (Magic Bath Books) Bath Book.* Yate, UK: Barron's Educational Series.

Touch and Feel

Brown, M. W. (2005). *Little fur family.* New York: HarperCollins Publishers.
Capucilli, A.S., & Schories, P. (2017). *Biscuit's Pet & Play Bedtime.* New York, NY: HarperFestival.
Coat, J. (2012). *Hippopposites.* New York: Abrams Appleseed.
Kunhardt, D. (2001). *Pat the bunny.* New York: Random House Children's Books.
Van Fleet, M. (2003). *Tails.* Orlando, FL: Houghton Mifflin Harcourt.
Watt, F. (2006). *That's not my kitten.* London: Usbourne.

Concept Books

Fleming, D. (2004). *The everything book.* New York: Holt.
George, L. B. (2006). *Inside mouse, outside mouse.* New York: HarperCollins Publishers.
Lehman, B. (2004). *The red book.* Boston: Houghton Mifflin.
Lomp, S., & Pixton, A. (2017). *Things that go!* New York, NY: Workman Publishing Co., Inc.
Mack, J. (2012). *Good news, bad news.* San Francisco, CA: Chronicle Books.
McMullan, J., & McMullan, K. (2005). *I stink.* New York: HarperFestival.
Seeger, L. V. (2007). *Black? White? Day? Night? A book of opposites.* New York: Roaring Brook Press.

Alphabet Books

Bonder, D. (2007). *Dogabet.* N. Vancouver, BC, Canada: Walrus.
Bruel, N. (2005). *Bad kitty.* New York: Roaring Brook Press.
Ernest, L. (2004). *The turn-around, upside down alphabet book.* New York: Simon & Schuster Children's Publishing.
Fleming, D. (2006). *Alphabet under construction.* New York: Henry Holt and Co.
Jeffers, O. (2017). *An alphabet.* New York, NY: Philomel Books, an imprint of Penguin Random House LLC.
Lionni, L. (2004). *The alphabet tree.* New York: Random House Children's Books.
Lluch, A. A. (2014). *alphabet: I like to learn the ABC's.* San Diego, CA: WS Publishing Group.
Martin, B. J. (2000). *Chicka chicka boom boom.* New York: Simon & Schuster Children's Publishing.
Van Fleet, M. (2008). *Alphabet.* New York: Simon & Schuster Children's Publishing.

Number Books

Ball, J. (2005). *Go figure! A totally cool book about numbers.* New York: DK.
Cyrus, K. (2016). *Billions of bricks: A counting book about building.* New York: Christy Ottaviano.
Ehlert, L. (2001). *Fish eyes: A book you can count on.* Orlando, FL: Houghton Mifflin Harcourt.
Fleming, D. (1992). *Count!* New York: Henry Holt and Co.
Fromental, J.-L. (2006). *365 penguins.* New York: Abrams.
Holub, J. (2012). *Zero the hero.* New York: Henry Holt and Company.
Menotti, A. (2012). *How many jelly beans? A giant book of giant numbers!* San Francisco, CA: Chronicle Books.

Morales, Y. (2003). *Just a minute: A trickster tale and counting book.* San Francisco, CA: Chronicle.

Sayre, J. (2006). *One is a snail, ten is a crab: A counting by feet book.* Cambridge, MA: Candlewick Press.

Schwartz, D. M. (1993). *How much is a million?* New York: HarperCollins Publishers.

Nursery Rhymes

Denton, K. (2004). *A child's treasury of nursery rhymes.* New York: Kingfisher.

Green, A. (2007). *Mother Goose's storytime nursery rhymes.* New York: Arthur A. Levine.

Grey, M. (2015). *The adventures of the dish and the spoon.* New York: Random House Children's Books.

Mathers, P. (2012). *The McElderry book of Mother Goose: Revered and rare rhymes.* New York: Margaret K. McElderry Books.

Rescek, S. (2006). *Hickory, dickory dock: And other favorite nursery rhymes.* New York: Tiger Tales.

Rhatigan, J. (2017). *Hey diddle diddle: classic nursery rhymes retold.* Lake Forest, CA: MoonDance.

Wordless Storybooks

Briggs, R. (1999). *The snowman.* New York: Random House Children's Books.

Cole, H. (2012). *Unspoken: A story from the underground railroad.* New York: Scholastic Inc.

dePaola, T. (1978). *Pancakes for breakfast.* Orlando, FL: Houghton Mifflin Harcourt.

Hutchins, P. (2005). *Rosie's walk.* New York: Simon & Schuster Children's Publishing.

Lawson, J., & Smith, S. (2015). *Sidewalk flowers.* Toronto, Ontario: Groundwood Books.

Mayer, M. (2003). *A boy, a dog, and a frog.* New York: Penguin Group.

Schories, P. (2004). *Breakfast for Jack.* Honesdale, PA: Boyd's Mill Press.

Tafuri, N. (1991). *Have you seen my duckling?* New York: HarperCollins Publishers.

Poetry Books

Degan, B. (2008). *Jamberry.* New York: HarperCollins Publishers.

Donaldson, J. (2006). *The Gruffalo.* New York: The Penguin Group.

Fogliano, J., & Morstad, J. (2016). *When green becomes tomatoes: Poems for all seasons.* NY, NY: Roaring Brook Press.

Pretlutsky, J. (1999). *The 20th century children's poetry treasury.* New York: Random House Children's Books.

Pretlutsky, J. (2007). *Good sports: Rhymes about running, jumping, throwing, and more.* New York: Random House Children's Books

Rammell, S. K. (2006). *City beats: A hip-hoppy pigeon poem.* Nevada City, CA: Dawn.

Silverstein, S. (2004). *Where the sidewalk ends.* New York: HarperCollins Publishers.

Wilson, K. (2014). *Outside the box.* New York: Margaret K. McElderry Books.

Traditional Literature (Fairy Tales, Fables, Myths, and Folktales)

Brett, J. (2009). *The mitten.* New York: Penguin Group.

Marshall, J. (1998). *Goldilocks and the three bears.* New York: Penguin Group.

Mosel, A. (2007). *Tikki Tikki Tembo.* New York: Square Fish.

Perkins, C., & Equihua, S. (2016). *Cinderella.* New York: Little Simon.

Pinkney, J. (2000). *Aesop's fables*. San Francisco, CA: Chronicle Books LLC.
Pinkney, J. (2009). *The lion and the mouse*. New York: Little, Brown & Co. Books for Young Readers.
Scieszka, J. (1992). *The stinky cheese man and other fairly stupid tales*. New York: Penguin Group.
Taback, S. (2000). *Joseph had a little overcoat*. New York: Penguin Group.
Williams, M. (2012). *Goldilocks and the three dinosaurs: As retold by Mo Williams*. New York: HarperCollins Publisher.

Easy-to-Read Books with Limited Vocabulary

Capucilli, A. S. (2003). *Biscuit loves school*. New York: HarperCollins Publishers.
Holub, J. (2003). *Why do horses neigh?* New York: Penguin Group.
Juster, N. (2006). *The hello, goodbye window*. New York: Hyperion Books for Children.
Karlin, N. (2006). *The fat cat sat on the mat*. New York: HarperCollins Publishers.
Parr, T. (2013). *The I love you book*. New York: Little, Brown Books for Young Readers.
Rocklin, J. (2003). *This book is haunted*. New York: HarperCollins Publishers.
Virj`an, E.J. (2016). *What this story needs is a pig in a wig*. New York: Scholastic Inc.

Books about Realistic Issues

Anholt, L. (2014). *Two nests*. Islington, London: Frances Lincoln Children's Books.
Brown, L. K., & Brown, M. T. (1998). *When dinosaurs die: A guide to understanding death*.
Buitrago, J., & Yockteng, R. (2015). *Two white rabbits*. Toronto, ON: Groundwood Books. New York: Little, Brown & Co. Books for Young Readers.
Buehner, C. (2000). *I did it, I'm sorry*. New York: Penguin Group.
Cohen, M. (2008). *Jim's dog muffins*. Long Island City, NY: Star Bright Books, Incorporated.
dePaola, T. (2000). *Nana upstairs and Nana downstairs*. New York: Penguin Group.
Katz, K. (2002). *The colors of us*. New York: Henry Holt & Co.
Levins, S., & Langdo, B. (2006). *Was it the chocolate pudding? A story for little kids about divorce*. Washington, DC: American Psychological Association.
Parr, T. (2009). *It's okay to be different*. New York: Little, Brown & Co. Books for Young Readers.
Penn, A. (2006). *The kissing hand*. Terre Haute, IN: Tanglewood Press.
Silverberg, C. (2013). *What makes a baby*. New York: Seven Stories Press.
Viorst, J., (1971). *The tenth good thing about Barney*. New York: Simon & Schuster.

Informational Books (Expository Texts Listed by Grade Level)

Pre-K

Bass, J. V. (2016). *Edible colors: See, learn, eat*. New York, NY: Roaring Brook Press.
Jordan, D. (2012). *Dream big: Michael Jordan and the pursuit of Olympic gold*. New York: Simon & Schuster Children's Books.
Rubbino, S. (2009). *A walk in New York*. Cambridge, MA: Candlewick Press.
Showers, P. (1991). *How many teeth?* New York: HarperCollins Publishers.
Ziefert, H. (2006). *You can't taste a pickle with your ear!* Maplewood, NJ: Blue Apple Books.
Zoehfeld, K. W. (1995). *What's alive?* New York: HarperCollins Publishers.

Grades K–1

Cousins, L. (2012). *Create with Maisy: A Maisy arts and crafts book.* Cambridge, MA: Candlewick Press.

dePaola, T. (1985). *The cloud book.* New York: Holiday House Inc.

DeWitt, L. (1993). *What will the weather be?* New York: HarperCollins Publishers.

Ehlert, L. (2005). *Leaf man.* Orlando, FL: Houghton Mifflin Harcourt.

Gibbons, G. (1992). *Weather words and what they mean.* New York: Holiday House Inc.

Pfeffer, W. (2004). *From seed to pumpkin.* New York: HarperCollins Publishers.

London, J., & So, M. (2016). *Otters love to play.* Somerville, MA: Candlewick Press.

Grades 1–2

Aliki. (1999). *My visit to the zoo.* New York: HarperCollins Publishers.

Bartoletti, S. C. (2004). *Flag maker.* Orlando, FL: Houghton Mifflin Harcourt.

Davies, N. (2004). *Oceans and seas.* New York: Kingfisher.

Gibbons, G. (2002). *Tell me, tree: All about trees for kids.* New York: Little, Brown & Co. Books for Young Readers.

Helfer, R., & Lewin, T. (2012). *The world's greatest lion.* New York: Philomel.

Pivon, H., & Thomson, S. L. (2004). *What presidents are made of.* New York: Simon & Schuster Children's Books.

Grades 2–3

Cole, J. (1990). *The magic school bus inside the human body.* New York: Scholastic, Inc.

Dorion, C. (2010). *How the world works: A hands-on guide to our amazing planet.* Cambridge, MA: Candlewick Press.

Frandin, J. B. (2002). *Who was Sacagawea?* New York: Penguin Group.

Fredericks, A. D. (2001). *Under one rock: Bugs, slugs, and other ughs.* Nevada City, CA: Dawn Publications.

George, J. S. (2004). *So you want to be president?* New York: Penguin Group.

Goldish, M. (2012). *Dolphins in the Navy.* New York: Bearport.

Markel, M., & Pham, L. (2016). *Hillary Rodham Clinton: Some girls are born to lead.* New York, NY: Balzer Bray.

Myers, L. (2002). *Lewis and Clark and me: A dog's tale.* New York: Henry Holt & Co.

National Geographic Kids. (2012). *5,000 awesome facts (about everything!)* Washington, DC: National Geographic Society.

Solheim, J. (2001). *It's disgusting and we ate it!: True food facts from around the world and throughout history.* New York: Simon & Schuster Children's Books.

Informational Text Series

Let's read and find out science. New York: HarperCollins Publishers.

My first Bob books series. New York: Scholastic Inc.

Science kids. Ashmore, Queensland, Australia: Kingfisher.

Sports Illustrated Kids rookie books series. New York: Sports Illustrated

Time for kids. New York: HarperCollins.

Who was. . . ? series. New York: Penguin Group.

Zoobooks series. Evanston, IL: Wildlife Education.

Biography

Abramson, A. (2007). *Who was Ann Frank?* New York: Penguin Group.

dePaola, T. (2001). *26 Fairmont Avenue.* New York: Penguin Group.

Fritz, J. (2002). *Double life of Pocahontas.* New York: Penguin Group.

Gerstein, M. (2007). *The man who walked between the towers.* New York: Square Fish.

Giovanni, N. (2007). *Rosa.* New York: Square Fish.

Kalman, M. (2012). *Looking at Lincoln*. New York: Nancy Paulsen Books.
Krull, K. (2003). *Harvesting hope: The story of Cesar Chavez*. Orlando, FL: Houghton Mifflin Harcourt.
Lakin, P. (2012). *Steve Jobs: Thinking differently*. New York: Aladdin.
Martin, J. B. (2009). *Snowflake Bentley*. Orlando, FL: Houghton Mifflin Harcourt.
Rhodes-Pitts, S., & Myers, C. (2015). *Jake makes a world: Jacob Lawrence, a young artist in Harlem*. New York: The Museum of Modern Art.

Magazines for Children

American Girl. 8400 Fairway Place, Middleton, WI 53562 (ages 8 to 12).
High Five. 803 Church Street, Honesdale, PA 18431 (ages 2 to 6).
Highlights. 803 Church Street, Honesdale, PA 18431 (ages 6 to 12).
Kids Discover. 149 Fifth Avenue, New York, NY (ages 6 and up).
Kiki Magazine. 118 W. Pike Street, Covington, KY 41011 (ages 8 to 14).
Ladybug Magazine. 7926 Jones Branch Drive McLean, VA 22102 (ages 3 to 6).
National Geographic's Kids. 1145 17th Street N. W., Washington, DC 20036 (ages 6 to 14).
National Geographic's Little Kids. 1145 17th Street N. W., Washington, DC 20036 (ages 3 to 6).
Nickelodeon. PO Box 1529, Elk Grove Village, IL 60009 (ages 6–14).
Ranger Rick. 1100 Wildlife Center Drive, Reston, VA (ages 7 and up).
Scholastic News. 557 Broadway, New York, NY 10012. (ages 5 to 11).
Time for Kids. 1271 Sixth Avenue, New York, NY 10020 (ages 5 to 12).
Zoobooks. PO Box 447, Peru, IL 61354 (ages 6–12.

Predictable Books

Repetitive Phrases

Brosgol, V. (2016). *Leave me alone!* New York: Roaring Brook Press.
Brown, M. W. (2007). *Goodnight moon*. New York: HarperCollins Publishers.
Dean, J. (2013). *Pete the cat: The wheels on the bus*. New York: HarperCollins Publishers.
Elliott, D. (2009). *And here's to you*. Cambridge, MA: Candlewick Press.
Gordon, J. R. (2000). *Two badd babies*. Honesdale, PA: Boyds Mills Press.
Guarino, D. (2004). *Is your mama a llama?* New York: Scholastic Inc.
Martin, B. J. (2007). *Brown bear, brown bear, what do you see?* New York: Henry Holt & Co.

Rhymes

Alborough, J. (2003). *Some dogs do*. Cambridge, MA: Candlewick Press.
Coat, J. (2015). *Rhymoceros*. New York: Abrams Appleseed.
Dewdney, A. (2009). *Llama llama misses mama*. New York: Penguin Group.
Donaldson, J. (2009). *Stick man*. New York: Scholastic Inc.
Lawrence, J. (2006). *This little chick*. Cambridge, MA: Candlewick Press.
Mayo, D. (2007). *House that Jack built*. Cambridge, MA: Barefoot Books.
Prelutsky, J. (2007). *Good sports: Rhymes about running, jumping, throwing, and more*. New York: Random House Children's Books.

Familiar Sequences (Days of the Week, Numbers, Letters, Months of the Year, and More)

Bang, M. (1996). *Ten, nine, eight*. New York: HarperCollins Publishers.
Carle, E. (2001). *Today is Monday*. New York: Penguin Group.
Carle, E. (2007). *The very hungry caterpillar*. New York: Penguin Group.

Litwin, E. (2012). *Pete the cat and his four groovy buttons.* New York: HarperCollins Publishers.
Reidy, J., & Timmers, L. (2016). *Busy builders, busy week!* New York: Bloomsbury.
Sendak, M. (1991). *Chicken soup with rice: A book of months.* New York: HarperCollins Publishers.
Ward, C. (2004). *Cookies week.* New York: Penguin Group.

Cumulative Patterns (As the Story Progresses, the Previous Line Is Repeated)

Adams, P. (2007). *There was an old lady who swallowed a fly.* England: Child's Play International.
Colandro, L. (2012). *There was an old lady who swallowed some books!* New York: Cartwheel Books.
Kalan, R., & Barton, B. (2003). *Jump, frog, jump!* New York: HarperCollins Publishers.
Stutson, C. (2009). *By the light of the Halloween moon.* Tarrytown, NY: Cavendish, Marshall Corporation.
Yolen, J. (2017). *On bird hill.* Apex, NC: Cornell Lab Publishing Group.

Books That Foster Critical Discussions

Cook, J. (2015). *But it's not my fault!* Boys Town, NE: Boys Town Press.
Cuyler, M. (2009). *Bullies never win.* Simon & Schuster Children's Books.
Green, J. (2005). *Why should I recycle?* Hauppauge, NY: Barron's Educational Series.
Lovell, P. (2001). *Stand tall, Molly Lou Melon.* New York: Penguin Group.
McCloud, C. (2012). *Will you fill my bucket? Daily acts of love around the world.* Northville, MI: Nelson Publishing and Marketing.
Polacco, P. (2012). *Bully.* New York: Penguin Group.
Polacco, P. (2001). *Thank you, Mr. Falker.* New York: Penguin Group.
Silverstein, S. (2004). *The giving tree.* New York: HarperCollins Publishers.

Favorite Well-Known Picture Storybooks

The following books represent a careful selection of some distinguished authors and excellent children's literature not to be missed.

Allsburg, C. V. (2009). *The polar express.* Orlando, FL: Houghton Mifflin Harcourt.
Bemelmans, L. (2000). *Madeline.* New York: Penguin Group.
Berenstain, S., & Berenstain, J. (2002). *The bears' picnic.* New York: Random House.
Brown, M. W. (2005). *Goodnight moon.* New York: HarperCollins.
Carle, E. (2007). *The very hungry caterpillar.* New York: Penguin Group.
Dean, J. (2013). *Freddy the frogcaster.* Washington, DC: Regnery Publishing, Inc.
Eastman, P. D. (2005). *Are you my mother?* New York: Random House.
Ellis, C. (2016). *Du iz tak?* London: Walker Books.
Freeman, D. (2008). *Corduroy.* New York: Penguin Group.
Henkes, K. (2007). *Chrysanthemum.* New York: Scholastic Inc.
Hoban, R. (2009). *Best friends for Frances.* New York: HarperCollins.
Johnson, C. (1981). *Harold and the purple crayon.* New York: Harper.
Kraus, R. (2008). *Leo the late bloomer.* New York: HarperCollins.
Lobel, A. (1974). *Frog and toad together.* Norristown, PA: Backpack Books.
McCloskey, R. (2010). *Blueberries for Sal.* New York: Penguin.
Miyares, D. (2015). *Float.* New York: Simon & Schuster Books for Young Readers.
Pinkney, J. (2006). *The little red hen.* Boston: Houghton Mifflin.
Piper, W. (2009). *The little engine that could.* New York: Penguin.
Potter, B. (2006). *The tale of Peter Rabbit.* New York: Warner.
Rey, H. A. (2006). *Curious George rides a bike.* Boston: Houghton Mifflin.

Scieszka, J. (1996). *The true story of the 3 little pigs.* New York: Penguin Group.
Sendak, M. (1988). *Where the wild things are.* New York: HarperCollins.
Seuss, Dr. (2000). *Horton hatches the egg.* New York: Random House.
Slobodkina, E. (2008). *Caps for sale.* Reading, MA: Addison-Wesley.
Steig, W. (2005). *Sylvester and the magic pebble.* New York: Simon & Schuster.
Tonatiuh, D. (2016). *The princess and the warrior: A tale of two volcanoes.* New York: Abrams Books For Young Readers.
Viorst, J. (1972). *Alexander and the terrible, horrible, no good, very bad day.* New York: Atheneum.
Wenzel, B. (2016). *They all saw a cat.* San Francisco, CA: Chronicle Books.
Willems, M. (2003). *Don't let the pigeon drive the bus.* New York: Hyperion Books for Children.
Willems, M. (2006). *Don't let the pigeon stay up late.* New York: Hyperion Books for Children.
Willems, M. (2007). *Knuffle Bunny.* New York: Scholastic, Inc.
Wood, A. (2010). *The napping house.* Orlando, FL: Houghton Mifflin Harcourt.

Books for Building Sound–Symbol Relationships

Consonants

B

Bottner, B. (1997). *Bootsie barker bites.* New York: Penguin Group.
James, S. (2008). *Baby brains: The smartest baby in the whole world.* Somerville, MA: Candlewick Press.
Martin, B. (2008). *Brown bear, brown bear, what do you see?* New York: Henry Holt & Co.
Vere, E. (2012). *Bedtime for monsters.* New York: Henry Holt and Company.

C (Hard)

Cain, S. (2006). *The crunching munching caterpillar.* Wilton, CT: Tiger Tales.
Edwards, P. D. (2004). *Clara caterpillar.* New York: HarperCollins.
Janni, R. (2012). *Every cowgirl loves a rodeo.* New York: Dial.
Numeroff, L. (2008). *If you give a cat a cupcake.* New York: HarperCollins Publishers.

C (Soft)

Dusen, C. V. (2009). *The circus ship.* Cambridge, MA: Candlewick Press.
Priceman, M. (2009). *Emeline at the circus.* New York: Random House Children's Books.
Rex, A. (2012). *Cold cereal.* New York: Balzar + Bray.
Ross, T. (2003). *Centipede's one hundred shoes.* New York: Henry Holt and Co.
Sanderson, R. (2002). *Cinderella.* New York: Little, Brown & Co. Books for Young Reader.

D

Graham, B. (2007). *Dimity Dumpty: The story of Humpty's little sister.* Cambridge, MA: Candlewick Press.
Hills, T. (2007). *Duck, duck, goose.* New York: Random House.
Rubin, A. (2012). *Dragons love tacos.* New York: Dial.

F

DeRubertis, B. (2010). *Frances frog's forever friend.* New York: Kane Press.
Duncan Edwards, P. (2010). *Four famished foxes and Fosdyke.* New York: Barnes & Noble.
Fox, M. (2000). *Feathers and fools.* Orlando, FL: Houghton Mifflin Harcourt.

Mack, J. (2012). *Frog and fly: Six slurpy stories.* New York: Philomel.
Stevens, J. (2005). *The great fuzz frenzy.* Orlando, FL: Houghton Mifflin Harcourt.

G (Hard)

Brown, M. W. (2005). *Goodnight moon.* New York: HarperCollins.
Clark, K. (2006). *Grandma drove the garbage truck.* Camden, ME: Down East Books.
Dewdney, A. (2006). *Grumpy Gloria.* New York: Penguin Group.
Dunrier, O. (2007). *Goosie and Gertie.* Orlando, FL: Houghton Mifflin Harcourt.
Eastman, P. (1997). *Go dog. Go!* New York: Random House.
Kann, V. (2009). *Goldilicious.* New York: HarperCollins.
Rathmann, P. (2004). *Good night, gorilla.* New York: Penguin.
Seeger, L.V. (2013). *Green.* New York: Roaring Brook Press.

G (Soft)

Andreae, G. (2008). *Giraffes can't dance.* New York: Scholastic.
Donaldson, J. (2005). *The spiffiest giant in town.* New York: Penguin Group.
Egielski, R. (2000). *The gingerbread boy.* New York: HarperCollins.
Geisert, A. (2012). *The giant seed.* Brooklyn, NY: Enchanted Lion Books.
Peck, J. (1998). *The giant carrot.* New York: Penguin Group.
Silverstein, S. (1964). *A giraffe and a half.* New York: HarperCollins.

H

Carle, E. (2009). *A house for hermit crab.* New York: Simon & Schuster.
Cecil, R. (2012). *Horsefly and honey.* New York: Henry Holt & Co.
Johnson, D. B. (2006). *Henry hikes to Fitchburg.* Orlando, FL: Houghton Mifflin Harcourt.
Seuss, Dr. (2000). *Horton hatches the egg.* New York: Random House.
Van Camp, K. (2009). *Harry and horsie.* New York: HarperCollins.

J

Davies, N. (2012). *Just ducks!* Cambridge, MA: Candlewick Press.
Degan, B. (2008). *Jamberry.* New York: Barnes & Noble.
Fischer, S. M. (2010). *Jump.* New York: Simon & Schuster.
Havill, J. (2009). *Jamaica's find.* Orlando, FL: Houghton Mifflin Harcourt.
Johnson, A. (2007). *Just like Josh Gibson.* New York: Simon & Schuster.
Van Allsburg, C. (1981). *Jumanji.* Orlando, FL: Houghton Mifflin Harcourt.

K

dePaola, T. (1994). *Kit and Kat.* New York: Penguin Group.
Fox, M. (1994). *Koala Lou.* Orlando, FL: Houghton Mifflin Harcourt.
Hillenbrand, W. (2012). *Kite day: A bear and mole story.* New York: Holiday House Inc.
Himmelman, J. (2008). *Katie loves the kittens.* New York: Henry Holt & Co.
Pilkey, D. (2003). *Kat Kong.* Orlando, FL: Houghton Mifflin Harcourt.

L

Bateman, T. (2012). *The leprechaun under the bed.* New York: Holiday House, Inc.
Blankenship, P. (2004). *Lulu's lost shoes.* Novato, CA: Treasure Bay.
Dewdney, A. (2005). *Llama, llama, red pajama.* New York: Penguin Group.
Gerth, M. (2006). *Ten little ladybugs.* Atlanta, GA: Dalmatian Press.
Horse, H. (2005). *Little rabbit lost.* Atlanta, GA: Peachtree Press.
Knudson, M. (2009). *Library lion.* Cambridge, MA: Candlewick Press.

M

Bemelmans, L. (2000). *Madeline.* New York: Penguin Group.
Cousins, L. (2007). *Maisy big, Maisy small.* Cambridge, MA: Candlewick Press.

Donofrio, B. (2007). *Mary and the mouse, the mouse and Mary.* New York: Random House.
Freeman, D. (2006). *Manuelo, the playing mantis.* New York: Penguin Group.
Kellogg, S. (2002). *The missing mitten mystery.* New York: Penguin Group.
Knudsen, M. (2012). *Big mean Mike.* Cambridge, MA: Candlewick Press.

N

Bunting, E. (1996). *No nap.* Orlando, FL: Houghton Mifflin Harcourt.
DaCosta, B., & Young, E. (2012). *Nightime ninja.* Guelph, Canada: Little, Brown Books for Young Readers.
O'Connor, J. (1993). *Nina, Nina, ballerina.* New York: Grosset.
Shannon, D. (1998). *No, David.* New York: Scholastic.
Wells, R. (2000). *Noisy Nora.* New York: Scholastic.
Wood, A. (2000). *The napping house.* Orlando, FL: Houghton Mifflin Harcourt.

P

Corey, S. (2006). *Players in pigtails.* New York: Scholastic.
Long, E. (2012). *Pig has a plan.* New York: Holiday House.
Munsch, R. (1992). *The paper bag princess.* Toronto, ON: Annick Press.
Numeroff, L. (2000). *If you give a pig a pancake.* New York: HarperCollins.
Palatini, M. (1997). *Piggie pie.* Orlando, FL: Houghton Mifflin Harcourt.
Wood, A. (2010). *Piggy pie po.* Orlando, FL: Houghton Mifflin Harcourt.

Q

Daywalt, D. (2013). *The day the crayons quit.* New York: Philomel.
Johnston, T. (1996). *The quilt story.* New York: Penguin Group.
Polacco, P. (2010). *The keeping quilt.* New York: Simon & Schuster.
Wood, A. (1998). *Quick as cricket.* New York: Child's Play-International.

R

Arnosky, J. (2001). *Rabbits and raindrops.* New York: Penguin Group.
Covell, D. (2012). *Rat & roach: Friends to the end.* New York: Viking Juvenile.
Pfister, M. (1999). *The rainbow fish.* New York: North-South Books.
Stewart, A. (2006). *Rabbit ears.* London: Bloomsbury.
Wells, R. (2004). *Ruby's beauty shop.* New York: Penguin Group.
Willis, N. C. (2002). *Raccoon moon.* Middletown, DE: Birdsong Books.
Wise Brown, M. (2005). *The runaway bunny.* New York: HarperCollins.

S

Arnold, T. (2009). *Super fly guy.* New York: Scholastic.
Duncan Edwards, P. (1998). *Some smug slug.* New York: HarperCollins.
Lionnni, L. (1973). *Swimmy.* New York: Random House.
McMullan, K., & McMullan, J. (2006). *I stink.* New York: HarperCollins.
Root, P. (2009). *Ten sleepy sheep.* Cambridge, MA: Candlewick Press.
Schachner, J. (2005). *Skippyjon Jones.* New York: Penguin Group.
Scotton, R. (2012). *Secret agent splat!* New York: HarperCollins.
Wright, M. (2010). *Sneezy the snowman.* Tarrytown, NY: Marshall Cavendish Corporation.

T

Bisset, J. (2008). *Tickle monster.* Seattle, WA: Compendium Inc.
Christian Anderson, H. (2004). *Thumbelina.* New York: Penguin Group.
Fleming, C. (2007). *Tippy-tippy-tippy, hide!* New York: Simon & Schuster.
Marino, G. (2012). *Too tall houses.* New York: Viking Juvenile.
Van Fleet, M. (2003). *Tails.* Orlando, FL: Houghton Mifflin Harcourt.
Zimmerman, A. (2007). *Trashy town.* New York: Weston Woods Studio.

V

Bauer Stamper, J. (2003). *Voyage the volcano.* New York: Scholastic.
Berenstain, J., & Berenstain, M. (2008). *Berenstain bears' Valentine party.* New York: HarperCollins.
Carle, E. (2007). *The very hungry caterpillar.* New York: Penguin Group.
McCue, L. (2004). *Corduroy's Valentine's day.* New York: Penguin Group.
Williams, M. (2011). *The velveteen rabbit.* Tarrytown, NY, Marshall Cavendish Corporation.

W

Bleiman, A. & Eastland, C. (2012). *Welcome to the world, zooborns!* New York: Simon Spotlight.
Hartman, B. (2004). *The wolf who cried boy.* New York: Penguin Group.
Henkes, K. (2010). *Wemberly worried.* New York: HarperCollins.
Keats, E. J. (1998). *Whistle for Willie.* New York: Penguin Group.
McGee, M. (2006). *Winston the bookwolf.* New York: Walker & Co.
Sendak, M. (1988). *Where the wild things are.* New York: HarperCollins.
Williams, S. (1996). *I went walking.* New York: Gulliver.

X

Fox, M. (1992). *Hattie and the fox.* New York: Simon & Schuster.
Harrison, H. (2014). *Extraordinary Jane.* New York: Dial.
Portis, A. (2006). *Not a box.* New York: HarperCollins.
Wells, R. (2002). *Max cleans up.* New York: Penguin Group.
Zonta, P. (2006). *Jessica's x-ray.* Tonawanda, NY: Firefly Books.

Y

Ashford Frame, J. (2008). *Yesterday I had the blues.* New York: Random House.
Barnett, M. (2012). *Extra yarn.* New York: Balzar + Bray.
Berger, C. (2008). *Little yellow leaf.* New York: HarperCollins.
Boynton, S. (2001). *Yay, you! Moving out, moving up.* New York: Simon & Schuster.
Bramsen, C. (2009). *The yellow tutu.* New York: Random House.
Van Fleet, M. (1992). *One yellow lion.* New York: Penguin Group.
Wells, R. (2009). *Yoko.* New York: Hyperion.

Z

Bingham, K. (2012). *Z is for moose.* New York: Greenwillow Books.
Campbell, R. (2007). *Dear zoo.* New York: Simon & Schuster.
Fontes, R. (2002). *How the zebra got its stripes.* New York: Random House Golden Books.
McDermott, G. (1996). *Zomo the rabbit. A trickster tale from West Africa.* New York. Scholastic.
Moss, L. (2000). *Zin! Zin! Zin! A violin.* New York: Simon & Schuster.
Wynne-Jones, T. (2009). *Zoom.* Toronto, ON: Groundwood Books.

Vowels (Long and Short)

A

Dorros, A. (1992). *Alligator shoes.* New York: Puffin.
Holabird, K. (2006). *Angelina and Alice.* New York: Penguin Group.
Holabird, K. (2008). *Angelina ballerina.* New York: Penguin Group.
Parish, H. (2010). *Amelia Bedelia's first apple pie.* New York: HarperCollins.
Stein, D. E. (2012). *Because Amelia smiled.* Cambridge, MA: Candlewick Press.

Van Allsburg, C. (1998). *Two bad ants.* Orlando, FL: Houghton Mifflin Harcourt.
Wellington, M. (2004). *Apple farmer Annie.* New York: Penguin Group.

E

Amani, M. J. (2012) *Excuse me, I'm trying to read.* Watertown, MA: Charlesbridge Publishing, Inc.
D'amico, C., & D'amico, S. (2004). *Ella the elegant elephant.* New York: Scholastic.
Knowles, S., & Clement, R. (1998). *Edward the emu.* New York: HarperCollins.
Lionni, L. (1998). *An extraordinary egg.* New York: Random House.
McPhail, D. *Emma's pet* (1993). New York: Puffin.
Munson, D. (2000). *Enemy pie.* San Francisco, CA: Chronicle Books.
Sakai, K. (2006). *Emily's balloon.* San Francisco, CA: Chronicle Books.

I

Beaty, A. (2007). *Iggy Peck, architect.* New York: Harry N. Abrams.
Dorros, A. (1999). *Isla.* New York: Puffin.
Gibbons, G. (2007). *Ice cream: The full scoop.* New York: Holiday House.
Hosford, K. (2012). *Infinity and me.* Minneapolis, MN: Lerner Publishing Group.
Lionni, L. (2010). *Inch by inch.* New York: Random House.
Orloff, K. (2004). *I wanna iguana.* New York: Penguin Group.
Reynolds, P. (2007). *Ish.* New York: Weston Woods Studios.

O

Cammuso, F. (2009). *Otto's orange day.* Cambridge, MA: Candlewick.
Dunrea, O. (2007). *Ollie.* Orlando, FL: Houghton Mifflin Harcourt.
Falconer, I. (2004). *Olivia.* New York: Simon & Schuster.
Fleming, C. (2012). *Oh no!* New York: Random House Children's Books.
Frasier, D. (2002). *Out of the ocean.* Orlando, FL: Houghton Mifflin Harcourt.
Middleton Elya, S. (2006). *Oh no! Gotta go!* New York: Penguin Group.
Parr, T. (2005). *Otto goes to school.* New York: Little Brown Books.

U

Anderson, H. C. (2008). *The ugly duckling.* New York: North-South Books.
Brett, J. (2011). *The umbrella.* New York: Penguin Group.
Disney, R. H. (2010). *Up.* New York: Random House Golden Books.
Lloyd, J. (2010). *Ella's umbrellas.* Vancouver, BC: Simply Read Books.
Monsell, E. M. (2010). *Underwear.* Park Ridge, IL: Albert Whitman & Company.
Redmond, E. S. (2012). *The unruly queen.* Cambridge, MA: Candlewick Press.
Yashima, T. (2004). *Umbrella.* New York: Penguin Group.

Digraphs

CH

Archambault, J., & Martin, B., Jr. (2000). *Chicka chicka boom boom.* New York: Simon & Schuster.
Black, I. M. (2009). *Chicken cheeks.* New York: Simon & Schuster.
Graves, K. (2010). *Chicken big.* San Francisco, CA: Chronicle Books.
Palanti, M. (2007). *Cheese.* New York: HarperCollins Publishers.
Ponti, C. (2013). *Chick and chickie play all day!* Cambridge, MA: Toon Books.
Yamada, U. (2007). *Story of Cherry the pig.* San Diego, CA: Kane Miller Book.

PH

Alter, A. (2011). *A photo for Greta.* New York: Random House.
Coleman, J. W. (2013). *Eight dolphins of Katrina: A true tale of survival.* New York: Houghton Mifflin Harcourt.

Foster, K. (2010). *A dolphin up a tree.* Los Angeles: Foster Branch Publishing.
Hill, S. (2006). *Punxsutawney Phyllis.* New York: Holiday House.

SH

Collins Berkes, M. (2002). *Seashells by the seashore.* Nevada City, CA: Dawn.
Davis, N. (2005). *Surprising sharks.* Cambridge, MA: Candlewick Press.
Hale, B. (2014). *Clark the shark dares to share.* New York: HarperCollins Publishers.
Shaw, N. (1997). *Sheep in a shop.* Boston: Houghton Mifflin.

TH

Bourgeois, P. (1986). *Franklin and the thunderstorm.* New York: Scholastic.
Craig, H. (2009). *Thirsty Thursday.* Cambridge, MA: Candlewick Press.
McElligott, M. (2007). *Bean thirteen.* New York: Penguin Group.
Milgrim, D. (2006). *Thank you, Thanksgiving.* Orlando, FL: Houghton Mifflin Harcourt.
Spinelli, J. (2012). *Third grade angels.* New York: Scholastic Inc.
Seuss, Dr. (2009). *Oh, the thinks you can think.* New York: Random House.

Word Families

Alborough, J. (2008). *Duck in the truck.* San Diego, CA: Kane Miller Books.
Edwards, D. (1998). *Some smug slug.* New York: HarperCollins.
Freeman, D. (2006). *Mop top.* Pine Plains, NY: Live Oak Media.
Karlin, N. (2006). *The fat cat sat on the mat.* New York: Barnes & Noble.
Kohuth, J. (2012). *Duck sock hop.* New York: Dial.
O'Connor, J. (1995). *Kate skates.* New York: Penguin Group.
Ryan, C. (2012). *Moo hoo.* New York: Walker Childrens.
Seuss, Dr. (1957). *The cat in the hat.* New York: Random House.
Shaw, N. E. (2009). *Sheep in a jeep.* Orlando, FL: Houghton Mifflin Harcourt.
Willis, R. (2002). *Raccoon moon.* Middletown, DE: Birdsong Books.
Wilson, K., & Randin, J. (2007). *A frog in the bog.* New York: Simon & Schuster.

Books for Following Directions

Betty Crocker Editors. (2007). *Betty Crocker's kids cook!* Hoboken, NJ: Wiley, & Sons.
Curtis, J. L. (2004). *It's hard to be five: Learning how to work my control panel.* New York: HarperCollins Publishers.
Gibbons, G. (1996). *How a house is built.* New York: Holiday House.
Gold, R. (2006). *Kids cook 1-2-3: Recipes for young chefs using only three ingredients.* New York: Bloomsbury.
Priceman, M. (1996). *How to make apple pie and see the world.* New York: Random House Publishers.
Robinson, N. (2006). *Origami adventures: Animals.* Hauppauge, NY: Barron's Educational Series.
Schafer, Albert. (2012). *Illusionology: The secret science of magic.* Somerville, MA: Candlewick Press.
Sturn, J., Arnold, A., & Frost, A. F. (2009). *Adventures in cartooning: How to turn your doodles into comics.* New York: First Second Books.
Takai, M., & Takai, H. (2017). *Fun Origami for children: Dino! 12 daring dinosaurs to fold!* London, UK: Ryland Peters & Small.

Series Books

Captain underpants series. New York: Scholastic.
Diary of a wimpy kid book series. New York: Amulet Books.

Elephant and piggie book series. New York: Disney-Hyperion.
Litwin, E. *Pete the cat series.* New York: HarperCollins Publishers.
McDonald, M. *Judy Moody series.* Cambridge, MA: Candlewick.
O'Connor, J. *Fancy Nancy series.* New York: HarperCollins Publishers.
Osborne, M. P. *Magic tree house series.* New York: Random House Publishers.
Parish, P. *Amelia Bedelia series.* New York: Scholastic Inc.
Park, B. *Junie B. Jones series.* New York: Random House Publishers.
Peppa Pig book series. New York: Scholastic Inc.
Rowling, J. K. *Harry Potter series.* New York: Scholastic Inc.
Rylant, C. *Henry and Mudge series.* New York: Simon & Schuster.
Stilton, G. *Geronimo Stilton series.* New York: Scholastic Inc.

Expository and Narrative Books Related to Themes

All about Me Books

Appelt, K. (2003). *Incredible me!* New York: HarperCollins Publishers.
Cain, J. (2006). *The way I feel.* Seattle, WA: Parenting Press.
Carlson, N. L. (1990). *I like me!* New York: Penguin Group.
Curtis, J. L. (2007). *I'm gonna like me: Letting off a little self-esteem.* New York: HarperCollins Publishers.
Estes, E. (2004). *The hundred dresses.* Orlando, FL: Houghton Mifflin Harcourt.
Howard, T. E. (2013). *All about me!* Bloomington, IN: Trafford Publishing.
Kingsbury, K. (2004). *Let me hold you longer.* Carol Stream, IL: Tyndale House.
Manushkin, F. (2015). *Happy in our skin.* Somerville, MA: Candlewick Press.
Mitchell, L. (2001). *Different just like me.* Watertown, MA: Charlesbridge.
Parr, T. (2009). *It's okay to be different.* New York: Little, Brown & Co. Books for Young Readers.

Animal Books

Bancroft, H., & Van Gelder, R. G. (1997). *Animals in winter.* New York. HarperCollins.
Becker, B. (2008). *A visitor for bear.* Cambridge, MA: Candlewick Press.
Collins, R. (2017). *This zoo is not for you.* London, UK: Nosy Crow.
Cusick, D. (2013). *Get the scoop on animal poop! From lions to tapeworms: 251 cool facts about scat, frass, dung, and more!* Watertown, MA: Imagine Publishing.
Hawes, J. (2000). *Why frogs are wet.* New York; HarperCollins.
Hickman, P. (2007). *How animals eat.* Tonawanda, NY: Kids Can Press.
Jenkins, S. (2008). *What do you do with a tail like this?* Orlando, FL: Houghton Mifflin Harcourt.
Larson, K., & Nethery, M. (2008). *Two Bobbies: A true story of Hurricane Katrina, friendship, and survival.* New York: Walker & Company.
Myron, V. (2009). *Dewey: There's a cat in the library.* New York: Little, Brown & Co. Books for Young Readers.
So, M. (2008). *Pale male: Citizen hawk of New York City.* New York: Random House Publishers.

Dinosaur Books

Brusatte, S. (2013). *Walking with dinosaurs encyclopedia.* New York: HarperFestival.
Carter, D. (2001). *Flapdoodle dinosaurs.* New York: Simon & Schuster.
Diggory-Shields, C. (2008). *Saturday night at the dinosaur stomp.* Cambridge, MA: Candlewick Press.

Gibbons, G. (2006). *Dinosaur discoveries.* New York: Holiday House.
Kudlinski, K. V. (2008). *Boy, were we wrong about the dinosaurs.* New York: Puffin.
Mitton, T. (2009). *Dinosaurumpus.* New York: Scholastic.
Willems, M. (2006). *Edwina, the dinosaur who didn't know she was extinct.* New York: Hyperion.
Viorst, J. (2010). *Lulu and the brontosaurus.* New York: Simon & Schuster.
Yolen, J., & Teague, M. (2000). *How do dinosaurs say good night?* New York: Scholastic.
Zoehfeld, K. W. (2003). *Did dinosaurs have feathers?* New York: HarperCollins.

Ecology

Cherry, L. (2000). *The great kapok tree: A tale of the Amazon rainforest.* Orlando, FL: Houghton Mifflin Harcourt.
Cherry, L. (2002). *River ran wild: An environmental history.* Orlando, FL: Houghton Mifflin Harcourt.
Fleming, D. (2000). *Where once there was a wood.* New York: Henry Holt & Co.
Fogliano, J. (2012). *And then it's spring.* New York: Roaring Book Press.
Green, J. (2005). *Why should I recycle?* Hauppauge, NY: Barron's Educational Series.
Kochanoff, P. (2009). *You can be a nature detective.* Missoula, MT: Mountain Press Publishing.
Rey, H. A. (2010). *Curious George plants a tree.* Orlando, FL: Houghton Mifflin Harcourt.
Wells, R. E. (2006). *Did a dinosaur drink this water?* Morton Grove, IL: Whitman, Albert & Company.
Woodman, N. (2007). *Dirt.* Des Moines, IA: National Geographic Society.

Five Senses

Cole, J. (2001). *The magic school bus explores the senses.* New York: Scholastic.
Johnson, J. (2011). *Discover Science: Senses.* New York: Kingfisher.
Miller, M. (1998). *My five senses.* New York: Simon & Schuster.
Roca, N. (2006). *The 5 senses.* Hauppauge, NY: Barron's Educational Series.
Rotner, S. (2012). *Body actions.* New York: Holiday House.

How Things Work

Macaulay, D. (1998). *The new way things work. New York:* Houghton Mifflin Harcourt.
Showers, P. (2001). *What happens to a hamburger?* New York: HarperCollins.
Sutton, S. (2012). *Demolition.* Somerville, MA: Candlewick.

Insects and Reptiles

Berger, M., & Berger, G. (2002). *Snap! A book about alligators and crocodiles.* New York: Scholastic.
Cronin, D. (2003). *Diary of a worm.* New York: HarperCollins.
Ehlert, L. (2001). *Waiting for wings.* Orlando, FL: Houghton Mifflin Harcourt.
Gibbons, G. (2010). *Snakes.* New York: Holiday House.
Heiligman, D. (1996). *From caterpillar to butterfly.* New York: HarperCollins.
Jenkins, S. (2012). *The beetle book.* Boston, MA: Houghton Mifflin Harcourt Publishing Company.
Kellog, S. (2004). *The mysterious tadpole.* New York: Penguin Group.
Orloff, K. K. (2004). *I wanna iguana.* New York: Penguin.
Rockwell, A. (2001). *Bugs are insects.* New York: HarperCollins.

Ocean Life

Carle, E. (2009). *A house for hermit crab.* New York: Simon & Schuster.
Jenkins, S. (2009). *Down, down, down: A journey to the bottom of the sea.* Orlando FL: Houghton Mifflin Harcourt.

Lionni, L. (1964). *Swimmy.* St. Louis, MO: Turtleback Books.
Pfeffer, W. (2009). *Life in a coral reef.* New York: HarperCollins.
Pfister, M. (1999). *The rainbow fish.* New York: North-South Books.
Sherry, K. (2007). *I'm the biggest thing in the ocean.* New York: Penguin Group.
Simon, S. (2013). *Coral reefs.* New York: HarperCollins.
Zoehfeld, W. K. (1994). *What lives in a shell?* New York: HarperCollins.

Space

Branley, F. M. (1998). *Floating in space.* New York: HarperCollins.
Curtis, C. (2008). *I took the moon for a walk.* Cambridge, MA: Barefoot Books.
Davis, K. C. (2001). *Don't know much about space.* New York: HarperCollins.
DeCristofano, C. C. (2012). *A black hole is not a black hole.* Watertown, MA: Charlesbridge Publishing Inc.
Floca, B. (2009). *Moonshot: The flight of Apollo 11.* New York: Simon & Schuster.
Gibbons, G. (2007). *The planets.* New York. Holiday House.
McNulty, F. (2005). *If you decide to go to the moon.* New York: Scholastic.
Rey, H. A. (2008). *Find the constellations.* Orlando, FL: Houghton Mifflin Harcourt.
Stott, C. (2003). *I wonder why stars twinkle and other questions about space.* New York: Kingfisher.

Seasons and Holidays

All Four Seasons

Bernard. (2001). *A tree for all seasons.* Washington, D.C.: National Geographic Society.
Branley, F. M. (2005). *Sunshine makes the seasons.* New York: HarperCollins.
Gibbons, G. (1996). *Reasons for seasons.* New York: Holiday House.
Rey, H. A. (2008). *Curious George seasons.* Orlando, FL: Houghton Mifflin Harcourt.
Rosenstiehl, A. (2010). *Silly Lilly and the four seasons.* Cambridge, MA: Candlewick Press.
Zoehfeld, K. W. (2014). *Secrets of the seasons: Orbiting the sun in our backyard.* New York: Knopf Books for Young Readers.

Autumn

dePaola, T. (2004). *Four friends in autumn.* New York: Simon & Schuster.
Ehlert, L. (2005). *Leaf man.* Orlando, FL: Houghton Mifflin Harcourt.
Ezra Stein, D. (2007). *Leaves.* New York: Penguin Group.
Houlb, J. (2012). *Pumpkin countdown.* Park Ridge, Illinois: Albert Whitman & Company.
Maestro, B. (1994). *Why do leaves change color?* New York: HarperCollins.
McNamara, M. (2007). *How many seeds in a pumpkin?* New York: Random House Children's Books.
Rawlinson, J. (2008). *Fletcher and the falling leaves.* New York: HarperCollins.
Rylant, C. (2008). *In November.* Orlando, FL: Houghton Mifflin Harcourt.
Tafuri, N. (2010). *The busy little squirrel.* New York: Simon & Schuster.

Winter

Brett, J. (2007). *The three snow bears.* New York: Penguin Group.
Briggs, R. (2000). *The snowman.* New York: Random House Children's Books.
Briggs Martin, J. (2009). *Snowflake Bentley.* Orlando, FL: Houghton Mifflin Harcourt.
Burton, V. L. (2009). *Katy and the big snow.* Orlando, FL: Houghton Mifflin Harcourt.
Ehlert, L. (2001). *Snowballs.* Orlando, FL: Houghton Mifflin Harcourt.
Fleming, D. (2001). *Time to sleep.* New York: Henry Holt & Co.
Keats, E. J. (1996). *The snowy day.* New York: Penguin Group.
Rylant, C. (2008). *Poppleton in winter.* New York: Scholastic.

Sams, C. R., & Stoick, J. (2000). *Stranger in the woods: A photographic fantasy.* Milford, MI: Carl R. Sams II Photography.

Stead, P. C. (2013). *Bear has a story to tell.* New York: Roaring Brook Press.

Yolen, J. (2005). *Owl moon.* New York: Scholastic.

Spring

Ehlert, L. (1992). *Planting a rainbow.* New York: Houghton Mifflin Harcourt.

Esbaum, J. (2010). *Everything spring.* Washington, DC: National Geographic Society.

Fleming, C. (2004). *Muncha! Muncha!* Muncha! Pine Plains, NY: Live Oak Media.

Hedlund, S. (2013). *Spring.* Minneapolis, MN: Magic Wagon.

Hubbell, P. (2005). *Hurray for spring!* Lanham, MD: Cooper Square Publishing LLC.

Ray, M.L. (2001). *Mud.* New York: Houghton Mifflin Harcourt.

Rylant, C. (2006). *Henry and Mudge in puddle trouble: The second book of their adventures.* Elmsford, NY: Spotlight.

Thompson, L. (2005). *Mouse's first spring.* New York: Simon & Schuster.

Wilson, K. (2008). *Bear wants more.* New York: Simon & Schuster.

Summer

Carter, D. A. (2008). *Beach bugs.* New York: Simon & Schuster.

DeGroat, D. (2009). *No more pencils, no more books, no more teacher's dirty looks.* New York: HarperCollins.

Ingalls Wilder, L. (2000). *Summertime in the big woods.* New York: HarperCollins.

Mayer, M. (2001). *Just grandma and me.* New York: Random House Children's Books.

Paraskevas, M. (2013). *Taffy saltwater's yummy summer day.* New York: Random House Children's Books.

Van Leeuwen, J. (2007). *Amanda pig and the really hot day.* New York: Penguin Group.

Wing, N. (2002). *The night before summer vacation.* New York: Penguin Group.

Cultural Diversity

African American

Andrews, T., & Collier, B. (2015). *Trombone shorty.* New York: Abrams Books.

Bridges, R. (1999). *Through my eyes.* New York: Scholastic.

Cole, H. (2013). *Unspoken: A story from the underground railroad.* New York: Scholastic Press.

Fitzgerald Howard, E. (2001). *Aunt Flossie's hats and crab cakes later.* Orlando, FL: Houghton Mifflin Harcourt.

Giovanni, N. (2007). *Rosa.* New York: Square Fish.

Hopkinson, D. (2005). *Under the quilt of night.* New York: Simon & Schuster.

King Mitchell, M. (1998). *Uncle Jed's barbershop.* New York: Simon & Schuster.

Levine, E. (2007). *Henry's freedom box: A true story from the underground railroad.* New York: Scholastic.

McKissack, P. C. (2008). *Goin' someplace special.* New York: Simon & Schuster.

Polacco, P. (1998). *Chicken Sunday.* New York: Penguin Group.

Rappaport, D. (2007). *Martin's big words: The life of Dr. Martin Luther King Jr.* New York: Hyperion Books.

Ringgold, F. (1996). *Tarbeach.* New York: Random House Children's Books.

Steptoe, J. (2001). *In daddy's arms I am tall: African Americans celebrating fathers.* New York: Lee & Low.

American

Bunting, E. (1999). *Smoky night.* Orlando, FL: Houghton Mifflin Harcourt.

Bunting, E. (2004). *October picnic.* Orlando, FL: Houghton Mifflin Harcourt.

Borden, L. (2005). *America is.* New York: Simon & Schuster.
Cheney, L. (2006). *Our 50 states: A family adventure across America.* New York: Simon & Schuster.
Keenan, S. (2007). *O, say can you see?* New York: Scholastic.
Lee-Tai, A. (2006). *A place where sunflowers grow.* San Francisco, CA: Children's Book Press.
McDonald, M. (2005). *Saving the Liberty Bell.* New York: Simon & Schuster.
Stewart, S. (2007). *The gardener.* New York: Square Fish.
Walker, D. (2010). *Hello, New York City.* New York: Sterling Publishing.
Wardlaw, L. (2012). *Red, white, and boom!* New York: Henry Holt and Co.
Wing, N., & Wummer, A. (2016). *The night before the Fourth of July.* New York: Grosset & Dunlap.

Asian

Bishop, C. H., & Wiese, K. (1996). *Five Chinese brothers.* New York: Penguin Group.
Coerr, E., & Himler, R. (2004). *Sadako and the thousand paper cranes, Vol 1.* New York: Penguin Group.
Demi. (2007). *The empty pot.* New York: Henry Holt & Co.
Lin, G. (2004). *Kite flying.* New York: Random House.
Lo, G. (2012). *Auntie Yang's great soybean picnic.* New York: Lee & Low Books, Inc.
Louie, A. L. (2009). *Yeh-Shen: A Cinderella story from China.* Darby, PA: Diane Publishing.
Mosel, A. (2010). *Tikki Tikki Tembo.* New York: Square Fish.
Mosel, A. (1993). *The funny little woman.* New York: Puffin.
Say, A. (2008). *Grandfather's journey.* Orlando, FL: Houghton Mifflin Harcourt.
Selby, D., & Leon, S. (2017). *Kids' travel guide—Japan* (Vol. 35). Flying Kids.
Yolen, J., & Young, E. (1998). *Emperor and the kite.* New York: Penguin Group.
Young, E. (1996). *Lon Po Po: A red riding hood story from China.* New York: Penguin Group.
Young, E., & Adams, T. (2004). *The lost horse: A Chinese folktale.* Orlando, FL: Houghton Mifflin Harcourt.

Irish

Climo, S. (2000). *Irish cinderlad.* New York: HarperCollins.
dePaola, T. (1994). *Patrick: Patron saint of Ireland.* New York: Holiday House.
dePaola, T. (2009). *Jamie O'Rourke and the big potato.* New York: Penguin Group.
Gleeson, B. (2005). *Finn McCoul.* Edina, MN: ABDO Publishing Co.
Heinrichs, A. (2013). *Saint Patrick's day.* North Mankato, MN: The Child's World, Incorporated.
McDermott, G. (2010). *Tim O'Toole and the wee folk.* New York: Penguin Group.
Wallace, A., & Elkerton, A. (2016). *How to catch a leprechaun.* Naperville, IL: Sourcebooks Jabberwocky.

Italian

Creech, S. (2005). *Granny Torrelli makes soup.* New York: HarperCollins.
dePaola, T. (1980). *The legend of old Befana.* Orlando, FL: Houghton Mifflin Harcourt.
dePaola, T. (1996). *Tony's bread.* New York: Penguin Group.
dePaola, T. (2010). *Strega Nona.* New York: Simon & Schuster.
Jacobson, R. (2005). *The Mona Lisa caper.* Plattsburgh, NY: Tundra.
Walker, D., & Teets, A. (2015). *Spaghetti & meatballs: Growing up Italian.* Terra Alta, WV: Headline Books.

Jamaican

Brent-Harris, A. (2011). *Sweet Jamaican summertime at grandma's.* Bloomington, IN: Xlibris Corp.
Fungchung, N., & Takashi, F. (2016). *Anya goes to Jamaica.* Nikko FungChung.

Medina, T. (2013). *I and I: Bob Marley*. New York: Lee & Low Books, Inc.
Pomerantz, C. (1989). *Chalk doll*. New York: HarperCollins.

Jewish

Gilman, P. (1993). *Something from nothing*. New York: Scholastic.
Halprin Wayland, A. (2009). *New year at the pier: A Rosh Hashanah story*. New York: Penguin Group.
Horowitz, D. (2007). *Five little gefiltes*. New York: Penguin Group.
Edwards, M. (2012). *Room for the baby*. New York: Random House.
Oberman, S. (2005). *Always prayer shawl*. Honesdale, PA: Boyds Mills Press.
Polacco, P. (2009). *Mrs. Katz and tush*. New York: Random House.
Polacco, P. (2010). *The keeping quilt*. New York: Simon & Schuster.
Simon, R., Simon, T., & Siegel, M. (2015). *Oskar and the eight blessings*. New York: Roaring Brook Press
Taback, S. (2000). *Joseph had a little overcoat*. New York: Penguin Group.

Latino

Alvarez, J. (2002). *How Tia Lola came to (visit) stay*. New York: Random House.
Dorros, A. (1997). *Abuela*. New York: Random House.
Engle, M., & Parisi, A. (2017). *Drum dream girl: how one girl's courage changed music*. New York: HMH Books for Young Readers.
Garza, C. L. (2000). *In my family en mi familia*. San Francisco, CA: Children's Book Press.
Gonzalez, L. (2008). *The storyteller's candle*. San Francisco, CA: Children's Book Press.
Krull, K. (2003). *Harvesting hope: The story of Cesar Chavez*. Orlando, FL: Houghton Mifflin Harcourt.
Mora, P. (2000). *Tomas and the library lady*. New York: Random House.
Negrin, F. (2002). *The secret footprints*. New York: Random House.
Roth, S. L. (2013). *Parrots over Puerto Rico*. New York: Lee & Low Books, Inc.
Soto, G. (1996). *Too many tamales*. New York: Penguin.

Middle Eastern

Khan, H. (2012). *Golden domes and silver lanterns: A Muslim book of colors*. San Francisco, CA: Chronicle Books.
Williams, K. L., & Mohammed, K. (2016). *Four feet, two sandals*. Grand Rapids, MI: Eerdmans Books for Young Readers.

Native Alaskans

Bania, M. (2002). *Kumak's house*. Portland, OR: Alaska Northwest Books.
Calie, D. (2013). *The little eskimo*. Albert Park, Australia: Wilkins Farago.
Dabcovich, L. (1999). *Polar bear son: An Inuit tale*. Orlando, FL: Houghton Mifflin Harcourt.
Gamble, A., Jasper, M., & Kelly, C. (2015). *Good night Alaska*. Dennis, MA: Good Night Books.
Herbet Scott, A. (2000). *On mother's lap*. Orlando, FL: Houghton Mifflin Harcourt.
Joosse, B. M. (1998). *Mama, do you love me?* San Francisco: Chronicle Books.

Native American

Bouchard, D. (2014). *The first flute*. Markham, ON: Fitzhenry & Whiteside.
dePaola, T. (1996). *The legend of Bluebonnet: An old Texas tale*. New York: Penguin Group.
Desimini, L. (1996). *How the stars fell into the sky*. Orlando, FL: Houghton Mifflin Harcourt.
Goble, P. (2001). *The girl who loved wild horses*. New York: Simon & Schuster.

Jeffers, S. (2002). *Brother eagle, sister sky: A message from Chief Seattle.* New York: Penguin Group.
Littlechild, G. (2003). *This land is my land.* San Francisco, CA: Children's Book Press.
Martin, R. (1998). *Rough face girl.* New York: Penguin Group.
Munsch, R. N. (1992). *A promise is a promise.* Vancouver BC: Annick Press.
Smith, M. G., & Flett, J. (2016). *My heart fills with happiness.* Victoria, BC: Orca Book.

Russian

Casey D., & Hall, A. (2015). *Babushka: a traditional tale.* Oxford, UK: Lion Children's Books.
Polacco, P. (1995). *Babushka's doll.* New York: Simon & Schuster.
Polacco, P. (1999). *Babushka Baba Yaga.* New York: Penguin Group.
Polacco, P. (2013). *The blessing cup.* New York: Simon & Schuster.
Ransome, A. (1987). *The fool of the world and the flying ship.* New York: Farrar, Straus & Giroux.
Tolstoy, A. (2006). *The gigantic turnip.* Cambridge, MA: Barefoot Books.

Children's Special Needs

Communication Problems (Speech and Language Differences)

Churnin, N., & Tuya, J. (2016). *The William Hoy story: How a deaf baseball player changed the game.* Chicago, IL: Albert Whitman & Company.
Heller, Lora (2012). *Sign language abc.* New York: Sterling Children's Books.
Kline, S. (1995). *Mary Marony and the chocolate surprise.* New York: Penguin Group.
Lester, H. (2002). *Hooway for Wodney Wat.* Orlando, FL: Houghton Mifflin Harcourt.
Moore-Malinos, J. (2007). *It's called dyslexia.* Hauppauge, NY: Barron's Educational Series.
Polacco, P. (2001). *Thank you, Mr. Falker.* New York: Penguin Group.

Physical Disabilities (Visual, Hearing, Physical)

Carlson, N. (1992). *Arnie and the new kid.* New York: Penguin Group.
Cowen-Fletcher, J. (1995). *Mama zooms.* New York: Scholastic.
Meyer, D. J. (1997). *Views from our shoes: Growing up with a brother or sister with special needs.* Bethesda, MD: Woodbine House.
Moore-Mallinos, J. (2008). *My friend has Down syndrome.* Hauppauge, NY: Barron's Educational Series, Inc.
Palacio, R.J. (n.d.). *We're all wonders.* New York: Knopf Books for Young Readers.
Palacio, R. J. (2012). *Wonder.* New York, NY: Random House.
Riggio Heelan, J. (2000). *Rolling along: The story of Taylor and his wheelchair.* Atlanta, GA: Peachtree Publishers.
Schaefer, L.M. (2008). *Some kids use wheelchairs.* North Mankato, MN: Capstone Press.
Thomas, P. (2002). *Don't call me special: A first look at disability.* Hauppauge, NY: Barron's Educational Series.
Willis, J., & Ross, T. (2000). *Susan laughs.* New York: Henry Holt & Co.

Learning Disabilities

Dahl, R. (1994). *Vicar of Nibbleswicke.* New York: Penguin.
Forgan, J. (2015). *Terrific Teddy's excessive energy* (Vol. 2). USA: Advocacy Consultants.
Fleming, V. (1993). *Be good to Eddie Lee.* New York: Penguin.
Hodge, D. (2007). *Lily and the mixed-up letters.* Plattsburgh, NY: Tundra.
Kraus, R. (2008). *Leo the late bloomer.* New York: Barnes & Noble.

Lears, L. (1998). *Ian's walk: A story about autism.* Morton Grove, IL: Albert Whitman & Co.

Lord, C. (2007). *Rules.* New York: Scholastic.

Milgrim, D. (2013). *Some monsters are different.* New York: Henry Holt & Co.

Shriver, M. (2001). *What's wrong with Timmy?* New York: Little, Brown Books.

Van Niekerk, C. (2008). *Understanding Sam and Asperger Syndrome.* Erie, PA: Skeezel Press.

Technology

Bedford, D., & Reeve, R. (2016). *Once upon a time. . . online.* New York: Parragon Inc.

Droyd, A. (2011). *Goodnight iPad: A parody for the next generation.* New York: Blue Rider Press.

Smith, L. (2010). *It's a book.* New York: Roaring Brook Press.

Appendix B

Integrated Language Arts Thematic Unit: Healthy Bodies, Healthy Minds

On the following pages, you will find a thematic unit dealing with "Healthy Bodies, Healthy Minds," written for children in preschool through third grade. This unit includes all content areas and weaves literacy instruction throughout. When using the unit, adapt and select the ideas for the children you teach, making sure to repeat activities to reinforce the concepts being taught. When carrying out the unit, samples from each student's work should be gathered through formal and informal assessment measures. This is an excellent way to track students' progress, and it can be used in portfolio assessment. Just before the activity section of this unit there are project-based ideas to do along with the theme. The projects involve people in the school and people in the outside world. With these projects children can help others. These types of projects are particularly appealing to children since they are doing something real for the community.

Factual Information

What Does It Mean To Be Healthy In Body and Mind?

Eating nutritious food, exercising regularly, getting enough sleep, keeping ourselves clean, are all very important to keeping fit and healthy in body and mind.

Why Should We Eat Healthy Foods?

Good foods are needed to supply your body and mind with the energy it needs to function and grow every day. All people need food to eat and water to drink to live. Food and water are also necessary for animals and most plants to live. Nutrients are the substances in food that give us the energy and strength we need to grow, work, and play.

What Are the Food Groups?

Eating properly, along with plenty of sleep and exercise, will keep a person's body healthy and strong. There are many types of food. Foods are separated into five categories and eating a proper amount of each daily will help ensure good health. Foods are categorized in the following manner:

1. **Vegetables:** Most vitamins and roughage are obtained from vegetables. A good diet should contain dark green, and yellow vegetables, like broccoli, lettuce, carrots, spinach, and squash. It is recommended that three to four servings be eaten daily from this group.
2. **Fruit:** Fruit is a healthy sweet treat, with plenty of vitamins and nutrients. Some examples include apples, oranges, pears, bananas, and strawberries. It is recommended that two to three servings be eaten daily from this group.

3. **Grains and cereal:** This group includes breads, rolls, bagels, crackers, cereals, such as oats and rice, and pastas. Carbohydrates, necessary for the energy to work and play, and fiber are the primary benefits of this group. Four daily servings are suggested.
4. **Meat, beans, poultry, fish, nuts, and eggs:** This category provides minerals and much of the protein in one's diet. Protein is essential for building and maintaining muscles. It is also important for overall growth. Two servings are suggested daily.
5. **Milk, cheese, yogurt, and cottage cheese:** These products are also high in protein and contain nutrients that build strong bones and teeth. Many of these products have a high fat content. Two to three servings are the recommended daily intake.
6. **Oils:** Oils are fats that are liquid at room temperature, like the vegetable oils that are commonly used in cooking, such as olive oil, corn oil, canola oil, and sunflower oil. Oils can come from many different plants and fish. Some foods are naturally high in oils, such as nuts, olives, some fish, and avocados.

A proper diet, including ample portions from the different food categories, is essential for a healthy, growing child. However, there are also foods known as *fats and sweets* or *junk foods*. These items provide no vitamins, minerals, or proteins and are not necessary for good health. These foods include soda, candy, and some seasonings and spices. On occasion these foods are fine in moderate amounts; however, a well-rounded diet is one containing items from the original groups discussed.

People from different cultures eat different food. Because the United States is home to people from many cultures, numerous American dishes have been influenced by Mexican, Asian, French, Italian, and Jamaican cooking, among others. It is fun to try ethnic foods and learn about different multicultural backgrounds.

Why Are Exercise, Rest, and Cleanliness Important?

Exercising by ourselves or with others can be fun. It gives us stronger muscles and healthier hearts, and it makes our bodies and minds feel good. It helps circulate our blood and makes us feel refreshed and relaxed.

People exercise regularly to keep healthy. Many of the sports or exercises here in the United States have been influenced by other cultures. For example, baseball was influenced by a British game called cricket, and American football was developed from rugby, a similar contact sport. Regular exercise helps to relieve stress and strengthen the body.

We spend a third of our lives sleeping. When we sleep, we give our bodies and minds time to rest, during which our heart rate and blood pressure decrease and breathing slows down. This is so our bodies and minds can work hard when we are awake. Getting too little sleep can affect how your body's and mind's ability to function and grow.

How Does Self-Esteem Affect Your Body and Positive Mind?

When people feel good about themselves we say that have a positive self-esteem. When we feel good about ourselves we are likely to take care of ourselves and avoid eating junk food.

Good mental health is important for coping with the demands of everyday life. Sometimes when you do not feel very good about yourself, it might help to make a list of all the things you can do such as riding a bike, reading a book, drawing a picture, or cooking a meal. People can also help us solve our problems and make us feel better. These people include parents, siblings, friends, and teachers. We all have strengths and weaknesses but we are most important in helping ourselves with problems.

It is healthy to express our feelings in appropriate ways. When someone does not take the time to think about his or her feelings and speak calmly in words, feelings may come out in other ways such as yelling, fighting, or staying alone. Getting plenty of sleep, eating nutritious meals, exercising outdoors, and keeping up personal hygiene will help you feel better about yourself.

Newsletter to Parents About Healthy Bodies, And Healthy Minds Theme

Your child will be participating in a unit that explores what it means to be healthy in body and mind. This unit will include the study of why we should eat healthy foods and what those foods are. We also will engage in activities to learn about exercise, rest, cleanliness, and the importance of self-esteem.

The good health unit will cover all subject areas—play, art, music, social studies, science, math, and literacy (reading, writing, listening, and oral language) that will be incorporated in the theme. Some of the activities we do at school may also be carried out at home with your child.

At School and at Home

Art: Your child will refine eye-hand coordination and visual discrimination skills and explore and experiment with different art materials. At school we will be creating food collages, and abstract bean mosaics. At home you can encourage your child to use his or her imagination by providing these and other food-related materials for art activities. Remember, that art is for exploring what can be done with different materials, rather than copying an adult model.

Science: We will be making applesauce, which will give the children an opportunity to listen, follow directions, and learn where apples come from and how they are grown, as well as how food changes as it's cooked. Making healthy snacks at home, such as fruit or salad, and involving your child in the preparation by using simple recipes will help to extend listening skills.

Literacy: Please assist at home by labeling healthy food items with the letters H and F (associated with health and food) or pointing out words that have these and other beginning sounds. Read signs and point out these letters when you are outside the home as well. Please read stories, poems, informational books, cookbooks, exercise magazines, and other literature related to our theme of good health to your child. Some books that will be featured in the unit include:

Achoo! by P. Demuth, 1997

Children Around the World by D. Montanari, D, 2001

Gregory, the Terrible Eater by M. Sharmat, 1984

No More Baths by B. Cole, 1989

Mooncake by F. Asch, 1983

We Need Your Help

We would like your assistance with our multicultural food of the week or your favorite food at home. If you are able to prepare a snack one day and discuss it, please sign your name and tell what type of snack you would like to prepare on the attached sheet.

If you can come in and read your child's favorite bedtime story to the class, please sign your name and tell what date you are available on the attached sheet.

If you have any other materials at home related to our theme, such as empty food containers, seeds, nuts, beans, or exercise or yoga magazines that we may use in our dramatic-play area, please send them in with your child.

Other Activities to Do with Your Child

Go to the supermarket with your child. Prepare a list beforehand of the food you need to purchase. Have your child check the things off as you put them in the cart. Try to purchase food from each food category.

Plant watermelon, avocado, and carrot seeds at home. Keep a diary or record of their growth, making comparisons between them.

Make simple, nutritious recipes at home, such as fruit salad, mixed green salad, butter, or peanut butter, to help our lessons carry over from class to home.

Take the time to engage in some exercise with your child each day. A brisk walk or bike ride will help your child learn that exercise is fun and should be done often. It is an activity your family will enjoy together.

Remind your child at bedtime that rest is important for our bodies. Share a special bedtime story each night with your child.

Child's Corner

Ask your child to write or draw something he or she did in school related to our theme. Help your child keep a journal of what foods he or she eats daily. Keep track of any exercises your child does. Keep track of how many hours of sleep your child gets, writing the number in the journal. Graph the numbers. Use a notebook for a journal. Have children bring their journals to school so we can compare similarities and differences in what children eat, how much they sleep and the type of exercise they do. If your child can improve his or her health to do more in any area, help them to figure that out and discuss how they will put that into action.

If you have any questions about the unit or you have additional ideas, please contact me. If you are in a profession that is related to our theme, such as a nutritionist, a fitness-related career, or know healthy recipes, please consider coming into class and talking to us.

Sincerely,

Lisa Mullin

I would like to prepare the following snack for your healthy bodies, healthy minds unit:

Snack:______________________________ Parent's Name:__________________

I am able to come in on the following date for a story reading:

Date:_____________

Book:________________________ Parent's Name:_______________________

Preparing the Classroom Environment

To begin the unit on healthy bodies, healthy minds, prepare the room so that the theme is evident to those who enter. Begin with some of the following suggestions and continue to add others as the unit progresses. Display environmental signs and labels about nutrition, personal hygiene, exercise, rest, and self-esteem wherever possible.

1. **Dramatic play:** The dramatic-play center can be turned into either a restaurant or a fitness center. As a restaurant, the center should include menus, receipts, order-taking slips, recipe cards, cookbooks, baking utensils, prop foods, signs commonly seen in restaurants, a cash register, play money, food posters, and waiter and waitress clothing. As a health club, the center could include light weights or dumbbells, jump ropes, balls, a balance beam, mats, gym membership cards, stop watches, heart-rate posters, sign-up sheets for aerobic classes, and towels.
2. **Block area:** To create places that food comes from such as farms and supermarkets, the following items can be added: farm props (animals and plants), supermarket props (play foods, receipts, money, and bags), environmental print signs and posters displaying food information, and cards for making signs.

3. **Outdoor play:** A health club/fitness center can be created outside by providing the following items: tables for stands or desks; exercise equipment including jump ropes, balls, a balance beam; play money; cash register; receipts; signs displaying the hours of business; and paper and pencils, so children learn that this is a place to go to keep our bodies healthy.
4. **Music:** Various songs on nutrition, exercise, personal hygiene, and good self-esteem can be added to the music center. All tapes should be accompanied by the written lyrics posted on the wall. Props to act out the songs may also be motivating. Students should also be encouraged to write and sing their own songs about good health.
5. **Art:** Include play dough and a poster with play dough recipes to make play foods. Include cooking and health magazines, dry foods to make collages, and fruit and vegetable-shaped sponges for printing with paint.
6. **Science:** Materials for various health and nutrition projects may be added: a stethoscope, a heart-rate chart, blood pressure device, foods to be classified into food groups, seed packages, and planting equipment. All these items should be accompanied with charts and journals to record ongoing progress. Posters of the human body showing the muscles and skeleton and informational books should also be added.
7. **Social studies:** Pictures of foods and the food pyramid, and maps that depict where certain food comes from, as well as where the children's families are from should be included. In addition, posters displaying various athletic events from around the world may appear in the center. Recipe books representing different cultures may also be added.
8. **Math:** Various foods can be used as counters, such as macaroni or dried beans. Charts and graphs to record various activities, such as eating favorite fruit, laps around the school yard, or number of hours slept per night, should be included. Black books for children to create their own number books are also needed.
9. **Literacy center**
   a. **Writing center:** Materials needed include a recipe box to share favorite recipes, food-shaped blank books, and a message board on which to share the morning message.
   b. **Library corner:** Include health and fitness magazines, cooking magazines, pamphlets about good nutrition and general health, and a collection of books pertaining to the unit from all genres. (See the following list and the bibliography at the end of the unit.)

Library Corner Booklist with Suggested Activities

Asch, F. (1983). *Mooncake.* Englewood Cliffs, NJ: Prentice Hall.

Bradenberg, F. (1976). *I wish I was sick, too.* NY: Greenwillow.

Carle, E. (1969). *The very hungry caterpillar.* New York: Philomel

Chambers, W. (1974). *The lip-smackin', joke-crackin' cookbook for kids.* New York: Golden Press.

Cole, J. (1988). *The magic school bus inside the human body.* New York: Scholastic.

Curtis, J. L. (2002). *I'm gonna like me: Letting off a little self-esteem.* New York: HarperCollins

De Brunhoff, L., & Weiss, E. (2002). *Babar's yoga for elephants.* New York: Harry N. Abrams.

Demuth, P. (1996). *Johnny Appleseed.* New York: Grosset & Dunlap.

Demuth, P. (1997). *Achoo!* New York: Grosset & Dunlap.
dePaola, T. (1975). *Strega Nona: An old tale.* Englewood Cliffs, NJ: Prentice Hall.
dePaola, T. (1978). *The popcorn book.* New York: The Holliday House.
Eberts, M. (1984). *Pancakes, crackers, and pizza.* Chicago: Children's Press.
Faulkner, M. (1986). *Jack and the beanstalk.* New York: Scholastic.
Hoban, R. (1976). *Bread and jam for Frances.* New York: Harper & Row.
Hopkins, L. B. (1985). *Munching: Poems about eating.* Boston: Little, Brown.
Irving, W. (1987). *Rip Van Winkle.* New York: Puffin Books.
Izawa, T. (1968). *The little red hen.* New York: Grosset & Dunlap.
Katzen, M., & Henderson, A. (1994). *Pretend soup and other real recipes: A cookbook for preschoolers and up.* Berkeley, CA: Ten Speed Press.
Kellogg, S. (1988). *Johnny Appleseed: A tall tale.* New York: Morrow Jr. Books.
Krauss, R. (1945). *The carrot seed.* New York: Scholastic.
Mayer, M. (1968). *There's a nightmare in my closet.* New York: Penguin.
McCloskey, R. (1948). *Blueberries for Sal.* New York: Penguin.
Montanari, D. (2001). *Children around the world.* Tonawanda, NY: Kids Can Press.
Numeroff-Joffe, L. (1985). *If you give a mouse a cookie.* New York: Scholastic.
Raffi. (1987). *Shake my sillies out.* New York: Random House.
Reid, M. (1996). *Let's find out about ice cream.* New York: Scholastic.
Ripley, C. (1997). *Why does popcorn pop? And other kitchen questions.* Toronto: Firefly Books.
Rockwell, L. (1999). *Good enough to eat: A kid's guide to food and nutrition.* New York: HarperCollins.
Seuss, Dr. (1960). *Green eggs and ham.* New York: Random House.
Shartmat, M. (1984). *Gregory, the terrible eater.* New York: Macmillan.
Shaw, C. (1947). *It looked like spilled milk.* New York: HarperCollins.
Showers, P. (1997). *Sleep is for everyone (Let's read-and-find-out science book).* New York: HarperCollins.
Silverstein, A., Silverstein, V. B., & Silverstein, Nunn, L. (2000). *Eat your vegetables! Drink your milk.* New York: Scholastic.
Simon, S. (1997). *The brain: Our nervous system.* New York: Scholastic.
Taylor, B. (1998). *A day at the farm.* New York: DK Publishing.
Thomas, P. (2002). *My amazing body: A first look at health and fitness.* Hauppauge, NY: Barron's Educational Series.
Westcott, M. B. (1980). *I know an old lady.* Boston: Little, Brown.
Zolotow, C. (1962). *Mr. Rabbit and the lovely present.* New York: Harper & Row.

Technology That Can Be Used During the Unit

Nutrition

Children's games about nutrition: www.mypyramid.gov/kids/

Games, presentations, and material for teachers about nutrition: www.facs.pppst.com/foodpyramid.html

Interactive food pyramid: www.nutritionexplorations.org/kids/nutrition-pyramid.asp

Flash games about nutrition: www.nourishinteractive.com/kids/gameroom.html

Exercise

Games and Rules that children can play outside: www.gameskidsplay.net/

Online games about exercise: www.kidnetic.com/kore/

New games for groups: http://wilderdom.com/games/PhysicalActivities.html

Hygiene

Dental Learning Games: www.learninggamesforkids.com/health_games_dental.html

Dental care games for kids by age: www.colgate.com/app/Kids-World/US/HomePage.cvsp

Personal Hygiene activities and ideas: www.hygiene-educ.com/en/learn/personal/guide/presentation2.html

Links to websites about hygiene: www.k12station.com/k12link_library html?subject=NHS&sub_cat=103496&final=103500

Project-Based Activities for This Unit

Good Food Project

In the chapter on motivation I describe a project based activity for good food. There are many children in the United States who go hungry. The students will search the Internet to find out where to find hungry children in the area in which they live. They will look for organizations that help to feed hungry children. They will create a pamphlet that informs their community about children who are hungry, and how they can help. For example, bring bags of food to a food pantry and provide addresses for them. The children decided to grow a vegetable garden on the school grounds and plant seeds to grow tomatoes, zucchini, cucumbers, carrots, and so on. After they planted, they took care of the garden by watering it, and harvesting it when there are grown vegetables ready to bring to the food pantry. They advertised their concerns and how others can help on Facebook, Instagram, and other sources of social media.

Project-Based Exercise Program

Knowing the importance of exercise the children decided that no one cares much about the elderly and exercise and that was a good project for them to tackle. They decided to write a small book about the importance of exercise for older people. The book would contain a lot of information about exercising and its importance. In addition the children would create an exercise program for seniors. They wrote a letter to directors of senior homes in their community. They asked if they would participate in the program after they created it and he approved of the program. They were delighted that there was at least one senior home that agreed to work with them.

They searched the Internet for information. They spoke with a physical therapist, a geriatric physician and to the director of the of the senior home where they would do the project They created a 15-minute exercise routine for the seniors and videotaped themselves doing the program. They selected some happy music for the background.

They took different parts of the book to write and their teacher proofed it before they sent it to Shutterfly to print. In addition to the book, people using the program would also get a DVD with the class modeling the routine. The children felt it would be beneficial to do it a week. The children made up a schedule so that students would go to conduct the sessions twice a week. The seniors loved it and so did the children. More books were published and DVDs burned since there were many requests for their publication.

Introductory Lesson for the Thematic Unit

Objective

A written message will provide for vocabulary development and sound-symbol associations. Print will be recognized as functional because it relays a message.

Activity: Morning message. Introduce the students to the good health unit by writing a message on the board. The message could look something like this:

"Today, we are going to begin learning about how to keep our bodies and our minds healthy. To take care of ourselves we need to eat good food, sleep, exercise, keep our bodies clean, and feel good about ourselves."

Read this message to the class using a pointer to track the print. Afterwards discuss the content of the message as well as the special words, letters, and sounds. Allow the children to add to the message. Do a morning message daily to inform students of new health facts, as well as any special events or questions that are related to the unit.

Concepts about Print

Objective 1

Increase oral and sight vocabulary through a discussion involving the seeing and writing of Very Own Words. Knowledge of nutrition will be gained.

Activity: Very Own Words. Before reading the story *I Know an Old Lady Who Swallowed a Fly* (Westcott, 1980), discuss with the children why it is dangerous to eat inappropriate food. After reading the story, children will discuss food they should not eat. Then ask them to name foods they like that are also good for them and the Old Lady. Write each child's favorite food on a 3-by-5 index card to be stored in their Very Own Word container.

Objective 2

Increase sight vocabulary and the ability to follow directions by using a chart with functional environmental print.

Activity: Environmental print. A helper chart will be made that lists jobs for students to perform in both English and Spanish with corresponding pictures. The chart should be located in a visible area and relate directly to the nutrition unit. Jobs may include cafeteria monitor, reading the lunch menu, and helping with the daily snack.

Objective 3

An alphabet book that reviews many nutrition words learned in the unit will be created. Knowledge of letters, both vowels and consonants, and words that are identified with specific letters and sounds will be demonstrated.

Activity: Nutrition alphabet book. An alphabet book will be made and photocopied for each child in the class. Each letter will relate to nutrition (i.e., A—Apple, B—bread, C—carrot, D—dairy, E—eggs, F—fish, etc.), and a complete sentence will be written with each letter (i.e., I like_____). The students will read the letters, words, and sentences with the teacher and with each other.

Oral Language

Objective 1

Speaking skills will be improved by speaking in complete sentences.

Activity: Show-and-tell. Have students bring in their favorite food from home representing different cultural backgrounds. Display and discuss with the class. Another activity would be to have children share a healthy habit they practice at home or at school.

Objective 2

Appropriate vocabulary for the level of maturity will be used when retelling a story.

Activity: Story retelling. Read a story related to nutrition, such as *The Very Hungry Caterpillar* (Carle, 1969), and allow the class to retell the story using food props that are in the book.

Objective 3

Language complexity will be increased through the use of adjectives. Students will gain knowledge about the different aspects of nutrition.

Activity: Webbing and creating poetry. Brainstorm the characteristics of nutritious food, such as milk, and provide a graphic presentation with a web (see below). List the characteristics of the food by writing adjectives to describe it. Create a web on the chalkboard. Encourage children to assist in putting together a poem by using the information on the web. Write the poem on chart paper. Encourage children to read it with you, tracking print from left to right as you read.

Motivating Reading and Writing

Objective 1

A story is read by a class parent to increase family literacy. Using the context of the story, outcomes will be predicted.

Activity: Prop story. A child's family member will read *If You Give a Mouse a Cookie* (Numeroff-Joffe, 1985) to the class. Use props such as a mouse doll, a plastic cup, an empty box of cookies, and so on to tell the story again to the class. Encourage participation by having the children use their knowledge of rhyme and context. Place the props in the library corner for the children to use.

Objective 2

A graphic organizer will be created to motivate interest and help children comprehend informational text.

Activity: The food pyramid. Read *Good Enough to Eat: A Kid's Guide to Food and Nutrition* (Rockwell, 1999) and discuss the food in the book. Next, have the children work together to create a food pyramid on the board, based on the information in the book. After they have drawn the pyramid, they can add the name of their favorite food to the appropriate food group. Discuss the nutritional value of the foods.

Concepts about Books

Objective 1

Learn to differentiate print from pictures and know what books are for.

Activity: Big Book. Create a class Big Book that contains pictures of and sentences about each child's favorite exercise or sport. Have English language learners write in both their home language and in English. When the book is completed, read the book together as a class. Place the Big Book in the library corner for repeated readings.

Objective 2

See and understand that print is read from left to right.

Activity: Poetry reading. Display a poem (such as "Shake My Sillies Out", Raffi, 1987) about movement or exercise on a large chart and read with the class. Use a pointer to show that print is read from left to right. Act out the poem and then create a class poem. Display and read it in the same manner.

Phonics

Objective 1

Learn about word families by writing a poem about nutrition.

Activity: Remind students about word families. Write a class poem about nutrition using word families such as day, way; bean, lean; eat, treat; and dine, fine.

Ask students to read the class poem aloud and together. Have individual students name the words that are in the same word family. Have students name other nutritional words that belong to word families, such as run, veggies, fruit, and list words that belong to the same word families. Challenge students who are able to write a new poem about nutrition using some of the rhyming words in the new list of word families.

Objective 2

Learn that words are made up of syllables. Gain phonemic awareness by listening to nutrition words and segmenting (clapping) syllables.

Activity: Syllable clap. Talk with children about why knowing about syllables can help them when they read and write. Ask them to clap with you as you say several words related to nutrition, making sure to also include words for exercise and being healthy. Begin with one-syllable words (e.g., run, eat, fruit, and sleep), then move on to two syllables (healthy, veggies, and apple), three syllables (exercise and banana), and so on. You may want to show pictures for the words for EL students. Then ask students to say other nutrition-related words with one syllable, then two, three, four, and so on, and ask the class to say and clap the syllables in these words. Include a few nutrition words in the home language(s) of your EL students and have them tell the class what the words mean and then have the class clap the syllables.

Comprehension

Objective 1

Learn about story structure by identifying story elements (setting, theme, characters, plot episodes, and resolution).

Activity: Story structure. The story *There's a Nightmare in my Closet* (Mayer, 1968) has been read to the children in the past. Before reading the story a second time, ask the children to try and remember the time the story takes place, and who the characters are. After reading the story a second time, have the children identify the three setting elements: time, place, and characters. Do the same thing with other story elements, such as the theme, plot episodes, and resolution. Have the children prepare a roll movie with five headings: setting, theme, characters, plot episodes, and resolution. Do one section of the roll movie at a time. Encourage them to draw pictures and include narrative for each of the sections. Repeat with other stories.

Objective 2

Create a K-W-L chart (what they **K**now, what they **W**ant to know, and what they have **L**earned).

Activity: K-W-L activity. Begin a discussion about exercise and how it affects the body. Ask what the children know about the importance of exercise. List their responses on chart paper under the heading "What We Know." Ask the students what they might want to learn about the subject and list those responses on chart paper as well under the heading "What We Want to Know." Introduce and read several informational books, posters, pamphlets, and magazines about exercise and a healthy body, such as *My Amazing Body: A First Look at Health and Fitness* (Thomas, 2002). After several days of discussion and activities in conjunction with these books, refer back to the lists you made at the beginning of the lesson. Create a new heading titled, "What We Learned" and ask the students to share things they learned about exercise over the past several days. Compare this list to the list of what they wanted to know about exercise. Ask questions like, how are they different? What could you do if you didn't learn something you wanted to know? Have the students complete similar charts before and after other lessons.

Writing

Objective 1

Emerging authors and illustrators: Learn that books are written by authors and that pictures are drawn by illustrators. Children will participate in brainstorming, drafting, conferencing, editing, and revising. An experience chart will be used as a prewriting activity.

Activity: Bed-Shaped Book. Read the books *Mooncake* (Asch, 1983) and *Sleep is for Everyone* (Showers, 1997). Create a story web on experience chart paper as students talk about characteristics of sleep (why it's important, what happens when you sleep). Each child will be writing a story about sleep while teacher conferences are taking place. Finished products will be written in books shaped like a bed. This activity can be extended to other topics related to the theme. For example, books may also be shaped like a bathtub or bar of soap if the story is about personal hygiene.

Objective 2

Communicate through writing about exercise and nutrition. See and use functional writing.

Activity: Notice bulletin board. A notice bulletin board with student and teacher sections will be prepared in the classroom. Children may display their work on the board, as well as leave and receive messages in their spaces. Students can share messages, such as what they had for lunch and what food group each item belonged to or what exercise or sports they played in gym or at home. They may also decorate their personal space by drawing pictures related to these topics.

Play

Objective 1

Follow written directions and use print in a functional manner in an outdoor play activity.

Activity: Outdoor play: Health Club. Set up a health club outside with different exercise stations. Have a sign-in sheet at each numbered station. Have children choose roles such as directing an exercise class, pouring water, filling in membership cards, or writing receipts. Encourage the children to name their club and hang posters as advertisements.

Objective 2

Engage in dramatic play, learning to listen to others, take turns, keep talk relevant, and build self-esteem.

Activity: Dramatic play: "I'm Glad I'm Me" Kingdom. Watch *Sesame Street's* "I'm Glad I'm Me" with Prince Charming Bird. Create an "I'm Glad I'm Me" Kingdom in the dramatic-play area. Hang flags the children have made to represent the things each child is proud of and likes about him- or herself. Supply crowns, robes, scepters, and so on. Place a basket of fairytale books in the center.

Art

Objective 1

Self-esteem and self-assessment will be fostered over the course of the unit.

Activity: I'm "thumb print" body books. Children will be given blank books to illustrate. On the cover they will put their thumb print and write the words "I'm (thumb print) body." Each week, they will draw a picture of something they have accomplished or are proud of. Encourage them to write beginning sounds or engage in invented spelling to accompany their pictures or take dictations in the books. After each entry, collect books and make motivational comments to the children. At the end of the unit, ask children to make a final comment on what they think their biggest accomplishment was.

Objective 2

Gain an appreciation for creativity and originality by designing collages and jewelry based on different cultures. Increase visual discrimination and enrich vocabulary through observation and discussion.

Activity: Macaroni art. Have students create collages using magazines, newspapers, macaroni, beads, markers, crayons, colored pencils, construction paper, and other various materials. Jewelry can also be made using macaroni and string. Macaroni can be dyed by placing it in food coloring and water for 3 minutes. Provide students with pictures, books, and real examples of multicultural jewelry, such as, Mexican or Native American necklaces, bracelets, or rings. Encourage children to design such types of jewelry. Students will observe and model each other's work and describe their own to the class.

Music

Objective 1

Recall skills will be enhanced as children relate their own bedtime experiences to the group.

Activity: Bedtime round. Listen to "Bedtime Round" by Tom Chapin. Post the lyrics and track from left to right as the children listen. Talk about bedtime and list other things children say in order to delay going to sleep. After practicing, try to sing the song in rounds as in the recording.

Objective 2

Increase sight word vocabulary. Talk about feelings and emotions in a supportive environment.

Activity: If you're happy and you know it. Sing the song "If You're Happy and You Know It." For each emotion, draw the corresponding face on a paper plate with the emotion written on it. Make a variety of plates—for example, if you're sad and you know it, if you're angry and you know it. Practice the song with the picture cards until the children can recognize the words without the drawings. Talk about each feeling. Make a list of things that make you feel each type of emotion.

Social Studies

Objective 1

The students should gain an appreciation for other cultures' influence on popular sports for exercise and should increase their knowledge of geography and other cultures.

Activity: Sports study. Students work in small groups to research the popular sports from other countries. Each group's contributions are added to a class Big Book about the topic. Play the different sports on the playground.

Objective 2

By introducing food and customs of different countries, an appreciation for the differences and contributions of other people and cultures will be developed. Oral and written communication skills will be increased.

Activity: Country of the week. Read *Children around the World* (Montanari, 2001). A "country of the week" will be focused on. Customs, foods, and major contributions of each will be highlighted. Children will discuss the differences and similarities among the countries, with an emphasis on foods and the healthfulness of each. The students may also write about their favorite food from each country. Different foods will be featured at snack time.

Science

Objective 1

The connection between oral and written language will be made through a discussion about how you catch a cold.

Activity: I wish I was sick, too. Read *I Wish I Was Sick, Too* (Brandenburg, 1976). Use an experience chart to record what the children know about catching a cold. Discuss the importance of cleanliness and the prevalence of germs in our lives. Allow each child to collect a sample of germs from objects and place on an agar Petri dish. Students can then predict which samples will grow faster than others. Children can then record their observations of any significant growth. Provide microscopes and/or magnifying glasses for more detailed observations.

Objective 2

Observe changes that occur in the form of food while following directions in preparing a recipe.

Activity: Making applesauce. Read *Johnny Appleseed* (Demuth, 1996) to the class. Discuss the nutritional value of apple products. Make applesauce with the class. Post the recipe and use it as a reference to point out all the steps involved in making applesauce.

Math

Objective 1

The connection between oral and written communication will be made by observing and recording the sleep patterns of animals.

Activity: Sleep patterns. Students will observe and record the sleep patterns of the class pet and graph daily results. Compare any differences on the graphs and discuss how animals need different amounts of sleep at different times of the day.

Objective 2

Relate pictures to text and see that pictures and print go together. Classify objects according to shape (triangles, circles, squares).

Activity: Sort a food. Read *Pancakes, Crackers, and Pizza* (Eberts, 1984) to the class. Emphasize the different shapes of food as you read: round pancakes, square crackers, and triangle shaped pieces of pizza. Create a chart with three columns (triangles, circles, squares). Encourage children to classify cutout pictures of food from magazines or newspapers in the appropriate columns on the chart. Provide three shoe boxes labeled with each shape so that children can continue to classify different foods on their own.

Culminating Activity

Objective 1

Share the products of the unit with children's family, friends, or other classes in the school.

Activity: Prepare a nutritious food, such as fruit salad and applesauce, for a snack to share with guests.

Activity: Sing a song related to the importance of rest from the unit, such as "Bedtime Round," or related to the importance of personal hygiene, such as "Brush Your Teeth."

Activity: Display art projects related to the unit. And describe how they were made.

Activity: Show plants from the science portion of the unit and discuss how they grew.

Appendix C
Technology

Discussion and Collaboration

PBS works: *www.pbworks.com/education*
Linoit: *http://en.linoit.com/*

International Collaboration

Childnet: *www.childnet.com*

iPhone/iPod/iPad Apps for Kids

21 Free Educational Apps for kids: *www.familyeducation.com/fun/mobile-apps/21-free-educational-apps-kids*

Music for Children

http://www.johnfarrell.net/meet-john-farrell
https://www.mtna.org/MTNA/Learn/Parent_and_Student_Resources/Websites_for_Kids.aspx

Resources for 21st Century Professional Development

Ed Web: *http://home.edweb.net/*
Thing Link: *www.thinglink.com/edu?showNavi=true*

Resources for Interactive Storybooks

Education.com: *www.education.com/stories/*
StoryPlace: *www.storyplace.org/*
Symbaloo: *www.symbaloo.com/mix/onlineinteractivebooks*

Resources for Podcasting

Podcast Generator: *www.podcastgenerator.net/*
Podmoatic: *www.podomatic.com/login*
PodBean: *www.podbean.com/start-podcast*

Resources for Reading

Oxford Owl: *www.oxfordowl.co.uk/*
Storyline online: *www.storylineonline.net/*

Resources for Teachers

TedEd: *http://ed.ted.com/*
Share My Lesson: *https://sharemylesson.com/*
Khan Academy: *www.khanacademy.org/*

Storytelling

Make-believe comix: *www.makebeliefscomix.com*
Storybird: *http://storybird.com/*
Folding Story: *http://foldingstory.com/*

Websites for Children

www.watchknowlearn.org
www.schooltube.com

Appendix D
Professional Associations and Related Journals Dealing with Early Literacy

What we have learned over the years concerning learning theory and early literacy development is the result of research by college professors and classroom teachers. Professional associations hold conferences and publish journals to inform and move the field forward. This appendix provides a list of groups and journals, along with other publications dealing with early literacy, for future study and reference.

American Library Association (ALA), 50 East Huron Street, Chicago, IL 60611, www.ala.org

American Montessori Society, Inc. (AMS), 116 East 16th Street, New York, NY 10003, https://amshq.org

Association for Childhood Education International (ACEI), 1200 18th Street, NW, Suite 700, Washington, DC 20036, https://www.acei.org (journals: *Childhood Education; Journal of Research in Childhood Education*)

Child Welfare League of America, Inc. (CWLA), 727 15th Street, NW, 12th floor, Washington, DC 20005, https://www.cwla.org (journal: *Child Welfare*)

Gordon and Breach Science Publishers, Inc., 325 Chestnut Street, Suite 800, Philadelphia, PA 19106

High/Scope Educational Research Foundation, 600 North River Street, Ypsilanti, MI 48198-2898, https://highscope.org (publications, videos, research, and professional development)

International Literacy Association (ILA), PO Box 8139, Newark, DE 19714, https://www.literacyworldwide.org/ (journals: *The Reading Teacher; Reading Research Quarterly;* brochures, pamphlets, and monographs)

Literacy Research Association (LRC), 7744 S. 13th Street, Oak Creek, WI 531154 (journal: *Journal of Literacy Research*)

National Association for the Education of Young Children (NAEYC), 1313 L Street, NW, Suite 500, Washington, DC 20005, https://naeyc.org (journals: *Young Children; Early Childhood Research Quarterly;* pamphlets and monographs)

National Center for Family Literacy, 325 West Main Street, Suite 300, Louisville, KY 40202-4237, https://www.familieslearning.org (newsletter: *Momentum*)

National Child Care Information Center, 9300 Lee Highway, Fairfax, VA 22031, www.nccic.org

National Council of Teachers of English (NCTE), 1111 W. Kenyon Road, Urbana, IL 61801, www.2.ncte.org (journal: *Language Arts*)

National Education Association, 1201 16th Street, NW, Washington, DC 20036, www.nea.org (journal: *NEA Today*; magazine: *Tomorrow's Teachers*)

National Head Start Association, 1651 Prince Street, Alexandria, VA 22314, www.nhsa.org (publication: *Children and Families Magazine*)

Office of Early Childhood Development, 330 C Street, NW, 4th floor, Washington, DC 20201

Reach Out and Read National Center, 89 South Street, Suite 201, Boston, MA 02111, www.reachoutandread.org

Reading Is Fundamental, 1730 Rhode Island Avenue, NW, Suite 1100, Washington DC 20036, www.rif.org (newsletter: *Read All about It*)

Society for Research in Child Development (SRCD), 1825 K Street, NW, Suite 325, Washington, DC 20006, www.srcd.org (journal: *Child Development*)

Appendix E

Suggestions for Instructors

Literacy Development in the Early Years: Helping Children Read and Write is written for students in graduate and undergraduate classes in courses such as Early Literacy Development and Reading in the Elementary School, or an Early Childhood Curriculum course that include literacy development as a major component. The book can also be used for professional development courses for classroom teachers. We suggest several activities to engage in with students. The following are a few that have been used successfully in class sessions or as assignments. Also, Appendix B includes an integrated language arts thematic unit that teachers can use as a model for beginning literacy programs in their preschool through third-grade classrooms. In addition to this brief guide for instructors, there is an online handbook that contains extensive ideas for assignments inside and outside the classroom, lesson plans, and both multiple-choice and short-answer tests. Access the instructor's online handbook using the password provided to adopters of the book.

Assignments and In-Class Activities

At the beginning of each chapter are focus questions that students should read prior to reading the chapter. At the end of every chapter are relevant activities contributed by classroom teachers. In addition there are activities to engage in. Read the activities; you might find that some of them are appropriate for class interaction in small groups and for discussion. Be sure in all planning that a discussion about English learners and issues of diversity is included.

Activities to participate in as you work your way through the book are as follows:

1. In Chapter 3, it is suggested that students select a child who they can study as they read the book. The child should be between 2 and 8 years old. The student should begin a portfolio for the child and meet with him or her from time to time to try strategies and assess and describe certain behaviors. Specifically, students should obtain a sample of writing, drawing, oral language, and a story retelling from the child. In addition, several of the measures provided in the book can be used to accumulate data about the child. For example:
    a. When reading Chapter 6 on language development, collect a language sample and analyze it for sentence length and numbers of different words. To elicit language from children, ask them to tell you about family, pets, TV shows they like, or games they play. Tape record the discussion and transcribe it for analysis.
    b. In Chapter 7, evaluate the child's knowledge about print using the checklist included.
    c. In Chapter 10, collect a writing sample from the child to determine the stage of writing, and analyze it for sense of story structure, the mechanics of writing, and so forth. To elicit a writing sample, you might have the child draw a picture and write about it. Talk about ideas to write before writing. Assure emergent writers that any way they can write is fine. Show them samples of children's writing from the text so they see that one-letter or scribble writing is fine.
    d. In Chapter 11, have the child retell a story that was read to him or her. Tape record the retelling and transcribe it. Analyze it using the measures that describe how to have the children retell and rewrite stories.

e. In Chapter 11, interview the child using using the form that measures motivation for reading and writing.

f. When studying the family, interview the child's parents using the English or Spanish form provided, which is a checklist concerning the home literacy environment.

2. At least three or four times during the semester, have the class break into groups to deal with special issues presented in the text. For example, in Chapter 9, the activity about Teachers A, B, and C is a good small-group activity. Have the students respond to the questions posed about the teachers and discuss which teacher each would wish to be. Discuss the pros and cons of each of the teachers presented.
3. Have students keep dialogue journals about readings that have made an impression on them. They can also include incidents in class that were particularly interesting, fun, or of concern. Respond to their journals with comments of your own.
4. Have your students take a vocabulary test using words from the glossary. Teachers need to be aware of the technical language associated with early literacy when talking with peers, interviewing for a job, and explaining issues to parents.
5. Have students bring six genres of children's literature to class to share in groups. Three books should be nonfiction or informational text and three should be fiction or narrative text. This assignment gives them the opportunity to browse through lots of books and see the variety of genres available. Set the books up as if your students were going into a classroom. They will gain a sense of the numbers and types of books that should be in a literacy center.
6. Ask students to draw a floor plan for their ideal classroom using the philosophy and strategies learned. Pay particular attention to the literacy center. Be sure they create plans to support literacy instruction for whole groups, small groups, and one-on-one settings.
7. Ask each student to be involved in a storytelling project. Give students a list of early literacy skills from those outlined on the checklists provided in the book. Have them select a skill they would like to teach. Ask them to find a picture storybook that will enable that skill to be taught. For example, if their skill is to teach sequencing, a story such as *I Know an Old Lady Who Swallowed a Fly* (Hoberman & Westscott, 2004) provides a sequence of events that are easily followed. The student then selects a technique for storytelling from those described in Chapter 11, such as a chalk talk, roll story, felt story, or other techniques they create themselves. A lesson plan is developed in which the teacher presents the story and teaches the skill through the use of the material created. The material is designed for children to use to practice the skill taught. In Chapter 11 the "Idea from the Classroom" concerning the story "A Bunny Called Nat" illustrates this type of assignment. Students present the storytelling in class.
8. Have the students select a group to work with. Ask the group to select a topic for a thematic unit. Using the guide for the unit in Chapter 8 and Appendix B, divide the sections and prepare a thematic unit for a classroom of children ages 2 through 8 years.
9. Have students participate in a teacher-researcher project. Each student selects a topic dealing with early literacy and carries out a mini-study. The study should include a statement of purpose, a short literature review related to the topic, a description of methods and procedures to follow during the study, a discussion of how the data will be analyzed, a report of the results of the data collection, and a discussion concerning the results. This is a large project that is introduced to students early in the semester in order for them to have ample time to carry it out. When writing the literature review, the students should be required to consult a few articles from professional journals. Some topics for study are literacy and play, computers and early literacy, family literacy, multicultural concerns in early literacy, and early intervention programs.

10. Have students bind their own books based on the directions provided in Chapter 10. Have them use the book for their dialogue journal or for writing their storytelling lesson plan.
11. Encourage students to join a professional organization such as the International Literacy Association or the National Association for the Education of Young Children.
12. Encourage your students to subscribe to a professional journal and a commercial teacher magazine.
13. One important activity to offer your students is to let them experience what it would be like to be a child learning to read. For this demonstration, we have provided materials and a plan for a class experience. This activity should take about 45 minutes of class time and should be done early in the semester when you are teaching theory. The lesson involves learning how to read with an alphabet called the *Confusabet*. Following is a plan for carrying out the Confusabet. Materials needed are provided in this appendix. Photocopy them for use in your lesson plan before beginning the lesson, or use the pages in the book.

The Confusabet Lesson

Objective: To experience how it feels to learn to read and write.

Materials

Confusabet alphabet and translation

Confusabet sight words and translation

Confusabet worksheets

Confusabet reading book and translation (books must be assembled)

Procedures

1. Before the lesson, ask students to think about and write answers to the following questions during the experience:
   a. What methods were used to teach reading? Which worked well and which did not work well?
   b. What emotions did you experience while learning to read and write the Confusabet?
   c. What strategies did you use to teach yourself how to read and write?
2. Hand out or turn to the Confusabet alphabet and pictures that have the names of the Confusabet characters on them.
3. Name the characters and have the students repeat their names.
4. Hand out or turn to worksheet 1. Ask students to find the character's name among other Confusabet words.
5. Hand out or turn to the list of Confusabet words. Provide students with context clues for each word—for example: The color of the traffic light that means you should stop is ________. Have the students fill in the word and point to the Confusabet word that is *red*.
6. Follow this step for all words and provide your own context clues.
7. Repeat the words with the students. You may repeat them all together, call on those who raise their hands, and call on students who do not raise their hands.
8. Turn to or hand out worksheet 2 with the Confusabet words just introduced, and ask students to underline and name the word in each list that is the same as the word at the top of the list.
9. Turn to or distribute the Confusabet primer. Call on students to read a line or a page at a time. Try round-robin reading as well.

During the Confusabet lesson, role-play as if you are a teacher of 6-year-olds. Praise students for doing well. Provide some positive reinforcement, and use some positive teaching techniques. Also try punitive techniques and phrases, such as "If you don't get this work correct, you won't get to take the book home to your parents," "You weren't listening; that's why you don't know the words," or "If you don't stop talking, you'll be sent to the principal's office."

During the Confusabet exercise, students should talk to each other naturally to try to work things out. When they do so, say, "Please do your own work and keep your eyes on your own paper," "Don't help each other; you have to learn to do it yourself," or "It's too noisy in here," or "We can't wait for you even though you haven't finished your work." When students have answers and are very anxious to give them, say, "You've already had your turn; give someone else a chance" or "Please settle down; you are disrupting the rest of the class." When students look ahead to preview materials handed out, say, "Please wait for me to tell you when to turn the page" or "Don't go ahead of me; we aren't up to that yet." This type of role-playing allows students to experience even more how children feel in the classroom, where these types of comments often occur.

10. After reading the Confusabet materials, ask students to write their names and then the sentence "I like to read and write" with Confusabet symbols.
11. At the end of the lesson, repeat the questions posed at the beginning:

    a. What methods did you use that worked well?
       What methods did you use that did not work well?
    b. What emotions did you experience?
    c. How did you teach yourself to learn to read?
    d. How did you go about learning to write?

Students will express that they experienced fear, anger, and frustration when they were having trouble. They will suggest that they wanted to tune out and not participate. Those who were succeeding will suggest that they were excited, they wanted to continue, and they wanted to share their excitement. Frequently students who are succeeding will be greeted with remarks such as "You've already had a turn. Settle down and let me give someone else a chance." When asked how they felt about this response, they will say that their feeling of excitement was cut short.

When students discuss the strategies they used to learn to read, they will often make comments similar to the following:

1. I used my past experience with knowledge from our real alphabet to help. For example, the Confusabet words have the same number of symbols as our alphabet. They also resemble some of the letters of our alphabet, and I was able to make associations.
2. I used the picture clues.
3. I used surrounding words or the context to figure out the word (contextual and syntactic clues).
4. I memorized symbols from one page to the next.
5. Some words were long or had an unusual shape, which helped me to figure out a word (configuration).
6. I looked at the first letter of a word to help figure it out.

When students are asked some of the things they did to help them read, they may say:

1. I pointed to the print to help me find my place.
2. I moved my eyes around the page to try and find clues.
3. I called out words one at a time, the way young children do.

What the students realize as a result of participating in the Confusabet experience is that they rely on meaning, past experience, associative strategies, and visual clues to figure out the words more than they do on individual skills such as phonics.

The Confusabet lesson presented here is adapted from materials created by Mildred Letton Wittock from the University of Chicago.

Confusabet Alphabet Letters

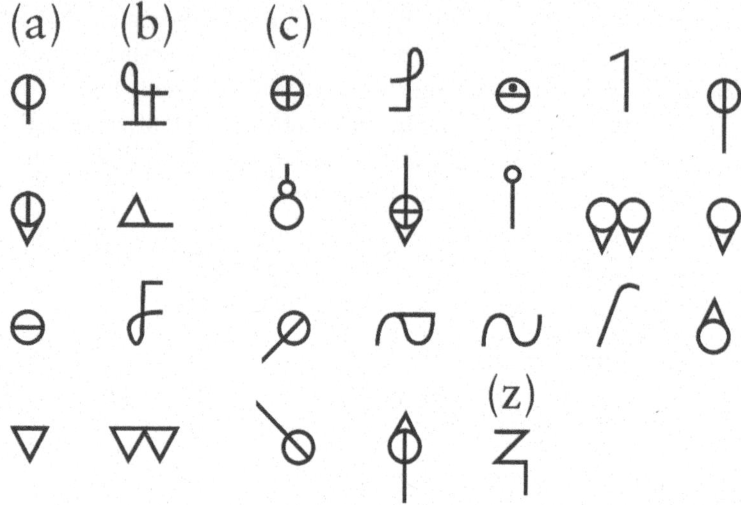

Confusabet Story Characters

Directions: Instructor names the characters for the students. Students repeat the names.

Confusabet Vocabulary Words

Directions: Instructor gives a context clue for each word to help students to read it. Students repeat the words.

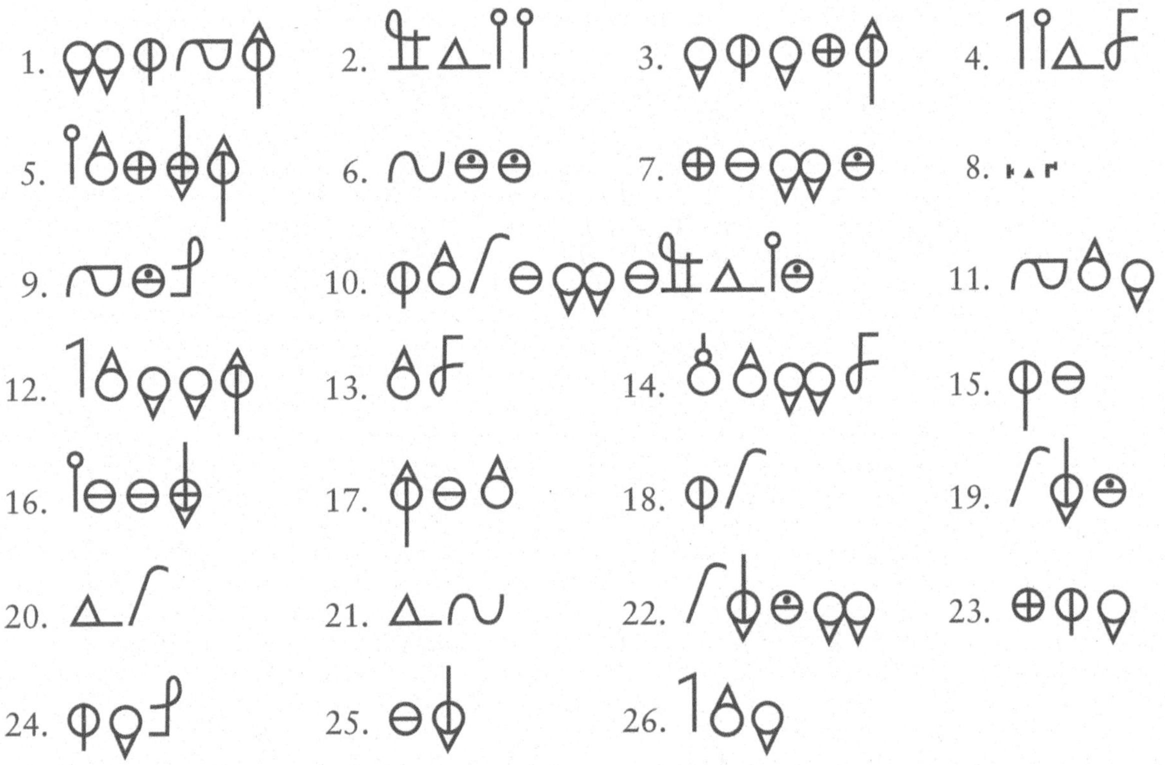

1. 2. 3. 4.
5. 6. 7. 8.
9. 10. 11.
12. 13. 14. 15.
16. 17. 18. 19.
20. 21. 22. 23.
24. 25. 26.

Confusabet Worksheet 1

Directions: Circle the name of the character in the list of words under his or her name. Say the name as you circle it.

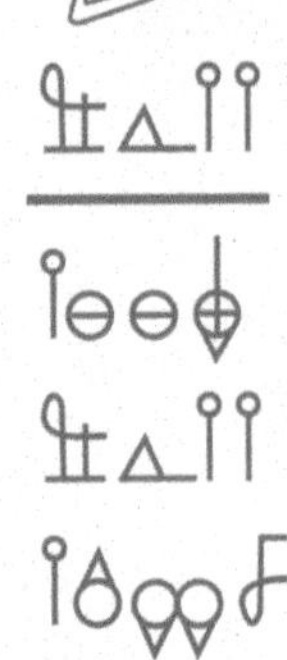

Confusabet Worksheet 2

Directions: Circle the underlined word in each column. Say the word as you circle it.

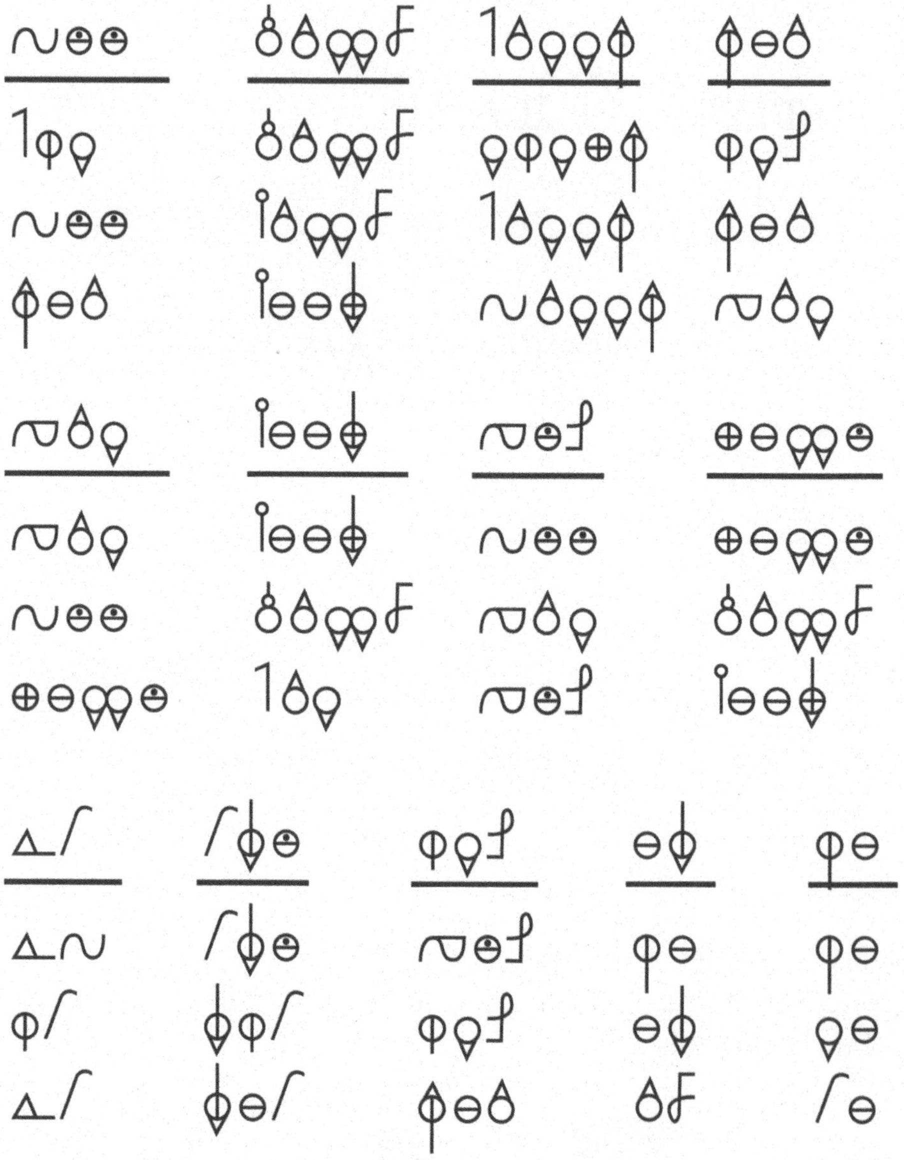

Confusabet Primer

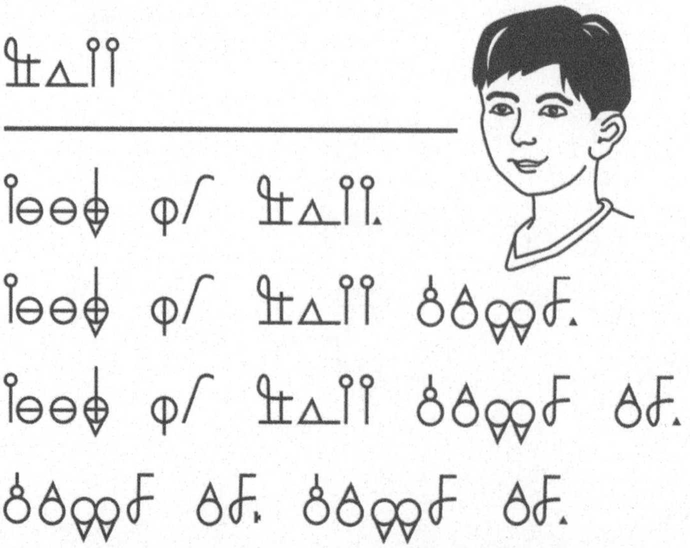

Confusabet Story 1

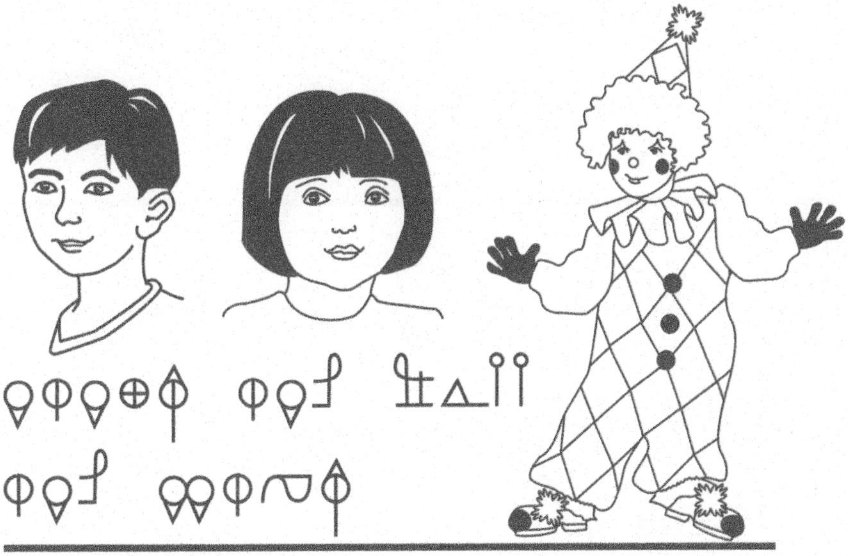

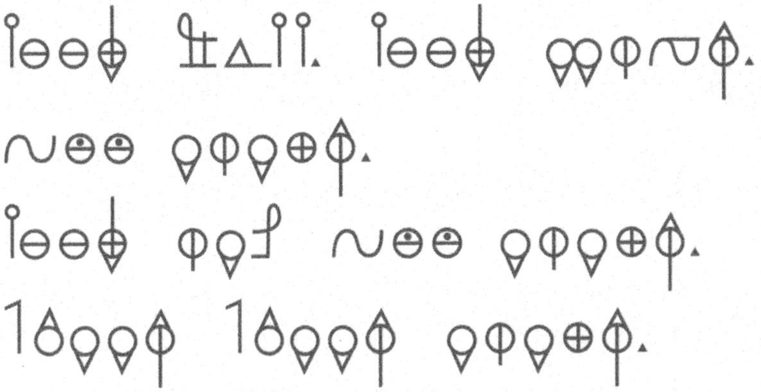

Confusabet Story 2

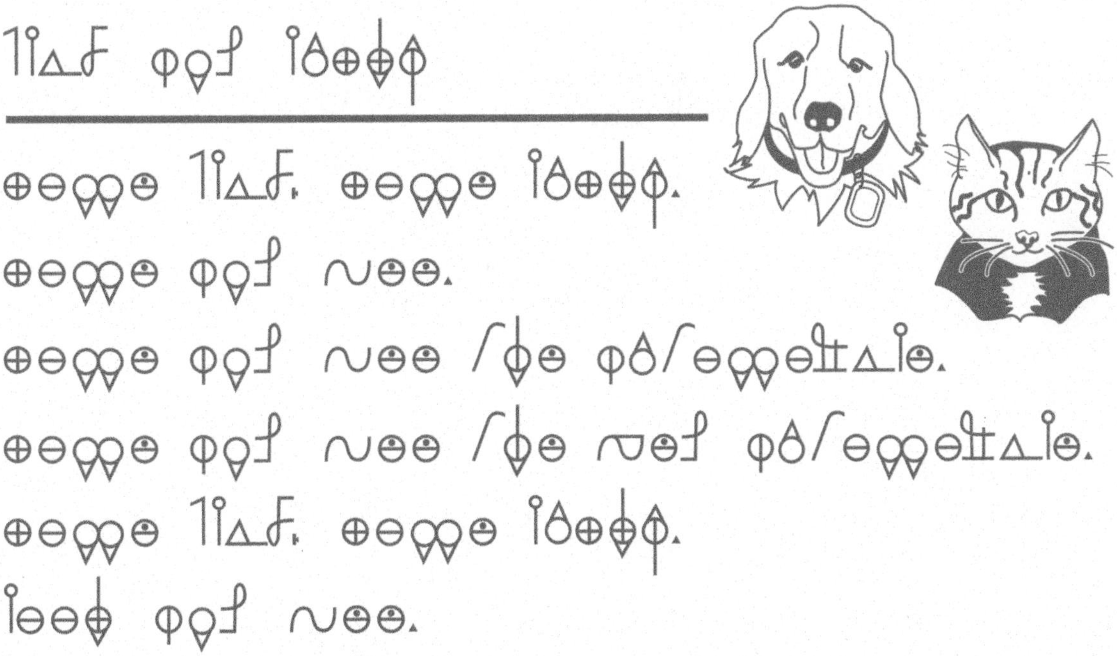

Confusabet Story 3

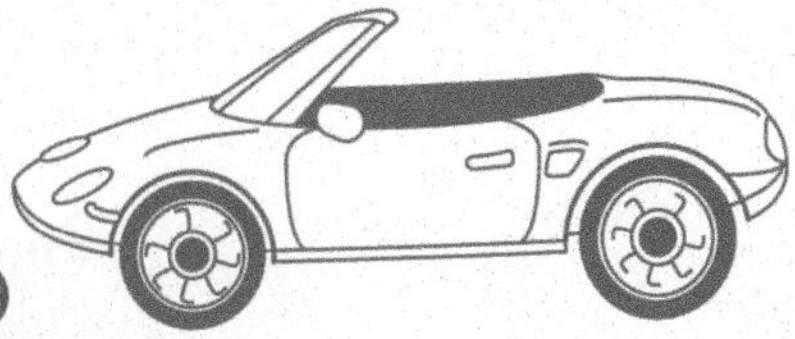

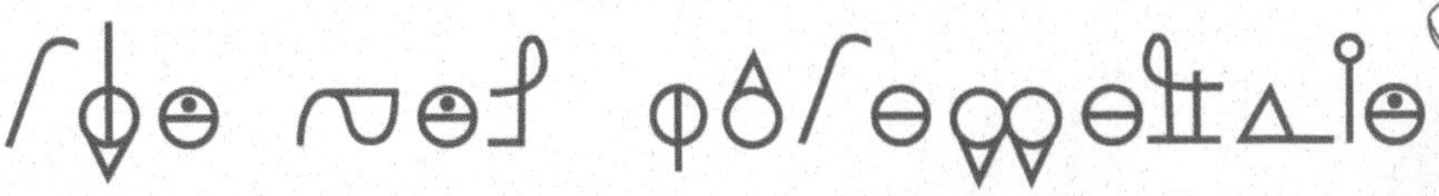

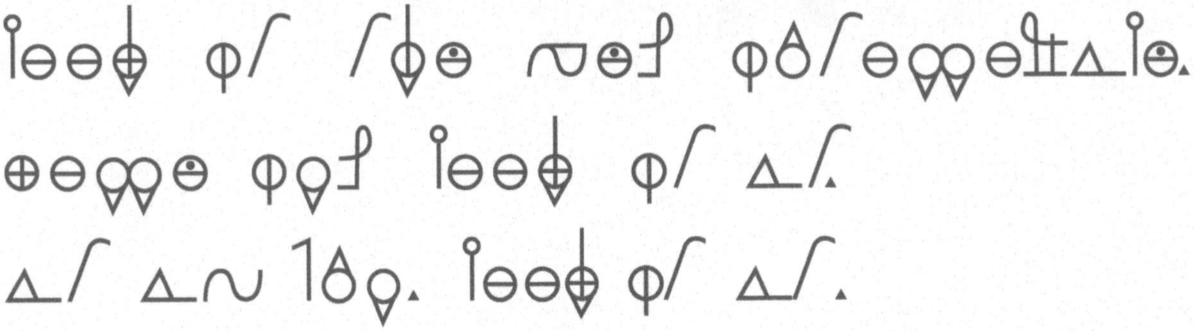

Confusabet Story 4

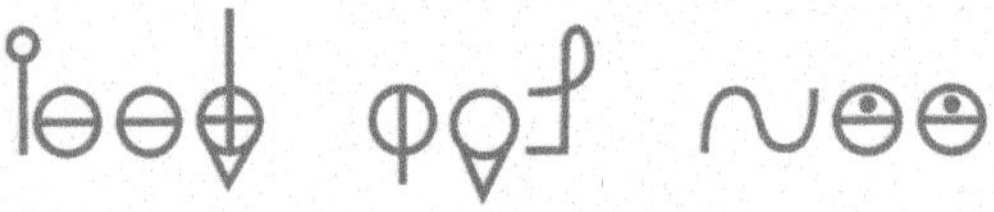

Confusabet Story 5

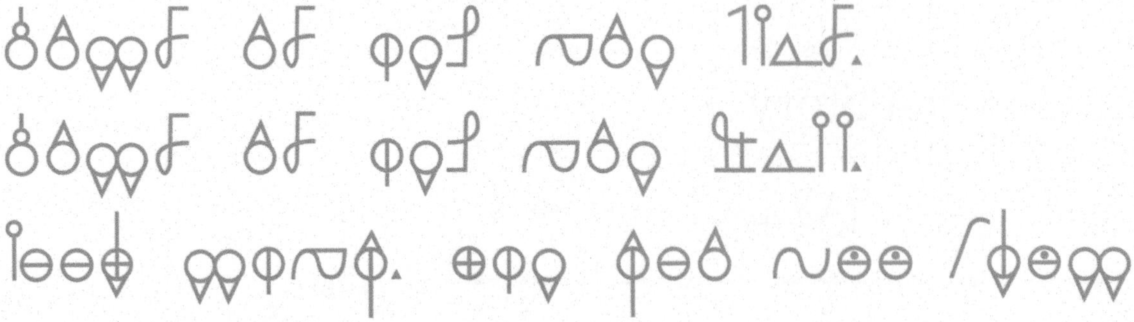

Confusabet Translations

Story Character Names

1. Mary 2. Bill 3. Nancy 4. Flip 5. Lucky

Vocabulary Translations with Context Clue Sentences

6. With my eyes I _________. see
7. Please _________ over here. come
8. , (comma) . (period) ? (question mark)
9. The top color light on a traffic signal is _________. red
10. Another name for a car is an _________. automobile
11. When I go fast on my feet I _________. run
12. A clown is _________. funny
13. When we take off in an airplane we go _________. up
14. When I play with a rope I _________ up. jump
15. The green traffic light means for us to _________. go
16. A word that rhymes with book and means to see is _________. look
17. Not me but _________. you
18. Come and look _________ it. at
19. _________ red automobile. the
20. Let's get into _________. it
21. It _________ fun to ride in. is
22. I'm going over there to be with _________. them
23. Yes I _________. can
24. Come _________ play with me. and
25. When I am surprised I say _________. oh
26. When I play with my friend I have _________. fun

Story Translations For Primer

Primer Title—*Look and See*

Story 1—*Bill*

Look at Bill.

Look at Bill jump.

Look at Bill jump up.

Jump up, jump up.

Story 2—*Nancy and Bill and Mary*

Look, Bill. Look, Mary.

See Nancy.

Look and see Nancy.

Funny funny Nancy.

Story 3—*Flip and Lucky*

Come, Flip. Come, Lucky.

Come and see.

Come and see the automobile.

Come and see the red automobile.

Come, Flip. Come, Lucky.

Look and see.

Story 4—*The Red Automobile*

Look at the red automobile.

Come and look at it.

It is fun. Look at it.

Story 5—*(Without pictures)*

Jump up and run, Flip.

Jump up and run, Bill.

Look, Mary. Can you see them?

Glossary

accommodation Changing existing schemes to incorporate new information.

aesthetic talk A form of conversation revolving around narrative literature in which children interpret and discuss what has been heard or read in relation to themselves.

alphabetic principle Knowing that words are composed of letters and that there is a systematic relationship between the letters and the sounds they make.

antiphonal reading A choral reading in which parts are taken by groups.

assimilation Incorporating information into already existing schemes.

Attention-Deficit Hyperactivity Disorder (ADHD) A problem with inattentiveness, overactivity, impulsivity, or a combination. For these problems to be diagnosed as ADHD, they must be out of the normal range for the child's age and development.

auditory discrimination The ability to hear, identify, and differentiate among familiar sounds, similar sounds, rhyming words, and letter sounds.

authentic assessment Assessment based on activities that represent and reflect the actual learning and instruction in the classroom.

balanced approach to literacy instruction The selection of theory and strategies to match learning styles of children. Constructivist and explicit strategies are both used.

behaviorist approach A learning theory in which adults provide a model and children learn through imitation encouraged by positive reinforcement.

Big Books Oversized books designed to allow children to see the print as it is being read.

biography A piece of children's literature that tells the story of a person's life.

blend A reader's ability to hear a series of isolated speech sounds and then recognize and pronounce them as a complete word.

blog A forum on the Internet for individuals to post feelings and /or respond to a topic. It is similar to a journal or diary, only it is made public by the author and is available on the Internet.

buddy reading The pairing of a child from an upper grade with a younger child for storybook reading.

child-centered curriculum (progressive education) An approach to education focusing on the needs of the students, rather than those of others involved in the educational process, such as teachers and administrators.

choral reading A small group or the entire class reads along with the teacher, who provides pacing and expression.

chunk Any group of letters within a word that is taught as a whole pattern; a chunk could be a phonogram, digraph, blend, and so on.

close reading a strategy used by teachers to ask children to read and analyze short text passages and thus practice critical reading skills.

comprehension An active process whereby a reader interprets and constructs meaning about the text based on prior knowledge and experience.

conference Meeting with the teacher or a peer to discuss work in progress.

consonant blends Two or three letters that, when placed together, merge into one sound while retaining representations of each letter sound (e.g., *bl* or *str*).

consonants All letters except *a, e, i, o, u*.

constructivist theory A theory that views learning as an active process by which children construct knowledge to learn by problem solving, guessing, and approximating.

content-area centers A place where materials for activities are kept for children to use independently for science, social studies, art, music, math, and so on.

context clues The use of syntax and semantic meaning of text to aid in word identification.

contracts Assignment sheets designating specific activities to be carried out by individual learners based on their needs, interests, and ability levels.

cooperative learning An instructional strategy in which children come together to learn through debate and discussion.

cultural diversity Reference to the wide variety of backgrounds, languages, customs, and environments represented within the larger society or a given classroom.

decoding Identifying words by using letter–sound and structural analysis.

descriptive writing Writing with language that describes precisely.

dialect An alternative form of one particular language used in different cultural, regional, or social groups.

differentiated instruction Designing instruction to meet the achievement needs of children in the same classroom. Often the assignment is the same for all, but less is expected of the child who is struggling (i.e., a shorter written story) and more of the sophisticated reader.

digraph Consonant digraphs are two consonants that, when placed together, make one new sound unlike the sound of either individual letter (e.g., *th* or *ch*). Vowel digraphs are two vowels together that make one sound that could be the sound of either vowel or a new sound (e.g., *ie, ai, oo, ou*).

direct instruction with a specific goal Children imitate adult models and adults offer positive reinforcement.

Directed Listening and Thinking Activity (DLTA) and Directed Reading and Thinking Activity (DRTA) A directed reading/listening framework that offers directions and strategies for organizing and retrieving information from a text that is read by or to a child. The steps in DLTA or DRTA include preparation for listening/reading with prequestions and discussion, setting a purpose for reading, reading the story, and a follow-up post-reading discussion based on the purpose set prior to reading.

Drop Everything and Read (DEAR) Time Quiet time for children to engage in silent reading.

early intervention Programs for children with special needs or those who are "at risk" in early childhood education intended to prevent potential problems in literacy development. The focus of the programs is on developmentally appropriate instruction using authentic reading and writing experiences. The program can be a pull-out or inclusion setting.

easy-to-read books High-interest books that have limited vocabulary, repeated vocabulary, vocabulary that is easy to read, short sentences, simple sentences, and pictures that help "read" the text.

echo reading The teacher reads a line of text and then the child reads the same line. The number of lines read is increased as the child's reading improves.

efferent talk A formal mode of conversation about expository text used to inform and persuade.

emergent literacy As coined by Marie Clay, refers to a child's early unconventional attempts at reading, writing, and listening.

English learner (EL) Children whose first language is not English. These children can have varying levels of English ability from no English to some.

environmental print Familiar print found in the surroundings, such as logos, food labels, and road signs.

explicit instruction A teacher-directed strategy with emphasis on teaching a task and the specific steps needed to master it.

expository text Text in any form that is informational and nonfiction.

expository writing Writing that includes many types of experiences and is usually about information that comes from content-area subjects such as social studies or science. This involves collecting information and summarizing it.

expressive language Putting words together to form thoughts or express oneself.

extrinsic motivation When individuals engage in an activity as a means to a particular end (i.e., reward, privilege, good grades), focusing on external rewards rather than the natural enjoyment of the process itself.

family literacy The different ways in which family members initiate and use literacy in their daily living.

fluency Level of reading ease and ability; a fluent reader is able to read on- or above-level books independently with high comprehension and accuracy.

formative feedback Feedback provided during the reading or writing process.

functional print Print for a purpose, such as informational signs, directions, greeting cards, lists, letters to pen-pals, and messages for the notice board.

functional writing Writing that serves clear, real-life purposes, including greeting cards and thank-you notes.

genre A specific type of literature, such as picture storybook, informational book, or poetry.

gifted Demonstrating exceptional ability.

graphemes Letters that make up individual sounds.

graphic organizers A comprehension strategy to help children understand the text by using a variety of visual charts to organize information.

guided reading Explicit reading instruction usually in small groups based on literacy needs.

high-frequency words Words that are frequently found in reading materials for children.

high-stakes assessment Standardized measures whose scores might determine major decisions about school districts, such as ratings of districts and promotion or retention decisions.

inclusion Special help, instruction and enrichment are offered in the regular classroom with the help of resource teachers and regular teachers planning together and teaching all children. This is in place of or in addition to pull-out programs for special help.

Independent Reading and Writing Periods (IRWP) A socially interactive time during which children select books and other literacy-related materials.

informal reading inventory Informal tests to determine a child's independent, instructional, and frustration level of reading.

informational writing A type of writing that is built on facts after collecting information and summarizing it. Informational writing does not include personal views.

informational text Books that are nonfiction about things that are real; also referred to as *expository text.*

integrated language arts An approach to literacy instruction that links reading, writing, listening, and language skills.

interdisciplinary literacy instruction Integration of content-area learning with literacy.

intergenerational literacy initiatives Planned, systematic programs specifically designed to improve the literacy development of both adults and children.

intrinsic motivation The desire to engage in particular behaviors or tasks for the sheer enjoyment of the task itself.

invented spelling Improvised spelling for words unknown in conventional spelling in which one letter often represents an entire syllable.

journal writing Written entries in notebooks by children, including *dialogue,* which is shared with teachers or peers who respond to what they read; *personal,* involving private thoughts related to children's lives or topics of special interest; *reading response,* writing in response to text reading; and *learning log,* a record of information usually involving other content areas.

K-W-L A cognitive strategy that enhances comprehension by assessing with students what they Know, what they Want to know, and what they Learned before and after reading.

language experience approach (LEA) A reading instruction method aimed at linking oral with written language on the premise that what is thought can be said, what is said can be written, and what is written can be read.

learning centers Spaces in the classroom filled with materials for independent student activity focusing on current topics of study within content areas and including literacy materials as well.

learning disabled Demonstrating significant difficulty in the acquisition and use of reading, writing, listening, speaking, and/or mathematical skills.

library corner A critical part of the literacy station that houses books or book collections on shelves.

literacy station A classroom area composed of a library corner and writing area.

literature-based instruction An approach to teaching reading in which varied genres of children's literature are used as the main source of reading material.

literature circles Discussion groups used to encourage critical discussions about literature among children.

maps and webs (mapping and webbing) Strategies for understanding text through the use of graphic representations for categorizing and structuring information. Maps deal with more detailed representations.

mental imagery Visualization of readings used to increase comprehension and clarify thought.

metacognition Awareness of one's own mental processes concerning how learning takes place.

morning message A daily message written by the teacher, on large chart paper about items of interest to the children. The teacher uses it for teaching skills.

motivation Initiating and sustaining a particular activity. It is considered the tendency to return to and continue working on a task with sustained engagement.

multimodal learning Alternative modes for learning, communicating, and making meaning. Multimodal theorists believe that communication can occur through various means (modes) such as a mix of print and technology that extend beyond traditional modes of reading and writing.

narrative literature Text that describes a sequence of events or gives an account of events.

narrative writing Writing stories.

nativist theory A theory that suggests that language development is innate to humans and that the environment has nothing to do with its acquisition.

neural shearing Loss of brain cells.

new literacy The concept of new literacies encompasses a wide domain of ideas. First, it referred to the use of technology to acquire literacy such as the Internet, cell phones, video games, email, podcasts, and so on. Now, it suggests that the acquisition of literacy can take place in multiple venues such as the use of print, technology, music, art, or in a particular setting.

nonstandard English A dialectal form of English that differs from the standard form in words, syntax, and language patterns.

one-to-one instruction Individualized instruction.

onsets Initial letter (or letters) before the first vowel in a word.

Padlet Added to a wiki, this online notice-board is ideal for making announcements, keeping notes, and so on.

paired reading A more able reader from the same class or another class acts as a tutor while reading with a less fluent student.

parent involvement programs Programs designed to involve and inform parents about activities that will promote their children's literacy development in school.

partner reading Peers reading together either simultaneously side by side or taking turns reading to each other.

persuasive writing Writing that involves trying to get someone to share your point of view.

phonemes Sounds made by individual letters and combinations of letters that make a single sound.

phonemic awareness Knowing that words are composed of a sequence of spoken sounds and being able to hear and identify these sounds. Phonemic awareness includes the ability to segment and blend individual sounds. Phonemic awareness is strictly an oral activity without association to symbols.

phonics A strategy that involves learning the alphabetic principles of language and knowledge of letter–sound relationships. Children learn to associate letters with the phonemes or basic speech sounds of English, to help them break the alphabetic code and become independent readers in the pronunciation of words.

phonogram A series of letters that begin with a vowel, often found together (for example, *ack, ed, ight, ock, ush*).

phonological awareness The ability to identify and manipulate individual speech sounds as well as syllables and whole words. Children can segment and blend single phonemes, syllables, and words.

picture concept books Books for very young children that have a theme such as animals. Each page will have a picture of an animal and possibly the name of the animal.

picture storybooks These books are the most well known type of children's literature. They usually are a fictional story where both the pictures and the print play a very important role in the book.

Podcast A digital media file containing audio and/or visual recordings that can be uploaded to the Internet.

poetry writing Poems can be rhymes or can follow other formulas, such as haiku or acrostics.

portfolio assessment A strategy for measuring student progress by collecting samples of their work that are placed into a folder called a *portfolio*. Materials include samples of a student's written work or drawings, anecdotal records, audiotapes, videotapes, checklists, and teacher-made and standardized test results, among others.

primary language instruction When a child is taught in the language learned first regardless of what that language may be.

process approach to writing Steps involved in the production of text, including prewriting, drafting, conferencing, revising, editing, and performing.

push-in programs Programs that provide special help for children in need by having a special teacher come into the classroom to work with a small group of children or one child who is in need of extra help.

pull-out programs Programs in which students are taken out of their classrooms for special help in literacy instruction or enrichment.

Reader's Theater The oral reading of a short play, in which children have parts and practice them for presentation.

reading readiness Various skills considered prerequisite in learning to read, such as auditory discrimination, visual discrimination, and motor skills.

reading recovery An early intervention program devised by Marie Clay in which first-graders who experience difficulties with reading receive intensive, one-on-one instruction using developmentally appropriate integrated language arts techniques.

reading workshop A period of time set aside for children to work on reading skills by reading books and conferencing with the teacher.

receptive language Ability to process, comprehend, or integrate spoken language; being able to understand what someone says to you.

reciprocal teaching Teaching that uses a scaffolded discussion technique that is built on four strategies that good readers use to comprehend text: questioning, clarifying, predicting, and summarizing.

repeated reading Reading the same book or story over and over until it is repeated or known. This familiarity offers the opportunity for fluent reading.

response groups A strategy for enhancing comprehension; students exchange or refine ideas and think critically about issues related to what they have listened to or read.

response to intervention (RTI) An approach that integrates assessment and intervention within a multilevel prevention system to maximize student achievement and to reduce behavior problems.

rich literacy environments Environments rich with materials that encourage reading and writing and support instruction.

rimes Ending parts of words that contain the vowel and the remainder of the word. Onsets and rimes make up words.

rubric A scoring guide that gives the student and teacher a sense of what they should strive for in their writing. It is an evaluation system for a teacher who ranks certain elements on the rubric, which then are listed, such as uses capitals and correct punctuation, writes neatly, stays on topic, gives details and examples, or writes things in an appropriate order.

running record An assessment strategy that involves the close observation and recording of a child's oral reading behavior; may be used for planning instruction.

scaffolding A strategy in which teachers provide children with modeling and support to help them acquire a skill.

schema A mental structure in which a person organizes and stores information he or she knows.

segment To divide words into segments based on their sound components; cat is "c-a-t."

self-monitoring A student's ability to read and self-correct words as they are read.

semantic cues Children try to figure out a word based on the meaning of the sentence it is in.

semantics Meaning that language communicates.

shared book experiences Whole- or small-group reading instruction through literature selections, in which Big Books are often used so that children can see the print and pictures. Big Books enable children to listen and participate in actual book readings.

sight words The words that are known immediately by a reader. Once a word becomes a sight word, the reader does not need to use word-attack skills to read it.

small-group instruction Close interaction occurs between the teacher and a few children for explicit instruction, based on needs and interests and for assessment.

standardized tests An assessment measure, commercially prepared and norm referenced, that reports results in terms of grade-level scores and percentile ranks.

standards Achievement goals that are defined at a state or national level and identify what students should know at the end of each grade level.

standards-based tests Tests developed by individual states based on the grade-level standards they designed for achievement in reading, math, and so on. These tests are scored based on how many answers are correct to be considered proficient or not. There is no curve on these tests; therefore, all children can pass as long as they get the designated number of questions correct.

story retellings The recital of familiar stories, in children's own words, in written or oral form to develop and assess comprehension of story.

story structure The elements of a well-constructed story, including setting, theme, plot episodes, and resolution.

summative feedback Feedback provided at the end of an assignment.

sustained silent reading (SSR) A time allocated for children to read silently.

synaptogenesis Connecting of brain cells or rapid development of neural connections.

syntax The structure of language or rules that governs how words work together in phrases, clauses, and sentences.

tape-assisted reading Listening to fluent reading samples on audiotapes while following the written text.

T-chart A graphic organizer that helps in comprehending expository and narrative text by classifying similarities and differences in characters, facts, and ideas.

telegraphic speech A form of speech used by children at about 12 months of age in which content words, such as nouns and verbs, are used (e.g., "Mommy cookie") but function words, such as conjunctions and articles, are omitted.

thematic unit A topic of study is learned through explorations across all areas of the curriculum.

think-aloud A comprehension strategy in which children talk about what they have read or other ideas they have about a story.

think, pair, share A discussion strategy that combines think time with cooperative learning. Following teacher-posed questions, the teacher first has children *think* about their answers; then children *pair* with a partner to discuss their responses; finally, during *share*, the students share responses with the group.

traditional literature Stories that are well known and passed down from families and from different countries. They are usually folktales, fables, and fairy tales.

t-unit An independent clause with all its dependent clauses attached that is helpful in measuring a child's ability to understand language complexity.

Very Own Words Favorite words generated by children, written on index cards, and kept in a container for them to read and write.

visual discrimination The ability to note similarities and differences visually between objects, including the ability to recognize colors, shapes, and letters.

vowels The letters *a, e, i, o, u*.

website A space on the Internet to store information. For classrooms, class websites are used to record classroom activities and engage in multiple online activities.

whole-group instruction Introduce information to the children with the whole class together, such as a lesson, discussion, reading a story, singing songs.

whole language instruction A philosophy from which strategies are drawn for literacy development. Strategies include the use of real literature, with the concurrent instruction of reading, writing, and oral language in meaningful, functional, and cooperative contexts, to help students become motivated to read and write.

wiki A type of website that can be set up by a teacher. A wiki can be your class website, as it is an online space to record classroom activities and engage in activities online.

word consciousness Word knowledge including nuances of word meaning, value of words, differences among school language, social language, and language used for play, and learning the meanings of unknown words.

word-study skills Knowledge about print, including the use of phonics context and syntax to decipher unknown words; the development of sight vocabulary; and the use of word configuration and structural analysis.

word wall A type of bulletin board or classroom display that features challenging and/or high-frequency words organized alphabetically.

wordless books Books that tell a story through illustrations. There are no words in the book. Children create the story using the pictures. These are not necessarily for very young children because often the stories are quite complicated.

writing corner An area in the classroom set aside for writing. There will be a table and chairs, various types of paper (large, small, lined, unlined, etc.) and lots of writing utensils (pencils, pens, colored pencils, crayons, markers).

writing mechanics Skills related to writing, such as spelling, handwriting, punctuation, and spacing.

writing workshop A period of time set aside for children to practice writing skills, work on writing projects, and confer with the teacher.

zone of proximal development Based on Vygotsky's theory, this refers to the period of time when a child has been guided by an adult and no longer needs the help. The adult retreats and allows the child to work on his or her own.

Children's Literature Bibliography

about scat, frass, dung, and more! Watertown, MA: Imagine Publishing.

Abramson, A. (2007). *Who was Ann Frank?* New York: Penguin Group.

Adams, P. (2007). *There was an old lady who swallowed a fly.* England: Child's Play International.

Aigner-Clark, J. (2003). *Baby Einstein: Water, water everywhere.* New York: Hyperion Books for Children.

Alborough, J. (2003). *Some dogs do.* Cambridge, MA: Candlewick Press.

Alborough, J. (2008). *Duck in the truck.* San Diego, CA: Kane Miller Books.

Aliki. (1999). *My visit to the zoo.* New York: HarperCollins Publishers.

Allsburg, C. V. (2009). *The polar express.* Orlando, FL: Houghton Mifflin Harcourt.

Alter, A. (2011). *A photo for Greta.* New York: Random House.

Alvarez, J. (2002). *How Tia Lola came to (visit) stay.* New York: Random House.

Amani, M. J. (2012) *Excuse me, I'm trying to read.* Watertown, MA: Charlesbridge Publishing, Inc.

Anderson, H. C. (2008). *The ugly duckling.* New York: North-South Books.

Andreae, G. (2008). *Giraffes can't dance.* New York: Scholastic.

Andrews, T., & Collier, B. (2015). *Trombone shorty.* New York: Abrams Books.

Anholt, L. (2014). *Two nests.* Islington, London: Frances Lincoln Children's Books.

Appelt, K. (2003). *Incredible me!* New York: HarperCollins Publishers.

Archambault, J., & Martin, B., Jr. (1989, 2000). *Chicka chicka boom boom.* New York: Simon & Schuster.

Arnold, T. (2009). *Super fly guy.* New York: Scholastic.

Arnosky, J. (2001). *Rabbits and raindrops.* New York: Penguin Group.

Asch, F. (1983). *Mooncake.* New York: Simon & Schuster.

Ashford Frame, J. (2008). *Yesterday I had the blues.* New York: Random House.

Avery, K., & McPhail, D. (1993). *The crazy quilt.* Glenview, IL: Scott Foresman.

Bachelet, G. (2006). *My cat, the silliest cat in the world.* New York: Abrams Books for Young Readers.

Ball, J. (2005). *Go figure! A totally cool book about numbers.* New York: DK.

Bancroft, H., & Van Gelder, R. G. (1997). *Animals in winter.* New York. HarperCollins.

Bang, M. (1996). *Ten, nine, eight.* New York: HarperCollins Publishers.

Bania, M. (2002). *Kumak's house.* Portland, OR: Alaska Northwest Books.

Barnett, M. (2012). *Extra yarn.* New York: Balzar 1 Bray.

Bartoletti, S. C. (2004). *Flag maker.* Orlando, FL: Houghton Mifflin Harcourt.

Base, G. (1986). *Animalia.* New York: Harry N. Abrams.

Bass, J. V. (2016). *Edible colors: See, learn, eat.* New York, NY: Roaring Brook Press.

Bateman, T. (2012). *The leprechaun under the bed.* New York: Holiday House, Inc.

Bauer Stamper, J. (2003). *Voyage the volcano.* New York: Scholastic.

Beaty, A. (2007). *Iggy Peck, architect.* New York: Harry N. Abrams.

Becker, B. (2008). *A visitor for bear.* Cambridge, MA: Candlewick Press.

Bedford, D., & Reeve, R. (2016). *Once upon a time. . . online.* New York: Parragon Inc.

Bemelmans, L. (1953). *Madeline's rescue.* New York: Viking.

Bemelmans, L. (2000). *Madeline.* New York: Penguin Group.

Berenstain, J., & Berenstain, M. (2008). *Berenstain bears' Valentine party.* New York: HarperCollins.

Berenstain, S., & Berenstain, J. (1987). *The Berenstain bears and too much birthday.* New York: Random House.

Berenstain, S., & Berenstain, J. (2002). *The bears' picnic.* New York: Random House.

Berger, C. (2008). *Little yellow leaf.* New York: HarperCollins.

Berger, M., & Berger, G. (2002). *Snap! A book about alligators and crocodiles.* New York: Scholastic.

Bernard. (2001). *A tree for all seasons.* Washington, D.C.: National Geographic Society.

Betty Crocker Editors. (2007). *Betty Crocker's kids cook!* Hoboken, NJ: Wiley, & Sons.

Bingham, K. (2012). *Z is for moose.* New York: Greenwillow Books.

Bishop, B. *My friend with autism.* Texas: Future Horizons.

Bishop C. H., & Wiese, K. (1996). *Five Chinese brothers.* New York: Penguin Group.

Bisset, J. (2008). *Tickle monster.* Seattle, WA: Compendium Inc.

Black, I. M. (2009). *Chicken cheeks.* New York: Simon & Schuster.

Blankenship, P. (2004). *Lulu's lost shoes.* Novato, CA: Treasure Bay.

Bleiman, A. & Eastland, C. (2012). *Welcome to the world, zooborns!* New York: Simon Spotlight.

Bonder, D. (2007). *Dogabet.* N. Vancouver, BC, Canada: Walrus.

Borden, L. (2005). *America is.* New York: Simon & Schuster.

Bottner, B. (1997). *Bootsie barker bites.* New York: Penguin Group.

Bouchard, D. (2014). *The first flute.* Markham, ON: Fitzhenry & Whiteside.

Bourgeois, P. (1986). *Franklin and the thunderstorm.* New York: Scholastic.

Boynton, S. (1984). *Doggies.* New York: Little Simon.

Boynton, S. (2001). *Yay, you! Moving out, moving up.* New York: Simon & Schuster.

Boynton, S. (2007). *Bath time.* New York: Workman Publishing.

Boynton, S. (2012). *Tickle time!* New York: Workman Publishing Co.

Bradenberg, F. (1976). *I wish I was sick, too.* NY: Greenwillow.

Bramsen, C. (2009). *The yellow tutu.* New York: Random House.

Branley, F. M. (1985). *Volcanoes.* New York: Harper & Row Junior Books.

Branley, F. M. (1998). *Floating in space.* New York: HarperCollins.

Branley, F. M. (2005). *Sunshine makes the seasons.* New York: HarperCollins.

Brenner, B. (1972). *The three little pigs.* New York: Random House.

Brent-Harris, A. (2011). Sweet Jamaican summertime at grandma's. Bloomington, IN: Xlibris Corp.

Brett, J. (1997). *The hat.* New York: Putnam & Grosset.

Brett, J. (2007). *The three snow bears.* New York: Penguin Group.

Brett, J. (2009). *The mitten.* New York: Penguin Group.

Brett, J. (2011). *The umbrella.* New York: Penguin Group.

Bridges, R. (1999). *Through my eyes.* New York: Scholastic.

Bridwell. N. (1963; 2015). *Clifford the big red dog.* New York: Scholastic.

Briggs, R. (2000). *The snowman.* New York: Random House Children's Books.

Briggs Martin, J. (2009). *Snowflake Bentley.* Orlando, FL: Houghton Mifflin Harcourt.

Brosgol, V. (2016). *Leave me alone!* New York: Roaring Brook Press.

Brown, L. K., & Brown, M. T. (1998). *When dinosaurs die: A guide to understanding death.*

Brown, M. (1957). *The three billy goats gruff.* New York: Harcourt Brace.

Brown, M. (1990). *Arthur's pet business.* New York: Little Brown.

Brown, M.W. (1945; 1975). *Goodnight moon.* Harper Collins.

Brown, M. W. (2005). *Little fur family.* New York: HarperCollins Publishers.

Bruel, N. (2005). *Bad kitty.* New York: Roaring Brook Press.

Brusatte, S. (2013). *Walking with dinosaurs encyclopedia.* New York: Harper Festival.

Buehner, C. (2000). *I did it, I'm sorry.* New York: Penguin Group.

Buitrago, J., & Yockteng, R. (2015). *Two white rabbits.* Toronto, ON: Groundwood Books. New York: Little, Brown & Co. Books for Young Readers.

Bunting, E. (1996). *No nap.* Orlando, FL: Houghton Mifflin Harcourt.

Bunting, E. (1999). *Smoky night.* Orlando, FL: Houghton Mifflin Harcourt.

Bunting, E. (2004). *October picnic.* Orlando, FL: Houghton Mifflin Harcourt.

Burton, V. L. (1943; 1971). *Katy and the big snow.* Boston: Houghton Mifflin.

Cain, J. (2006). *The way I feel*. Seattle, WA: Parenting Press.

Cain, S. (2006). *The crunching munching caterpillar*. Wilton, CT: Tiger Tales.

Calie, D. (2013). *The little eskimo*. Albert Park, Australia: Wilkins Farago.

Cammuso, F. (2009). *Otto's orange day*. Cambridge, MA: Candlewick.

Campbell, R. (2007). *Dear zoo*. New York: Simon & Schuster.

Capucilli, A. S. (2003). Biscuit loves school. New York: HarperCollins Publishers.

Capucilli, A.S., & Schories, P. (2017). *Biscuit's Pet & Play Bedtime*. New York, NY: HarperFestival.

Carle, E. (1969). *The very hungry caterpillar*. New York: Philomel

Carle, E. (2001). *Today is Monday*. New York: Penguin Group.

Carle, E. (2007). *The very hungry caterpillar*. New York: Penguin Group.

Carle. E. (2007). *Brown bear, brown bear: What do you see?. (Anniversary edition)* New York: Puffin Books.

Carle, E. (2009). A house for hermit crab. New York: Simon & Schuster.

Carlson, N. (1992). *Arnie and the new kid*. New York: Penguin Group.

Carlson, N. L. (1990). *I like me!* New York: Penguin Group.

Carter, D. (2001). *Flapdoodle dinosaurs*. New York: Simon & Schuster.

Carter, D. A. (2008). *Beach bugs*. New York: Simon & Schuster.

Casey D., & Hall, A. (2015). *Babushka: a traditional tale*. Oxford, UK: Lion Children's Books.

Cecil, R. (2012). *Horsefly and honey*. New York: Henry Holt & Co.

Chambers, W. (1974). *The lip-smackin', joke-crackin' cookbook for kids*. New York: Golden Press.

Cheney, L. (2006). *Our 50 states: A family adventure across America*. New York: Simon & Schuster.

Cherry, L. (2000). *The great kapok tree: A tale of the Amazon rainforest*. Orlando, FL: Houghton Mifflin Harcourt.

Cherry, L. (2002). *River ran wild: An environmental history*. Orlando, FL: Houghton Mifflin Harcourt.

Christian Anderson, H. (2004). *Thumbelina*. New York: Penguin Group.

Churnin, N., & Tuya, J. (2016). *The William Hoy story: how a deaf baseball player changed*

Clark, K. (2006). *Grandma drove the garbage truck*. Camden, ME: Down East Books.

Climo, S. (2000). *Irish cinderlad*. New York: HarperCollins.

Coat, J. (2012). *Hippopposites*. New York: Abrams Appleseed.

Coat, J. (2015). *Rhymoceros*. New York: Abrams Appleseed.

Coerr, E., & Himler, R. (2004). *Sadako and the thousand paper cranes, Vol 1*. New York: Penguin Group.

Cohen, M. (1980). *First grade takes a test*. New York: Dell.

Cohen, M. (2008). *Jim's dog muffins*. Long Island City, NY: Star Bright Books, Incorporated.

Colandro, L. (2012). *There was an old lady who swallowed some books!* New York: Cartwheel Books.

Cole, B. (1989). *No more baths*. New York: Farrar, Straus & Giroux.

Cole, H. (2013). *Unspoken: A story from the underground railroad*. New York: Scholastic Press.

Cole, J. (1987). *The magic school bus inside the earth*. New York: Scholastic.

Cole, J. (1990). *The magic school bus inside the human body*. New York: Scholastic, Inc.

Cole, J. (2001). *The magic school bus explores the senses*. New York: Scholastic.

Coleman, J. W. (2013). *Eight dolphins of Katrina: A true tale of survival*. New York: Houghton Mifflin Harcourt.

Collins Berkes, M. (2002). *Seashells by the seashore*. Nevada City, CA: Dawn.

Collins, R. (2017). *This zoo is not for you*. London, UK: Nosy Crow.

Cook, J. (2015). *But it's not my fault!* Boys Town, NE: Boys Town Press.

Corey, S. (2006). *Players in pigtails*. New York: Scholastic.

Cousins, L. (2007). *Maisy big, Maisy small*. Cambridge, MA: Candlewick Press.

Cousins, L. (2012). *Create with Maisy: A Maisy arts and crafts book*. Cambridge, MA: Candlewick Press.

Covell, D. (2012). *Rat & roach: Friends to the end*. New York: Viking Juvenile.

Cowen-Fletcher, J. (1995). *Mama zooms*. New York: Scholastic.

Cowley, J. & Bishop, N. (2006) *Red tree-eyed frog*. New York: Scholastic.

Cowley, J., & Fuller, E. (2006). *Mrs. Wishy-Washy's farm*. New York: Penguin Young Readers Group.

Craig, H. (2009). *Thirsty Thursday*. Cambridge, MA: Candlewick Press.

Creech, S. (2005). *Granny Torrelli makes soup*. New York: HarperCollins.

Cronin, D. (2000). *Click, clack, moo: Cows that type*. New York: Simon & Schuster.

Cronin, D. (2003). *Diary of a worm*. New York: HarperCollins. CT: Straight Edge Press.

Curtis, C. (2008). *I took the moon for a walk*. Cambridge, MA: Barefoot Books.

Curtis, J. L. (2002). *I'm gonna like me: Letting off a little self-esteem*. New York: HarperCollins

Curtis, J. L. (2004). *It's hard to be five: Learning how to work my control panel*. New York: HarperCollins Publishers.

Cusick, D. (2013). *Get the scoop on animal poop! From lions to tapeworms: 251 cool facts*

Cuyler, M. (2009). *Bullies never win*. Simon & Schuster Children's Books.

Cyrus, K. (2016). *Billions of bricks: A counting book about building*. New York: Christy Ottaviano.

D'amico, C., & D'amico, S. (2004). *Ella the elegant elephant*. New York: Scholastic.

Dabcovich, L. (1999). *Polar bear son: An Inuit tale*. Orlando, FL: Houghton Mifflin Harcourt.

DaCosta, B., & Young, E. (2012). *Nightime ninja*. Guelph, Canada: Little, Brown Books for Young Readers.

Dahl, R. (1994). *Vicar of Nibbleswicke*. New York: Penguin.

Daley, A., & Russell, C. (1999). *Goldilocks and the three bears*. London: Ladybird Books.

Davies, N. (2004). *Oceans and seas*. New York: Kingfisher.

Davies, N. (2012). *Just ducks!* Cambridge, MA: Candlewick Press.

Davis, C. (2009). *Animals on the farm: My first noisy bath book*. Hauppauge, NY: Barron's Educational Series.

Davis, K. C. (2001). *Don't know much about space*. New York: HarperCollins.

Davis, N. (2005). *Surprising sharks*. Cambridge, MA: Candlewick Press.

Daywalt, D. (2013). *The day the crayons quit*. New York: Philomel.

Dean, J. (2013). *Freddy the frogcaster*. Washington, DC: Regnery Publishing, Inc.

Dean, J. (2013). *Pete the cat: The wheels on the bus*. New York: HarperCollins Publishers.

DeBeer, H. (1996). *Little polar bear, take me home!* New York: North-South Books.

De Brunhoff, L., & Weiss, E. (2002). *Babar's yoga for elephants*. New York: Harry N. Abrams.

DeCristofano, C. C. (2012). *A black hole is not a black hole*. Watertown, MA: Charlesbridge Publishing Inc.

Degan, B. (2008). *Jamberry*. New York: Barnes & Noble.

DeGroat, D. (2009). *No more pencils, no more books, no more teacher's dirty looks*. New York: HarperCollins.

Demi. (2007). *The empty pot*. New York: Henry Holt & Co.

Demuth, P. (1996). *Johnny Appleseed*. New York: Grosset & Dunlap.

Demuth, P. (1997). *Achoo!* New York: Sagebrush Educational Resources.

Denton, K. (2004). *A child's treasury of nursery rhymes*. New York: Kingfisher.

dePaola, T. (1975). *Strega nona*. New York: Simon & Schuster.

dePaola, T. (1978). *Pancakes for breakfast*. Orlando, FL: Houghton Mifflin Harcourt.

dePaola. T. (1978). *The popcorn book*. New York: Holiday House.

dePaola, T. (1980). *The legend of old Befana*. Orlando, FL: Houghton Mifflin Harcourt.

dePaola, T. (1985). *The cloud book*. New York: Holiday House Inc.

dePaola, T. (1994). *Kit and Kat*. New York: Penguin Group.

dePaola, T. (1994). *Patrick: Patron saint of Ireland*. New York: Holiday House.

dePaola, T. (1996). *The legend of Bluebonnet: An old Texas tale*. New York: Penguin Group.

dePaola, T. (1996). *Tony's bread*. New York: Penguin Group.

dePaola, T. (2000). *Nana upstairs and Nana downstairs*. New York: Penguin Group.

dePaola, T. (2001). *26 Fairmont Avenue*. New York: Penguin Group.

dePaola, T. (2004). *Four friends in autumn*. New York: Simon & Schuster.

dePaola, T. (2009). *Jamie O'Rourke and the big potato*. New York: Penguin Group.

dePaola, T. (2010). *Strega Nona*. New York: Simon & Schuster.

DePaulo, T. (1978). *The popcorn book*. Upper Saddle River, NJ: Prentice Hall.

DeRubertis, B. (2010). *Frances frog's forever friend*. New York: Kane Press.

Desimini, L. (1996). *How the stars fell into the sky*. Orlando, FL: Houghton Mifflin Harcourt.

Dewdney, A. (2005). *Llama, llama, red pajama*. New York: Penguin Group.

Dewdney, A. (2006). *Grumpy Gloria.* New York: Penguin Group.

Dewdney, A. (2009). *Llama llama misses mama.* New York: Penguin Group.

DeWitt, L. (1993). *What will the weather be?* New York: HarperCollins Publishers.

Diary of a wimpy kid book series. New York: Amulet Books.

Diggory-Shields, C. (2008). *Saturday night at the dinosaur stomp.* Cambridge, MA: Candlewick Press.

Disney, R. H. (2010). *Up.* New York: Random House Golden Books.

DK Board Books. (2004). *My first farm board book.* New York: DK.

DK Publishing. (2004). *Farm animals.* New York: DK Publishing.

Donaldson, J. (2005). *The spiffiest giant in town.* New York: Penguin Group.

Donaldson, J. (2006). *The Gruffalo.* New York: The Penguin Group.

Donaldson, J. (2009). *Stick man.* New York: Scholastic Inc.

Donofrio, B. (2007). *Mary and the mouse, the mouse and Mary.* New York: Random House.

Dorion, C. (2010). *How the world works: A hands-on guide to our amazing planet.* Cambridge, MA: Candlewick Press.

Dorros, A. (1992). *Alligator shoes.* New York: Puffin.

Dorros, A. (1997). *Abuela.* New York: Random House.

Dorros, A. (1999). *Isla.* New York: Puffin.

Droyd, A. (2011). *Goodnight iPad: A parody for the next generation.* New York: Blue Rider Press.

Duncan Edwards, P. (1998). *Some smug slug.* New York: HarperCollins.

Duncan Edwards, P. (2010). *Four famished foxes and Fosdyke.* New York: Barnes & Noble.

Dunrea, O. (2007). *Ollie.* Orlando, FL: Houghton Mifflin Harcourt.

Dunrier, O. (2007). *Goosie and Gertie.* Orlando, FL: Houghton Mifflin Harcourt.

Dusen, C. V. (2009). *The circus ship.* Cambridge, MA: Candlewick Press.

Duvoisin, R. (2002). *Petunia.* New York: Dragonfly.

Eastman, P. (1997). *Go dog. Go!* New York: Random House.

Eastman, P. D. (2005). *Are you my mother?* New York: Random House.

Eberts, M. (1984). *Pancakes, crackers, and pizza.* Chicago: Children's Press.

Edwards, D. (1998). *Some smug slug.* New York: HarperCollins.

Edwards, M. (2012). *Room for the baby.* New York: Random House.

Edwards, P. D. (2004). *Clara caterpillar.* New York: HarperCollins.

Egielski, R. (2000). *The gingerbread boy.* New York: HarperCollins.

Ehlert, L. (1992). *Planting a rainbow.* New York: Houghton Mifflin Harcourt.

Ehlert, L. (2001). *Fish eyes: A book you can count on.* Orlando, FL: Houghton Mifflin Harcourt.

Ehlert, L. (2001). *Snowballs.* Orlando, FL: Houghton Mifflin Harcourt.

Ehlert, L. (2001). *Waiting for wings.* Orlando, FL: Houghton Mifflin Harcourt.

Ehlert, L. (2005). *Leaf man.* Orlando, FL: Houghton Mifflin Harcourt.

Elephant and piggie book series. New York: Disney-Hyperion.

Elliott, D. (2009). *And here's to you.* Cambridge, MA: Candlewick Press.

Ellis, C. (2016). *Du iz tak?* London: Walker Books.

Engle, M., & Parisi, A. (2017). *Drum dream girl: how one girl's courage changed music.* New York: HMH Books for Young Readers.

Ernest, L. (2004). *The turn-around, upside down alphabet book.* New York: Simon & Schuster Children's Publishing.

Esbaum, J. (2010). *Everything spring.* Washington, D.C.: National Geographic Society.

Estes, E. (2004). *The hundred dresses.* Orlando, FL: Houghton Mifflin Harcourt.

Ezra Stein, D. (2007). *Leaves.* New York: Penguin Group.

Falconer, I. (2004). *Olivia.* New York: Simon & Schuster.

Faulkner, M. (1986). *Jack and the beanstalk.* New York: Scholastic.

Fischer, S. M. (2010). *Jump.* New York: Simon & Schuster.

Fitzgerald Howard, E. (2001). *Aunt Flossie's hats and crab cakes later.* Orlando, FL: Houghton Mifflin Harcourt.

Fleming, C. (2004). *Muncha! Muncha!* Muncha! Pine Plains, NY: Live Oak Media.

Fleming, C. (2007). *Tippy-tippy-tippy, hide!* New York: Simon & Schuster.

Fleming, C. (2012). *Oh no!* New York: Random House Children's Books.

Fleming, D. (1992). *Count!* New York: Henry Holt and Co.

Fleming, D. (2000). *Where once there was a wood.* New York: Henry Holt & Co.

Fleming, D. (2001). *Barnyard banter.* New York: Henry Holt.

Fleming, D. (2001). *Time to sleep.* New York: Henry Holt & Co.

Fleming, D. (2004). *The everything book.* New York: Holt.

Fleming, D. (2006). *Alphabet under construction.* New York: Henry Holt and Co.

Fleming, V. (1993). *Be good to Eddie Lee.* New York: Penguin.

Floca, B. (2009). *Moonshot: The flight of Apollo 11.* New York: Simon & Schuster.

Fogliano, J. (2012). *And then it's spring.* New York: Roaring Book Press.

Fogliano, J., & Morstad, J. (2016). *When green becomes tomatoes: Poems for all seasons.* NY, NY: Roaring Brook Press.

Fontes, R. (2002). *How the zebra got its stripes.* New York: Random House Golden Books.

Forgan, J. (2015). *Terrific Teddy's excessive energy* (Vol. 2). USA: Advocacy Consultants.

Foster, K. (2010). *A dolphin up a tree.* Los Angeles: Foster Branch Publishing.

Fowler, A. (1992). *Frogs and toads and tadpoles, too!* Chicago: Children's Press.

Fowler, A. (1993). *Chicken or the egg?* New York: Scholastic.

Fox, M. (1992). *Hattie and the fox.* New York: Simon & Schuster.

Fox, M. (1994). *Koala Lou.* Orlando, FL: Houghton Mifflin Harcourt.

Fox, M. (2000). *Feathers and fools.* Orlando, FL: Houghton Mifflin Harcourt.

Fox, M. (2000). *Harriet, you'll drive me wild.* New York: Harcourt.

Frandin, J. B. (2002). *Who was Sacagawea?* New York: Penguin Group.

Frasier, D. (2002). *Out of the ocean.* Orlando, FL: Houghton Mifflin Harcourt.

Fredericks, A. D. (2001). *Under one rock: Bugs, slugs, and other ughs.* Nevada City, CA: Dawn Publications.

Freeman, D. (2006). *Manuelo, the playing mantis.* New York: Penguin Group.

Freeman, D. (2006). *Mop top.* Pine Plains, NY: Live Oak Media.

Freeman, D. (2008). *Corduroy.* New York: Penguin Group.

Fritz, J. (2002). *Double life of Pocahontas.* New York: Penguin Group.

Fromental, J.-L. (2006). *365 penguins.* New York: Abrams.

Fujikawa, A. (1980). *Jenny learns a lesson.* New York: Grosset & Dunlap.

Fungchung, N., & Takashi, F. (2016). *Anya goes to Jamaica.* Nikko FungChung.

Galdone, P. (1983). *The gingerbread boy.* Boston: Houghton Mifflin.

Gamble, A., Jasper, M., & Kelly, C. (2015). *Good night Alaska.* Dennis, MA: Good Night Books.

Garza, C. L. (2000). *In my family en mi familia.* San Francisco, CA: Children's Book Press.

Geisert, A. (2012). *The giant seed.* Brooklyn, NY: Enchanted Lion Books.

George, J. S. (2004). *So you want to be president?* New York: Penguin Group.

George, L. B. (2006). *Inside mouse, outside mouse.* New York: HarperCollins Publishers.

Gerstein, M. (2007). *The man who walked between the towers.* New York: Square Fish.

Gerth, M. (2006). *Ten little ladybugs.* Atlanta, GA: Dalmatian Press.

Gibbons, G. (1992). *Weather words and what they mean.* New York: Holiday House Inc.

Gibbons, G. (1996). *How a house is built.* New York: Holiday House.

Gibbons, G. (1996). *Reasons for seasons.* New York: Holiday House.

Gibbons, G. (2002). *Tell me, tree: All about trees for kids.* New York: Little, Brown & Co. Books for Young Readers.

Gibbons, G. (2006). *Dinosaur discoveries.* New York: Holiday House.

Gibbons, G. (2007). *Ice cream: The full scoop.* New York: Holiday House.

Gibbons, G. (2007). *The planets.* New York. Holiday House.

Gibbons, G. (2010). *Snakes.* New York: Holiday House.

Gilman, P. (1993). *Something from nothing.* New York: Scholastic.

Giovanni, N. (2007). *Rosa.* New York: Square Fish.

Gleeson, B. (2005). *Finn McCoul.* Edina, MN: ABDO Publishing Co.

Goble, P. (2001). *The girl who loved wild horses.* New York: Simon & Schuster.

Gold, R. (2006). *Kids cook 1-2-3: Recipes for young chefs using only three ingredients.* New York: Bloomsbury.

Golden Books. (2003). *Sleep bunny.* New York: Random House Children's Books.

Goldish, M. (2012). *Dolphins in the Navy*. New York: Bearport.

Gonzalez, L. (2008). *The storyteller's candle.* San Francisco, CA: Children's Book Press.

Gordon, J. R. (2000). *Two badd babies.* Honesdale, PA: Boyds Mills Press.

Graham, B. (2007). *Dimity Dumpty: The story of Humpty's little sister.* Cambridge, MA: Candlewick Press.

Graves, K. (2010). *Chicken big.* San Francisco, CA: Chronicle Books.

Green, A. (2007). *Mother Goose's storytime nursery rhymes.* New York: Arthur A. Levine.

Green, J. (2005). *Why should I recycle?* Hauppauge, NY: Barron's Educational Series.

Grey, M. (2015). *The adventures of the dish and the spoon.* New York: Random House Children's Books.

Guarino, D. (2004). *Is your mama a llama?* New York: Scholastic Inc.

Hale, B. (2014). *Clark the shark dares to share.* New York: HarperCollins Publishers.

Halprin Wayland, A. (2009). *New year at the pier: A Rosh Hashanah story.* New York: Penguin Group.

Harlem. New York: The Museum of Modern Art.

Harrison, H. (2014). *Extraordinary Jane.* New York: Dial.

Hartman, B. (2004). *The wolf who cried boy.* New York: Penguin Group.

Havill, J. (2009). *Jamaica's find.* Orlando, FL: Houghton Mifflin Harcourt.

Hawes, J. (2000). *Why frogs are wet.* New York; HarperCollins.

Hazen, B. S. (1983). *Tight times.* New York: Picture Puffins.

Hedlund, S. (2013). *Spring.* Minneapolis, MN: Magic Wagon.

Heiligman, D. (1996). *From caterpillar to butterfly.* New York: HarperCollins.

Heinrichs, A. (2013). *Saint Patrick's day.* North Mankato, MN: The Child's World, Incorporated.

Helfer, R., & Lewin, T. (2012). *The world's greatest lion.* New York: Philomel.

Heller, Lora (2012). *Sign language abc.* New York: Sterling Children's Books.

Henkes, K. (2007). *Chrysanthemum.* New York: Scholastic Inc.

Henkes, K. (2010). *Wemberly worried.* New York: HarperCollins.

Hennesey, B. G., & Pearson, T. C. (1989). *The queen of hearts.* New York: Picture Puffins.

Herbet Scott, A. (2000). *On mother's lap.* Orlando, FL: Houghton Mifflin Harcourt.

Hickman, P. (2007). *How animals eat.* Tonawanda, NY: Kids Can Press.

Hill, S. (2006). *Punxsutawney Phyllis.* New York: Holiday House.

Hillenbrand, W. (2012). *Kite day: A bear and mole story.* New York: Holiday House Inc.

Hills, T. (2007). *Duck, duck, goose.* New York: Random House.

Himmelman, J. (2008). *Katie loves the kittens.* New York: Henry Holt & Co.

Hoban, R. (1964). *Bread and jam for Frances.* New York: Harper & Row.

Hoban, R. (2009). *Best friends for Frances.* New York: HarperCollins.

Hoberman, M. A. (2001). *You read to me, I'll read to you.* New York: Little Brown.

Hoberman, M. A., & Westcott, N. B. (2004). *I know an old lady who swallowed a fly.* New York: Little Brown.

Hodge, D. (2007). *Lily and the mixed-up letters.* Plattsburgh, NY: Tundra.

Holabird, K. (2006). *Angelina and Alice.* New York: Penguin Group.

Holabird, K. (2008). *Angelina ballerina.* New York: Penguin Group.

Holub, J. (2003). *Why do horses neigh?* New York: Penguin Group.

Holub, J. (2012). *Zero the hero.* New York: Henry Holt and Company.

Hopkins, L. B. (1985). *Munching: Poems about eating.* Boston: Little, Brown.

Hopkinson, D. (2005). *Under the quilt of night.* New York: Simon & Schuster.

Horowitz, D. (2007). *Five little gefiltes.* New York: Penguin Group.

Horse, H. (2005). *Little rabbit lost.* Atlanta, GA: Peachtree Press.

Hosford, K. (2012). *Infinity and me.* Minneapolis, MN: Lerner Publishing Group.

Houlb, J. (2012). *Pumpkin countdown.* Park Ridge, Illinois: Albert Whitman & Company.

Howard, T. E. (2013). *All about me!* Bloomington, IN: Trafford Publishing.

Hubbell, P. (2005). *Hurray for spring!* Lanham, MD: Cooper Square Publishing LLC.

Hurd, E. (1980). *Under the lemon tree.* Boston: Little Brown.

Hutchins, P. (2005). *Rosie's walk.* New York: Simon & Schuster Children's Publishing.

Ingalls Wilder, L. (2000). *Summertime in the big woods.* New York: HarperCollins.

Irving, W. (1987). *Rip Van Winkle.* New York: Puffin Books.

Izawa, T. (1968). *The little red hen.* New York: Grosset & Dunlap.

Jacobson, R. (2005). *The Mona Lisa caper.* Plattsburgh, NY: Tundra.

James, S. (2008). *Baby brains: The smartest baby in the whole world.* Somerville, MA: Candlewick Press.

Janni, R. (2012). *Every cowgirl loves a rodeo.* New York: Dial.

Jeffers, O. (2017). *An Alphabet.* New York, NY: Philomel Books, an imprint of Penguin Random House LLC.

Jeffers, S. (2002). *Brother eagle, sister sky: A message from Chief Seattle.* New York: Penguin Group.

Jenkins, S. (2008). *What do you do with a tail like this?* Orlando, FL: Houghton Mifflin Harcourt.

Jenkins, S. (2009). *Down, down, down: A journey to the bottom of the sea.* Orlando FL: Houghton Mifflin Harcourt.

Jenkins, S. (2012). *The beetle book.* Boston, MA: Houghton Mifflin Harcourt Publishing Company.

Johnson, A. (1993). *Do like Kyla.* New York: Scholastic.

Johnson, A. (2007). *Just like Josh Gibson.* New York: Simon & Schuster.

Johnson, C. (1981). *Harold and the purple crayon.* New York: Harper.

Johnson, D. B. (2006). *Henry hikes to Fitchburg.* Orlando, FL: Houghton Mifflin Harcourt.

Johnson, J. (2011). *Discover Science: Senses.* New York: Kingfisher.

Johnston, T. (1996). *The quilt story.* New York: Penguin Group.

Joosse, B. M. (1998). *Mama, do you love me?* San Francisco: Chronicle Books.

Jordan, D. (2012). *Dream big: Michael Jordan and the pursuit of Olympic gold.* New York: Simon & Schuster Children's Books.

Juster, N. (2006). *The hello, goodbye window.* New York: Hyperion Books for Children.

Kalan, R., & Barton, B. (2003). *Jump, frog, jump!* New York: HarperCollins Publishers.

Kalman, M. (2012). *Looking at Lincoln.* New York: Nancy Paulsen Books.

Kann, V. (2009). *Goldilicious.* New York: HarperCollins.

Karlin, N. (2006). *The fat cat sat on the mat.* New York: HarperCollins Publishers.

Katz, K. (2002). *The colors of us.* New York: Henry Holt & Co.

Katz, K. (2007). *Baby's day.* New York: Little Simon.

Katzen, M., & Henderson, A. (1994). *Pretend soup and other real recipes: A cookbook for preschoolers and up.* Berkeley, CA: Ten Speed Press.

Keats, E. (1966). *Jenny's hat.* New York: Harper & Row.

Keats, E. (1996). *The snowy day.* New York: Viking.

Keats, E. J. (1967). *Peter's chair.* New York: Harper & Row.

Keats, E. J. (1974). *Pet show.* New York: Aladdin Books.

Keats, E. J. (1996). *The snowy day.* New York: Penguin Group.

Keats, E. J. (1998). *A letter to Amy.* New York: Puffin.

Keats, E. J. (1998). *Whistle for Willie.* New York: Penguin Group.

Keenan, S. (2007). *O, say can you see?* New York: Scholastic.

Kellog, S. (2004). *The mysterious tadpole.* New York: Penguin Group.

Kellogg, S. (1989). *Is your mama a llama?* New York: Scholastic.

Kellogg, S. (1988). *Johnny Appleseed: A tall tale.* New York: Morrow Jr. Books.

Kellogg, S. (2002). *The missing mitten mystery.* New York: Penguin Group.

Khan, H. (2012). *Golden domes and silver lanterns: A Muslim book of colors.* San Francisco, CA: Chronicle Books.

King Mitchell, M. (1998). *Uncle Jed's barbershop.* New York: Simon & Schuster.

Kingsbury, K. (2004). *Let me hold you longer.* Carol Stream, IL: Tyndale House.

Kline, S. (1995). *Mary Marony and the chocolate surprise.* New York: Penguin Group.

Knowles, S., & Clement, R. (1998). *Edward the emu.* New York: HarperCollins.

Knudsen, M. (2012). *Big mean Mike.* Cambridge, MA: Candlewick Press.

Knudson, M. (2009). *Library lion.* Cambridge, MA: Candlewick Press.

Kochanoff, P. (2009). *You can be a nature detective.* Missoula, MT: Mountain Press Publishing.

Kohuth, J. (2012). *Duck sock hop.* New York: Dial.

Kraus, R. (2008). *Leo the late bloomer.* New York: HarperCollins.

Krull, K. (2003). *Harvesting hope: The story of Cesar Chavez.* Orlando, FL: Houghton Mifflin Harcourt.

Kubler, A. (2002). *Head, shoulders, knees and toes.* New York: Children's Play International.

Kubler, A. (2003). *Ten little fingers.* New York: Children's Play International.

Kudlinski, K. V. (2008). *Boy, were we wrong about the dinosaurs.* New York: Puffin.

Kunhardt, D. (2001). *Pat the bunny*. New York: Random House Children's Books.

La Reau, K., & Magoon S. (2006). *Ugly fish.* Orlando, FL: Harcourt.

Lakin, P. (2012). *Steve Jobs: Thinking differently*. New York: Aladdin.

Larson, K., & Nethery, M. (2008). *Two Bobbies: A true story of Hurricane Katrina, friendship, and survival.* New York: Walker & Company.

Lawrence, J. (2006). *This little chick.* Cambridge, MA: Candlewick Press.

Lawson, J., & Smith, S. (2015). *Sidewalk flowers*. Toronto, Ontario: Groundwood Books.

Lears, L. (1998). *Ian's walk: A story about autism.* Morton Grove, IL: Albert Whitman & Co.

Lee-Tai, A. (2006). *A place where sunflowers grow.* San Francisco, CA: Children's Book Press.

Lehman, B. (2004). *The red book.* Boston: Houghton Mifflin.

LeSieg, T. (1961). *Ten apples up on top.* New York: Random House.

Lester, H. (2002). *Hooway for Wodney Wat.* Orlando, FL: Houghton Mifflin Harcourt.

Let's read and find out science. New York: HarperCollins Publishers.

Levine, E. (2007). *Henry's freedom box: A true story from the underground railroad.* New York: Scholastic.

Levins, S., & Langdo, B. (2006). *Was it the chocolate pudding? A story for little kids about divorce.* Washington, DC: American Psychological Association.

Lin, G. (2004). *Kite flying.* New York: Random House.

Lionni, L. (1998). *An extraordinary egg.* New York: Random House.

Lionni, L. (2004). *The alphabet tree.* New York: Random House Children's Books.

Lionni, L. (2010). *Inch by inch.* New York: Random House.

Lionnni, L. (1973). *Swimmy.* New York: Random House.

Littlechild, G. (2003). *This land is my land.* San Francisco, CA: Children's Book Press.

Litwin, E. (2012). *Pete the cat and his four groovy buttons.* New York: HarperCollins Publishers.

Litwin, E. *Pete the cat series.* New York: HarperCollins Publishers.

Lloyd, J. (2010). *Ella's umbrellas.* Vancouver, BC: Simply Read Books.

Lluch, A. A. (2014). *Alphabet: I like to learn the ABC's*. San Diego, CA: WS Publishing Group.

Lo, G. (2012). *Auntie Yang's great soybean picnic*. New York: Lee & Low Books, Inc.

Lobel, A. (1974). *Frog and toad together.* Norristown, PA: Backpack Books.

Lobel, A. L. (1979). *Frog and toad are friends.* New York: HarperCollins.

Lomp, S., & Pixton, A. (2017). *Things that go!* New York, NY: Workman Publishing Co., Inc.

London, J., & So, M. (2016). *Otters love to play*. Somerville, MA: Candlewick Press.

Long, E. (2012). *Pig has a plan*. New York: Holiday House.

Lord, C. (2007). *Rules.* New York: Scholastic.

Louie, A. L. (2009). *Yeh-Shen: A Cinderella story from China.* Darby, PA: Diane Publishing.

Lovell, P. (2001). *Stand tall, Molly Lou Melon*. New York: Penguin Group.

Lum, K., & Johnson, A. (2008). *What cried granny: An almost bedtime story*. New York: Puffin Books.

Maass, R. (1993). *When winter comes.* New York: Scholastic.

Macaulay, D. (1998). *The new way things work. New York:* Houghton Mifflin Harcourt.

Mack, J. (2012). *Frog and fly: Six slurpy stories.* New York: Philomel.

Mack, J. (2012). *Good news, bad news*. San Francisco, CA: Chronicle Books.

Maestro, B. (1994). *Why do leaves change color?* New York: HarperCollins.

Magsamen, S. (2007). *Messages from the heart: Good night, little one: Huggable, lovable,*

Manushkin, F. (2015). *Happy in our skin*. Somerville, MA: Candlewick Press.

Marino, G. (2012). *Too tall houses*. New York: Viking Juvenile.

Markel, M., & Pham, L. (2016). *Hillary Rodham Clinton: Some girls are born to lead*. New York, NY: Balzer Bray.

Marshall, J. (1998). *Goldilocks and the three bears*. New York: Penguin Group.

Martin, B. J. (2000). *Chicka chicka boom boom*. New York: Simon & Schuster Children's Publishing.

Martin, B. J. (2007). *Brown bear, brown bear, what do you see?* New York: Henry Holt & Co.

Martin, J. B. (2009). *Snowflake Bentley*. Orlando, FL: Houghton Mifflin Harcourt.

Martin, R. (1998). *Rough face girl.* New York: Penguin Group.

Mathers, P. (2012). *The McElderry book of Mother Goose: Revered and rare rhymes.* New York: Margaret K. McElderry Books.

Mayer, M. (1968). *There's a nightmare in my closet.* New York: Penguin.

Mayer, M. (2001). *Just grandma and me.* New York: Random House Children's Books.

Mayer, M. (2003). *A boy, a dog, and a frog.* New York: Penguin Group.

Mayo, D. (2007). *House that Jack built.* Cambridge, MA: Barefoot Books.

McCloskey, R. (1941). *Make way for ducklings.* New York: Viking Books.

McCloskey, R. (1948; 2010). *Blueberries for Sal.* New York: Penguin.

McCloud, C. (2012). *Will you fill my bucket? Daily acts of love around the world.*

McCue, L. (2004). *Corduroy's Valentine's day.* New York: Penguin Group.

McDermott, G. (1996). *Zomo the rabbit. A trickster tale from West Africa.* New York. Scholastic.

McDermott, G. (2010). *Tim O'Toole and the wee folk.* New York: Penguin Group.

McDonald, J. (2017). *Hello, World! Backyard Bugs.* Doubleday Books for Young Readers.

McDonald, M. (2005). *Saving the Liberty Bell.* New York: Simon & Schuster.

McDonald, M. *Judy Moody series.* Cambridge, MA: Candlewick.

McElligott, M. (2007). *Bean thirteen.* New York: Penguin Group.

McGee, M. (2006). *Winston the bookwolf.* New York: Walker & Co.

McGovern, A. (1967; 1992). *Too much noise.* Boston: Houghton Mifflin.

McKissack, P. C. (2008). *Goin' someplace special.* New York: Simon & Schuster.

McMullan, K., & McMullan, J. (2006). *I stink.* New York: HarperCollins.

McNamara, M. (2007). *How many seeds in a pumpkin?* New York: Random House Children's Books.

McNulty, F. (1979). *How to dig a hole to the other side of the world.* New York: Harper & Row.

McNulty, F. (2005). *If you decide to go to the moon.* New York: Scholastic.

McPhail, D. *Emma's pet* (1993). New York: Puffin.

Medina, T. (2013). *I and I: Bob Marley.* New York: Lee & Low Books, Inc.

Menotti, A. (2012). *How many jelly beans? A giant book of giant numbers!* San Francisco, CA: Chronicle Books.

Merriam, E., & DeGroat, D. (1989). Where is everybody? An animal alphabet. New York: Simon & Schuster Books for Young Children.

Meyer, D. J. (1997). *Views from our shoes: Growing up with a brother or sister with special needs.* Bethesda, MD: Woodbine House.

Meyer, M. n.d. *Dazzle Dots and the Missing Spots.* Taggies Soft Book.

Middleton Elya, S. (2006). *Oh no! Gotta go!* New York: Penguin Group.

Milgrim, D. (2006). *Thank you, Thanksgiving.* Orlando, FL: Houghton Mifflin Harcourt.

Milgrim, D. (2013). *Some monsters are different.* New York: Henry Holt & Co.

Miller, M. (1998). *My five senses.* New York: Simon & Schuster.

Mitchell, L. (2001). *Different just like me.* Watertown, MA: Charlesbridge.

Mitton, T. (2009). *Dinosaurumpus.* New York: Scholastic.

Miyares, D. (2015). *Float.* New York: Simon & Schuster Books for Young Readers.

Monsell, E. M. (2010). *Underwear.* Park Ridge, IL: Albert Whitman & Company.

Montanari, D. (2001). *Children around the world.* New York: Kids Can Press.

Moore-Malinos, J. (2007). *It's called dyslexia.* Hauppauge, NY: Barron's Educational Series.

Moore-Mallinos, J. (2008). *My friend has down syndrome.* Hauppauge, NY: Barron's Educational Series, Inc.

Mora, P. (2000). *Tomas and the library lady.* New York: Random House.

Morales, Y. (2003). *Just a minute: A trickster tale and counting book.* San Francisco, CA: Chronicle.

Mosel, A. (1993). *The funny little woman.* New York: Puffin.

Mosel, A. (2010). *Tikki Tikki Tembo.* New York: Square Fish.

Moss, L. (2000). *Zin! Zin! Zin! A violin.* New York: Simon & Schuster.

Munsch, R. (1992). *The paper bag princess.* Toronto, ON: Annick Press.

Munsch, R. N. (1992). *A promise is a promise.* Vancouver BC: Annick Press.

Munson, D. (2000). *Enemy pie.* San Francisco, CA: Chronicle Books.

My first Bob books series. New York: Scholastic Inc.

Myers, L. (2002). *Lewis and Clark and me: A dog's tale.* New York: Henry Holt & Co.

Myron, V. (2009). *Dewey: There's a cat in the library.* New York: Little, Brown & Co. Books for Young Readers.

National Geographic Kids. (2012). *5,000 awesome facts (about everything!)* Washington, DC: National Geographic Society.

Negrin, F. (2002). *The secret footprints.* New York: Random House.

Neitzel, S. (1991). *The jacket I wear in the snow.* New York: Greenwillow Books.

Northville, MI: Nelson Publishing and Marketing.

Numeroff-Joffe, L. (1985). *If you give a mouse a cookie.* New York: Scholastic.

Numeroff, L. (2000). *If you give a pig a pancake.* New York: HarperCollins.

Numeroff, L. (2008). *If you give a cat a cupcake.* New York: HarperCollins Publishers.

O'Connor, J. (1993). *Nina, Nina, ballerina.* New York: Grosset.

O'Connor, J. (1995). *Kate skates.* New York: Penguin Group.

O'Connor, J. *Fancy Nancy series.* New York: HarperCollins Publishers.

Oberman, S. (2005). *Always prayer shawl.* Honesdale, PA: Boyds Mills Press.

Orloff, K. K. (2004). *I wanna iguana.* New York: Penguin.

Osborne, M. P. *Magic tree house series.* New York: Random House Publishers.

Palacio, R. J. (2012). *Wonder.* New York, NY: Random House.

Palacio, R. J. (2017). *We're all wonders.* New York: Knopf Books for Young Readers.

Palanti, M. (2007). *Cheese.* New York: HarperCollins Publishers.

Palatini, M. (1997). *Piggie pie.* Orlando, FL: Houghton Mifflin Harcourt.

Paraskevas, M. (2013). *Taffy saltwater's yummy summer day.* New York: Random House Children's Books.

Parish, H. (2010). *Amelia Bedelia's first apple pie.* New York: HarperCollins.

Parish, P. *Amelia Bedelia series.* New York: Scholastic Inc.

Park, B. *Junie B. Jones series.* New York: Random House Publishers.

Parr, T. (2005). *Otto goes to school.* New York: Little Brown Books.

Parr, T. (2009). *It's okay to be different.* New York: Little, Brown & Co. Books for Young Readers.

Parr, T. (2013). *The I love you book.* New York: Little, Brown Books for Young Readers.

Parrish, P. (1970). *Amelia Bedelia.* New York: Avon Books.

Peck, J. (1998). *The giant carrot.* New York: Penguin Group.

Penn, A. (2006). *The kissing hand.* Terre Haute, IN: Tanglewood Press.

Peppa Pig book series. New York: Scholastic Inc.

Perkins, C., & Equihua, S. (2016). *Cinderella.* New York: Little Simon.

Pfeffer, W. (2004). *From seed to pumpkin.* New York: HarperCollins Publishers.

Pfeffer, W. (2009). *Life in a coral reef.* New York: HarperCollins.

Pfister, M. (1999). *The rainbow fish.* New York: North-South Books.

Pilkey, D. Captain underpants book series. New York: Scholastic.

Pilkey, D. (2003). *Kat Kong.* Orlando, FL: Houghton Mifflin Harcourt.

Pinkney, J. (2000). *Aesop's fables.* San Francisco, CA: Chronicle Books LLC.

Pinkney, J. (2006). *The little red hen.* New York: Dial Press.

Pinkney, J. (2009). *The lion and the mouse.* New York: Little, Brown & Co. Books for Young Readers.

Piper, W. (2009). *The little engine that could.* New York: Penguin.

Pivon, H., & Thomson, S. L. (2004). *What presidents are made of.* New York: Simon & Schuster Children's Books.

Polacco, P. (1995). *Babushka's doll.* New York: Simon & Schuster.

Polacco, P. (1998). *Chicken Sunday.* New York: Penguin Group.

Polacco, P. (1999). *Babushka Baba Yaga.* New York: Penguin Group.

Polacco, P. (2001). *Thank you, Mr. Falker.* New York: Penguin Group.

Polacco, P. (2009). *Mrs. Katz and tush.* New York: Random House.

Polacco, P. (2010). *The keeping quilt.* New York: Simon & Schuster.

Polacco, P. (2012). *Bully.* New York: Penguin Group.

Polacco, P. (2013). *The blessing cup.* New York: Simon & Schuster.

Polacio, R.J. (2017). *We're all wonders.* New York: Random House.

Pomerantz, C. (1989). *Chalk doll.* New York: HarperCollins.

Ponti, C. (2013). *Chick and chickie play all day!* Cambridge, MA: Toon Books.

Portis, A. (2006). *Not a box.* New York: HarperCollins.

Potter, B. (2006). *The tale of Peter Rabbit.* New York: Warner.

Pretlutsky, J. (1999). *The 20th century children's poetry treasury.* New York: Random House Children's Books.

Pretlutsky, J. (2007). *Good sports: Rhymes about running, jumping, throwing, and more.* New York: Random House Children's Books

Priceman, M. (1996). *How to make apple pie and see the world.* New York: Random House Publishers.

Priceman, M. (2009). *Emeline at the circus.* New York: Random House Children's Books.

Priddy, R. (2003). *Fuzzy bee and friends.* New York: Priddy Books

Priddy, R. (2003). *Squishy turtle and friends.* New York: Priddy Books.

Priddy, R. (2013). *Hello baby: Bathtime bath book.* New York: Priddy Books.

Quackenbush, R. (1972). *Old MacDonald had a farm.* New York: Lippincott.

Quackenbush, R. (1973). *Go tell Aunt Rhody.* New York: Lippincott.

Raffi. (1987). *Shake my sillies out.* New York: Random House.

Rankin, L. (1996) *The handmade alphabet.* New York: Puffin Books.

Rammell, S. K. (2006). *City beats: A hip-hoppy pigeon poem.* Nevada City, CA: Dawn.

Ransome, A. (1987). *The fool of the world and the flying ship.* New York: Farrar, Straus & Giroux.

Rappaport, D. (2007). *Martin's big words: The life of Dr. Martin Luther King Jr.* New York: Hyperion Books.

Rathmann, P. (2004). *Good night, gorilla.* New York: Penguin.

Rawlinson, J. (2008). *Fletcher and the falling leaves.* New York: HarperCollins.

Ray, M.L. (2001). *Mud.* New York: Houghton Mifflin Harcourt.

Redmond, E. S. (2012). *The unruly queen.* Cambridge, MA: Candlewick Press.

Reid, M. (1996). *Let's find out about ice cream.* New York: Scholastic.

Reid, S., & Fernandes, E. (1992). *The wild toboggan ride.* New York: Scholastic.

Reidy, J., & Timmers, L. (2016). *Busy builders, busy week!* New York: Bloomsbury.

Rescek, S. (2006). *Hickory, dickory dock: And other favorite nursery rhymes.* New York: Tiger Tales.

Rex, A. (2012). *Cold cereal.* New York: Balzar 1 Bray.

Rey, H. A. (1941). *Curious George.* Boston: Houghton Mifflin.

Rey, H. A. (2006). *Curious George rides a bike.* Boston: Houghton Mifflin.

Rey, H. A. (2008). *Curious George seasons.* Orlando, FL: Houghton Mifflin Harcourt.

Rey, H. A. (2008). *Find the constellations.* Orlando, FL: Houghton Mifflin Harcourt.

Rey, H. A. (2010). *Curious George plants a tree.* Orlando, FL: Houghton Mifflin Harcourt.

Reynolds, P. (2007). *Ish.* New York: Weston Woods Studios.

Rhatigan, J. (2017). *Hey diddle diddle: classic nursery rhymes retold.* Lake Forest, CA: MoonDance.

Rhodes-Pitts, S., & Myers, C. (2015). *Jake makes a world: Jacob Lawrence, a young artist in*

Riggio Heelan, J. (2000). *Rolling along: The story of Taylor and his wheelchair.* Atlanta, GA: Peachtree Publishers.

Ringgold, F. (1996). *Tarbeach.* New York: Random House Children's Books.

Ripley, C. (1997). *Why does popcorn pop? And other kitchen questions.* Toronto: Firefly Books.

Robinson, N. (2006). *Origami adventures: Animals.* Hauppauge, NY: Barron's Educational Series.

Roca, N. (2006). *The 5 senses.* Hauppauge, NY: Barron's Educational Series.

Rocklin, J. (2003). *This book is haunted.* New York: HarperCollins Publishers.

Rockwell, A. (2001). *Bugs are insects.* New York: HarperCollins.

Rockwell, L. (1999). *Good enough to eat: A kid's guide to food and nutrition.* New York: HarperCollins.

Romendik, I. (2002). *The musical Mary had a little lamb (rub-a-dub book).* Westport, CT: Straight-Edge Press.

Root, P. (2009). *Ten sleepy sheep.* Cambridge, MA: Candlewick Press.

Rosenstiehl, A. (2010). *Silly Lilly and the four seasons.* Cambridge, MA: Candlewick Press.

Ross, T. (2003). *Centipede's one hundred shoes*. New York: Henry Holt and Co.

Roth, S. L. (2013). *Parrots over Puerto Rico*. New York: Lee & Low Books, Inc.

Rotner, S. (2012). *Body actions*. New York: Holiday House.

Rowling, J. K. *Harry Potter series*. New York: Scholastic Inc.

Rubbino, S. (2009). *A walk in New York*. Cambridge, MA: Candlewick Press.

Rubin, A. (2012). *Dragons love tacos*. New York: Dial.

Ryan, C. (2012). *Moo hoo*. New York: Walker Children's Books.

Rylant, C. (2006). *Henry and Mudge in puddle trouble: The second book of their adventures*. Elmsford, NY: Spotlight.

Rylant, C. (2008). *In November*. Orlando, FL: Houghton Mifflin Harcourt.

Rylant, C. (2008). *Poppleton in winter*. New York: Scholastic.

Rylant, C. *Henry and Mudge series*. New York: Simon & Schuster.

Sakai, K. (2006). *Emily's balloon*. San Francisco, CA: Chronicle Books.

Sams, C. R., & Stoick, J. (2000). *Stranger in the woods: A photographic fantasy*. Milford, MI: Carl R. Sams II Photography.

Sanderson, R. (2002). *Cinderella*. New York: Little, Brown & Co. Books for Young Reader.

Say, A. (2008). *Grandfather's journey*. Orlando, FL: Houghton Mifflin Harcourt.

Sayre, J. (2006). *One is a snail, ten is a crab: A counting by feet book*. Cambridge, MA: Candlewick Press.

Schachner, J. (2005). *Skippyjon Jones*. New York: Penguin Group.

Schaefer, L. M. (2008). *Some kids use wheelchairs*. North Mankato, MN: Capstone Press.

Schafer, Albert. (2012). *Illusionology: The secret science of magic*. Somerville, MA: Candlewick Press.

Schories, P. (2004). *Breakfast for Jack*. Honesdale, PA: Boyd's Mill Press.

Schwartz, D. M. (1993). *How much is a million?* New York: HarperCollins Publishers.

Science kids. Ashmore, Queensland, Australia: Kingfisher.

Scieszka, J. (1992). *The stinky cheese man and other fairly stupid tales*. New York: Penguin Group

Scieszka, J. (1996). *The true story of the 3 little pigs*. New York: Penguin Group.

Scotton, R. (2012). *Secret agent splat!* New York: HarperCollins.

Seeger, L. V. (2007). *Black? White? Day? Night? A book of opposites*. New York: Roaring Brook Press.

Seeger, L.V. (2013). *Green*. New York: Roaring Brook Press.

Selby, D., & Leon, S. (2017). *Kids' travel guide—Japan* (Vol. 35). Flying Kids.

Sendak, M. (1962). *Chicken soup with rice*. New York: Harper & Row.

Sendak, M. (1963; 1988). *Where the wild things are*. New York: HarperCollins.

Sendak, M. (1962; 1991). *Chicken soup with rice: A book of months*. New York: HarperCollins Publishers.

Sendak, M. (1991). *Pierre*. New York: HarperCollins.

Seuss, Dr. (1957). The cat in the hat. New York: Random House.

Seuss, Dr. (1960). *Green eggs and ham*. New York: Random House.

Seuss, Dr. (1971). *The lorax*. New York: Random House.

Seuss, Dr. (1996). *Mr. Brown can moo! Can you?* New York: Random House.

Seuess, Dr. (1957; 2017). *How the Grinch stole Christmas*. New York: Random House.

Seuss, Dr. (2000). *Horton hatches the egg*. New York: Random House.

Seuss, Dr. (2009). *Oh, the thinks you can think*. New York: Random House.

Shannon, D. (1998). *No, David*. New York: Scholastic.

Sharmat, M. (1984). *Gregory, the terrible eater*. New York: Scholastic.

Shaw, C. (1947). *It looked like spilt milk*. New York: HarperCollins.

Shaw, N. (1997). *Sheep in a shop*. Boston: Houghton Mifflin.

Shaw, N. E. (2009). *Sheep in a jeep*. Orlando, FL: Houghton Mifflin Harcourt.

Seuess, Dr. (1957; 2017). *How the Grinch stole Christmas*. New York: Random House.

Shelby, A. & Travis, I. (1991). *Potluck*. UK: Orchard Books.

Sherry, K. (2007). *I'm the biggest thing in the ocean*. New York: Penguin Group.

Showers, P. (1991). *How many teeth?* New York: HarperCollins Publishers.

Showers, P. (1997). *Sleep is for everyone (Let's read-and-find-out science book)*. New York: HarperCollins.

Showers, P. (2001). *What happens to a hamburger?* New York: HarperCollins.

Shriver, M. (2001). *What's wrong with Timmy?* New York: Little, Brown Books.

Silverberg, C. (2013). *What makes a baby*. New York: Seven Stories Press.

Silverstein, S. (1964). *A giraffe and a half*. New York: HarperCollins.

Silverstein, S. (2004). *The giving tree*. New York: HarperCollins Publishers.

Silverstein, S. (2004). *Where the sidewalk ends*. New York: HarperCollins Publishers.

Silverstein, A., Silverstein, V. B., & Silverstein, Nunn, L. (2000). *Eat your vegetables! Drink your milk*. New York: Scholastic.

Simon, R., Simon, T., & Siegel, M. (2015). *Oskar and the eight blessings*. New York: Roaring Brook Press

Simon, S. (1997). *The brain: Our nervous system*. New York: Scholastic.

Simon, S. (2013). *Coral reefs*. New York: HarperCollins.

Slobodkina, E. (1987). *Caps for sale*. New York: HarperCollins

Small World Creations ltd. (2017). *Splish Splash (Magic Bath Books) Bath Book*. Yate, UK: Barron's Educational Series.

Smith, L. (2010). *It's a book*. New York: Roaring Brook Press.

Smith, M. G., & Flett, J. (2016). *My heart fills with happiness*. Victoria, BC: Orca Book.

snuggable books. New York: Little, Brown & Co. Books for Young Readers.

So, M. (2008). *Pale male: Citizen hawk of New York City*. New York: Random House Publishers.

Solheim, J. (2001). *It's disgusting and we ate it!: True food facts from around the world and throughout history*. New York: Simon & Schuster Children's Books.

Soto, G. (1996). *Too many tamales*. New York: Penguin.

Spinelli, J. (2012). *Third grade angels*. New York: Scholastic Inc.

Sports Illustrated Kids Rookie Books series. New York: Sports Illustrated

Stead, P. C. (2013). *Bear has a story to tell*. New York: Roaring Brook Press.

Steig, W. (2005). *Sylvester and the magic pebble*. New York: Simon & Schuster.

Stein, D. E. (2012). *Because Amelia smiled*. Cambridge, MA: Candlewick Press.

Steptoe, J. (2001). *In daddy's arms I am tall: African Americans celebrating fathers*. New York: Lee & Low.

Stevens, J. (2005). *The great fuzz frenzy*. Orlando, FL: Houghton Mifflin Harcourt.

Stewart, A. (2006). *Rabbit ears*. London: Bloomsbury.

Stewart, S. (2007). *The gardener*. New York: Square Fish.

Stilton, G. *Geronimo Stilton series*. New York: Scholastic Inc.

Stott, C. (2003). *I wonder why stars twinkle and other questions about space*. New York: Kingfisher.

Sturn, J., Arnold, A., & Frost, A. F. (2009). *Adventures in cartooning: How to turn your doodles into comics*. New York: First Second Books.

Stutson, C. (2009). *By the light of the Halloween moon*. Tarrytown, NY: Cavendish, Marshall Corporation.

Sutton, S. (2012). *Demolition*. Somerville, MA: Candlewick.

Taback, S. (2000). *Joseph had a little overcoat*. New York: Penguin Group.

Tafuri, N. (1991). *Have you seen my duckling?* New York: HarperCollins Publishers.

Tafuri, N. (2010). *The busy little squirrel*. New York: Simon & Schuster.

Takai, M., & Takai, H. (2017). *Fun Origami for Children: Dino!: 12 Daring Dinosaurs to Fold*. London, UK: Ryland Peters & Small.

Taylor, B. (1998). *A day at the farm*. New York: DK Publishing.

Tchin (1997). *Rabbit's wish for snow: A Native American legend*. New York: Scholastic.

The game. Chicago, IL: Albert Whitman & Company.

Thomas, P. (2002). *Don't call me special: A first look at disability*. Hauppauge, NY: Barron's Educational Series.

Thomas, P. (2002). *My amazing body: A first look at health and fitness*. Hauppauge, NY: Barron's Educational Series.

Thompson, L. (2005). *Mouse's first spring*. New York: Simon & Schuster.

Time for kids. New York: HarperCollins.

Tolstoy, A. (2006). *The gigantic turnip*. Cambridge, MA: Barefoot Books.

Tonatiuh, D. (2016). *The princess and the qarrior: A tale of two volcanoes*. New York: Abrams Books For Young Readers.

UK: Barron's Educational Series.

Van Allsburg, C. (1981). *Jumanji*. Orlando, FL: Houghton Mifflin Harcourt.

Van Allsburg, C. (1998). *Two bad ants*. Orlando, FL: Houghton Mifflin Harcourt.

Van Camp, K. (2009). *Harry and horsie*. New York: HarperCollins.

Van Fleet, M. (1992). *One yellow lion*. New York: Penguin Group.

Van Fleet, M. (2003). *Tails*. Orlando, FL: Houghton Mifflin Harcourt.

Van Fleet, M. (2008). *Alphabet*. New York: Simon & Schuster Children's Publishing.

Van Leeuwen, J. (2007). *Amanda pig and the really hot day*. New York: Penguin Group.

Van Niekerk, C. (2008). *Understanding Sam and Asperger Syndrome*. Erie, PA: Skeezel Press.

Vere, E. (2012). *Bedtime for monsters*. New York: Henry Holt and Company.

Viorst, J. (1972). *Alexander and the terrible, horrible, no good, very bad day*. New York: Atheneum.

Viorst, J. (2010). *Lulu and the brontosaurus*. New York: Simon & Schuster.

Viorst, J., (1971). *The tenth good thing about Barney*. New York: Simon & Schuster.

Virj`an, E.J. (2016). *What this story needs is a pig in a wig*. New York: Scholastic Inc.

Walker, D. (2010). *Hello, New York City*. New York: Sterling Publishing.

Walker, D., & Teets, A. (2015). *Spaghetti & meatballs: Growing up Italian*. Terra Alta, WV: Headline Books.

Wallace, A., & Elkerton, A. (2016). *How to catch a leprechaun*. Naperville, IL: Sourcebooks Jabberwocky.

Ward, C. (2004). *Cookies week*. New York: Penguin Group.

Wardlaw, L. (2012). *Red, white, and boom!* New York: Henry Holt and Co.

Watt, F. (2006). *That's not my kitten*. London: Usbourne.

Wellington, M. (2004). *Apple farmer Annie*. New York: Penguin Group.

Wells, R. (2000). *Noisy Nora*. New York: Scholastic.

Wells, R. (2002). *Max cleans up*. New York: Penguin Group.

Wells, R. (2004). *Ruby's beauty shop*. New York: Penguin Group.

Wells, R. (2009). *Yoko*. New York: Hyperion.

Wells, R. E. (2006). *Did a dinosaur drink this water?* Morton Grove, IL: Whitman, Albert & Company.

Wenzel, B. (2016). *They all saw a cat*. San Francisco, CA: Chronicle Books.

Westcott, N. B. (1980). *I know an old lady*. Boston: Little, Brown.

White, E. B. (1952). *Charlotte's web*. New York: Scholastic.

Who was. . . ? series. New York: Penguin Group.

Willems. M. (2003). *Don't let the pigeon drive the bus*. New York: Hyperion Books for Children

Willems, M. (2006). *Don't let the pigeon stay up late*. New York: Hyperion Books for Children.

Willems, M. (2006). *Edwina, the dinosaur who didn't know she was extinct*. New York: Hyperion.

Willems, M. (2004). *Knuffle Bunny*. New York: Scholastic, Inc.

Williams, K. L., & Mohammed, K. (2016). *Four feet, two sandals*. Grand Rapids, MI: Eerdmans Books for Young Readers.

Williams, M. (2011). *The velveteen rabbit*. Tarrytown, NY, Marshall Cavendish Corporation.

Williams, M. (2012). *Goldilocks and the three dinosaurs: As retold by Mo Williams*. New York: HarperCollins Publisher.

Williams, S. (1996). *I went walking*. New York: Gulliver.

Willis, J., & Ross, T. (2000). *Susan laughs*. New York: Henry Holt & Co.

Willis, N. C. (2002). *Raccoon moon*. Middletown, DE: Birdsong Books.

Wilson, K. (2008). *Bear wants more*. New York: Simon & Schuster.

Wilson, K. (2014). *Outside the box*. New York: Margaret K. McElderry Books.

Wilson, K., & Randin, J. (2007). *A frog in the bog*. New York: Simon & Schuster.

Wing, N. (2002). *The night before summer vacation*. New York: Penguin Group.

Wing, N., & Wummer, A. (2016). *The night before the Fourth of July*. New York: Grosset & Dunlap.

Wood, A. (1998). *Quick as cricket*. New York: Child's Play-International.

Wood, A. (2010). *Piggy pie po*. Orlando, FL: Houghton Mifflin Harcourt.

Wood, A. *Silly Sally* (series). Orlando, FL: Houghton Mifflin Harcourt.

Wood, A. (2010). *The napping house*. Orlando, FL: Houghton Mifflin Harcourt.

Woodman, N. (2007). *Dirt*. Des Moines, IA: National Geographic Society.

Wright, B.F. (1984). *The real mother goose*. Chicago: Rand McNally

Wright, M. (2010). *Sneezy the snowman*. Tarrytown, NY: Marshall Cavendish Corporation.

Wynne-Jones, T. (2009). *Zoom*. Toronto, ON: Groundwood Books.

Yamada, U. (2007). *Story of Cherry the pig*. San Diego, CA: Kane Miller Book.

Yashima, T. (2004). *Umbrella*. New York: Penguin Group.

Yolan, J., & Teague, M. (2005). *How do dinosaurs eat their food?* New York: Scholastic.

Yolen, J. (2005). *Owl moon.* New York: Scholastic.

Yolen, J. (2017). *On bird hill.* Apex, NC: Cornell Lab Publishing Group.

Yolen, J., & Teague, M. (2000). *How do dinosaurs say good night*? New York: Scholastic.

Yolen, J & Teague, M. (2005). *How do dinosaurs eat their food?* New York: Scholastic

Yolen, J., & Young, E. (1998). *Emperor and the kite.* New York: Penguin Group.

Young, E. (1996). *Lon Po Po: A red riding hood story from China.* New York: Penguin Group.

Young, E., & Adams, T. (2004). *The lost horse: A Chinese folktale.* Orlando, FL: Houghton Mifflin Harcourt.

Zemach, M. (1991). *The three little pigs.* New York: Tandem Library.

Ziefert, H. (2006). *You can't taste a pickle with your ear!* Maplewood, NJ: Blue Apple Books.

Zimmerman, A. (2007). *Trashy town.* New York: Weston Woods Studio.

Zoehfeld, K. W. (1994). *Manatee winter.* Hartford, CT: Trudy Corporation.

Zoehfeld, K. W. (1995). *What's alive?* New York: HarperCollins Publishers.

Zoehfeld, K. W. (2003). *Did dinosaurs have feathers?* New York: HarperCollins.

Zoehfeld, K. W. (2014). *Secrets of the seasons: Orbiting the sun in our backyard.* New York: Knopf Books for Young Readers.

Zoehfeld, W. K. (1994). *What lives in a shell?* New York: HarperCollins.

Zolotow, C. (1977). *Mr. Rabbit and the lovely present.* New York: Harper & Row.

Zonta, P. (2006). *Jessica's x-ray.* Tonawanda, NY: Firefly Books.

Zoobooks series. Evanston, IL: Wildlife Education.

References

Abuhamdeh, S., & Csikszentmihalyi, M. (2009). Intrinsic and extrinsic motivational orientations in the competitive context: An examination of person-situation interactions. *Journal of Personality, 77*(5), 1615–1635.

Adams, M. J. (1990). *Beginning to read: Thinking and learning about print.* Urbana, IL: University of Illinois Center for the Study of Reading.

Adams, M. J. (2001). Alphabetic anxiety and explicit, systematic phonics instruction: A cognitive science perspective. In S. B. Neuman & D. K. Dickinson (Eds.), *Handbook of early literacy research* (pp. 66–80). New York: Guilford Press.

Akhavan, L. L. (2006). *Help! My kids don't all speak English: How to set up a language workshop in your linguistically diverse classroom.* Portsmouth, NH: Heinemann.

Allen, J. K. (2017). Exploring the role teacher perceptions in the underrepresentation of culturally and linguistically diverse students in gifted programming. *Gifted Child Today, 40*(2).

Allen, R. V. (1976). *Language experience in communication.* Boston: Houghton Mifflin.

Allington, R. L. (2009). *What really matters in fluency: Research-based practices across the curriculum.* Boston: Allyn & Bacon.

Allington, R. L., & Cunningham, P. M. (2006). *Schools that work* (3rd ed.). New York: Longman.

Allison, D. T., & Watson, J. A. (1994). The significance of adult storybook reading styles on the development of young children's emergent reading. *Reading Research and Instruction, 34*(1), 57–72.

Almasi, J. F., & Fullerton, S. K. (2013). *Teaching Strategic Processes in Reading* (2nd ed.). New York, NY: Guilford.

Almasi, J. F., & Hart, J. (2011). Best practices in comprehension. In L. M. Morrow & L. B. Gambrell (Eds.), *Best practices in literacy instruction* (4th ed.). New York: Guilford Press.

Anderson, J., Anderson, A., Friedrich, N., & Ji Eun, I. (2010). Taking stock of family literacy: Some contemporary perspectives. *A Journal of Early Childhood Literacy, 10*(1), 33–53.

Anderson, R. C., & Pearson, P. D. (1984). A schema-theoretic view of basic processing in reading. In P. D. Pearson (Ed.), *Handbook of reading research* (pp. 255–292). New York: Longman.

Anderson, R. C., Fielding, L. G., & Wilson, P. T. (1988). Growth in reading and how children spend their time outside of school. *Reading Research Quarterly, 23*, 285–303.

Anderson, R. C., Hiebert, E. H., Scott, J. A., & Wilkinson, I. A. G. (1985). *Becoming a nation of readers.* Washington, DC: National Institute of Education.

Ankrum, J., Genest, M., & Belcastro, E. (2014). The power of verbal scaffolding: "Showing" beginning readers how to use reading strategies. *Early Childhood Education Journal, 42*(1), 39.

Anthony, J. L., & Lonigan, C. J. (2004). The nature of phonological awareness: Converging evidence from four studies of preschool and early grade school children. *Journal of Educational Psychology, 96*(1), 1–18.

Antonacci, P., & O'Callaghan, C. (2003). *Portraits of literacy development: Instruction and assessment in a well-balanced literacy program, K–3.* Upper Saddle River, NJ: Merrill/Prentice Hall.

Applebee, A. N., & Langer, J. A. (1983). Instructional scaffolding: Reading and writing as natural language activities. *Language Arts, 60*, 168–175.

Applebee, A. N., Langer, J. A., & Mullis, M. (1988). *Who reads best? Factors related to reading achievement in grades 3, 7, and 11.* Princeton, NJ: Educational Testing Service.

Applegate, M. D., Applegate, A. J., & Modla, V. B. (2009). "She's my best reader; she just can't comprehend": Studying the relationship between fluency and comprehension. *The Reading Teacher, 62*(6), 512–521.

Armstrong, T. (2009). *Multiple intelligences in the classroom.* Alexandria, VA: Association for Supervision and Curriculum Development.

Ashton-Warner, S. (1963). *Spinster.* New York: Simon & Schuster.

Ashton-Warner, S. (1986). *Teacher.* New York: Bantam.

Assel, M. S., Landry, S. H., Swank, P. R., & Gunnewig, S. (2007). An evaluation of curriculum setting, and mentoring on performance of children enrolled in pre-kindergarten. *Reading and writing: An interdisciplinary journal, 20*(5), 463–494.

Au, K. (1998). Constructivist approaches, phonics, and the literacy learning of students of diverse backgrounds. In T. Shanahan & F. V. Rodriguez-Brown (Eds.), *Forty-seventh yearbook of the National Reading Conference* (pp. 1–21). Chicago: National Reading Conference.

Au, K. (2001, July–August). Culturally responsive instruction as a dimension of new literacy. *Reading Online 5*(1).

Auerbach, E. (1989). Toward a social–contextual approach to family literacy. *Harvard Educational Review, 56*, 165–181.

Axelrod Y., Hall A. H., & McNair J. C., (2015). Kindergarten through grade 3: A is burrito and B is Sloppy Joe: Creating print-rich environments for children in K–3 classrooms. *YC: Young Children*, (4), 16.

Bandeira de Mello, A. (2011). Mapping state proficiency standards onto NAEP scales: Variation and change in state standards for reading and mathematics, 2005–2009. National Assessment of Educational Progress. Washington, DC: National Center for Educational Statistics. Retrieved from http://nces.ed.gov/nationsreportcard/pdf/studies/2011458.pdf.

Banks, J., & Banks, C. (2009). *Multicultural education: Issues and perspectives* (4th ed.). Boston: Allyn and Bacon.

Barone, D. (1998). How do we teach literacy to children who are learning English as a second language. In S. Neuman & K. Roskos (Eds.), *Children achieving: Best practices in early literacy* (pp. 56–76). Newark, DE: International Reading Association.

Barone, D. (2011). Welcoming Families: A parent literacy project in a linguistically rich, high-poverty school. *Early Childhood Education Journal, 38*(5), 377–384.

Barone, D. M., Mallette, M. H., & Xu, S. H. (2004). *Teaching early literacy: Development, assessment, and instruction.* New York: Guilford Press.

Barone, D., & Morrow, L. M. (2003). *Literacy and young children: Research based practices.* New York: Guilford Press.

Bauer, E. B., & Manyak, P. C. (2008). Creating language-rich instruction for English-language learners. *The Reading Teacher, 62*(2), 176–178.

Bauer, E. B., & Mesmer, H. A. E. (2008). Response to Intervention (RTI): What teachers of reading need to know. *The Reading Teacher, 62*(2), 176–178.

Baumann, J. F. (1992). Effect of think aloud instruction on elementary students' comprehension monitoring abilities. *Journal of Reading Behavior, 24*(2), 143–172.

Baumann, J. F., Hoffman, J. V., Duffy-Hester, A. M., & Ro, J. M. (2000). The first R: Reading in the early grades. *Reading Teacher, 54,* 84–98.

Bear, D.R., Invernizzi, M., Templeton, S., & Johnston, F. (2012). *Words their way: Word study for phonics, vocabulary, and spelling instruction* (5th ed.). Upper Saddle River, NJ: Pearson.

Beauchat, K. A., Blamey, K. L., & Walpole, S. (2010). *The building blocks of preschool success.* New York, NY: Guilford.

Beauchat, K., Blamey, K., & Walpole, S. (2009). Building preschool children's language and literacy one storybook at a time. *Reading Teacher, 63*(1), 26–39.

Beck, I. L., & McKeown, M. G. (2001). Text talk: Capturing the benefits of read-aloud experiences for young children. *Reading Teacher,* 55, 10–20.

Beck, I. L., & McKeown, M. G. (2007). Increasing young children's oral vocabulary repertoires through rich and focused instruction. *The Elementary School Journal, 107*(3), 251–273.

Beck, I. L., McKeown, M. G., & Kucan, L. (2013). *Bringing words to life: Robust vocabulary instruction* (2nd ed.). New York: Guilford Press.

Beck, I. L., Perfetti, C., & McKeown, M. (1982). The effects of long-term vocabulary instruction on lexical access and reading comprehension. *Journal of Educational Psychology, 74,* 506–521.

Bedford, D., & Reeve, R. (2016). *Once upon a time . . . online.* New York: Parragon Inc.

Bellinger, J. M., & DiPerna, J. C. (2011). Is fluency-based story retell a good indicator of reading comprehension? *Psychology in the Schools,* 48, 416–426.

Berk, L. E. (2007). *Infants, children, and adolescents.* Upper Saddle River, NJ: Prentice Hall.

Berk, L. E. (2008). *Child development.* Boston: Allyn and Bacon.

Blachowicz, C. L. Z., & Fisher, P. J. (2002). Best practices in vocabulary instruction: What effective teachers do. In L. M. Morrow, L. Gambrell, & M. Pressley (Eds.), *Best practices in literacy instruction* (2nd ed., pp. 87–110). New York: Guilford Press.

Blachowicz, C., & Fisher, P. (2015). *Teaching vocabulary in all classrooms* (5th ed.). Upper Saddle River, NJ: Pearson.

Blanch, N., Forsythe, L. C., Roberts, S. K., & Van Allen, J. H. (2017). Reigniting writers: Using the literacy block with elementary students to support authentic writing experiences. *Childhood Education, 93*(1), 48.

Blau, S., Elbow, P., Killgallon, D., & Caplan, R. (1998). *The writer's craft.* Evanston, IL: McDougal Littell.

Bloom, L. (1990). Development in expression: Affect and speech. In N. Stein & T. Trabasso (Eds.), *Psychological and biological approaches to emotion* (pp. 215–245). Hillsdale, NJ: Erlbaum.

Boling, E. (2007). Linking technology, learning, and stories: Implications from research on hypermedia video-cases. *Teaching and Teacher Education, 23*(2), 189–200.

Boling, E., Castek, J., Zawilinski, L., Barton, K., & Nierlich, T. (2008). Collaborative literacy: Blogs and Internet projects. *Reading Teacher, 61*(6), 504–506.

Bond, G. L., & Dykstra, R. (1967a). The cooperative research program in first-grade reading instruction. *Reading Research Quarterly, 2,* 5–142.

Bond, G. L., & Dykstra, R. (1967b). *Coordinating center for first grade reading instruction programs.* (Final Report of Project No. x-001, Contact No. OES10–264). Minneapolis, MN: University of Minnesota.

Bouch, M. (2005). *Comprehension strategies for English language learners.* New York: Scholastic.

Boushey, G. & Moser, J. (2006). *The daily five: Fostering literacy independence in the elementary grades.* Portland, ME: Stenhouse.

Boushey, G. & Moser, J. (2009). *CAFÉ book: Engaging all students in daily literacy assessment and instruction.* Portland, ME: Stenhouse Publishers.

Bowman, B. T., Donovan, M. S., & Burns, M. S. (Eds.). (2000). *Eager to learn: Educating our preschoolers.* Washington, DC: National Academy Press.

Brock, C. H., & Raphael, T. E. (2005). *Windows to language, literacy, and culture.* Newark, DE: International Reading Association.

Bromley, K. (2003). Building a sound writing program. In L. M. Morrow, L. B. Gambrell, & M. Pressley (Eds.), *Best practices in literacy instruction* (2nd ed., pp. 243–263). New York: Guilford Press.

Bromley, K. (2006). From drawing to digital creations: Graphic organizers in the classroom. In D. S. Strickland & N. Roser (Eds.). *Handbook on teaching literacy through the communicative and visual arts,* Vol. II. Mahwah, NJ: Lawrence, Erlbaum.

Bromley, K. (2007). Assessing student writing. In J. Paratore & McCormack (Eds.), *Classroom literacy assessment* (pp. 210–226). New York: Guilford Press.

Bromley, K. (2011). Best practices in writing. In L. M. Morrow & L. B. Gambrell (Eds.), *Best practices in literacy instruction* (4th ed.). New York: Guilford Press.

Brophy, J. (2004). *Motivating students to learn* (2nd ed.). Mahwah, NJ: Erlbaum.

Brophy, J. (2008). Developing students' appreciation for what is taught in school. *Educational Psychologist, 43*(3), 132–141.

Brown, R. (2008). The road not yet taken: A transitional strategies approach to reading instruction. *The Reading Teacher, 61*(7). 538–547.

Brown, R., Cazden, C., & Bellugi-Klima, U. (1968). The child's grammar from one to three. In J. P. Hill (Ed.), *Minnesota symposium on child development.* Minneapolis: University of Minnesota Press.

Brownell, R. (Ed.). (2000). *Expressive one-word picture vocabulary test, 2 to 18 years.* Novato, CA: Academic Therapy Publications.

Bryant, D., & Maxwell, K. (1997). The effectiveness of early intervention for disadvantaged children. In M. Guralnick (Ed.), *The effectiveness of early intervention* (pp. 23–46). Baltimore: Paul H. Brookes.

Bufalino, J., Wang, C., Gómez-Bellengé, F. X., & Zalud, G. (2010). What's possible for first grade at-risk literacy learners receiving early intervention services. *Literacy Teaching and Learning 15*(1), 1–15.

Bulfin, S. A., & North, S. M., (2007). Negotiating digital literacy practices across school and home: case studies of young people in Australia. *Language and Education, 21*(3) 247–263.

Burke, A., & Rowsell, J. (2007). Assessing new literacies: Evaluating multimodal practice. *E-Learning Journal, Special Edition,* Oxford, UK: Symposium Journals.

Burns, M. S., Snow, C. E., & Griffin, P. (Eds.). (1999). *Starting out right: A guide to success.* Washington, DC: National Academy Press.

Bus, A. G. (2001). Joint caregiver–child storybook reading: A route to literacy development. In S. B. Neuman & D. K. Dickinson (Eds.), *Handbook of early literacy research* (pp. 179–191). New York: Guilford Press.

Byrne, B., & Fielding-Barnsley, R. (1993). Evaluation of a program to teach phonemic awareness to young children: A one-year follow-up. *Journal of Educational Psychology, 85,* 104–111.

Byrne, B., & Fielding-Barnsley, R. (1995). Evaluation of a program to teach phonemic awareness to young children: A two- and three-year follow-up and a new preschool trial. *Journal of Educational Psychology, 87,* 488–503.

Caesar, L. G., & Nelson, N. W. (2014). Parental involvement in language and literacy acquisition: A bilingual journaling approach. *Child Language Teaching & Therapy, 30*(3), 317–336.

Calkins, L. M. (1994). *The art of teaching writing*. (2nd Ed.) Portsmouth, NH: Heinemann.

Callcott, D., Hammond, L., & Hill, S. (2015). The synergistic effect of teaching a combined explicit movement and phonological awareness program to preschool aged students. *Early Childhood Education Journal, 43*(3), 201.

Cappellini, M. (2005). *Balancing reading and language learning: A resource for teaching English language learners, K–5*. Portland, ME: Stenhouse; Newark, DE: International Reading Association.

Carter, D., Chard, D., & Pool, J. (2009). A family strengths approach to early language and literacy development. *Early Childhood Education Journal, 36*(6), 519–526.

Caspergue, R. (2017). Ready for kindergarten? Rethinking early literacy in the Common Core era. *The Reading Teacher, 7*(6), 643–648.

Cavanaugh, D., Clemence, K., Teale, M., Rule, A., & Montgomery, S. (2016). Kindergarten scores, storytelling, executive function, and motivation improved through literacy-rich guided play. *Early Childhood Education Journal*, 1–13.

Cazden, C. B. (2005). The value of conversations for language development and reading comprehension. *Literacy Teaching and Learning, 9*(1), 1–6.

CCSS; Common Core State Standards, 2011, Common Core State Standards Initiative. Retrieved from www.corestandards.org.

Center for the Improvement of Early Reading Achievement. (2001). *Put reading first; The research building blocks for teaching children to read*. Washington, DC: National Institute for Literacy.

Cepada, N. J., Vul, E., Rohrer, D., Wixted, T., & Pashler, H. (2008). Spacing effects in learning: A temporal ridgeline of optimal retention. *Psychological Science 19*(11), 1095–1102.

Chomsky, C. (1965). *Aspects of a theory of syntax*. Cambridge, MA: MIT Press.

Christ, T., Chiu, M. M., & Wang, X. C. (2014). Preschoolers' engagement with reading behaviours: A statistical discourse analysis of peer buddy-reading interactions. *Journal of Research in Reading, 37*(4), 375–408.

Clay, M. M. (1966). *Emergent reading behavior*. Doctoral dissertation, University of Auckland, New Zealand.

Clay, M. M. (1987). Implementing reading recovery: Systematic adaptations to an educational innovation. *New Zealand Journal of Educational Studies, 22*, 35–38.

Clay, M. M. (1991). *Becoming literate: The construction of inner control*. Portsmouth, NH: Heinemann.

Clay, M. M. (1993a). *An observation survey of early literacy achievement*. Portsmouth, NH: Heinemann.

Clay, M. M. (1993b). *Reading Recovery: A guidebook for teachers in training*. Portsmouth, NH: Heinemann.

Clay, M. M. (2000). *Concepts about print: What have children learned about the way we print language?* Portsmouth, NJ: Heinemann.

Cloud, N., Genesee, F., & Hamayan, E. (2009). *Literacy instruction for English language learners: A teacher's guide to research-based practices*. Portsmouth, NH: Heinemann.

Cobb, J. B. (2017). Investigating reading metacognitive strategy awareness of elementary children: A developmental continuum emerges. *Journal of Research in Childhood Education, 31*(3), 401–418.

Cochran-Smith, M. (1984). *The making of a reader*. Norwood, NH: Ablex.

Coiro, J., & Dobler, E. (2007). Exploring the online reading comprehension strategies used by sixth-grade skilled readers to search for and locate information on the Internet. *Reading Research Quarterly, 42*(2), 214–257.

Collins, N. L. D., & Shaeffer, M. B. (1997). Look, listen, and learn to read. *Young Children, 52*(5), 65–67.

Combs, M. (2009). *Readers and writers in primary grades: A balanced literacy approach K–3* (3rd ed.). Upper Saddle River, NJ: Pearson Education.

Connell, R. W. (1994). Poverty and education. *Harvard Educational Review, 64*, 125–149.

Cook-Cottone, C. (2004). Constructivism in family literacy practices: Parents as mentors. *Reading Improvement, 41*(4), 208–216.

Cooter, K. S. (2006). When mama can't read: Counteracting intergenerational illiteracy. *The Reading Teacher, 59*(7), 698–702.

Corgill, A. M. (2008). *Of primary importance: What's essential in teaching young writers*. Portland, ME: Stenhouse.

Council of Chief State School Officers. (2010). *Common core state standards for English language arts & literacy in history/social studies, science, and technical subjects*. Washington, DC. www.corestandards.org/articles/8-national-governors-association-and-state-education-chiefs.

Cox, C. (2007). *Teaching language arts: A student- and response-centered classroom* (6th ed.). Boston: Allyn and Bacon.

Crosby, S. A., Rasinski, T., Padak, N., & Yildirim, K. (2015). A 3-year study of a school-based parental involvement program in early literacy. *Journal of Educational Research, 108*(2), 165–172.

Cullinan, B. E. (1992). *Invitation to read: More children's literature in the reading program*. Newark, DE: International Reading Association.

Cunningham, P. (2013). *Phonics they use: Words for reading and writing* (6th ed.). Boston, MA: Pearson.

Cunningham, P. M., & Cunningham, J. W. (1992). Making words: Enhancing the invented spelling–decoding connection. *Reading Teacher, 46*, 106–115.

Cunningham, P., & Hall, D. (2001). *Making words*. Torrance, CA: Good Apple.

Dahl, K., & Farnan. N. (1998). *Children's writing: Perspectives from research*. Newark, DE: International Reading Association & National Reading Conference.

Daniels, H. (1994). *Literature circles: Voice and choice in the student centered classroom*. Portland, ME: Stenhouse.

Delgado-Gaitan, C. (1992). School matters in the Mexican-American home: Socializing children to education. *American Educational Research Journal, 29*, 459.

Delpit, L. (1995, December). *Other people's children*. Presentation at the National Reading Conference, New Orleans, LA.

Dennis, L. R., Rueter, J. A., & Simpson, C. G. (2013). Authentic assessment: Establishing a clear foundation for instructional practices. *Preventing School Failure, 57*(4), 189–195.

Dewey, J. (1966). *Democracy and education*. New York: First Press.

Dewitz, P., Jones, J., & Leahy, S. (2009). Comprehension strategy instruction in core reading programs. *Reading Research Quarterly, 44*(2), 102–126.

Dickinson, D. K., & Tabors, P. O. (Eds.). (2001). *Beginning literacy with language*. Baltimore: Paul H. Brookes.

Dickinson, D. K., De Temple, J. M., Hirschler, J. A., & Smith, M. W. (1992). Book reading with preschoolers: Co-construction of text at home and at school. *Early Childhood Research Quarterly, 7*, 323–346,

Dickinson, D. K., McCabe, A., & Essex, M. J. (2006). A window of opportunity we must open to all: The case for preschool with high-quality support for language and literacy. *Handbook of Early Literacy Research, 2*, 11–28.

Donahue, P. L., Finnegan, R. J., Lutkus, A. D., Allen, N. L., & Campbell, J. R. (2001). *The nation's report card: Reading 2000*. Washington, DC: U.S. Department of Education, Office of Educational Research and Improvement.

Donahue, P., Doane, M., & Grigg, W. Educational Testing Service. (2000). *Nation's report card.* National Assessment of Educational Progress. http://nces.ed.gov/nationsreportcard/.

Dorerty Stahl, K. A., & Stahl, S. A. (2012). Young word wizards!: Fostering vocabulary development in preschool and primary education. In *Vocabulary instruction: Research to practice* (2nd ed., pp. 72–91). New York, NY: Guilford Press.

Droyd, A. (2011). *Goodnight iPad: A parody for the next generation.* New York: Blue Rider Press.

Duke, N. (2000). 3.6 minutes per day: The scarcity of information texts in first grade. *Reading Research Quarterly, 35,* 202–224.

Duke, N. (2004). The case for informational text. *Educational Leadership, 6,* 40–44.

Duke, N. K. (2016). Project based instruction: A great match for informational text. American Federation of Teachers.

Duke, N. K. (2014). *Inside information: Developing powerful readers and writers of informational text through project based instruction.* New York: Scholastic

Duke, N. K., & Kays, J. (1998). Can I say "Once upon a time?" Kindergarten children developing knowledge of information book language. *Early Childhood Research Quarterly, 13*(2), 295–318.

Duke, N. K., & Pearson, P. D. (2002). Effective practices for developing reading comprehension. In A. E. Farstrup & S. J. Samuels (Eds.), *What research has to say about reading instruction* (3rd ed., pp. 205–242). Newark, DE: International Reading Association.

Dunn, L. M., & Dunn, L. M. (1997). *The Peabody picture vocabulary test: 2 years to 18 years.* Circle Pines, MN: American Guidance Service.

Dunsmore, K., & Fisher, D. (2010). *Bring literacy home.* Newark, DE: International Reading Association.

Durkin, D. (1966). *Children who read early.* New York: Teachers College Press.

Durkin, D. (1978–1979). What classroom observations reveal about reading instruction. *Reading Research Quarterly, 14,* 481–533.

Dyson, A. H. (1985). Individual differences in emerging writing. In M. Farr (Ed.), *Advances in writing research.* Vol. 1: *Children's early writing development.* Norwood, NJ: Ablex.

Dyson, A. H. (1986). Children's early interpretations of writing: Expanding research perspectives. In D. Yoden & S. Templeton (Eds.), *Metalinguistic awareness and beginning literacy.* Exeter, NH: Heinemann.

Dyson, A. H. (1993). *Social worlds of children learning to write in an urban primary school.* New York: Teachers College Press.

Dweck, C.S. (2007) Mindset: The new psychology of success. New York, NY: Ballantine Books.

Educational Research Service. (1997). *Promoting early literacy through family involvement* (ERS Information Folio No. C98-F0226). Arlington, VA: Author.

Edwards, P. (1995). Combining parents' and teachers' thoughts about storybook reading at home and school. In L. M. Morrow (Ed.), *Family literacy connections in schools and communities* (pp. 54–69). Newark, DE: International Reading Association.

Edwards, P. (2010). The role of family literacy programs in the school success or failure of African American families and children. In K. Dunsmore & D. Fisher (Eds.), *Bring literacy home* (pp. 184–202). Newark, DE: International Reading Association.

Edwards, S. A., Maloy, R. W., & Verock-O'Loughlin, R. (2003). *Ways of writing with young kids: Teaching creativity and conventions unconventionally.* Boston: Allyn and Bacon.

Ehri, L., & Roberts, T. (2006). The roots of learning to read and write: Acquisition of letters and phonemic awareness. *Handbook of Early Literacy Research, 2,* 113–131.

Englemann, S., & Bruner, E. (1969). *DISTAR: Direct Instruction System for Teaching Arithmetic and Reading.* Chicago: Science Research Associates.

Enz, B., & Morrow, L. M. (2009). *Assessing preschool literacy development: Informal and formal measures to guide instruction.* Newark, DE: International Reading Association.

Erickson, K. A., & Koppenhaver, D. A. (1995). Developing a literacy program for children with severe disabilities. *Reading Teacher, 48,* 676–684.

Fields, M. V., Groth, L. A., & Spangler, K. L. (2007). *Let's begin reading right: A developmental approach to emergent literacy* (6th ed.). Upper Saddle River, NJ: Pearson.

Fingon, J. (2005). The words that surround us. *Teaching PreK–8, 35,* 54–56.

Fitzpatrick, J. (1997). *Phonemic awareness.* Cypress, CA: Creative Teaching Press.

Fletcher, R., & Portalupi, J. (2001). *Writing workshop: The essential guide.* Portsmouth, NH: Heinemann.

Flewitt, R., Messer, D., & Kucirkova, N. (2015). New directions for early literacy in a digital age: The iPad. *Journal of Early Childhood Literacy, 15*(3), 289–310.

Flippo, R. R., Holland, D. D., McCarthy, M. T., & Swinning, E. A. (2009). Asking the right questions: How to select an informal reading inventory. *The Reading Teacher, 63*(1), 79–83.

Flynn, E. E. (2016). Language-rich early childhood classroom: Simple but powerful beginnings. *Reading Teacher, 70*(2), 159–166.

Foorman, B., Dombek, J., & Smith, K. (2016). *Seven elements important to successful implementation of early literacy intervention.* Hoboken, NJ: Wiley-Blackwell Publishing.

Fountas, I. C., & Pinnell, G. S. (1996). *Guided reading: Good first teaching for all children.* Portsmouth, NH: Heinemann.

Fountas, I. C., & Pinnell, G. S. (2012). Guided Reading: The Romance and the Reality. *The Reading Teacher, 66*(4), 268–284.

Fox, B. J. (2014). *Phonics and word study for the teacher of reading: Programmed for self-instruction* (11th ed.). Boston: Pearson

Freedman, P. (2007). Writing with the wind. *Encounter, 20*(1), 7–9.

Freeman, Y. S., & Freeman, D. E. (2006). *Teaching reading and writing in Spanish and English in bilingual and dual language classrooms* (2nd ed.). Portsmouth, NH: Heinemann.

Frey, N., & Fisher, D. B. (2006). *Language arts workshop: Purposeful reading and writing instruction.* Upper Saddle River, NJ: Pearson.

Froebel, F. (1974). *The education of man.* Clifton, NJ: Augustus M. Kelly.

Fromkin, V., & Rodman, R. (2010). *An introduction to language* (9th ed.). Fort Worth, TX: Harcourt Brace.

Galda, G. (1995). Language change in the history of English: Implications for teachers. In D. Durkin (Ed.), *Language issues: Readings for teachers* (pp. 262–272). White Plains, NY: Longman.

Gambrell, L. B., & Almasi, J. (1994). Fostering comprehension development through discussion. In L. M. Morrow, J. K. Smith, & L. C. Wilkinson (Eds.), *Integrated language arts: Controversy to consensus* (pp. 71–90). Boston: Allyn and Bacon.

Gambrell, L. B., & Gillis, V. R. (2007). Assessing children's motivation for reading and writing. In J. R. Paratore & R. L. McCormack (Eds.), *Classroom literacy assessment: Making sense of what students know and do.* New York: Guilford Press.

Gambrell, L. B., & Koskinen, P. S. (2002). Imagery: A strategy for enhancing comprehension. In C. C. Block & M. Pressley (Eds.), *Comprehension instruction: Research-based best practices* (pp. 305–319). New York: Guilford Press.

Gambrell, L. B., Almasi, J. F., Xie, Q., & Heland, V. (1995). Helping first graders get off to a running start in reading: A home-school-community program that enhances family literacy. In L. Morrow

(Ed.), *Family literacy connections at school and home* (pp. 143–154). Newark, DE: International Reading Association.

Gambrell, L., Morrow, L. M., & Pressley, M. (2007). *Best practices in literacy instruction.* New York: Guilford Press.

Gambrell, L., Palmer, B., Codling, R., & Mazzoni, S. (1996). Assessing motivation to read. *Reading Teacher, 49,* 518–533.

Garcia, E., & McLaughlin, B. (Eds.), with Spodek, B., & Soracho, O. (1995). *Meeting the challenge of linguistic and cultural diversity in early childhood education.* New York: Teachers College Press.

Gardner, H. (Ed.). (2006). *Multiple intelligences: New Horizons in theory and practice.* New York: Basic Books.

Gaskins, I. W. (2003). A multidimensional approach to beginning literacy. In D. M. Barone & L. M. Morrow (Eds.), *Literacy and young children: Research-based practices* (pp. 45–60). New York: Guilford Press.

Gee, J. P. (2007). *What videogames have to teach us about language and literacy.* New York: Palgrave.

Gelzheiser, L., Hallgren-Flynn, L., Connors, M., & Scanlon, D. (2014). Reading thematically related texts to develop knowledge and comprehension. *Reading Teacher, 68*(1).

Genishi, C., & Dyson, A. (1984). *Language assessment in the early years.* Norwood, NJ: Ablex.

George, M, Raphael, T. E., & Florio-Ruane, S. (2003). Connecting children, culture, curriculum, and text. In G. G. Garcia (Ed.), *English learners: Reading the highest level of literacy* (pp. 308–332). Newark, DE: International Reading Association.

Gersten, R., Scott, B., Shanahan, T., Linan-Thompson, Collins, P., & Scarcella, R. (2007). *LES practice guide: Effective literacy and English language instruction for English learners, elementary grades.* Washington, DC: NCEE 2007-401-1. U.S. Department of Education, Institute of Education Sciences, National Center for Education Evaluation and Regional Assistance.

Gesell, A. (1925). *The mental growth of the preschool child.* New York: Macmillan.

Gignoux, P., & Wilde, S. (2005). The power of collaboration. *Teaching Artist Journal, 3*(2), 99–105.

Gollnick, D. M., & Chinn, P. C. (2008). *Multicultural education in a pluralistic society* (8th ed.). Upper Saddle River, NJ: Merrill/Prentice Hall.

Goodman, K. S. (1967). Reading: A psycholinguistic guessing game. *Journal of the Reading Specialist, 4,* 126–135.

Gorman, B., Fiestas, C., Peña, E.D., & Clark, M. (2011). Creative and stylistic devices employed by children during a storybook narrative task: A cross-cultural study. *Speech, Language, Hearing Services in Schools, 42,* 167–181.

Graves, D. (1994). *A fresh look at writing.* Portsmouth, NH: Heinemann.

Graves, D. H. (1983). *Writing: Teachers and children at work.* Exeter, NH: Heinemann.

Graves, D., & Hansen, J. (1983). The author's chair. *Language Arts, 60,* 176–183.

Graves, M. F., Juel, C., & Graves, B. B. (2006). *Teaching reading in the 21st century.* Boston: Allyn and Bacon.

Gregory, A., & Cahill, M. (2010). Kindergartners can do it, too!: Comprehension strategies for early readers. *Reading Teacher, 63*(6), 515–520.

Grieshaber, S., Shield, P., Luke, A., & Macdonald, S. (2012). Family literacy practices and home literacy resources: An Australian pilot study. *Journal of Early Childhood Literacy, 12*(2), 113–138.

Griffin, M. (2001). Social contexts of beginning reading. *Language Arts, 78*(4), 371–378.

Gullo, D. F. (2013). Improving instructional practices, policies, and student outcomes for early childhood language and literacy through data-driven decision making. *Early Childhood Education Journal, 41*(6), 413–421.

Gundlach, R., McLane, J., Scott, F., & McNamee, G. (1985). The social foundations of early writing development. In M. Farr (Ed.), *Advances in writing research. Vol. 1: Children's early writing development.* Norwood, NJ: Ablex.

Gunning, T. G. (2012). *Creating literacy instruction for all children* (8th ed.). Boston, MA: Pearson.

Guthrie, J. T. (2002). Engagement and motivation in reading instruction. In M. L. Kamil, J. B. Manning, & H. J. Walberg (Eds.), *Successful reading instruction* (pp. 137–154). Greenwich, CT: Information Age.

Guthrie, J. T. (2004). *Motivating reading comprehension: Concept-oriented reading instruction.* Mahwah, NJ: Erlbaum.

Guthrie, J. T. (2004). Teaching for literacy engagement. *Journal of Literary Research, 36*(1), 1–28.

Guthrie, J. T. (2011). Best practices for motivating students to read. In L. M. Morrow & L. B. Gambrell (Eds.), *Best practices in literacy instruction* (4th ed.). New York: Guilford Press.

Hadaway, N. L., & Young, T. A. (2006). Changing classrooms: Transforming instruction. In T. A. Young & N. Hadaway (Eds.), *Supporting the literacy development of English language learners: Increasing success in all classrooms* (pp. 6–18). Newark, DE: International Reading Association.

Hall, M. A. (1976). *Teaching reading as a language experience.* Columbus, OH: Merrill.

Halliday, M. A. K. (1975). *Learning how to mean: Exploration in the development of language.* London: Edward Arnold.

Hallinan, M. T., & Sorenson, A. B. (1983). The formation and stability of instructional groups. *American Sociological Review, 48,* 838–851.

Hannon, B. (2012). Understanding the relative contributions of lower-level word processes, higher-level processes, and working memory to reading comprehension performance in proficient adult readers. *Reading Research Quarterly, 47*(2), 125–152.

Hansen, J. (1987). *When writers read.* Portsmouth, NH: Heinemann.

Harp, W. (2000). Assessing reading and writing in the early years. In S. Strickland & L. M. Morrow (Eds.), *Beginning reading and writing, kindergarten to grade 2* (pp. 154–167). New York: Teachers College Press.

Harris, J., Golinkoff, R. M., & Hirsh-Pasek, K. (2011). Lessons from the crib for the classroom: How children really learn vocabulary. In S. B. Neuman & D. K. Dickinson (Eds.) *Handbook of early literacy research,* Vol. 3 (pp. 49–65). NY: Guilford Press.

Hart, B., & Risley, T. (1995). *Meaningful differences in the everyday experiences of young American children.* Baltimore: Paul H. Brookes.

Hart, B., & Risley, T. R. (1999). *The social world of children learning to talk.* Baltimore: Paul H. Brookes.

Hasbrouck, J., & Tindal, G. (2006). Oral reading fluency norms: A valuable assessment tool for reading teachers. *Reading Teacher, 59,* 636–644.

Hastings, K. (2016). Leveled reading and engagement with complex texts. *Reading Improvement, 53*(2), 65–71.

Heath, S. B. (1982). What no bedtime story means. *Language in Society, 11,* 49–76.

Heath, S. B. (1983). *Ways with words: Language, life, and work in communities and classrooms.* Cambridge, England: Cambridge University Press.

Hedgcock, J. S., & Ferris, D. R. (2009). *Teaching readers of English: Students, texts, and contexts.* New York: Routledge.

Herrell, A. & Jordan, M. L. (2011). *50 strategies for teaching english language learners* (4th Ed.). New York, Pearson.

Herrera, S., Perez, D. & Escamilla, K. (2010). *Teaching reading to english language learners*. New York: Pearson.

Hiebert, E. H., & Raphael, T. E. (1998). *Early literacy instruction*. Fort Worth, TX: Harcourt Brace.

Hiebert, E. H., & Taylor, B. (1994). *Getting reading right from the start*. Newark, DE: International Reading Association.

Hill, S. (1997). *Reading manipulatives*. Cypress, CA: Creative Teaching Press.

Hindin, A., Steiner, L. M., & Dougherty, S. (2017). Building our capacity to forge successful home-school partnerships: Programs that support and honor the contributions of families. *Childhood Education, 93*(1), 10–19.

Hoff, E. (2012). *Language development*. Stamford, CT: Cengage Learning.

Holdaway, D. (1979). *The foundations of literacy*. Sydney: Ashton Scholastic.

Hoover, J. J., & Patton, J. R. (2005, March). Differentiating curriculum and instruction for English-language learners with special needs. *Intervention in School and Clinic, 40*(4), 231–235.

Hoover-Dempsey, K. V., & Whitaker, M. C. (2010). The Parental Involvement Process: Inclinations for literacy development. In K. Dunsmore & D. Fisher (Eds.), *Bring literacy home* (pp. 53–82). Newark, DE: International Reading Association.

Horn, M., & Giacobbe, E. (2007). *Talking, drawing, writing: Lessons for our youngest writers*. Portland, ME: Stenhouse.

Howard, S. J., Woodcock, S., Ehrich, J., & Bokosmaty, S. (2017). What are standardized literacy and numeracy tests testing? Evidence of the domain general contributions to students' standardized educational test performance. *British Journal of Educational Psychology, 87*(1), 108–122.

Hresko, W., Reid, D. K., & Hammill, D. (1999). *Test of language development: Primary, 4 through 8 years*. Austin, TX: Pro-Ed.

Huck, C. S. (1992). Books for emergent readers. In B. E. Cullinan (Ed.), *Invitation to read: More children's literature in the reading program*. Newark, DE: International Reading Association.

Hullinger-Sirken, H., & Staley, L. (2016). Understanding writing development: Catie's continuum. *YC Young Children, 71*(5), 74–78.

Hunt, K. W. (1970). *Syntactic maturity in children and adults*. Monograph of the Society for Research in Child Development (vol. 25). Chicago: University of Chicago Press.

Im, H. (2017). Kindergarten standardized testing and reading achievement in the U.S.: Evidence from the early childhood longitudinal study. *Studies in Educational Evaluation, 55*, 9–18.

International Reading Association & National Association for the Education of Young Children. (1998). *Learning to read and write: Developmentally appropriate practices for young children*. Newark, DE: Author.

International Reading Association & National Council of Teachers of English. (1996). *Standards for the English language arts*. Newark, DE: Author.

International Reading Association. (1998). *Phonemic awareness and the teaching of reading: A position statement of the board of directors of the International Reading Association*. Newark, DE: Author.

International Reading Association. (1999). *Position statement: Using multiple methods of beginning reading instruction*. Newark, DE: Author.

International Reading Association. (2001). Association issues position statement on second-language literacy instruction. *Reading Today*. Retrieved on May 14, 2003, from www.findarticles.com.

International Reading Association. (2006). *Reading in preschool*. Newark, DE: Author.

Invernizzi, M. (2003). Concepts, sounds, and the ABCs: A diet for a very young reader. In D. M. Barone & L. M. Morrow (Eds.), *Literacy and young children: Research-based practices* (pp. 140–157). New York: Guilford Press.

Irving, A. (1980). *Promoting voluntary reading for children and young people*. Paris: UNESCO.

Ivey, G. (2002). Building comprehension when they're still learning to read the words. In C. C. Block & M. Pressley (Eds.), *Comprehension instruction: Research-based best practices* (pp. 234–247). New York: Guilford Press.

Jalongo, M. R. (2007). *Early childhood language arts* (4th ed.). Boston: Allyn and Bacon.

Jewell, M., & Zintz, M. (1986). *Learning to read naturally*. Dubuque, IA: Kendall/Hunt.

Johns, J. (2012). *Basic reading inventory; Pre-primer through grade twelve and early literacy assessment*. Dubuque, IA: Kendal Hunt Publishing Company.

Johns, J., & Berglund, R. L. (2002). *Fluency: Evidence-based strategies*. Dubuque, IA: Kendall/ Hunt.

Johns, J., Lenski, S. D., & Elish-Piper, L. (1999). *Early literacy assessments and teaching strategies*. Dubuque, IA: Kendall/Hunt.

Johnson, D., & Pearson, P. D. (1984). *Teaching reading vocabulary* (2nd ed.). New York: Holt.

Johnston, P., & Costello, P. (2005). Principles of literacy assessment. *Reading Research Quarterly, 40*(2), 256–267.

Juel, C. (1989). The role of decoding in early literacy instruction and assessment. In L. Morrow & J. Smith (Eds.), *Assessment for instruction in early literacy* (pp. 135–154). Upper Saddle River, NJ: Prentice Hall.

Juel, C. (1994). Teaching phonics in the context of the integrated language arts. In L. Morrow, J. K. Smith, & L. C. Wilkinson (Eds.), *Integrated language arts: Controversy for consensus* (pp. 133–154). Boston: Allyn and Bacon.

Justice, L. M., Pence, K., Bowles, R. B., & Wiggins, A. (2006). An investigation of four hypotheses concerning the order by which 4-year-old children learn the alphabet letters. *Early Childhood Research Quarterly, 21*(3), 374–389.

Karmiloff, M., & Karmiloff-Smith, A. (2001). *Pathways to language: From fetus to adolescent*. Cambridge, MA: Harvard University Press.

Katz, L. G., & Chard, S. C. (2000). *Engaging children's minds: The project approach* (2nd ed.). Norwood, NJ: Ablex.

Kelly, D. (2004). *1001 best web sites for kids*. New York: Teacher Created Materials.

Kersten, S. (2017). Becoming nonfiction authors: Engaging in science inquiry. *The Reading Teacher, 71*(1), 33–41.

Kesler, T., Gibson, L. J., & Turansky, C. (2016). Bringing the book to life: Responding to historical fiction using digital storytelling. *Journal of Literacy Research, 48*(1), 39–79.

Kindzierski, C. M. (2009). I like it the way it is: Peer-revision writing strategies for students with emotional and behavioral disorders. *Preventing School Failure, 54*(1), 51–59.

King, R., & McMaster, J. (2000). *Pathways: A primer for family literacy program and development*. Louisville, KY: National Center for Family Literacy.

Kinzer, C. K., & McKenna, M. C. (1999, May). *Using technology in your classroom literacy program: Current and future possibilities*. Paper presented at the Annual Convention of the International Reading Association, San Diego, CA.

Kissel, B. (2008). Promoting writing and preventing writing failure in young children. *Preventing School Failure, 52*(4), 53–56.

Knobel, M., & Lankshear, C. (2006). Weblogs worlds and constructions of effective and powerful writing: Cross with care, and only where signs permit. In K. Pahl & J. Rowsell (Eds.), *Travel notes from new literacy studies: Instances of practice* (pp. 72–95). Clevedon, UK: Multilingual Matters.

Knobel, M., & Lankshear, C. (2007). *The new literacies sampler*. New York: Peter Lang.

Krashen, S. (2003). *Explorations in language acquisition and use*. Portsmouth, NH: Heinemann.

Kress, G. (1997). *Before writing*. London: Routledge.

Kucirkova, N., Messer, D., & Whitelock, D. (2012). Parents reading with their toddlers: the role of personalisation in book engagement. *Journal of Early Childhood Literacy*.

Kuhl, P. (1994). Learning and representation in speech and language. *Current Opinion in Neurobiology, 4*, 812–822.

Kuhn, M. (2007). Effective oral reading assessment (or why round robin reading doesn't cut it). In J. R. Paratore & R. L. McCormack (Eds.), *Classroom literacy assessment: Making sense of what students know and do* (pp. 101–112). New York: Guilford Press.

Kuhn, M. R., & Stahl, S. A. (2003). Fluency: A review of developmental and remedial strategies. *Journal of Educational Psychology, 95*, 3–21.

Kuhn, M., Schwanenflugel, P., Morris, R., Morrow, L. M., Woo, D., Meisinger, E., et al. (2006). Teaching children to become fluent and automatic readers. *Journal of Literacy Research, 38*(4), 357–387.

Kuhn, M.R., Schwanenflugel, P. J. & Meisinger, E. B. (2010). Aligning theory and assessment of reading fluency: Automaticity, prosody, and definitions of fluency. *Reading Research Quarterly, 45*, 230–251.

Labbo, L. D., & Ash, G. E. (1998). What is the role of computer related technology in early literacy? In S. B. Neuman & K. A. Roskos (Eds.), *Children achieving: Best practices in early literacy* (pp. 180–197). Newark, DE: International Reading Association.

Lassonde, C. (2006). You oughta have my life! The story of Jaime, a resistant writer. *Support for Learning, 21*(3), 135–140.

Lennenberg, E. (1967). *Biological foundations of language*. New York: Wiley.

Lepper, M. R., Corpus, J. H., & Iyengar, S. S. (2005). Intrinsic and extrinsic motivational orientations in the classroom: Age differences and academic correlates. *Journal of Educational Psychology, 97*(2), 184–196.

Leseman, P. P. M., & de Jong, P. F. (1998). Home literacy: Opportunity, instruction, cooperation and social-emotional quality predicting early reading achievement. *Reading Research Quarterly, 33*, 294–318.

Leslie, L. & Caldwell, J. S. (2010). *Qualitative reading inventory-5*. Boston, MA: Allyn & Bacon.

Leu, D. J., & Kinzer, C. K. (2003). *Effective literacy instruction, K-8*. Upper Saddle River, NJ: Merrill/Prentice Hall.

Leu, D. J., Jr., Kinzer, C. K., Coiro, J., & Cammack, D. (2004). Toward a theory of new literacies emerging from the Internet and other information and communication technologies. In R. Ruddell & N. Unrau (Eds.), *Theoretical models and processes of reading* (5th ed., pp. 1568–1611). Newark, DE: International Reading Association.

Levin, I., Snatil-Carmon, S., & Asif Rave, O. (2006). Learning of letter names and sounds and their contribution to word recognition. *Journal of Experimental Child Psychology, 93*(2), 139–165.

Lindfors, J. (1989). The classroom: A good environment for language learning. In P. Rigg & V. Allen (Eds.), *When they don't all speak English: Integrating the ESL student into the regular classroom* (pp. 39–54). Urbana, IL: National Council of Teachers of English.

Li-Yuan, W. (2009). Children's graphical representations and emergent writing: Evidence from children's drawings. *Early Child Development & Care, 179*(1), 67–79.

Lonigan, C. (2006). Conceptualizing phonological processing skills in prereaders. *Handbook of Early Literacy Research, 2*, 77–89.

Lonigan, C., & Whitehurst, G. (1998). Relative efficacy of parent and teacher involvement in a shared-reading intervention for preschool children from low-income backgrounds. *Early Childhood Research Quarterly, 23*(2), 263–290.

Lou, Y., Abrami, P. C., Spence, J. C., Poulsen, C., Chambers, B., & d'Apollonia, S. (1996). Within-class grouping. A meta-analysis. *Review of Educational Research, 66*(4), 423–458.

Manning, M., Manning, G., & Long, R. (1994). *Theme immersion: Inquiry-based curriculum in elementary and middle schools*. Portsmouth, NH: Heinemann.

Marinak, B. A., Gambrell, L. B., & Mazzoni, S. A. (2012). *Maximizing motivation for literacy learning: Grades K–6*. New York: Guilford Press.

Marinak, B. A., Gambrell, L. B., & Mazzoni, S.A. (2013). *Maximizing motivation for literacy learning grades K–6*. New York: Guilford Press.

Mariotti, A. & Homan, S. (2009). *Linking reading assessment to instruction: An application worktext for elementary classroom teachers* (5th ed.). New York: Routledge.

Marriott, D. (1997). *What are the other kids doing?* Cypress, CA: Creative Teaching Press.

Marsh, J., Hannon, P., Lewis, M., & Ritchie, L. (2017). Young children's initiation into family literacy practices in the digital age. *Journal of Early Childhood Research, 15*(1), 47–60.

Martinez, M., & Teale, W. (1987). The ins and outs of a kindergarten writing program. *Reading Teacher, 40*, 444–451.

Martinez, M., & Teale, W. (1988). Reading in a kindergarten classroom library. *Reading Teacher, 41*(6), 568–572.

McAfee, O., & Leong, D. (1997). *Assessing and guiding young children's development and learning*. Boston: Allyn and Bacon.

McCarrier, A., Pinnell, G. S., & Fountas, I. C. (2000). *Interactive writing: How language & literacy come together, K–2*. Portsmouth, NH: Heinemann.

McCormick, C., & Mason, J. (1981). What happens to kindergarten children's knowledge about reading after summer vacation? *Reading Teacher, 35*, 164–172.

McElveen, S. A., & Dierking, C. C. (2001). Children's books as models to teach writing. *The Reading Teacher, 54*(4), 362–364.

McGee, L. (2007). Language and literacy assessment in preschool. In J. Paratore & R. McCormack (Eds.), *Classroom literacy assessment: Making sense of what students know and do* (pp. 65–84). New York: Guilford Press.

McGee, L. M., & Morrow, L. M. (2005). *Teaching literacy in kindergarten*. New York: Guilford Press.

McGee, L. M., & Richgels, D. J. (2008). *Literacy's beginnings: Supporting young readers and writers* (5th ed.). Boston: Allyn and Bacon.

McGeown, S., & Medford, E. (2014). Using Method of Instruction to Predict the Skills Supporting Initial Reading Development: Insight from a Synthetic Phonics Approach. *Reading and Writing, 27*(3), 591–608.

McKenna, M. C. (2001). Development of reading attitudes. In L. Verhoeven & C. Snow (Eds.), *Literacy and motivation: Reading engagement in individuals and groups* (pp. 135–158). Mahwah, NJ: Erlbaum.

McKenna, M. C., & Dougherty-Stahl, K. A. (2009). *Assessment for reading instruction*. New York: Guilford Press.

McKenna, M., Labbo, L., Conradi, K., & Baxter, J. (2010). Effective use of technology in literacy instruction. In L. Morrow & L. B. Gambrell (Eds.), *Best practices in literacy instruction* (4th ed.). New York: Guilford Press.

McLaughlin, M. (2010). *Guided comprehension in the primary grades* (2nd ed.). Newark, DE: International Reading Association.

McNaughton, S. (2006). Considering culture in research-based interventions to support early literacy. *Handbook of Early Literacy Research, 2*, 113–131.

McNeil, D. (1970). *The acquisition of language: The study of developmental psycholinguistics.* New York: Harper & Row.

Meier, D. R. (2004). *The young child's memory for words: Developing first and second language and literacy.* New York: Teachers College Press.

Melekoglu, M. A. & Wilkerson, K. L. (2013). Motivation to read: How does it change for struggling readers with and without disabilities? *International Journal of Instruction, 6*(1), 77–88.

Meller, W. B., Richardson, D., & Hatch, J. A. (2009). Using reading-alouds with critical literacy literature in K-3 classrooms. *Young Children, 11*, 76–78.

Melzi, G., Paratore, J. R., & Krol-Sinclair, B. (2000). Reading and writing in the daily lives of Latino mothers participating in an intergenerational literacy project. *National Reading Conference Yearbook, 49*, 178–193.

Mendelsohn, A. L. (2002). Promoting language and literacy through reading aloud: The role of the pediatrician. *Current Problems in Pediatric and Adolescent Health Care, 32*(6), 183–210.

Mendelsohn, A. L., Huberman, H. S. Berkule, S. B., Brockmeyer, C. A., Morrow, L. M., Dreyer, B. P. (2011). Primary care strategies for promoting parent-child interactions and school readiness in at-risk families: The Bellevue project for early language, literacy, and education success. *Archives of Pediatrics & Adolescent Medicine (165)*, 33–41.

Mendelsohn, A. L., Mogilner, L. N., Dreyer, B. P., Forman, J. A., Weinstein, S. C., Broderick, M., Cheng, K. J., Magloire, T., Moore, T., & Napier, C. (2001). The impact of a clinic-based literacy intervention on language development in inner-city preschool children. *Pediatrics, 107*(1), 130–134.

Mendelsohn, A. L., Valdez, P. T., Flynn, V., Foley, G. M., Berkule, S. B., Tomopoulos, S., Fierman, A. H., Tineo, W., & Dreyer, B. P. (2007). Use of videotaped interactions during pediatric well-child care: Impact at 33 months on parenting and on child development. *Journal of Developmental & Behavioral Pediatrics, 28*(3), 206–212.

Mesmer, E. M., & Mesmer, H. A. E. (2008). Response to Intervention (RTI): What teachers of reading need to know. *The Reading Teacher, 62*(4), 280–290.

Miller, L. C. (2010). *Make me a story: Teaching writing through digital storytelling.* Portland, ME: Stenhouse.

Miramontes, O. B., Nadeau, A., & Commins, N, L. (1997). *Restructuring schools for linguistic diversity: Linking decision making to effective programs.* New York: Teachers College Press.

Moats, L. C. (2005–2006). How spelling supports reading: And why it is more regular and predictable than you may think. *American Educator*, 12–22, 42–43.

Montessori, M. (1965). *Spontaneous activity in education.* New York: Schocken Books.

Moore, G. (1986). Effects of the spatial definition of behavior settings on children's behavior: A quasi-experimental field study. *Journal of Environmental Psychology, 6*(3), 205–231.

Morgan, B., & Smith, R. D. (2008). A wiki for classroom writing. *Reading Teacher, 62*(1), 80–82.

Morphett, M. V., & Washburne, C. (1931). When should children begin to read? *Elementary School Journal, 31*, 496–508.

Morris, D., & Slavin, R. (Eds.). (2003). *Every child reading.* Boston: Allyn and Bacon.

Morrison, G. S. (2008). *Fundamentals of early childhood education* (5th ed.). Upper Saddle River, NJ: Prentice Hall.

Morrison, T. G. & Wilcox B. (2013.) *Developing literacy: Reading and writing to, with and by children.* Boston: Pearson.

Morrison, V., & Wlodarczuk, L. (2009). Revisiting read-aloud: Instructional strategies that encourage students' engagement with texts. *The Reading Teacher, 63*(2), 110–188.

Morrow, L. M. & Enz, B. J. (2009). *Assessing preschool literacy development: Informal and formal measures to guide instruction.* Newark, DE: International Reading Association.

Morrow, L. M. (1978). Analysis of syntax in the language of six-, seven-, and eight-year-olds. *Research in the Teaching of English, 12*, 143–148.

Morrow, L. M. (1982). Relationships between literature programs, library corner designs, and children's use of literature. *Journal of Educational Research, 75*, 339–344.

Morrow, L. M. (1983). Home and school correlates of early interest in literature. *Journal of Educational Research, 76*, 221–230.

Morrow, L. M. (1984). Reading stories to young children: Effects of story structure and traditional questioning strategies on comprehension. *Journal of Reading Behavior, 16*, 273–288.

Morrow, L. M. (1985). Retelling stories: A strategy for improving children's comprehension, concept of story structure, and oral language complexity. *Elementary School Journal, 85*, 647–661.

Morrow, L. M. (1986). *Promoting responses to literature: Children's sense of story structure.* Paper presented at the National Reading Conference, Austin, TX.

Morrow, L. M. (1987). Promoting voluntary reading: The effects of an inner city program in summer day care centers. *Reading Teacher, 41*, 266–274.

Morrow, L. M. (1988). Young children's responses to one-to-one story readings in school settings. *Reading Research Quarterly, 23*(1), 89–107.

Morrow, L. M. (1990). Preparing the classroom environment to promote literacy during play. *Early Childhood Research Quarterly, 5*, 537–554.

Morrow, L. M. (1992). The impact of a literature-based program on literacy achievement, use of literature, and attitudes of children from minority backgrounds. *Reading Research Quarterly, 27*, 250–275.

Morrow, L. M. (1995). *Family literacy connections at school and home.* Newark, DE: International Reading Association.

Morrow, L. M. (1996). Story retelling: A discussion strategy to develop and assess comprehension. In L. B. Gambrell & J. F. Almasi (Eds.), *Lively discussions: Fostering engaged reading* (pp. 265–285). Newark, DE: International Reading Association.

Morrow, L. M. (2002). *The literacy center: Contexts for reading and writing* (2nd ed.). York, ME: Stenhouse.

Morrow, L. M. (2003). *Organizing and managing the language arts block.* New York: Guilford Press.

Morrow, L. M. (2004). *Children's literature in preschool: Comprehending and enjoying books.* Newark, DE: International Reading Association.

Morrow, L. M. (2005). Language and literacy in preschools: Current issues and concerns. *Literacy Teaching and Learning, 9*(1), 7–19.

Morrow, L. M. (2007). *Developing literacy in preschool.* New York: Guilford Press.

Morrow, L. M. (2012). *Interactive behavior between parents and children during storybook reading and dramatic play.* Literacy Research Association, San Diego, CA.

Morrow, L. M. (2012). *Teaching the alphabet.* Huntington Beach, CA: Shell Educational Publishing.

Morrow, L. M., & Asbury, E. (2003). Best practices for a balanced early literacy program. In L. M. Morrow, L. Gambrell, & M. Pressley (Eds.), *Best practices in literacy instruction* (2nd ed., pp. 49–67). New York: Guilford Press.

Morrow, L. M., & O'Connor, E. (1995). Literacy partnerships for change with "at risk" kindergartners. In R. Allington & S. Walmsley

(Eds.), *No quick fix: Rethinking literacy programs in America's elementary schools* (pp. 97–115). New York: Teachers College Press.

Morrow, L. M., & Smith, J. K. (1990). The effect of group setting on interactive storybook reading. *Reading Research Quarterly, 25,* 213–231.

Morrow, L. M., & Tracey, D. (1997). Strategies for phonics instruction in early childhood classrooms. *Reading Teacher, 50*(8), 2–9.

Morrow, L. M., & Tracey, D. H. (1997). Instructional environments for language and learning. Considerations for young children. In J. Flood, S. B. Heath, & D. Lapp (Eds.), *Handbook for literacy educators: Research on teaching the communicative and visual arts,* 475–485. New York: Macmillan.

Morrow, L. M., & Weinstein, C. S. (1986). Encouraging voluntary reading: The impact of a literature program on children's use of library centers. *Reading Research Quarterly, 21,* 330–346.

Morrow, L. M., & Young, J. (1997). A family literacy program connecting school and home: Effects on attitude, motivation, and literacy achievement. *Journal of Educational Psychology, 89,* 736–742.

Morrow, L. M., Applegate, M. D., Applegate, A. J., & Molda, V. B. (2009). Promoting literacy during play by designing early childhood classroom environments. *Reading Teacher, 44,* 396–405.

Morrow, L. M., Berkule, S. M., Mendelsohn, A., Healey, K. M., & Cates, C. B. (2013). Learning through play. In R. Reutzel (Ed.). *The Handbook of Research-Based Practice in Early Childhood Education.* New York, NY: Guilford Press.

Morrow, L. M., Gambrell, L. B., & Freitag, E. (2009). *Using children's literature in preschool to develop comprehension: Understanding and enjoying books.* Newark, DE: International Reading Association.

Morrow, L. M., Kuhn, M. R., & Schwanenflugel, P. J. (2006). The family fluency program. *Reading Teacher, 60*(4), 322–333.

Morrow, L. M., Mendelsohn, A. L., Berkule, S. B., Healey, K. (2012). Modeling interactive story book reading and play with high-needs mothers and their preschoolers to enhance language and literacy: A video interactive program (VIP). San Diego, CA: Literacy Research Association national conference.

Morrow, L. M., Mendelsohn, A., & Kuhn, M. (2010). Characteristics of three family literacy programs that work. In K. Dunsmore & D. Fisher (Eds.), *Bring literacy home* (pp. 83–103). Newark, DE: International Reading Association.

Morrow, L. M., O'Connor, E. M., & Smith, J. (1990). Effects of a story reading program on the literacy development of at-risk kindergarten children. *Journal of Reading Behavior, 20*(2), 104–141.

Morrow, L. M., Paratore, J. R., & Tracey, D. H. (1994). *Family literacy: New perspectives, new opportunities.* Newark, DE: International Reading Association.

Morrow, L. M., Pressley, M., Smith, J., & Smith, M. (1997). The effects of integrating literature-based instruction into literacy and science programs. *Reading Research Quarterly, 32,* 54–77.

Morrow, L. M., Reutzel, D. R., & Casey, H. (2006). Organization and management of language arts teaching: Classroom environments, groping practices, and exemplary instruction. In C. Evertson (Ed.), *Handbook of classroom management* (pp. 559–582). Mahwah, NJ: Erlbaum.

Morrow, L. M., Scoblionko, J., & Shafer, D. (1995). The family reading and writing appreciation program. In L. M. Morrow (Ed.), *Family literacy connections in schools and communities* (pp. 70–86). Newark, DE: International Reading Association.

Morrow, L. M., Sharkey, E., & Firestone, W. (1994). Collaborative strategies in the integrated language arts. In L. M. Morrow, J. K. Smith, & L. C. Wilkinson (Eds.), *Integrated language arts: Controversy to consensus* (pp. 155–176). Boston: Allyn and Bacon.

Morrow, L. M., Strickland, D. S., & Woo, D. G. (1998). *Literacy instruction in half- and whole-day kindergarten: Research to practice.* Newark, DE: International Reading Association.

Moss, B., Leone, S. & Dipillo, M. L. (1997). Exploring the literature of fact: Linking reading and writing through information trade books. *Language Arts, 74*(6), 418–429.

Moustafa, M. (1997). *Beyond traditional phonics: Research discoveries and reading instruction.* Portsmouth, NH: Heinemann.

Muhonen, H., Rasku-Puttonen, H., Pakarinen, E., Poikkeus, A., & Lerkkanen, M. (2016). Scaffolding through dialogic teaching in early school classrooms. *Teaching And Teacher Education, 55,* 143–154.

Nagy, W. (1988). *Teaching vocabulary to improve reading comprehension.* Newark, DE: International Reading Association.

National Center for Family Literacy. (1993). Parents and children together. In *Creating an upward spiral of success* (pp. 6–8). Louisville, KY: Author.

National Center for Family Literacy. (2004). *Report of the National Early Literacy Panel.* Washington DC: National Institute for Literacy.

National Center on Education and the Economy and the Learning Research and Development Center at the University of Pittsburgh. (1999). *Reading and writing grade by grade: Primary literacy standards for kindergarten through third grade.* Washington, DC: National Center on Education and the Economy.

National Early Literacy Panel. (2008). *Developing early literacy: Report of the national early literacy panel.* Washington, DC: National Institute for Literacy.

National Reading Panel Report. (2000). *Teaching children to read.* Washington, DC: National Institute of Child Health and Human Development.

Neuman, S. B., & Celano, D. (2006). The knowledge gap: Implications of leveling the playing field for low-income and middle-income children. *Reading Research Quarterly, 41*(2), 176–201.

Neuman, S., & Roskos, K. (1992). Literary objects as cultural tools: Effects on children's literacy behaviors in play. *Reading Research Quarterly, 27*(3), 203–225.

Neuman, S., & Roskos, K. (1994). Building home and school with a culturally responsive approach. *Childhood Education, 70,* 210–214.

Neuman, S., & Roskos, K. (1997). Knowledge in practice: Contexts of participation for young writers and readers. *Reading Research Quarterly, 32,* 10–32.

Neuman, S., & Roskos, K. (Eds.). (1998). *Children achieving: Best practices in early literacy.* Newark, DE: International Reading Association.

Neumann, M., Hood, M., & Ford, R. (2013). Using environmental print to enhance emergent literacy and print motivation. *Reading And Writing, 26*(5), 771–793.

New Jersey State Department of Education. (1998). *Test specification booklet.* Trenton, NJ: Author.

New Jersey State Department of Education. (2004). *N.J. standards for the English language.* Trenton, NJ: Author.

Newberger, J. J. (1997). New brain development research: A wonderful window of opportunity to build public support for early childhood education. *Young Children, 52*(4), 4–9.

Newman, J. (1984). *The craft of children's writing.* Exeter, NH: Heinemann.

Ninio, A. (1980). Picture book reading in mother–infant dyads belonging to two subgroups in Israel. *Child Development, 51,* 587.

O'Connor, R. E., Harty, K. R., & Fulmer, D. (2005 November/December). Tiers of intervention in kindergarten through third grade. *Journal of Learning Disabilities, 38*(6), 532–538.

O'Flahavan, J., Gambrell, L. B., Guthrie, J., Stahl, S., & Alverman, D. (1992, April). Poll results guide activities of research center. *Reading Today*, 12.

Ogle, D. (1986). K-W-L: A teaching model that develops active reading of expository text. *Reading Teacher, 39*, 564–570.

O'Kelley Wingate, K., Rutledge, V. C., & Johnston, L. (2014). Choosing the right word walls for your classroom. *YC: Young Children, 69*(1), 52.

Orellana, M. E., & Hernandez, A. (1999). Talking with the walk: Children reading urban environmental print. *Reading Teacher, 51*, 612–619.

Ortiz, C., Stowe, R. M., & Arnold, D. H. (2001). Parental influence on child interest in shared picture book reading. *Early Childhood Research Quarterly, 16*(2), 263–281.

Otto, B. (2006). *Language development in early childhood* (2nd ed.). Upper Saddle River, NJ: Merrill/-Prentice Hall.

Overturf, B., Montgomery, L., & Smith, M. (2013). Word nerds: Teaching all students to learn and love vocabulary.

Pappas, C., Kiefer, B., & Levstik, L. (1995). *An integrated language perspective in the elementary school: Theory into action.* New York: Longman.

Paratore, J. R., Homza, A., Krol-Sinclair, B., Lewis-Barrow, T., Melzi, G., Stergis, R., et al. (1995). Shifting boundaries in home and school responsibilities: Involving immigrant parents in the construction of literacy portfolios. *Research in the Teaching of English, 29*, 367–389.

Paratore, J. R., Melzi, G., & Krol-Sinclair, B. (2003). Learning about the literate lives of Latino families. In D. M. Barone & L. M. Morrow (Eds.), *Literacy and young children: Research-based practices* (pp. 101–120). New York: Guilford Press.

Paris, A. H., & Paris, S. G. (2007). Teaching narrative comprehension strategies to first graders. *Cognition and Instruction, 25*(1), 1–44.

Park, J. Y. (2012). A different kind of reading instruction: Using visualizing to bridge reading comprehension and critical literacy. *Journal of Adolescent & Adult Literacy, 55*(7), 629–640.

Parker, E. L., & Pardini, T. H. (2006). *The words came down: English language learners read, write, and talk across the curriculum, K-2.* Portland, ME: Stenhouse.

Pearson, P. D., Roehler, L. R., Dole, J. A., & Duffy, G. G. (1992). Developing expertise in reading comprehension. In S. J. Samuels & A. E. Farstrup (Eds.), *What research has to say about reading instruction* (2nd ed., pp. 145–199). Newark, DE: International Reading Association.

Pelatti, C. Y., Schmitt, M. B., & Justice, L. M. (2013). Talk it out: Building oral language. In R. Reutzel (Ed.) *Handbook of Research-Based Practice in Early Education.* New York: Guilford Press.

Pellegrini, A., & Galda, L. (1982). The effects of thematic fantasy play training on the development of children's story comprehension. *American Educational Research Journal, 19*, 443–452.

Pflaum, S. (1986). *The development of language and literacy in young children* (3rd ed.). Columbus, OH: Merrill.

Piaget, J., & Inhelder, B. (1969). *The psychology of the child.* New York: Basic Books.

Pilonieta, P., & Medina, A. (2009). Reciprocal teaching for the primary grades: We can do it, too! *Reading Teacher, 63*(2), 120–129.

Pinker, S. (2007). *The language instinct: How the mind creates language.* New York: Harper Perennial Modern Classics.

Pinnell, G. S., Freid, M. D., & Estice, R. M. (1990). Reading recovery: Learning how to make a difference. *Reading Teacher, 43*(4), 282–295.

Pittelman, S. D., Heimlich, J. E., Berglund, R. L., & French, M. P. (1991). *Semantic feature analysis: Classroom applications.* Newark, DE: International Reading Association.

Pole, K. (2015). Why downt you riyt back to me? *Reading Teacher, 69*(1), 119–128.

Polikoff, M. S., Porter, A. C., & Smithson, J. (August 2011). How well aligned are state assessments of student achievement with state content standards? *American Educational Research Journal, 48*(4), 965–995.

Porath, S. (2014). Talk less, listen more. *Reading Teacher, 67*(8), 627–635.

Pratt, S. M., & Urbanowski, M. (2016). Teaching early readers to self-monitor and self-correct. *Reading Teacher, 69*(5), 559–567.

Prensky, M. (2001). Digital natives, digital immigrants. *On the Horizon, 9*(5), 1–6.

Prescott, O. (1965). *A father reads to his child: An anthology of prose and poetry.* New York: Dutton.

Pressley, M. (1998). *Reading instruction that works: The case for balanced teaching.* New York: Guilford Press.

Pressley, M., & Hilden, K. (2002). How can children be taught to comprehend text better? In M. L. Kamil, J. B. Manning, & H. J. Walberg (Eds.), *Successful reading instruction* (pp. 33–53). Greenwich, CT: Information Age.

Pressley, M., Allington, R. L., Wharton-McDonald, R., Block, C. C., & Morrow, L. (2001). *Learning to read: Lessons from exemplary first-grade classrooms.* New York: Guilford Press.

Purcell-Gates, V., Duke, N. K., & Martineau, J. A. (2007). Learning to read and write genre-specific text: Roles of authentic experience and explicit teaching. *Reading Research Quarterly, 42*(1), 8–45.

Rand Reading Study Group. (2002). *Reading for understanding: Toward a research and development program in reading comprehension.* Washington, DC: Author/OERI/Department of Education.

Rand, M. (1993). Using thematic instruction to organize an integrated language arts classroom. In L. M. Morrow, J. K. Smith, & L. C. Wilkinson (Eds.), *Integrated language arts: Controversy to consensus* (pp. 177–192). Boston: Allyn and Bacon.

Rasinski, T. (1990). Effects of repeated reading and listening while reading on reading fluency. *Journal of Educational Research, 83*, 147–150.

Read, S. (2005). First and second graders writing information text. *The Reading Teacher, 59*(1), 36–44.

Reese, L. (2012). Storytelling in Mexican homes: Connections between oral and literacy practices. *Bilingual Research Journal, 35*(3), 277–293.

Report of the National Early Reading Panel. (2004). Washington, DC: National Institute for Literacy.

Reutzel, D. R., & Cooter, R. B. (2009). *Teaching children to read: Putting the pieces together* (4th ed.). Upper Saddle River, NJ: Pearson/Merrill/Prentice Hall.

Risko, V. J., & Walker-Dalhouse, D. (2010). Making the most of assessments to inform instruction. *The Reading Teacher, 63*(5) 420–422.

Risko, V. J., & Walker-Dalhouse, D. (2011). Drawing on text features for reading comprehension and composing. *The Reading Teacher, 64*(5), 376–378.

Ritchie, S., James-Szanton, J., & Howes, C. (2003). Emergent literacy practices in early childhood classrooms. In C. Howes (Ed.), *Teaching 4- to 8-year-olds* (pp. 71–92). Baltimore: Paul H. Brookes.

Robertson, C., & Salter, W. (2007). *Phonological awareness test E.* Moline, IL: LinguiSystems, Inc.

Rodríguez-Brown, F. V. (2009). *The home-school connection: Lessons learned in a culturally and linguistically diverse community.* Taylor & Francis.

Rodriguez-Brown, F. V. (2010). Latino culture and schooling: Reflections on family literacy with a culturally and linguistically different community. In K. Dunsmore & D. Fisher (Eds.), *Bring literacy home* (pp. 203–226). Newark, DE: International Reading Association.

Rog, L. J. (2007). *Marvelous minilessons for teaching beginning writing, K–3*. Newark, DE: International Reading Association.

Rosenblatt, L. M. (1988). *Writing and reading: Transactional theory* (Report No. 13). University of California, Berkeley, CA: Center for the Study of Writing.

Rosencrans, G. (1998). *The spelling book: Teaching children how to spell, not what to spell*. Newark, DE: International Reading Association.

Roser, N. (2010). Talking over books at home and in school. In K. Dunsmore & D Fisher (Eds.), *Bringing literacy home* (pp. 104–135). Newark, DE: International Reading Association.

Roskos, K. A., & Christie, J. F. (Eds.). (2000). *Play and literacy in early childhood: Research from multiple perspectives*. Mahwah, NJ: Erlbaum.

Roskos, K. A., Christie, J. F., & Richgels, D. J. (2003). The essentials of early literacy instruction. *Young Children*, *58*(2), 52–60.

Roskos, K. A., Tabors, P., & Lenhart, L. (2009). *Oral language and early literacy in preschool: Talking, reading and writing*. Newark, DE: International Reading Association.

Rossi, R., & Stringfield, S. (1995). What we must do for students placed at risk. *Phi Delta Kappan*, *77*, 73–76.

Rousseau, J. (1962). *Emile* (ed. and trans. William Boyd). New York: Columbia University Teachers College (original work published 1762).

Routman, R., (2005). *Writing essentials: Raising expectations and results while simplifying teaching*. Portsmouth, NH: Heinemann.

Rowe, D., & Neitzel, C. (2010). Interest and agency in 2- and 3-year-olds' participating in emergent writing. *Reading Research Quarterly*, *45*(2), 169–195.

Rowsell, J., & Lapp, D. (2010). Best practices in new literacies. In L. M., Morrow & L. B. Gambrell (Eds.), *Best practices in literacy instruction*. New York: Guilford Press.

Rusk, R., & Scotland, J. (1979). *Doctrines of the great educators*. New York: St. Martin's Press.

Salinas, M., Pérez-Granados, D. R., Feldman, H. M., & Huffman, L. C. (2017). Beyond immigrant status: Book-sharing in low-income Mexican-American families. *Journal of Early Childhood Research*, *15*(1), 17–33.

Sampson, M. B. (2002). Confirming K-W-L: Considering the source. *Reading Teacher*, *55*(6), 528–532.

Santoro, L. E., Baker, S. K., Fien, H., Smith, J. M., & Chard, D. J. (2016). Using read-alouds to help struggling readers access and comprehend complex, informational text. *TEACHING Exceptional Children*, *48*(6), 282–292.

Schickedanz, J. & Collins, M. F. (2013). *So much more than the ABCs: The early phases of reading and writing*. Washington, D.C.: National Association for the Education of Young Children.

Schickedanz, J. A., & Casbergue, R. M. (2009). *Writing in preschool: Learning to orchestrate meaning and marks*. Newark, DE: International Reading Association.

Schickedanz, J. A., York, M. E., Stewart, I. S., & White, A. (1990). *Strategies for teaching young children*. Upper Saddle River, NJ: Prentice Hall.

Schrodt, K., Fain, J. G., & Hasty, M. (2015). Exploring culturally relevant texts with kindergartners and their families. *Reading Teacher*, *68*(8), 589–598.

Schwanenflugel, P., Meisinger, E., Wisenbaker, J., Kuhn, M., Strauss, G., & Morris, R. (2006). Becoming a fluent and automatic reader in the early elementary school years. *Reading Research Quarterly*, *41*(4), 496–522.

Seefeldt, C., & Barbour, N. (1998). *Early childhood education: An introduction*. Columbus, OH: Merrill/Prentice Hall.

Seglem, R. & Witte, S. (2009). You gotta see it to believe it: Teaching visual literacy in the English classroom. *Journal of Adolescent & Adult Literacy*, *53*(3), 216–226.

Sénéchal, M., & LeFevre, J. A. (2002). Parental involvement in the development of children's reading skill: A five-year longitudinal study. *Child development*, *73*(2), 445–460.

Shanahan, T. (2006). Relations among oral language, reading, and writing development. In C. MacArthur, S. Graham, & J. Fitzgerald (Eds.), *Handbook of writing research* (pp. 171–186). New York: Guilford Press.

Shaywitz, S. (2003). *Overcoming dyslexia*. New York: Knopf.

Sheridan, M., & Rowsell, J. (2010). *Design literacies: Learning and innovation in a digital age*. London: Routledge.

Shonkoff. J., & Meisels, S. J. (2000). *Handbook of Early Childhood Intervention* (2nd ed.). Cambridge: Cambridge University Press.

Shore, K. (2001). Success for ESL students: 12 practical tips to help second-language learners. *Instructor*, *1*(110), 30–32, 106.

Short, K. G., Lynch-Brown, C., & Tomlinson, C. M. (2018) Essentials of Children's Literature (9th ed.). Hoboken, NJ: Pearson.

Shubitz, S. (2016). *Craft moves: lesson sets for teaching writing with mentor texts*. Portland, ME: Stenhouse.

Siegle, D. (2012). Embracing e-books: Increasing students' motivation to read and write. *Gifted Child Today (35)*2, 137–143.

Silvaroli, N. J. (2001). *Classroom reading inventory* (9th ed.). Blacklick, OH: McGraw-Hill.

Sipe, L. (2008). *Storytime: Young children's literacy understanding in the classroom*. New York: Teachers College Press.

Skinner, B. F. (1954). The science of learning and the art of teaching. *Harvard Educational Review*, *24*, 86–97.

Skinner, B. F. (1992). *Verbal behavior*. Acton, MA: Copley Publishing Group.

Slavin, R. E. (1987). Ability grouping and student achievement in elementary schools: A best-evidence synthesis. *Review of Educational Research*, *57*, 292–336.

Slavin, R. E. (1997). *Educational psychology: Theory and practice* (5th ed.). Boston: Allyn and Bacon.

Slavin, R. E., & Madden, N. A. (1989). What works for students at risk: A research synthesis. *Educational Leadership*, *46*, 4–13.

Smith, F. (1971). *Understanding reading*. New York: Holt.

Smith, L. (2010). *It's a book*. New York: Roaring Brook Press.

Snow, C. E., & Matthews, T. J. (2016). Reading and language in the early grades. *Future of Children*, *26*(1), 57–74.

Snow, C. E., Burns, M. S., & Griffin, P. (1998). *Preventing reading difficulties in young children*. Washington, DC: National Academy Press.

Soderman, A. K., Gregory, K. S., & McCarty, L. T. (2005). *Scaffolding emergent literacy: A child-centered approach for preschool through grade 5* (2nd ed.). Boston: Allyn and Bacon.

Soderman, A., & Farrell, P. (2008). *Creating literacy-rich preschools and kindergartens*. Boston: Pearson Education.

Sorenson, A. B., & Hallinan, M. T. (1986). Effects of ability grouping on growth in academic achievement. *American Educational Research Journal*, *23*, 519–542.

Spandel, V. (2008). *Creating young writers: Using six traits to enrich writing process in primary classrooms*. Boston: Allyn and Bacon.

Spandel, V. (2012). *Creating writers through six-trait writing assessment and instruction*. (6th ed.) Boston, MA: Pearson.

Spencer, B. H., & Guillaume, A. M. (2006). Integrating curriculum through the learning cycle: Content-based reading and vocabulary instruction. *Reading Teacher*, *60*(3), 206–219.

Spiegel, D. L. (1992). Blending whole language and systematic direct instruction. *Reading Teacher, 46,* 38–44.

Spielberg, S. (1987). Acceptance speech at the Academy Award Ceremonies, Los Angeles.

Stahl, S. A. (2003). No more "madfaces": Motivation and fluency development with struggling readers. In D. M. Barone & L. M. Morrow (Eds.), *Literacy and young children: Research-based practices* (pp. 195–209). New York: Guilford Press.

Stahl, S. A. (2008). The effects of three instructional methods on the reading comprehension and content acquisition of novice readers. *Journal of Literacy Research, 40*(3) 359–393.

Stahl, S. A., & Heubach, K. M. (2005). Fluency-oriented reading instruction. *Journal of Literacy Research, 37,* 25–60.

Stanovich, K. E. (1986). Mathew effects in reading: Some consequences of individual differences in the acquisition of literacy. *Reading Research Quarterly, 21,* 360–407.

Stauffer, R. G. (1980). *The language-experience approach to the teaching of reading* (2nd ed.). New York: Harper & Row.

Stine, H. A. (1993). *The effects of CD-ROM interactive software in reading skills instructions with second grade Chapter I students.* Doctoral dissertation, George Washington University. Ann Arbor, MI: University Microfilms International.

Strickland, D., & Schickedanz, J. (2009). *Learning about print in preschool: Working with letters, words, and beginning links with phonemic awareness.* Newark, DE: International Reading Association.

Strickland, D., & Snow, C. (2002). *Preparing our teachers: Opportunities for better reading instruction.* Washington, DC: Joseph Henry Press.

Sullivan, N. W., & Buchanan, C. D. (1963). *Programmed reading series.* New York: McGraw-Hill.

Sulzby, E. (1985a). Children's emergent reading of favorite storybooks. *Reading Research Quarterly, 20,* 458–481.

Sulzby, E. (1985b). Kindergartners as writers and readers. In M. Farr (Ed.), *Advances in writing research. Vol. 1: Children's early writing* (pp. 127–199). Norwood, NJ: Ablex.

Sylvester, R., & Greenidge, W. (2009–2010). Digital storytelling: Extending the potential for struggling writers. *The Reading Teacher, 63,* 284–285.

Tabors, P. (1998). What early childhood educators need to know: Developing effective programs for linguistically and culturally diverse children and families. *Young Children, 53*(6), 20–26.

Tafa, E. (2001). *Reading and writing in preschool education.* Athens, Greece: Ellinika Grammata.

Tamis-LeMonda, C. S., Baumwell, L. B., & Cristofaro, T. (in press). Parent-child conversations during play. *First Language.*

Tamis-LeMonda, C. S., Bornstein, M. H., & Baumwell, L. (2001). Maternal responsiveness and children's achievement of language milestones. *Child Development, 72*(3), 748–767.

Taylor, B. M. (2008). Tier 1: Effective classroom reading instruction in the elementary grades. In D. Fuchs, S. Fuchs, & S. Vaughn (Eds.), *Response to intervention: A framework for reading education* (pp. 5–25). Newark, DE: International Reading Association.

Taylor, B. M., Frye, B. J., & Maruyama, M. (1990). Time spent reading and reading growth. *American Educational Research Journal, 27,* 351–362.

Taylor, B. M., Strait, J., & Medo, M. A. (1994). Early intervention in reading: Supplemental instruction for groups of low-achieving students provided by first-grade teachers. In E. H. Hiebert & B. Taylor (Eds.), *Getting reading right from the start* (pp. 107–123). Newark, DE: International Reading Association.

Taylor, L., & Adelman, H. S. (1999). Personalizing classroom instruction to account for motivational and developmental differences. *Reading & Writing Quarterly, 15*(4), 255–276.

Teale, W. (2003). Questions about early literacy learning and teaching that need asking—And some that don't. In D. M. Barone & L. M. Morrow (Eds.), *Literacy and young children: Research-based practices* (pp. 140–157). New York: Guilford Press.

Teale, W. H., & Gambrell, L. B. (2007). Raising urban students' literacy achievement by engaging in authentic, challenging work. *Reading Teacher, 60*(8), 728–739.

Temple, C., Nathan, R., Burris, N., & Temple, F. (1988). *The beginnings of writing.* Boston: Allyn and Bacon.

Templeton, S. & Gehsman, K. M. (2014). *Teaching reading and writing. The developmental approach.* Boston: Pearson.

Templeton, S. (1996). *Teaching the integrated language arts.* Belmont, CA: Wadsworth Publishing.

Tomlinson, C. A. (2004). *How to differentiate instruction in mixed-ability classrooms* (2nd ed.). Alexandria, VA: Association for Supervision and Curriculum Development.

Tompkins, G. E. (2007). *Literacy for the 21st century: Teaching reading and writing in prekindergarten through grade 4* (2nd Ed.). Upper Saddle River, NJ: Pearson Education.

Tompkins, G. E. (2001). *Language arts content and teaching strategies* (5th Ed.). Upper Saddle River, NJ: Prentice Hall.

Tompkins, G.E. (2011). *Teaching writing: Balancing process and product* (6th ed.). Boston, MA: Pearson.

Treiman, R., & Kessler, B. (2003). The role of letter names in the acquisition of literacy. In R. V. Kail (Ed.), *Advances in child development and behavior* (3rd ed., pp. 105–135). Oxford, UK: Academic Press.

Treiman, R., Schmidt, J., Decker, K., Robins, S., Levine, S. C., Demir, Ö. E., & Demir, Ö. E., (2015). *Parents' Talk About Letters With Their Young Children. Child Development, 86*(5), 1406–1418.

Turbill, J., & Bean, W. (2006). *Writing instruction K–6: Understanding process, purpose, audience.* Katonah, NY: Richard C. Owen.

U.S. Department of Education. (2001). *No child left behind legislation.* www.nochildleftbehind.gov.

Veatch, J., Sawicki, F., Elliot, G., Barnett, E., & Blackey, J. (1973). *Key words to reading: The language experience approach begins.* Columbus, OH: Merrill.

Vukelich, C., & Christie, J. (2009). *Building a foundation for preschool literacy: Effective instruction for children's reading and writing development.* Newark, DE: International Reading Association.

Vukelich, C., Christie, J., & Enz, B. (2007). *Helping young children learn language and literacy.* Boston: Allyn and Bacon.

Vukelich, C., Evans, C., & Albertson, B. (2003). Organizing expository texts: A look at the possibilities. In D. M. Barone & L. M. Morrow (Eds.), *Literacy and young children: Research-based practices* (pp. 261–290). New York: Guilford Press.

Vygotsky, L. S. (1978). *Mind in society: The development of psychological processes.* Cambridge, MA: Harvard University Press.

Walmsley, S. A. (1994). *Children exploring their world: Theme teaching in elementary school.* Portsmouth, NH: Heinemann.

Walpole, S., & McKenna, M. C. (2007). *Differentiated reading instruction strategies for primary grades.* New York: Guilford Press.

Ward, M., & McCormick, S. (1981). Reading instruction for blind and low vision children in the regular classroom. *Reading Teacher, 34,* 434, 444.

Wasik, B. A. & Iannone-Campbell, C. (2012/January 2013). Developing vocabulary through purposeful, dtrategic conversations. *The Reading Teacher, 66*(4), 321–332.

Wasik, B. A., & Bond, M. A. (2001). Beyond the pages of a book: Interactive book reading and language development in preschool classrooms. *Journal of Educational Psychology, 93*(2), 243–250.

Wasik, B. H., Dobbins, D. R., & Herrmann, S. (2001). Intergenerational family literacy: Concepts, research, and practice. In S. B. Neuman & D. K. Dickinson (Eds.), *Handbook of early literacy research* (pp. 444–458). New York: Guilford Press.

Weinstein, C. S., & Mignano, A. J., Jr. (2003). *Elementary classroom management* (3rd ed.). Boston: McGraw-Hill.

Weitzman, E., & Greenberg, J. (2002). *Learning language and loving it: A guide to promoting children's social, language, and literacy development in early childhood settings* (2nd ed.). Toronto: Hanen Centre.

Wentzel, K. R. (2009). Students' relationships with teachers as motivational contexts. In K. R. Wentzel & Wigfield, A. (Eds.), *Handbook of motivation at school* (pp. 301–322). New York: Routledge/Taylor & Francis Group.

Wepner, S., & Ray, L. (2000). Sign of the times: Technology and early literacy learning. In D. S. Strickland & L. M. Morrow (Eds.), *Beginning reading and writing* (pp. 168–182). New York: Teachers College Press.

Wheelock, W., Silvaroli, J. & Campbell, C. (2012). *Classroom reading inventory* (12th ed.). New York: McGraw-Hill.

Whitehurst, G. J., & Lonigan, C. J. (2001). Emergent literacy: Development from prereaders to readers. In S. B. Neuman & D. K. Dickinson (Eds.), *Handbook of early literacy research* (pp. 11–29). New York: Guilford Press.

Wilson, A. A. (2008). Motivating young writers through write-talks: Real writers, real audiences, real purposes. *Reading Teacher, 61*(6), 485–487.

Wise Lindeman, K. (2013). Response to intervention and early childhood best practices: Working hand in hand so all children can learn. *YC: Young Children, 68*(2), 16.

Woods, M. J. & Moe, A. (2011). Analytical reading inventory: Comprehensive standards-based assessment for all students including gifted and remedial (9th ed.). Boston, MA: Allyn & Bacon.

Worthy, J., Maloch, B., Pursley, B., Hungerford-Kresser, H., Hampton, A., Jordan, M., & Semingson, P. (2015). What are the rest of the students doing? Literacy work stations in two first-grade classrooms. *Language Arts, 92*(3), 173–186.

Wright, S. (2010). *Understanding creativity in early childhood*. London: Sage Publications.

Xu, H. (2003). The learner, the teacher, the text, and the context: Sociocultural approaches to early literacy instruction for English language learners. In D. M. Barone & L. M. Morrow (Eds.), *Literacy and young children: Research-based practices* (pp. 61–80). New York: Guilford Press.

Xu, S. H. (2010). *Teaching English language learners: Literacy strategies & resources for K–6*. New York: Guilford.

Xu, S. H., & Rutledge, A. L. (2003). Chicken starts with ch!: Kindergartners learn through environmental print. *Young Children, 58*, 44–51.

Xu, Y., & Drame, E. (2008). Culturally appropriate content: Unlocking the potential of response to intervention for English language learners. *Early Childhood Educational Journal, 35*(4), 305–311.

Yopp, H. K. (1992). Developing phonemic awareness in young children. *The Reading Teacher, 45*(9), 696–703.

Yopp, R. H., & Yopp, H. K. (2000). Sharing informational text with young children. *Reading Teacher, 53*(5), 410–423.

Young, C., & Rasinski, T. (2009). Implementing readers' theatre as an approach to classroom fluency instruction. *The Reading Teacher, 63*(1), 4–13.

Zecker, L. (1999). Different texts, different emergent written forms. *Language Arts, 76*(1), 483–484.

Zeece, P., & Wallace, B. (2009). Books and good stuff: A strategy for building school to home literacy connections. *Early Childhood Education Journal, 37*(1), 35–42.

Index

C

G

H

I

J

K

L

Q

R

Y

Z